REI[illegible] ARROWS

OXFORD STUDIES IN EARLY EMPIRES

Series Editors
Nicola Di Cosmo, Mark Edward Lewis, and Walter Scheidel

The Dynamics of Ancient Empires
State Power from Assyria to Byzantium
Edited by Ian Morris and Walter Scheidel

Rome and China
Comparative Perspectives on Ancient World Empires
Edited by Walter Scheidel

Trouble in the West
The Persian Empire and Egypt, 525–332 BCE
Stephen Ruzicka

Sui-Tang China and Its Turko-Mongol Neighbors
Culture, Power, and Connections, 580–800
Jonathan Karam Skaff

State Correspondence in the Ancient World
From New Kingdom Egypt to the Roman Empire
Edited by Karen Radner

State Power in Ancient China and Rome
Edited by Walter Scheidel

The Confucian-Legalist State
A New Model for Chinese History
Dingxin Zhao

The Jiankang Empire in Chinese and World History
Ethnic Identity and Political Culture
Andrew Chittick

Reign of Arrows
The Rise of the Parthian Empire in the Hellenistic Middle East
Nikolaus Leo Overtoom

Reign of Arrows

The Rise of the Parthian Empire in the Hellenistic Middle East

Nikolaus Leo Overtoom

Syrian ceramic relief plaque of a Parthian horse archer drawing a composite bow while riding.

OXFORD
UNIVERSITY PRESS

OXFORD
UNIVERSITY PRESS

Oxford University Press is a department of the University of Oxford. It furthers the University's objective of excellence in research, scholarship, and education by publishing worldwide. Oxford is a registered trade mark of Oxford University Press in the UK and certain other countries.

Published in the United States of America by Oxford University Press
198 Madison Avenue, New York, NY 10016, United States of America.

First issued as an Oxford University Press paperback, 2023

CIP data is on file at the Library of Congress
ISBN 978–0–19–088832–9 (hardback)
ISBN 978–0–19–768022–3 (paperback)

1 3 5 7 9 8 6 4 2

Paperback printed by Marquis, Canada

To my family,
Janet, Ian, Brie, and Stacey

Contents

Maps

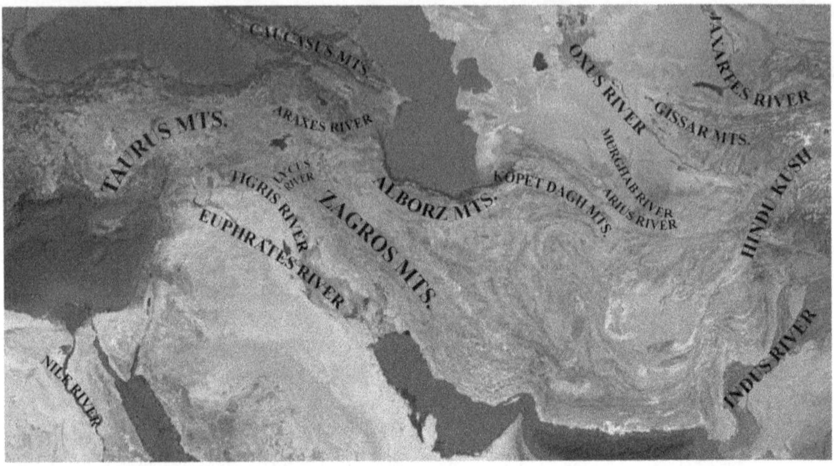

Map 1. Important Rivers and Mountains

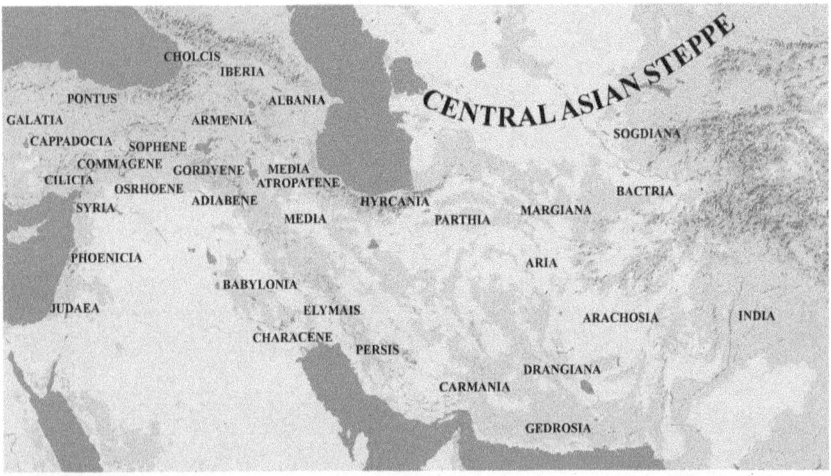

Map 2. Important Regions

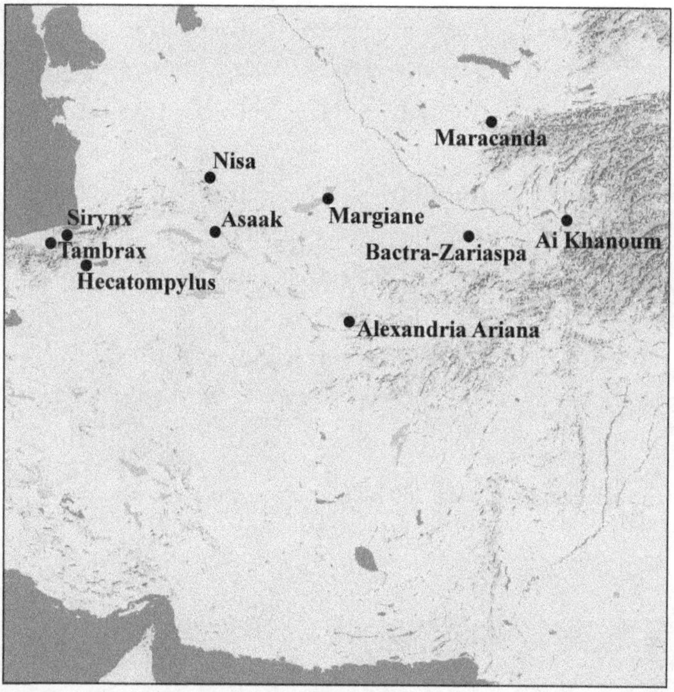

MAP 3. Important Cities to the East

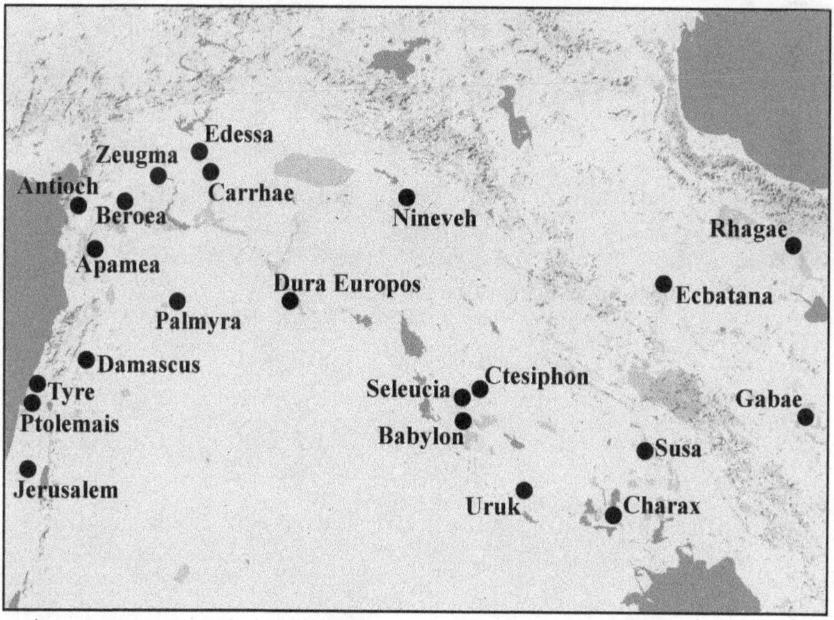

MAP 4. Important Cities to the West

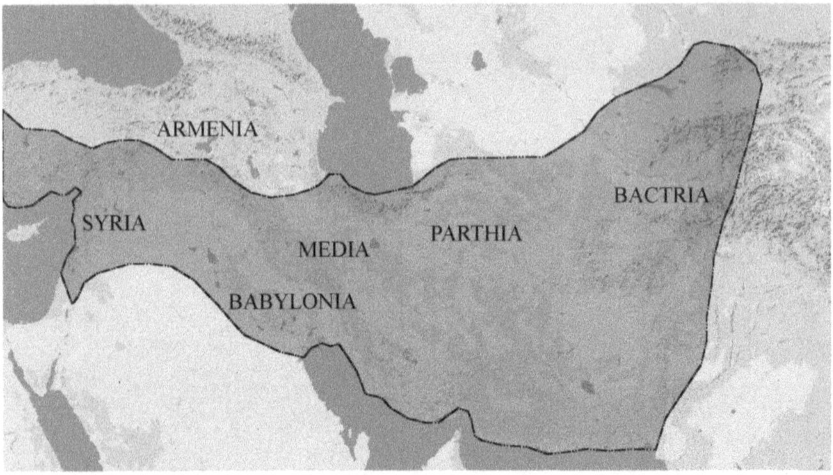

MAP 5. The Seleucid Empire ca. 280 BCE

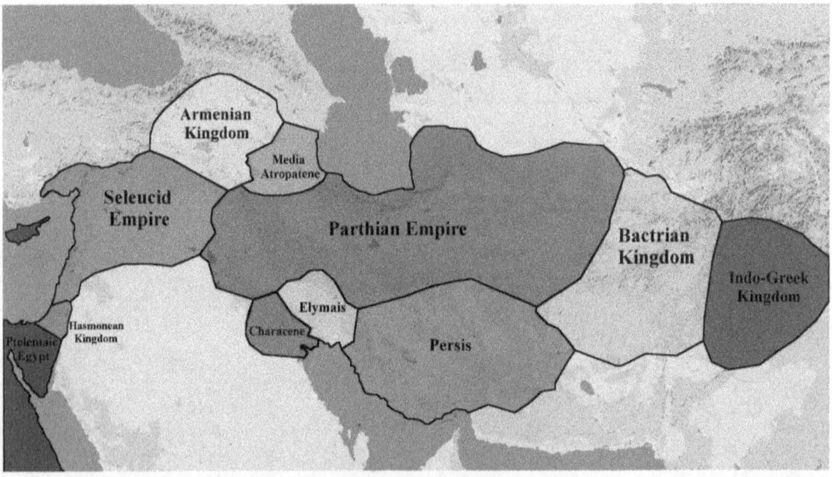

MAP 6. The Hellenistic Middle East ca. 140 BCE

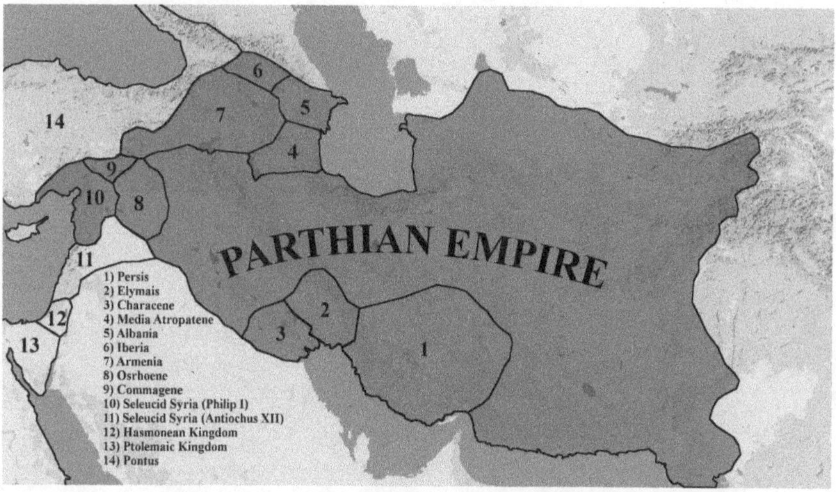

Map 7. The Parthian Empire ca. 87 BCE (numbers 1–10 denote vassal states)

Preface

When I decided to begin investigating the geopolitics of the Hellenistic world, I knew that I wanted to examine the somewhat surprising success of the little-known Parthians. Their later rivalry with the Romans garners the attention; however, I found the origin and early expansion of the Parthians a fascinating subject worthy of greater scholarly consideration. What began as research for a single chapter quickly blossomed into an entire book project as I came to realize the potential and need for a new account of this overshadowed people in this underappreciated part of the world. The ability of the Parthians to rival Rome is noteworthy; however, their ability to survive the numerous threats that they faced in the Hellenistic Middle East and, in fact, to thrive within such a competitive and hostile environment is the true feat. I have tried to make this interdisciplinary study compelling not only to specialists in history and political science, but also to general readers interested in the ancient world or international relations.

This book introduces the Seleucid Empire's hegemony over the Hellenistic Middle East in the early third century before investigating the rapidly changing geopolitical climate in this region in the 240s–230s.[1] It is a reconstruction of early Parthian history from the founding of the Parthian state to the reign of Mithridates II (ca. 121–91). Yet not all of the events of Mithridates' reign are detailed in this study. The focus of this book is the rise of the Parthian Empire within the Hellenistic Middle East, and it concludes with Mithridates II's successful policy to subjugate the Seleucids under Parthian hegemony. I am presently working on a second book project that focuses on the subsequent struggles of the Parthians to maintain their hegemony and their budding rivalry with Rome during the first century.

1. All dates in this study are BCE unless otherwise indicated.

In the following pages, the term "Hellenistic" represents the much-expanded Greek-influenced world that flourished from Italy to the Indus in the wake of Alexander the Great's conquests and the partitioning of his empire by his companions after his death. Although the Parthians certainly were not Greek, they existed within this Hellenistic world, and they were heavily influenced by it. Meanwhile, the term "Hellenistic Middle East" represents a territorial space roughly defined by the Levantine coast, Syria, northern Mesopotamia, and Armenia in the west, and the Central Asian steppe and the Indus River valley in the east. Further, note that there has been a recent scholarly trend to abandon the term "Parthian" in favor of the dynastic eponym "Arsacid" because it better represents the ruling class of the state during this period. It also fits more appropriately within the tradition of labeling Middle Eastern empires by dynastic names (for example, the Achaemenids, the Seleucids, and the Sasanians). Although I generally agree with this new emphasis and utilize the terms "Arsacid" and "Arsacids" where appropriate, I have chosen to favor the terms "Parthian" and "Parthians" in this work for the sake of clarity and familiarity for the general reader. I refer to all Parthian coins using the Sellwood type number index (for example, S1.1 [Figure 1]). Where possible, I acquired images of select coins; however, images of all coins referenced in this study are not included because of the difficulty and cost of acquiring them.[2] Finally, I quote a broad range of ancient sources in this book. I have provided information on the various Greek and Roman sources and translations utilized in this study in the section "Greek and Roman Literary Sources." Although I generally utilize well-established available translations, my analysis is based upon an examination of the various original Greek and Latin passages in every case, and I vouch for all the following translated passages. When the translation is my own, I have noted it. My understanding of material in other ancient languages or in cuneiform depends entirely upon the cited translator.

2. For a comprehensive digital collection of descriptions and images of Parthian coins referenced, but not included, in this study, see www.parthia.com/parthia_sellwood.htm.

Acknowledgments

This book is the culmination of several years of research and writing. It would not have been possible without the encouragement and support of numerous people and institutions. As a result, my debts are numerous.

I have been fortunate in the selflessness, direction, and inspiration of my advisors. I would like to begin by thanking Steven Ross at Louisiana State University (LSU) for the considerable time and energy he put forth in helping me shape and revise this project in its early stages. His unyielding energy and support made this research possible. I must thank Arthur Eckstein at the University of Maryland (UMD) for guiding my scholarship. His pioneering effort to incorporate international relations theory into the study of ancient geopolitics has been a crucial influence on my work. I also must thank Christopher Fuhrmann at the University of North Texas for his unrivaled influence on my love for the study and teaching of ancient history. His many years of guidance and friendship have been fundamentally important to my success as a student, teacher, and scholar.

I have benefited greatly from the guidance and input of numerous esteemed scholars and friends. From my time at LSU, Maribel Dietz, Suzanne Marchand, Victor Stater, and John Poirot contributed significantly, and from my time at UMD, Judith Hallett, Will Burghart, and Joe Frechette provided necessary encouragement. At the University of New Mexico, Lorenzo Garcia offered helpful suggestions on how to better interpret Polybius' Greek, and Timothy Graham has been a most generous colleague, mentor, and friend.

The enthusiasm and warm welcome of leading scholars in Parthian and Hellenistic studies have been immensely encouraging and appreciated. I am aware that my research in many ways stands on the shoulders of giants. I especially thank Gholamreza Assar, Adrian Bivar, Malcolm Colledge, Vesta Curtis, Edward Dąbrowa, Neilson Debevoise, Arthur Eckstein, Richard Frye, Jerome Gaslain, John Grainger, Leonardo Gregoratti, Stefan Hauser, Frank Holt,

Hermann Hunger, Paul Kosmin, Jeffrey Lerner, Charlotte Lerouge-Cohen, Valery Nikonorov, Marek Olbrycht, Abraham Sachs, Gareth Sampson, David Sellwood, Rahim Shayegan, Rolf Strootman, Robartus van der Spek, Josef Wiesehöfer, and Jozef Wolski for their influential scholarship. I cannot thank enough Edward Dąbrowa, Leonardo Gregoratti, Jeffrey Lerner, and Marek Olbrycht for their notes and advice. I sincerely apologize if I have omitted anyone inadvertently. It has been an honor to contribute to the burgeoning field of Parthian studies in recent years, and a primary purpose of this book is to create more awareness and further the discussion. Any shortcomings herein are solely the fault of the author.

The support of Louisiana State University, Missouri State University, the University of New Mexico, and Washington State University also deserves acknowledgment. The libraries and their staffs at these universities were indispensable. Meanwhile, the history departments at each of these institutions offered me vital funding as a young professional to conduct research and present my work at numerous conferences. The 2015–2016 Louisiana State University Graduate School Dissertation Year Fellowship Award made the early stages of this project possible. A New Mexico Humanities Council Grant provided me with the funding necessary to secure photography and distribution rights. Finally, the Gorham Fund Grant for the Advancement of Ancient History at the University of New Mexico helped support the progress of my research.

I would like to thank the Classical Association of the Middle West and South for the Mason A. Stewart Travel Award to present research at the 2018 meeting in Winston-Salem, the Association of Ancient Historians for two subvention grants to attend the 2015 meeting in Santa Barbara and present research at the 2016 meeting in Tacoma, the AAH grant committee for the 2012 Scott R. Jacobs Fellowship Grant for the Advancement of Alexander Studies, and the association's continued support of the AAH affiliate panels at the American Historical Association annual meetings. Audiences at two dozen conference presentations over the past few years have provided valuable questions and comments. I also would like to thank the editorial staffs and readers of *Acta Antiqua Academiae Scientiarum Hungaricae*, *Anabasis. Studia Classica et Orientalia*, *Classical World*, *The International History Review*, the *Journal of Ancient History*, *Parthica. Incontri di culture nel mondo antico*, and *Studia Iranica* for their continued support of my research.

As senior classics editor at Oxford University Press, New York, Stefan Vranka has been dependable, supportive, and patient. I cannot thank Stefan and OUP enough for their interest in my research and their eagerness to include my book in the Oxford Studies in Early Empires Series. I also must thank the series editors, Nicola Di Cosmo, Mark Edward Lewis, and Walter Scheidel, for their support. Similarly, the anonymous readers for the Press offered useful comments and encouragement, for which I thank them.

Such an ambitious project would not have been possible without the love and support of a wide network of friends and family. I thank you all. I feel most fortunate for the love and support of my in-laws, Mike and Norma Williams; my sister, Gabrielle Gormley; my brother, Ian Overtoom; and my mother, Janet Farrow. They provide me with encouragement and motivation, which is more important than I can express. My wife, Stacey Overtoom, has been my greatest companion for the better part of two decades. Her efforts to help me complete this project were invaluable. The greatest of thanks goes to her.

Timeline

(All dates are as exact as possible.)

323—Alexander the Great dies in Babylon, beginning the struggle of the Diadochi

312/311—Seleucus I seizes Babylon, founding the Seleucid state and subsequently securing the eastern satrapies of Alexander's former empire

306/305—Seleucus concludes a treaty with the Mauryan Emperor, Chandragupta, ceding the Indus River valley and Arachosia in exchange for 500 war elephants

305—Seleucus declares himself king

301—Seleucus helps win the Battle of Ipsus, gaining Syria

281—Seleucus wins the Battle of Corupedium, gaining Anatolia and Thrace; Seleucus assassinated

280—A Seleucid general, Demodamas, successfully counterattacks against the Parni in response to their attacks on Margiana

274–271—First Syrian War, Seleucus' successor, Antiochus I, loses southern Anatolia to Ptolemaic Egypt

260–253—Second Syrian War, Antiochus I's successor, Antiochus II, fights a mostly indecisive war against Ptolemaic Egypt; marries Ptolemy II's daughter, Berenice, repudiating his former wife, Laodice

250—Traditional founding of the Parthian state (now defunct)

248/247—Beginning of the Parthian era; Arsaces I crowned king of the Parni

246—Antiochus dies, leaving a succession crisis; Berenice and her son assassinated; Laodice helps secure the Seleucid throne for her son, Seleucus II

246–241—Third Syrian War, Ptolemy III invades Syria and Mesopotamia, temporarily seizing Babylon and gaining southern Syria

246/245–236—First civil war of Seleucus and Antiochus Hierax, Seleucus' brother declares independence in Anatolia, defeating Seleucus at the Battle of Ancyra; the brothers agree to a truce, leaving Antiochus Hierax in control of Anatolia

246/245—Arsaces unsuccessfully invades Margiana

245—Seleucid satraps of Parthia and Bactria rebel

245–239/238—Andragoras rules independently over Parthia

239—Seleucus loses the Battle of Ancyra

239/238—Arsaces invades and seizes Parthia; subsequently invades and seizes Hyrcania

238—Attalus I declares himself king in western Anatolia; Diodotus I declares himself king in Bactria

236/235—Diodotus II becomes king of Bactria; subsequently makes peace and an alliance with Arsaces

235/234–229/228—Seleucus begins his eastern campaign; Arsaces defeats Seleucus, possibly capturing him; Seleucus returns to the west

229/228–226—Second civil war of Seleucus and Antiochus Hierax; Seleucus wins

223/222—Antiochus III becomes king of the Seleucid Empire

221—Euthydemus I murders Diodotus, seizing the throne of Bactria

220—Antiochus defeats the usurper Molon and subdues Media Atropatene

219–217—Fourth Syrian War, Antiochus regains portions of southern Syria but loses the Battle of Raphia to Ptolemy IV

216–213—Antiochus expands his holdings in Anatolia

212—Antiochus subdues Armenia

211—Arsaces II becomes king of Parthia

210—Antiochus begins his eastern campaign

209–208—Antiochus invades Parthia, capturing Hecatompylus; he wins the Battle of Mount Labus and the siege of Sirynx, annexing much of Parthia and forcing Arsaces to become his subordinate ally

208–206—Antiochus invades Bactria, winning the Battle of the Arius River; he besieges Bactra-Zariaspa for two years before forcing Euthydemus to become his subordinate ally

206–205—Antiochus invades India, forcing Sophagasenus to become his subordinate ally

202–195—Fifth Syrian War, Antiochus wins the Battle of Panium, annexing Coele-Syria from Ptolemy V

192–188—Romano-Seleucid War, Antiochus unsuccessfully invades Greece; Romans decisively defeat Antiochus at the Battle of Magnesia; Antiochus agrees to the Treaty of Apamea, costing him control over all his possessions in Anatolia

187—Antiochus launches a second eastern campaign but dies trying to loot the Temple of Bel in Elymais; Seleucus IV becomes king of the Seleucid Empire

185—Phriapatius becomes king of Parthia

180—Indo-Greek Kingdom emerges as a rival to Bactria in northern India

175—Seleucus is assassinated; Antiochus IV becomes king of the Seleucid Empire

170—Arsaces IV becomes king of Parthia

170–168—Sixth Syrian War, Antiochus nearly captures Alexandria in Egypt before Roman intervention

168—Phraates I becomes king of Parthia; Eucratides I becomes king of Bactria

167–160—Maccabean Rebellion, Antiochus' religious persecution of the Jews causes a revolt that eventually leads to the founding of the Hasmonean Kingdom

165—Parthians reconquer Hyrcania; Antiochus initiates his eastern campaign

165/164—Mithridates I becomes king of Parthia, consolidating Parthian gains in Hyrcania

164—Antiochus dies in southern Iran after failing to loot a temple in Elymais

163/162–158—Mithridates annexes most of Aria and Margiana from Eucratides

162/161—Demetrius I seizes the Seleucid throne, murdering Antiochus V; Timarchus rebels in Media

161–160—Timarchus occupies Babylonia but Demetrius defeats and kills him

158–155—Mithridates begins his conquest of Media

152–150—Alexander Balas usurps the Seleucid throne, defeating and killing Demetrius

147—Parthians complete their conquest of Media; Demetrius II contests the Seleucid throne; Elymais and perhaps Persis declare independence from the Seleucid Empire

146/145—Ai Khanoum in Bactria likely falls to Central Asian invaders

145—Alexander Balas assassinated, making Demetrius king; Diodotus Tryphon contests the Seleucid throne, championing the cause of Antiochus VI; Eucratides assassinated

145–138—Civil war of Demetrius and Diodotus Tryphon

141—Characene declares independence from the Seleucid Empire; Parthians occupy Babylonia and Persis

141/140—Elymais unsuccessfully invades Babylonia

140—Mithridates occupies Elymais

140/139—Demetrius prepares an eastern expedition

138—Demetrius invades Mesopotamia; Mithridates defeats and captures Demetrius in Babylonia; Mithridates becomes severely ill; Antiochus VII challenges Tryphon's position in Syria

138/137—Elymais unsuccessfully invades Babylonia

137—Antiochus defeats Tryphon, gaining control of Syria

134—Antiochus invades Judaea, besieging Jerusalem

133—Elymais and Characene unsuccessfully invade Babylonia

133/132—Parthians conquer Elymais, establishing a vassal state; Parthians also perhaps vassalize Persis

132—Jews agree to terms of surrender; Mithridates dies of illness, making Phraates II king of Parthia

130—Antiochus invades Mesopotamia, occupying Babylonia and Elymais

129—Antiochus invades Media; Phraates releases Demetrius from captivity to contest the throne in Syria; Babylonian communities rebel against Seleucid occupation; Phraates ambushes and kills Antiochus; Demetrius seizes the Seleucid throne

128—Demetrius unsuccessfully invades Egypt; Syria rebels against his rule; Alexander Zabinas emerges as a rival to his throne; the Saka plunder the Iranian plateau; Characene declares autonomy

127—Alexander invades Syria, occupying Antioch; Characene briefly occupies Babylonia; Elymais rebels; Phraates dies fighting the Saka; Phraates' uncle, Artabanus I/II, named king of the Parthians

126—Alexander defeats Demetrius near Damascus; Characene briefly occupies Babylonia; Artabanus dies; his son, Artabanus II/III, becomes king of the Parthians

125—Demetrius killed near Tyre; Seleucus V becomes king of the Seleucids but is killed by his mother; Antiochus VIII becomes king of the Seleucids; Characene forced to pay tribute to the Parthians

124—Parthians install a governor in Characene; they also put down the rebellion in Elymais, capturing Susa

123—The Tochari invade Parthia, ravaging the Iranian plateau

123/122—Antiochus defeats and kills Alexander, becoming the sole king of the Seleucids

122—Artabanus dies fighting the Tochari; the young Arsaces X perhaps becomes king of Parthia

121—Mithridates II becomes king of Parthia; he subdues Characene and undertakes an eastern campaign against the Central Asian invaders

120—Arab tribes plunder Babylonia; Characene and Elymais rebel

119—Parthians regain control of Babylonia; Mithridates conducts major eastern campaign, decisively defeating the "Guti"

119–112—Mithridates defeats the Central Asian tribal confederations, successfully subduing their strongholds and restoring the eastern frontier of the Parthian Empire; he annexes Bactria, Sogdiana, and Arachosia and resettles the Iranian plateau

116/115—Parthians and Chinese make first contact

115—Antiochus IX contests his half-brother Antiochus VIII's throne

113—Parthians continue their conquest of northern Mesopotamia with occupation of Dura Europos

113/112—Successful Parthian operations in Media Atropatene against the Armenians

111—Mithridates defeats the Armenians; Tigranes II becomes a Parthian hostage; Babylonian scribes begin using the title "King of Kings" in association with Mithridates

96—Antiochus VIII dies, whose sons, Seleucus VI, Philip I, and Demetrius III, contest Antiochus IX's throne

96/95—Mithridates establishes Tigranes in Armenia as a Parthian vassal

95—Seleucus defeats and kills Antiochus IX, whose son, Antiochus X, contests the claims of the sons of Antiochus VIII to the throne; Tigranes annexes Sophene and invades Cappadocia

94—Antiochus X defeats and kills Seleucus, whose brother, Antiochus XI, contests Antiochus X's position at Antioch; the Roman general Sulla liberates Cappadocia; Parthians and Romans make first contact

93—Antiochus X defeats and kills Antiochus XI; he continues his wars against Philip and Demetrius; Sinatruces rebels in the east against Mithridates

93/92—Sinatruces, having gained control of most of the Iranian plateau, seizes Susa

92—Tigranes invades Cappadocia

91—Mithridates dies fighting Sinatruces; Mithridates' son, Gotarzes I, becomes king of the Parthians, contesting Sinatruces' claim

89/88—Parthians defeat and kill Antiochus X

87—Gotarzes defeats Sinatruces, forcing him into exile; however, Gotarzes soon after dies; his brother, Mithridates III, becomes king of the Parthians; Parthians defeat and capture Demetrius; Parthians establish Philip at Antioch as a Parthian vassal; Antiochus XII contests Philip's throne from Damascus

Greek and Roman Literary Sources

Ael. *NA*	Claudius Aelianus (Roman rhetorician, ca. early third century CE), *On the Nature of Animals*
Ael. *VH*	Aelianus, *Various History*
Aesop	Aesop (Greek fabulist, ca. early sixth century)
Amm. Mar.	Ammianus Marcellinus (Roman soldier and historian, ca. late fourth century CE). Trans. J. Rolfe, 1939–1950
Ampelius	Lucius Ampelius (Roman tutor, dates unknown, perhaps late second or early third century CE)
Appian *Mithr.*	Appian of Alexandria (Roman historian of Greek background, ca. middle second century CE), *The Mithridatic Wars*
Appian *Syr.*	Appian, *The Syrian Wars*. Trans. H. White, 1899
Arnob.	Arnobius (Roman Christian writer, ca. early fourth century CE)
Arr. *Anab.*	Arrian of Nicomedia (Roman general and historian of Greek background, ca. middle second century CE), *Anabasis of Alexander*
Arr. *Parth.*	Arrian, *Parthica*
Athen.	Athenaeus of Naucratis (Roman rhetorician and grammarian of Greek background, ca. late second century CE). Trans. C. Yonge, 1854
Caes. *BG*	Gaius Julius Caesar (Roman general and statesman, ca. middle first century), *The Gallic War*
Callim.	Callimachus (Greek poet, ca. middle third century)
Cat.	Gaius Valerius Catullus (Roman poet, ca. middle first century)

ChronPasc.	Paschale Chronicle (Byzantine chronicle of world history, ca. early seventh century CE)
ChronSynt.	Chronographeion Syntomon (Byzantine chronicle of rulers, ca. middle ninth century CE)
Cic. *Man.*	Marcus Tullius Cicero (Roman politician and orator, ca. middle first century), *For the Manilian Law*
Cic. *Ver.*	Cicero, *Against Verres.*
Cosmas Indicop.	Cosmas Indicopleustes (Catholic monk and geographer, ca. middle fifth century CE)
Ctesias	Ctesias of Cnidus (Greek historian, ca. early fourth century)
Curt.	Quintus Curtius Rufus (Roman historian, ca. middle first century CE). Trans. J. Rolfe, 1946
Dio	Cassius Dio (Roman historian of Greek background, ca. early third century CE). Trans. E. Cary, 1914–1927
Diod.	Diodorus Siculus (Greek historian, ca. late first century). Trans. R. Geer, 1947; C. Welles, 1963; F. Walton, 1957–1967
Dion. Hal.	Dionysius of Halicarnassus (Greek historian, ca. late first century to early first century CE)
Eus. *Chron.*	Eusebius of Caesarea (Roman historian and Christian bishop of Greek background, ca. early fourth century CE), *Chronicle*. Trans. A. Smith, 2008
Eutrop.	Flavius Eutropius (Roman historian, ca. late fourth century CE)
ExcBarb.	Excerpta Latina Barbari (Latin chronicle of world history poorly translated from Greek, ca. middle eighth century CE)
Florus	Florus (Roman historian, ca. early second century CE). Trans. E. Forster, 1929
Front. *Strat.*	Sextus Julius Frontinus (Roman statesman and general, ca. late first century CE), *Stratagems*
Herod.	Herodotus (Greek historian, ca. middle fifth century). Trans. A. Godley, 1920
Herodian	Herodian (Roman historian, ca. early third century CE)
Hieron. *Chron.*	Eusebius Sophronius Hieronymus or St. Jerome (Roman theologian and historian, ca. early fifth century CE), *Chronicle*
Hieron. *Daniel*	Hieronymus or St. Jerome, *Commentary on Daniel*
Hor. *Od.*	Horace (Roman poet, ca. late first century), *Odes*

Isid.	Isidore of Charax (Greek geographer, ca. late first century or early first century CE)
Jo. Antioch.	John of Antioch (Byzantine monk and chronicler, ca. early to middle seventh century CE). Trans. S. Mariev, 2008
Jo. Mal.	John Malalas (Byzantine chronicler, ca. middle to late sixth century CE)
Jos. *Ant.*	Flavius Josephus (Roman historian of Jewish background, ca. late first century CE), *Antiquities of the Jews.* Trans. W. Whiston, 1895
Jos. *Bell.*	Josephus, *The Jewish Wars*
Justin	Justinus (Roman historian, dates unknown, perhaps late second century to late fourth century CE), *Epitome (of Pompeius Trogus,* ca. *early first century* CE). Trans. J. Watson, 1853
Justin *Prol.*	Justinus, *Prologi*
Livy	Titus Livius (Roman historian, ca. early first century CE), *Ab Urbe Condita*
Livy *Epit.*	Livy, *Periochae Epitome*, ca. fourth century CE
Livy *Obseq.*	Livy, *Obsequens*
Lucan *Phar.*	Marcus Annaeus Lucan (Roman poet, ca. middle first century CE), *Pharsalia*
Lucian *Hist. Conscr.*	Lucian of Samosata (Roman rhetorician of Greek background, ca. middle to late second century CE), *How to Write History*
Lucian *Macr.*	Lucian, *Long Livers*
I–II, IV–V Maccabees	(Deuterocanonical books of the Bible, ca. late second century), *Books of the Maccabees.* Trans. H. Cotton, 1832; J. Lendering, 2006
Memnon	Memnon of Heraclea (Roman historian of Greek background, dates unknown, perhaps first or second century CE)
Moses	Moses of Chorene (Armenian historian, ca. middle to late fifth century CE)
Orosius	Paulus Orosius (Christian historian, ca. early fifth century CE), *Seven Books of History against the Pagans*
Ovid *Ars Am.*	Publius Ovidius Naso (Roman poet, ca. early first century CE), *The Art of Love*
Paus.	Pausanias (Roman geographer of Greek background, ca. middle second century CE)

Phaed.	Phaedrus (Roman fabulist, ca. early to middle first century CE)
Phlegon	Phlegon of Tralles (Roman author of Greek background, ca. second century CE)
Photius *Bib.*	Photius of Constantinople (Byzantine church leader and chronicler, ca. middle to late ninth century CE), *The Library*
Plaut. *Truc.*	Plautus, *Truculentus* (Roman playwright, ca. early second century)
Pliny *NH*	Gaius Plinius Secundus (Roman writer and natural philosopher, ca. middle first century CE), *Natural History*. Trans. J. Bostock and H. Riley, 1855
Plut. *Alex.*	Plutarch (Roman biographer and essayist of Greek background, ca. early second century CE), *Life of Alexander*. Trans. B. Perrin, 1919
Plut. *Ant.*	Plutarch, *Life of Antony*
Plut. *Apophtheg. Rom.*	Plutarch, *Sayings of the Romans*
Plut. *Crass.*	Plutarch, *Life of Crassus*. Trans. B. Perrin, 1916
Plut. *Demet.*	Plutarch, *Life of Demetrius*
Plut. *Luc.*	Plutarch, *Life of Lucullus*
Plut. *Mor.*	Plutarch, *Moralia*
Plut. *Nic. and Crass.*	Plutarch, *Comparison of Nicias and Crassus*
Plut. *Pomp.*	Plutarch, *Life of Pompey*
Plut. *Reg. Imp.*	Plutarch (attributed), *Sayings of Kings and Commanders*
Plut. *Sul.*	Plutarch, *Life of Sulla*
Polyaen.	Polyaenus (Roman military strategist, ca. middle to late second century CE)
Polyb.	Polybius (Roman historian and Greek statesman, ca. middle second century), *The Histories*. Trans. W. Paton, 1922–1927
Pomp. Mela	Pomponius Mela (Roman geographer, ca. early to middle first century CE)
Porph.	Porphyry (Roman philosopher, ca. late third century CE)
Posid.	Posidonius (Greek philosopher and historian, ca. early first century)
Ruf. Fest.	Rufus Festus (Roman historian, ca. late fourth century CE)
Sebeos	Sebeos (Armenian bishop, ca. seventh century CE). Trans. R. Thomson, 1978.
Solinus	Gaius Julius Solinus (Roman grammarian, ca. early to middle third century CE)

Strabo	Strabo (Roman historian, geographer, and philosopher of Greek background, ca. early first century CE). Trans. H. Jones, 1917–1932. Note also D. Roller, 2014
Suet. *Caes.*	Gaius Suetonius Tranquillus (Roman biographer, ca. early second century CE), *Life of Caesar*
Suet. *Dom.*	Suetonius, *Life of Domitian*
Syncellus	George Syncellus (Byzantine chronicler and ecclesiastic, ca. early ninth century CE)
Tac. *Agr.*	Publius Cornelius Tacitus (Roman statesman and historian, ca. early second century CE), *Agricola*
Tac. *Ann.*	Tacitus, *Annals*
Tac. *Hist.*	Tacitus, *Histories*. Trans. C. Moore and J. Jackson, 1925–1937
Thuc.	Thucydides (Greek historian, ca. late fifth century). Trans. C. Smith, 1919–1923
Val. Max.	Valerius Maximus (Roman rhetorician, ca. early first century CE)
Vell. Pat.	Marcus Velleius Paterculus (Roman soldier and historian, ca. early first century CE)
Virg. *Geog.*	Publius Vergilius Maro (Roman poet, ca. late first century), *Georgics*
Xen. *Cyrop.*	Xenophon (Greek general and historian, ca. middle fourth century), *Cyropaedia*
Xen. *Hell.*	Xenophon, *Hellenica*
Zos.	Zosimus (Byzantine historian, ca. late fifth to early sixth centuries CE), *New History*

Genealogical Table of the Early Arsacids

(This table offers a possible, perhaps likely reconstruction; however, the full genealogy of the early Arsacids remains indefinite.)

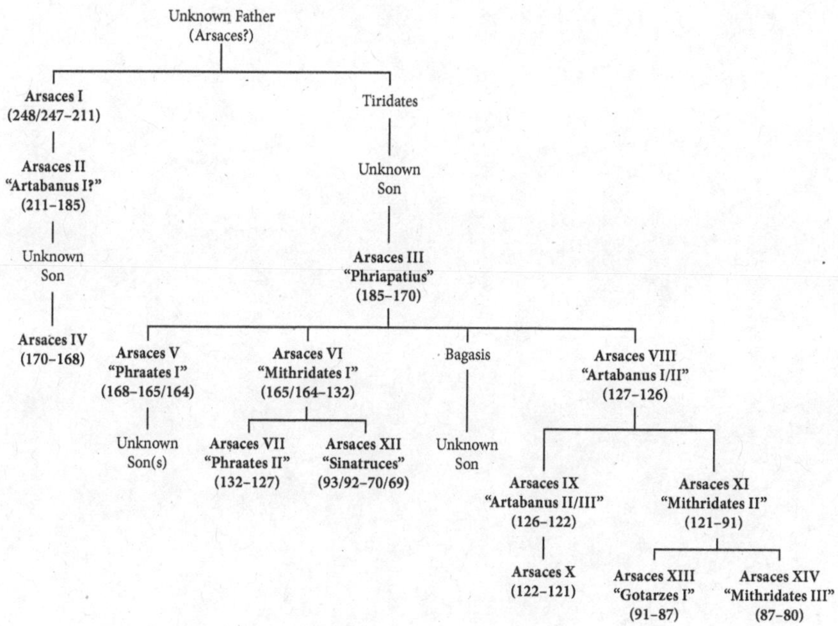

Parthian Kings and Select Coins

(For more information regarding all coins referenced in this study, note the Sellwood Type Numbers Index with accompanying images at www.parthia.com/parthia_sellwood.htm.)

Arsaces I (248/247–211)

FIGURE 1
S1.1—Silver Hemidrachm, Nisa (?), Greek inscription: "[the coin] of Arsaces, Autocrat (ΑΡΣΑΚΟΥ [Α]ΥΤΟΚΡΑΤΟΡΟΣ)."

FIGURE 2
S2.1—Silver Drachm, Nisa (?), Greek inscription: "[the coin] of Arsaces, Autocrat (ΑΡΣΑΚΟΥ ΑΥΤΟΚΡΑΤΟΡΟΣ)."

Arsaces II "Artabanus I?" (211–185)

FIGURE 3
S6.1—Silver Drachm, Rhagae (?), Greek inscription: "[the coin] of Arsaces (ΑΡΣΑΚΟΥ)."

FIGURE 4
S7.1—Silver Drachm, Hecatompylus, Greek inscription: "[the coin] of Arsaces (ΑΡΣΑΚΟΥ)."

Arsaces III "Phriapatius" (185–170)

Figure 5

S8.2—Bronze Chalkous, Hecatompylus, Greek inscription: "[the coin] of Arsaces (ΑΡΣΑΚΟΥ)."

Figure 6

S9.1—Silver Drachm, Hecatompylus, Greek inscription: "[the coin] of King Arsaces (ΒΑΣΙΛΕΩΣ ΑΡΣΑΚΟΥ)."

Figure 7

S10.1—Silver Drachm, Hecatompylus, Greek inscription: "[the coin] of the Great King Arsaces (ΒΑΣΙΛΕΩΣ ΜΕΓΑΛΟΥ ΑΡΣΑΚΟΥ)."

FIGURE 8
S10.15—Silver Drachm, Hecatompylus, Greek inscription: "[the coin] of the Divine King Arsaces (ΒΑΣΙΛΕΩΣ ΘΕΟΥ ΑΡΣΑΚΟΥ)."

Arsaces IV (170–168)

FIGURE 9
S9.2—Silver Drachm, Nisa, Greek inscription: "[the coin] of King Arsaces (ΒΑΣΙΛΕΩΣ ΑΡΣΑΚΟΥ)."

Arsaces V "Phraates I" (168–165/164)

FIGURE 10
S9.3—Silver Drachm, Syrinx, Greek inscription: "[the coin] of King Arsaces (ΒΑΣΙΛΕΩΣ ΑΡΣΑΚΟΥ)."

FIGURE 11
S10.9—Silver Drachm, unknown mint, Greek inscription: "[the coin] of the Great King Arsaces (ΒΑΣΙΛΕΩΣ ΜΕΓΑΛΟΥ ΑΡΣΑΚΟΥ)."

Arsaces VI "Mithridates I" (165/164–132)

FIGURE 12
S10.17—Silver Drachm, Hecatompylus, Greek inscription: "[the coin] of the Great King Arsaces, Son of a Divine Father (ΒΑΣΙΛΕΩΣ ΜΕΓΑΛΟΥ ΑΡΣΑΚΟΥ ΘΕΟΠΑ ΤΟΡ[ΟΣ])."

FIGURE 13
S12.6—Bronze Octochalkous, Ecbatana, Greek inscription: "[the coin] of King Arsaces (ΒΑΣΙΛΕΩΣ ΑΡΣΑΚΟΥ)."

FIGURE 14
S13.2—Silver Tetradrachm, Seleucia, Greek inscription: "[the coin] of the Great King Arsaces, Admirer of the Greeks (ΒΑΣΙΛΕΩΣ ΜΕΓΑΛΟΥ ΑΡΣΑΚΟΥ ΦΙΛΕΛΛΗΝΟΣ)."

FIGURE 15
S13.10—Silver Drachm, Seleucia, Greek inscription: "[the coin] of the Great King Arsaces (ΒΑΣΙΛΕΩΣ ΜΕΓΑΛΟΥ ΑΡΣΑΚΟΥ)."

Arsaces VI "Mithridates I" (165/164–132) and Bagasis

FIGURE 16
S12.4—Silver Obol, Ecbatana, Greek inscription: "[the coin] of the Great King Arsaces (Β[ΑΣΙΛΕΩΣ ΜΕΓ]ΑΛ[Ο]Υ ΑΡΣΑΚΟΥ)."

Arsaces VII "Phraates II" (132–127)

FIGURE 17
S17.1—Silver Tetradrachm, Seleucia, Greek inscription: "[the coin] of the Great King Arsaces, Bearer of Victory" (ΒΑΣΙΛΕΩΣ ΜΕΓΑΛΟΥ ΑΡΣΑΚΟΥ ΝΙΚΙΦΟΡΟΥ)."

FIGURE 18
S16.10—Silver Drachm, Nisa, Greek inscription: "[the coin] of the Great King Arsaces, Son of a Divine Father (ΒΑΣΙΛΕΩΣ ΜΕΓΑΛΟΥ ΑΡΣΑΚΟΥ ΘΕΟΠΑΤΟΡΟΣ)."

Arsaces VIII "Artabanus I/II" (127–126)

FIGURE 19
S18.1—Silver Tetradrachm, Seleucia, Greek inscription: "[the coin] of King Arsaces (ΒΑΣΙΛΕΩΣ ΑΡΣΑΚΟΥ)."

Arsaces IX "Artabanus II/III" (126–122)

Figure 20
S19.2—Silver Drachm, Ecbatana (?), Greek inscription: "[the coin] of the Great King Arsaces, Son of a Divine Father (ΒΑΣΙΛΕΩΣ ΜΕΓΑΛΟΥ ΑΡΣΑΚΟΥ ΘΕΟΠΑΤΟΡ [ΟΣ])."

Figure 21
S21.3—Silver Tetradrachm, Seleucia, Greek inscription: "[the coin] of King Arsaces (ΒΑΣΙΛΕΩΣ ΑΡΣΑΚΟΥ)."

Figure 22
S20.1—Silver Drachm, Ecbatana, Greek inscription: "[the coin] of the Great King Arsaces, Brother-Loving (ΒΑΣΙΛΕΩΣ ΜΕΓΑΛΟΥ ΑΡΣΑΚΟΥ ΦΙΛΑΔΕΛΦΟΥ)."

FIGURE 23
S22.4—Silver Drachm, Margiane, Greek inscription: "[the coin] of King Arsaces, Brother-Loving, Admirer of the Greeks ([Β]ΑΣΙΛΕΩ[Σ] ΑΡΣΑΚΟ[Υ] ΦΙΛΑΔΕΛΦΟΥ ΦΙΛΕΛΛΗΝΟΣ)."

Arsaces X (122–121)

FIGURE 24
S23.2—Silver Tetradrachm, Seleucia, Greek inscription: "[the coin] of King Arsaces, Illustrious, Admirer of the Greeks (ΒΑΣΙΛΕΩΣ ΑΡΣΑΚΟΥ ΕΠΙΦΑΝΟΥΣ ΦΙΛΕΛΛ ΗΝΟΣ)."

Arsaces XI "Mithridates II" (121–91)

FIGURE 25
S24.4—Silver Tetradrachm, Seleucia, Greek inscription: "[the coin] of the Great King Arsaces, Illustrious (ΒΑΣΙΛΕΩΣ ΜΕΓΑΛΟΥ ΑΡΣΑΚΟΥ ΕΠΙΦΑΝΟΥΣ)."

FIGURE 26
S27.1—Silver Drachm, Rhagae, Greek inscription: "[coin of] the Great King of Kings Arsaces, Illustrious (ΒΑΣΙΛΕΩΣ ΒΑΣΙΛΕΩΝ ΜΕΓΑΛΟΥ ΑΡΣΑΚΟΥ ΕΠΙΦΑΝΟ ΥΣ)."

FIGURE 27
S28.5—Silver Drachm, Rhagae, Greek inscription: "[coin of] the Great King of Kings Arsaces, Illustrious (ΒΑΣΙΛΕΩΣ ΒΑΣΙΛΕΩΝ ΜΕΓΑΛΟΥ ΑΡΣΑΚΟΥ ΕΠΙΦΑΝΟ ΥΣ)."

Arsaces XII "Sinatruces" (93/92–70/69)

FIGURE 28
S33.5—Silver Drachm, Rhagae, Greek inscription: "[coin of] the Great King Arsaces, Son of a Defied Father, Conqueror (ΒΑΣΙΛΕΩΣ ΜΕΓΑΛΟΥ ΑΡΣΑΚΟΥ ΘΕΟΠΑΤΡΟΥ ΝΙΚΑΤΟΡΟΣ)."

Arsaces XIII "Gotarzes I" (91–87)

FIGURE 29
S29.2—Silver Drachm, Rhagae, Greek inscription: "[coin of] the King of Kings Arsaces, Just, Beneficent, and Admirer of the Greeks (ΒΑΣΙΛΕΩΣ ΒΑΣΙΛΕΩΝ ΑΡΣΑΚΟΥ ΔΙΚΑΙΟΥ ΕΥΕΡΓΕΤΟΥ ΚΑΙ ΦΙΛΕΛΛΗΝ[ΟΣ])."

Arsaces XIV "Mithridates III" (87–80)

FIGURE 30
S31.6—Silver Drachm, Rhagae, Greek inscription: "[the coin] of the Great King Arsaces, Autocrat, Father-Loving, Illustrious, Admirer of the Greeks (ΒΑΣΙΛΕΩΣ ΜΕΓΑΛΟΥ ΑΡΣΑΚΟΥ ΑΥΤΟΚΡΑΤΟΡΟΣ ΦΙΛΟΠΑΤΟΡΟΣ ΕΠΙΦΑΝΟΥΣ ΦΙΛΕ ΛΛΗΝΟΣ)."

Introduction: Sources and Theory

Alexander the Great's victory at the Battle of Gaugamela in 331 BCE was a stunning upset.[1] After Alexander and his famed Companion cavalry pierced the heart of Darius III's battle lines upon the flat plains of northern Mesopotamia, the Persian king fled the field, destined never again to offer significant resistance to the invaders. For nearly three years, Alexander and his army of well-trained Greek and Macedonian soldiers had won a series of major victories against the Achaemenid Persians and absorbed the lands of Anatolia, the Levant, and Egypt into the expanding Macedonian Empire. Although he was outnumbered considerably, Alexander won his most decisive victory at Gaugamela, which opened the rest of the Middle East to conquest. Over the next seven years, Alexander fought difficult campaigns in what is today Iran, Turkmenistan, Afghanistan, and Pakistan before returning to Babylon as the king of Macedon, pharaoh of Egypt, king of Persia, and leader of a much-expanded Greek world.

Under Alexander, the Macedonians seized the Middle East and ushered in the Hellenistic era. They did not completely relinquish their dominant hold over the region for over two centuries. Yet Alexander's sudden death in 323 ended any hope of a universal empire as his generals quickly turned to violent confrontations to divide his expansive kingdom. The wars of the Diadochi or "Successors" were endemic and destructive; however, Macedonian rule over the Middle East endured in the form of the largest of the Successor kingdoms, the Seleucid Empire, founded by one of Alexander's former commanders, Seleucus I Nicator ("the Victor"), when he seized Babylon in 312/311.

At its greatest extent in the late fourth and early third centuries, the Seleucid Empire stretched from western Anatolia and the Levant to the Central Asian steppe and the Hindu Kush. It was a massive, heterogeneous kingdom that relied on the military power and political prestige of its Greek-speaking kings to survive. From its power base in Syria, the Seleucid dynasty looked to exert control over its various Greek, Macedonian, and indigenous peoples. This was no simple task as external pressures from Hellenistic rivals in the Eastern Mediterranean and tribal confederations from the Central Asian steppe threatened the stability

1. Again, all dates in this study are BCE unless otherwise indicated.

Reign of Arrows. Nikolaus Leo Overtoom, Oxford University Press (2020). Oxford University Press.
DOI: 10.1093/oso/9780190888329.001.0001.

and indeed the viability of the kingdom. By the middle of the third century, a series of external challenges and internal disputes set the stage for a new and revolutionary phase of history in the Hellenistic Middle East. Over the next century and a half, a new power arose in the east to dominate the region, the Parthians. As Alexander had foreseen on his deathbed, hegemony over the Middle East once again fell "τῷ κρατίστῳ (to the strongest)."[2]

This study at its core is a reevaluation of the political and military encounters that helped shape the international environment of the Hellenistic world from the middle third to the early first centuries. This study combines traditional historical approaches, such as source criticism and the integration of material evidence, with the incorporation of modern international relations theory to help reconstruct the rise of the Parthians (or Arsacids) to dominance over their Greek, Iranian, and Central Asian neighbors in the Hellenistic Middle East. This new theoretical approach will help illuminate different spatial and geographical perspectives of the ancient world and provide a fresh perspective on ancient international relations in this period. It is a major effort to synthesize a wide array of especially recent scholarship across numerous fields of study to present the reader with the most cogent, well-rounded, and up-to-date account of the intersections of Hellenistic and Parthian history possible in this period. Its primary focus is the volatile development of the Parthian state from the humblest of origins to the heights of empire. Yet much effort also has been put forth to reinvestigate the important geopolitical developments of the numerous competing major, middling, and minor states within the Hellenistic Middle East, especially the Seleucid Empire and Bactria, to illustrate the highly militarized and competitive international environment of the Hellenistic Middle East and emphasize its wide-ranging influence on international relations and state decision-making in this period. The territorial and thematic expanse of this study will lend itself not only to Hellenistic, Parthian, and ancient Middle Eastern studies, but also to ancient Near Eastern, Central Asian, Indian, and even Roman studies.

The main points of emphasis in this study are as follows. It provides a comprehensive reevaluation of early Parthian political and military history through a new interdisciplinary approach to provide new perspectives on spatial realities, international relations, and state decision-making in the Hellenistic Middle East. It investigates how the Parthians balanced security threats and geopolitical concerns both internally and along their frontiers to become a major imperial power. It explores the formation of the Arsacids' imperial identity and the motivations behind it. Further, it aims to demonstrate that the adaptability and distinctiveness of the Parthians' social, political, and military makeup allowed them to excel against stronger, often better-situated competitors.

2. Diod. 17.117.4. Note Antela-Bernardez 2011.

This work also emphasizes the considerable agency of a wide range of states and statesmen within the Hellenistic Middle East to avoid more Rome-centric understandings of the decline of Greek and Macedonian rule in the east. For instance, it rejects the Rome-centric scholarly tradition that the Romans, rather than the Parthians, were responsible for the "irreversible weakening of the Seleukid Kingdom."[3] This tradition stems largely from the biased and misinformed perspectives of our surviving Greek and Roman sources. However, by making a concerted effort to understand state decision-making from an alternate point of view than the generally accepted western tradition, this study attempts to offer a more inclusive and better representative account of the motivations and methods of eastern states in this period. The picture that emerges is one of eastern states often acting aggressively and proactively, rather than passively and reactively, in their international relations. Only recently have scholars begun to place Parthia within a broader Eurasian perspective and appreciate the considerable geopolitical concerns that the Parthians had to confront along their vast and vulnerable frontiers.[4] As the Parthians undertook efforts to expand their power on both their western and eastern frontiers, multiple security concerns both fed Parthian ambitions and imposed limitations.

Unfortunately, there are unavoidable textual and material limitations to our definitive understanding of early Parthian history and the history of the larger Hellenistic Middle East in this period. Our sources for Parthian history are few, scattered, and almost all from a Greek and Roman perspective.[5] Therefore, this study is a new interpretation of the political and military history of the Hellenistic Middle East based upon what can be considered the most compelling and probable reconstruction of the available evidence. This study offers a well-conceived, well-researched assessment of the rise of the Parthian state within the Hellenistic Middle East to help create a platform for further scholarly debate on the topic. Compared to scholarly attention paid to the other major pre-Islamic empires of the Middle East—the empires of the Achaemenids, Seleucids, and Sasanians—the Parthians receive little appreciation. This led one scholar recently to describe the Parthian era as "among the least known in Oriental history and archaeology."[6] Meanwhile, in the contexts of world history, one historian recently noted, "It is this region [Parthia] and ruling power [the Arsacids] that has been missed in the coverage of world history, as Rome and China have been the main focus for world historians."[7] Thus, this study helps bring the Parthian Empire further

3. Gabelko 2009: 52. Note Coşkun and Engels 2019.

4. See Dąbrowa 1983; Wolski 1993; Wiesehöfer 1998; Olbrycht 1998a; id. 1998b; id. 1998c; Wheeler 2002: 287; Olbrycht 2003; Dąbrowa 2013; Olbrycht 2015a; id. 2016a; Overtoom 2016a; id. 2016d; Gregoratti 2017b: 125–27.

5. Lerouge-Cohen 2007: 21–39; Hackl, Jacobs, and Weber 2010b.

6. See Hauser 2013: 728–30; Gregoratti 2015a: 203–4; Sampson 2015: xvi, 32.

7. Daryaee 2015: 286.

out of the shadows of history and sheds new light on the Parthians' important contributions to the geopolitical developments of the Middle Eastern world.[8]

With the sometimes severe limitations of our available sources in mind, the potential insights that the theoretical framework of modern international relations theory offers to the study of Parthian political history are quite exciting. In fact, this study is the first comprehensive attempt to apply modern international relations theory to the interpretation of Parthian expansionism and interactions with neighboring states.[9] The application of international relations theory helps provide a fuller appreciation of the geopolitical developments of the Parthian state and may help us overcome some of the limitations of our sources; however, it must be said that it is not a panacea and must be utilized carefully within the parameters of our surviving literary and physical evidence. Therefore, recent work in archaeology and numismatics is invaluable to the historical reconstruction of the Hellenistic Middle East, and this study is in line with other recent efforts to reevaluate the growth of the Parthian state through the investigation of new evidence, such as cuneiform records, archaeological evidence, and numismatics.[10]

There have been relatively few comprehensive studies of the formation, growth, and international relations of the Parthian state. Most studies of this sort are either outdated, cursory, or, in the case of numerous recent attempts, of limited or questionable academic merit.[11] Furthermore, interest in much later Roman and Parthian interactions dominates the field.[12] Although there is growing interest

8. Colledge called the Arsacids "mostly shadowy figures." Colledge 1967: 176.

9. Note also Overtoom 2016a; id. 2019a.

10. See Lerner 1999; Assar 2000; id. 2001a; id. 2001b; id. 2004; id. 2005a; id. 2006c; id. 2006d; Dąbrowa 2008 [2009]; id. 2009; id. 2010; Olbrycht 2010a; id. 2010b; Hackl, Jacobs, and Weber 2010b; id. 2010c; Shayegan 2011; Dąbrowa 2011a; id. 2012; Ellerbrock and Winkelmann 2012; Hauser 2013; Faghfoury 2020. Grajetzki challenges the narrow view of Parthian history and culture as an afterthought or degeneration of Roman or Greek examples, demonstrating that the major cultural transformations of the east occurred under the Parthians, not their Hellenistic predecessors or Sasanian successors. Grajetzki 2011. Note Lerouge-Cohen 2007; id. 2009b; id. 2010; id. 2013; Gregoratti 2015b: 14–15; Olbrycht 2017b: 4–5. For reevaluations of Romano-Parthian relations, note Kennedy 1996; Wheeler 2002; Ferguson 2005, Schlude 2009; Overtoom 2016c; id. 2017a; Schlude and Rubin 2017; Sampson 2020; Curtis and Magub 2020; Schlude 2020; Overtoom 2021b.

11. Although widely available to general readers, several recent accounts of Parthian history are self-published and unreliable. Collins 2002; Graham 2013; Rea 2013; id. 2014; Charles River Editors 2015; id. 2016; id. 2017; Marić 2018. For available narratives of various periods of Parthian history, note Lewis 1728; Lindsay 1852; Rawlinson 1873; id. 1876 (2002); Tarn 1932; Rostovzteff 1936; Cameron 1936; Debevoise 1938; Ziegler 1964; Stark 1966; Colledge 1967; id. 1977; Schippmann 1980; Bivar 1983; Frye 1984; Lepper and DeVoto 1985; Colledge 1986; Wilcox 1986; Shahbazi 1986a; id. 1986b; Schippmann 1986; Wolski 1993; Campbell 1993; Koshelenko and Pilipko 1999; Frye 2000; Schlude 2009; Sheldon 2010; Assar 2011; Dąbrowa 2012; Hauser 2013; Grainger 2013a; Meulenbroek 2014; Poirot 2014; Sampson 2015; Grainger 2016; McLaughlin 2016: Ch. 12–13; Gregoratti 2016a; id. 2017b; Barnett 2017; Syvänne 2017; Balakhvantsev 2017; Bishop 2018; Fratantuono 2019; Sampson 2020; Curtis and Magub 2020; Sheppard 2020; Schlude 2020; Ellerbrock 2021/2022. The quality of these studies ranges widely from excellent to serviceable; however, few address Parthian history primarily, and those that do are either introductions, summaries, or outdated.

12. In recent years note Schlude 2009; Sheldon 2010; Graham 2013; Rea 2014; Poirot 2014; Sampson 2015; Charles River Editors 2015; id. 2016; McLaughlin 2016: Ch. 12–13; Gregoratti 2017b; Barnett 2017; Syvänne 2017; Bishop 2018; Fratantuono 2019; Sampson 2020; ; Curtis and Magub 2020; Sheppard 2020; Schlude 2020; Overtoom 2021b.

in Parthian studies, no comprehensive monograph dedicated entirely to early Parthian history prior to contact with Rome exists.

Archaeological research on the Parthian era only began to elicit comprehensive attention in the past half-century, severely handicapping Parthian studies prior to the 1970s.[13] In fact, one of the first archaeologists to examine the archaeological traces of the Parthians, Edward Keall, originally described them in the 1960s and 1970s as "lesser mortals" when compared to the other imperial dynasts of the Middle East and referred to the Arsacids as the "political clowns of the millennium."[14] Fortunately, Parthian studies has been a growing field, particularly since the 1990s, and scholars continue to work diligently to discredit such unfounded and negative portrayals of the Parthians.[15] Yet scholars still generally consider Neilson Debevoise's 1938 study of the Parthians to be the best available summary of Parthian political history, despite the acknowledgment that his history "begs for revision."[16] Moreover, scholarly attention has been lacking or inadequate in deciphering Parthian motives for expansion and reasons for Parthian success within the larger contexts of the international environment of the Hellenistic Middle East. Scholarship on early Parthian history often suffers from what international relations theorists call "unit-attribute" theory, which is the belief that the internal forces of a single state determine external outcomes. Unfortunately, such an approach generally overlooks possible external explanations from the larger international environment. Although the internal characteristics of states and statesmen remain important since the answers to state (or unit) success ultimately lie within them, on their own they lack scope.[17] States exist within competitive interstate systems, and by overlooking a system-level analysis of geopolitical developments, scholars ignore half the picture.

A good example of misguided "unit-attribute" theory in Parthian studies is the notion that Parthian success stemmed from a "nationalistic" Iranian backlash against the Hellenistic Seleucids. Theodor Mommsen described the Parthian rebellion and war against the Seleucids as a nationalistic crusade against Hellenism.[18] George Rawlinson described the Parthian rebellion as a barbarian, nationalistic slave uprising against Greek masters in an attempt to reclaim Asia for the Asians.[19] Eshan Yarshater argued that an ethnic nationalism emerged under the Parthians as a reaction to Hellenism.[20] Alireza Shahbazi describes the

13. Sherwin-White and Kuhrt 1993: 88; Dąbrowa 2012: 25; Callieri and Chaverdi 2013: 690; Hauser 2013: 728–30.

14. Keall 1967; id. 1975; id. 1977a; id. 1977b; id. 1982.

15. Keall eventually offered a more favorable and balanced account of the Parthians. Id. 1994. However, the legacy of the disparagement of the Parthians continues to motivate Parthian scholarship. See Gregoratti 2017a.

16. Wheeler 2002: 291; Hauser 2013: 744.

17. Geller and Singer 1998: 47, 50–51, 67; Eckstein 2006: 27–28. Note Ñaco del Hoyo and Sánchez 2018.

18. Mommsen 1856 (1903): iii 286–90, iv 421, 433; v 157. Manandyan rejected Mommsen and Reinach's depictions of "national reactions" in the east against Rome. Manandyan 1940 (2007): 4. Note Reinach 1890.

19. Rawlinson 1876 (2002): 21, 24, 41, 97–98, 105, 118–19.

20. Yarshater 1983: xxix, xxxviii.

Parthians as having a "strong national identity" and argues that the first king of the Parthians, Arsaces I (Figures 1–2), wanted "to emphasize his nationalistic and royal aspirations."[21] Moreover, Elias Bickerman argues that with the openness of Greek civilization, the Seleucids "decapitated the native nationalism" of the Iranians.[22] Finally, Gareth Sampson calls Arsaces I's creation of the Parthian state a "native" uprising against the Seleucids.[23] Yet the success of the Parthians was not the result of an eastern reaction against and rejection of Hellenism. In fact, the early Parthian rulers often were *philhellenes* (or friends of the Greeks), and many incorporated this designation into their coinage and titulature.[24] Thus, the "nationalism" theory to explain Parthian success is inaccurate and inappropriate.[25]

Another good example of "unit-attribute" theory in Parthian studies is Joseph Wolski's argument that Parthian success stemmed from the Parthians' eager "restoration" of the image of the Achaemenid Persian Empire.[26] Although the Parthians came to embrace much of Persian culture as they occupied the Middle East, they also adopted Hellenistic cultural aspects and maintained a unique identity of their own.[27] Thus, the "restoration" theory is dismissive and inadequate.[28]

Furthermore, there are other problematic "unit-attribute" explanations worth considering briefly. There is a misguided tradition that describes the Parthians as feeble or passive, blaming the incompetence or weakness of Parthia's enemies, especially the Seleucids, to explain Parthian successes; however, this theory unjustifiably robs the Parthians of their agency and accomplishment.[29] Additionally,

21. Shahbazi 1986a; id. 1990.

22. Bickerman 1983: 17–18. Bickerman's belief that "the Greeks were no racists, and everybody was free to choose the Greek way of life" is simplistic and mistaken. The Greeks developed some of the harshest prejudices and stereotypes of eastern peoples. Note Isaac 2006: Ch. 4.

23. Sampson 2015: 35–41.

24. Wiesehöfer 1994b; Dąbrowa 1998; Frye 2000: 18; Curtis 2000: 25; Dąbrowa 2005 [2006]; id. 2006–2007 [2008]; id. 2008 [2009]; id. 2010a; id. 2010b; id. 2011a; id. 2011d; Assar 2011; Fowler 2013: 5072; Dąbrowa 2014a; Thonemann 2015: 87, 91–96, 105, 114; Grainger 2016: 201–2; Lerner 2017; Olbrycht 2017b. For example, the Arsacids even continued to patronize Greek athletic contests as "friends of the Greeks" at Babylon. *THI* 218 ("The Gymnasium Inscription").

25. Compare Neusner 1963; Wolski 1976a; Schippmann 1986; Shipley 2000: 321; Lerner 2017: 14; Engels 2018: 190. A modern concept such as nationalism is incompatible with the realities of ancient societies and cannot explain the success of the Parthians. Note Overtoom 2016a: 989; Strootman 2018: 140. Colledge noted that subjects of the Parthians "were bound together by no ties of elaborately graded citizenship." Colledge 1967: 75–76. Hoyland similarly rejects the rise of the Arab state in the seventh century CE as a "nationalist enterprise." Hoyland 2015: 61.

26. See esp. Wolski 1966; id. 1976a; id. 1983a; id. 1985a; id. 1993. Note also Chahin 1987: 225; Arnaud 1998: 31; Grainger 2013a: 136; id. 2016: 172. For the Arsacids' use of Persian titulature, note Sellwood 1983: 285; Olbrycht 2013a.

27. Note Shayegan 2011: 210–25; Dąbrowa 2011a; Strootman 2018.

28. Overtoom 2016a: 989.

29. Lindsay 1852: 15–16; Mommsen 1856 (1903): iii 288; Rawlinson 1876 (2002): 24, 33–34, 41, 97–98, 105, 118–19; Breasted 1914 (1944): 752; Vogt 1955: 74; Wolski 1956–1957; Syme 1958: 47, 493–97; Ward 1977: 287, 289; Yarshater 1983: xlix–l; Garlan 1984: 359; Campbell 1993; Warry 1995: 157; Potter 2010: 157–60; Sheldon 2010: 1–2, 6, 10, 21–23, 36–40, 61, 177; Edwell 2013a: 191, 194, 206; id. 2013b: 6051; Grainger 2013a: 185–86; id. 2014: 199, 210; Sampson 2015: 44–45; Grainger 2016. For the supposed weakness of the Seleucids, see Will 1967: i 264ff.; Walbank 1981: 123ff.; Musti 1984. Contra Briant 1987: 42–52; Sancisi-Weerdenburg 1987; Sherwin-White 1987: 2–3; Sherwin-White and Kuhrt 1993: 217, 228–29; Shipley 2000: 291, 321, 324–25, 340; Grainger 2016; Coşkun and Engels 2019.

John Curtis tries to argue that a desire to control the lucrative trade-routes between the eastern and western worlds was a primary motivation for Parthian expansion; however, the sources do not support this conclusion.[30] Greater economic prosperity was a welcome, although arguably inadvertent result of Parthian expansion, and the sources clearly demonstrate that the political security of the state and the military reputation of the Arsacids principally motivated expansion.[31] Finally, the arguments of Susan Sherwin-White and Amélie Kuhrt that the Parthians' expansionism and aggression toward neighbors was endemic and stemmed from their cavalry-based army and their need to find more land for their cavalry-based aristocracy makes Parthian belligerence appear unique and ignores the considerable outside dangers that the Parthians faced from highly militarized and aggressive neighbors.[32] John Poirot's recent conclusion that the Parthians' desires to remain independent motivated early Parthian imperialism, rather than explanations of Parthian land hunger or imperial envy, is a step in the right direction.[33] Yet none of these theories considers Parthian motivations and exceptionalism within the larger context of the international system of states in the ancient world. Ultimately, the great benefit of applying international relations theory to an evaluation of geopolitical developments in the ancient world is that it allows us to gain greater perspective and avoid myopic conclusions through the investigation of systemic pressures within interstate systems, which affected all state decision-making. Thus, this project will fill the above-mentioned gaps in Hellenistic and Parthian studies through a new, more comprehensive, and more interdisciplinary approach to the development of the Parthian state within the larger contexts of the international environment of the Hellenistic Middle East.

I have divided this study into an introduction and six main chapters that chart the development of the Parthian state from a fledgling minor kingdom to an unrivaled world empire within the Hellenistic Middle East, placing emphasis on political, military, and cultural interactions that the Parthians had with their numerous Greek, Iranian, and Central Asian neighbors. Chapter 1, "From Migrants to Masters of the Middle East," considers the reasons for the success of the Parthians in their rise from a minor nomadic group to a dominant imperial force. It analyzes the most important cultural factors of the early Parthian state, namely the versatility of Parthian society, the innovations of the Parthian military, and the early Arsacids' ability to manage and exploit these qualities to the benefit of the state through their capable leadership and dynastic stability. These important qualities of the Parthian state established the exceptional advantages the Parthians needed to create, maintain, and expand their power and influence

30. Curtis 2000: 24–25. Compare Colledge 1967: 80–1; Sellwood 1991; Daryaee 2015: 287; McLaughlin 2016: Chs. 5, 11–13; Gregoratti 2016b.

31. Eckstein comes to similar conclusions regarding Roman imperialism. Eckstein 2007.

32. Sherwin-White and Kuhrt 1993: 89.

33. Poirot 2014: 18 n.37.

within the hotly contested and dangerously competitive international environment of the Hellenistic Middle East.

Chapter 2, "The Emergence of the Parthian State," introduces the establishment of the Parthian state on the Iranian plateau in the middle third century. The unexpected decline of the power of the Seleucid Empire in the 240s because of dynastic turmoil caused a crisis in the Hellenistic Middle East. This crisis encouraged eastern satraps to rebel and the nomadic Parni tribe (known afterward as the Parthians) to invade northeastern Iran. The successful invasion of the Parni to seize Parthia and establish a new kingdom, paired with the sudden rise of their regional power and the failure of the Seleucids to eliminate this new threat, helped create a new interstate system in which the Seleucids, Parthians, and the newly independent Bactrians shared power. The sweeping success of the first Parthian king, Arsaces I, established Parthia as a limited regional power; however, its existence for several decades remained precarious.

Chapter 3, "The Empire Strikes Back," investigates the initial failure of the Seleucids in their attempt to reclaim the lost lands of the east. It discusses the failed eastern expedition of Seleucus II; however, its focus is the sudden renewal of Seleucid power under the determined ruler, Antiochus III, who desired to reestablish Seleucid hegemony over the Iranian plateau. Under Antiochus, the Seleucids retaliated against the recent efforts of the Parthians and Bactrians to establish strong independent kingdoms. His campaign throughout the Middle East in the 200s was the greatest since Alexander the Great. Antiochus took advantage of Parthian and Bactrian disorganization, reclaiming much of Parthia and establishing the new king of the Parthians, Arsaces II (Figures 3–4), as his subordinate allied ruler. This campaign in many ways stunted the growth of the Parthian state for decades; however, Antiochus did not destroy the Arsacids entirely, which allowed them eventually to reassert their power in the region.

Chapter 4, "The Fall of Bactria, the Rise of Parthia," considers the decline of Greek rule in Bactria under the mounting weight of external and internal pressures. Antiochus III successfully subdued Bactria as another subordinate allied kingdom; however, the devastation of nomadic incursions and growing Parthian aggression further undermined the power and authority of the Bactrian kings. The decline of Bactria was in stark contrast to the recovery and consolidation of Parthian power in the first half of the second century. By the latter half of the century, these factors and the sudden decline of Seleucid power to the west once again facilitated the rapid expansion of the Parthian state under a new ambitious ruler, Mithridates I (Figures 12–16). The efforts of the Seleucid king, Demetrius II, in the early 130s to quell the rising threat of the Parthians failed spectacularly, and for the first time the Parthian realm extended into Mesopotamia. The Parthians established an empire and emerged as the only major rival to Seleucid power in the Hellenistic Middle East.

Chapter 5, "The Climax of the Seleucid-Parthian Rivalry," focuses on the contexts and consequences of the last great Seleucid campaign in the Middle East. The new rivalry of the Seleucids and Parthians was highly volatile. Yet the potential strength of the Seleucid state remained considerable under a strong ruler. The enthusiastic Seleucid king, Antiochus VII, became determined to reestablish the undisputed power of the Seleucid Empire throughout Mesopotamia and the Iranian plateau. His grand campaign against the Parthians in the early 120s was the greatest threat to the survival of the Parthian state since the campaign of Antiochus III almost a century before. Unfortunately for the Seleucids, it also culminated in the greatest defeat in their history. With their decisive victory, the Parthians were poised to push their advantage against the Seleucids into the lands of the Near East for the first time. However, a near catastrophic series of nomadic invasions along the eastern frontier of the Parthian Empire demanded the full attention of the Parthians. Once more the Parthians faced a considerable threat to the survival of their state as they suffered multiple severe defeats in their efforts to repulse nomadic incursions into the Iranian plateau. It was not until arguably the greatest of the Parthian monarchs, Mithridates II (Figures 25–27), became the new leader of the Parthians that they emerged as a world power.

Chapter 6, "Parthian Hegemony," emphasizes the efforts of Mithridates II to consolidate and expand his power and prestige to establish the Parthians as an unrivaled imperial force. Through a determined war against the Central Asian tribal confederations, Mithridates emerged as the savior of the empire. After restoring the eastern frontier, he turned his attention to expanding Parthian power and influence over the remaining Hellenistic rivals to the west, particularly Armenia and the dwindling Seleucid state. Mithridates utilized diplomacy and military force to dominate these rivals, expanding the network of vassal kings under his authority and taking the title "King of Kings." The hegemonic campaign he began against the Seleucids eventually culminated in the temporary submission of the Seleucids to Parthian dominance under his immediate successors, ending a century-and-a-half-long rivalry. In the late second and early first centuries, Mithridates established the Parthians for the first time as the undisputed masters of the Hellenistic Middle East.

The Sources and Their Challenges

This study covers a wide range of peoples, places, and events, and therefore it utilizes a considerable array of surviving literary sources on Hellenistic and Parthian history; however, epigraphic and numismatic sources also are of importance because so little of the historical record of the Parthians has survived. In reconstructing Parthian history, we must maneuver through Greek and Roman literary sources that dominate the narrative and often treat the Parthians hostilely or cursorily and mostly from a foreign perspective.[34] Meanwhile, the Armenians, Arabs, and Chinese offer some evidence of Parthian history and culture; however, these sources also often suffer from the above limitations.[35] Scholars must supplement the historical record of the Parthians with material evidence to help recreate acceptable and plausible reconstructions of Parthian history. Therefore, it is appropriate here to discuss briefly the usefulness and restrictiveness of our literary, archaeological, epigraphic, and numismatic evidence on the rise of the Parthian state and the geopolitical developments in the Hellenistic Middle East in the third to the first centuries as they relate specifically to this study.[36]

Unfortunately, no account of the Parthians' history survives from their perspective. The late Roman epitomizer Justin notes that the Augustan Age writer Pompeius Trogus stressed the reserved and taciturn nature of the Parthians, recording that they were "readier to act than speak, and consequently shrouding both their successes and failures in silence."[37] Justin's account of Trogus' work, which attempted in part to record a history of the Parthians up to the reign of Augustus, indicates that Trogus appeared frustrated at this "silence" of the Parthians.[38] The Parthians tended to rely on oral traditions for legends and stories, and therefore many of these were lost or drastically altered before being written down.[39] It is quite possible that the Parthians had not created a thorough or readily available historical record of their rise to power in the Hellenistic Middle East by the Augustan Age at least, leaving Trogus to rely on a collection of Greek authors and Roman observations.[40] Moreover, the succeeding Sasanian Persians viewed the Parthians as unworthy interlopers and the Muslims viewed them as contemptible infidels, and therefore whatever Parthian documents survived in the east into the third century CE were ignored or suppressed in the following centuries.[41] Thus, to attempt to understand the Parthians one must engage the Graeco-Roman literary tradition; however, scholars also rely heavily on

34. Note Wiesehöfer 1998; Dąbrowa 2010a: 123; id. 2012: 21–25; Overtoom 2016c.

35. For Armenian sources, see Hackl, Jacobs, and Weber 2010c: 175–455. For Arabic sources, see id. 455–72. For Chinese sources, see Tao 2007; Hackl, Jacobs, and Weber 2010c: 482–512.

36. For discussions of Parthian sources, note Widengren 1983: 1261–69; Boyce 1983; Wiesehöfer 1998; Wolski 2003; Lerouge-Cohen 2007: 26–37; Dąbrowa 2010a: 123; id. 2012: 21–25; Ellerbrock and Winkelmann 2012: Chs. 1, 8; Hauser 2013: 729–30; Sampson 2015: 186–99; Rezakhani 2016; Wiesehöfer and Müller 2017. For Parthian art and architecture, see Colledge 1967: 115–65; id. 1977; Schlumberger 1983; Mathiesen 1992; Curtis and Stewart 2007; Ellerbrock and Winkelmann 2012: Chs. 5, 12; Invernizzi 2016; Kaim 2016; Wiesehöfer 2016: 217–18; Anderson 2016; Wiesehöfer and Müller 2017.

37. Justin 41.3.8. Scholars continue to debate the dates of Justin, ranging from the second to fourth centuries CE. Note Popov-Reynolds 2013.

38. For a brief introduction to Trogus, see Beck 2013.

39. Curtis and Stewart 2007: 2; Wiesehöfer 2016: 217; Dąbrowa 2016b: 573–75.

40. Yardley 2003; Lerouge-Cohen 2009a; Beck 2013; Müller 2017b.

41. Colledge 1967: 103–4, 174; Nikonorov 2005; Dignas and Winter 2007: 56–62; Hauser 2013: 729–30; Invernizzi 2013; Klein and Wirtz 2013: 5069; Gregoratti 2015b: 14; Wiesehöfer 2016: 217; Overtoom 2016c; Olbrycht 2016d; Ghodrat-Dizaji 2016; Gariboldi 2016; Gyselen 2016. Little was known of the Parthians in the Middle East by the Middle Ages. For example, the tenth and eleventh century CE Persian poet Firdawsī lamented the obscurity of the Arsacids. See Warner and Warner 1912: 211; Assar 2011: 164.

three major alternative sources of information, namely archaeological records, the Babylonian *Astronomical Diaries*, and Parthian coinage.

Material evidence in the form of inscriptions, ostraca, art, architecture, and urban planning helps scholars reconstruct cultural, political, and economic developments within the Parthian state to broaden our understanding of the intricacy and multiculturalism of Parthian society.[42] Field surveys in Iraq, Iran, Afghanistan, and Pakistan, and in particular excavations at Merv, Nisa, Hecatompylus, Susa, Uruk, Babylon, Seleucia-Ctesiphon, Nineveh, Hatra, and Dura Europos, continue to yield valuable evidence that enhances the historical record. Yet interest in the field is relatively new and important sites are difficult to access because of the ongoing instability of the modern Middle East.

The *Astronomical Diaries* are a collection of cuneiform tablets that record a long series of astronomical observations and important events and weather. These tablets offer a rare internal voice to the developments of the Parthian state. For this study they provide invaluable evidence of Parthian rule in Mesopotamia from the 140s to 90s; however, their small geographical focus and restricted detail limit their overall usefulness on their own.[43]

Finally, much Parthian coinage has survived, which helps scholars reconstruct the structure and chronology of the Arsacid dynasty. Moreover, the quality, abundance, and features of these coins provide important insights into periods of internal strife and external conflict, helping scholars identify the objectives of Parthian imperial propaganda.[44] Numismatics is also invaluable to the reconstruction of the history of Parthia's rivals, such as Hellenistic Bactria.[45] Much

42. Note Rostovtzeff 1935; id. 1938; Robert 1963: 76; Pigulevskaja 1963; Diakonoff and Livshits 1966: 143–44 n.28, pls. X–Xa; Robert 1967: 283, 291; Keall 1967; Chaumont 1968: 16–18; id. 1971: 145–47; Sellwood 1972; Keall 1975; Pilipko 1976; Keall 1977a; id. 1977b; Simonetta 1979; Pilipko and Loginov 1980; Keall 1982; Bivar 1983: 33; Lukonin 1983: 687–89; Vogelsang 1985; Koshelenko 1985b; Usmanova, Filanovich, and Koshelenko 1985: 226–42; Colledge 1986; Kawami 1987; Downey 1988; Herrmann 1989; Schmitt 1990; Olbrycht 1993; Herrmann, Kurbansakhatov, et al. 1994: 62; Huyse 1995; id. 1996; Eiland 1996; Bader 1996: 264; Koshelenko, Giabov, and Bader 1996: 308–13, 316–17; Curtis, Hillenbrand, and Rogers 1998; Nikitin 1998; Eiland 1998; Nikonorov 1998b; Potts 1999; Lerner 1999; Curtis 2000; Assar 2000; id. 2001a; id. 2001b; Diakonoff and Livshits 1976–2001; Bernard, Pinault, and Rougemont 2004; Canali De Rossi 2004; Assar 2004; id. 2005a; Merkelbach and Stauber 2005; Rose 2005; Bopearachchi and Boussac 2005; Assar 2006c; id. 2006d; Nokandeh et al. 2006; Invernizzi 2007; Bennison and Gascoigne 2007; Errington and Curtis 2007; Smirnova 2007: 382–83; Dąbrowa 2008 [2009]; id. 2009; id. 2010; Olbrycht 2010a; id. 2010b; Curtis and Stewart 2010; Schippmann 2011; Dąbrowa 2011a; Shayegan 2011; Grajetzki 2011; Ellerbrock and Winkelmann 2012; Rougemont 2012a; id. 2012b; id. 2012c; Wójcikowski 2013; Hauser 2013; Gholami and Assar 2013; Callieri and Chaverdi 2013: 690; Hauser 2013: 728–30; James 2013: 108; Dirven 2013; Canepa 2014a; Nikonorov; 2014; Wiesehöfer 2014; Simpson 2014; Dąbrowa 2014b: 62; Menegazzi 2014; Boucharlat 2014; Canepa 2015; Gregoratti 2015b: 14–15; Dąbrowa 2016a; Olbrycht 2016c; Jakubiak 2016; Kaizer 2016; Olbrycht 2017b; Canepa 2017a; Schlude and Rubin 2017; Canepa 2018; Porada 2019.

43. Note Sachs 1955; Neugebauer 1955a; id. 1955b; Sachs and Hunger 1988; id. 1989; id. 1996; van der Spek 1997–1998; Hunger and Sachs 2001; Potts 2002; Hackl, Jacobs, and Weber 2010c: 1–175; Dąbrowa 2014b: 62; Corò 2017; Haubold, Steele, and Stevens 2019.

44. Note Dąbrowa 2008 [2009]; id. 2010a; Hackl, Jacobs, and Weber 2010b: 589–638; Dąbrowa 2011a; Sinisi 2012; id. 2014.

45. Note Bopearachchi 1991; id. 1991–1992; id. 1993; id. 1998a; Holt 1999; Bopearachchi and Boussac 2005; Holt 2012a; Bopearachchi 2015; Thonemann 2015: 96–102; Kritt 2015; Sinisi 2015; Lerner 2015a; Militký and Mašek 2019.

like the available archaeological record and the surviving *Astronomical Diaries*, the usefulness of Parthian coinage to the reconstruction of Parthian history on its own is limited.[46] Yet, although the relative ambiguity of these eastern sources makes definitive conclusions based upon them difficult, they are important supplements to our Greek and Roman literary evidence.[47]

The Greeks and, particularly, the Romans came to view the Parthians as major rivals and found the Parthians and their history of interest.[48] Although it is fragmentary, Polybius provides our earliest surviving account of Parthian history. He briefly chronicles the eastern campaign of Antiochus III against the Parthians and Bactrians (211–205) from now lost Hellenistic sources.[49] Apollodorus and Posidonius, whose works are lost, and Diodorus Siculus and Isidore of Charax were other Greeks who chronicled aspects of early Parthian society and history.[50] Parthian history eventually became a vibrant and popular literary genre during the Roman imperial period, especially at times of conflict between Rome and Parthia, and the Roman audience became familiar with the eastern foe of Rome. For instance, Cassius Dio, writing in the early third century CE, states, "Now about their [that is, the Parthians'] race and their country and their peculiar customs many have written, and I have no intention of describing them."[51] It is not a coincidence that Livy, Pompeius Trogus, Strabo, Nicolaus of Damascus, Quintus Dellius, and Apollonius wrote their accounts on Parthian history after the defeats of Crassus (54–53) and Antony (36–35) and during Augustus' rivalry with the Parthians.[52] Nor is it a coincidence that Lucan found the Parthians of interest in his poetry during the war between the Romans and Parthians under Nero, nor that Plutarch, Tacitus, Appian, and Arrian wrote their accounts on the Parthians during and after Trajan's Parthian war (114–117 CE), nor that Lucian made mention of new works on the Parthians written after Verus' Parthian war (161–166 CE), nor that Cassius Dio, Asinius Quadratus, and perhaps Justin wrote their accounts on Parthian history after the Severans' wars against Parthia severely damaged the Parthian state (195, 197–198, 216–217 CE), nor, finally, that

46. For Parthian coinage, see Scott 1854; Gardner 1877; Wroth 1903; Petrowicz 1904; Sellwood 1962; Simonetta 1966; Sellwood 1972; id. 1976; Simonetta and Sellwood 1978; Simonetta 1979; Sellwood 1980; Mørkholm 1980; Sellwood 1983; Dilmagnani 1986; Alram 1986b; Shore 1993; Loginov and Nikitin 1996; Nikitin 1998; Simonetta 2001; Assar 2004; id. 2005a; id 2009b; id. 2011; Nelson 2011; Rezakhani 2013; Gholami and Assar 2013; Meadows 2014.

47. Hackl, Jacobs, and Weber 2010b: 492–589; id. 2010c; Dąbrowa 2014b: 62; Sampson 2015: 194.

48. Olbrycht 2004b; Lerouge-Cohen 2007; Overtoom 2016c; Wiesehöfer and Müller 2017.

49. Polyb. 10.27–31. For Polybius, note Walbank 1957–1979; id. 1990; Eckstein 1995; Walbank 2002; Champion 2004; McGing 2010; Hackl, Jacobs, and Weber 2010b: 346–52; Overtoom 2011; id. 2013; Gibson and Harrison 2013; Parmeggiani 2014; Overtoom 2016e.

50. Note Chaumont 1986c; Nikonorov 1998a; Yarrow 2006; Lerouge-Cohen 2007: 26–29; Hackl, Jacobs, and Weber 2010b: 143–47, 190–99, 354–55; McLaughlin 2016: 173–74; Schuol 2017; Hartmann 2017; Hauser 2017; Schmitt 2017; Engels 2017; Nawotka 2017; Müller 2017a.

51. Dio 40.15.1.

52. Lerouge-Cohen 2007: 29–32; Hackl, Jacobs, and Weber 2010b; Sampson 2015: 195–98; Overtoom 2016c; Babnis 2017; Olbrycht 2018. For Nicolaus of Damascus, note Shahin 2018.

Ammianus Marcellinus found the Parthians of interest after Julian's failed invasion of Mesopotamia (363 CE).[53] Unfortunately, the destruction of the Parthian Empire by the Sasanian Persians in the middle 220s CE meant that later Roman writers devoted less attention to Parthian history, and as the European and Middle Eastern worlds drifted apart once more by the end of late antiquity, no Greek or Roman history of the Parthians survived the Middle Ages remotely intact.[54] What remains is a limited and often random collection of references to Parthian society and history based upon various known and unknown lost works of antiquity, which provides a broken and often cursory account of the Parthians through the eyes of their rivals.[55]

The most important and well-rounded of the surviving accounts of early Parthian history is Justin's third century CE epitome of Pompeius Trogus' *Historiae Philippicae*, which was a universal history of the eastern world from the ancient Assyrians to the Parthians into the reign of Augustus in forty-four books and which was written during Augustus' reign.[56] Nothing of Trogus' original work survives; however, he appears to have integrated several Greek authors, such as Apollodorus, Timagenes, Ephors, Timaeus, Duris, Posidonius, and Polybius, into his narrative, while maintaining his own conclusions on the subject matter.[57] Scholars continue to debate the extent to which Justin retained the original language and ideas of Trogus in his epitome; however, most scholars now accept that Justin used Trogus' work extensively as a framework but reworked it to his own moralistic ends.[58] In particular, Justin was not interested in Trogus' philosophy or historical approach, abbreviating or omitting what did not fit his own rhetorical objectives and ignoring historical accuracy and chronological precision when it suited him.[59] Although scholars can identify two voices within the epitome, it is difficult to determine with certainty all of the occasions where Justin inserted his own opinions into the narrative, and to my knowledge no modern commentary addresses this issue in detail for Books 41–42 on the Parthians.[60] This

53. Lerouge-Cohen 2007: 32–39; Hackl, Jacobs, and Weber 2010b; Overtoom 2016c; Wiesehöfer and Müller 2017; Nabel 2019; Schlude 2020. Note Lucian *Hist. Conscr.* 14, 15, 16, 29, 32. For Lucian, note Hackl, Jacobs, and Weber 2010b: 280–85. For Asinius Quadratus, note Cornell 2013: 615–16.

54. Sampson 2015: 188–91, 197–98. There remained some interest in the Parthians in late antiquity because many Romans viewed the conflict with the Sasanian Persians as a continuation of the long-standing Romano-Parthian rivalry. Overtoom 2016c.

55. Note Kennedy 1996: 69; Overtoom 2016c; id. 2017a; id. 2017b; Wiesehöfer and Müller 2017.

56. For Trogus and Justin, note Watson 1853; Brunt 1980; Jal 1987; Alonso-Núñez 1987; Syme 1988; Alonso-Núñez 1992; Heckel 1997; Comploi 2002; Yardley 2003; Yarrow 2006; Lerouge-Cohen 2009a; Hackl, Jacobs, and Weber 2010b: 244–71; Wheatley and Heckel 2012; Ballesteros-Pastor 2013; Bartlett 2014; Borgna 2015, Mineo and Zecchini 2016; Galimberti and Zecchini 2016; Müller 2017b; Mineo and Zecchini 2018.

57. Yardley 2003; Lerouge-Cohen 2009a; Beck 2013; Müller 2017b.

58. Goodyear 1992; Yardley and Develin 1994; Yardley and Heckel 1997; Yardley, Heckel, and Wheatley 2011; Popov-Reynolds 2013; Bartlett 2014.

59. Bartlett 2014: 278–80.

60. A new French translation of Books 24–44 from the Collection des Universités de France with accompanying notes is planned for 2020.

means that we must cite Justin extensively in this work but acknowledge that the sentiments of Justin toward the Parthians also perhaps reflect those of Trogus and his Augustan Age peers.[61]

Justin's emphasis on eastern developments and peoples makes his work unique and invaluable within the surviving Graeco-Roman tradition. Although Justin provides us with only an outline, Trogus originally recorded the formation and rise of the Parthian state to dominance over the Hellenistic Middle East in detail because he viewed Rome and Parthia as the successors of the old world order and because he wanted to portray the Romans, although not completely dominant, as superior.[62] Justin's epitome of Trogus is more detailed and far more engaging than Florus' epitome of Livy, making it a vital source of information for the geopolitical developments of the Parthian state despite its condensed narrative.[63]

A contemporary of Trogus, the historian and geographer Strabo, whose more extensive accounts of Parthian history regrettably are now lost, offers information on the background of the Parthians and on their later struggle with Armenia that is an important supplement to Justin's epitome and our other literary sources.[64] Both Trogus and Strabo utilized the Parthian history of Apollodorus, who was a Greek subject of the Parthians in the early first century, as an important source; however, Strabo in particular incorporated Apollodorus' conclusions in his sections on Parthian culture, ethnography, and militarism.[65] Trogus and Strabo also appear to have shared Apollodorus' opinion that the Parthians and Romans had split the inhabited world between their rival hegemonies.[66]

The other three main literary sources of information on the Parthians are Plutarch (ca. early second century CE), Appian (ca. middle second century CE), and Cassius Dio (ca. early third century CE). Plutarch offers some of our most detailed accounts of certain Parthian events during the Mithridatic Wars and Crassus' invasion of Mesopotamia in his *Lives* on Lucullus, Pompey, and Crassus.[67] For instance, his detailed account of the Battle of Carrhae is unrivaled.[68] However, Plutarch only was interested in the Parthians as they related to his Roman subjects, and therefore he rarely addressed earlier Parthian history.

Appian's history of Rome's wars against the Parthians unfortunately has not survived, and this means that his histories, the *Syrian Wars* and the *Mithridatic*

61. Note Sonnabend 1986; Rose 2005; Lerouge-Cohen 2009a; Hill 2013; Schlude 2015; Overtoom 2016c.

62. Lerouge-Cohen 2009a; Beck 2013; Sampson 2015: 198; Overtoom 2016c.

63. Popov-Reynolds 2013. For the Parthians in Livy and Florus, see Hackl, Jacobs, and Weber 2010b: 160–66, 271–74.

64. Strabo 11.9.2–3. For Strabo, see Jones, 1917–1932; Diller 1975; Dueck 2000; Hackl, Jacobs, and Weber 2010b: 369–84; Dąbrowa 2015; Engels 2017.

65. For Apollodorus, note Chaumont 1986c; Nikonorov 1998a; Engels 2017; Nawotka 2017; Müller 2017a. Compare Strabo 2.5.12, 11.7.3, 15.1.3.

66. Overtoom 2016c; Engels 2017: 55–57.

67. For Plutarch, note Perrin 1914; id. 1916; id. 1917; Lamberton 2001; Duff 2002; Hartmann 2008; Hackl, Jacobs, and Weber 2010b: 314–44; Pelling 2011; Stadter 2011; Beck 2014; Stadter 2015.

68. Sampson 2015: 186.

Wars, only mention the Parthians in passing. Sallust (ca. middle first century) in his *Histories* and Memnon of Heraclea (ca. first or second century CE) similarly offer only a few passing references to the Parthians in their accounts of the Mithridatic Wars.[69] Although Appian's surviving accounts rarely offer any detail on Parthian events, his generally straightforward, matter-of-fact writing style makes his accounts usually more reliable than the more rhetorical accounts of Plutarch, and his focus on eastern kings allowed him to discuss how the Arsacids became major players in the Hellenistic Middle East.[70]

Cassius Dio wrote a monumental work, *Roman History*, which in eighty books covered the entire history of Rome from Aeneas to the Severans. He too considered the Parthians worthy rivals of the Romans, and he offers valuable and relatively detailed accounts of Parthian events in his books on the Mithridatic Wars and Crassus' invasion, namely Books 30–37 and 40, often with more of a reliable historical focus than does Plutarch.[71] However, again the Parthians were only important to Dio as they related to the concerns of Rome, making his work of limited value to the reconstruction of early Parthian history.

There are other minor sources worth brief consideration. Pliny the Elder wrote in the late 70s CE, and like Strabo, inserted snippets of Parthian history and culture into his *Natural History* when he found them interesting and relevant.[72] Tacitus, writing in the early second century CE, offers important insights into the Romano-Parthian conflict during the reign of Nero that include portions of Parthian history.[73] Arrian wrote a Parthian history, *Parthica*, in the middle second century CE; however, only fragments of this work survive in much later Byzantine collections. Although Arrian idealized the Parthians and described them as justified in their rebellion against the Seleucids, he followed well-established Graeco-Roman literary traditions in his portrayal of the Parthians, emphasizing their nomadic origins and unique militarism.[74] Ammianus viewed the Roman rivalry with the Sasanian Persians under Julian in the 360s CE as a continuation of the Romano-Parthian conflict, and therefore the origin and militarism of the Parthians interested him.[75] Finally, Josephus, writing in the late first century CE,

69. For Sallust, note Rolfe 1921; McGushin 1992; id. 1994; Adler 2006; Ramsey 2015. For Memnon, note Smith 2004; Yarrow 2006; Hackl, Jacobs, and Weber 2010b: 292–93.

70. For Appian, note White 1899; id. 1912–1913; Chaumont 1986d; Brodersen 1989; Carsana 2007; Hackl, Jacobs, and Weber 2010b: 28–36.

71. Dio 40.14.3–4. For Dio, note Cary 1914–1927; Millar 1964; Chaumont 1995; Murison 1999; Hackl, Jacobs, and Weber 2010b: 53–140; Lange and Madsen 2016.

72. For Pliny the Elder, note Bostock and Riley 1855; Murphy 2004; Carey 2006; Hackl, Jacobs, and Weber 2010b: 307–13; Gibson and Morello 2011.

73. For Tacitus, note Hackl, Jacobs, and Weber 2010b: 388–427; Overtoom 2016c; Heil 2017; Dąbrowa 2017a.

74. For Arrian, note Lepper and DeVoto 1985; Hackl, Jacobs, and Weber 2010b: 37–47; Stehle 2013; Bucciantini 2017; Lerouge-Cohen 2017.

75. Emperor Julian shared this view in his own writings. Overtoom 2016c: 155, 158–59, 163, 165–68; id. 2016g. For Ammianus, note Syme 1968; Matthews 1989; Barnes 1998; Kelly 2008; Hackl, Jacobs, and Weber 2010b: 23–25; Jenkins 2016; Overtoom 2016c; id. 2016f.

offers a unique Jewish perspective of the rapidly changing geopolitical situation in the Near East in his works *Antiquities of the Jews* and *The Jewish Wars*.[76] Again, his references to the Parthians are scattered and often hostile; however, Josephus' sources included writers, presumably including Jewish ones, who had a different and more intimate knowledge of geopolitics in the Hellenistic Middle East and of Parthian rule since a large Jewish community remained in Mesopotamia.[77]

Thus, the source difficulties facing scholars of early Parthian history and of the Hellenistic Middle East are considerable. It is vital to utilize all available literary, epigraphic, and numismatic evidence to establish the most probable reconstruction of events; however, reasonable speculation grounded in the available evidence is necessary and unavoidable. This study offers a reconstruction of early Parthian history and the interactions of the Parthian state with its Greek, Iranian, and Central Asian neighbors with a critical eye toward the Greek and Roman perspective of our sources. Such an analysis should help balance our generally "western" perception of these events and challenge considerably our current conceptualization of the international environment in the Hellenistic Middle East in the third to first centuries. As the field of Parthian studies continues to grow and more material evidence is brought to light, our understanding and reconstruction of Parthian society and history will continue to evolve.

Realist Theory and the Ancient World

This study is an interdisciplinary effort to reconstruct ancient international relations and geopolitics. It introduces the concepts of modern political theory to the historical analysis of ancient state interactions in the Hellenistic Middle East. This allows for a new interpretation of the available evidence to expand our understanding of an often underappreciated and enigmatic period of history. This study employs Realist Theory (specifically a Neorealist or "structural" approach to international relations, which is the study of how system structures affect international behaviors and outcomes) as a framework to help provide greater perspective and a more expansive understanding of state decision-making and interaction in the ancient world.[78] Therefore, this work is an effort to bridge the unfortunate gap between historians and political scientists in considering ancient international relations and should be of interest to both academic communities.[79]

76. For Josephus, note Whiston 1895; Täubler 1904; Cohen 1979; Mason 2000; Hackl, Jacobs, and Weber 2010b: 202–44; Pastor, Stern, and Mor 2011; Gruen 2017.

77. Note Neusner 1965; id. 1983; Daryaee 2015: 288; Gruen 2017. Josephus states that he translated several works and sent them to Jewish communities within the Parthian Empire. Jos. *Bell.* 1.1–7; id. *Ant.* 15.14, 21, 18.310–79, 20.34–37.

78. Waltz was the most influential advocate of Neorealism. See Waltz 1979: Ch. 5–6. Compare Evans and Newnham 1998: 364–65. Note Eckstein 2005; id. 2006; id. 2012; id. 2013; Overtoom 2016a; id. 2016d; id. 2019a; id. 2019b; id. 2019c; id. 2019/2020; id. 2020; id. 2021.

79. For the potential benefits and challenges of blending historical analysis and political science theory, note Schroeder 1997. Compare Levy 1988; Elman and Elman 1997. Political scientists have made few notable efforts to

Realist Theory (also known as Political Realism or simply Realism) is a predominant school of thought in modern international relations theory and, in general, is completely foreign to historians.[80] I share Arthur Eckstein's preference for the sub-school of Realist Theory called "offensive" Realism, because of the comparatively primitive and violent characteristics of international environments in the ancient world.[81] Offensive Realism maintains that states seek to maximize their security and power through domination and hegemony because of the anarchic nature of many interstate systems (or international communities in which states interact and compete).[82] Systems of militarized interstate anarchy were common in the ancient world, including the systems that developed in the Hellenistic Middle East. Therefore, it is necessary to introduce the main themes of Realism to this audience to help familiarize them with its concepts and how their application to ancient international relations studies is beneficial.[83] This theoretical approach allows us to consider with more precision the structural factors that influenced ancient states and statesmen within particular interstate systems.[84]

Realism emphasizes the unforgiving and competitive nature of interactions between states within an international system of states that lacks enforceable international law and/or central authority, known as interstate anarchy.[85] In Realist Theory, under the conditions of interstate anarchy, war always remains a threat to the survival of states. Further, short-term self-preservation, through the acquisition of power at the expense of one's neighbors, is the primary goal of states. An emphasis on power acquisition provides states with security, and this emphasis is fundamentally important because states can rely only upon themselves to acquire that security. Thus, in an effort to survive in an unforgiving and violent international environment, states often turn to grim self-help policies in

utilize ancient examples. Eckstein 2006: 7–8. For good efforts, see Fliess 1966; Lebow and Strauss 1991. For cursory or error prone efforts, see Liska 1978: 11–14; Gilpin 1981: 99–100, 146–7; Doyle 1986: 82–91; Little 1993: 144–50; Zack 2017.

80. For competing theories and criticisms, see esp. Keohane and Nye 1987: 745–49; Kegley 1993: 133–35; Frankel 1996a; id 1996b; Lynn-Jones 1998; Eckstein 2006: 6 n.9, 29–33; Viotti and Kauppi 2011: 39–76; Eckstein 2012: 10–11.

81. Eckstein 2006: 6 n.9, 10 n.18.

82. For offensive Realism, see Labs 1997; Rose 1998; Mearsheimer 2001: Ch. 2; Taliaferro 2000–2001. For the applicability of offensive Realism to China in the tenth to seventeenth centuries CE, see Wang 2011: 21–23, 21 n.55–56.

83. For Realist theorists' arguments that their paradigms about the anarchic character of international politics are enduring, timeless, and unchanging, see Waltz 1979: 66; Doyle 1991: 175; Glaser 1997: 171; Elman and Elman 1997: 9 and n.11, 13–14; Keeley 1999: 16–17; Copeland 2000: Ch. 8; Eckstein 2006: 9–10. For recent investigations of international relations in the Hellenistic world and the Roman Republic, see Billows 2007; Ñaco del Hoyo and Sánchez 2018.

84. Note Ñaco del Hoyo and Sánchez 2018.

85. For interstate anarchy, see Waltz 1959: 159–60; Hobbes 1959: 65; Schuman 1969: 485; Aron 1973: 6; Wight 1978: 101; Waltz 1979: 76, 102, 127; Gilpin 1981: 7; Schelling 2000: 182. For the absence of international law in the ancient world, see Eckstein 2006: 1, 12, 20–22, 32, 39; Grainger 2017b. Compare Aron 1973: 98–99. Contra Bederman 2001; Sartre 2007: 619–20, 624.

an ongoing competition for limited resources.[86] Hence, for instance, Thucydides, whom many consider the founder of Realist thought, argues that fear of growing Athenian power, which threatened Sparta indirectly and more importantly directly threatened Spartan allies, such as Corinth, encouraged Sparta to declare war on Athens to protect its international standing and network of allies.[87] This of course began the devastating Peloponnesian War (431–404). In fact, Corinth's crucial role in bringing Sparta and Athens to blows in this hegemonic conflict demonstrates that middling and minor states within these volatile international environments also acted aggressively to maximize their power and security with considerable unintended geopolitical ramifications.[88]

The systemic pressures of an international system of states, especially in times of interstate anarchy, impose these harsh realities upon all states. Therefore, all states tend to pursue power-maximizing conduct in their own self-interest, de facto making all successful states (those that survive within a system of violent interstate anarchy) aggressive and militaristic. Consequently, since all states must become militarized and warlike to survive, especially in the ancient world, the main difference between states within this type of an interstate system is their *capability* to pursue power-maximizing policy, not their *desire* to do so.[89] This is a crucial distinction since few scholars have recognized that the Parthians shared the desire to act aggressively and expand their territory at the expense of their main rivals.[90]

Realist Theory maintains that the need for states to maximize their security and strength at the expense of their competitive neighbors through self-interested, self-help policies is a byproduct of the systemic pressures of highly competitive international environments, and in this sense, all states tend to become similar in their drive for security and power or else they do not survive. Thucydides' Melian Dialogue, where the Athenians demand that the Melians submit to their power or face destruction, is perhaps the best example of this difficult reality in the context of antiquity.[91] However, these harsh yet pragmatic

86. For self-help, see Aron 1973: 64–65, 130; Taylor 1978: 130; Liska 1978: 4–6; Waltz 1979: 104; id. 1988: 616; Mearsheimer 1994–1995: 11–12; Sheehan 1996: 8; Eckstein 2006: 14–23. Contra Wendt 1992. Geographical location also is an important factor in the potential vulnerability of states to systemic pressures. Note Gourevitch 1978: 896. For the local application of self-help policies in the Roman Empire, see Fuhrmann 2012: Ch. 3.

87. Thuc. 1.23.6. For Thucydides, see Connor 1987; Allison 1989; Price 2001; Shanske 2006; Kagan 2009; Mynott 2013; Parmeggiani 2014; Thauer and Wendt 2016. For Thucydides and Realist thought, see Waltz 1979: 66, 127, 186–87; Gilpin 1981: 93, 226–27; id. 1988: 592–606; Doyle 1991: 181–82; Kauppi 1991: 102; Lebow 1991: 125; Crane 1998: Ch. 2; Eckstein 2003; id. 2006: 37, 48–58; Lendon 2006; Ñaco del Hoyo and Sánchez 2018.

88. When Thucydides states that Sparta feared the growth of Athens, he means, at least in part, that Sparta feared that Corinth feared the growth of Athens. See Thuc 1.67–71, 119–24.

89. For power-maximizing, see Huntington 1993: 68–83; Mearsheimer 1994-1995: 11–12; Zakaria 1998: 29; van Evera 1998: 13–14; Taliafero 2000: 128–29. This was common in the ancient world; see Eckstein 2006: 12, 15, 18, 49–50, 52, 118, 143–44, 149, 162–63, 174, 176, 179, 234, 241–42, 268, 315; id. 2012: 7. Note van Wees 2004: 145, 150; Seaman 2013: 644, 652.

90. See Wheeler 2002: 287–8.

91. Thuc. 5.84–116. Although Thucydides had strong moral reservations about the actions of the Athenians against Melos, as a well-informed Athenian and pragmatist, "he had arrived at an empirical conclusion as to how

concepts of power relations were a geopolitical reality that most ancient writers recognized and accepted.[92]

Since, according to Realism, all successful states ultimately follow a selfish, self-help regime, the vital variable in state success is the distribution of capabilities in power across units within a system of states. In a competitive interstate system, such as all the interstate systems in antiquity, superiority of power, not balance of power is the ultimate goal for states. Hence, states look to dominate vulnerable or potentially dangerous neighbors to expand their power and to ensure their survival.[93] Balance of power within an interstate system is unstable and the geopolitical stakes for polities could not be higher, which helps explain the numerous major military conflicts found throughout history, particularly in the ancient world.

Realist theorists argue that interactions between states become increasingly tense because the understanding of power capabilities between states is opaque. In a system of interstate anarchy, warfare is the only way to determine actual state power and its relation to the power capabilities of other states.[94] The dilemma, known as the "uncertainty principle," forces states to work continually to identify and counteract potential or perceived threats to their security through efforts to maximize power at the expense of the security of neighbors.[95] Further, this opaque awareness of power capabilities throughout an interstate system forces states to consider and prepare for "worst-case scenarios."[96] Thus, tensions are high, and stakes are higher as competing states maneuver for opportunity and advantage within interstate systems.

The crudeness and infrequency of diplomatic interaction among ancient polities added to their opaque awareness of one another's power capabilities and intentions, which led to heightened tension between states and oftentimes war throughout antiquity. There were no permanent ambassadors in the ancient world, and when ambassadors were utilized, it was only on an ad hoc basis.[97] The primary purpose of modern diplomatic representation and dialogue is the alleviation of tension and ambiguity between nations before the escalation of potential conflicts of interest. However, no such system was in place to aid ancient states.[98]

states in general actually act." Eckstein 2006: 49. Compare Cohen 1984: 37; Doyle 1991: 172–73; Johnson-Bagby 1994: 133–34; Rahe 1996: 106–41; Crane 1998: 64.

92. For example, note Livy 5.48.9, 27.44, 42.50, 45.26.7–8; Caes. *BG* 1.36; Dion. Hal. 6.6.2; Jos. *Bell.* 2.345–401, Tac. *Hist.* 4.17; id. *Ann.* 12.12.1, 15.1.4–5, 14.1, 25; id. *Agr.* 30; Dio 37.6.1; Strabo 16.1.26; Plaut. *Truc.* 4.3.30; Phaed. 1.5, 30, 4.6; Aesop 12, 14, 31, 32, 53, 455 in Gibbs 2002.

93. Treves 1970; Morgenthau 1973: 208; Sheehan 1996: 14; Eckstein 2006: 16.

94. Note Morgenthau 1973: 208; Gilpin 1981: 9; Levy 1983: 24; Blainey 1988: 114; Thompson 1988: 41; Waltz 1993: 73; Wohlforth 1994–1995: 104–5, 123, 127; Jervis 2001: 282 and n.2; Eckstein 2006: 17.

95. For the uncertainty principle, see Jervis 1976: 58–113; Taylor 1978: 130; Waltz 1988: 619; Sheehan 1996: 8; Glaser 1997: 184; Eckstein 2006: 17.

96. For worst-case scenario preparation, see Morgenthau 1973: 208; van Evera 1998: 13–14; Eckstein 2006: 17.

97. Grant 1962: 262; Ziegler 1964; Eckstein 2006: 58–59; id. 2012: 12–13. Note Lendon 2002; Ager 2009; Eilers 2009; Grainger 2017b.

98. For modern surprise at the lack of ancient diplomacy, see Aron 1973: 15; Lebow 1991: 144–45; Kauppi 1991: 119.

In fact, diplomatic missions in the ancient world rarely were utilized until after a conflict of interest had escalated to the threshold of armed conflict. Hence, there was little chance for ancient diplomacy to succeed in defusing situations since conflicts had usually already escalated and since power relations and reputation were at stake.

This lack of diplomatic access in the ancient world went hand-in-hand with the reliance of ancient states on crisis diplomacy, what international relations theorists call "compellence diplomacy."[99] Compellence diplomacy often took the form of ultimatums. In situations where the power balance between states is drastically in favor of one state over another, the weaker state might submit to compellence diplomacy. Yet the objective of the lesser state in this scenario is self-preservation, not the preservation of peace. Thus, ancient states tried to use compellence diplomacy as "a less directly violent means of interstate coercion."[100] However, this process often created further tension and resentment between ancient states, and it made interstate violence more likely in the future. In fact, since compellence diplomacy was intertwined with power relations and reputation among states, the coercive, arrogant demands of states could not in fact be a bluff. States that delivered an ultimatum of war, such as the Athenians at Melos in Thucydides' account, had to be and were ready to go to war. Compellence diplomacy reflects the brutal realities of power relations within ancient international environments, and its use was yet another motivation for states to maximize their power.[101]

Realist Theory also maintains that in times of interstate anarchy, the competitiveness of the international environment drives all states toward self-interested, power-maximizing policies to expand state strength in the face of genuine threats of destruction. Moreover, in systems of militarized interstate anarchy, which again were common in the ancient world, there rarely was an international or central authority available to mediate or compel peaceful resolutions of conflicts, nor could such a central authority assure the compliance of states involved in disputes. Legally trained scholars, such as Karl-Heinz Ziegler, have exaggerated the force of international law in the ancient world.[102] Norms of international conduct certainly existed in the ancient world; however, ancient states simply ignored them when it was convenient.[103] Thus, although we should not completely deny

99. Eckstein 2006: 60; id. 2012: 14. For compellence diplomacy, see Ferrar 1981: 194–200; Questor 1988: 704–6; Mercer 1993: 166–67; Stevenson 1997: 134–35.

100. Eckstein 2006: 60. Compare Strauss 1991: 203; Lebow 1991: 144–45. For the applicability of compellence diplomacy to Confucian China under the Song Dynasty (960-1279 CE) and the Ming Dynasty (1368-1644 CE), see Wang 2011: 162.

101. Eckstein 2006: 61; id. 2012: 15.

102. Wheeler 2002: 287–88. Ziegler's legalistic approach to Roman and Parthian relations is too often anachronistic and misleading. Ziegler 1964.

103. Wheeler 2011: 86.

the existence of international law in the ancient world, there were no enforceable international laws that could curtail aggression between determined ancient states. Consequently, pressures to seek power were high in antiquity since state survival was fragile, and conflict between rival states often became inevitable and remained frequent.[104]

Friction between states is made worse by what international relations theorists call the "security dilemma."[105] The security dilemma is a process whereby one state that successfully increases its security does so at the cost of the security of its neighbors. This in turn pushes those neighboring states toward further efforts to maximize their own power and to expand state security. Within systems of interstate anarchy, like the interstate systems of the ancient Mediterranean and Middle East, power was a zero-sum game and resources were finite. These harsh realities encouraged states to act aggressively or face the threat of destruction. Hence, as Thucydides relates, just prior to the Peloponnesian War the Athenians refused to abandon their expanding empire even though the Spartans threatened immediate war if they did not.[106] For the Athenians the risk of backing down in the face of Spartan demands to Athens' long-term state security was simply too great and outweighed the more immediate threat of war. The famous Athenian statesman Pericles captured this sentiment explicitly when he said, "From this empire, however, it is too late for you even to withdraw, if any one at the present crisis, through fear and shrinking from action does indeed seek thus to play the honest man; for by this time the empire you hold is a tyranny, which it may seem wrong to have assumed, but which certainly it is dangerous to let go."[107] Pericles then continues, "For men of peace are not safe unless flanked by men of action; nor is it expedient in an imperial state, but only in a vassal state, to seek safety by submission."[108] The Athenians' belief that it was necessary to maintain and expand their power at the expense of neighboring states to preserve their safety was not unique to Athens. This was an endemic problem in the ancient world, and unfortunately this emphasis on the pursuit of security made conflict among states increasingly necessary and unavoidable.[109] These various defects of the international system of states in antiquity made war a normal aspect of state interactions.[110]

104. See Brecher and Wilkenfeld 1982: 380–417; Holsti 1991: 20; Geller and Singer 1998: 99; Keeley 1999: 160–1; Eckstein 2006: 1, 12, 20–2, 32, 39. For the impact of growing tension between states on eventual conflict, see Midlarsky 1988: 6, 20–44; Thompson 1999: 3–28.

105. Note Glaser 1997.

106. Thuc. 1.72, 75–6.

107. Id. 2.63.

108. Ibid.

109. For the uncertainty principle and security dilemma, see Herz 1950: 157–80; Jervis 1978: 167–214; Waltz 1988: 619; Glaser 1997: 177 and n.29. For its impact, see Liska 1990: 482; Copeland 2000: 12, 17, 145–47, 165–68; Eckstein 2006: 21–22, 242 n.217.

110. See Waltz 1959: 160; Wight 1978: 137; Waltz 1979: 102; id. 1988: 620–21; id. 2000: 8. For the ancient world, note Eckstein 2005: 484–85; Rawlings 2013: 5; Millett 2013: 51; Overtoom 2016a; id. 2016c; id. 2016d; id 2017a; id. 2017b; id. 2019a; id. 2019b; id. 2019c; id. 2019/2020; id. 2020; id. 2021.

In international relations theory, the balance of power within an interstate system often heavily determines the frequency of war. Modern studies suggest that a system of multipolarity, where several states of relatively equivalent power capabilities interact in a precarious competition for security, is the most war-prone system.[111] The Italian peninsular system of the fifth and fourth centuries and much of the geopolitical history of Classical Greece are good examples of multipolarity in antiquity.[112] A system of bipolarity, where two major states dominate all others, although vulnerable to the threat of system-wide war between the two polar powers, generally is more stable than multipolarity.[113] We find good examples of bipolarity in the ancient world in the conflict between Sparta and Athens in the Peloponnesian War, in the struggle between Rome and Carthage in the Punic Wars, and in the rivalry that emerged between Rome and Parthia after the invasion of Crassus in 54–53.[114] Finally, a system of unipolarity, wherein one state dominates the entire interstate system, generally is the least war-prone; however, unipolarity is difficult to obtain and often unstable.[115] This study discusses various phases of balance of power in the Hellenistic Middle East and how the evolving arrangement of interstate systems in the region helped influence state decision-making.

International relations theory also maintains that dramatic shifts in the power balance of an interstate system, namely the sudden rise or decline of a state within that system, destabilize the international system of states and usually result in hegemonic war (a large-scale war that reorders or creates a new interstate structure that better reflects the realities of power distribution and balance of power within the system).[116] A good example of hegemonic war in antiquity and its potentially drastic consequences is the destruction of the Carthaginian Empire in the Second Punic War by Rome, which allowed the Romans to then dominate the Western Mediterranean. The sudden and dramatic fluctuation of a state's power within an interstate system causes what international relations theorists call a "power-transition crisis." Although a power-transition crisis does not in and of itself cause war, it makes hegemonic war more likely because it destabilizes the interstate system and brings power relations into question.[117] One example of power-transition crisis in this study is the sudden decline of Seleucid power in

111. Gochman and Maoz 1984: 592–93; Geller and Singer 1998: 128; Keeley 1999: 118–21; Eckstein 2006: 20, 23, 67.

112. Note Strauss 1991: 198–201; Eckstein 2006: Ch. 3 and 118–58.

113. Waltz 1979: 161–70; Geller and Singer 1998: 115–17; Eckstein 2006: 23, 67. Contra Copeland 1996.

114. Note Eckstein 2006: 158–80.

115. Layne 1993; Geller and Singer 1998: 115–17; Motyl 2001. Note Wilkinson 1999.

116. Note Levy 1985: 365–66; Gilpin 1988: 591–606.

117. For power-transition theory, see Lemke and Kugler 1996: 3–33; Geller and Singer 1998: 72–5; Tammen 2000. For power-transition crisis because of a deteriorating state, see Organski and Kugler 1980. For power-transition crisis because of an ascending state, see Gilpin 1981; id. 1988: 602. For examples of power-transition crisis in antiquity, see Eckstein 2006: 23–24, 105, 114, 269; id. 2012: 4 *et passim*; Overtoom 2016a; id. 2019a.

the 240s and 230s and the major geopolitical repercussions that followed this decline.[118] The pressures created by a power-transition crisis are dangerous because they narrow the choices of action available to states, a process known as "cognitive closure."[119] States acting under the pressures of cognitive closure feel more impelled by circumstance to act forcefully.

Political theorists argue that in the process of power-transition, polities are considered either "status quo states," those that wish to maintain the current distribution of power within the interstate system, or "revisionist states," those that wish to redress the distribution of power within the system in their favor.[120] There are varying degrees of status quo and revisionist states, and the position of a state can be variable from situation to situation. Yet due to the systemic pressures of interstate anarchy, namely the drive of polities to maximize power for state security, few polities are status quo states. In fact, almost every polity in a system of interstate anarchy is at least a "limited revisionist state."[121] In certain, rare instances, a polity presented with favorable circumstances may become an "unlimited revisionist state," known also as a "revolutionary state." Unlimited revisionist states desire the complete overthrow of the distribution of power within the current interstate system in favor of their own hegemony or empire.[122] Persia under Cyrus the Great and Macedon under Alexander the Great are perhaps the best examples of unlimited revisionist states in antiquity.[123] Yet the Parthian state also experienced periods during its early development where it acted like an unlimited revisionist state.

Apart from providing a useful and rewarding theoretical framework for the study of geopolitical history in the ancient world, especially in the third to first centuries, the structural Realist approach to international relations helps us reevaluate the reasons for Parthian success within the larger international environment of the Hellenistic Middle East. It helps us determine which state characteristics (or unit-attributes) were in fact significant to Parthian imperialism within the wider contexts of system-level analysis. Unit-attribute theory, which again is the belief that the internal forces of a single state determine external outcomes, remains important; however, explanations that rely solely upon internal state factors without considering the pressures of the international

118. Overtoom 2016a.

119. For cognitive closure, see Levy 1991: 261; Kauppi 1991: 115–16; Eckstein 2006: 25.

120. For status quo and revisionist states, see Carr 1939; Glaser 1992: 501 n.4; Schweller 1994: 72–107; id. 1996: 90–121; id. 1998: 19–26; Geller and Singer 1998: 65–67; Lyall 2005; Eckstein 2006: 25–26, 108–10. Compare Jervis 1978.

121. Note Wolfers 1962: 84–86, 125; Aron 1973: 75; Glaser 1992: 501 and n.4; Taliaferro 2000–2001: 129; Eckstein 2006: 26.

122. For unlimited revisionist states, see Kissinger 1957; Schweller 1994: 93–95, 100, 107; id. 1996: 106–7; id. 1998: 75–89; id. 2015: 8–10. Unlimited revisionist states are quite rare in world history (although they seem to occur in antiquity with more frequency). Eckstein 2006: 26; Overtoom 2019a; id. 2019b.

123. Overtoom 2016a: 985, 987.

environment in which that state operated ignore half of the picture.[124] Therefore, system-level analysis does not attempt to replace unit-level explanations of state actions, such as cultural or economic factors or the individual personalities of state leaders; rather, it utilizes the explanatory power of structural pressures and opportunities to enhance our understanding of geopolitical developments and the motivations of states and statesmen.

In this study the human element within state decision-making and the personalities of state leaders remain fundamentally important to our understanding of geopolitical developments in this period.[125] The great statesmen of the Hellenistic Middle East were not robotic; their emotions and desires affected state policy and sometimes had severe geopolitical consequences.[126] However, again we should also recognize that their actions and policies were not made in a vacuum. The systemic pressures of the international environment encouraged these men toward making certain decisions. Thus, with a better understanding of systemic pressures in the ancient world through the application of Realist Theory, we can better understand the decision-making of state leaders in the ancient world as well.

Unit-level variables, such as cultural peculiarities or even the personalities of unique state leaders, are factors that can and did have a significant impact on international developments. However, this study acknowledges that states exist under similar systemic pressures that we cannot fully appreciate without a system-level analysis of the international environment. Instead, we should filter explanations drawn from the unit-level through an understanding of the shared systemic pressures and geopolitical realities of the international system of states. What becomes increasingly apparent from this process is that unit-level variables have more to do with the unique *capabilities* of states rather than with the *will* of states since all successful states within a harsh, competitive system of interstate anarchy develop similar ruthless motives to survive and prosper, namely the fierce pursuit of state security and strength through aggressive, self-interested power-maximizing policies.[127]

In recent years there has been growing interest in the application of modern international relations theory to the geopolitical developments of the ancient world. Arthur Eckstein in his pioneering study *Mediterranean Anarchy, Interstate War, and the Rise of Rome* uses the theoretical framework of Realism to challenge William Harris' popular unit-attribute theory that Rome came to dominate the Mediterranean world because Rome was exceptionally and pathologically more

124. Geller and Singer 1998: 47, 50–51, 67; Eckstein 2006: 27–28.

125. Note Eckstein 2006: 8–9. Compare Waltz 2000: 24.

126. Note Ñaco del Hoyo and Sánchez 2018.

127. For the emphasis on different capabilities but not motives, see Waltz 1979: 96–97. For expansionist tendencies in the pursuit of security, see Niebuhr 1932: 42; Hobbes 1959: 67; Wolfers 1962: 84–86, 125; Glaser 1992: 501 and n.4; Labs 1997: 1–49; Waltz 2000: 33.

aggressive and warlike than its neighbors.[128] Eckstein demonstrates through a system-level analysis of the interactions of states within the Mediterranean world from the fifth to the early second centuries that Rome was in fact not unique in its bellicosity and aggression. Rather, all major, middling, and minor states in the ancient Mediterranean world displayed harsh, militarized characteristics. This was because they all existed within an exceptionally cruel interstate anarchy, the systemic pressures of which had shaped their outlooks on and approaches to the international environment. Hence, Eckstein demonstrates that Rome certainly was a highly militarized and belligerent power, but so were all its neighbors.[129]

To account for the success of Roman imperialism during this period, Eckstein instead emphasizes the unique cultural and logistical capabilities of the Roman state to pursue self-interested, power-maximizing policies. Ultimately, there was nothing unique about Roman violence and aggression; their success did not develop from something pathological in Roman society.[130] Rather, Rome's success in the hegemonic struggle to dominate the Mediterranean world was due primarily to its willingness and ability to assimilate non-Romans into the Roman polity and thus to create a state that had greater military resources and was better socially integrated than were its competitors.[131] The ability of the Romans to assimilate and integrate non-Romans into the Roman state structure meant that Rome came to possess an exceptional competitive advantage over neighboring states in the struggle for security and power in the ancient Mediterranean world. The emphasis here for Eckstein is that Rome's intentions were not unique; its capabilities were.[132]

Such an understanding of Roman expansion and consolidation of power during the Middle Republic was only possible through the introduction of system-level analysis, utilizing the theoretical framework of Realism to gain a fresh and more thorough perspective.[133] This study applies a similar approach to the early developments of the Parthian state and its many interactions with its Greek, Iranian, and Central Asian neighbors. The introduction of Realist Theory to our understanding of the geopolitical developments within the Hellenistic

128. Harris 1979. Note also id. 2016.

129. Eckstein 2006. Compare id. 2003; id. 2005; id. 2007; id. 2012.

130. Id. 2006: 2–4.

131. This was something Mommsen had argued in the middle nineteenth century. Mommsen 1856 (1903); Eckstein 2012: 20 n.60.

132. Eckstein 2006: 33–35.

133. Unfortunately, Eckstein's work has not yet had the intended impact. Id. 2006: 7–8; id. 2012: 23–24, 27–28. Few historians have proven willing to engage Eckstein's use of modern international relations theory and his system-level analysis directly, and some have forcefully rejected it. Note Harris 2016. Meanwhile, even fewer political scientists appear to be aware of Eckstein's work. See Quillin 2009; Wheeler 2011: 86; Ramsey 2013. Gera praises Eckstein's work for its interdisciplinary efforts but calls it "a very challenging read." Gera 2010. Meanwhile, Hölkeskamp expresses discomfort at Eckstein's "political-science jargon" and "American hidden agenda" in his use of Realist theory. Hölkeskamp 2009. Yet some scholars, including myself, argue that Eckstein's work demands recognition and further interdisciplinary attention. Sartre 2007; Culham 2008; Erskine 2008; Scheidel 2008; Champion 2009; Frechette 2009; Dixon 2009. Note Ñaco del Hoyo and Sánchez 2018.

Middle East from the third to the first centuries offers us the opportunity to gain a similarly fresh and more well-rounded perspective of international relations and state decision-making in a compelling yet less-appreciated part of the world. It can help us determine how the Parthian state emerged, survived, and thrived, and it is to this subject that we now turn.

From Migrants to Masters of the Middle East

From the middle third to the early first centuries, the Parthians went from a minor migratory group on the southern fringes of the Central Asian steppe to the dominant power throughout the Hellenistic Middle East. Their rise to hegemony within one of antiquity's most volatile, vulnerable, and violent international environments is nothing short of remarkable. Throughout their early existence, the Parthians had to navigate tenuous and obscure foreign relations with numerous aggressive and highly militarized neighbors, while developing a strong state and military that could secure their survival within the Iranian plateau. The Parthians rarely had more resources or soldiers than their major rivals the Bactrians, Seleucids, and Romans. Yet they found ways to outlast and outperform a long series of competitors in the Hellenistic Middle East. Before this study concentrates on a reassessment of the geopolitical history of the early Parthian state from its humble beginnings to its hegemonic dominance, it is worthwhile to consider the critical characteristics of the Parthian state that not only allowed the Parthians to compete with bigger, stronger, and better-situated neighboring powers, but also allowed them to surpass these rivals to establish one of the world's greatest empires.

Considering Parthian "Exceptionalism"

Although many scholars have doubted the comparative militarism or hegemonic desires of the Parthians, the ancient Greeks and Romans respected the Parthians' military capabilities and imperial aggression.[1] In particular, the budding rivalry of the Romans and Parthians became a primary focus of Rome's foreign policies in the latter half of the first century and drastically expanded the Romans'

1. Note Lindsay 1852: 15–16; Mommsen 1856 (1903): iii 288; Rawlinson 1876 (2002): 24, 33–34, 41, 97–98, 105, 118–19; Breasted 1914 (1944): 752; Vogt 1955: 74; Wolski 1956–1957; Syme 1958: 47, 493–97; Ward 1977: 287, 289; Yarshater 1983: xlix–l; Garlan 1984: 359; Campbell 1993; Warry 1995: 157; Potter 2010: 157–60; Sheldon 2010: 1–2, 6, 10, 21–23, 36–40, 61, 177; Edwell 2013a: 191, 194, 206; id. 2013b: 6051; Grainger 2013a: 185–86; id. 2014: 199, 210; Sampson 2015: 44–45; Grainger 2016.

Reign of Arrows. Nikolaus Leo Overtoom, Oxford University Press (2020). Oxford University Press.
DOI: 10.1093/oso/9780190888329.001.0001.

perceptions of the world in which they interacted.[2] Even after the fall of the Parthians to the rebellious Sasanian Persians in the 220s CE, the Romans continued to find their three-century-long rivalry with the Parthians of interest and relevant to the changing world of late antiquity.[3]

Justin, our leading authority on the Parthians, in his epitome of Trogus' Augustan Age work considered Parthia to be the last true rival of Rome, and described the Parthians as bold, tough, and warlike, stating:

> The disposition of the [Parthian] people is proud, quarrelsome (*seditiosa*), faithless, and insolent (*procacia*); for a certain roughness of behavior (*violentiam*) they think becoming to men, and gentleness (*mansuetudinem*) only to women. They are always restless (*inquieti*), and ready for any commotion (*dicendum*), at home or abroad; taciturn by nature; more ready to act than speak, and consequently shrouding both their successes and failures in silence. They obey their princes, not from humility, but from fear (*metu*). They are libidinous, but frugal in diet. To their word or promise they have no regard, except as far as suits their interest.[4]

Although Justin here utilizes some well-established ancient stereotypes about eastern duplicity, cruelty, and despotism to describe the Parthians, which he emphasizes elsewhere in his history (36.1.5, 38.9.2, 38.10.5–6, 42.1.2, 42.1.4, 42.2.5–6) and which distort the realities of Parthian society and culture, the Romans' treatment of the Parthians in their literature and propaganda was unique because it did not adhere to the standard pattern of environmental theory, where a people's climate determined their qualities.[5] To the Romans, the Parthians were not typical easterners, and they shared respectable military qualities with the Gauls and Germans. Benjamin Isaac argues, "The reason for this, presumably, is the persistent ability by the Parthian Empire to remain independent of Roman power. This made it impossible to describe them as effeminate, fickle, weak, and subject to debilitating practices."[6] Dio also praises the Parthians as "especially formidable in warfare (ἄλλως ἰσχυροὶ τὰ πολέμια)," considering them a match for the Romans militarily because "even to this day [they] hold their own in the wars they wage against us, whenever they become involved in them."[7] In an example from late antiquity, Ammianus describes the Parthians as the most

2. Overtoom 2016d; id. 2021.

3. Id. 2016c.

4. Justin 41.3.7–10. Overtoom 2016c: 142–50.

5. Wolski was the first Parthian scholar to emphasize the influence of Greek and Roman stereotypes of easterners on the image of the Parthians. Wolski 1965; id. 1967; id. 1975; id. 1981; id. 1983b; id. 1985b; id. 1989. Justin utilized the juxtaposition of courage and corruption in his depiction of the Parthians to portray the Romans as morally and politically superior. Müller 2017b.

6. Isaac 2006: 377–78.

7. Dio 40.14.3–4. Translation slightly altered.

fearsome warriors in the east, which is an opinion several earlier Greek and Roman authors shared.[8] Ammianus continues, "There [in the Parthians' homeland] the inhabitants of all the districts are savage and warlike, and take such pleasure in war and conflict, that one who loses his life in battle is regarded as happy beyond all others. For those who depart from this life by a natural death they assail with insults, as degenerate and cowardly."[9] Thus, the Graeco-Roman tradition vividly illustrates the considerable militarism of the Parthians, and recently scholars have begun to emphasize the significant scope and tradition of that militarism within Parthian society.[10]

Yet the combativeness of the Parthians and their highly militarized society was not unique in antiquity. Scholars such as Gareth Sampson have gone too far in trying to incorporate the Parthians into the discussion of larger geopolitical developments in the third to first centuries by portraying them as rivals to the Romans' supposed unique bellicosity. For example, Sampson recently compared the Parthians' conquests in the east to "Rome's relentless push across the Hellenistic world."[11] Although the Romans and Parthians were warlike and aggressive, they were not uniquely so when we also consider their numerous highly militarized competitors. As mentioned previously, Arthur Eckstein has argued quite convincingly that the Romans in fact were not uniquely bellicose in the violent and unforgiving international environment of the Mediterranean.[12] Further, Eckstein has demonstrated that states in ancient China and India also were highly militarized and warlike and that they too existed in harsh international environments that encouraged heightened militarism and endemic conflict.[13] Meanwhile, numerous tribes on the Central Asian steppe had a well-established military tradition that stemmed largely from their highly bellicose societies, which developed in an unstable and dangerous international environment.[14]

This study stresses that several major, middling, and minor states throughout the Hellenistic Middle East developed similar highly militarized characteristics, placing a similar emphasis on developing strong military societies and aggressive foreign policies, in part because of the harsh and unforgiving realities of international environments in the ancient world. All ancient states needed to be hypermilitarized to maintain their autonomy and to secure their survival, and therefore, unique bellicosity, along with other aforementioned "unit-attribute" theories, such as Parthian anti-Greek "nationalism," Persian revivalism, inept rivals, imperial envy, land hunger, and domination of trade routes, do not satisfactorily

8. Amm. Mar. 23.6.28. Compare Lucan *Phar.* 8.211–455; Dio 40.15; Plut. *Crass.* 24–28; Pliny *NH* 16.159–62.
9. Amm. Mar. 23.6.44.
10. Note Hauser 2006; Olbrycht 2016a; Overtoom 2017b.
11. Sampson 2015: 32.
12. Eckstein 2003; id. 2006; id. 2012; id. 2013.
13. Id. 2005: 481–97.
14. Wolski 1996; Cosmo 2004; Golden 2011: 21–34; Mair 2014: 22–23, 159, 161, 168, 170, 178, 646.

account for the Parthians' exceptional success. Instead, the crucial factors that most accurately help explain the eventual triumph of the early Parthian state are the versatility of Parthian society, the innovations of the Parthian military, and the early Arsacids' ability to manage and exploit these qualities to the benefit of the state through their capable leadership and dynastic stability.[15]

One of the Parthians' critical cultural characteristics, namely the adaptability of their society, materialized in their flexible internalization of Greek, Persian, and nomadic elements into their social, administrative, and political identity. Diodorus emphasizes the inclusiveness of Parthian society, which internalized the "best (ἄριστα)" of foreign customs.[16] Moreover, Trogus and Justin viewed the Parthians as a powerful and resilient people, who had benefited from great leadership, determination, and adaptability, allowing them to survive their humble origins, outlast numerous better-situated competitors, and emerge as the last rivals of Rome.[17] Thus, the Graeco-Roman tradition identifies one of the fundamental advantages of the Parthians within the competitive international environment of the Hellenistic Middle East. They were willing to draw upon and adapt the successful social characteristics and strategies of all the peoples with whom they came into contact and conflict. As Strabo argued, the Parthians never lost touch with their nomadic origin; however, to this identity they incorporated important elements of Persian and Greek rule that allowed the Arsacids to create and maintain a massive empire.[18] This unique social versatility, which the Arsacids cultivated and encouraged, heavily influenced the Parthians' more diverse and inclusive form of imperialism that allowed the Parthians to dominate the Middle East for a longer period than their Persian and Macedonian predecessors.

Social Versatility and Parthian Imperialism

Scholars have portrayed the Parthians as "Scythian" nomads, Persian "revivalists," and Hellenistic successors.[19] Yet Parthian society was an amalgamation of nomadic, Persian, and Greek elements.[20] Under the leadership of the Arsacids, the flexible cultural identity of the Parni (after they settled within the Iranian plateau and integrated themselves within Parthian communities) facilitated their incorporation of influential Irano-Hellenistic customs into their new and expanded society, while in many ways maintaining the roots of their nomadic past, for

15. Overtoom 2019a. Compare Sherwin-White and Kuhrt 1993: 85.

16. Diod. 33.18.

17. Justin 41.1–3. Note Olbrycht 2003; Hill 2013; Overtoom 2016c: 143; id. 2017a; Engels 2017: 55–56; Müller 2017b.

18. Strabo 11.9.2.

19. See Lozinski 1959: 36–37; Paratore 1966: 526–27; Wolski 1966; Colledge 1967: 57–76; Wolski 1976a; id. 1983a; id. 1984; id. 1985a; id. 1990b; id. 1991; id. 1993; Warry 1995: 154–56; Olbrycht 1998b; Koshelenko and Pilipko 1999; Hauser 2013.

20. See Curtis 2000: 25; Olbrycht 2003: 98–99.

instance their horse-based culture.[21] While some scholars reject the impact of nomadic components on the development of the Parthian state, others simply emphasize that the Parthians had lost their nomadic lifestyle by the middle of the third century.[22] Certainly, the association of the Parthians primarily with "Scythian" nomadic or barbarian characteristics is partly inaccurate and a misguiding legacy of our Greek and Roman sources.[23] Yet the fundamental importance of the horse to Parthian society and warfare demonstrates that they did not abandon all of their nomadic roots in favor of Persian or Greek customs, and in fact, in recent years the importance of nomadic roots to the identity of the Parthians has found many advocates.[24] In fact, although the Parthians endured periods of severe tension with the Central Asian tribal confederations, they maintained a working relationship with these peoples, especially the leaders within these tribes.[25]

Although elements of their steppe origin were important to the development of Parthian society, the Arsacids quickly recognized the usefulness of adopting aspects of Irano-Hellenistic tradition to support their rule, especially in the development of their coinage, art, and language.[26] The Parthians successfully melded aspects of nomadic, Persian, and Greek traditions into their multicultural, multilinguistic, and multireligious society to create a uniquely diverse identity within the Hellenistic Middle East that gave the Parthians important advantages in their competition with numerous neighboring powers.[27] The Parthians utilized their social versatility to establish and expand their imperialism, absorbing diverse and disparate communities into a lasting empire through the consolidation of power under the guidance of the early Arsacids and their flexible imperial ideology.[28]

21. Note Frye 1984: 208; Shahbazi 1986a; Olbrycht 2003: 73–75; Hauser 2005; Dąbrowa 2011a; id. 2014c; Olbrycht 2017b: 18–19, 22. See Justin 41.3.4. For the complexity and vibrancy of horse-based cultures on the Central Asian steppe, note Di Cosmo 2004.

22. For the former, see Wolski 1964b: 380; Schippmann 1986; Boyce 1994: 249; Hauser 2013. For the latter, see Grajetzki 2011: 9–10. Compare Lerner 1999: 13–19.

23. Strabo 7.3.12, 11.7.1, 8.2–3, 9.2–3; Justin 2.1.3, 2.3.6, 41.1.1f., 10, 41.2.3–4; Pliny *NH* 6.19.50, 29.112; Arr. *Parth.* Fr. 2–3; Curt. 4.12.11, 6.2.13f.; Pomp. Mela 3.4, 33; Lucan *Phar.* 2.50, 553, 8.178, 216, 302, 353, 432. Note Lerouge-Cohen 2017. For this portrayal in scholarship, see Rawlinson 1876 (2002): 11, 24, 29; Lozinski 1959: 36–37; Poirot 2014: 17 n.33. Contra Hauser 2013.

24. Koshelenko 1980: 193–95; id. 1985a: 344; Nikonorov 1987a; id. 1987b; id. 1994; id. 1995; Olbrycht 1996; id. 1998a; id. 1998b; Nikonorov 1998b; Zadneprovskiy 1999; Koshelenko and Pilipko 1999; Olbrycht 1999; id. 2000a; id. 2000b; Nikonorov 2000a; Olbrycht 2003; Hauser 2005; Lerouge-Cohen 2007: 15–21; Nikonorov 2010; Grainger 2015: 64–65. Compare Justin 41.2.2, 3.4, 42.2.5–6; Plut. *Crass.* 21.7, 27.2; Jos. *Bell.* 1.255; Jos. *Ant.* 14.342.

25. Wolski 1980b; id. 1996; Gregoratti 2013b. Compare Tao 2007: 95; Dąbrowa 2011a; Olbrycht 2013a; id. 2015a.

26. Note Curtis 2000: 25, 34; Olbrycht 2003; Dąbrowa 2011a; id. 2011d; Hauser 2013: 739–43; Dąbrowa 2014a; Thonemann 2015: 87, 91–96, 105, 114. For the flexible use of language under the Arsacids (Greek, Aramaic, Parthian, and Middle Persian), see Olbrycht 2003: 74; Ellerbrock and Winkelmann 2012: Chs. 8–9; Haruta 2013: 781–85, 788; Rougemont 2013: 798–800; Wiesehöfer 2016: 217; Olbrycht 2017b: 21.

27. See Olbrycht 2003; Hackl, Jacobs, and Weber 2010a; Dąbrowa 2012; Olbrycht 2015a; Sampson 2015: 32; Wiesehöfer 2016: 217, 227; Overtoom 2016a; id. 2016d; id. 2019a; id. 2019b; id. 2019c; id. 2019/2020; id. 2020; id. 2021 .

28. Note Dąbrowa 2010a; id. 2010b; id. 2010c; id. 2011a; id. 2014a; Wiesehöfer 2016: 217; Overtoom 2019a;

Although not a "restoration" of the Achaemenid Persian Empire, nor an Iranian "nationalistic" movement against Hellenism, the Parthians came to embrace much of Persian culture within their society as they occupied the Hellenistic Middle East.[29] The Sasanian Persians, who replaced Parthian power in the 220s CE, saw themselves as the true Persian revivalists in the Middle East, and although there was in fact much continuation between Arsacid and Sasanian Iran, they mostly viewed the Parthians as imposters.[30] Yet it was the Parthians, not the Sasanian Persians, who reintroduced Iranian elements into post-Seleucid Persia.[31] The early Arsacids helped develop this Irano-Parthian identity to further integrate their expanding empire, eventually going so far as to adopt Greek and Persian titulature into their imperial identity.[32] The early Arsacids also seamlessly integrated their expanding Irano-Parthian imperial identity into already established Hellenistic parameters of their dynastic rule, such as the creation of a new calendrical era beginning in 248/247 and the establishment of a Hellenistic ruler-cult.[33]

Therefore, the Arsacids found success in part by embracing elements of Persian culture and connecting the Parthian Arsacid royal line to the Persian Achaemenid royal line.[34] However, the Parthians also were willing to adopt Seleucid administrative precedents, while including Greek communities and statesmen in the administration of local government.[35] The Parthians employed administrators who initially functioned similarly to a satrap, regional strategos, garrison commander (φρούραρχος), citadel commander (ἀκροφύλαξ), and viceroy; however, they did so unsystematically with an openness to altering their administrative or military functions.[36] For example, Rahim Shayegan recently has argued that perhaps the supreme commander in Babylonia in the early Arsacid period was similar to the Seleucid viceroy in Anatolia and the Achaemenid *karanoi*.[37] This

id. 2019b.

29. See Wolski 1966; id. 1976a; id. 1983b; id. 1985a; id. 1993. Note Daryaee 2015: 286–87; Strootman and Versluys 2017; Shayegan 2017. Note also Pliny *NH* 6.16.41.

30. Note Colledge 1967: 103–4, 174; Nikonorov 2005; Dignas and Winter 2007: 56–62; Hauser 2013: 729–30; Invernizzi 2013; Klein and Wirtz 2013: 5069; Gregoratti 2015b: 14; Wiesehöfer 2016: 217; Overtoom 2016c; Olbrycht 2016d; Ghodrat-Dizaji 2016; Gariboldi 2016; Gyselen 2016.

31. See Curtis 2000: 34; Shayegan 2011: 332, 369–70; Gregoratti 2015b: 14–15.

32. See Sellwood 1983: 285; Wolski 1990b; id. 1991; Dąbrowa 2011a; Shayegan 2011: 334–49; Dąbrowa 2014a; Canepa 2017b; Engels 2018; Shayegan 2017; Strootman 2018.

33. Dąbrowa 2009; id. 2010a; id. 2010b; id. 2010c; id. 2011a; id. 2011b; id. 2011c; id. 2014c; Grainger 2015: 65; Daryaee 2015: 286; Wiesehöfer 2016: 217; Gaslain 2016; Olbrycht 2016e; Nabel 2017a; Dąbrowa 2016b; id. 2017a. Note Kosmin 2018.

34. See Colledge 1967: 33; Dąbrowa 1983: 103–17; Wolski 1984: 373–79; Wiesehöfer 1986: 177–81; Panitschek 1990: 459–61; Wolski 1990a: 8–9; id. 1990b: 15; id. 1990c: 108–9; id. 1991: 53–55; id. 1993: 152–60; Wiesehöfer 1994a: 39; id. 1994b: 55–66; id. 2000: 714; Wheeler 2002: 288–89; Wiesehöfer 2002a: 112–13; id. 2002b: 296; id. 2005: 120; Fowler 2005: 125–55; Assar 2006c: 143–44; Wiesehöfer 2007b: 128; Shayegan 2011: 41–60; Dąbrowa 2012; Lerner 2017.

35. Dąbrowa 1994; Shipley 2000: 322; Dąbrowa 2005; id. 2005 [2006]; id. 2006-2007 [2008]; id. 2011a; id. 2011d; Shayegan 2011: 137–39; Wiesehöfer 2014; Lerouge-Cohen 2014; Olbrycht 2017b. Note Bickerman 1938.

36. Note Colledge 1967: 57–60; Dąbrowa 2011a.

37. Shayegan 2011: 210–25; id. 2017.

Parthian supreme commander presided over the general of Babylonia, the governor of Babylonia, the mayor of Babylon, and the guard commander of Babylon. Meanwhile, the second-in-command to the Parthian king, who became known as the satrap of satraps, was the governor of Media, and he presided over the supreme commander in Babylonia. Although it remains partly speculative, Shayegan concludes that these offices within the Arsacid power structure were not limited to Babylonia.[38] Far from being "a discrepant and sometimes grotesque blend of Greek and barbaric traditions," the Parthians were able to apply their versatile social identity to the administration of their expanding empire with precision and nuance, which made their imperialism familiar to subject communities and encouraged them to participate more readily in the maintenance of the Parthian state.[39]

Throughout much of the third to first centuries, the Parthians came to represent the interests of the multicultural communities of the Hellenistic Middle East better than their Greek and Macedonian rivals. The cultural flexibility of the Parthians helped encourage indigenous communities to support the early Arsacids, which in turn allowed the Parthians to occupy large sections of the Middle East quickly under capable and charismatic leaders, such as Arsaces I, Mithridates I, and Mithridates II.[40] For example, as the Parthians annexed the territories of Mesopotamia from the Seleucids in the 140s–100s, they offered more local representation and autonomy to the communities within this region.[41] Although the Achaemenids utilized administrative inclusiveness and cultural flexibility to gain and maintain support within their massive empire, the Seleucids mostly failed to persuade sufficiently "indigenous elites to identify imperial interest with their own."[42] The more dismissive and exploitative occupation of the multicultural eastern territories by the Seleucids, which in the examples of Seleucus II, Antiochus III, Antiochus IV, and Antiochus VII resulted in disaster, created local resentment on a scale that the Parthians rarely encountered.[43] Thus, compared to the Seleucid occupation of the Middle East, indigenous aristocrats had heightened regional autonomy and power under the Parthians with greater access to authority and participation within the Parthian imperial system.[44]

38. Id. 224–25.

39. Warry 1995: 155.

40. See Dąbrowa 1994; Frye 2000: 18; Dąbrowa 2008 [2009]; id. 2011a; Grajetzki 2011: 14; Overtoom 2016a; Olbrycht 2016e; id. 2017b; Dąbrowa 2017a; Lerner 2017; Overtoom 2019a; id. 2019b; id. 2019c; id. 2020.

41. Dąbrowa 2005; id. 2005 [2006]; Tao 2007: 91; Dąbrowa 2006–2007 [2008]; id. 2008 [2009]; id. 2011a. For Parthian officials in lower Mesopotamia, note Teixidor 1987.

42. Kosmin 2013a: 686. Note Chrubasik 2016: Ch. 1. For the Achaemenids, note Wiesehöfer 1996: 66–101; Briant 2002: 873–76; Lerner 2015a: 304–5.

43. Note Justin 32.2.1-2, 38.10.8-10, 39.1.6, 41.4.4-5; Appian *Syr.* 11.65-66; Diod. 28.3.1, 29.15.1, 34/35.15-17; Strabo 16.1.18; Polyb. 31.9; Jos. *Ant.* 12.354-9; *II Maccabees* 9.1-3; Porph. 56; Athen. 5.38; Posid. 16 (F. H. G. III.258); Sebeos in Thomson 1978: 364-65; Eus. *Chron.* (Smith ed.): 255; Moses 2.2.

44. Wolski 1989; Olbrycht 2010b: 147; Grajetzki 2011: 11, 15; Dąbrowa 2012; Wiesehöfer 2016: 217–18, 227; Gregoratti 2016a: 5; Olbrycht 2017b. For the Babylonian elite under the Seleucids, note Stevens 2016; Haubold 2016. Compare Graslin-Thomé 2012.

A major factor in the ability of the Parthians to establish, maintain, and expand their hegemony throughout the Hellenistic Middle East was the inclusiveness of their society, which the Arsacids utilized to embrace regional aristocracies and incorporate them into a more flexible structure of empire.[45] Arsaces I helped establish this precedent when he quickly convinced the Parthian aristocracy in northeastern Iran to support him and his dynasty against the interests of the Seleucid state and its officials.[46] Although the increasingly diverse Parthian aristocracy did not always elect the king, it played an progressively pivotal role in the support of the regime and the military.[47] The Parthians even established an advisory body of kinsmen, wise men, and religious leaders, similar to the Roman Senate, to help guide the policies of the state.[48] Thus, the Parthian state from its conception built upon the social flexibility of a multicultural union of regional leaders under the ultimate authority of the Arsacids. This made the high command of the Parthian state versatile and eclectic, allowing the Arsacids to develop a more inclusive system of administration that emphasized, utilized, and internalized the capabilities and strengths of local leaders.[49]

Although the power of the Parthian kings was primary, the Parthians implemented a system of tributary vassal kingdoms under their suzerainty that gave local leaders enough security and freedom that they generally supported the regime. For instance, the kings of Elymais dedicated many large rock reliefs symbolizing the authority of their rule alongside Parthian examples.[50] Scholars generally have viewed the administrative system of the Parthians differently from the examples of other Persian and Greek rulers of the Middle East because of the Arsacids' support of and reliance upon vassals, referring to the Parthians as "feudal" warlords.[51] Although the imperialism of the Parthians was unique and a major factor in their ultimate success, terms like "feudal state," "feudalization," or "system of feudalism," when discussing the Parthians, create an inappropriate association between the structure of the Parthian state and the much later and vastly different political and social systems of medieval Europe. The term "feudalism" traditionally has been used as a pejorative to compare the barbarous and backward reputation of medieval Europe to that of Rome.[52] Thus, associating the Parthians with "feudalism" reinforces the false narrative that

45. Dąbrowa 2011a; Wiesehöfer 2016: 227; Gregoratti 2016b: 86–89; id. 2017a; Overtoom 2019a.

46. Frye 1984: 208; Shahbazi 1986a; Olbrycht 2003: 73–75; Overtoom 2016a.

47. Olbrycht 2016a.

48. Strabo 11.9.3; Plut. *Crass.* 32.3. Note Lerouge-Cohen 2007: 245–55.

49. Keall 1994: 271–72; Dąbrowa 2013; Wiesehöfer 2016: 217–18; Gregoratti 2017a; Olbrycht 2017b.

50. Kawami 2013; Dąbrowa 2014b: 62–63. Compare Mehrkiyan 1997.

51. Note Debevoise 1938: xxxviii; Wolski 1967; Colledge 1967: 63–64, 66, 86, 175; id. 1986: 3; Assar 2006c: 143; Jones and Ereira 2006: 164–66; Goldsworthy 2009: 88–89; Sheldon 2010: 2–3; Assar 2011: 121; Engels 2011; Sampson 2015: 32, 118; Daryaee 2015: 287; Shahbazi 2019. For the differences between Parthian vassal kingdoms and Roman client states, see Hartmann 2015.

52. Note Bull 2005. For the numerous problems surrounding the use of the term "feudalism," see Brown 1998: 148–69.

the Parthians also were barbarous and backward when compared to Rome and the other major empires of the Middle East. To avoid this problem, Wolfram Grajetzki describes the Parthian Empire as a "kind of federal state."[53] Although this term also carries with it problems of modern perception, the terminology of a "federal system" appears more suitable than that of a "feudal system." Moreover, Leonardo Gregoratti recently described the Parthian Empire "as a network or confederacy of political and cultural realities."[54] Ultimately, it is difficult to associate the Parthian Empire with other systems of political organization because the early Arsacids created a uniquely flexible imperial system supported by a diverse network of regional vassal kings and aristocratic families who were willing to support the regime for four and a half centuries in large part because of the inclusivity and adaptability of that system.[55] This was not a detrimental system of "institutional weakness," but rather a source of strength.[56]

The Parthians eventually divided their empire into eighteen districts and appointed vassal kings or governors (*shahrdars*) to manage these regions; however, partly because of the limitations of their military capabilities and partly for reasons of expediency, the Parthians created a more extensive vassalage system to support their imperialism, which generally allowed greater local autonomy and political representation in subject regions in exchange for royal support.[57] For example, the Arsacids often allowed their vassals to issue their own coinage.[58] The Arsacids also allowed their vassals, such as Queen Helena of Adiabene, to secure hereditary succession for their dynasties.[59] In fact, several scholars recently have argued that this administrative strategy was deliberate and fairly unique, advocating that it was a leading reason for the longevity of the Parthian Empire.[60] For instance, as the Parthians expanded their hegemony westward under Mithridates II in the 110s–90s, these vassal kingdoms allowed the Parthians swiftly to consolidate their authority over wide-ranging and often peripheral regions. Moreover, since the Parthians' professional standing army was relatively small, the Arsacids increasingly utilized their network of strong aristocratic families and vassal kingdoms to raise necessary levies and share the military burden of controlling such a large imperial territory.[61] This meant that, first, as their empire expanded,

53. Grajetzki 2011: 11.

54. Gregoratti 2017a.

55. Wolski 1967; id. 1981; Keall 1994: 271–72; Olbrycht 2016a; Gregoratti 2017a.

56. Grainger is often dismissive and critical of Parthian imperialism. Note Grainger 2016: 115.

57. Pliny *NH* 4.112. The central authority of the Arsacids over their empire is much debated. See Dąbrowa 2012; Hauser 2013: 734–39; Gregoratti 2017a. Note Tacitus' exaggerated description of the relative autonomy of Seleucia under the Parthians. Tac. *Ann.* 6.42, 11.9. Strabo's account is more acceptable. Strabo 16.1.16. Compare Plut. *Crass.* 32.3–5.

58. Bernard 1990: 41–43; Olbrycht 2010b: 147; Rezakhani 2013.

59. Shayegan 2011: 222. For Adiabene as a vassal of Parthia, note Luther 2015.

60. Keall 1994; Olbrycht 2003: 98–99; id. 2010b: 147; Grajetzki 2011: 11; Daryaee 2015: 287; Wiesehöfer 2016: 217–18; Gregoratti 2017a.

61. Note Wilcox 1986: 6; Hauser 2006; id. 2013; Olbrycht 2016a; Overtoom 2017b; id. 2019a. Some scholars suggest the Arsacids only maintained weak control over the army or that the Parthian military was an inexperienced

the Parthians could conduct quick, successful campaigns with their limited military and yet maintain their territorial gains without the need for a costly, drawn-out occupation, and second, during their intense rivalries with the Seleucids and Romans, the Parthians could vigorously defend their territory against invaders with a loyal and determined army.

By establishing tributary kingdoms in the peripheral regions of the Parthian Empire, such as Media Atropatene, Persis, Elymais, Characene, and Armenia, the Parthians delegated many of the responsibilities and costs of maintaining these regions to their vassals, while preserving a flexible approach to encouraging the loyalty and participation of vassal rulers by utilizing threats of invasion, occupation, and replacement.[62] Thus, the Parthians created a nuanced imperial system that afforded them many of the benefits of direct empire, such as military resources and tax revenue, while avoiding the difficult tasks of provincial administration, management of major urban centers, and frontier defense. This allowed the Parthians to maintain a consistent strategy for western expansion, especially in the late second and early first centuries, through a network of tributary kingdoms and marriage alliances. Shayegan captured the value of this new system to the Parthians' imperial aggression when he stated, "Arsacid indirect rule was therefore not necessarily a sign of the empire's inability to impose its political will, but a major tenet of its strategy—including the *hostage* and *matrimonial policies*—which perceived expansionism not merely in terms of conquest, but as the projection of Arsacid influence by dint of clientage and alliances."[63] This nuanced approach to imperialism significantly aided the standing and longevity of the Arsacids politically and militarily.

The generally good leadership and relative stability of the early Arsacids is a focus of this study, and the strength of the Arsacid dynasty went hand-in-hand with the success of the Parthian state from the third to the first centuries. Unlike the Seleucids and Bactrians, who became crippled by dynastic strife in this period, the Arsacids did not experience a civil war until the late 90s.[64] The stability of the monarchy during their early history gave the Parthians another important advantage in their struggle to dominate the Hellenistic Middle East.[65] When the Parthian king was a capable and commanding figure, the state prospered; however, when the king was weak, or the throne was contested, something that

militia. Colledge 1967: 66, 75; Sheldon 2010: 175. Such notions have been dismissed in recent years. See Hauser 2006; id. 2013: 734–39; Olbrycht 2016a; Overtoom 2017b. Even at the end of Arsacid rule in the early third century CE, after centuries of conflict with Rome, the Parthian military relied heavily upon annual levies. Herodian 3.1.2, 6.5.3–4, 6.7.1. Herodian views the Sasanian Persian army as a continuation of the Parthian army. Overtoom 2016c: 166.

62. Note Gregoratti 2017a; Overtoom 2019a.

63. Shayegan 2011: 328. Compare Wiesehöfer 2007a; Gregoratti 2011b; id. 2017a. See Tac. *Ann.* 13.34; Strabo 11.13.1; Jos. *Ant.* 20.54–92.

64. Note Assar 2005a: 53; id. 2005b; id. 2006d: 56–62; id. 2011: 121–22.

65. Overtoom 2016a; id. 2019a; id. 2019b; id. 2020.

occurred far too frequently after the late 90s, the power of the state dwindled. The expanding power of the Parthian aristocracy played an important role in the long cycle of civil wars that sapped the strength of the Arsacids from the first century onward.[66] Yet the capable and ambitious early Arsacids were indispensable to the formation and expansion of the Parthian state from a minor kingdom to a major empire, and the innovations of the Parthian military were the final crucial element that the Parthians needed to survive and overcome their numerous rivals.

The Parthians' Unique Mode of Warfare

The innovations of the Parthian army were indeed exceptional in the Hellenistic Middle East. Although the Parthians settled on the Iranian plateau and came to embrace many cultural influences from Greek and Persian neighbors, they did not adopt the military traditions of the Greeks and Persians. Instead, the Parthians continued to emphasize the asymmetric cavalry tactics and organization of their nomadic roots.[67] The Parthians recruited their cavalry largely from settler-soldiers, who offered service in exchange for land; however, the Parthians' cavalry-focused militarism was of steppe origin, and the social structure of the Parthian state remained closely connected to its military organization.[68]

The Parthians were the first major world power to introduce and maintain nomadic cavalry-based hit-and-run tactics and strategies into a successful, long-term empire, an achievement the Graeco-Roman tradition recognizes.[69] Strabo states, "The cause of this [that is, the Parthians' success at empire building and in their rivalry with Rome] is their mode of life, and also their customs, which contain much that is barbarian and Scythian in character, though more that is conducive to hegemony and success in war (πλέον μέντοι τὸ χρήσιμον πρὸς ἡγεμονίαν καὶ τὴν ἐν τοῖς πολέμοις κατόρθωσιν)."[70] The composition of the Parthian military, its use in the field, and its ability to maintain a major imperial state gave the Parthians perhaps their greatest advantage in their struggle to dominate the Hellenistic Middle East, and the Parthians' asymmetric mode of warfare meant that smaller, more logistically limited, and lighter-armed Parthian armies could resist and annihilate the more professionalized and heavier-armed

66. Wolski 1967; id. 1989; Dąbrowa 2013; Gregoratti 2013b.

67. See Olbrycht 2003; Hauser 2005; Olbrycht 2016a; Overtoom 2016a; id. 2017b; id. 2019a; id. 2019b; id. 2019c; id. 2020; id. 2021. Compare Wolski 1956-1957; id. 1964b; id. 1965; id. 1966; id. 1967; id. 1976b; id. 1981; id. 1983a; id. 1984; id. 1985b; id. 1991; id. 1993; id. 1996.

68. Colledge 1967: 65; Nikonorov 1987c; id. 1995; Goldsworthy 1998: 74; Nikonorov 1998b; id. 2000a; id. 2000b; Olbrycht 2001; Nikonorov 2002; Olbrycht 2003; Nikonorov 2005; Roth 2009: 114; Nikonorov 2010; id. 2014; Olbrycht 2016a; Overtoom 2016a.

69. Although Rawlinson unfairly disparaged the Parthians' mode of warfare with racial criticism, he recognized that the Parthians' mode of warfare had an important strategic emphasis and that the use of this mode of warfare within a "civilized," that is, a traditional state, was unique. Rawlinson 1876 (2002): 32.

70. Strabo 11.9.2.

armies of the Seleucids and Romans through speed, maneuverability, flexibility, and deception.[71]

By at least the middle 230s, the Parthians under Arsaces I had developed a mode of warfare that incorporated their distinctive cavalry-based army and tactics into their wider strategic thinking. Although the Parthians came to include infantry forces in the maintenance of their empire, for over four hundred years the horse remained the focus of the Parthian military.[72] There never was a serious attempt by the Arsacids to overhaul their cavalry-based army to reform it to more Persian, Greek, or Roman standards.[73] Peter Brunt argued, "The capacity of the Parthians almost to annihilate his [Crassus'] forces was the result of developments in Iran entirely extraneous to the factors that operated in Italy or the Roman empire."[74] The Parthians emphasized an asymmetric approach to warfare, which was at the core of their tactical and strategic thinking in part because of their unique military and tactical developments both on the Central Asian steppe and the Iranian plateau.[75] It was a variation and improvement of nomadic asymmetric warfare, which Herodotus called "invincible and unapproachable (ἄμαχοί τε καὶ ἄποροι προσμίσγειν)."[76] Often outnumbered by better-equipped and stronger Macedonian and Roman enemies, the Parthians developed a calculated military withdrawal strategy that allowed them throughout their recorded history to deceive and outmaneuver more conventional Hellenistic and Roman armies.[77]

Similar to other aspects of Parthian history, surviving accounts of the Parthian army on campaign are scattered and often cursory. Plutarch's account of the clash between the Parthians and Romans at Carrhae in 53 is our most detailed description of Parthian warfare, making it an invaluable piece of evidence.[78] However, instead of viewing the Carrhae campaign and indeed the battle itself as the near flawless execution of a well-developed Parthian mode of warfare, scholarly tradition generally has attempted to portray the Parthian tactics and strategy utilized during the Carrhae campaign as somehow anomalous and, therefore, has attempted to portray the Parthian general Surena as an unrivaled Parthian military genius and reformer.[79] This study calls this assumption into question, arguing

71. Overtoom 2017b; id. 2019a.

72. Although the figures are largely theoretical and represent a "best-case scenario," for the most recent account of the composition and potential manpower of the Parthian army, note Olbrycht 2016a.

73. For the Achaemenid and Sasanian armies, note Farrokh 2017; Wozniak 2018. The Parthians eventually had a much larger effect on Roman warfare. Coulston 1986.

74. Brunt 1988: 83.

75. Note Olbrycht 2015a.

76. Herod. 4.46.2–3. Note Kosmin 2014: 43; Grainger 2015: 64–65.

77. Overtoom 2017b.

78. For Plutarch and Carrhae, see Frendo 2007; Overtoom 2017a.

79. The scholarly tradition that the Carrhae campaign was an aberration is long-standing. For example, note Mommsen 1856 (1903): v 157, 164; Sampson 2015: 111–13, 117–21, 147, Ch. 6, 166, 177. Compare Timpe 1962; Koshelenko 1980; Nikonorov 1995; Sheldon 2005: 86–99; Frendo 2007; Lerouge-Cohen 2007: 282–95; Sheldon 2010: 13–64; Weggen 2011; Traina 2010; id. 2011: 209–17, Suren-Pahlav 2019.

instead that the Parthians' military actions during the Carrhae campaign were merely a variation and continuation of a long-standing unique mode of warfare. Consideration of the Parthians' campaigns against Seleucus II, Antiochus III, Demetrius II, and Antiochus VII in relation to the Carrhae campaign is paramount to establishing a more nuanced understanding of the implementation of a unique Parthian mode of warfare over a period of two centuries rather than two years (54–53). Thus, in this section we shall consider the events recorded in Plutarch's account of the Battle of Carrhae, not as an anomaly, but as a representation of Parthian military tradition.

The Parthian army primarily remained a cavalry force under the Arsacids for centuries in part because of heavy influences from its nomadic Parni roots.[80] Justin records, "The manner of their arms is that of their fatherland and Scythia (*armorum patrius ac Scythicus mos*)."[81] Here Justin recognizes the flexibility of the Parthian army in its incorporation and alteration of nomadic warfare. He continues, "They ride on horseback on all occasions; on horses they go to war, and to feasts; on horses they discharge public and private duties; on horses they go abroad, meet together, traffic, and converse. Indeed, the difference between slaves and freemen is, that slaves go on foot, but freemen only on horseback."[82] Moreover, Josephus indicates that the horse was so important to Parthian society that the "greatest dishonor (ἀτιμιῶν μεγίστη)" possible for a Parthian nobleman was to be forced to ride a donkey in the nude.[83] Thus, the horse was fundamental to the identity of Parthian society and warfare. Parthian nobles illustrated their status through the quality and quantity of their horses and retainers.[84]

Justin also provides a glimpse into how the Parthians trained for war from a young age and prepared for campaigns. He states:

> They have an army, not like other nations, of free men, but chiefly consisting of slaves, the numbers of whom daily increase, the power of manumission being allowed to none, and all their offspring, in consequence, being born slaves. These bondmen they bring up as carefully as their own children, and teach them, with great pains, the arts of riding and shooting with the bow. As any one is eminent in wealth, so he furnishes the king with a proportionate number of horsemen for war. Indeed, when fifty thousand cavalry encountered [Marcus] Antonius, as he was making war upon Parthia, only four hundred of them were free men.[85]

80. Note Wolski 1981; Olbrycht 2016a; Overtoom 2016a. For the use of war elephants in the Partho-Sasanian period, see Daryaee 2016.

81. Justin 41.2.4. Translation slightly altered.

82. Id. 41.3.4. For the importance of the horse to the nomadic peoples of the Central Asian steppe, note Sinor 1972; id. 1981; Shahbazi 1987; Hyland 2003; Di Cosmo 2004; Anthony 2007; Noble 2015; Willekes 2016; Anderson 2016.

83. Jos. *Ant.* 18.356–59. My translation. Compare Dio 40.15.2–6.

84. See Coulston 1986; Shahbazi 1987; Kennedy 1996: 83–84; Olbrycht 2003; id. 2015a; id. 2016a; id. 2016d.

85. Justin 42.2.5–6. Compare Herodian 6.5.4.

Although Josephus corroborates this depiction of the Parthians utilizing a small group of free men to lead their army, the Graeco-Roman tradition exaggerate the Parthians' use of slaves as soldiers, utilizing Greek and Roman stereotypes of servile easterners to explain the composition of the Parthian military.[86] Justin and Josephus likely illustrate a wider misunderstanding of the Parthians' system of dependency with military obligations by Greek and Roman observers, where "free men" actually represent leading Parthian aristocrats serving in the name of the king and "slaves" actually represent the retainers of those aristocrats.[87] Yet, in the above passage, Justin highlights the importance of riding and archery to Parthian military training, and he demonstrates that in times of war the Parthian king called upon his nobles to provide the horsemen he needed for a campaign.[88]

Justin also discusses the style of Parthian warfare. He records, "Of engaging with the enemy in close fight, and of taking cities by siege, they [the Parthians] know nothing. They fight on horseback, either galloping forward or turning their backs. Often, too, they counterfeit flight, that they may throw their pursuers off their guard against being wounded by their arrows."[89] Here Justin underscores what I call the Parthians' "Feign Retreat, Defeat in Detail" mode of warfare.[90] After the Parthians had established a secure state in what is today northeastern Iran under Arsaces I and had begun expanding that state at the expense of their neighbors, the Parthian army came to possess a marked advantage in mobility and flexibility over more traditionally armed and organized Hellenistic armies.[91] Justin continues, "In general they [the Parthians] retire before the enemy in the very heat of the engagement, and, soon after their retreat, return to the battle afresh; so that, when you feel most certain that you have conquered them, you have still to meet the greatest danger from them."[92] Justin illustrates that the Parthians utilized aggressive hit-and-run and deceptive feigned retreat maneuvers as the core of their innovative mode of warfare in the Hellenistic Middle East. When implemented correctly the Parthians' unique mode of asymmetric warfare was devastating, giving them an important military advantage that aided in their survival and eventual rise to power.

The Parthians became famous for a military maneuver commonly known as the "Parthian Shot."[93] Although it is likely the Parni, before establishing themselves

86. Jos. *Bell.* 1.255; id. *Ant.* 14.342. Note Wolski 1965; id. 1967; id. 1975; id. 1981; id. 1983b; id. 1985b; id. 1989; Isaac 2006: Chs. 4–5, 8. Compare Dąbrowa 2011a; Gregoratti 2011a; id. 2015a: 203–4; Gruen 2017; Shahbazi 2019.

87. Note Dąbrowa 2013; Olbrycht 2016a.

88. Dio also argues that the Parthians excelled in horsemanship and archery from boyhood, arguing that "they are almost invincible in their own country and in any that has similar characteristics." Dio 40.15.2, 4. Note Olbrycht 2016a: 296, 303–6, 312–13.

89. Justin 41.2.7. Compare Hor. Od. 2.13; Tac. *Ann.* 15.4, 7, 13, 16. Parthian noblewomen also perhaps learned to ride and fight and maintained personal armies. Note the story of Princess Rhodogune suppressing a rebellion. Polyaen. 27. Compare Appian *Syr.* 11.68. For Parthian women, note Brosius 2010; Farrokh and Karamian 2018.

90. Note Overtoom 2017b.

91. Note id. 2016a.

92. Justin 41.2.9. Compare Herodian 6.3.7.

93. For efforts to explain the tactics of the Parthians, including the use of the "Parthian Shot," see Wilcox 1986;

in Parthia in the middle third century, were one of several Central Asian steppe tribes developing this asymmetric approach to combat, they were responsible for introducing it to the wider Graeco-Roman world in the Middle East and Near East and for perfecting its use in battle.[94] Parthian horse archers developed a highly effective system of delivering fire upon an enemy while advancing and withdrawing. The "Parthian Shot" was the process by which a rider gripped and maneuvered his horse away from the enemy with his lower body, while turning his upper body back toward the enemy to deliver precise fire. It was one of the most effective military techniques developed in the ancient world. Added to this effectiveness, at least according to the Greek and Roman sources, was the unique structure and devastating power of the Parthian composite bow, giving the Parthians a technological advantage as well.[95] The Parthians adapted and developed a complex production process, allowing large-scale manufacturing of the renowned Parthian composite bow, while importing and casting high-quality steel for their arms and armor.[96] With these advantages the Parthians successfully developed the "Parthian Shot" technique into a highly synchronized and potentially devastating battlefield tactical maneuver that they could deliver aggressively or defensively to great effect.

Yet the use of lightly armed horse archers on their own in battle was not a reliable way for the Parthians to secure victory, especially against the heavily armored and numerically superior armies of the Seleucids and Romans. Since the arms and armor (or the lack thereof) of horse archers were inadequate for close combat, this posed serious tactical and strategic problems for nomadic horse archer-based armies in ancient warfare. We know from various images of Parthian archers in sculpture and coinage that they rode to battle in little to no armor.[97] Thus, horse archers were relatively useless in hand-to-hand combat on the battlefield, as Justin emphasized.[98] If an enemy could manage to engage the Parthian horse archers, the result was usually disastrous for the Parthians. For instance, Justin relates a story where Seleucid soldiers destroyed an army

Nikonorov 1995; Warry 1995: 154–56; Lerouge-Cohen 2007: 285–313; Sheldon 2010; Traina 2010; Sampson 2015; Overtoom 2017b; id. 2019a; id. 2019b; id. 2019c; id. 2020; id. 2021. Compare Plut. *Crass.* 24.4–5, 25, 27.1–2; Tac. *Ann.* 6.35, 13.40.5–6, Ovid *Ars Am.* 1.201–12.

94. For example, Chinese sources record that the Hsiung-nu were using similar armaments, training, and tactics at this time. Di Cosmo 2004: 276–78. Note McLaughlin 2016: 4–5. For the long tradition of horse-based warfare, note May 2007; Noble 2015.

95. Plut. *Crass.* 18.2–3, 24.4–5; Dio 40.22.4; Amm.. Mar. 22.8.37. For the image of Parthian horse archers in Greek and Roman sources, see Lerouge-Cohen 2007: 296–300. War iconography, especially the archer, featured heavily on Parthian coinage. See Sellwood 1980; Rezakhani 2013: 767, 769–71; Lerner 2017. Iconography such as this on Parthian coinage helps emphasize the militarism of Parthian society. For information on Parthian coinage practices and styles, see Rezakhani 2013: 766–72; Dąbrowa 2014a. According to Plutarch, the Arsacids took pride in their archery. Plut. *Demet.* 20.2. Note Burriș-Davis 2014.

96. Note Sheldon 2010: 36; McLaughlin 2016: 5, 154–61.

97. Note Gaslain 2006. The Parthians wore riding clothes similar to other nomadic peoples at the time. Olbrycht 2003: 89–92.

98. Justin 41.2.7.

of Parthian cavalry in melee.[99] Meanwhile, Tacitus recounts a much later battle, where an enemy army forced the Parthian horse archers to fight in close range and destroyed them.[100] Moreover, the bow itself is a problematic weapon, first, because it requires good weather to fire correctly, limiting its effectiveness in winter, and, second, because it relies on supplies of ammunition. For example, Dio records that the Parthians avoided warfare in "the dead of winter" because it was too wet.[101] He also notes that the Parthians at Carrhae finally had to retire because their "bowstrings snapped under the constant shooting, [and] the missiles were exhausted."[102] In theory, well-equipped and organized armies could hope simply to wait out a force of enemy horse archers until the riders had exhausted their limited supply of arrows and had to withdraw. These glaring combat deficiencies generally restricted the effectiveness and sustainability of nomadic forces in battle and on campaign. If the Parthians hoped to develop into a more effective military force that could contend with the superior size, equipment, and organization of the Hellenistic and later Roman armies in the Near East and Middle East, then they had to develop logistical and military innovations to make their armies more competitive.[103]

First, the Parthians addressed the supply restrictions facing their horse archers. For example, at the Battle of Carrhae, Plutarch tells us that Crassus had hoped to outlast the barrage of the Parthian horse archers until they had exhausted their supply of arrows; however, "when they [the Romans] perceived that many camels laden with arrows were at hand, from which the Parthians who first encircled them took a fresh supply, then Crassus, seeing no end to this, began to lose heart, and sent messengers to his son with orders to force an engagement with the enemy before he was surrounded."[104] Scholars generally assume without good reason that this extra supply of arrows delivered to the Parthian horse archers at the Battle of Carrhae was a unique and singular innovation of the Parthian commander Surena; however, such a scenario is highly unlikely, and no ancient writer makes such a claim.[105]

Plutarch's emphasis in this passage is not that the sudden logistical innovation of Surena confounded the Romans; rather, his moralistic, rhetorical emphasis

99. Id. 42.1.5.

100. Tac. *Ann.* 6.35.

101. Dio 40.15.4.

102. Id. 40.24.1.

103. Colledge's claims that, first, the Parthians adopted Seleucid tactics and armaments once they settled in Iran, making this the source of their early success, and that, second, the Parthians abandoned Hellenistic style warfare after a tactical "revolution" under Mithridates II in the late second century, developing their army "along traditional Iranian lines," are unsubstantiated and in almost complete opposition to our available evidence. Colledge 1967: 65. Although Rawlinson unfairly disparaged the Parthian mode of warfare as offensively ineffective and not adaptive, he recognized that, despite minor improvements, the Parthians' mode of warfare was "essentially the same system" for over four centuries. Rawlinson 1876 (2002): 109.

104. Plut. *Crass.* 25.1.

105. For example, note Colledge 1967: 66–7; Sampson 2015: 128–9.

is to portray Crassus as an ill-prepared and woefully outmaneuvered foil to his wiser and more capable subordinate, Cassius.[106] By the middle 50s, the Roman army recently had gained experience fighting against the Scythian mercenaries of Mithridates VI of Pontus and Tigranes II of Armenia; however, the Pontic and Armenian armies, which were more traditionally organized and equipped, had recruited and utilized horse archers sparingly.[107] The Parthian army was quite different from these contemporary Near Eastern powers because it utilized horse archers as a fundamental portion of its military force and as a crucial factor in its tactics. Yet Crassus and his contemporaries, who had never fought a major battle against the Parthians, made no clear distinction between the military forces of the Parthians and those of other Irano-Hellenized peoples in the Near East in large part because of ignorance and prevalent Roman stereotypes about eastern peoples.[108] Therefore, at Carrhae the heavy contingent of horse archers and the logistical capabilities of the Parthians surprised Crassus, not because they were the sudden innovations of a unique military genius as Gareth Sampson recently has argued, but rather because the Romans were unfamiliar with the different composition and capabilities of the Parthian army because they assumed the Parthians fought like all other eastern peoples.[109] Again, instead of viewing the Parthian army at Carrhae atypically, we should instead consider that Surena merely executed a variation of the Parthians' traditional mode of warfare.

It is highly unlikely that the Parthians, who won several decisive victories and experienced unparalleled military success against their rivals within the Hellenistic Middle East, had not developed a logistical solution as simple as bringing along extra arrows in a baggage train to resupply their horse archers in battle prior to 53. The size of Surena's baggage train was perhaps unusual because of his exceptional affluence and power; however, the concept of resupplying horse archers on the battlefield should hardly be considered unique to him, especially since even Plutarch does not make this claim.[110] Meanwhile, although Plutarch is the only ancient writer who mentions supplies of arrows on the battlefield explicitly, it is illogical to argue, as Sampson does, that Surena implemented a sudden logistical innovation at Carrhae, which was crucial to the success of the Parthian army against the Romans, that the Parthians after Carrhae abruptly abandoned without thought.[111] We should not consider the Parthian baggage train at Carrhae an isolated innovation simply because only Plutarch, with his unusually detailed

106. Overtoom 2016d; id. 2017a; id. 2021.

107. Appian *Mithr.* 9.64, 11.78, 12.85; Memnon 29.6; Dio 36.5–6.1; Plut. *Luc.* 26; id. *Apophtheg. Rom.* 203; Eutrop. 6.9; Phlegon, Frag. 12, in Hansen 1996: 62. Note Matyszak 2008: 128–29; Mayor 2010: 298.

108. Plut. *Crass.* 18.3–4, 20.1; id. *Luc.* 36.6–7. For Graeco-Roman stereotypes of eastern peoples, see Isaac 2006: Chs. 4–8. Compare Sonnabend 1986; Gruen 2007; Kennedy, Roy, and Goldman 2013: Ch. 10; Gregoratti 2016b: 82–86; Müller 2017b; Lerouge-Cohen 2017.

109. Sampson 2015. Compare Warry 1995: 156.

110. Plut. *Crass.* 21.6.

111. Sampson 2015: 119–20.

account, makes a specific record of it. We must consider the likely possibility that the Parthians in fact already had developed a mobile method to resupply their horse archers on the battlefield during their rise to supremacy within the Hellenistic Middle East, which Surena later adapted and which the Parthians continued to use long after Carrhae.[112]

Second, to make their army more competitive and threatening, the Parthians developed heavily armored cavalrymen, commonly known as cataphracts, to supplement their force of horse archers and to enhance the offensive capabilities of their army considerably.[113] The Parthian cataphracts (κατάφρακτοι, meaning encased in armor) paired the armored cavalry of the Central Asian tribes with the Macedonian-style long lance, and because of the Parthians this new form of "shock" cavalry became increasingly popular in the west.[114] Over the course of the third to first centuries, the Parthian military maintained and expanded its access to sources of high-quality mounts, acquiring, breeding, and training Central Asian Akhal-Teke and Iranian Nisaean horses.[115] As the Parthians expanded further into the Iranian plateau, they came to favor Iranian horses, which were known for their outstanding speed, strength, and beauty, while importing superior steel from Central Asia to arm and armor their cavalry.[116] The Parthians' access to abundant supplies of high-quality mounts and superior steel afforded them another advantage on the battlefield over their Greek and Roman rivals.

The Parthians used their heavy cavalry in battle to protect their horse archers and to exploit weak points in enemy formations. This method of warfare was so successful that the Parthian military barely changed for four centuries.[117] Dio, writing in the early third century CE around the time of the fall of the Parthian

112. Olbrycht argues that the logistical capabilities of the Parthian army were efficient and considerable. Olbrycht 2016: 298–9.

113. Dio 40.15.1–2; Justin 41.2.10.

114. The Massagetae and Dahae developed armored cavalry long before Arsaces I invaded Parthia, and when Alexander the Great campaigned in Bactria and Sogdiana against these tribes, they found the longer Macedonian spear more effective and adopted it. See Olbrycht 2003: 94–95. Compare Koshelenko 1980; Nikonorov 1987c; id. 1994; Warry 1995: 154–56; Olbrycht 1996; id. 1998a; id. 1998b; id. 1998c; Nikonorov 1998b; Mielczarek 1998; Olbrycht 1999; id. 2000a; id. 2000b; Nikonorov 2000a; Olbrycht 2001; Nikonorov 2010; Olbrycht 2015a; Anderson 2016. Thus, other nomadic peoples had developed heavy cavalry similar to the cataphract and had used similar hit-and-run tactics as the Parthians in battle; however, the logistical and strategic capabilities of the Parthian state compared to the Central Asian tribal confederations and the Parthians' introduction of the cataphract to the west were unique. Note Shahbazi 1987. Sampson's conclusion that the Parthians did not become a "devastating fighting machine" until they "perfected" the use of cataphracts in the 130s is exaggerated and unconvincing. Sampson 2015: 46. Note Gaslain 2008; Ellerbrock and Winkelmann 2012: Ch. 11; Overtoom 2017b; id. 2019a; id. 2019b; id. 2019c; id. 2020.

115. For the Parthians' breeding of horses, see Shahbazi 1987; Olbrycht 2001; Davis 2007: 28–41; Burris-Davis 2014.

116. Strabo 3.4.15, 11.13.7; Pliny *NH* 34.41; Hor. *Od.* 3.2; Plut. *Crass.* 24, 27. Note Olbrycht 2001; Ellerbrock and Winkelmann 2012: Ch. 10; McLaughlin 2016: 4–5; Farrokh et al. 2017.

117. This was a pre-stirrup period of cavalry warfare. Thus, the Parthians developed a saddle that probably had Eurasian steppe origins, which anchored heavily armored riders and allowed them to use "shock" tactics in battle. Shahbazi 1987; Nikonorov 2002; James 2013: 113. For the image of Parthian cataphracts in Greek and Roman sources, see Lerouge-Cohen 2007: 300–3.

Empire, succinctly illustrates the makeup and fighting style of the Parthians in similar terms to those of Plutarch in the second century CE and Pompeius Trogus in the Augustan Age. Dio records:

> They [the Parthians] make no use of a shield, but their forces consist of mounted archers and pikesmen, mostly encased in armor (κατάφρακτοι). Their infantry is small, made up of the weaker men; but even these are all archers. They practice from boyhood, and the climate and the land combine to aid both horsemanship and archery. The land, being for the most part level, is excellent for raising horses and very suitable for riding about on horseback; at any rate, even in war they lead about whole droves of horses, so that they can use different ones at different times, can ride up suddenly from a distance, and also retire to a distance speedily.[118]

Here Dio emphasizes the Parthians' asymmetric, hit-and-run tactics; however, he also records that the Parthians maintained a large reserve of fresh horses while on campaign to utilize in battle. Although he does not mention supplies of arrows explicitly, he clearly demonstrates that the Parthians understood the importance of resupplying their soldiers on the battlefield. The "droves of horses" mentioned by Dio illustrate that the Parthian army developed a mobile supply train for battle that was in fact not unique to Carrhae. The Parthians used these fresh mounts to harass the enemy with quick strikes and withdrawals. It is difficult to deny that these fresh mounts also would have carried supplies of arrows for the new assaults and feigned retreats of the Parthian horse archers. Dio soon after claims that the Parthians, who were "almost invincible" when defending their territory, struggled with "offensive war . . . because they encounter an entirely different condition of land and sky and because they do not lay in supplies of food or pay."[119] Although he ignores the Parthians' numerous successful conquests from their earlier history, Dio's criticism of the logistical limitations of the Parthians emphasizes the feeding and paying of their soldiers during prolonged campaigns. He does not claim that the Parthians struggled to supply ammunition to their soldiers. Rather, he recognizes that the Parthians' ability to reequip their soldiers on the battlefield, especially when the terrain was favorable, was exemplary.[120]

Without the development of a system to supply fresh mounts and arrows to the soldiery, the Parthian army could not have sustained major campaigns or endured extended battles offensively or defensively against the Seleucids and Romans on several occasions over the course of multiple centuries. Additionally, it seems highly likely that this logistical innovation occurred under the early Arsacids. For example, Polybius records that the Parthian army under Arsaces II

118. Dio 40.15.2–3. Translation slightly altered. Compare Tac. *Ann.* 6.35.
119. Dio 40.15.4–6.
120. Id. 40.15.3–5.

assaulted the vastly superior army of Antiochus III in 209 near Mount Labus with great determination for an entire day.[121] The duration and vigor of the Parthians' assaults would not have been possible without a way to resupply their horse archers.

Thus, the establishment of a strong military identity and infrastructure under the early Arsacids and the implementation of a logistical system to resupply their horse archers, paired with the development of perhaps the most devastating and versatile heavy cavalry in the world in this period, made the Parthian military more sustainable on campaign and in battle than its nomadic contemporaries. The Parthians emerged as the major rival of the more professionally organized Seleucids and Romans in large part because of their unique military and approach to warfare. It was this pairing of speed and strength within the Parthian army that allowed the Parthians to develop their unique "Feign Retreat, Defeat in Detail" mode of warfare.

The Parthians' mode of warfare had three fundamental and interchangeable tactical aspects, what I call the "Massed Assault Tactic," the "Hit-and-Run Tactic," and the "Feigned Retreat Tactic."[122] In battle the Parthians could attempt to overwhelm an enemy with the blunt force of their heavy cavalry. Justin notes, "They would be irresistible, if their vigor and perseverance were equal to the fury of their onset."[123] Thus, it appears the Parthians preferred to test an enemy formation with a sudden onslaught early in an engagement. As discussed below in detail, Plutarch's account of Carrhae also supports this conclusion. Yet if the Massed Assault Tactic was unsuccessful or unfavorable, then the Parthians turned to their other, more nuanced tactics. Justin, and indeed most of our surviving Greek and Roman sources, viewed the asymmetrical aspects of Parthian warfare as successful but devious or cowardly; however, the Parthians' mode of warfare derived its uniqueness and effectiveness from these nontraditional approaches to combat.[124]

When their Massed Assault Tactic was not viable to carry the day, the Parthians could utilize their Hit-and-Run Tactic to harass the enemy formation and to manipulate it into disorder. If the enemy broke its formation, the Parthian cataphracts once again could mount devastating charges and overwhelm isolated enemy detachments. Yet if the enemy formation did not react to the Parthians' coordinated, aggressive assaults, then the Parthians could implement their Feigned Retreat Tactic, where the Parthians "feigned" becoming disorganized

121. Polyb. 10.31.1–3.
122. Overtoom 2017b.
123. Justin 41.2.8.
124. Note Justin's condemnation of the Parthians' victory over the Seleucid king, Demetrius II, in 138. Id. 36.1.5, 38.9.2. For Greek and Roman thoughts on the military success and power of the Parthians, see Overtoom 2016c: 150; id. 2017a.

and routing in the face of the enemy to encourage the enemy to break formation and pursue them.

Within our discussion of the tactical aspects of the Parthians' mode of warfare it is necessary to make a clear distinction between the latter two tactical maneuvers. Although the Parthians utilized the "Parthian Shot" technique effectively in both tactical approaches to battle, the Hit-and-Run Tactic was an aggressive and offensive maneuver meant to force an enemy into exposing gaps within its defensive formation for the Parthian army (particularly the cataphracts) to exploit.[125] While executing the Hit-and-Run Tactic, the Parthian army remained organized and determined. Meanwhile, the Parthian Feigned Retreat Tactic was a deceptive and defensive maneuver meant to encourage an enemy to break its formation in mistaken pursuit. While executing the Feigned Retreat Tactic, the Parthian army appeared disorganized and defeated; however, in actuality it remained a well-coordinated unit. By feigning a general rout, the Parthians hoped to encourage overconfidence in the enemy so that they could isolate and destroy separated enemy detachments.[126] Plutarch's unparalleled depiction of the Parthian army at the Battle of Carrhae serves as a necessary point of reference when trying to illustrate these Parthian tactics in use, and therefore, we must consider this account in detail.

Before the momentous Battle of Carrhae in 53, reports began to reach the Romans that the Parthian army was stronger and more of a threat than expected.[127] Plutarch states:

> But from the cities of Mesopotamia in which the Romans had garrisons, certain men made their escape at great hazard and brought tidings of serious import. They had been eyewitnesses both of the numbers of the enemy and of their mode of warfare (τῶν ἀγώνων ὧν ἠγωνίσαντο) when they attacked their cities, and, as is usual, they exaggerated all the terrors of their report (οἷα δὲ φιλεῖ πάντα πρὸς τὸ δεινότεπον ἐξαγγέλλοντες). "When the [Parthian] men pursued," they declared, "there was no escaping them, and when they fled, there was no taking them; and strange missiles are the precursors of their appearance, which pierce through every obstacle before one sees who sent them; and as for the armor of their mail-clad [cataphract] horsemen, some of it is made to force its way through everything, and some of it to give way to nothing."[128]

125. Plutarch describes the Parthians utilizing the "Parthian Shot" technique aggressively against the defensive position of the Romans at Carrhae. Plut. *Crass.* 24.5–6.

126. Justin also emphasizes the Parthians' approach to feigned retreat tactics. Note Justin 41.2.7, 9. Compare Florus 2.20.3–10.

127. Dio provides our other surviving account of the battle; however, his summary suffers from a lack of comparable detail, conflated events, and periodic confusion. Note Sampson 2015: 186–87. Yet Sampson's recent depiction of the battle exaggerates the innovativeness of the Parthians' battle plan and their military objectives. Note id. 122–44.

128. Plut. *Crass.* 18.2–3.

Plutarch here exaggerates the sudden timing of these events in 53 to help portray Crassus as an incompetent fool, whose greed and lack of preparation led to the disaster at Carrhae.[129] In reality, Crassus had been quite successful in securing northern Mesopotamia as an important bridgehead in 54, and the Parthians had abandoned the region temporarily.[130] In fact, later in Book 20 Plutarch records:

> The country was destitute of [Parthian] men [during Crassus' advance into Mesopotamia in 53], but they [the Roman scouts] had come upon the tracks of many horses which had apparently wheeled about and fled from pursuit (οἷον ἐκ μεταβολῆς ὀπίσω διωκομενων). Wherefore Crassus himself was all the more confident, and his soldiers went so far as to despise the Parthians utterly, believing that they would not come to close quarters.[131]

Again, Plutarch exaggerates Crassus' reaction to portray him negatively; however, in both passages Plutarch emphasizes the mobility of the Parthian army and its asymmetric fighting style.

In the former passage (18.2–3), Roman scouts apparently identified some of the aspects of the Parthians' unique "mode of warfare," which they described as a series of inescapable assaults and unstoppable withdrawals that harassed the Roman garrisons with horse archers and heavy cavalry utilizing superior arms and armor. Meanwhile in the latter passage (20.1), Roman scouts discovered evidence of large formations of Parthian cavalry that had suddenly "fled from pursuit." Moreover, Plutarch in Book 18 continues:

> When the [Roman] soldiers heard this [that is, the effectiveness of the Parthians' mode of warfare], their courage ebbed away. For they had been fully persuaded that the Parthians were not different at all from the Armenians or even the Cappadocians, whom Lucullus had robbed and plundered till he was weary of it, and they had thought that the most difficult part of the war would be the long journey and the pursuit of men who would not come to close quarters; but now, contrary to their hopes, they were led to expect a struggle and great peril. Therefore, some of the officers thought that Crassus ought to call a halt [to the campaign] and reconsider the whole undertaking.[132]

This passage (18.4) demonstrates that the Romans had almost no knowledge of the Parthian military as late as the middle 50s and that they associated the Parthians' military with traditional eastern stereotypes. The Romans had never

129. Note Overtoom 2017a.
130. Dio 40.12.2.
131. Plut. *Crass.* 20.1.
132. Id. 18.4.

before fought the Parthians in a major engagement, and therefore, despite access to eastern guides and the experience of eastern clients, the Romans had little appreciation of how the Parthian military actually operated in the 50s. Moreover, passage 18.4 particularly is of interest because it plainly states that the Parthians' mode of warfare remained unique among those of other eastern peoples. The Romans had incorrectly assumed that the Parthians fought like the other peoples of the Hellenistic Near East.

Plutarch in these three passages also inadvertently illustrates the important psychological aspects of the Parthians' asymmetric approach to warfare. Initially in passages 18.2–3 and 18.4 the Romans were shocked at the aggression and determination of the Parthian army and became fearful; however, this fear quickly turned to contempt in passage 20.1 after the Romans observed that the Parthians had "fled from pursuit." Even Plutarch in the first passage calls the frenzied Roman reports of the terrifying Parthian army "exaggerated." Yet the sudden, seemingly frantic retreat of the Parthians in the face of Crassus' advance was a well-established military strategy to manipulate the enemy, which the Parthians had utilized against the Seleucids on multiple occasions since the reign of Arsaces I.[133] The abrupt, but calculated withdrawal of the Parthians in 53 ultimately inspired overconfidence in Crassus and his soldiers and encouraged them to pursue this "fleeing" enemy further into Mesopotamia. In its pursuit the Roman army became increasingly isolated and vulnerable, allowing the Parthians to wheel around and fight at Carrhae on favorable terms. Surena's campaign in 54–53 was a deliberate and successful strategy by the Parthians to harass, deceive, and overwhelm the Romans based upon the strengths of the Parthians' unique "Feign Retreat, Defeat in Detail" mode of warfare.[134]

Within this long-standing military tradition, the Parthians applied their tactical approaches to battle to their larger strategic objectives. Mobility, flexibility, deception, intimidation, and concentration of force were at the core of their campaign strategies. The Parthians had three fundamental strategic approaches, what I call the "Overwhelm Strategy," the "Harass Strategy," and the "Deceptive Withdrawal Strategy."[135] Similar to their tactical approaches to war, these strategies were flexible and interchangeable over the course of a campaign, and since the Parthians rarely possessed a numerical advantage in a conflict, they tended to favor the latter two strategies.

In campaigns where an enemy became vulnerable through miscalculation, coercion, or deception, the Parthians utilized their Overwhelm Strategy to engage

133. Note Strabo 11.8.8; Justin 36.1.5, 38.9.2, 10.7–10, 41.4.9–10; id. *Prol.* 35–36; Polyb. 10.28.5–6, 29.1–2, 31.1–3; Jos. *Ant.* 13. 186, 218–19, 253; *I Maccabees* 14.2–3; *V Maccabees* 21.23–24; Appian *Syr.* 11.67–68; Diod. 33–35, 34/35.16–17; Amm. Mar. 23.6.3; Jo. Mal. 8.198; Athen. 5.38; Posid. 16 (F. H. G. III.258); Sachs and Hunger 1996: no. -137A; Eus. *Chron.* (Smith ed.): 255.

134. Overtoom 2016d: Ch. 6; id. 2017b; id. 2021.

135. Id. 2017b.

the enemy aggressively with overwhelming force and defeat that enemy in detail. For example, the Parthians implemented their Overwhelm Strategy to attack Crassus at Carrhae and later to destroy Marc Antony's baggage train during his invasion of Media. In 36 the Parthians surrounded and annihilated around 10,000 Roman soldiers along with Antony's legate, Oppius Statianus, and the crucially important Roman siege engines.[136] Yet the Parthians also had utilized the Overwhelm Strategy to defeat the armies of Seleucus II, Demetrius II, and Antiochus VII.[137] The mobility, flexibility, and sustainability of the Parthian army on campaign generally was an effective, often devastating approach to warfare that frustrated many of the Parthians' numerous enemies.

If the Parthians faced an enemy that could not be overcome with brute force, they preferred to act aggressively with an asymmetric style of strategic warfare that distressed, hounded, and confused that enemy. The Parthians' Harass Strategy attempted to force an enemy through coercion into making mistakes during its advance or retreat that might create an opportunity for the Parthians to exploit. It was similar to the Hit-and-Run Tactic in its use of mobility, coordination, and psychological warfare to demoralize and weaken an enemy. For example, the Parthians implemented their Harass Strategy especially during the retreats of Crassus and Antony. The Parthians outmaneuvered, isolated, and enveloped Roman detachments numerous times during Antony's advance and retreat from Media as they aggressively pursued the Roman army.[138] Yet the Parthians also had utilized the Harass Strategy to manipulate the armies of Antiochus III and Demetrius II.[139]

If the more aggressive Harass Strategy did not work or was not applicable, the Parthians could turn to their Deceptive Withdrawal Strategy, which mimicked the execution and objectives of the Feigned Retreat Tactic almost completely except for its strategic scope. Because of their superior mobility, the Parthians deceptively could withdraw deep into their territory in the hope that they could encourage overconfidence or complacency in an enemy. For example, the Parthians implemented the Deceptive Withdrawal Strategy to persuade Crassus to advance toward Carrhae and to encourage Antony to leave his baggage train in a vulnerable position. Yet the Parthians also had utilized the Deceptive Withdrawal Strategy to outmaneuver and deceive the armies of Seleucus II, Antiochus III, and Antiochus VII.[140] Once the enemy had relaxed its guard or made a dangerous

136. Vell. Pat. 2.82; Plut. *Ant.* 38.2–3; Dio 49.25–6; Florus 2.20.3; Livy *Epit.* 130. For recent accounts of Antony's Median war, note Dąbrowa 2006b; Sheldon 2010: 65–80; McLaughlin 2016: 163–67; Taylor 2017: 212–13; Jones 2017.

137. Justin 36.1.5, 38.9.2, 10.7–10, 41.4.9–10; id. *Prol.* 35–36; Diod. 34/35.16; Jos. *Ant.* 13. 186, 218–9, 253; *I Maccabees* 14.2–3; *V Maccabees* 21.23–24; Appian *Syr.* 11.67–68; Diod. 33–35, 34/35.16–17; Amm. Mar. 23.6.3; Jo. Mal. 8.198; Athen. 5.38; Posid. 16 (F. H. G. III.258).

138. Plut. *Ant.* 39.2–50.1; Florus 2.20.4–10.

139. Polyb. 10.29.3–31.3; Justin 36.1.4, 38.92.

140. Strabo 11.8.8; Justin 38.10.6–10, 41.4.9–10; Polyb. 10.28.5–7, 31.3–5; Jos. *Ant.* 13.251.

blunder, the Parthians could counterattack with their Overwhelm or Harass strategies.

Some might wonder if the strategic deceptive withdrawals of the Parthians in these various campaigns simply could be *real* retreats. A military retreat is not necessarily a surrender or a defeat; it can be part of a policy of strategic withdrawal, the main intent of which is to preserve one's forces and to reengage later under circumstances that are more favorable. However, first, the Parthian style of retreat was unique compared to more conventionally armed Persian, Hellenistic, or Roman examples because of its more mobile and flexible nomadic elements. Ancient armies traditionally sought out climactic, decisive battles with face-to-face strength of arms as the determining factor. Yet the Parthians rarely did this because their style of warfare was nontraditional, and they never developed the heavy infantry necessary to match Hellenistic or Roman armies on more traditional terms. This major difference in military philosophy helps explain the confusion and frustration of the Seleucids and Romans in their numerous unsuccessful conflicts with the Parthians. The strategic deceptive withdrawals and the tactical feigned retreats of the Parthians, because of their vastly superior mobility and different military philosophy, were indeed unique compared to the more standard understanding of retreats by other contemporary militaries in the Graeco-Roman world.

Second, it is clear from the sources that the Parthians wanted their enemies to assume that they were not only retreating but also *fleeing*. The Parthians went through great difficulties to implement a system of organized chaos during their strategic withdrawals and tactical retreats. They wanted to create the impression of disorder and weakness, while maintaining strict discipline and awareness, to capitalize on opportunities. Thus, the Parthians *feigned* weakness at the tactical and strategic levels to accomplish similar objectives, namely the defeat of an overconfident and vulnerable enemy in detail. When the Parthians "fled" an important territory in the face of a major invasion, they were not *really* abandoning it. They ultimately wanted to lure their enemies into making poor military decisions so that the Parthians could isolate, harass, and overwhelm them.

Finally, there is enough evidence to suggest that the Parthians' strategic approach to warfare, including their policy of strategic deceptive withdrawals, was fairly uniform over the course of two centuries. The Parthians could apply their asymmetric mode of warfare in a well-developed strategy over many months and over hundreds of miles. The Parthians' unique approach to implementing a retreat in the form of strategic deceptive withdrawals and tactical feigned retreats complemented their military advantages. It also helps explain their ability to withstand major efforts on several occasions by the Seleucids and Romans to subdue them.

Dio, Florus, and especially Plutarch each explain in similar terms how the Parthians deceived, harassed, and then overwhelmed Crassus and Antony tactically and strategically utilizing their "Feign Retreat, Defeat in Detail" mode of warfare. In particular, Florus provides an illuminating summary of the Parthians' strategic approach to Marc Antony's later invasion of Media. He states:

> But such was the exceeding vanity of the man [Antony] that, in his desire for fresh titles of honor, he longed to have the Araxes and Euphrates [rivers] inscribed beneath his statues, and, without any pretext or design and without even a pretended declaration of war, just as if it were part of the art of generalship to attack by stealth, he left Syria and made a sudden attack upon the Parthians. The Parthians, who were crafty as well as confident in their arms, pretended to be panic-stricken and to fly across the plains (*simulat trepidationem et in campos fugam*). Antonius immediately followed them, thinking that he had already won the day, when suddenly a not very large force of the enemy unexpectedly burst forth, like a storm of rain, upon his troops in the evening when they were weary of marching, and overwhelmed two legions with showers of arrows from all sides.[141]

In this campaign the Parthians implemented strategic withdrawals to inspire overconfidence in the enemy, encouraging that enemy to make military blunders that the Parthians could then turn to their advantage. Florus' brief account succinctly underscores how the Parthians successfully implemented their Deceptive Withdrawal, Harass, and Overwhelm strategies in concert to defeat Antony and his army physically and psychologically.

Plutarch in passages 18.2–3, 18.4, and 20.1 with the benefit of almost two centuries of hindsight also emphasizes the Parthians' military concepts of utilizing deceptive withdrawals as a military strategy and the tactical use of interchanging light-missile cavalry and heavily armored cavalry to break up and isolate enemy formations.[142] Despite Plutarch's mostly negative portrayal of Crassus foolishly walking into a trap in 53, in actuality Crassus and his army knew little about the Parthians, their tactics, or their larger strategic goals prior to the Battle of Carrhae.[143] The military prowess of the Parthians in this decisive battle understandably surprised the Roman soldiers, many of whom were inexperienced, and the Romans soon came to fear the unique Parthian mode of warfare as the long-standing rivalry between the Romans and Parthians emerged in the late first century.[144]

141. Florus 2.20.2–3. Compare Dio 49.24–9.
142. Compare Plut. *Crass.* 21.2.
143. See id. 25.1. Note Overtoom 2017a; id. 2021.
144. Sampson 2015: 96; Overtoom 2016c; id. 2017a; Sampson 2020; Overtoom 2021b.

The Example of Carrhae

Just prior to the Battle of Carrhae, Plutarch states that the Parthians utilized the hilly terrain in the region to veil the size of their army and used deception to conceal the makeup of their forces, both of which were important aspects of the Parthians' mode of warfare.[145] Dio also states that the Parthians kept "most of their army hidden; for the ground was uneven in spots and wooded."[146] The Parthians had a well-established tradition of utilizing terrain to mask their troop deployment to surprise enemy formations.[147]

Plutarch's account of the battle underscores that the Parthians especially emphasized psychological warfare in their tactics and strategy. Misdirection, deception, and confusion were fundamentally important to the Parthians' concept of war. In fact, Plutarch remarks that the Parthians utilized topography and unique instruments to intimidate enemies. He states:

> But when they [the Parthians] were near the Romans and the signal was raised by their commander, first of all they filled the plain with the sound of a deep and terrifying roar. For the Parthians do not incite themselves to battle with horns or trumpets, but they have hollow drums of distended hide, covered with bronze bells, and on these they beat all at once in many quarters, and the instruments give forth a low and dismal tone, a blend of wild beast's roar and harsh thunder peal. They had rightly judged that, of all the senses, hearing is the one most apt to confound the soul, soonest rouses its emotions, and most effectively unseats the judgment.[148]

Plutarch here emphasizes that the Parthians had developed a drum that allowed them to create a unique and terrifying cacophony to unnerve their enemies.[149] He writes that this commotion had the desired effect on Crassus' men and that it was at this moment that the Parthians revealed their military strength and position.[150] The Battle of Carrhae helps demonstrate that the psychological impact of the Parthians' mode of warfare was considerable.[151]

Plutarch then emphasizes the flexibility of Parthian tactics at the start of the battle. Prior to this clash the Parthians had never fought the Romans in a major

145. Plut. *Crass.* 23.6.

146. Dio 40.21.2.

147. Compare the depiction of similar Parthian tactics in the third and second centuries. Polyb. 10.29.3–4, 30.1–9; Diod. 34/35.16.

148. Plut. *Crass.* 23.6–7.

149. Justin also stresses that the Parthians did not utilize trumpets but rather favored drums to signal battle. Justin 41.2.8. Note Nikonorov 2000b.

150. Plut. *Crass.* 24.1.

151. A psychological element to ancient warfare was common. Most ancient militaries attempted to utilize weapons, armor, equipment, and animals on the battlefield to intimidate the enemy. For example, Mattern argues that the Romans had a "prominent psychological element" in their warfare. Mattern 1999: 119. However, the Parthians developed a distinctive approach to psychological warfare.

engagement, and the Parthians were equally uncertain of Roman tactics, equipment, and capabilities. Much as the Romans had assumed the Parthians fought like the other peoples of the Near East, the Parthians likely expected the Romans to fight much like the conventional Hellenistic armies they had encountered for centuries. Contrary to recent scholarly conclusions, neither the Parthians nor the Romans altered their tactics or strategy in any significant way prior to this first engagement.[152]

Therefore, the Parthians and the Romans implemented their different modes of warfare at Carrhae and attempted to direct the battle in favor of their different combat styles. What emerged from the conflict was that, although the Roman military was superior in manpower, defensive combat, and traditional battlefield organization, the Parthian military had two crucial advantages over the Roman military: its superior flexibility and mobility. By the 50s these key advantages had allowed the Parthians to compete successfully within the Hellenistic Middle East for centuries against other rivals, who had possessed similar characteristics of size, structure, and style of combat to those of the Romans.

At the start of the battle, the Parthians, who were uncertain of the Romans' military capabilities, implemented the Massed Assault Tactic. The Parthian cataphracts, utilizing the momentum of the Parthians' psychological warfare, at first charged en masse against the Roman formation in an attempt to shatter the Roman army through blunt force. Plutarch records, "At first they purposed to charge upon the Romans with their long spears and throw their front ranks into confusion."[153] Yet the Parthians quickly recognized the strong defensive capabilities of the Roman infantry and their defensive square formation. Therefore, the Parthians quickly turned to their Feigned Retreat Tactic to test the discipline of the Roman formation. Plutarch states:

> But when they [the cataphracts] saw the depth of their formation [that is, the Roman battle line], where shield was locked with shield, and the firmness and composure of the men, they [the cataphracts] drew back, and while seeming to break their ranks and disperse, they surrounded the hollow square in which their enemy stood before he [Crassus] was aware of the maneuver. And when Crassus ordered his light-armed troops to

152. Sampson's conclusions that, first, the Parthians in 54–53 implemented an ancient version of the German "Schlieffen Plan" of pre–World War I Europe and that, second, the Parthian king, Orodes II, wanted to sacrifice Surena and his army at Carrhae is unconvincing. Sampson 2015: 112–13, 144. In reality, the Parthians' strategy was more like the classic double envelopment or pincer movement. Orodes and Surena wanted either to force Crassus to withdraw back into Syria or to isolate and trap Crassus between their two aggressive forces. To accomplish this objective, Orodes occupied Armenia, threatening Crassus from the north, and Surena harassed and delayed the Romans in Mesopotamia with his mobile army. See Plut. *Crass.* 21.4–5. Note Overtoom 2016d: Ch. 6; id. 2021. In fact, the Parthian strategy in 54–53 almost in no way relates to the Schlieffen Plan, which tried to avoid a two-front war (something the Parthians did not face) and required a passive enemy (something Crassus was not). For the Schlieffen Plan, see Zuber 2014; Ehlert et al. 2014.

153. Plut. *Crass.* 24.3.

> make a charge, they did not advance far, but encountering a multitude of arrows, abandoned their undertaking, and ran back for shelter among the men-at-arms, among whom they caused the beginning of disorder and fear, for these now saw the velocity and force of the arrows, which fractured armor, and tore their way through every covering alike, whether hard or soft.[154]

Plutarch highlights the maneuverability of the Parthian army, which adjusted to the battle as it unfolded far quicker than the Romans. The Parthians quickly recognized that the Roman army was in too strong of a defensive position to overwhelm it through blunt force, and therefore the cataphracts appeared to break their ranks and flee. This had the intended effect of encouraging the Romans to advance their light troops away from the protection of the main formation, and it allowed the Parthians to outmaneuver the Romans. Once Crassus committed his light troops to a charge, the Parthians quickly transitioned back to their Massed Assault Tactic. The cataphracts turned about and maneuvered into position, surrounding the main Roman formation, and the Parthian horse archers advanced to capitalize on the isolated light-armed Roman soldiers. The Parthians easily routed these detachments with the precision of their attacks and the quality of their arms and armor, and as the defeated light troops retreated back into the main formation, they spread fear and disorder. This added to the psychological impact of the Parthians' mode of warfare and made the Roman army increasingly vulnerable to further attacks.

From the beginning of the battle, the Parthians maintained freedom of movement and gained the initiative in the conflict, while the Romans became increasingly isolated and reactive. This meant that the Parthians could play to the strengths of their mode of warfare. After the initial engagement, the Parthians learned that the defensive capabilities of the Roman army were considerable; however, the Romans also had proved vulnerable to reacting brashly when the Parthians appeared to be in retreat. Thus, the Parthians could hope to force the Romans into making further tactical mistakes through coercion and deception.

The Roman general Lucullus had experienced the long-range effectiveness of the equipment of horse archers during cavalry skirmishes in Armenia in 68; however, the dense formation of the Romans at Carrhae made the Parthians' horse archers even more effective.[155] With the Roman army once again massed together, the Parthians continued to alter their tactics rapidly and effectively. Plutarch continues:

> The Parthians now stood at long intervals from one another and began to shoot their arrows from all sides at once, not with any accurate aim (for

154. Id. 24.3–4.
155. Compare Dio 36.5–6.1; Florus 1.46.8.

> the dense formation of the Romans would not suffer an archer to miss even if he wished it), but making vigorous and powerful shots from bows which were large and mighty and curved so as to discharge their missiles with great force. At once, then, the plight of the Romans was a grievous one [as they were surrounded and showered with arrows]; for if they kept their ranks, they were wounded in great numbers, and if they tried to come to close quarters with the enemy, they were just as far from effecting anything and suffered just as much. For the Parthians shot as they fled, and next to the Scythians, they do this most effectively; and it is a very clever thing to seek safety while still fighting, and to take away the shame of flight.[156]

Here Plutarch offers the first example of the Parthians implementing their Hit-and-Run Tactic. The horse archers, utilizing the "Parthian Shot" technique, peppered the Romans relentlessly with their superior bows and arrows while advancing and withdrawing in good order, again hoping to force the Romans to break formation. The Romans who tried to advance took heavy losses and had to fall back. Plutarch even recognizes that the coordinated movements of the Parthian horse archers were a traditional tactic of nomadic warfare that the Parthians had perfected. Since the Hit-and-Run Tactic was aggressive and determined, it kept up the fight against an enemy. As long as the densely formed Roman army was immobilized, the Parthian horse archers could harass it at will and wait for the Romans to make a critical mistake.

Crassus had hoped to simply outlast the barrage of the Parthian horse archers; however, the Romans eventually realized that the Parthians were resupplying their men from a mobile baggage train.[157] Crassus began to fear that the Parthians might surround and overwhelm his army completely, and therefore, he decided to attempt to regain the initiative in the battle. Plutarch states:

> Crassus, seeing no end to this [that is, the Parthians' Hit-and-Run Tactic], began to lose heart, and sent messengers to his son [Publius] with orders to force an engagement (προσμῖξαι βιάσεται) with the enemy before he was surrounded; for it was his wing especially which the enemy were attacking and surrounding with their cavalry, in the hope of getting in his rear. Accordingly, the young man took thirteen hundred horsemen, of whom a thousand had come from Caesar, five hundred archers, and eight cohorts of the men-at-arms who were nearest him and led them all to the charge.[158]

156. Plut. *Crass.* 24.5–6.
157. Id. 25.1.
158. Id. 25.1–2.

The Parthians had used their superior flexibility and mobility to begin condensing, encircling, and isolating sections of the Roman army, which was a common tactical and strategic goal of the Parthians.[159] Crassus out of desperation played directly into the hands of the Parthians when he instructed his son Publius to "force an engagement" with a sizable portion of the available Roman cavalry. This decision divided the Roman army further and left the Roman infantry dangerously isolated. The charge of Publius was the military opportunity on the battlefield that the Hit-and-Run Tactic was meant to create for the mobile Parthian army.

Initially, Publius' charge appeared successful, driving the Parthians from the field. This gave the Roman infantry under Crassus a much-needed respite from combat. However, Plutarch captures in his account that Publius' success in fact was not as it appeared. With Publius advancing from the main Roman formation, the Parthians once again quickly shifted their tactics. Plutarch records:

> The Parthians who were trying to envelop him [that is, Publius], either because, as some say, they encountered marshes, or because they were maneuvering to attack Publius as far as possible from his father, wheeled about and ran off (ἐδίωκον). Then Publius, shouting that the [Parthian] men did not stand their ground, rode after them.... The [Roman] cavalry followed after him, and even the infantry kept pace with them in the zeal and joy (προθυμίᾳ καὶ χαρᾷ) which their hopes inspired; for they thought they were victorious and in pursuit of the enemy, until, after they had gone forward a long distance, they perceived the trick (τὴν ἀπάτην). For the seeming fugitives wheeled about and were joined at the same time by others more numerous still.[160]

Early in the battle, the Romans had experienced the considerable challenge of trying to break out of their defensive position against the Parthian cavalry. The Parthians had met every advance with a quick counterattack. Publius expected similar resistance from the Parthians during his charge, and therefore, his initial advance appears to have been fairly restrained. Yet the Parthians recognized a major opportunity, and therefore, they turned to their Feigned Retreat Tactic, seemingly fleeing the field.

159. Note Ruf. Fest. 17.2. Antony especially fell victim to the Parthians' asymmetric mode of warfare. See Vell. Pat. 2.82; Plut. *Ant.* 38.2–3, 39.2–50.1; Dio 49.25–26; Florus 2.20.3–10; Livy *Epit.* 130. Antony, whose Parthian campaign lost more Roman lives than that of Crassus, mostly escaped the harsh censure endured by the legacy of Crassus because our accounts of Antony's expedition, particularly Strabo's and Plutarch's, are based upon the pro-Antony history written by Quintus Dellius. Note Gutschmid 1888: 97 n.3; Bengtson 1974: 10–11; Chaumont 1986b; Overtoom 2017a. For the Parthians and the Seleucids, see Strabo 11.8.8; Justin 36.1.5, 38.9.2, 10.7–10, 41.4.9–10; id. *Prol.* 35–36; Polyb. 10.28.5–6, 29.1–2, 31.1–3; Jos. *Ant.* 13. 186, 218–19, 253; *I Maccabees* 14.2–3; *V Maccabees* 21.23–24; Appian *Syr.* 11.67–68; Diod. 33–35, 34/35.16–17; Amm. Mar. 23.6.3; Jo. Mal. 8.198; Athen. 5.38; Posid. 16 (F. H. G. III.258); Sachs and Hunger 1996: no. -137A; Eus. *Chron.* (Smith ed.): 255.

160. Plut. *Crass.* 25.2–3. Translation slightly altered.

The Parthians needed to isolate Publius and his men if they hoped to annihilate this vital portion of Crassus' army. Publius' force of 1,300 cavalry, 500 archers, and 4,000 infantry was much larger and more mobile than any previous Roman detachment sent to pursue the Parthians, and the Parthians wanted to draw out Publius and his men to destroy them in detail. If Publius remained too close to the main Roman army, he could rely on reinforcements or retreat easily into the main line. Therefore, the Parthians feigned a general rout to encourage overconfidence in Publius. The isolation and destruction of enemy detachments through coercion and deception was the primary objective of the Parthians' mode of warfare and had been for centuries.[161] At Carrhae the Romans experienced this firsthand for the first time. Publius mistakenly assumed that he had gained the initiative, and he took the bait. Plutarch emphasizes the overconfidence of the Romans as they eagerly chased the fleeing Parthians and moved farther away from the safety of the main army. The Romans mistook cunning for weakness because the Parthians' Feigned Retreat Tactic was well-coordinated and convincing. Dio adds that Publius misjudged the strength and intentions of the Parthians so he "led out his cavalry against them, and when they turned purposely to flight, pursued them, thinking the victory was his; thus, he was drawn far away from the main army, and was then surrounded and cut down."[162] By the time the Romans realized their mistake, it was too late. The Parthians suddenly wheeled around and closed their trap.

Before continuing our analysis of Publius' charge, we should note the affect that the sudden change in Parthian tactics had on Crassus' larger force. Plutarch records:

> After ordering his son to charge the Parthians and receiving tidings that the enemy were routed to a great distance and hotly pursued, and after noticing also that his own immediate opponents were no longer pressing him so hard (since most of them [that is, the Parthians] had streamed away to where Publius was), he [Crassus] recovered a little courage, and drawing his troops together, posted them for safety on sloping ground, in immediate expectation that his son would return from the pursuit.[163]

Crassus and his officers also did not recognize that the Parthians were conducting a tactical maneuver to isolate Publius. In fact, Publius had been so confident in his initial success that he sent messengers to his father detailing the rout of the enemy and his successful pursuit. This false sense of accomplishment further lulled the main Roman army into making another tactical mistake. Although

161. The Parthians' destruction of Antiochus VII and his isolated vanguard in 129 is perhaps the best example prior to Carrhae. Diod. 34/35.16–17; Justin 38.10.7–10; Jos. *Ant.* 13.253; Appian *Syr.* 11.68; *V Maccabees* 21.23–4.

162. Dio 40.21.3.

163. Plut. *Crass.* 26.1.

Crassus protected his men by reforming them on sloping ground, he further isolated his son. In the time it took Crassus to reorganize his soldiers, the entire weight of 10,000 Parthian horsemen could press upon Publius. Once again, because of overconfidence the main Roman force seemingly took no precautions to follow up on Publius' apparent success or to monitor the continued movements of the Parthians.

Publius quickly realized that he had made a critical mistake once the Parthians began to renew their attack. Plutarch states:

> Then the Romans [under Publius] halted, supposing that the enemy would come to close quarters with them, since they were so few in number. But the Parthians stationed their mail-clad [cataphract] horsemen in front of the Romans, and then with the rest of their cavalry in loose array rode around them, tearing up the surface of the ground, and raising from the depths great heaps of sand which fell in limitless showers of dust, so that the Romans could neither see clearly nor speak plainly, but, being crowded into a narrow compass and falling upon one another, were shot, and died no easy nor even speedy death. . . . Thus, many died, and the survivors also were incapacitated for fighting.[164]

Here we find the Parthians once again emphasizing the use of psychological warfare. They intentionally clouded the air with dust to blind and suffocate the Romans. Dio records, "The heat and thirst (it was midsummer, and this action took place at noon) and the dust, of which the barbarians raised as much as possible by all riding around them, told fearfully upon the survivors, and many succumbed from these causes, even though unwounded."[165] These actions not only disoriented the Roman formation, but also helped conceal the movements of the Parthian cavalry. In a short time, Publius found himself completely isolated and increasingly vulnerable as the Parthians seamlessly reverted to their more aggressive Hit-and-Run Tactic.

Plutarch here also offers some insight into how the cataphracts factored into the continually shifting tactics of the Parthian army. If needed, the cataphracts could make a massed assault; however, they also were meant to support the horse archers during their attacks. Here they acted as a pinning force to protect the horse archers and to keep Publius' cavalry in place so that the horse archers could surround and confuse Publius' men. If Publius tried to break out of this closing trap, the cataphracts could counterattack with devastating force. Plutarch continues:

164. Id. 25.3–6.
165. Dio 40.23.4.

> Publius himself, accordingly, cheered on his cavalry, made a vigorous charge with them, and closed with the enemy. But his struggle was an unequal one both offensively and defensively, for his [men's] thrusting was done with small and feeble spears against breastplates of raw hide and steel, whereas the thrusts of the enemy [cataphracts] were made with pikes against the lightly equipped and unprotected bodies of the Gauls.[166]

Publius' Gallic light cavalry, although swift and skilled, ultimately was no match for the heavily armed and armored Parthian cataphracts within the confined space of the closing Parthian trap.[167] Once again, the Romans had lost the initiative in the battle, and what emerged was a microcosm of the engagement earlier in the day. The Parthian horse archers harassed Publius' men, raining arrows down upon the Romans as they advanced and withdrew. Meanwhile, the cataphracts exploited any break in the Roman formation with devastating and well-timed charges.

Out of desperation Publius attempted to form a defensive position on a small hill.[168] Plutarch relates, "But here [on the small hill], where the inequality of the ground raised one man above another, and lifted every man who was behind another into greater prominence, there was no such thing as escape, but they were all alike hit with arrows, bewailing their inglorious and ineffectual death."[169] The sudden reversal of their fortune, the determination of the Parthian attacks, and the deadly force of the Parthians' weapons crushed the confidence of Publius and his men. Unable to break out against the Parthian heavy cavalry and unable to protect themselves against the unrelenting barrage of arrows, the Romans began to despair. Plutarch records that Publius refused to abandon his men but abandoned hope of victory, stating:

> Then he himself [Publius], being unable to use his hand, which had been pierced through with an arrow, presented his side to his shield-bearer and ordered him to strike home with his sword. In like manner also Censorinus is said to have died; but Megabacchus took his own life, and so did the other most notable men. The survivors fought on until the Parthians mounted the hill and transfixed them with their long spears, and they say that not more than five hundred were taken alive. Then the Parthians cut off the head of Publius and rode off at once to attack Crassus.[170]

Once the Parthian horse archers had weakened Publius' force to the point of collapse, the Parthians once more turned to their Massed Assault Tactic and

166. Plut. *Crass*. 25.7.
167. Id. 25.7–9.
168. Id. 25.9–10.
169. Id. 25.10.
170. Id. 25.11–12.

overwhelmed the Roman survivors, delivering the coup de grâce through blunt force. All three fundamental tactical aspects of the Parthians' mode of warfare had overwhelmed Publius and his men physically and psychologically. The Battle of Carrhae helps illustrate how the Parthians' concept of warfare was meant to inflict severe psychological agony upon an enemy force through perceived reversals of fortune because of Parthian mobility, aerial superiority, and ambuscades.[171]

With the death of Publius and his men, the Parthians placed further emphasis on psychological warfare, cutting off the head of Crassus' son and taking it back to the main Roman force. Dio describes a similar scene worth noting for its emphasis on the effects of Parthian psychological warfare and the devastation of the Parthians' coordinated cavalry assaults. He records:

> For if they [the Romans] decided to lock shields for the purpose of avoiding the arrows by the closeness of their array, the pikemen [that is, the cataphracts] were upon them with a rush, striking down some, and at least scattering the others; and if they extended their ranks to avoid this, they would be struck with the arrows. Hereupon many died from fright at the very charge of the pikemen, and many perished hemmed in by the horsemen. Others were knocked over by the pikes or were carried off transfixed. The missiles falling thick upon them from all sides at once struck down many by a mortal blow, rendered many useless for battle, and caused distress to all. They flew into their eyes and pierced their hands and all the other parts of their body and, penetrating their armor, deprived them of their protection and compelled them to expose themselves to each new missile. Thus, while a man was guarding against arrows or pulling out one that had stuck fast, he received more wounds, one after another. Consequently, it was impracticable for them to move, and impracticable to remain at rest. Neither course afforded them safety, but each was fraught with destruction, the one because it was out of their power, and the other because they were then more easily wounded.[172]

The cunning, brutality, and relentlessness of the Parthians' mode of warfare created feelings of disbelief, frustration, hopelessness, and fear. Plutarch and Dio illustrate that the Parthians had executed their asymmetric approach to warfare to perfection in the second phase of the battle. Not only had the Parthians successfully deceived and destroyed a vital portion of the Roman army, but also the

171. Note the later situation of Antony and his army as the psychological warfare of the Parthians took its toll. Plut. *Ant.* 39.5–50.1. Perhaps the best example from the Parthians' conflict against the Seleucids is their annihilation of Demetrius II's army in 138. Justin 36.1.4–5, 38.9.2. Compare id. *Prol.* 35–36; Appian *Syr.* 11.67; Jos. *Ant.* 13.186, 218–19; *I Maccabees* 14.2–3; Diod. 33.28.1; Eus. *Chron.* (Smith ed.): 255. See Dąbrowa 1999 [2000].

172. Dio 40.22.2–5.

death and disfigurement of Publius was an important factor in the third and final phase of the engagement.

With great difficulty a messenger had warned Crassus of the deteriorating position of his son, and Plutarch states, "Crassus was a prey to many conflicting emotions, and no longer looked at anything with calm judgement. His fear for the whole army drove him to refuse, and at the same time his yearning love for his son impelled him to grant assistance; but at last he began to move his forces forward."[173] Although Plutarch again likely exaggerates the situation to censure Crassus for giving into passion over reason, he illustrates the toll that the Parthians' psychological warfare was beginning to take on Crassus.[174] Plutarch then records that the Parthian army suddenly returned "with clamor and battle cries which made them more fearful than ever, and again many of their drums began bellowing about the Romans, who awaited the beginning of a second battle."[175] Thus, the main Roman force also suddenly experienced a severe reversal of fortune with the news of Publius' defeat and the return of the Parthians, and the Parthians wasted no time in returning to their distinctive emphasis on surprise and sensory deprivation to undermine the confidence of their enemy. Plutarch continues:

> Besides, those of the enemy who carried the head of Publius fixed high upon a spear, rode close up and displayed it, scornfully asking after his parents and family, for surely, they said, it was not possible that Crassus, most base and cowardly of men, should be the father of a son so noble and of such splendid valor. This spectacle shattered and unstrung the spirits of the Romans more than all the rest of their terrible experiences, and they were all filled, not with a passion for revenge, as was to have been expected, but with shuddering and trembling.[176]

Here again Plutarch likely exaggerates the notion of Crassus' cowardice to criticize him for the disaster at Carrhae; however, Plutarch captures the serious consequences of the Parthians' psychological warfare.[177] The destruction of Publius' force, the terrifying appearance and noise of the Parthians, and the dismemberment of Publius' body devastated Roman morale. The Romans went from believing that the battle was over and that victory was assured to the visceral realization that, not only were the Parthians ready to renew the fight, but they had obliterated Publius and his men. Once again, the rapidly shifting tactics of the Parthians had inspired overconfidence, hubris, and a false sense of security

173. Plut. *Crass.* 26.2–3.
174. Note Overtoom 2017a.
175. Plut. *Crass.* 26.3.
176. Id. 26.4.
177. Note Overtoom 2017a.

followed by fear, confusion, and a sense of hopelessness. The "zeal and joy" of the Romans shattered once the Parthians renewed their attacks with voracity.

In a rare example of Plutarch praising Crassus, he writes that Crassus "showed more brilliant qualities in that awful hour than ever before" as Crassus tried to encourage his men and accept blame for the unfolding disaster.[178] However, Plutarch continues, "Even as he spoke such words of encouragement, Crassus saw that not many of his men listened with any eagerness, but when he also bade them raise the battle cry, he discovered how despondent his army was, so weak, feeble, and uneven was the shout they made, while that which came from the Barbarians was clear and bold."[179] Crassus' efforts to accept blame for the defeat, to remind his soldiers of their need for revenge, and to encourage them with tales of Roman valor in battle all failed to overcome his soldiers' fear and despair.[180] Various effective Parthian psychological devices, paired with the devastation of the Parthians' weapons, had nearly broken the spirit of the Roman army.[181]

The Parthians sensed the vulnerability of the Romans and continued to press their advantage, bolstering their fighting spirit.[182] Plutarch records:

> Then, as the enemy got to work, their light cavalry rode around on the flanks of the Romans and shot them with arrows, while the mail-clad [cataphract] horsemen in front, plying their long spears, kept driving them together into a narrow space, except those who, to escape death from the arrows, made bold to rush desperately upon their foes. These did little damage but met with a speedy death from great and fatal wounds, since the spear that the Parthians thrust into the horses was heavy with steel, and often had impetus enough to pierce through two men at once. After fighting in this manner until night came on, the Parthians withdrew.[183]

Without Publius' soldiers Crassus' larger force found itself isolated and mostly immobile. The Parthians immediately returned to their Hit-and-Run Tactic. The Roman army remained too large to overwhelm in a massed assault; however, the vulnerability of the Roman formation meant the horse archers could deliver their fire continually and with devastating effect. As had happened at the beginning of the battle and in the fight against Publius, the cataphracts organized to protect the horse archers and exploit breakouts and gaps in the Roman line. Crassus' army

178. Plut. *Crass.* 26.5–6.

179. Id. 27.1.

180. Id. 26.5–6.

181. Dio argues that the Romans tried to avenge Publius' death but that the numbers and tactics of the Parthians overwhelmed them. Dio 40.22.1.

182. Dio includes an account of Abgarus of Osrhoene betraying Crassus and assaulting the rear of the Roman lines. Id. 40.23.1–2. Plutarch makes no mention of such an event. It is highly likely that Dio, writing a century later, here adds a fictional event into the battle narrative. Sampson 2015: 136.

183. Plut. *Crass.* 27.1–2.

became entirely pinned down.[184] Coordinated cataphract formations with their terror-inspiring weapons manipulated the Roman soldiers into dense formations that became ideal targets for the horse archers. Only darkness saved the Roman army from total destruction on that day.

The Battle of Carrhae is an exemplary example of the Parthians' "Feign Retreat, Defeat in Detail" mode of warfare on the battlefield, and the larger campaign demonstrates the mobility, cunning, and deadly force that the Parthians also could exercise strategically. Plutarch records that Crassus lost 30,000 men and eventually his own life over the course of the battle and the subsequent contested retreat back to Syria.[185] However, although Carrhae is the most well-known and best-documented victory of the Parthians, the eastern campaigns of Seleucus II, Antiochus III, Demetrius II, Antiochus VII, and Marc Antony demonstrate that the Parthian tactical and strategic actions depicted in Plutarch's account were not atypical. Although Surena may have implemented a variation of the Parthians' mode of warfare in 54–53, it owed itself to a tried-and-true military tradition, one which the Parthians had developed and implemented under the early Arsacids for almost two centuries and one which they continued to implement against the Romans.[186]

The rise of the Parthians from minor nomadic tribe to world superpower, dominating the Hellenistic Middle East for three centuries, is one of the greatest and yet least-known examples of imperial success in world history. The Parthians' balance of flexibility and force in their cultural identity, administration, and military gave them important advantages in the competitive, hostile, and perilous international environment of the Hellenistic Middle East that allowed them to overcome numerous highly militarized and aggressive neighbors. Their story is one of adapting to circumstances and overcoming obstacles better than all their peer competitors from the third to the first centuries. From Arsaces I to Mithridates II, the early Arsacids carved out a mighty imperial state that endured far longer than the previous hegemonies of the Achaemenids, Argeads, and Seleucids. This unexpected success created a legacy that inadvertently influenced the early relationship of the Parthians and Romans and eventually led to one of the longest-standing rivalries in history.[187] For too long the Parthians have been overlooked, underappreciated, and misunderstood; it is time for them to start taking their rightful place in the conversation of "exceptional" ancient peoples. In Parthia's rise to power and enduring success, it truly was one of the world's most outstanding early empires, and it is to the creation of that empire that we now turn.

184. Dio offers a similar conclusion. Dio 40.23.3–24.3.

185. Plut. *Crass.* 27.2–31. Compare Dio 40.25–27. Plutarch concludes his negative portrayal of Crassus by giving Crassus credit that he at least died with some dignity. Plut. *Nic. and Crass.* 5.2; id. *Pomp.* 76.6.

186. Note Olbrycht 1998d.

187. Note Overtoom 2016c; id. 2016d; id. 2017a; id. 2017b; id. 2019b; id. 2021.

The Emergence of the Parthian State

By the early third century, the Middle East had become a Hellenistic world. The massive Successor state, the Seleucid Empire, dominated the largest expanse of Alexander the Great's former conquests. From Syria to Afghanistan one power ruled the Middle Eastern world. There was nothing to suggest that a new power would emerge to dominate this region for three hundred years. Powerful Hellenistic armies and militaristic Hellenistic kings knew no rival; this was the height of Macedonian imperialism. Yet a century and a half later, the once mighty Hellenistic kingdoms of the Diadochi (or Successors) had faltered as the Romans in the west and the Parthians in the east expanded their hegemony at the expense of Greek and Macedonian rule.

There was never a guarantee that the Parthians would emerge as the dominant force in the Middle East. Yet they eventually achieved this impressive feat through a long, costly process of continual conflict with neighboring states. This study examines the numerous challenges the Parthians faced during their struggles to establish a kingdom, consolidate their security, and expand their power from the middle third to the early first centuries to better understand the factors that allowed the Parthians to be successful. From minor nomadic tribe to major world empire, the story of Parthian success is nothing short of remarkable. In their early history, the Parthians benefited from strong leadership, a flexible and accommodating cultural identity, and innovative military characteristics that allowed them to compete against and indeed eventually overcome rivals who were often more powerful.

The international environment of the Hellenistic Middle East was harsh and unforgiving. States were highly militarized, bellicose, and diplomatically aggressive in their struggle for power, security, and limited resources. The Parthians, like their many Greek, Iranian, and Central Asian neighbors, maintained their kingdom through bloodshed and compromise, just trying to survive in a dangerous and unforgiving environment where massacre, mass enslavement, or even total destruction were continual concerns.[1] In the following pages, the security

1. The Parthians were ruthless when necessary. For example, note their execution of the Greek population of Sirynx in the early 200s, their mass enslavement of thousands of Greek soldiers and their suppression of Seleucia and Babylonia in the early 120s, and their destruction of Central Asian tribes in the early 110s. Polyb. 10.31.10–13; Justin 38.10.8, 42.1.4; Diod. 34/35.15; Sachs and Hunger 1996: no. -118A. Note Overtoom 2019b; id 2019c.

Reign of Arrows. Nikolaus Leo Overtoom, Oxford University Press (2020). Oxford University Press.
DOI: 10.1093/oso/9780190888329.001.0001.

threats, power relations, and warfare of ancient states will be familiar themes. To appreciate fully how the Parthians succeeded in creating one of the largest and longest-lasting empires in world history, we must first investigate the environment in which they developed and the challenges they had to overcome.

Seleucid Crisis

Two years after the death of Alexander the Great, Seleucus I, one of Alexander's infantry commanders, became governor of Babylonia; however, the destructive wars of the Diadochi made his position vulnerable.[2] From 316 to 301 he waged a series of wars against another Successor, Antigonus Monophthalmus ("the One-Eyed"), who had come to dominate much of the eastern portion of Alexander's former empire.[3] Finally in 301 at the Battle of Ipsus, Seleucus and his ally, another Successor, Lysimachus, decisively defeated Antigonus, killing him in the battle and dividing his lands.[4] Seleucus retained his possessions in the Middle East (lands encompassing what is modern Iraq and Iran and portions of Turkmenistan, Afghanistan, Pakistan, Uzbekistan, Tajikistan, and Kyrgyzstan) and gained control of Syria, while Lysimachus received Anatolia. Yet the alliance between the two ambitious men was short-lived, and with the defeat of Lysimachus at the Battle of Corupedium in 281, Seleucus added Anatolia and Thrace to his vast domain. What international relations theorists call an interstate system of "tripolarity" (or the rivalry of three dominant states) between the Hellenistic power centers in Macedon, Egypt, and Syria emerged in the Hellenistic world.

At the tip of a spear, Seleucus I had created the largest, wealthiest, and most diverse Hellenistic Successor state. Appian describes Seleucus as a great and opportunistic conqueror, who was second only to Alexander the Great.[5] However, despite Seleucus' success in building a mighty empire, such a vast domain proved consistently and increasingly difficult to maintain for his successors.[6] Tax revenues and war spoils fueled the Seleucid economy; however, the silver revenue needed to administer the empire and pay the army was a constant source of concern for the Seleucid kings.[7] Under the Seleucids, production and distribution of commodities and coinage was mostly regional, and although Mesopotamia was an important economic center of the Seleucid Empire, inter-regional trade

2. For Seleucus, see Bevan 1902; Bikerman 1938; Rostovtzeff 1941; Will 1967; Mehl 1986; Kuhrt and Sherwin-White 1987; Sherwin-White and Kuhrt 1993; Bennett and Roberts 2012a; Grainger 2013b; Ogden 2016.

3. For Antigonus, see Briant 1973; Billows 1997; Champion 2014.

4. For Lysimachus, see Lund 1992.

5. See Appian *Syr.* 9.55.

6. Note Grainger 2013b; id. 2014; id. 2016.

7. For the structure of the Seleucid royal economy and the argument that the Seleucid state had similar economic priorities to modern states, see Aperghis 2004. Compare van der Spek 2000; Davis 2006; id. 2011; Thonemann 2015: Chs. 6–7; Grainger 2017a: Chs. 6, 9.

was quite limited.[8] Thus, the wealth of the Seleucid state was potentially vast, and regionally in places like Syria, Mesopotamia, Media, Parthia, and Bactria, there was considerable wealth that could be turned into state revenue; however, the Seleucid economy functioned mostly at a regional level, where the production and revenues of each region often went to support that region. This meant that the Seleucids had a financial incentive to protect these wealthy regions to guard their ability to rule and pay the army; however, the regional structure of the economy also created great potential wealth and power for usurpers and breakaway kingdoms.[9]

Further, the Seleucid state was primarily western-focused. That is, the geopolitical developments of the Eastern Mediterranean were the main concern of the Seleucids and generally separate from the geopolitical developments on the Iranian plateau. The Seleucids mostly ruled from Antioch, their imperial capital in Syria, and spent the next two and a half centuries fighting against the other Hellenistic polities of the Eastern Mediterranean.[10] Western wars dominated the attention of the Seleucid kings and drained the Seleucid treasury. Strabo states, "The Macedonians [that is, the Seleucids] did indeed rule over the country [of the Iranian plateau] for a short time, but they were so occupied with wars that they could not attend to their remote possessions [in the east]."[11] Although Seleucus I and his son Antiochus I undertook major efforts to stabilize and develop the eastern frontier in the 290s and 280s, the lands of Iran, Afghanistan, and Pakistan became relatively neglected and marginalized, eventually allowing strong regional powers to exert more autonomy and regional influence.[12] The Seleucids' prioritizing of their western front, where their enemies generally used massed Macedonian tactics, also meant that the Seleucids' military structure and concepts were not well suited to combat the asymmetric warfare of the Parthians in the east. Unless the Seleucids were to maintain two armies trained for radically different styles of warfare, their ability to adapt to Parthian tactics was limited, helping create several opportunities for the Parthians to outmaneuver and overwhelm Seleucid forces.

8. See Aperghis 2011; van der Spek and van Leeuwen 2014; Grainger 2015: 56; Thonemann 2015.

9. Chrubasik 2016.

10. The Seleucids never lost their Macedonian identity and, in fact, embraced it; however, they also created a dynastic identity deeply embedded in northern Syria. See Kosmin 2014: Chs. 3–4. The economic focus of the Seleucid Empire also was the Mediterranean. See Manning 2015.

11. Strabo 11.7.2.

12. Antiochus strengthened the defenses in Babylonia and prepared military resources in the east during his father's reign. Finkel, van der Spek, Pirngruber 2020g; id. 2020h. For the efforts of Seleucus and Antiochus in Bactria, note Holt 1999: 24–29; Bing and Sievers 2011; Grainger 2014: Chs. 5, 8. For the relative neglect of the eastern lands of the Seleucid Empire, see Kosmin 2013a; Plischke 2014: 315–34; Grainger 2015: 56; Overtoom 2016a; van der Spek 2018. Contra Sherwin-White and Kuhrt 1993: 73–74, 90, 108; Holt 1999: 25. Although I generally agree with Sherwin-White, Kuhrt, and Holt that the Seleucids took interest in maintaining their eastern empire, there should be no doubt that western affairs took precedence over eastern affairs and that Syria was the center of the empire. Overtoom 2016a; id. 2019a.

Further, communication and travel between Syria and the empire's eastern frontier was too slow and difficult to manage effectively, and Seleucid governors along the eastern frontier increasingly found themselves isolated and threatened by well-organized tribal confederations from the Central Asian steppe.[13] These men gained a great deal of local autonomy and began to think of themselves as independent rulers. Meanwhile, the western focus of the Seleucid state meant that eastern campaigns were costly, dangerous, and infrequent. A major disadvantage of the Seleucid Empire, and the later Parthian Empire, was that unlike the Roman Empire, they lacked a large body of water to facilitate movement and communication from one edge of their empires to the other. In fact, communication from Syria to the eastern frontier could take multiple months.[14] Eastern campaigns were massive investments of money, materials, men, and time. Moreover, Seleucid kings who conducted years of campaigning in the east left themselves vulnerable, first, to invasion by other Hellenistic states into the wealthy lands of Syria and Anatolia and, second, to internal, dynastic rebellion in the form of usurpers to the throne. For example, Polybius records that Antiochus III's advisor Hermeias "was afraid of an expedition into the interior [of the east] owing to its danger and continued to yearn for the campaign against Ptolemy [IV] which he had originally planned."[15] Hermeias did not want Antiochus to fight a difficult war in the east and instead favored the more traditional rivalry against the Ptolemies in the west. Only the strongest of kings at the best of times could hold such an extensive and diverse empire together.[16] Unfortunately for the Seleucids, such men were a rarity.

Seleucid control of the eastern satrapies declined suddenly in the middle third century as a series of costly wars against Ptolemaic Egypt and dynastic disputes sapped Seleucid strength. In particular the sudden death of Antiochus II (246), the Seleucid defeat in the Third Syrian War (246–241), and the subsequent civil war for the throne (ca. 246/245–236) severely damaged the reputation and military might of the Seleucid Empire.[17] This unexpected decline of Seleucid power in the 240s caused what international relations theorists call a "power-transition crisis" in the Hellenistic Middle East, which temporarily ended Seleucid hegemony and allowed rival states to emerge in Parthia and Bactria.

13. For the development of pastoral nomadism and the evolution of nomadic cultures in Central Asia in the first millennium, particularly as concerns Chinese perceptions of and interactions with these nomadic peoples, see Di Cosmo 2004. Compare Cribb and Errington 1992; Anthony 2007; Herrmann and Cribb 2007; Beckwith 2009.

14. Taylor 2013: 11, 14.

15. Polyb. 5.55.3.

16. Grainger recognized that without a strong king the Seleucid Empire could "collapse into component parts and vanish." He then emphasizes that this "almost happened in the 240s." Grainger 2015: 66–67. Note Chrubasik 2016.

17. Lerner attributes the decline of Seleucid authority over eastern Iran directly to these two conflicts. Lerner 1999: 30. Recently, Coşkun has attempted to shift the civil war to ca. 245–241. Coşkun 2018. Note also Erickson 2018.

Before the Crisis

To understand better the power-transition crisis of the 240s–230s and its consequences, it is important first to provide a concise account of the evolving international environment in the ancient Middle East prior to this crisis. Before the rise of Persian (or Achaemenid) power under Cyrus the Great in the middle sixth century, there existed what international relations theorists call an international environment of "multipolar interstate anarchy" over the Middle Eastern world, which we may call the "Middle Eastern interstate system."[18] In the sixth century, numerous competing states, such as the Median Empire, the Neo-Babylonian Empire, the Kingdom of Egypt, and the Kingdom of Lydia, shared this fractured, dangerous, and violent interstate system, which stretched from Anatolia and Egypt in the west to the Iranian plateau in the east. Yet under the charismatic and capable Cyrus the Great, the hitherto minor Persian state in southwestern Iran became what international relations theorists call an "unlimited revisionist state." That is, Persia under Cyrus' leadership came to desire the complete overthrow of the distribution of power within the current interstate system in favor of its own hegemony and empire. Moreover, the sudden rise of Persian power created another example of a power-transition crisis as Cyrus quickly conducted successful hegemonic war against the Medians, Lydians, and Neo-Babylonians.[19]

Cyrus created an unrivaled state, establishing what international relations theorists call "unipolar" hegemony over the Middle Eastern interstate system. He even expanded the geographical bounds of this interstate system by incorporating more eastern lands, namely large portions of what is modern Turkmenistan, Uzbekistan, Tajikistan, and Afghanistan, attacking the tribal confederations of the Central Asian steppe and extending his eastern frontier.[20] Thus began the precarious relationship between the imperial powers of the Middle East and the peoples of the Central Asian steppe, in which the later Parni and then the Parthians are included.[21] Cyrus' eastern campaign extended the spatial boundaries of the Middle Eastern interstate system over the southern portion of the Central Asian steppe; however, Cyrus' sudden death in battle against these tribes ended the conflict abruptly and put a halt to Persian ambitions in the region.[22]

Even after Cyrus' death, the Persians consolidated and expanded their power over the remaining independent polities within the Middle East. Cyrus' son,

18. In a previous article, I referred to this interstate system as the "old Eastern system"; however, I now prefer to call it the "Middle Eastern system" for better organization and clarity. See Overtoom 2016a: 985–87.

19. For the rise of Persia, see Dandamaev 1989; Vogelsang 1992; Briant 2002; Allen 2005; Waters 2014; Daryaee 2015: 278–80.

20. Herod. 1.214; Ctesias fr. 9.7–8. Compare Xen. *Cyrop.* 8.7; Strabo 11.11.6.

21. The Persian Empire was the first imperial Middle Eastern state to initiate major conflict in Central Asia, and violence between Middle Eastern and Central Asian peoples continued for over 2,000 years. See Baumer 2012: 198–203. Compare Dąbrowa 2016a.

22. Cyrus likely died in battle; however, the evidence is not definitive. See Dandamaev 1989: 66–67; Waters 2014: 52.

Cambyses II, established Persian dominion over Egypt in the 520s, and Darius I expanded eastward, incorporating much of what is modern Pakistan into the empire. In fact, Darius' successful invasion of the Indus River valley caused a process known to international relations theorists as "system overlap," where two contemporary, yet separate interstate systems extend over a similar frontier zone.[23] The Middle Eastern interstate system came to overlap with the contemporary, yet separate "Indian interstate system."[24] However, the Persians chose not to pursue conflict into the Indian subcontinent, and therefore the Middle Eastern and Indian systems continued to overlap but did not merge.[25] Instead, the Persians established a strong eastern frontier with the Central Asian tribes and Indian kingdoms that protected the wealthy lands of the Iranian plateau.[26]

Unlike the later Macedonians, the Persians ruled over the lands along their eastern frontier for almost two centuries without much difficulty and maintained close relations with the nomadic and Indian elements on their eastern periphery.[27] In fact, a major factor in the success of the Persian Empire along its eastern frontier was its support of local subject rulers in exchange for their recognition of Persian hegemony.[28] Another main advantage was that the Persian center of power was the royal cities of Persepolis, Susa, and Ecbatana in western Iran. That is, unlike Alexander the Great, whose power base was in Macedonia, or the Seleucids, whose power base was in Syria, the Persian monarchy, and later the Parthians, had easier and more direct access to the regions along their eastern frontier.[29] In fact, Athenaeus illustrates that the Parthians shared the Persians' emphasis on maintaining eastern palaces as bases of operation.[30] He states, "And in like manner the kings of the Parthians spend their spring in Rhagae [northern Iran], their winter in Babylon, and the rest of the year at Hecatompylus [northeastern Iran]."[31] Under the Persians, eastern regions, such as Bactria, Aria, Arachosia, and Drangiana, remained important centers of power until the end of the empire.[32]

It appears that Alexander the Great came to understand the importance of an eastern capital to the viability of his massive new empire. In fact, Alexander's

23. Note Aron 1973: 87–88; Buzan, Jones, and Little 1993: 66–80; Eckstein 2006: 116; Klotz and Lynch 2007: 104; Kuranga 2010: 200–1; Quinn 2010: 92, 93, 113, 121; Shiping 2014: 484–86; Overtoom 2016d.

24. Overtoom 2016a: 986.

25. Id. 986, 997.

26. Note Lyonette 1990; Vogelsang 1990.

27. The Persians faced only one major rebellion along their eastern frontier. For the insurrection of the Margians under Frada, see Dandamaev 1989: 125–26. Compare Daryaee 2015: 278–82. For interactions between the Persians and various Central Asian peoples, see Olbrycht 2015b. For early Seleucid interactions with the Mauryan Empire in India and with Central Asian peoples, see Kosmin 2014: Chs. 1–2; Grainger 2014: Chs. 5, 8.

28. Vogelsang 1992: 241–44. Compare Meadows 2005.

29. Colburn argues there was good connectivity and communication in the Achaemenid Empire. Colburn 2013. For Alexander at Susa, see Olbrycht 2016f.

30. For Athenaeus and the Parthians, see Hackl, Jacobs, and Weber 2010b: 48–49.

31. Athen. 12.8. Compare Strabo 11.13.1, 13.5, 15.3.3; Jos. *Ant.* 10.263–65.

32. Vogelsang 1992: 221.

soldiers feared that "he would establish the permanent seat of his kingdom in Asia."[33] Plutarch even records that Alexander received advice on how to rule a vast empire from Calanus, a Brahman sage, stating, "[Calanus] demonstrated to Alexander how important it was for him to concentrate his authority at the middle of his empire and not to travel far away from it."[34] Perhaps to accomplish this goal, Alexander attempted to favor Babylon as an important administrative capital and military base.[35] Onesicritus and Strabo tell us that Alexander favored Babylon above all other eastern cities and that he intended to build it up still further.[36] Alexander's decision to move the body of his best friend, Hephaestion, from Ecbatana to Babylon for a lavish state burial also demonstrates that he favored the city.[37] Later, the founder of the Seleucid Empire, Seleucus I, established an imperial capital, Seleucia, near Babylon; however, within a generation the Seleucid capital and court had shifted to Antioch on the coast of the Eastern Mediterranean.[38] Antiochus II (261–246) was the first Seleucid king who did not travel to the eastern frontier during his reign, and no Seleucid king visited the eastern frontier after 281 until Antiochus III's campaign in the 200s.[39] The Seleucids quickly favored an imperial identity and established an imperial focus more connected to the Greek world of the Eastern Mediterranean.

In addition to their eastern power bases, the Achaemenids appear to have maintained a more integrated eastern frontier. Unlike the later Seleucid satraps in Bactria, who served mostly to protect the northeastern frontier of the empire and to keep the aggressive peoples of the Central Asian steppe at arm's length, the Persian satraps of Bactria were the key representatives of the Achaemenids to these peoples and maintained a close relationship with them.[40] This favorable relationship between the Persians and the Central Asian tribal confederations helps explain the fierce resistance Alexander faced during his invasions of Bactria and Sogdiana.[41] Moreover, the ongoing rivalry of the Seleucids with other Hellenistic dynasts in the Eastern Mediterranean made the maintenance of the eastern frontier of their empire of secondary importance, and the increasingly western focus of the Seleucid dynasty was a main factor in the power-transition crisis of the 240s–230s.[42]

33. Curt. 10.2.12.
34. Plut. *Alex.* 65.
35. Id. 68.1–2; Curt. 10.1.19; Arrian *Anab.* 7.19.3–5.
36. See Strabo 15.3.8–10.
37. Arrian *Anab.* 7.14.8; Diod. 17.110.8. Compare Plut. *Alex.* 72; Justin 12.12.11; Polyaen. 4.3.31.
38. For the royal cities of the Seleucid Empire, see Kosmin 2014: Chs. 7–8.
39. Grainger 2014: 196. Seleucus II attempted to visit the eastern frontier in the 230s; however, the Parthians defeated his invasion of the Iranian plateau. Overtoom 2016a: 998–1000; id. 2020.
40. Vogelsang 1992: 234–5. Compare Lyonnet 1990; Lerner 2015a: 304.
41. See Holt 2005. Compare Worthington 2014: Ch. 11; Rapin 2017; Crescioli 2017; Gorshenina 2017.
42. Overtoom 2016a.

Another major obstacle obstructing the Seleucids' attempts to control the vast lands of the Middle East was that their incorporation of these lands and peoples was mostly superficial instead of careful and detailed.[43] John Grainger argues, "The lightness of the administration was therefore a necessary result of the size and difficulty of administering the kingdom, and of the priority of the army in the allocation of resources; but, of course, this also meant that the kingdom necessarily remained less than fully integrated since the provincial administrators were largely independent of the centre."[44] Although the power of the Seleucid king was extensive, he relied on a limited and variable group of the king's Friends (*philoi*), a royal council, and governors to administer the extensive empire. The comparatively small and limited Seleucid government was a deliberate reaction to the geopolitical and financial realities of ruling over such a disparate empire, rather than a result of the inability or incompetence of the Seleucid state; however, it made integration of subject peoples and leaders into the Seleucid state difficult. The Diadochi as a whole did not share Alexander's openness to foreign cultures or his movement toward administrative inclusiveness.[45]

Although the Persians could have expanded their northern and eastern frontiers further, their eastern frontier was relatively stable, and therefore geopolitical concerns to the west increasingly garnered their attention. Egypt was a hotbed of unrest and rebellion, while Persian expansion into western Anatolia and Thrace had increased the scope of the Middle Eastern interstate system once more.[46] The Persian-dominated Middle Eastern interstate system came to overlap with the contemporary, yet separate Greek-dominated "Aegean interstate system" of the Classical Greek city-states.[47] With Darius I's successful western campaigns, the mounting tension between the Persians and the Greeks soon led to hegemonic war in the form of the Graeco-Persian Wars. The Persian invasions of Greece in the early fifth century and the subsequent concerted Greek military response to the threat of Persia caused what international relations theorists call "system merger."[48] The Middle Eastern and Aegean systems merged violently in the early fifth century and created a new, more expansive, and further integrated

43. Grainger 2007: 186–88; id. 2015: 80–81; id. 2017a: Chs. 6–8. Compare Kosmin 2014: Chs. 7–8.

44. See Grainger 2015: 81–85. Compare Sekunda 2010; Kosmin 2014; id. 2018.

45. The openness of the Seleucids to foreign cultures is subject to debate. Sherwin-White and Kuhrt maintain that the Seleucids were an influential heir of the Persians in the Middle East and were much more open to indigenous cultures than is commonly assumed. See Sherwin-White and Kuhrt 1993. Compare Olbrycht 2004a; id. 2011; id. 2013b; id. 2014; Canepa 2014b; Olbrycht 2017a; Engels 2017.

46. Note Ruzicka 2012.

47. Zack recently referred to the Aegean interstate system as the "Hellenic state system." Zack 2017: 9–26. Yet I find the geographical association more appropriate. Note Overtoom 2016a: 986–87.

48. Sometimes contemporary, yet separate interstate systems merged into a single, larger system because of a process Buzan called "the increased interaction capacity" between the polities in the two regions. Buzan determined that the enlargement and merger of interstate systems occurred periodically in international political history. Yet it occurred more frequently in the premodern world. For the expansion and merger of interstate systems, see Buzan, Jones, and Little 1993: 66–80; Eckstein 2006: 116; Overtoom 2016a; id. 2019a. Compare Aron 1973: 87–88.

interstate system that better reflected the new geopolitical realities of the international environment.[49] This new interstate system, which we may call the "Graeco–Middle Eastern interstate system," incorporated all the Greek lands of the Eastern Mediterranean and the Persian held regions of the Middle East.[50]

The Graeco-Persian Wars damaged Persian prestige and the perception of Persian power and gave the Greeks an opportunity to expand their power extensively at the expense of Persia. Athens in particular threatened to establish a bipolar rivalry within the new and extended international environment of the Graeco–Middle Eastern interstate system in the middle fifth century through its aggression against Persia and its growing imperialism. Yet the destructive Peloponnesian War squandered Athens' opportunity, and Greece descended into geopolitical turmoil. The Persians used the divisiveness of the Greek city-states to reestablish their holdings in Anatolia and interfere diplomatically and financially in Greek affairs for decades.[51] The Persian Empire remained the only major power in the Graeco–Middle Eastern interstate system as Athens, Sparta, and Thebes sapped their strength in the regional conflicts of Greece.

With the rise of Macedon under Philip II, the Macedonian defeat of the Greeks at Chaeronea in 338, and the subsequent Macedonian invasion of Anatolia, Macedon emerged as a hegemonic threat to the Persian Empire. Macedon then became another example of an unlimited revisionist state under the ambitious command of Alexander the Great. The Persian Empire faced its own power-transition crisis in the 330s–320s when Alexander began to conduct successful hegemonic war against the Persians and eventually established unrivaled but short-lived Macedonian hegemony (or unipolarity) over the extensive Graeco–Middle Eastern interstate system.[52] Although the transition of power between the Persians and Macedonians was swift and total, Alexander's efforts to expand the limits of the Macedonian-dominated Graeco–Middle Eastern interstate system into the Indian subcontinent failed, and his sudden death cut short his plans to expand it into Arabia and the Western Mediterranean.[53]

Alexander's death created another power-transition crisis in the late 320s–300s as the Diadochi fought to control portions of Alexander's former empire, introducing multipolar anarchy into the Graeco–Middle Eastern interstate system.[54] One of his generals, Seleucus I, was able to consolidate control over a

49. Overtoom 2016a: 986–97.

50. In a previous article, I referred to this interstate system as the "Greek-Eastern system;" however, I now prefer to call it the "Graeco–Middle Eastern system" for better organization and clarity. See id. 986–88, 992, 995, 997–98.

51. Most notably the Persians used threat of force to help end the Corinthian War and implement the King's Peace in 387/386. See Xen. *Hell.* 5.1.29–31.

52. Overtoom 2016a: 987.

53. See id. 2012. Compare id. 2013; Crescioli 2017; Olbrycht 2017a; Prontera 2017; Biagi 2017.

54. Note Bosworth 2005; Grainger 2007; Waterfield 2011; Romm 2012; Anson 2016; Troncoso 2016; Müller 2016; Ogden 2016; Mari 2016; Pownall 2016; Prandi 2016. Zack recently concluded that the death of Alexander and the wars of the Successors created "a geographically extensive, new system—the Hellenistic." Zack 2017: 39. Yet the

large section of the Hellenistic Middle East, incorporating lands from Anatolia and Syria in the west to Afghanistan and Pakistan in the east under the newly founded Seleucid Empire.[55] By the middle 270s a system of tripolar rivalry between the Antigonids in Greece, the Ptolemies in Egypt, and the Seleucids in Syria had emerged.

The Seleucids controlled the largest empire, establishing themselves as the imperial successors of Alexander and the Persians in the Middle East; however, they appear to have had a slightly different outlook on their hegemony in the east than their predecessors. Alexander and the Persians had viewed their imperial space as limitless on the Central Asia steppe and in the Indian subcontinent; however, Paul Kosmin recently has argued that the Seleucids formed stricter limitations on their imperial space, especially along their eastern frontier, with "explicit and formal recognition of equal peer kingdoms."[56] Although, at least in theory, it is unlikely that the Seleucid kings abandoned their royal ideology of unlimited, universal rule, practical concerns in the west encouraged the Seleucids to develop a more restricted policy in the east.[57] Therefore, Kosmin's arguments for the limitation of Seleucid hegemony in the east, where the Seleucids actually restricted and shrank the limits of the Graeco–Middle Eastern interstate system when they created an "ideological *limes*" along the frontier of the Central Asian steppe and in 306/305 ceded the Indus River valley and Arachosia to the Mauryan Emperor, Chandragupta, in exchange for 500 war elephants, generally appear sound.[58]

As discussed in this study, the Seleucids took an inconsistent and reactive interest in eastern geopolitical developments. They decided to establish Bactria as a bulwark to protect the eastern edge of their empire and turned their attention to the geopolitical developments of the Eastern Mediterranean.[59] Meanwhile, in the west they took an active and aggressive interest in the tripolar rivalry that emerged with the Antigonids and Ptolemies.[60] These different western and eastern spatial perspectives of their hegemony played an important part in the

term "Hellenistic" in this context is too broad and undefined, and an extensive interstate system already was in place throughout the Eastern Mediterranean and Middle East. Overtoom 2016a.

55. Note Grainger 2014. Compare Capdetrey 2007.

56. Kosmin 2014: 123.

57. Strootman puts forth strong arguments that "claims to unlimited power were central to Seleukid ideology, and conquest was a principal duty of the king" and that Seleucid kings had to balance royal ideology about universal hegemony against political pragmatism. Strootman 2004. Compare Engels 2017. Yet the western focus of the Seleucid state helped create a different, more distant approach to the geopolitics of the east for the Seleucids. Overtoom 2016a; id. 2019a.

58. For the new Seleucid boundary with the steppe, see Kosmin 2014: 59–61. Compare Holt 1999: 28; Strootman 2014; Grainger 2014: Chs. 5, 8; Lerner 2015a: 307; Strootman 2019. For Seleucus I's arrangement with the Mauryans, see Appian *Syr.* 9.55; Strabo 15.2.9. Antiochus III later made a similar agreement with the new regional king, Sophagasenos. See Polyb. 11.34.11–12. For Arachosia, see Schmitt 1986c.

59. Holt 1988; id. 1999: 28–9; id. 2012a; Lerner 2013; id. 2016.

60. See Ager 2003. The focus of Seleucid military operations was to contain Ptolemaic expansion and dominate the coast of the Eastern Mediterranean. For a more detailed account of the recurring, destructive conflicts between the Seleucids and Ptolemies known as the Syrian Wars, see Grainger 2010.

formation of a new interstate system in the Hellenistic Middle East after the crisis of the 240s–230s.

Seleucid Decline

Seleucus I had been an experienced and capable leader with an extensive diplomatic and military record. He was the sort of strong central figure that the disparate Seleucid Empire needed to flourish. He had initiated what we may call the "First Seleucid Cycle" of hegemony over the Hellenistic Middle East (300s–240s). Yet a series of serious mishaps began to plague his successors and weaken the kingdom he had founded. The endemic warfare and dynastic rivalries of the Diadochi were exhausting and deleterious to the Hellenistic Successor states.[61] The Seleucid Empire was particularly susceptible to periods of weakness and decline because of its massive size, and the power-transition crisis of the 240s–230s was a consequence of one of these periods of Seleucid decline.[62]

Seleucus I's successor, Antiochus I, lost large portions of southern Anatolia to Ptolemy II in the First Syrian War (274–271). Antiochus I's successor, Antiochus II, fought the mostly indecisive Second Syrian War (260–253) against Ptolemy II to reclaim these lost territories. Yet the greatest consequence of this second war was the dynastic chaos that it indirectly created within the Seleucid state. To seal the peace agreement between Egypt and Syria after the second war, Antiochus agreed to take a new wife. He repudiated his first wife, Laodice I, who already had borne him two sons, aptly named Seleucus and Antiochus, sending her to Ephesus, and he married Ptolemy's daughter, Berenice, who also would bear him a son.[63] When Antiochus suddenly died in 246, perhaps poisoned on the order of Laodice, Berenice tried to place her son on the throne with herself as regent. As a Ptolemaic princess, she called upon her brother, Ptolemy III, the new king of Egypt, to come to her aid. Unfortunately for her and her son, aid did not materialize swiftly enough. Laodice returned to Syria, likely arranged the murder of Berenice and her son, and supported her eldest son, Seleucus II, as king. Ptolemy III sought revenge for the murder of his sister and nephew and initiated the Third Syrian War (246–241), which was a disaster for the Seleucid Empire. Ptolemy campaigned successfully in Syria and Mesopotamia, even seizing Babylon temporarily in early 245.[64] Meanwhile, Seleucus' younger brother and co-ruler in

61. Ogden argues that dynastic conflicts were the primary factor in the decline of all Hellenistic kingdoms. Ogden 1999.

62. Overtoom 2016a.

63. For a recent attempt to reassess the reputation and role of Laodice in these events, see Martinez-Sève 2003. Compare Grainger 2014: 181–82, 186; Coşkun 2016; id. 2018. For Seleucid royal women, see Coşkun and McAuley 2016. For Hellenistic royal marriage alliances, see Grainger 2017b: Ch. 2. For the Parthian's use of dynastic marriages, see Dąbrowa 2018.

64. Monerie 2019. For the death of Antiochus and the violent aftermath of his death, see Appian *Syr.* 11.65–66; Porph. 43; Justin 27.1.1–10; id. *Prol.* 26; Polyaen. 8.50; Hieron. *Daniel* 11: 7–9; Polyb. 5.58.11; Cat. 66.12, 36; Callim. 110.40–78; Val. Max. 9.10e1; Cosmas Indicop. (OGIS 54); *Papyri Haunienses* 6.14–17; Finkel, van der Spek, Pirngruber 2020e; id. 2020f.

Anatolia, Antiochus Hierax, declared independence, causing a major distraction for Seleucus. Although setbacks in the Aegean forced Ptolemy to relinquish his gains in Mesopotamia, Seleucus lost important coastal towns in Anatolia and Syria to Ptolemaic Egypt, which devastated Seleucid prestige and the perception of Seleucid power.[65]

Two periods of civil war against Antiochus Hierax (ca. 246/245–236 and 229/228–226) proved equally disastrous for Seleucid prestige and power.[66] Early in the first conflict at the Battle of Ancyra, Seleucus II lost to Antiochus and had to relinquish his control of all Seleucid lands in Anatolia, which Antiochus ruled independently for several years as a rival Seleucid king.[67] The Seleucid satraps along the eastern frontier found themselves increasingly isolated during this extended period of turmoil.

The satraps of Parthia and Bactria had power and wealth; however, the neglect of the royal government in Syria meant that the eastern forces of the Seleucid Empire lost the ability to conduct preemptive campaigns against potential threats, making Seleucid military policy in the east more defensive and reactionary. Although the isolation of the eastern satraps encouraged greater military pressure from the tribes on the Central Asian steppe, as long as the Seleucid king was capable to respond to nomadic invasions in the east with convincing force, the integrity of the empire's frontiers remained intact. However, when the power of the monarchy faltered during the crisis of the 240s–230s, the powerful eastern satraps decided to break away from the empire, destabilizing the Hellenistic Middle East and overturning Seleucid hegemony. This chaos encouraged the nomadic Parni to invade northeastern Iran with the intention of establishing a new kingdom.[68]

New Kingdoms Form

In the west, growing Seleucid weakness caused by the devastating Third Syrian War and subsequent civil war allowed Attalus, the dynast of Pergamon, to declare himself king in western Anatolia in 238.[69] The Attalid Kingdom remained an important player in the geopolitical developments of the Eastern Mediterranean until its absorption into the Roman state in 133.[70] However, in the east the sudden

65. See Justin 27.1.1–3.12, 41.4.4–5; Appian *Syr.* 11.65; Plut. *Reg. Imp. Apophtheg.* 184A; Eus. *Chron.* (Smith ed.): 251. Note Grainger 2014: 194.

66. In ancient international relations, the reputation of state power and leadership was of the utmost importance. Wheeler 2002: 287.

67. Justin 27.2.6–12, 41.4.7; Plut. *Mor.* 184A, 489A–B, 508D–E; Polyaen. 4.9.6, 8.61.1; Eus. *Chron.* (Smith ed.): 251; Athen. 13.64. For more on the civil war between Seleucus II and Antiochus Hierax, see Tarn 1928: 717–20; Newell 1938a: 392–95; Bickerman 1944: 76 n.23; Wolski 1947: 40; Frye 1984: 178–80; Brodersen 1986: 378–81; Grainger 2014: Chs. 14–15; Overtoom 2016a; Coşkun 2018; Olbrycht 2020/2021.

68. Note Overtoom 2016a: 988.

69. Lerner 1999: 30. Compare Bevan 1902: i 194 n.5, 285 n.2, 288; Macdonald 1922: 440; Bickerman 1944: 76ff.; Mitchell 2018.

70. For Attalus and the Attalid Kingdom, see Hansen 1971; Allen 1983; Thonemann 2013.

decline of the power of the Seleucid state in the 240s caused a crisis that eventually led to the complete overthrow of Seleucid imperial dominion and the rise of Parthia and Bactria as regional powers within a new interstate system.

The formation of new rival kingdoms in Parthia and Bactria drastically changed the international environment in the Hellenistic Middle East and altered Seleucid policy toward its eastern frontier. A new tripolar rivalry emerged on the Iranian plateau and established a new interstate system, which we may call the "Iranian interstate system."[71] The Iranian interstate system paralleled those found in the Mediterranean. It was a harsh international environment with multiple militarized, bellicose, and aggressive polities. There was no enforceable international law, a lack of ameliorative diplomacy, and no way to understand the realities of power relations between states short of open conflict. The Parthians faced serious threats to their security and survival from Hellenistic kings, native Iranian dynasties, and Central Asian tribes. This chaotic and dangerous international environment helped influence their policy as the Parthians struggled, first, to survive within the Iranian interstate system and, later, to expand and dominate that system.

The Parni

The people later collectively recognized as the Parthians began as a nomadic tribe known as the Parni, who in the early third century came to settle in what is today western Turkmenistan.[72] Traditional scholarship maintains that the foundation of the Parthian state occurred in 250, with the Parthian (or Arsacid) era beginning in ca. 248/247.[73] However, in a recent study Jeffrey Lerner argues convincingly that these traditional dates are too early to represent actual geopolitical developments in the region, and he rejects that the Parthian era corresponds to the Parni's seizure of the Seleucid satrapy of Parthia in northeastern Iran.[74] Instead, he uses coinage and Justin's account of events to establish the independent reign of a rebellious Seleucid satrap named Andragoras over Parthia from ca. 245–239/238, at which point the Parni invaded and claimed the region.[75] Thus, Lerner

71. In a previous article, I referred to this interstate system as the "new Eastern system"; however, I now prefer to call it the "Iranian system" for better organization and clarity. Note Overtoom 2016a: 985–7, 999–1001.

72. The Parni likely were a part of the larger Dahae confederacy on the southern Central Asian steppe. See Olbrycht 2003: 71–72; id. 2015b: 257–58; id. 2019a. Compare Lozinski 1959: 9; Jettmar 1967: 214; Gardiner-Garden 1987: 15–16; Assar 2011: 113; Balakhvantsev 2017: 24–61.

73. For the traditional dating system, see Saint-Martin 1850: i–ii; Scott 1854: 131–39; Gardner 1877: 3; Cunningham 1888: 79; Tarn 1932: 576; Debevoise 1938: 9; Bickerman 1944: 80–83; Tolstov 1948: 232 ff.; Wolski 1956–1957: 42–3; Narain 1957: 13–14; Schmitt 1964: 73ff; Assar 2011: 113–14. For problems with this system, see Bivar 1969: 9ff.; Frye 1984: 208; Wiesehöfer 2013b. For a historiographical survey of the debate, see Lerner 1999: 14–16.

74. Lerner 1999: 13–23. Unfortunately, some recent scholarship has overlooked or ignored Lerner's sound conclusions. See Garthwaite 2005: 67; Katouzian 2009; Grainger 2014: 196–8; Sampson 2015: 35–41.

75. Lerner 1999: 23–26. Compare Frye 1985; Assar 2004: 77; Brosius 2006: 85; Curtis 2007: 7; Lerouge-Cohen 2007: 12–13; Assar 2011: 114; Dąbrowa 2012: 26; Daryaee 2015: 286; Balakhvantsev 2017: 61–70.

argues that the coronation of Arsaces I as king of the Parni, ten years prior to their invasion of Parthia—not the invasion itself—established the Parthian era.[76] With this new understanding, the expansion of the Parni into Parthia occurred after the Third Syrian War and during the first phase of the civil war of Seleucus II and Antiochus Hierax, and it corresponds directly with the power-transition crisis of the 240s–230s in the Hellenistic Middle East.[77]

Lerner argues that, in the early third century, the nomadic Parni unsuccessfully attempted to seize the satrapy of Margiana.[78] Incursions into Iran and Afghanistan by Central Asian peoples were a continual threat to the stability and security of polities in the Middle East throughout the premodern period, and the Parni were simply one of many aggressive, expansionistic tribes in the region in the Hellenistic period.[79] The militarized and violent societies and lifestyles of Asiatic tribes were a product of the harsh systemic pressures of the international environment in the region. Life on the steppe was unforgiving and tribal warfare endemic. Justin records the precariousness of life on the steppe and the long history of conflict that the Parthians endured. He states:

> The Parthians, in whose hands the empire of the east now is, having divided the world, as it were, with the Romans, were originally exiles from Scythia [the Central Asian steppe]. This is apparent from their very name; for in the Scythian language exiles are called Parthi. During the time of the Assyrians and Medes, they were the most obscure of all the people of the east. Subsequently, too, when the empire of the east was transferred from the Medes to the Persians, they were but as a herd without a name, and fell under the power of the stronger. At last they became subject to the Macedonians, when they conquered the east; so that it must seem wonderful to everyone, that they [the Parthians] should have reached such a height of good fortune as to rule over those nations [that is, Persia and the Seleucid Empire] under whose sway they had been merely slaves.[80]

76. For the argument that the coronation of Arsaces began the Parthian era, see Lerner 1999: 17, 29. Compare Wroth 1903: 273ff.; Debevoise 1938: 9; Dąbrowa 2012: 26. For opposing views, see Lerner 1999: 18–19. For Lerner's criticisms of Wolski's reconstruction, see id. 19–22. Note Wolski 1947: 13ff.; id. 1956–1957: 35–39; id. 1959: 222–25; id. 1960: 110ff.; id. 1962: 136ff; id. 1974: 159ff.; id. 1976b: 439–44; id. 1982: 131ff.; id. 1991: 49–55; id. 1996. Compare Neusner 1963: 48–50; Schmitt 1964: 64ff.; Will 1967: i 301–8; Altheim and Stiehl 1970; Bivar 1983: 28–30; Frye 1984: 207–8; Musti 1984: 213–20; Brodersen 1986; Shahbazi 1986b; Gardiner-Garden 1987: 13. It appears that Arsaces was crowned in Asaak, which contained a guarded everlasting fire. Isod. 11.

77. Grainger puts forth an inventive, yet poorly supported conclusion that Arsaces conducted two invasions of Parthia, one in 247/246 and the other in 237. Grainger 2014: 196–98.

78. Lerner 1999: 13–14, 29.

79. For background on the regions of the Central Asian steppe in this period, see Negmatov 1999; Boardman 2007. For the concept of Central Asia and its geographical characteristics, see Sinor 1990a; Taaffe 1990. For background information on the movement of peoples in this region over numerous centuries, see Abdullaev 2007; Stride 2007; Golden 2011: 9–20; Baumer 2012. For background on the various tribes in the area after Alexander's conquests, see Zadneprovskiy 1999.

80. Justin 41.1.1–6.

Justin here incorrectly conflates the history of the Parthians prior to Arsaces I's conquest of Parthia with that of the Parni and the subsequent Arsacid Parthian period; however, he clearly illustrates the instability and vulnerability of this region and recognizes the considerable political and military accomplishments of the Parthians in establishing dominion over the Hellenistic Middle East. He continues:

> The Parthians [that is, the Parni], being forced to quit Scythia by discord at home, gradually settled in the deserts betwixt Hyrcania, [and the lands of] the Dahae, the Arei, the Sparni, and the Margiani. They then advanced their borders, though their neighbors, who at first made no opposition, at length endeavored to prevent them, to such an extent, that they not only got possession of the vast level plains, also of steep hills, and heights of the mountains.[81]

Justin here returns to the volatility of life on the Central Asian steppe and the determination of the Parni to establish a secure power base despite the growing opposition of their competing neighbors, emphasizing again the Parthians' political and military success.

The organization of various Central Asian peoples into tribal confederations, like the Dahae confederacy, was an attempt to create greater strength and security against neighboring tribes on the steppe and against the Persian and Hellenistic kingdoms on the Iranian plateau. In settling western Turkmenistan (northern Parthia), the Parni came to live directly on the periphery of the Seleucid Empire. This proximity, paired with a lack of diplomatic communication and restricted awareness of power capabilities, caused mounting tension along the frontier and made conflict between the Parni and the Seleucids increasingly likely.

Although Alexander the Great had left a large force to occupy Bactria and the surrounding territories, the restlessness of these Greek soldiers and Alexander's sudden death in 323 severely disrupted the region, forcing Seleucus I to campaign there between 308 and 305.[82] In the middle 290s–280s, Seleucus committed himself to establishing Bactria as a strong frontier region, even appointing his son, Antiochus I, as viceroy in the east to supervise the development of firm Seleucid control over the new frontier.[83] Frank Holt argues that, although the efforts of Seleucus and Antiochus in this period created a prosperous and strong eastern frontier, these efforts encouraged aggression from the Central Asian tribes, especially the Parni, first, because attacking these prosperous frontier regions created opportunities to gain considerable status and wealth and, second, because the increasingly defensive stance of the Seleucids in the east generated doubt about

81. Id. 41.1.10–11. Note Olbrycht 2019a.
82. Holt 1999: 24; Lerner 2015a: 306; Olbrycht 2017a.
83. Holt 1999: 26–7; Lerner 2016.

the capabilities and intentions of the Seleucids in these regions.[84] After settling in the area, the Parni's subsequent invasion of neighboring Seleucid-held Margiana was, in part, a result of these opportunities and uncertainties.[85]

Margiana was a wealthy and relatively urbanized region of what is today eastern Turkmenistan. Alexander the Great had settled the region with Greek colonies and fortifications, including the prosperous oasis city of Alexandria-in-Margiana or Margiane (later known as Merv, which remained an important eastern city until the Mongol invasions of the thirteenth century CE).[86] The addition of Margiana to the holdings of the Parni would have been a great boon to their regional power and security. Meanwhile, the loss of Margiana would have undermined Seleucid authority in the region severely and compromised the eastern frontier of the Seleucids.

Parni attacks on Margiana in the late 280s challenged the regional standing of the Seleucid state and the integrity of its frontier, and therefore, the Seleucids had to respond to the Parni invasion of Margiana with force to restore the perception of Seleucid strength in the region or else risk encouraging further aggression against them. The Seleucids quickly dispatched an army to neutralize the Parni threat. Thus, one of the most noticeable difference in the capabilities of the Seleucid state between the 280s and 240s is the Seleucids' ability to respond to eastern threats to their hegemony with decisive force.

The Parni invasion of Margiana failed, and the Seleucid general, Demodamas, counterattacked against the Parni in ca. 280.[87] This campaign appears to have been successful enough to tamper the expansionistic capabilities of the Parni for a few decades; however, domination of the tribes of the Central Asian steppe was not a strategic goal for the Seleucids. Once Demodamas had retaliated against the Parni and restored the strength of the Seleucid frontier, it appears that he ended his campaign abruptly. He did not completely remove the threat of the Parni, and therefore, by 248/247 a new king, Arsaces I, came to lead a resurgent Parni tribe, introducing the Parthian era.[88] Arsaces was determined to expand the power and

84. Holt 1999: 29.

85. Note Lerner 1999: 13–14, 29; Holt 1999: 29. Although unlikely, Wolski argued that Arsaces invaded Margiana on the way to settling northern Parthia. Wolski 1947: 26–31; id. 1969: 253–4; id. 1974: 159ff.

86. For Alexander's settlement of the region, see Fraser 1996: 31, 91, 116–18. Compare Holt 1999: 27; Zavyalov 2007; Olbrycht 2017a. Note Pliny *NH* 6.18.47; Strabo 9.10.2; Curt. 7.10.15. For the development of Central Asia after Alexander and before the Islamic conquests, see Herrmann and Cribb 2007. For archaeological surveys of the region, see Usmanova, Filanovich, and Koshelenko 1985: 226–42; Koshelenko, Giabov, and Bader 1996: 308–13, 316–17; Simpson 2014. For the regional importance of Merv, see Williams 2002; Brun 2005; Williams 2007. For the importance of Merv in the Sasanian and early Islamic periods, see Kennedy 2006: 6–9, 83–84, 86–96, 200; id. 2008: 170 *et passim*; Hoyland 2015: 86, 116, 120, 125, 205.

87. Pliny *NH* 6.18. See Hennig 1944: 222–23; Robert 1984: 467–82; Frye 1984: 208; Lerner 1999: 29; id. 2017. For the efforts of Seleucid generals, such as Demodamas and Patrocles, to stabilize and strengthen the eastern frontier, note Holt 1999: 27–28; Lerner 2017.

88. For recent evaluations of Arsaces I's reign, see Assar 2005a: 32–35; id. 2011: 113–14; Balakhvantsev 2017: 65–70. Arsaces' father perhaps also was named Arsaces, and his grandfather perhaps was named Phriapetes. Arr. *Parth*. Fr. 3.

security of his people, and it was under Arsaces that the Parni assumed the identity of the Parthians.[89]

Within the first three years of his reign, Arsaces I appears to have led a new Parni invasion of Margiana, fighting an unsuccessful campaign against the Seleucid satrap of Bactria, Diodotus.[90] At this time Diodotus' responsibilities as satrap appear potentially to have included administrative and military command over not only Bactria but also Sogdiana, Margiana, and Aria.[91] This was an enormous command with wide-ranging responsibilities, and threats to the northeastern frontier of the Seleucid Empire were considerable; the recent invasions of the Parni make this evident. Diodotus' isolation and expanded role in the administration of the northeastern frontier of the Seleucid Empire illustrates the neglect of the central government in Syria and its continued distraction with western wars. Although Diodotus was successful in repulsing Arsaces' invasion of Margiana in ca. 246/245, Seleucus II did not send an army to punish the Parni and quash their military ambitions as his predecessors had done.[92] Seleucus II was too involved in the dynastic conflicts of the west.

The Third Syrian War had begun because of these conflicts in 246, initiating the power-transition crisis of the 240s–230s throughout the Eastern Mediterranean and Middle East, and the subsequent civil war between Seleucus II and Antiochus Hierax perpetuated that crisis. The eastern satraps of the Seleucid Empire had already endured years of neglect and isolation. This lack of support from the central government, along with Seleucus' contested succession to the throne, the destructive war against Ptolemy III, and the growing threat of Arsaces I, led the two major satraps along the eastern frontier of the Seleucid Empire, Diodotus and Andragoras, to rebel in 245.[93]

Lerner put forward a similar reconstruction of events, associating the Third Syrian War with the rebellion of Andragoras and Diodotus.[94] Yet his account does not fully appreciate why these events coincided within the rapidly evolving international environment at this time. Here we can utilize the theoretical framework of Realism to further our understanding of the geopolitical developments of this period. The power-transition crisis of the 240s–230s made the rebellions of Diodotus and Andragoras possible and understandable. Appian makes this

89. The Parni quickly assimilated within Parthia in the middle of the third century. Note Shahbazi 1986a; Olbrycht 2003: 73.

90. This is also Lerner's reconstruction of Strabo and Justin's accounts. Lerner 1999: 13. Note Strabo 11.9.3; Justin 41.4.9. For a recent evaluation of Diodotus, see Holt 1999:19, 24–25, 67–74, 77, 82, 85, 94–101. For recent studies of Hellenistic Bactria, see id. 1999; Lerner 1999; Sidky 2000; Holt 2005; Omar 2009; Holt 2012a; Lerner 2015a; Bordeaux 2018.

91. See Schmitt 1964: 64–65, 68, 75.

92. Assar's suggestion that Arsaces defeated Seleucus in 247, while he was still "the junior ruler in charge of the 'Upper Satrapies' under his father Antiochos II" is untenable. Assar 2011: 114.

93. Note Overtoom 2016a: 984–85. Diodotus possibly made his eldest son co-ruler at about this time. Holt 1999: 19.

94. Lerner 1999: 29.

connection when he records, "He [Ptolemy III] invaded Syria and advanced as far as Babylon. The Parthians [that is, the people of the satrapy of Parthia under Andragoras] now began their revolt, taking advantage of the confusion in the house of the Seleucids."[95] The rebellion Appian here describes was that of Andragoras, not of Arsaces I as Gareth Sampson argues. Sampson unfortunately conflates the actions of the people of Parthia prior to Arsaces' invasion of the region with the actions of the Parni under Arsaces, which leads him to hypothesize incorrectly that Arsaces rebelled from the still loyal Andragoras, seized his satrapy, and declared independence in the middle 240s.[96]

With the rebellions of Andragoras in Parthia and Diodotus in Bactria, Seleucid imperial dominion over the Hellenistic Middle East fractured and the Graeco–Middle Eastern interstate system returned to a temporary state of multipolar anarchy. The decline of Seleucid power in the west in the middle 240s created a power void in the east. Justin captures the consequences of the crisis, stating:

> For their revolt [that is, the Parthians under Andragoras], the dispute between the two brothers, Seleucus [II] and Antiochus [Hierax], procured them impunity; for while the brothers sought to wrest the throne from one another, they neglected to suppress the rebellion. At the same period, also, Theodotus [that is, Diodotus], governor of the thousand cities of Bactria, revolted, and assumed the title of king; and all the other people of the east, influenced by his example, fell away from the Macedonians [that is, the Seleucids].[97]

Justin here indicates that the Parthians under Andragoras rebelled prior to Arsaces I's invasion. In fact, he soon after continues that Arsaces subsequently rose to power by invading Parthia.[98] Unfortunately, Justin confuses the year of the rebellion of Parthia, placing it either in 256 during the consulship of Lucius Manlius Vulso and Marcus Atilius Regulus or, more likely, in 250 during the consulship of Lucius Manlius Vulso and Gaius Atilius Regulus; however, both of these dates are impossible because, as Justin notes in the same sentence, Parthia rebelled against Seleucus II, who was not king until 246.[99] Further, Justin was unsure of Arsaces' tribal affiliation with the Parni, stating that Arsaces was "a man of uncertain origin."[100] Justin's uncertainty here perhaps helps explain his mistaken association of the Parni with the history of the Parthians prior to Arsaces' invasion. Gholamreza Assar also argues that Justin here refers to a rebellion in

95. Appian *Syr.* 11.65. Compare id. 8.48; Strabo 15.1.3.
96. Sampson 2015: 38–41. Compare Justin 41.1.1–6; Herodian 6.2.7.
97. Justin 41.4.4–5. Compare Strabo 15.1.3.
98. Justin 41.4.6–7.
99. Id. 41.4.3. Justin records the consul Marcus Atilius Regulus, but Justin likely substituted Marcus for Gaius mistakenly. Note Wenghofer 2018: 153.
100. Justin 41.4.6.

Parthia that occurred prior to the Parni invading, and therefore Justin recognized that the dynastic chaos that followed the death of Antiochus II and the inability of the Seleucids to demonstrate their power in the east made the rebellions of Andragoras and Diodotus possible.[101] Thus, the crisis of the 240s–230s threatened the hegemony of the Seleucid Empire in the Hellenistic Middle East and made the eastern frontier increasingly vulnerable.

With his extensive eastern command and resources, Diodotus likely appeared to be the front runner to become the major rival to Seleucid authority in the east.[102] Meanwhile, Andragoras commanded a wealthy and geographically well-situated region in northeastern Iran.[103] However, the sudden deterioration of Seleucid power and the state's inability to retaliate against the Parni's second attack on Margiana meant that this hereto insignificant nomadic tribe from the Central Asian steppe also had an excellent opportunity to exploit the power void forming in the Hellenistic Middle East. By the early 230s, Arsaces I had recovered from his setback in Margiana, and he was ready to capitalize on Seleucid weakness by turning his attention to the isolated satrapy of Parthia and its rebellious satrap, Andragoras.

After the successful defense of his lands in ca. 246/245, Diodotus did not pursue the Parni as they retreated from Margiana. There are several possible reasons for his lack of action. First, Diodotus already possessed an extensive command, and the Parni were not the only Central Asian tribe that threatened his satrapies. Pursuit of the Parni would have made his extensive frontier vulnerable to other nomadic incursions. Second, before 245 Diodotus still was acting as an administrator of the Seleucid state, albeit an isolated one. He likely received no official command from the central government to pursue a war outside of his territories, nor any supplies or money to pursue such a war. Third, Diodotus rebelled against Seleucus II soon after his victory in Margiana. In fact, Diodotus' defeat of Arsaces I likely motivated and legitimized his rebellion, allowing him to adopt the epithet *Soter* ("Savior").[104] Diodotus knew that after rebelling, an eventual military showdown with the Seleucid state was likely, and therefore an offensive campaign against the Parni was a risky endeavor, and one that was not worth pursuing while he prepared for rebellion. Finally, although the Seleucid central government was strong enough to punish the Parni for raiding the empire in the 280s, in the 240s the Bactrian governor was not strong enough to do so on his own.

There clearly was a considerable difference in power relations within the Hellenistic Middle East by the middle 240s that encouraged the actions of the

101. Assar 2006e: 27, 31; id. 2011: 113.

102. Strabo notes Diodotus' military success and expanding power. Strabo 11.9.3.

103. Andragoras controlled at least two mints and struck numerous official and personalized coins. See Diakonoff and Zeimal 1988.

104. Holt 1999: 19.

eastern satraps and the Parni. Prior to their rebellions, Diodotus and Andragoras were not the most important Seleucid officials, nor were they part of the central Seleucid regime. Moreover, they were not united or allied; rather, each fended for himself. The result was a decline in the coordination and retaliatory power of the Seleucid state against the Central Asian tribal confederations.

Once Diodotus had repulsed Arsaces I's invasion of Margiana, the Parni became someone else's problem, namely Andragoras' problem in Parthia. Although there is no reason to believe that Diodotus considered Andragoras an enemy, it is plausible that Diodotus viewed Andragoras, who commanded a large neighboring satrapy and who also was cultivating thoughts of rebellion, as a potential rival. Lerner questions recent interpretations of a series of gold coins produced by Andragoras that claim the coins illustrate an alliance between Andragoras and Diodotus against the Seleucids.[105] He concludes that, although an alliance between the two men was possible, nothing of note came of it, including a record of the alliance through coinage.[106] Ultimately, Diodotus had his own troubles and was glad to rid himself of the Parni menace. The deflection of that menace onto the lands of Andragoras, although perhaps not the design of Diodotus, could not have upset him.

Diodotus' unwillingness or inability to conduct an offensive campaign against the Parni, paired with the inability of Seleucus II to avenge the new Parni penetration of the Seleucid frontier, allowed Arsaces I to recover quickly from his military setbacks in Margiana during the latter half of the 240s. Arsaces was an ambitious man with a resilient army, pursuing aggressive policies. He was determined to expand his territory and began, seemingly for the first time, to expand southwestward into Iran by the early 230s. This change of strategy for Arsaces reflected the geopolitical realities of the Hellenistic Middle East at this time.

Seleucid authority within the Iranian plateau had collapsed with the rebellions of Diodotus and Andragoras. Moreover, Diodotus' defense of Margiana had demonstrated that eastern expansion would be difficult for the Parni without greater resources. Yet the power of Andragoras in Parthia was untested. From his rebellion in 245 to his overthrow in 239/238, Andragoras' position within Parthia and his influence over his subjects was precarious. Lerner argues that Andragoras abandoned Greek coinage, the use of Greek names, and began associating himself with Iranian deities to win local favor since his position in Parthia had become vulnerable.[107] This was an act of political desperation that ultimately failed since Arsaces I soon after invaded and conquered the region. External threats to the rebellious satrapy, namely Seleucid retaliation or nomadic invasion, were considerable.[108]

105. Lerner 1999: 23–24. Compare Diakonoff and Zeimal 1988: 16–18; Alram 1998: 370.
106. Lerner 1999: 25.
107. Id. 25–26.
108. Mattern's investigation of the importance of the perception of strength and revenge in Roman imperial

Arsaces I understood the potential threat of the Seleucids and by the 230s became aware of Andragoras' vulnerability. In fact, Justin emphasizes Arsaces' fears of Seleucid power, the opportunity that the crisis provided, and the precarious position of Andragoras. He records, "He [Arsaces], who was accustomed to live by plunder and depredations, hearing a report that Seleucus [II] was overcome by the Gauls in Asia [Minor], and being consequently freed from dread of that prince, invaded Parthia with a band of marauders, overthrew Andragoras the governor, and, after putting him to death, took upon himself the government of the country."[109] Justin here emphasizes the importance of perceptions of power and weakness and the difficult and perilous existence of ancient states.

In the years since Arsaces I's invasion of Margiana in ca. 246/245, Seleucus II had reclaimed most of the lands lost to Ptolemy III in the Third Syrian War, halted the momentum of his brother in Anatolia, and adopted the epithet Callinicus ("Beautiful Victor").[110] As long as Seleucus appeared strong in the latter half of the 240s, Arsaces was reluctant to invade the lands of the empire, in part seemingly because of the threat of imminent Seleucid retaliation. However, after Seleucus' further setbacks in the civil war against his brother in the late 240s and early 230s, Arsaces was "freed from dread" and emboldened to act aggressively. The natural target became Andragoras' untested and vulnerable territory.

Marek Olbrycht also argues that the Parni, and other Dahae tribes, were aware of geopolitical developments within the Seleucid Empire and that "it is not surprising that in the middle of the 3rd century BC when the state of the Seleucids suffered from internal and external conflicts, the nomads living on the north-eastern border immediately took advantage of that situation."[111] The geopolitical development that Olbrycht discusses here was in fact the power-transition crisis of the 240s–230s, and the aggressive reaction of the Parni was a predictable reaction under the pressures of interstate anarchy. Thus, Seleucus II's defeat in Anatolia at Ancyra (ca. 239) perpetuated the power-transition crisis in the Hellenistic Middle East, allowing Arsaces I to seize his opportunity to invade the isolated satrapy of Parthia, defeat and kill the rebellious Andragoras, and establish his own power in the region.[112]

Another major motivation for Arsaces I's invasion of Parthia in 239/238 was the dangerous and unstable existence of the Parni on the Central Asian steppe.[113]

foreign policy can be applied to this earlier period and to other ancient states. See Mattern 1999: 4, 22–23, 69, 108, 117, 119, 120–22, 171–202, 211–22. Compare Fuhrmann 2012: 43, 83, 135, 158, 168–69, 176–77; Rawlings 2013: 5.

109. Justin 41.4.7. Compare Zos. 1.13; Photius *Bib*. 58; Syncellus in Adler and Tuffin 2002: 412.

110. Lerner 1999: 37; Olbrycht 2020/2021. Compare Strootman 2015; Coşkun 2018.

111. Olbrycht 2003: 72–3.

112. The proposed date of the Battle of Ancyra ranges from 246 to 234. For 246, see Heller 2013; Coşkun 2016; id. 2018. For 234, see Beloch 1927. Generally, scholars accept Bickerman's proposed date of 239; however, Olbrycht in a forthcoming article is attempting to move the date back to 244/243. Olbrycht 2020/2021. Since this article is not yet published, its arguments and content could evolve.

113. For a new investigation of interactions along the Eurasian steppe in antiquity, see Bemmann and Schmauder 2015.

At the time of the crisis, the Parni tribe had been moving southward and westward for decades in search of a secure and prosperous home.[114] Their attacks on the regions of Margiana and Parthia were not simply raids for status and loot. Their displacement on the steppe made them vulnerable, and therefore, they implemented a calculated strategy to create a protected and permanent kingdom within the wealthier, more secure lands of the Seleucid Empire. Under Arsaces' strong leadership, this plan came to fruition in large part because of the opportunities that the crisis provided, and therefore we should not rely primarily on cultural or economic explanations for the creation of the Parthian state, as many previous historians have done.[115] Ultimately, the Parni were not migrating toward the Seleucid Empire simply because they desired to raid the wealthy lands of Parthia and Bactria; rather, they were trying to gain access to the well-positioned, wealthy lands of the Iranian plateau for protection from violent neighbors, increased state security, political opportunity, and the ability to establish and cultivate a strong power base.

Arsaces and the Parthians

The sudden instability of the eastern frontier of the Seleucid Empire, brought on by the recent political and military failures of the Seleucids in the west, and the new vulnerability of the independent eastern satraps had inspired Arsaces I to invade Parthia and establish a new kingdom. The emergence of the Kingdom of Parthia under Arsaces further destabilized the international environment in the Hellenistic Middle East and encouraged Diodotus to declare himself king of Bactria.[116] With Arsaces' defeat of Andragoras, the Parthian aristocracy joined forces with the Parni, which allowed Arsaces to integrate the Parni into the local community and create a new base of power in northeastern Iran that was well-situated geographically for further expansion in all directions.[117]

Gareth Sampson recently has attempted to divide our surviving accounts of the formation of the Parthian state under Arsaces I into two categories, a rebellion scenario and an invasion scenario, before attempting to reconcile them with a new but vague reconstruction. Sampson concludes rather puzzlingly, first, that only Diodotus rebelled in 245 from the Seleucids; second, that Diodotus hired Arsaces as a mercenary to win his independence; third, that Diodotus had a falling out with Arsaces, which forced Arsaces to flee Bactria; fourth, that

114. Justin 41.1.10–11.

115. Note Mommsen 1856 (1903): iii 286–90, iv 421, 433; v 157; Rawlinson 1876 (2002): 21, 24, 41, 97–98, 105, 118–19; Wolski 1966; id. 1976a; id. 1983a; Yarshater 1983: xxix, xxxviii; Bickerman 1983: 17–18; Wolski 1985a; Shahbazi 1986a; id. 1990; Wolski 1993; Sherwin-White and Kuhrt 1993: 89; Curtis 2000: 24–25; Grainger 2013a: 136; id. 2016: 172.

116. See Bopearachchi 1995; Lerner 1999: 30, 33. Compare Holt 1999: 19.

117. Arsaces successfully gained the support of the indigenous population. Frye 1984: 208; Shahbazi 1986a; Olbrycht 2003: 73–75.

the Seleucid governor of Parthia then enlisted Arsaces as a mercenary to fight Diodotus; fifth, that Arsaces then had a falling out with the Seleucid governor in Parthia and killed him; and sixth, that Arsaces finally declared independence from the Seleucids in Parthia through a "native" rebellion.[118] Despite calling the reconstruction of the history of the early Parthian state "impossible" and criticizing other scholars for making "great leaps of logic that are not supported by the remaining evidence," Sampson's reconstruction contains surprising omissions, makes great leaps of logic itself, and too often distorts the available evidence.[119]

Sampson inexplicably ignores the rebellion of Andragoras in 245. He also insists on connecting Arsaces I to Bactria even though Strabo clearly favors the evidence supporting Arsaces' connection to the Parni and his invasion and conquest of Parthia. Strabo records:

> But when revolutions were attempted by the countries outside the Taurus, because of the fact that the kings of Syria and Media, who were in possession also of these countries, were busily engaged with others, those who had been entrusted with their government first caused the revolt of Bactriana and of all the country near it, I mean Euthydemus [actually Diodotus] and his followers; and then Arsaces, a Scythian, with some of the Dahae (I mean the Parni, as they were called, nomads who lived along the Oxus), invaded Parthia and conquered it.[120]

Strabo continues in the next section:

> They say that the Parni Dahae were emigrants from the Dahae [confederacy] above Lake Maeotis [that is, the Sea of Azov], who are called Xandii or Parii. But the view is not altogether accepted that the Dahae are a part of the Scythians who live about Maeotis. At any rate, some say that Arsaces derives his origin from the Scythians, whereas others say that he was a Bactrian, and that when in flight from the enlarged power of Diodotus and his followers he caused Parthia to revolt.[121]

The surviving accounts of Arsaces' humble beginnings and eventual rise to power share common thematic literary elements with the mythical origin stories of other eastern dynasts, such as Cyrus and Sasan.[122] Strabo and Justin demonstrate that the history of the origin of Arsaces and the Parthians was fragmentary and inconsistent even by the Augustan Age; however, they do not favor a

118. Sampson 2015: 39–41. Chahin makes a similarly convoluted and unlikely reconstruction. Chahin 1987: 239.

119. Sampson 2015: 39.

120. Strabo 11.9.2.

121. Id. 11.9.3.

122. Shahbazi 1986a.

rebellion model.[123] Moreover, although Arsaces' first coinage (S1–S2 [Figures 1–2]) contained the title "Autokrat," which Assar identifies as an "elected general" in Seleucid protocol, these early coins purposefully were modeled closely on Seleucid prototypes while including Persian and nomadic imagery to illustrate Arsaces' legitimacy and multiculturalism.[124] There simply is no conclusive evidence that Arsaces served as a mercenary for the Seleucids, Bactrians, or Parthians. Meanwhile, passage 35.43–45 of the Bundahišn, which is a collection of Zoroastrian writings on cosmogony and cosmology, further connects Arsaces as a leader of the Parni.[125] Similarly, there is no evidence that Diodotus and Andragoras ever were at war, making Sampson's reconstruction even more speculative.

Finally, although Sampson cites Strabo, Appian, Dio, Herodian, and the often-unreliable fragments of Arrian found in Zosimus, Syncellus, and Photius as evidence for a "native rebellion theory," none of these sources actually substantiates his conclusions, which do not refer to any supporting scholarship from this century.[126] For example, Appian clearly refers to Andragoras' rebellion in 245, not to the actions of Arsaces I in 239/238.[127] Further, the theatrical Arrian-based accounts in Zosimus, Syncellus, and Photius do not inspire confidence in this instance because of their factual inconsistencies and their unbalanced rhetorical emphasis on passionate emotions driving the motives of Diodotus, Andragoras, and Arsaces.[128] Ultimately, Sampson's recent reconstruction is too hypothetical and not inclusive enough of other important recent scholarship to alter the traditional narrative. Arsaces did not lead a native rebellion against the Seleucids, rather he and his Parni took the rebellious satrapy of Parthia by force in 239/238 from the usurper Andragoras and convinced the Parthians to support him in establishing a new, independent kingdom.

Arsaces I's sudden position of power within Parthia offered him new access to neighboring lands as the invigorated Parthians looked to establish their regional power and state security, and his prompt conquest of Hyrcania by 235 to the west demonstrates his swift integration of the Parni into the larger Parthian population and established aristocracy. Although Susan Sherwin-White and Amélie Kuhrt contend that the Parthians did not settle much south of the Alborz Mountains and that Parthian power remained centered on Turkmenistan until the second century, this minimalist approach is in opposition to much of the

123. Justin 41.4.6–7.

124. Gaslain 2005b: 9–25; Assar 2011: 114.

125. See Frye 1984: 206; Shahbazi 1986a. For the Roman association of the Parthians with the Scythians, see Isaac 2006: 373–75.

126. Sampson 2015: 35–39. Note that Dio's account says nothing of a rebellion. Dio 40.14.3. For the Parthians in Herodian and Zosimus, see Hackl, Jacobs, and Weber 2010b: 174–90, 433–35.

127. Appian *Syr.* 11.65.

128. Zos. 1.13; Photius *Bib.* 58; Syncellus in Adler and Tuffin 2002: 412.

surviving evidence.[129] The Parni originally occupied the lands north of the Kopet Dagh mountain range, which is a continuation of the Alborz, and centered their power on the important cities of Nisa and Asaak; however, by the time of Seleucus II's eastern campaign in the late 230s, Arsaces clearly had occupied Hyrcania in northern Iran south of the Caspian Sea and the important region around Hecatompylus (near modern Damghan, Iran) south of the Alborz.[130]

Arsaces I's sudden achievements, paired with Diodotus' successful rebellion in Bactria and the recent setbacks of Seleucus II, created an unsettled and volatile international environment in the Iranian plateau, encouraging a budding rivalry between Parthia and Bactria. Diodotus, who was a long-standing enemy of Arsaces, commanded great resources and influence in the region, and under his authority Bactria was the leading power in the east. However, Arsaces' conquest of Parthia and then his sudden expansion into Hyrcania made the Parthians a regional power and potential rival of Bactria. The successful efforts of Arsaces to maximize the power of his new kingdom increasingly made the Parthians a threat to the security of Diodotus' territories.[131] Meanwhile, the regional power of Diodotus and the looming threat of Seleucid retaliation encouraged the Parthians to increase their own security through aggressive military measures. Justin records, "Not long after, too, he [Arsaces] made himself master of Hyrcania, and thus, invested with authority over two nations, raised a large army, through fear (*metu*) of Seleucus [II] and Theodotus [that is, Diodotus], king of the Bactrians."[132] Arsaces' "fear" of Seleucid or Bactrian aggression and his response to that fear was a function of the character of the chaotic and dangerous international environment, which helps explain why the Parthians immediately implemented a self-help regime to maximize their power, including the conquest of Hyrcania and the expansion of their army.[133]

Arsaces I's successful invasion of Parthia during the crisis, his conquest of Hyrcania, and the expansion of the Parthian army in turn threatened the exposed Seleucid Empire to the west and the newly independent Kingdom of Bactria to the east. The Parthians' efforts to mitigate their vulnerability and alleviate their security concerns through expansion intensified friction with neighboring states because increased Parthian strength and security came at the detriment of their neighbors. For the Seleucids, the crisis had destabilized the lands they still held in the east. For instance, there were military disturbances in Babylonia in 238, 235, and 229.[134] It became increasingly urgent for Seleucus II to address the rising

129. Sherwin-White and Kuhrt 1993: 88–89, 197; Strootman 2015. Compare Lerouge-Cohen 2007: 228–29.

130. Polyb. 10.28.6–7; Justin 41.4.8.

131. Note Lerner 1999: 30–31.

132. Justin 41.4.8. Note Strabo 11.9.2.

133. Arsaces expanded his army in part by creating new pasturelands for his cavalry and recruiting the sedentary, indigenous population into the Parthian ranks. Olbrycht 2003: 74–75.

134. Sachs and Hunger 1989: no. -237, no. -234, no. -229. It is possible the disturbance in 238 was a reaction to Seleucus' setbacks in Anatolia. Note Overtoom 2016a; id. 2016d: Ch. 1; id. 2020.

threat of the Parthians and Bactrians to protect Seleucid holdings in Media and Mesopotamia. Meanwhile for the Bactrians, Lerner convincingly argues that it was the growing threat of Parthia under Arsaces in the first half of the 230s "that led Diodotus among others to assert his formal independence from the Seleucid kingdom."[135] That is, the drastic rise of Parthian power in the region under Arsaces had undermined Diodotus' position as the front runner to dominate the Iranian plateau after the collapse of Seleucid authority in the 240s. In response to this threat, Diodotus attempted to solidify his position and power by assuming the title of king in ca. 238, officially breaking all ties to the Seleucid Empire.[136] With the establishment of the Parthian and Bactrian kingdoms, tension between the Seleucid Empire, Bactria, and Parthia was at an all-time high by the middle 230s, and their individual efforts to increase the security of their own states made their competitors feel increasingly insecure. Further open conflict was all but assured.

New Interstate Systems Emerge

In an international environment of interstate anarchy, such as the one in the Hellenistic Middle East after the sudden decline of Seleucid power in the 240s–230s, war always is a threat to state security and thus states emphasize short-term, self-help policies to secure self-preservation. States must pursue what international relations theorists call "power-maximizing policies," such as the strengthening of defenses, the expansion of the military, or the conquest of new territory, in the face of uncertain but serious security threats. Hence, the systemic pressures of the international environment encourage states to seek security through the maximization of power and influence by dominating other states in the interstate system. Ammianus, who wrote a brief account of the powers of the Middle East in his description of the much later Roman invasion of Mesopotamia by Emperor Julian, describes the militaristic spirit of the Hellenistic Bactrians and the threat they posed to the early Parthians. Ammianus states:

> The lands next to these the Bactriani possess, a nation formerly warlike and very powerful, and always at odds with the Persians [that is, the Parthians], until they [the Parthians] reduced all the peoples about them to submission and incorporated them under their own name. In ancient times they [the Bactrians] were ruled by kings who were formidable even to Arsaces [that is, the Parthian kings].[137]

135. Lerner 1999: 30, 33.

136. In ca. 238, Diodotus issued new coinage that replaced the portrait and title of the Seleucid king with his own, signaling his coronation and the creation of a completely independent kingdom. See Bopearachchi 1995. Holt places this event as late as 235. Holt 1999: 19.

137. Amm. Mar. 23.6.55. For the Romans' use of the terms "Parthian" and "Persian" interchangeably in late antiquity, see Overtoom 2016c: 165–70.

Thus, we see in Ammianus' account a glimpse of the harsh and violent conditions facing states in the Hellenistic Middle East, the fluidity of ancient power relations, and the rivalry of the Parthians and Bactrians.

The swift expansion of Parthia's strength and perceived power under Arsaces I drastically increased what international relations theorists call the "uncertainty principle" and the "security dilemma" in the Hellenistic Middle East. With the power-transition crisis of the 240s–230s and the emergence of Parthia as a regional power under Arsaces, substantial uncertainty of power relations and fear of the ambitions of neighboring states permeated the Iranian plateau and affected the decision-making of state leaders. Arsaces' efforts to mitigate the vulnerability of his new kingdom and alleviate its security concerns encouraged Diodotus I and Seleucus II to do the same, and this cycle of insecurity made conflict between these states increasingly likely.[138] Therefore, it is not surprising that the Seleucids, as soon as they were able, responded to the rising threat of the Parthians with two major retaliatory expeditions led by Seleucus II and Antiochus III discussed in Chapter 3.

Yet the rapid transformation of the international environment throughout the Hellenistic Middle East in the 240s–230s allowed two new interstate systems to emerge. The Parni originally operated within the limitations of the Central Asian steppe; however, as they migrated farther south and began to come into contact and conflict with the Seleucid Empire, they entered a volatile area on the periphery of the Iranian plateau. For decades the Seleucids had attempted to create a defined and stable eastern frontier, with firmer spatial barriers along the extensive boundaries of the Graeco–Middle Eastern interstate system.[139] As long as Andragoras and Diodotus simply remained rebellious satraps and potential usurpers to the Seleucid throne, the territorial integrity of the Seleucid Empire remained essentially intact, at least abstractly, and the lands of the Iranian plateau remained directly connected to the geopolitical developments of the Eastern Mediterranean. That is, Andragoras and Diodotus in the middle 240s to the early 230s were no different from a long line of other usurpers who entered civil wars against Seleucid monarchs, and therefore their rebellions alone did not create a new interstate system within the Hellenistic Middle East. However, when Arsaces I successfully penetrated the traditional Seleucid frontier, killing Andragoras and creating a new foreign kingdom in northeastern Iran, and when Diodotus I declared himself king of Bactria, officially proclaiming separate sovereignty

138. This cycle of insecurity is the "perpetual tragedy of relations between and among states" that Realist theoreticians emphasize. See Butterfield 1951: 19; Waltz 1959: 160; Arendt 1970: 5; Holsti 1972; Wight 1978: 101–2, 137; Waltz 1979: 102; Thompson 1988: xviii; Liska 1990: 482; Holsti 1991; Little 1993: 150; Spirtas 1996; Glaser 1997: 177; Geller and Singer 1998; Waltz 2000: 8; Copeland 2000: 12, 17, 145–47, 165–8, Ch. 8. Hence, "war is normal" under an international structure of militarized anarchy. Waltz 1988: 620–21.

139. Kosmin 2014: 59–61, 123.

from the Seleucid Empire, the international environment within the Hellenistic Middle East changed drastically.

Suddenly, two sovereign states had emerged to challenge Seleucid hegemony within the Iranian plateau, and the geopolitical limitations and focus of these new polities shifted immediately eastward and separated from those of the Eastern Mediterranean. The Graeco–Middle Eastern interstate system, which had been in place since the Persian Wars, abruptly and effectively split. Tripolarity between Antigonid Macedon, Ptolemaic Egypt, and the Seleucid power base in Syria remained in place in the west in the new, more focused "Eastern Mediterranean interstate system."[140] Yet a turbulent and rather ambiguous tripolarity between Parthia, Bactria, and the Seleucid Empire also emerged in the east in the newly formed Iranian interstate system.[141]

After the emergence of the Iranian interstate system in the early 230s, Parthia and Bactria no longer concerned themselves directly with the geopolitical developments and rivalries of the Eastern Mediterranean, which remained the focus of the traditional Hellenistic Successor states until the rise of Roman unipolar hegemony over the entire Mediterranean from the 190s–160s.[142] Moreover, the geopolitical developments of the Iranian interstate system were only intermittently and indirectly related to those of the Eastern Mediterranean interstate system through sporadic Seleucid efforts to reclaim their lost eastern lands in the 230s, 200s, 180s, 160s, 130s, and 120s. The Seleucid approach to their imperialism in the east also changed as the policy of direct Seleucid control over the Iranian plateau gave way to a system of loose hegemony over subordinate allied kingdoms.

Thus, the Seleucid Empire came to operate simultaneously in separate major interstate systems, which is a geopolitical distinction shared by several other large, powerful empires throughout history.[143] A good illustration of this separation between the geopolitical developments in the west and those in the east is the fact that all of our surviving sources view events in Syria and Babylonia as separate from one another in this period.[144] The geopolitical developments in the east, especially those concerning Parthia, had no direct connection to the emerging international environment of the Graeco-Roman Mediterranean world. They instead belonged to a separate interstate system in the east that was only indirectly affected by western developments.

140. Eckstein 2006: Ch. 4; id. 2012.

141. Overtoom 2016a: 997–98.

142. Note Eckstein 2012; Overtoom 2016a; id. 2016d: Chs. 1–3; id 2019a.

143. See Overtoom 2016a: 1011 n.106. It is worth noting that the Seleucids in fact stood at the intersection of several smaller international systems as well, including the Levantine bipolar rivalry with the Ptolemies, the Asia Minor multipolar cluster before 188, the Caspian axis of petty kingdoms, and even a Red Sea nexus of cities and tribes. Note Kosmin 2013b.

144. Grainger 2013a: 179.

The major difference between the participation of the Seleucids in the Eastern Mediterranean interstate system and the Iranian interstate system was the political, cultural, and economic focus of the Seleucids. Since the Seleucids had come to favor western geopolitical developments and rivalries, their participation in the Eastern Mediterranean interstate system was active, aggressive, and frequent. Meanwhile, their participation in the Iranian interstate system was reactive, inconsistent, and sporadic.[145] Although the Seleucid state remained an important power in the east, possessing the potential strength to threaten the survival of Parthia and Bactria, the Parthians and Bactrians continually took advantage of the Seleucids' western distractions to maximize their regional security and power, adding to their own regional rivalry.

The newly formed Iranian interstate system had a precarious early existence. The Parthians immediately were surrounded by strong and potentially hostile neighbors. Arsaces I and Diodotus I already had established a violent rivalry, making the relationship between Parthia and Bactria unstable. Yet the extent of the threat of the Seleucids remained uncertain. If a Seleucid king could settle the affairs of the state in the west, war in the east to reclaim the Iranian plateau was sure to follow. To legitimize their position and ensure their survival, the Parthians would have to weather this storm.

145. Note Kosmin 2013a; Plischke 2014: 315–34; Grainger 2014; id. 2015; id. 2016.

3

The Empire Strikes Back

The international environment of the Iranian plateau had suddenly changed with the emergence of the Parthians under Arsaces I as a rising power. Although Arsaces had defeated the rebellious Seleucid satrap, Andragoras, and had seized the neighboring territory of Hyrcania, Parthia remained vulnerable between the Seleucid power base in Media and the new Kingdom of Bactria. Both the Seleucids and Bactrians also had good reason to find Arsaces' success concerning. Diodotus I commanded a vast territory with multiple precarious frontiers. Moreover, he was openly hostile toward Arsaces. For the next century, the Parthians and Bactrians remained regional rivals and often viewed one another as enemies. Yet the two new powers on the Iranian plateau had a mutual enemy in the form of the Seleucid Empire. Despite the recent success of Diodotus and Arsaces in establishing new kingdoms, the Seleucid Empire remained the primary power in the Hellenistic Middle East. The power-transition crisis of the 240s–230s had weakened the Seleucid state and had distracted the Seleucid kings, fracturing the eastern frontier; however, the potential power of the Seleucid state remained considerable.[1] All that was needed was a strong leader to put an end to the vicious cycle of civil wars and devastating foreign invasions.

Vengeance against the Parthians became a priority for Seleucus II and his son, Antiochus III, and at the height of Antiochus' power Seleucid hegemony stretched from Greece to India. Antiochus' eastern expedition in the late third century forced the temporary submission of Parthia, and although the results of Antiochus' campaign were not permanent, for a generation the Parthians were unable to challenge Seleucid hegemony directly. This chapter will investigate the initial military and political challenges that the Seleucid Empire experienced in trying to assert and maintain its hegemony over the newly formed Iranian interstate system in the east, while examining the efforts of the Parthians to resist and survive Seleucid retaliation.

1. Strootman argues that Seleucus II's reign was merely a setback and not the "beginning of the end." Strootman 2011; id. 2015; id. 2018.

Reign of Arrows. Nikolaus Leo Overtoom, Oxford University Press (2020). Oxford University Press.
DOI: 10.1093/oso/9780190888329.001.0001.

Sins of the Father

Arsaces I's attack against Andragoras and his subsequent conquests of Parthia and Hyrcania had compromised the eastern frontier of the Seleucid Empire and had facilitated the further fracturing of Seleucid power in the Hellenistic Middle East by encouraging Diodotus I to declare his independent kingship. When the Parni violated the Seleucid frontier in ca. 280, the Seleucids had responded with Demodamas' retaliatory campaign. The emphasis of the campaign was to punish the Parni and reestablish the perception of Seleucid power in the region to dissuade further aggression against the frontier. The inability of the Seleucids to punish the Parni for their renewed aggression in the first half of the 240s helped encourage the rebellions of Andragoras and Diodotus and inspire the invasion of Parthia by Arsaces.

Yet in the 230s, despite their recent success, the Parthians under Arsaces I could expect some form of imminent Seleucid retaliation. The disintegration of the eastern frontier made a Seleucid campaign to reconquer the region and punish the Parthians and Bactrians increasingly necessary. In terms of international relations theory, in a system of interstate anarchy, like the Iranian interstate system, where power relations are fluid and state capabilities are uncertain, reputation is linked directly to perceptions of state power. Damage to a state's perceived power, regardless of its actual power capabilities, encourages further aggression by competitors within the anarchic system. Thus, states must take challenges to their authority and slights to their reputation with the utmost seriousness and repay them with the utmost severity. By the 230s, Seleucus II could no longer afford to ignore the growing crisis in the east. Justin tells us that Seleucus "came to take vengeance on the rebels (*ad defectores persequendos veniente*)."[2] Seleucus mounted the first royal campaign into the east since his great-grandfather but with much different results.[3]

A Pact between Rivals

In ca. 238–236, with Seleucus II still embroiled in civil war against his brother in the west, the newly crowned Diodotus I of Bactria was the immediate threat to the young Parthian state. Diodotus and Arsaces I had been long-standing enemies ever since Arsaces' failed invasion of Margiana in the middle 240s, which had allowed Diodotus to establish himself as the "Savior" of Bactria.[4] Meanwhile, Diodotus' kingdom was much larger than Arsaces' and his military had proved effective against Arsaces' cavalry-based army, at least while on the defensive. Even

2. Justin 41.4.9.
3. Overtoom 2021a.
4. Holt 1999: 19.

with the addition of Hyrcania, the Kingdom of Parthia was vulnerable along its entire western and eastern frontiers.

The central geographical position of Parthia, which allowed the Parthians numerous avenues of expansion in all directions throughout the Iranian plateau, also presented the dangerous prospect of multiple front wars. A two-front war against the Seleucids in the west and the Bactrians in the east likely would have proved fatal to Arsaces I's young kingdom. This helps explain the "fear" Arsaces felt of outside aggression in the early 230s and his own aggressive expansion into Hyrcania and swift military recruitment.[5]

Yet before Arsaces I's enemies could overwhelm him, fate intervened for the Parthians. A difficult civil war delayed the looming retaliation of the Seleucids, and before Diodotus I could pursue a war against the Parthians, he suddenly died. His son, Diodotus II, became the new king of Bactria in ca. 236/235, and he quickly abandoned his father's hostility toward the Parthians.[6] Diodotus II and Arsaces not only came to make peace, but they also declared themselves allies.[7]

An end to hostilities and a military alliance between Parthia and Bactria in the middle of the 230s made sense for several reasons. First, as the new king of the young Bactrian state, Diodotus II lacked the prestige and influence of his father to rule his new kingdom without opposition.[8] His father had been a gifted administrator, working in relative isolation on the fringe of the Seleucid Empire for many years. Diodotus I had expanded his administrative control beyond his official satrapy in Bactria and had ruled so effectively that the indigenous population seems to have supported his bid for independence. Moreover, Diodotus I had a proven military record. He had successfully defended his extensive frontier and repulsed Arsaces I's invasion of Margiana. Diodotus II had none of these accolades. A peace treaty and alliance with Parthia allowed Diodotus II the opportunity to consolidate his political power and position. Second, it provided Arsaces with the time he needed to settle his people and reorganize his new kingdom. It is impressive how quickly the Parni transformed from their nomadic tribal organization to an integrated monarchy in Parthia with Iranian and Hellenistic influences.[9] The willingness and ability of the Arsacid Parthians to maintain a flexible political and cultural identity became a major advantage for them in their efforts to dominate the Hellenistic Middle East. Third, an alliance between Parthia and Bactria relieved some of the mounting tension between the

5. Justin 41.4.8. Sampson claims Seleucus II and Diodotus I formed an "anti-Parthian pact" without any evidence of such an agreement. Sampson 2015: 42–43. Such a pact seems highly unlikely since Seleucus would not have wanted to recognize Diodotus' legitimacy by forming a military alliance with him.

6. For Diodotus II, see Holt 1999: 19, 25, 66–69, 71, 74–75, 83, 101–7, 125–27.

7. Justin 41.4.9. Note Holt 1999: 62–64. Grainger incorrectly asserts that Diodotus II was a Seleucid "governor of Baktria" in 235 before declaring himself king. Grainger 2014: 200; id. 2015: 65.

8. In fact, a rival, Euthydemus I, eventually overthrew Diodotus II. See Holt 1999: 55, 104, 106, 118; Bivar 2012.

9. See Keshelenko 1966: 12–47, 214–18; Olbrycht 1996: 167; id. 1998a: 31–34; Lerner 1999: 34.

two polities that had built up because of Arsaces' recent military expansions. For Bactria it removed the dangerous prospect of an abrupt war with the rising Parthian state. Meanwhile, for Parthia the alliance removed the immediate threat of a two-front war, which had been a great concern of Arsaces. Finally, the alliance served to counter the threat of an impending Seleucid retaliatory campaign. Arsaces and Diodotus II understood that the Seleucid civil war would not last forever, and therefore the Parthians and Bactrians could anticipate that whoever won the Seleucid civil war likely would look to reestablish his prestige and the power of the empire through an anabasis (a campaign into the interior of the Middle East).

Parthia was the more vulnerable region because it shared a long frontier along the central Iranian plateau with the Seleucid Empire. The full force of Seleucid reprisal would fall first upon the Parthians. Yet Bactria also had every reason to fear Seleucid retaliation. The rebellion of Diodotus II's father and the formation of the Kingdom of Bactria had been a betrayal of the Seleucid king and a direct challenge to Seleucid hegemony. Diodotus II could expect that if the Seleucids were successful in reconquering Parthia, he would be left isolated against a Seleucid invasion of Bactria. Therefore, Arsaces I and Diodotus II decided to put aside their differences to shift the balance of power in the Hellenistic Middle East more in their favor.

Parthian and Bactrian fears of Seleucid aggression quickly began to materialize when Seleucus II and Antiochus Hierax signed an uneasy truce in ca. 236. With a temporary cessation of conflict in the western theater, Seleucus prepared an invasion of the east. Unfortunately, there is little information available on Seleucus' anabasis; however, the invasion likely occurred during the truce between Seleucus and Antiochus (ca. 236–229/228).[10] This truce also likely helped encourage the alliance of Arsaces I and Diodotus II.

Military disturbances in Babylonia may provide a further clue as to the dates for Seleucus II's anabasis. The Babylonian *Astronomical Diaries* tell of fighting between two different factions within the Seleucid army during the truce.[11] The disturbance in 235 likely preceded Seleucus' arrival in the region, and the disturbance in 229 could have been a reaction to his failed campaign. The most recent argument that Seleucus perhaps began his anabasis in 241/240 appears far too early because it assumes the Parthians held Seleucus captive throughout the 230s; however, it is impossible that the Seleucid throne in Syria was vacant for this long without major conflict throughout the decade.[12] Meanwhile, the often-cited dates 231–227 are too late.[13] Jeffrey Lerner's preference to end the campaign no

10. Note Lerner 1999: 33; Shipley 2000: 290; Strootman 2015; Overtoom 2021a. Compare Will 1967: i 278–81, 308–11.
11. See Sachs and Hunger 1989: no. -234, no. -229.
12. Olbrycht 2020/2021.
13. See Frye 1984: 168; Schippmann 1986; Drijvers 1998: 285. Compare Holt 1999: 64.

later than 229/228 seems more plausible since the truce between Seleucus and Antiochus Hierax ended at this time.[14] It seems unlikely that Seleucus would have remained campaigning in the east against the Parthians once his brother openly threatened the security of his more important western lands. Therefore, the most likely time frame for Seleucus' invasion of the Iranian plateau is 235/234–229/228.

It appears that the initial stages of the eastern campaign went well for Seleucus II. He pacified Babylonia, strengthened Media, and reclaimed much of Parthia, temporarily forcing Arsaces I to withdraw toward the Central Asian steppe. Strabo records, "Later Arsaces, when he fled (φεύγων) from Seleucus Callinicus, withdrew into the country of the Apasiacae."[15] Yet there is no record of a military victory over the Parthians by Seleucus, despite Gareth Sampson's unsubstantiated claim that Seleucus obtained "the total defeat of Arsaces" or Rolf Strootman's assumption that Seleucus restored Seleucid hegemony in the east by establishing Parthia as a "vassal principality."[16] Moreover, the Roman tradition is clear that Arsaces later defeated Seleucus.[17]

Arsaces I's resources were quite limited. If Seleucus II had defeated the Parthians decisively, this would have devastated Arsaces' position. It would have been almost impossible for him to then raise another army strong enough to defeat Seleucus later in the campaign. If there was a military engagement in the early stages of the invasion, it must have been minor.

Thus, Strabo's brief account is peculiar and requires further consideration. Arsaces I had been readying for a Seleucid invasion for years by the time Seleucus II entered Parthia, levying soldiers, expanding his territory, and forging the alliance with Bactria. It perhaps seems odd then that Arsaces would "flee" Parthia without a major engagement. Strabo's passage directly connects the flight of Arsaces from Seleucus to the flight of the Persian general Spitamenes from Alexander the Great.[18] In Strabo's account both eastern commanders appear cowardly, desperate, and inferior compared to their Macedonian counterparts. Yet Strabo here follows a well-established Graeco-Roman literary tradition of portraying easterners as inferior, and therefore these stereotyped characteristics of easterners in this passage likely are a superficial exaggeration of the actual motives of Arsaces.[19]

14. Lerner 1999: 33. Note also Dąbrowa 2012: 26.

15. Strabo 11.8.8. For the Apasiacae and the relationship of Parthia with other Central Asian tribes, see Lerner 1999: 34 n.6.

16. Sampson 2015: 42; Strootman 2015; id. 2018.

17. Justin 41.4.9–10; Amm. Mar. 23.6.3; Jo. Mal. 8.198.

18. Strabo 11.8.8. Compare Arr. *Anab.* 3.28.16, 29.12, 30.1.

19. The Greeks and Romans viewed the Parthians as a mixture between the Scythians and Persians. Thus, for the Romans the Parthians were fiercer than the Persians, but they too suffered from eastern despotism and duplicity. See Isaac 2006: Chs. 4–5, 8. Compare Overtoom 2011; id. 2012; Kennedy, Roy, and Goldman 2013: Ch. 10; Gregoratti 2015a: 203–4; Overtoom 2016c; id. 2017a; id. 2017b; Müller 2017b; Engels 2017.

Instead of viewing Arsaces I as a weak easterner, fleeing in the face of the superior Macedonian general, Seleucus II, I prefer to consider the actions of Arsaces in a more constructive light. If we view Seleucus' anabasis within the larger contexts of a long series of asymmetrical defensive wars waged by the Parthians against more traditionally armed Macedonian and Roman invaders over the next two centuries, then we get a sense that Arsaces' withdrawal in the face of Seleucus' advance was in fact a planned Parthian strategy, rather than a cowardly escape. Strabo here inadvertently appears to record the first surviving reference to a unique mode of warfare developed by the Parthians, their "Feign Retreat, Defeat in Detail" mode of warfare, which gave them another important advantage in their long-standing efforts to dominate the Hellenistic Middle East.[20]

Seleucus Fails in the East

After agreeing to a truce with his brother in ca. 236, Seleucus II came to the east to take vengeance on the Parthians and Bactrians. Although Arsaces I and Diodotus II had formed a military alliance against this impending threat, Parthia was the most immediate and vulnerable target of the Seleucids. When Seleucus invaded Parthia sometime in the latter half of the 230s, the Parthians were not able to overwhelm him in a conventional battle. Strabo records that Arsaces fled in the face of Seleucus' invasion to his allies on the Central Asian steppe; however, Strabo's biased portrayal of weak easterners in direct comparison to Alexander the Great and Seleucus disregards any strategic objectives on the part of the Parthians.[21] There is no evidence for a major engagement early in this conflict, and therefore we should consider why Arsaces chose to "flee."

If we consider the anabasis of Seleucus II within the context of the Parthians' asymmetric mode of warfare, Arsaces I's withdrawal into the Central Asian steppe does not appear to be a cowardly or disorganized rout; rather, it appears to be a calculated, strategic maneuver. Despite Arsaces' recent efforts to solidify his regional strength and expand his army, he quickly recognized that his force was no match for the royal Seleucid army in a conventional battle, and therefore he did not risk a major engagement at this time. Arsaces decided to conserve his strength and attempted to deceive Seleucus into thinking the Parthians were weak. Arsaces implemented the first possible example that we have of the Parthians' Deceptive Withdrawal Strategy. The Parthians feigned retreat toward the Central Asian steppe to encourage Seleucus to become complacent or overconfident. Therefore, Strabo unknowingly captured the Parthians utilizing their unique asymmetric mode of warfare.

The Parthian army had the mobility and the flexibility to avoid enemy forces, which allowed them to maintain the initiative during campaigns even though

20. Overtoom 2017b.
21. Strabo 11.8.8.

they were in retreat. With experience from years of interactions along the Seleucid eastern frontier and after watching the recent crisis in the Hellenistic Middle East unfold, Arsaces I understood that in the latter half of the 230s Seleucus II could not maintain a static campaign in the far-off eastern lands of the Iranian plateau for an extended period. Tensions with Seleucus' brother, Antiochus Hierax, who ruled from Anatolia, remained considerable and a renewal of the civil war was looming. In fact, Justin states that after Seleucus suffered a defeat at the hands of the Parthians he was "recalled into Asia [Minor] by new disturbances."[22] Meanwhile, Arsaces was not Seleucus' only target. Seleucus also wanted to punish the Bactrians while he was in the east.

With a clear understanding of the many obstacles that Seleucus II faced, Arsaces I could afford to be cautious and bide his time. Seleucus could not force a major engagement with the more mobile Parthians, but he also could not remain in Parthia permanently. Whether the Seleucids returned to Syria or invaded Bactria, the position of Arsaces remained strong on the southern edge of the Central Asian steppe if he could retain control over his army. Arsaces could wait for the Seleucids to leave southern Parthia, and he was in a great position to take advantage of any military opportunities in the meantime. If we accept that the militarily experienced and capable Arsaces did not simply flee in panic in the face of Seleucus' advance, then his attempt to lull the Seleucids into a state of dangerous complacency and his calculations about the pressures facing Seleucus were correct. Arsaces would demonstrate the effectiveness of the Parthians' mode of warfare.

Unfortunately, only a brief outline of the campaign has survived; however, two events are certain. After the initial withdrawal of the Parthians, they soon after defeated the Seleucids decisively in battle. Justin records, "Engaging with king Seleucus [II], who came to take vengeance on the rebels [in Parthia and Bactria], he [Arsaces] obtained a victory; and the Parthians observe the day on which it was gained with great solemnity, as the date of the commencement of their liberty."[23] Moreover, although Ammianus confuses Seleucus II with his great-grandfather Seleucus I, he similarly records, "After many glorious and valiant deeds, and after he [Arsaces I] had conquered Seleucus [I] Nicator [in reality, Seleucus II], successor of the said Alexander [the Great], on whom his many victories had conferred that surname, and [after Arsaces] had driven out the Macedonian [that is, the Seleucid] garrisons [from Parthia], he passed his life in quiet peace, and was a mild ruler and judge of his subjects."[24] Justin and Ammianus are clear that the defeat of Seleucus II's anabasis was swift and unexpected.

22. Justin 41.4.9–5.1.

23. Id. 41.4.9–10. Note Strabo 11.8.8.

24. Amm. Mar. 23.6.3. John Malalas offers a similar account and makes the same mistake as Ammianus. See Jo. Mal. 8.198. For the Parthians in John Malalas, see Hackl, Jacobs, and Weber 2010b: 285–92.

It is also possible that the Parthians even captured Seleucus II in the aftermath of their victory. The principal evidence supporting the conclusion that the victorious Arsaces I also captured Seleucus is a brief account in Athenaeus, who states, "And in his [Posidonius'] eleventh book [but perhaps his sixteenth book], speaking of Seleucus [II] the king, and relating how he came against Media, and warred against Arsaces, but was taken prisoner by the barbarian, and how he remained a long time in captivity to Arsaces, being treated like a king by him."[25] Some scholars discount this passage by arguing that Athenaeus and Posidonius here mistake Seleucus II either for Demetrius II, whom the Parthians later captured, or simply for *a Seleucus*, who they claim was a little-known son of the later king, Antiochus VII.[26] There is a further speculative argument that Seleucus II launched two eastern expeditions, one that succeeded in driving off Arsaces I and another that resulted in defeat at the hands of Arsaces.[27] Yet it is highly unlikely that Seleucus II had the time or resources to conduct two major eastern expeditions; rather, the sources simply emphasize two phases of Seleucus' anabasis. In the first phase, Seleucus encountered initial success, or at least what appeared to be success since the Parthians looked to have fled.[28] Then in the second phase, Seleucus suffered a considerable defeat against the Parthians, after which he returned to the west.[29]

What remains to be considered is the fate of Seleucus II during his anabasis.[30] Athenaeus and Posidonius state that he became a prisoner, and Seleucus' adopted personal image and coinage perhaps also supports the conclusion that the Parthians held him in captivity, at least briefly.[31] Seleucus adopted the epithet *Pogon* ("Bearded"), and he and Demetrius II, whom the Parthians later captured, produced coinage portraying themselves with a full beard (an image that became standard in Parthian coinage).[32] It is perhaps most likely that Seleucus

25. Athen. 5.38; Posid. 16 (F. H. G. III.258).

26. For Demetrius' capture, which admittedly bears several similarities, see Justin 36.1.5, 38.9.2; id. *Prol.* 35–36; Appian *Syr.* 11.67; Jos. *Ant.* 13.186, 218–19; *I Maccabees* 14.2–3; Diod. 33.28.1; Eus. *Chron.* (Smith ed.): 255; Sebeos in Thomson 1978: 364–65. Note Kidd 1988: 303; Nabel 2017a.

27. See Schippman 1980: 22ff.; Wolski 1996: 182–83; Lerner 1999: 36–37. Assar suggests an even more unlikely scenario that Seleucus originally fought Arsaces unsuccessfully in 247 before conducting an inconclusive invasion of Parthia again in 229. Assar 2011: 114.

28. Seleucus minted coins in Media before invading Parthia depicting the weapons of the Parthians to symbolize his supposed dominance over them. Lorber and Iossif 2009: 95.

29. Strootman suggests Seleucus successfully vassalized Parthia. Strootman 2011; id. 2013b: 6121; id. 2015; id. 2018. However, there is no evidence that Arsaces served as Seleucus' vassal, and the sources are clear that Seleucus' eastern campaign was a failure. Justin 41.4.9–5.1; Amm. Mar. 23.6.3; Jo. Mal. 8.198; Athen. 5.38; Posid. 16 (F. H. G. III.258).

30. For those who argue that Seleucus was a Parthian captive, see Froelich 1744: 30–31, 66; Clinton 1881: 311–13; Cunningham 1884: 113–14; Eckhel 1888: 218; Head 1911: 639; Linfert 1976: 160; Lerner 1999: 35; Olbrycht 2020/2021. For those who attempt to reject this argument, see Visconti 1808: 298–99; Babelon 1890: lxv; Newell 1938a: 64, 135, 200–3; Will 1967: i 311–13; Kidd 1988: 304; Lorber and Iossif 2009: 90; Strootman 2011; id. 2015; id. 2018. For the Seleucid hostages of the Parthians, note Nabel 2017a.

31. For Seleucus' bearded coinage, see Newell 1938a: 64, 135, 200–3; Lorber and Iossif 2009: 95–96.

32. For the use of beards in Seleucid coinage, see Lorber and Iossif 2009. For Seleucus adopting the epithet *Pogon*, see Polyb. 2.71.4.

and later Demetrius adopted their bearded identities to reflect the length and emphasize the religious importance of their eastern campaigns.[33] Yet it is highly unlikely that their bearded images marked major victories over the Parthians, which they did not gain, or symbolized an attempt to associate themselves directly with senior Greek gods, such as Zeus.[34] After returning to the west, their beards likely served as a reminder of their unfinished business in the east against the Parthians, and therefore, "the beard would have been a damaging symbol of failure—yet the alternative of impiety was perhaps even more unacceptable."[35] Apart from Athenaeus' account of Posidonius, the evidence admittedly is circumstantial; however, the capture of Seleucus by the Parthians remains possible and should not be rejected out of hand.

Although Seleucus II may or may not have become a captive of Arsaces I, the Parthians under Arsaces' guidance unequivocally gained a significant military victory over the Seleucids, and Seleucus fell victim to the Parthians' unique mode of warfare. The sudden reversal of Seleucus' fortune and the swiftness of his defeat makes it likely that he made a military or logistical error that left his army vulnerable to a Parthian counterattack. With a unified force, the Seleucids had been too strong for the Parthians to confront in battle, and therefore Seleucus' defeat appears to have been a consequence of dividing his army and his attention.[36]

Ammianus and Photius state that Arsaces I had to remove Seleucid garrisons from Parthia after his defeat of Seleucus II.[37] Therefore, after the Parthians under Arsaces "fled" and appeared not to be a threat, Seleucus apparently attempted to reoccupy southern Parthia by dividing a portion of his army into garrisons.[38] Once Seleucus had divided his main force, Arsaces saw his opportunity and successfully counterattacked against what remained of Seleucus' divided field army.[39] It is quite plausible that, misunderstanding the purpose of the Parthians' unique mode of warfare, Seleucus viewed Arsaces' withdrawal to the north as a sign of weakness and an assurance of his victory.[40] By not pursuing Arsaces and by dividing his army to reoccupy Parthia, Seleucus demonstrated that he did not consider the Parthians a serious threat. Further, this complacency could have encouraged Seleucus to turn his attention toward Bactria, which at the time was considered the stronger regional rival. Yet a march toward Bactria would have

33. Lorber and Iossif 2009: 105, 111–12.

34. Id. 87, 105, 107–11. Seleucus also adopted the epithet Callinicus ("Beautiful Victor"); however, this appellation celebrated his victory over his western rivals, not the Parthians. Lerner 1999: 37; Coşkun 2018: 221–22; Olbrycht 2020/2021.

35. Lorber and Iossif 2009: 105.

36. Overtoom 2021a.

37. Amm. Mar. 23.6.3; Photius *Bib.* 58.

38. These garrisons might have been necessary winter quarters. Antiochus VII later had to divide his army into garrisons during his campaign against the Parthians as well. See Justin 38.10.8; Diod. 34/35.17.2.

39. Antiochus VII suffered a similar defeat. Justin 38.10.8–10; Diod. 34/35.15–17; Appian *Syr.* 11.68.

40. Note Lorber and Iossif 2009: 95.

exposed the flanks of Seleucus' divided army to Arsaces' decisive counterattack. In fact, some scholars argue that Arsaces' new ally, Diodotus II, sent troops from Bactria to aid the Parthians.[41] If Bactrian troops played any role in the climactic battle between Arsaces and Seleucus, then the conflict likely occurred closer to Bactria in eastern Parthia.

Seleucus II never reached Bactria, and therefore, his anabasis ended in disaster at the hands of the Parthians somewhere in between his invasion of Parthia and his planned invasion of Bactria. It appears that the Parthians' Deceptive Withdrawal Strategy accomplished two key objectives. First, it inspired complacency in Seleucus, who began reoccupying Parthia instead of pursuing the Parthians, and second, it encouraged overconfidence in Seleucus, who decided to divide his army and turn his attention toward the Bactrians without first defeating the Parthians.

By dividing his army, ignoring the threat of the Parthians, and increasingly isolating himself between Arsaces I and Diodotus II as he continued east, Seleucus II created a major opportunity for his enemies. Arsaces shifted from the Parthians' Deceptive Withdrawal Strategy to their Overwhelm Strategy. The vulnerability of the Seleucid army made the sudden victory of Arsaces possible. Thus, our first recorded instance of the Parthians implementing their "Feign Retreat, Defeat in Detail" mode of warfare demonstrates its early association with the Arsacids and its effectiveness.[42] Arsaces executed the Parthians' asymmetric approach to warfare to perfection because Seleucus played directly into its strengths.

Seleucus II's defeat and possible capture in the latter half of the 230s had enormous geopolitical ramifications.[43] The reputation of the already reeling Seleucid state was damaged considerably and the prestige of the Seleucid king significantly diminished. This military defeat against the Parthians, paired with the possible shameful capture of the Seleucid king, severely threatened the stability of the Seleucid state in the west and further weakened Seleucid authority. This encouraged other regions like Persis, Elymais, and Media Atropatene to challenge Seleucid hegemony and helped cause another cycle of civil wars.[44]

Seleucus II's failures in the east also suddenly left Mesopotamia and Syria vulnerable. Power relations within the Eastern Mediterranean interstate system established by the ca. 236 truce between Seleucus and Antiochus Hierax no longer reflected the realities of power distribution across that system of states. International relations theory demonstrates that power relations are continually fluid, and the defeat of Seleucus drastically and suddenly reduced the power of the Seleucid Empire and Seleucus' authority. This helps explain from

41. Wolski 1996: 182–83; Lerner 1999: 36.
42. Overtoom 2017b.
43. Lerouge-Cohen unfairly belittles the Parthians' struggle against Seleucus. Lerouge-Cohen 2007: 274.
44. Grainger 2015: 20, 56; id. 2016: 52. For Elymais under the Seleucids, note Dąbrowa 2004 [2005]; id. 2014b.

a system-level analysis why Antiochus renewed the civil war against Seleucus in 229/228 with the invasion of Syria and Mesopotamia.[45] The sudden weakness of Seleucus and his regime because of his failed anabasis encouraged further pressure from competitors.

Meanwhile, in the east the failure of Seleucus II to subdue Parthia and Bactria reinforced the tripolar structure of the newly formed Iranian interstate system between the Seleucids, Parthians, and Bactrians.[46] It also helped further solidify Parthian power regionally and expanded Arsaces I's regional influence.[47] Finally, it allowed Arsaces to establish a solid economic and military foundation in Parthia that his successors continued to develop over the next century.[48]

The defeat and possible capture of Seleucus II appears also to have led to the establishment of formal and recognized independence for Parthia and Bactria.[49] Justin records, "The Parthians observe the day on which it [victory over Seleucus II] was gained with great solemnity, as the date of the commencement of their liberty (*libertatis*)."[50] By defeating Seleucus and repulsing his anabasis the Parthians and Bactrians had reassured their sovereignty in direct opposition to the Seleucid state. Yet Arsaces I and Diodotus II still would have desired formal recognition of their independence by Seleucus to enhance their legitimacy and international standing. They did not want to remain "rebels" within the Hellenistic Middle East, and the defeat of Seleucus gave them the opportunity they needed to demand formal recognition of their independence.

There were practical reasons for Seleucus II to recognize the sovereignty of Parthia and Bactria as well. It appears Seleucus conducted his anabasis in the latter half of the 230s, perhaps entering Babylonia as early as 235/234 to prepare the campaign.[51] After settling affairs in Babylonia, Elymais, and Media, he attempted to reoccupy Parthia before suffering his defeat.[52] This expedition seemingly spanned several years, lasting long enough for Seleucus to grow his iconic large beard. Whether or not Seleucus was a captive of the Parthians for a portion of his time in the east, it does not appear he returned to Babylonia until 229/228.[53]

45. Justin 41.5.1. Compare Lerner 1999: 37. Contra Coşkun 2018.

46. Overtoom 2016a: 985, 987–88, 992, 998–99.

47. In fact, Justin compares Arsaces' military success to Cyrus the Great and Alexander the Great, each of whom capitalized on hegemonic war during a power-transition crisis. Justin 41.5.1–6. Note Overtoom 2016a: 985–87. For the reception of Alexander in Iranian and Roman traditions, see Overtoom 2011; id. 2012; id. 2013; Nabel 2017b; Moore 2017.

48. Note Olbrycht 1998b: 51–76; id. 2003: 74–75; id. 2010a: 229; Overtoom 2019a; id. 2019b; id. 2019c; id. 2019/2020; id. 2021.

49. Lerner 1999: 36–37. Compare Schippmann 1980: 22ff.; Wolski 1996: 182. Contra Strootman 2015; id. 2018; Wenghofer 2018.

50. Justin 41.4.10.

51. Note Sachs and Hunger 1989: no. -234.

52. Seleucus minted coins in Nisibis, Susa, Seleucia, and Ecbatana for his eastern campaign. Lorber and Iossif 2009: 95.

53. Note Sachs and Hunger 1989: no. -229.

Seleucus II's long absence and eventual defeat in the east encouraged his brother, Antiochus Hierax, to renew the civil war in the west and to invade Syria and Mesopotamia. Antiochus' aggression in the west created a grave situation for Seleucus. If Seleucus remained at odds with the Parthians and Bactrians (or, more desperately, if he remained a prisoner), he risked losing the western portion of the empire to his hostile brother. By 229/228 Seleucus needed to come to terms with Arsaces I and Diodotus II to avoid a two-front war, to deter further expansion by the Parthians and Bactrians against Seleucid lands, and to pursue the civil war against his brother in the west. After his defeat against the Parthians, Seleucus had little choice but to acquiesce to the demands of Arsaces and Diodotus, and if Seleucus had become a captive, he had even less leverage. Lerner argues, "There is also nothing to preclude the possibility that one of the conditions for Seleucus' release was his formal recognition of the sovereignty of Arsaces I and that of Diodotus II."[54] If Seleucus had in fact become a Parthian prisoner, it is hard to imagine that Arsaces would have released Seleucus without such assurances. Yet Seleucus' defeat in the east and the renewal of civil war in the west was enough on its own to force Seleucus' hand in recognizing the sovereignty of Parthia and Bactria. By agreeing to peace with Arsaces, Seleucus was able to take the garrisons he had established throughout Parthia with him back to Babylonia. This allowed Seleucus to consolidate his remaining forces to pursue the war against his brother and freed the Parthians of the burden of attacking fortified garrisons, allowing Arsaces to reoccupy southern Parthia with ease.[55]

Although Seleucus II and the Seleucids did not abandon the possibility of future eastern campaigns to subdue the Parthians and Bactrians, the focus of the empire was in the west, and the renewed civil war against Antiochus Hierax took precedence. Justin criticizes Seleucus and Antiochus for not putting aside their differences to face outside threats to the empire, stating, "Leaving their foreign enemies unmolested, [they] continued the [civil] war for the destruction of each other."[56] Western conflicts consumed Seleucus' attention for the remained of his reign, and it fell to his son, Antiochus III, to avenge Seleucus' failures in the east.

Even after forming an alliance with Bactria and defeating the Seleucids in battle, Arsaces I still understood the dangers of the international environment in the Hellenistic Middle East and the potential power and threat of his neighbors. Once Seleucus II returned to the west to fight his brother, Arsaces immediately set into motion policies to maximize his power and the security of his kingdom. Justin records:

54. Lerner 1999: 36.
55. Note Amm. Mar. 23.6.3; Photius *Bib.* 58; Justin 41.4.10.
56. Justin 27.3.6.

> Respite being thus given to Arsaces, he settled the Parthian government, levied soldiers, built fortresses, and strengthened his towns. He founded a city also, called Dara, in Mount Zapaortenon [or Mount Apaortenon, near modern Dargaz, Iran], of which the situation is such, that no place can be more secure or more pleasant; for it is so encircled with steep rocks, that the strength of its position needs no defenders; and such is the fertility of the adjacent soil, that it is stored with its own produce. Such too is the plenty of springs and wood that it is amply supplied with streams of water and abounds with all the pleasures of the hunt. Thus Arsaces, having at once acquired and established a kingdom, and having become no less memorable among the Parthians than Cyrus [the Great] among the Persians, Alexander [the Great] among the Macedonians, or Romulus among the Romans, died at a mature old age; and the Parthians paid this honor to his memory, that they called all their kings thenceforward by the name of Arsaces.[57]

Thus, these actions by Arsaces were a continuation of his earlier policy, when he had seized Hyrcania and enlarged his army.[58] Yet, despite the recent victory against the Seleucids, Parthian power remained fragile.[59] The Seleucid threat had been defeated but not destroyed. Moreover, Bactria, although recently an ally, was a potential rival in the east that could return to its former hostility. Meanwhile, the uncertainty and volatility of the Central Asian steppe meant that nomadic raids or invasions remained a constant threat.

The pressures of the interstate anarchy within the Hellenistic Middle East made complacency dangerous, and therefore Arsaces I spent the rest of his reign securing his new kingdom, emphasizing political stability, military growth, and frontier security. Ammianus adds, "Finally, after all the neighboring lands had been brought under his [Arsaces'] rule, by force, by regard for justice, or by fear, and he had filled Persia with cities, with fortified camps, and with strongholds, and to all the neighboring peoples, which she [the Parthian state] had previously feared, he had made her a constant cause of dread, he died a peaceful death in middle life."[60] Again, we see the importance of the perception of power in ancient international relations and an emphasis on the creation of state stability and security. Photius in his summary of Arrian's *Parthica* also records that Arsaces set up his government and established a powerful state.[61]

57. Id. 41.5.1–6. Note Strabo 15.1.36.

58. Justin 41.4.8.

59. Rawlinson's conclusion that after the Parthians defeated Seleucus "they had nothing to fear" and that they were assured of their strength "to preserve their freedom" is incorrect. Rawlinson 1876 (2002): 28, 33.

60. Amm. Mar. 23.6.3–4.

61. Photius *Bib.* 58. For Arsaces' titulature and concept of government, note Gaslain 2005a: 221–23; id. 2009: 27–39; Assar 2011: 114; Olbrycht 2013a.

Fear was an important aspect of ancient geopolitical interactions between states. The uncertainty of power relations and power capabilities in interstate politics meant that fear of neighboring states and the use of fear to project power was common in ancient interstate systems.[62] One of Arsaces I's principle policies after his defeat of Seleucus II's anabasis was to establish a fearful reputation for the Parthians. In so doing he enhanced the perceived power of the Parthians in the region, deterring aggression from warlike neighbors and increasing the security of Parthia. Arsaces' militarized policies in part were a reaction to the harsh realities of the international environment in the Hellenistic Middle East. Arsaces had made Parthia's position stronger as one of the three leading powers within the newly formed Iranian interstate system, but he recognized the need to maximize that strength. The remainder of Arsaces' reign was a period of stability and prosperity; however, this period of peace did not last.

The Seleucid Backlash

Within a generation of his death, the diligent efforts of Arsaces I to increase the power and security of the Parthians were put to the test against the largest threat the new Parthian state had yet faced. John Grainger's bleak opinion that "the Seleukid kingdom appeared in 222 to be as complete a political failure as Alexander's" is far too dismissive of the longevity and considerable geopolitical accomplishments of the Seleucids.[63] Despite the power-transition crisis of the 240s–230s and the failure of Seleucus II's eastern campaign, the Seleucid Empire remained a powerful, aggressive, and wealthy state in the Eastern Mediterranean and Middle Eastern worlds for another century.[64] Heavy militarism remained essential to the prestige of the king and the viability of the state. The Seleucid army went on campaign every year, countering internal disturbances, fighting external enemies, or using show of force to maintain power relations with neighboring states.[65] Moreover, the Seleucid kings established and maintained an administration system designed to maximize the states' ability to collect tax revenues to run the government and pay the army.[66] What the Seleucid state too often lacked was strong central leadership.

62. For the prominent role of fear in the decision-making of ancient states, see Thuc. 1.23.6, 88. For an example of the prominent role of fear and hatred in ancient warfare, see Vell. Pat. 1.12. For examples of the power of fear in antiquity, especially under a system of interstate anarchy, see Eckstein 2006: 22 *et passim*; id. 2012: 9 *et passim*. Compare Wheeler 2002: 288.

63. Grainger 2014: 213.

64. Note Strootman 2011–2012; id. 2013b; id. 2014; Overtoom 2016d: Chs. 2–3; Coşkun and Engels 2019; Strootman 2019; Overtoom 2019a; id. 2019/2020.

65. In fact, Anțiochus was the longest reigning Seleucid king and only experienced at most four years of peace. Taylor 2013; Grainger 2015: 82; id. 2017a: 137; Feyel and Graslin-Thomé 2017.

66. See Aperghis 2004; id. 2011. Compare Houghton and Lorber 2002. It cost about 7,000–8,000 talents a year to support the Seleucid field army of 70,000–80,000 soldiers. Grainger 2015: 60–61.

Antiochus III, later known as Antiochus the Great, came to the Seleucid throne after his father, Seleucus II, died suddenly in 226/225 and soldiers assassinated his elder brother, Seleucus III, in 223/222.[67] Antiochus was a military man with grand ambitions. At the height of his power, Antiochus ruled over nearly 1.5 million square miles of territory; his army was around 120,000 soldiers strong; and he collected roughly 600 tons of silver bullion in annual revenues.[68] He eventually used the considerable funds of the Seleucid state to organize an expeditionary force of 70,000 men to avenge his father and subdue the Seleucids' rivals in the east, namely the Parthians and Bactrians.[69] His successful eastern campaign allowed him to restore Seleucid hegemony throughout the Hellenistic Middle East, and under Antiochus the Seleucid Empire came to play an important role in the separate and evolving interstate systems within the Mediterranean basin and Iranian plateau, bringing Seleucid power to its pinnacle. In the face of Antiochus' invasion, the Parthians confronted the real possibility of total annihilation, and without their great leader, Arsaces I, the Parthians had to survive the Seleucid backlash.

Antiochus Aspires to Be Great

The sudden death of Antiochus III's father and the murder of his brother further damaged the reputation of the Seleucid dynasty and the perceived power of the state. The Seleucids had lost control of important lands in the east, and dynastic weakness threatened to create further internal chaos. The perceived weakness of the Seleucid state and the vulnerability of the monarchy encouraged two more satraps in the east to revolt against Seleucid authority. Much like the earlier rebellions of Andragoras and Diodotus, in 222 the satrap Molon seized the opportunity to declare himself independent in Media, while his bother Alexander declared independence in Persia.[70] Media, located in western Iran, was one of the most important satrapies in the Seleucid Empire. Control of this region provided control of several of the important passes through the Zagros Mountains.[71] The region allowed direct access to Parthia and Bactria, and it was the last eastern defense of the vulnerable, yet valuable Mesopotamian valley. The Seleucid Empire could not hope to protect Mesopotamia or reassert its influence in the

67. Appian *Syr.* 11.66. Compare Finkel, van der Spek, Pirngruber 2020f. Assar has argued recently that the death of Seleucus II occurred in 225/4 and the death of Seleucus III occurred in 222. Assar 2007. Antiochus earned the epithet "Great" because of his successful conquests in the east. Appian *Syr.* 1.1.

68. Aperghis 2004: 57, 201, 251. Compare Strootman 2011; Taylor 2013: 1.

69. For Antiochus' army, see Bar-Kochva 1987: 10; Taylor 2013: 72; Grainger 2015: 60–63. Note Justin 41.5.7.

70. For recent accounts of the revolt of Molon and the war against Antiochus, see Taylor 2013: Ch. 2; Grainger 2015: Ch. 1; Richter 2017.

71. There perhaps were two main routes from Media into the distant lands of the Hellenistic Middle East. The first route was in the north via Hyrcania, and the second route looped south of Hyrcania. This has led some scholars to argue that the Parthian state did not in fact cut off Seleucid access to the distant lands of the Hellenistic Middle East until the middle of the second century. See Sherwin-White and Kuhrt 1993: 73, 79, 84–85, 89, 110, 223; Strootman 2015; id. 2018.

east without control of Media. In fact, the region was so important to the empire that its satraps often held the title of governor of the Upper Satrapies, which gave them wide-ranging administrative and military powers in the east and, in a military sense, made them second in command to the king.[72] Molon utilized this position of considerable power to challenge Antiochus.

The rebellion of Molon against Antiochus III further illustrates the importance of the perception of power and the fragility and fluidity of power relations in the ancient world. Polybius emphasizes the force that Molon wielded and the fear that he inspired. He records:

> Molon therefore being master of the country, which might rank as a kingdom, was already, as I said sufficiently formidable owing to his superior power; but now that the royal generals, as it seemed, had retired from the field before him, and that his own troops were in high spirits, owing to their expectation of success having been so far fulfilled, he seemed absolutely terrible and irresistible to all the inhabitants of Asia.[73]

With his sizable army and the ineffectiveness of Antiochus' generals, Molon was in a stronger position than had been Andragoras, Diodotus I, or Arsaces I to challenge the Seleucid king directly. He was not content with regional independence; rather, Molon wanted to dominate the Seleucid Empire by replacing Antiochus.

At the height of Molon's rebellion, he had seized much of Mesopotamia from Antiochus III's unsuccessful generals.[74] Moreover, the rebellions of Molon in Media and Alexander in Persia coincided with another Seleucid war against the Ptolemies in Coele-Syria, which distracted Antiochus.[75] Antiochus had hoped to enhance his military reputation through the defeat of the Seleucids' main rival, the Ptolemies; however, the seriousness of Molon's growing threat finally forced Antiochus to act against him with force.[76] Fortunately for the Seleucid state, in 220 Antiochus decisively defeated Molon in Mesopotamia, and Antiochus' victory allowed him to recover the center of his empire.[77]

With the death of Molon, internal resistance to Antiochus III's rule mostly subsided. Conquests in the east became a focus of his policy to restore Seleucid authority and heighten the security of the empire. Polybius states, "Elated by his success and wishing to overawe and intimidate the barbarous princes whose dominions bordered on and lay beyond his own provinces, so as to prevent their

72. For a recent survey of the Upper Satrapies, especially under the Seleucids, see Plischke 2014: 22–172. Compare Brüggemann 2017; Lerner 2018.

73. Polyb. 5.45.1–2.

74. Id. 5.45.3–48.16.

75. Id. 5.45.5–6.

76. Id. 5.48.17–51.11.

77. Id. 5.52.1–54.13. Antiochus had visited Babylon in 224/223 as a representative of his brother Seleucus III. See Bing and Sievers 2011; Finkel, van der Spek, Pirngruber 2020d. Antiochus' familiarity with the region perhaps helps explain his military success against Molon. Note Graslin-Thomé 2017; Richter 2017; Monerie 2019.

furnishing anyone who rebelled against him with supplies or armed assistance, the king decided to march against them and in the first place against Artabarzanes [the king of Media Atropatene]."[78] Antiochus saw the need to strike fear into the hearts of the eastern kings through force of arms. After he reclaimed Babylonia, Elymais, Media, and Persia from his rebellious satraps, Antiochus invaded the small region of Media Atropatene in northwestern Iran and forced its king to become his subordinate ally.[79] Michael Taylor notes that this created "an important precedent for future deals with breakaway kingdoms."[80] In his eastern dealings, Antiochus continually favored creating subordinate allied states in peripheral regions over the restoration of direct Seleucid imperial dominion.[81]

Although Antiochus III spent most of the 210s fighting western wars of expansion, he seems never to have lost his desire to avenge his father's failed eastern campaign.[82] He fought Ptolemy IV to a stalemate in the Fourth Syrian War (219–217) and reclaimed large sections of Anatolia.[83] This allowed Antiochus to secure his western lands with strong frontiers and freed him to take an enormous force of around 70,000 men to reclaim the east.

Antiochus III had several personal reasons for campaigning in the east, especially the desire to avenge his father, seek glory, and enhance his prestige; however, there were pressing geopolitical reasons for his grand eastern campaign as well. As Polybius states, an anabasis was necessary to reestablish the dominance of the Seleucid state over the Hellenistic Middle East through force and fear.[84] Antiochus particularly needed to punish Parthia and Bactria for damaging the reputation of the Seleucid dynasty and for challenging the power of the Seleucid state. Further, the policies of the Parthians and Bactrians to maximize their own power and security had come at the direct expense of the Seleucids, and these military policies increasingly had made the Parthians and Bactrians a threat to the Seleucid state.[85] Antiochus was determined to make all the major eastern rivals of the Seleucids subservient to his authority. In 212 Antiochus forced Armenia to become another subordinate allied kingdom of the resurgent Seleucid Empire

78. Polyb. 5.55.1.

79. Id. 5.55.6–10.

80. Taylor 2013: 35.

81. Strootman suggests Antiochus' father established this new eastern policy. Strootman 2015; id. 2018.

82. The Seleucids, even under Antiochus, maintained a primarily western focus in their geopolitical activities. Eckstein 2012; Kosmin 2013a; Plischke 2014: 315–34; Kosmin 2018; Coşkun and Engels 2019.

83. For the role of Antiochus during the Fourth Syrian War and in particular within Anatolia, see Ma 2000; Grainger 2015: Ch. 2–3, 5, 7, 10. For wide-ranging scholarly opinions on why Antiochus undertook his anabasis, see Rostovtzeff 1941: i 459; Schmitt 1964: 86–90; Will 1967: ii 51ff.; Bernard 1985: 85–95; Narain 1989: 397–98; Green 1990: 295; Sherwin-White and Kuhrt 1993: Ch. 7; Lerner 1999: 52; Taylor 2013: 72; Plischke 2014: 265–75; Grainger 2015: 56–57; Coloru 2017; Dumke 2017; Brüggemann 2017.

84. Polyb. 5.55.1.

85. Some scholars contend that the Parthians recognized Seleucid suzerainty in the late third century. Sherwin-White and Kuhrt 1993: 197; Strootman 2015. Yet it is hard to imagine why Antiochus would have conducted such an extensive campaign against the Parthians and Bactrians if they already recognized Seleucid suzerainty and posed no serious threat to the Seleucid state. Overtoom 2016a; id. 2016d: Ch. 2; id. 2020.

and then readied his army to conduct a major war to reestablish Seleucid hegemony over the Iranian plateau.[86]

The Battle for Parthia

After Seleucus II's defeat and before Antiochus III's invasion, the Parthians attempted to solidify their regional power and security. Arsaces I had begun organizing the government, securing the frontier, and expanding the army.[87] Arsaces also had secured an important alliance with Diodotus II of Bactria; however, after the immediate threat of the Seleucid invasion had dissipated with the defeat of Seleucus, it appears that Parthia and Bactria quickly returned to their previously hostile relationship.[88] Although the two states had banded together in the face of Seleucid aggression in the middle 230s, no such military alliance remained in place when Antiochus invaded the east in 210. Lerner argues that over this twenty-year period diplomatic relations between the two states had deteriorated to the point that "political hostilities between Parthia and Bactria had reignited and that the situation was similar to what had existed between Arsaces I and Diodotus I."[89] If so, this is yet another example of the pressures of interstate anarchy pushing states to adopt and maintain a constantly bellicose posture. As Ammianus notes, the Parthians' rivalry with the Bactrians was one of their most fierce.[90]

Parthia and Bactria had formed an alliance out of necessity in the middle 230s to balance against Seleucid aggression. However, once the Parthians defeated the Seleucid army and forced Seleucus II to abandon his anabasis, the Seleucids were no longer an immediate threat to either power, encouraging the rivalry between the Parthians and Bactrians to reemerge. Moreover, Parthia had become a major regional power under Arsaces I. The Parthians' victory over Seleucus gave a considerable boost to their military prestige and power. Therefore, although the potential threat of the Seleucid Empire remained in the distance, Parthia suddenly became Bactria's greatest competitor in the east in the 220s. The rapid expansion of the Parthians, their success in war, and the efforts of Arsaces to consolidate his power were all reasons to make Bactria wary.

Meanwhile, the Parthians could not ignore the potential threat of the Bactrians. Despite the recent military and political success of the Parthians, Bactria remained at this time the leading regional power. In fact, Antiochus III eventually had more difficulty subduing Bactria than Parthia, and in the 220s, Bactria reemerged as the primary competitor of Parthia. Moreover, this powerful neighbor of the Parthians became unreliable in this period because of dynastic

86. Polyb. 8.23. Note Bing and Sievers 2011; Grainger 2015: 57–59; id. 2017a: 37.
87. Amm. Mar. 23.6.3–4. Photius *Bib.* 58.
88. Justin 41.4.9.
89. Lerner 1999: 42.
90. Amm. Mar. 23.6.55.

instability. The murder of Diodotus II and the usurpation of the Bactrian throne by the ambitious Euthydemus I in the late 220s helped dissolve the alliance between Parthia and Bactria and made relations between the two powers increasingly tense.[91]

To understand the end of the Partho-Bactrian alliance further, one must also appreciate the structure and limitations of diplomacy in the Hellenistic world. The alliance between Arsaces I and Diodotus II had served its immediate purpose by the middle 220s, and the threat of the Seleucids had dissipated, at least temporarily. Grainger has argued extensively that treaties made by Hellenistic kings traditionally were agreements between two men, not binding agreements between two states.[92] Yet even these treaties were easily broken with regularity without a strong central authority or the power of international law to enforce them.[93] Thus, the personalities of various kings could play an important role in diplomacy. The successors of Arsaces I and Diodotus II were not obligated to maintain the temporary alliance. In fact, the death of either king nullified the treaty unless his successor renewed the arrangement, and neither Euthydemus I of Bactria nor Arsaces II of Parthia made such an arrangement.

There is one more important factor in the dissolution of the Partho-Bactrian alliance. The Parthians, and in particular Arsaces I, had developed an amenable relationship with Diodotus II. Diodotus had been less hostile than his father and more vulnerable within Bactria itself. Diodotus' friendly actions toward the Parthians made him appear less of a threat, and relations between Arsaces I and Diodotus II appear to have been stable and comfortable. Thus, when Euthydemus I had Diodotus murdered and seized the Bactrian throne in the late 220s, the Parthians, and in particular Arsaces I, had good reason to dislike and distrust this usurper. Euthydemus was ambitious and unpredictable, causing growing uncertainty and concern about the potential threat of Bactria to Parthia.

The failure of the Parthians and Bactrians to put aside their differences in the face of another, more powerful Seleucid invasion in 210 speaks to the considerable friction and distrust that had developed between the two states. The Parthians and Bactrians were at a great disadvantage, and the Seleucids were the primary beneficiaries of the renewed Partho-Bactrian rivalry. Antiochus III did not face an allied resistance as had his father, and Antiochus planned to take full advantage of the disunity of the eastern kings to isolate them against his grand

91. For the scholarly debate surrounding the usurpation of the Bactrian throne by Euthydemus I and the conclusion that it occurred at the same time as Molon's rebellion, see Lerner 1999: 38–41. For Euthydemus, see Holt 1999: 126–33; Bivar 2012; Mairs 2013b; Plischke 2014: 276–78. Note Polyb. 11.34.

92. Grainger 2013a: 65–67; id. 2015: 70, 78–81, 190, 193–95; id. 2016: 1–2; id. 2017a: 36–40, 138; id. 2017b. The Parthian kings appear to have followed a similar diplomatic policy. See Dąbrowa 2010a; id. 2010c; Schlude and Rubin 2017.

93. Polybius was a major advocate for the pragmatic choices of states and statesmen in foreign relations; however, he also had a strong moral viewpoint that one should act nobly. See Eckstein 1995.

army.[94] The unwillingness of the Parthians and Bactrians to cooperate in the 200s gave Antiochus the opportunity he needed to establish Seleucid hegemony over the east.

After a year of organizing his soldiers and supplies in Babylonia, Antiochus III began his grand eastern expedition by entering Media in 210.[95] His first objective was to secure the money he needed to fund his anabasis. Therefore, he looted about 4,000 talents of gold and silver from the Temple of Aene in Ecbatana.[96] With this money, Antiochus could direct his full attention against his first military objective, the reconquest of Parthia and Hyrcania.[97] Yet Antiochus remembered his father's failure and understood the potential danger of his anabasis. The health and military ability of the king were indispensable to Hellenistic monarchies. The Seleucids especially relied on competent, charismatic kings to hold together their disparate empire. When the king was weak or died suddenly, as occurred during the power-transition crisis of the 240s–230s, the empire suffered considerable loses. These risks worried Antiochus and his advisors, and therefore Antiochus secured the succession in 209 just before invading Parthia by making his young son, who was also named Antiochus, his co-ruler so that the boy and his mother could help manage the court and empire in the west while Antiochus fought a hegemonic war in the east.[98]

At the time of Antiochus III's invasion, Parthia was vulnerable. The Parthians no longer could rely on the military aid of Bactria, and Arsaces I had died of old age in 211, making his son, Arsaces II (211–185), otherwise possibly known as Artabanus I, the new king of Parthia only one year before Antiochus' anabasis began.[99] There is much confusion surrounding the identity and reigns of the early Arsacids. For example, in a new study about Antiochus' war against Parthia, Grainger, despite citing a recent, well-argued article by Gholamreza Assar, states that Tiridates, the son of Arsaces I, became the second Parthian king.[100] However, it is now clear that Tiridates was Arsaces I's brother and never ruled.[101] Arsaces II

94. Grainger 2015: 66.

95. Id. 60–63; Graslin-Thomé 2017.

96. Polyb. 10.27.12–13. Note Dumke 2017.

97. Holleaux 1930: 140; Walbank 1967: ii 231–32; Koshelenko 1976: 33–34; Lerner 1999: 45.

98. Bing and Sievers 2011; Grainger 2015: 66–67. Note Polyb. 5.55.3–4.

99. Assar 2005a: 29–35; 2011: 114–15. For the traditional numbering system that identified Arsaces II as Artabanus I and the later Artabanus as Artabanus II, see Foy-Vaillant 1725: 16; Lewis 1728: 17–23; Lindsay 1852: 4–6, 133–35; Rawlinson 1873: 54; Gardner 1877: 4–5, 26–27; Gutschmid 1888: 36 n.4, 81; Justi 1895: 31, 412; Allotte de la Fuÿe 1904: 320–22; Minns 1915: 40 and n.58; Sykes 1915: 336–37; Tarn 1930: 119 and n.4; id. 1932: 575–76; Debevoise 1938: 16; Kahrstedt 1950: 11 n.1; Colledge 1967: 27–28; Bivar 1983: 31; Frye 1983: 209–10; Lukonin 1983: 687f.; Sherwin-White and Kuhrt 1993: 198; Assar 2008: 1–7; id. 2009a: 119–34; id. 2011: 114. For an alternative numbering system that removes the association of Arsaces II with the name Artabanus I and therefore names Artabanus, who ruled ca. 126–122, Artabanus I, see Wolski 1962: 138ff.; Schmitt 1964: 62 n.2, 63; Le Rider 1965: 313ff.; Bengston 1969: 417; Altheim and Stiehl 1970: 445ff.; Volkmann 1972: 533–34; Lerner 1999: 26–28; Assar 2005a. Note also Overtoom 2019b: 16; id. 2019c: 101.

100. Grainger 2015: 65.

101. See Assar 2004; id. 2005a; id. 2011: 113–14. Note Photius' summary of Arrian's *Parthica*, Photius *Bib.* 58. Dąbrowa argues Tiridates is non-historical. Dąbrowa 2012: 27. For the uncertainty surrounding the identity of Arsaces II and the conclusion that Justin's Artabanus in *Prologue* 41 is in fact Arsaces II, see Assar 2008; id. 2009a; id. 2011: 114.

became king; however, he did not possess his father's keen sense of political and military timing, and he was not well prepared to challenge Antiochus' massive invasion.

Arsaces II from the start of the campaign misjudged the objectives and determination of his enemy. Polybius records that Antiochus III outmaneuvered Arsaces as he entered Parthia by crossing difficult terrain. He states, "Arsaces [II] had expected Antiochus [III] to advance as far as this region [that is, western Parthia], but he did not think he would venture with such a large force to cross the adjacent desert, chiefly owing to the scarcity of water."[102] When Arsaces realized his mistake, he attempted to regain the initiative by destroying the water supply in the region. Polybius continues:

> Arsaces, however, when he saw that Antiochus was attempting to march across the desert, endeavored instantly to fill up and destroy the wells. The king when this news reached him sent off Nicomedes with a thousand horse, who, finding that Arsaces had retired (ὑποκεχωρηκότα) with his army, but that some of his cavalry were engaged in destroying the mouths of the channels, attacked and routed these, forcing them to fly (τρεψάμενοι φυγεῖν ἠνάγκασαν), and then returned to Antiochus.[103]

Once again, we find the Parthians withdrawing or "fleeing" in the face of a superior approaching army. The Parthians in fact abandoned their new capital, Hecatompylus, and withdrew northwest into Hyrcania.[104] Arsaces here likely tried to follow the example of his father, implementing the Parthians' Deceptive Withdrawal Strategy in the face of Antiochus' massive invasion. Not only did Arsaces II understand that his army was no match for Antiochus' immense force in a conventional fight, but he also quickly realized that Antiochus had outmaneuvered him and had gained the initiative in the campaign. Therefore, Arsaces withdrew with his main force and left detachments to frustrate the Seleucids by destroying the wells.

A main objective of the Parthian mode of warfare was to encourage an enemy to break formation and over pursue, at which point the Parthians could counterattack and destroy isolated sections of a much larger force. Antiochus III unknowingly played into the strengths of the Parthians' mode of warfare when he sent Nicomedes with 1,000 horsemen to attack the Parthian detachments near the wells. This was a great opportunity for the Parthians to isolate and destroy an important portion of Antiochus' army early in the campaign. Instead of accepting Polybius' negative portrayal of the Parthians as weak and cowardly, once again

102. Polyb. 10.28.1.
103. Id. 10.28.5–6.
104. Id. 10.28.6–7. Note Appian *Syr.* 9.57.

I prefer to view this campaign more constructively, putting forth the argument that the Parthians actively were trying to deceive and overwhelm the Seleucids through cunning and speed.

Polybius records that the Parthian detachments "routed," "forcing them to fly;" however, this was a common, calculated aspect of Parthian warfare that Polybius and his contemporaries either did not understand or did not care to appreciate. Instead, it is possible that the Parthians pretended to "flee" to encourage Nicomedes and his vulnerable detachment to pursue them. The Parthian detachments lacked the force necessary to overwhelm the Seleucid cavalry, and therefore their only hope to destroy Nicomedes was to encourage him to give chase toward the main Parthian army. Unfortunately for the Parthian detachments, this feigned retreat did not further draw out Nicomedes, who remained disciplined and returned to the main Seleucid force after securing the wells. Yet the actions of Arsaces II also appear to be key in this initial failure by the Parthians.

As important as the experienced generalship of Antiochus III was to the success of the Seleucids during his eastern expedition, the inexperience of Arsaces II was a key factor in the shortcomings of the Parthians during this campaign. For a second time, Arsaces allowed himself to be outmaneuvered. Nicomedes reported that Arsaces had "retired with his army," moving a good distance from his detachments near the wells. Arsaces had not anticipated Antiochus striking at the wells with such speed. Deprived of access to these wells, Antiochus could not have crossed the broad northern deserts of Iran in pursuit of the Parthians without dividing his immense force. Arsaces' decision to retreat was meant either to lull Antiochus into a false sense of security or to encourage Antiochus into offering an ill-advised chase. Although Antiochus' decision to divide his force initially played directly into the hands of the Parthians, Arsaces failed to capitalize upon it. Arsaces left too few men near the wells to destroy them once Nicomedes arrived, and he had moved too far away from these detachments to come to their aid. Thus, Nicomedes was able to save the wells from destruction and to avoid destruction himself. After the Seleucids secured these wells, they could move northeast and pursue the Parthians en masse. Arsaces no longer could hope to overwhelm separated portions of Antiochus' army as the Seleucids moved across Parthia, and therefore, he abandoned his isolated capital, Hecatompylus, and retreated into the mountains of Hyrcania.[105]

Polybius next offers an interesting perspective on some fundamental differences between the conventional warfare of the Seleucids and the asymmetric warfare of the Parthians. Polybius states:

> Here [at Hecatompylus] he [Antiochus III] gave his army a rest, and now came to the conclusion that had Arsaces [II] been able to risk a battle

105. Polyb. 10.28.7.

> he would not have withdrawn from his own country and could not have chosen a place more favorable to his army for the struggle than the neighborhood of Hecatompylus. It was evident then to anyone who gave proper consideration to the matter that as he was retreating (ἐκχωρεῖ) he had other intentions (γνώμης). Antiochus therefore decided to advance into Hyrcania.[106]

After a march of some 350 miles over arid terrain, which took Antiochus' enormous army over a month to complete, Antiochus observed the strength of Hecatompylus and expected the Parthians to fight in the traditional manner of defending their well-placed capital.[107] That is, Antiochus expected the Parthians to fight him on terms that he understood. He also failed to recognize the exact purpose of the Parthians' retreat. Although Polybius makes the obvious conclusion that the Parthians "had other intentions," he offers no explanation as to what those intentions were. The ambiguity of Polybius' remark helps illustrate that, despite several conflicts against the Parthians by the time Polybius was writing his history in the middle second century, the Greeks continued to have either little understanding or appreciation of the Parthians' asymmetric mode of warfare.

As we have seen, the Parthians' mode of warfare, if executed correctly, was highly effective. It allowed the Parthians to use their smaller but more mobile army to outmaneuver larger, better-equipped enemy forces. Antiochus III during his eastern campaign did not appreciate that the Parthians did not have to risk conventional climactic battles early in the campaign because they had developed different tactical and strategic methods to obtain military victories. Their style of warfare was more flexible, deceptive, and opportunistic than anything Antiochus had encountered, and although it is perhaps unreasonable to censure the Greeks and Romans for not drastically reforming their military and conventional modes of warfare to better combat the Parthians, they continually misunderstood or disregarded the different function of the Parthians' mode of warfare. Even though Arsaces I had outmaneuvered and overwhelmed Antiochus' father using similar strategies and tactics, Antiochus also assumed that the Parthians were weak and vulnerable, and without hesitation he immediately decided to pursue Arsaces II into Hyrcania.

Before continuing with our discussion of Antiochus' invasion, we must consider briefly the crucial factors that helped undermined the Parthian war effort under Arsaces II. First, Arsaces proved to be a better warrior than a general. His early mismanagement of the campaign had forced him to abandon Parthia because he continued to try to deceive the Seleucids and manipulate them into making a mistake through a series of feigned retreats. The Parthians' reliance on

106. Id. 10.29.1–2.

107. Antiochus' army covered around ten miles a day. Taylor 2013: 75.

feigned retreats, especially strategically, was unique within the contexts of the Graeco-Roman world in large part because it was inherently risky, both politically and militarily, since the Parthians willingly abandoned resources and fortified positions to an enemy force. A talented military commander was vital to its success.

The Parthians' Deceptive Withdrawal Strategy encouraged an enemy army to penetrate their frontier in the hope of creating an opportunity to overwhelm an overstretched or isolated enemy force. In essence, the Parthians temporarily abandoned the short-term security of their state for potential long-term rewards. This asymmetric approach to warfare was at odds with the more conventional Greek and Roman modes of warfare. This different military philosophy made the Parthians appear weak or cowardly to the Greeks and Romans, thus encouraging the Greeks and Romans to underestimate the Parthians in war. In theory, this led to overconfidence and military mistakes that benefited the smaller, more mobile Parthian army. Hence, Antiochus III placed Nicomedes' detachment in considerable danger as he entered western Parthia; he thought the abandonment of Hecatompylus was a major strategic mistake; and he felt no reservations in pursuing Arsaces II into the mountains of Hyrcania.

Although the Parthians had spent years fortifying their kingdom, Arsaces II decided against a strategy of siege defense in Parthia when faced with Antiochus III's immense invasion. A policy of siege defense might have worn down Antiochus' army through attrition, as did the later siege of Bactra-Zariaspa, and in fact, the Parthians later in the campaign attempted to implement a siege defense strategy out of desperation.[108] Yet drawn-out siege warfare against a concentrated force was not the strength of the mobile Parthian military, and the potential benefits for the Parthians of ambushing the Seleucid army, utilizing deception and speed, had manifested itself only a generation prior. If the Parthians could execute a strategic feigned retreat effectively, the results could be tremendous as Arsaces I had demonstrated against Seleucus II; however, if the Parthians failed to execute this strategy effectively, the results could be ruinous because it sacrificed the structural integrity of their kingdom.

The Parthians' Deceptive Withdrawal Strategy was meant to create the *appearance* of weakness and vulnerability so that the Parthians could turn this deception to their advantage; however, if they executed this risky strategy incorrectly, the *appearance* of weakness and vulnerability quickly manifested itself as *actual* weakness and vulnerability. In ancient international relations, where power relations, military reputation, and the projection of strength were fundamentally important to state interactions, the unique Parthian mode of warfare was a considerable gamble because it encouraged enemies to act more aggressively. Again,

108. Note Polyb. 10.31.6–13, 49.15, 29.12.8.

the actions of Antiochus III as he entered Parthia and occupied Hecatompylus support this conclusion. The continued retreat of the Parthians had convinced Antiochus that they were vulnerable, and therefore, he pursued them eagerly into Hyrcania. If the Parthians were able to outmaneuver and defeat an invader, such as Seleucus II, then they restored their military reputation and security within the international environment despite initially appearing to have abandoned large portions of their kingdom. Yet if the Parthians failed to overwhelm an invader, they had only aided in making themselves weak and vulnerable. This then encouraged other competitors to challenge them, allies to abandon them, and the soldiers to lose heart.

Parthian commanders, often the king, had to be able to hold together the loyalty and confidence of their soldiers and allies in the face of seemingly abandoning territory and wealth to an enemy without a fight, making a talented and decisive general imperative to overcoming these considerable political and military risks. Arsaces I had been a battle-hardened, charismatic leader, and therefore he added considerably to the success of the Parthians' asymmetric mode of warfare against Seleucus II. Yet Arsaces II, who proved to be a brave warrior, also proved to be militarily and politically inadequate against the more resolute and capable Antiochus III.[109]

Second, the Parthians were not prepared for the size, scale, and determination of Antiochus III's invasion. Antiochus' army was massive. Justin places the figures at 100,000 infantry and 20,000 cavalry, although modern estimates place the figure around 70,000 men.[110] This was one of the largest armies assembled by any Hellenistic ruler, and it was undoubtedly much larger than the force brought to the east by Antiochus' father. Because of the unsuccessful war against Ptolemy III in Syria and the ongoing conflict with Antiochus Hierax in Anatolia, Seleucus II did not have the full resources of the empire in the west at his disposal. Moreover, he did not have the ability to concentrate such an immense force in the east; Antiochus III, however, did. Antiochus, despite his considerable setback at the Battle of Raphia in 217, settled his southern border in Coele-Syria with Ptolemy IV, who was eager for peace.[111] Antiochus then subdued much of Anatolia from 216–213, defeating his rival Achaeus and securing his western frontier.[112] Finally, Antiochus forced Armenia, like Media Atropatene before it, to become his subordinate ally, securing his northern border.[113] By the end of the 210s, Antiochus was prepared to focus nearly the full might of his expanded empire against Parthia

109. Justin describes Arsaces II as a man who "fought with the greatest of bravery against Antiochus." Justin 41.5.7.

110. Ibid.

111. For the battle of Raphia, see Polyb. 5.80–86. For the subsequent peace, see id. 5.87. Note Taylor 2013: Ch. 4; Grainger 2015: Ch. 2; Gerardin 2017; Apicella 2017; Ecker et al. 2017.

112. Polyb. 5.57, 107.4, 7.15–18, 8.17–23. Note Bing and Sievers 2011; McAuley 2018; D'Agostini 2018.

113. Polyb. 5.55, 8.23. Note Bing and Sievers 2011; Grainger 2017a: 37–39.

and Bactria in an extended eastern expedition. Even with Arsaces I's major efforts to expand the size of the Parthian army, Arsaces II found himself at a tremendous disadvantage militarily.

The Parthians also underestimated the capabilities of Antiochus III as a commander. Antiochus was a more competent and capable leader than his father. He had defeated major uprisings in Media, Mesopotamia, and Anatolia, he had used threat of force and diplomacy to subdue Media Atropatene and Armenia, and he had learned from his shortcomings at Raphia. His style of command was aggressive but instinctive, and this allowed him to gain the initiative and retain it throughout the campaign against Arsaces II. Arsaces found himself outmanned and outmatched by Antiochus' army and military expertise.

Third, the deterioration of the relationship between the Parthians and their former allies, the Bactrians and the Central Asian tribal confederations, left Parthia isolated. In the war against Seleucus II, the alliance between Parthia and Bactria had served as a crucial balance against Seleucid power. The two states had fought the Seleucids as a unified front, and it is possible that Diodotus II had sent troops to aid Arsaces I in his major victory over Seleucus.[114] In the war against Antiochus III, Parthia and Bactria decided to face the Seleucids separately. This was a major advantage for Antiochus since he could focus on subjugating Parthia first without fear of Bactrian aggression. The isolation of the Parthians allowed Antiochus to pursue Arsaces II immediately into Hyrcania after occupying western Parthia. Seleucus II had not been able to ignore Bactria, and therefore, he had to split his attention, complicating his strategy. Arsaces I took advantage of Seleucus' vulnerability; however, Arsaces II never had the same opportunity against Antiochus.

Meanwhile, at the height of the war against Seleucus II, Arsaces I had withdrawn northeast into the lands of his nomadic allies within the Central Asian steppe; however, in the war against Antiochus III, Arsaces II chose to withdraw northwest into Hyrcania. Arsaces II's decision to avoid the steppe appears to have been out of necessity rather than by choice. Lerner argues that the efforts of the Parthians under Arsaces I to fortify their new domain for decades had increasingly isolated them from their former nomadic allies.[115] Thus, in terms of international relations theory, the power-maximizing policies of the Parthians to strengthen the defenses of their kingdom and to expand the size of their army had perpetuated the security dilemma throughout the region, causing increased anxiety about growing Parthian power that helped drive a wedge between Parthia and its former Bactrian and Central Asian allies, who came to view Parthia increasingly as a threat. Because of the harsh nature of the interstate anarchy in the Iranian interstate system, the diligent efforts of the Parthians to expand the security of their

114. See Lerner 1999: 35.
115. Id. 46.

state in turn threatened the security of their neighbors, progressively alienating the Parthians' former allies.

Unlike Arsaces I in the first war, Arsaces II in the second war was less able to take advantage of the vast Central Asian steppe to bide his time and wait for Antiochus III to return to the west or to make a mistake. Without Bactrian allies to the east or Central Asian allies to the north, Arsaces II had little choice but to withdraw into Hyrcania; however, because of the mountainous terrain and Antiochus' swift advance, this decision severely limited the range of movement of the Parthian army, nullifying the Parthians' advantage of mobility.

Ultimately, the situation that the Parthians faced in 209 was dire, and Arsaces II was not a skilled enough general to overcome it. From the beginning of the campaign, Arsaces made critical mistakes. He had blundered in his efforts to cut off the water supply while Antiochus III crossed the deserts of northern Iran with his immense army, and he had missed his opportunity to crush Nicomedes' isolated detachment.[116] This forced Arsaces to abandon his well-placed and fortified capital in the hope that he could still overwhelm the Seleucids in Hyrcania. Unfortunately for the Parthians, Arsaces' efforts in Hyrcania fared little better.

Access to Hyrcania, located in what is today northeastern Iran and southwestern Turkmenistan, from Hecatompylus is difficult because of the Alborz Mountains. Taylor argues that Antiochus III chose to invade Hyrcania to resupply his army because his army was too vulnerable in the arid lands south of the Alborz.[117] Although the more fertile lands of Hyrcania would have made foraging less difficult for Antiochus' army, the task of crossing the Alborz was daunting and risky. The region created numerous logistical concerns for Antiochus and his enormous army. Ultimately, Antiochus invaded Hyrcania because he was in pursuit of the Parthians.

The Parthians knew that the Seleucid army could not cross this difficult terrain en masse, which helps explain Arsaces II's decision to withdraw into this region. Arsaces was trying to recapture the initiative in the campaign. Polybius records:

> Upon reaching Tagae and learning from the inhabitants what a difficult country he [Antiochus III] would have to pass through before reaching the pass over Mount Labus, which leads down to Hyrcania, and how great numbers of barbarians [that is, the Parthians] were posted at different spots where his march would be particularly hard, he decided to break up his light-armed troops into several bodies and divide their officers among them, with instructions as to the route they should take. He also resolved to break up the army servants (τοὺς λειτουργούσ) whose duty it was to

116. Polyb. 10.28.5–6.
117. Taylor 2013: 75.

> march together with the light-armed troops and make the ground occupied by these passable for the phalanx and the pack-train.[118]

The difficult terrain forced Antiochus to divide his large army into several bodies. This was the opportunity the Parthians needed to counterattack and even the odds. Polybius even emphasizes that the phalanx and baggage train of the Seleucid army were vulnerable. When the Parthians defeated Marc Antony's massive invasion almost two centuries later, they utilized the mountainous terrain of northwestern Iran in a similar strategy to destroy the Roman baggage train.[119] This forced Antony to abandon his campaign, losing tens of thousands of soldiers in the process.

With its grain supplies, pack animals, and siege equipment, Antiochus III's baggage train was enormous and cumbersome.[120] Arsaces II saw his opportunity to recover from his earlier mistakes, and he quickly implemented the Parthians' Harass Strategy. Yet Antiochus was well-prepared to mitigate the vulnerability of his army as he moved toward Hyrcania. He had brought along a considerable force of army servants, essentially engineers and workers, that he used to clear the mountain passes over the Alborz. This meant that his vulnerable phalanx and baggage train could remain close to the advanced light divisions. Therefore, Antiochus was able to avoid stretching his army too thin. Even though Arsaces began placing his men into strong positions to ambush the Seleucids, Antiochus' preparedness and Arsaces' continued miscalculations meant that the Parthians failed to capitalize on this critical opportunity.

In addition to the army servants that Antiochus III had commissioned to clear the mountain passes for his phalanx and baggage train, Antiochus decided to screen his main force with fast-moving, lightly armed troops. Polybius states:

> Having made this plan, he gave the command of the first division to Diogenes, entrusting him with archers and slingers and those of the mountaineers who were expert in throwing javelins and stones, who also, whenever time and place called for it, fought singly and rendered most useful service on difficult ground. After these he placed about two thousand Cretans armed with shields under the command of Polyxenidas of Rhodes, and lastly the light troops armed with breastplate and shield under Nicomedes of Cos and Nicolaus the Aetolian.[121]

The speed of the light troops and their adaptability on rough terrain made them a tremendous screen to protect Antiochus' divided main force. Even if the Parthians

118. Polyb. 10.29.3–4. Translation slightly altered.

119. Vell. Pat. 2.82; Plut. *Ant.* 38.2–3, 39.2–50.1; Dio 49.25–26; Florus 2.20.3–10; Livy *Epit.* 130.

120. Antiochus' army easily consumed over thirty-five tons of grain a day. Taylor 2013: 75. For the logistical capabilities of Hellenistic armies, see Engels 1980.

121. Polyb. 10.29.5–6. Translation slightly altered.

were able to isolate and attack one of these divisions, the Seleucids could send reinforcements quickly, all while keeping their slower, heavily armed infantry safe. Moreover, the javelineers, slingers, and archers in these light divisions could match the firepower of the Parthians. In the tight mountain passes of the Alborz, facing Antiochus' swift light divisions, the Parthians could not utilize superior speed or aerial power to overwhelm the Seleucids.

Arsaces II had not anticipated Antiochus III's calculated advance into the Alborz, and in so doing, he made another considerable blunder. The Parthians had made major defensive preparations to trap and destroy Antiochus and his army, and therefore, they had mitigated their own speed and maneuverability because they knew the terrain was to their advantage if the Seleucids fought conventionally. Polybius records:

> As these separate [Seleucid] bodies advanced they found the road much rougher and narrower than the king [Antiochus] had expected. For the total length of the ascent was about three hundred stades [or about thirty-four miles], and for the greater part of this distance it was through a deep torrent bed, in which progress was rendered difficult by quantities of rock and trees that had fallen of their own accord from the precipices above, while numerous other obstacles placed there by the barbarians [that is, the Parthians] contributed to the result. For they had constructed a series of barricades of felled trees and had collected a quantity of huge rocks, while they themselves along the whole defile had occupied favorable positions on the heights where they fancied themselves in security. So that Antiochus would have found it perfectly impossible to execute his project had they not miscalculated.[122]

Had Antiochus been less prepared, he would have found himself blocked by the rough terrain, which was even more difficult than he had anticipated, by a series of barricades, and by the well-placed Parthian soldiers. Arsaces had meant for his retreat toward Hyrcania to draw in an overconfident enemy into a mountain pass ambush that very well could have annihilated the Seleucid army by isolating it in sections and destroying it with concentrated fire.[123]

Polybius continues to underscore the pivotal role that Arsaces II's miscalculations played. Polybius states:

> For these preparations had been made and these positions occupied under the idea that the whole enemy army must necessarily ascend through the defile itself; but they never saw that though the phalanx and pack-train could not march by any other route than the one they supposed, since it

122. Id. 10.30.1–3.

123. Note the Parthians' later defeat of Antiochus VII. Justin 38.10.8–10; Diod. 34/35.15–17; Appian *Syr.* 11.68.

> was impossible for that part of the army to attack the mountain slopes, yet it was by no means beyond the power of unburdened and light-armed troops to ascend over the bare rocks. So that as soon as Diogenes, advancing outside the defile, came in contact with the first barbarian [that is, Parthian] post the face of things was entirely changed. For at once upon encountering the enemy he acted as circumstances suggested and making a further flank movement uphill got on higher ground, and by throwing showers of javelins and stones from the hand inflicted severe punishment on them, the greatest damage being done by the stones slung from a distance.[124]

Arsaces knew that Antiochus III's massive army could not pass the Alborz with concentrated strength. The terrain was so difficult that the phalanx and baggage train could only move slowly along one path in a long, drawn-out line. As Polybius remarks, it should have been impossible for the Seleucids to cross the Alborz in this fashion because of the strong defensive positions of the Parthians. Yet Arsaces incorrectly assumed that Antiochus would act brashly, and the Parthians apparently were completely unprepared for assaults by concentrated light-armed troops. Antiochus yet again had outmaneuvered Arsaces.

Arsaces II's miscalculations lost him his greatest opportunity to defeat the Seleucid invasion, and the Parthians again quickly lost the initiative as the light-armed divisions began to roll up the Parthians' ambush positions. Polybius continues:

> As soon as they had forced this first post to withdraw and occupied their position the army servants had time to clear and level the ground in front of them at their ease, a task soon accomplished owing to their large numbers. In fact, by this means, with the slingers, archers, and javelineers marching along the high ground in loose order, but closing up and occupying favorable positions, and with the Cretans covering their movements and marching parallel to them close to the defile slowly and in good order, the barbarians [that is, the Parthians] no longer stood their ground, but abandoning their positions collected on the actual summit of the pass.[125]

Antiochus III's foresight and careful preparation nullified the threat of the Parthians' ambush. The light-armed divisions flushed out the isolated Parthian detachments, which had no advantage of speed or firepower. This allowed the army servants to clear the obstacles barring the pass, permitting the entire Seleucid army to advance slowly but safely. The dismounted Parthian cavalry had no advantage in the mountain pass against the Seleucid light divisions, and the

124. Polyb. 10.30.4–7.
125. Id. 10.30.8–9. Translation slightly altered.

Parthians were unable to disrupt the main Seleucid force. Arsaces realized his mistake and ordered his forces to withdraw and regroup.

Arsaces II understood that, despite his failed ambush, the best chance he had to defeat Antiochus III remained while the Seleucids were isolated and hemmed in by the mountains. Yet Arsaces also had witnessed the ineffectiveness of his soldiers in the isolated mountain skirmishes. The strength of the Parthian army was speed and maneuverability, and therefore Arsaces decided to concentrate his forces on the more open ground of the summit of the pass, where his cavalry could be more operational.

In the subsequent Battle of Mount Labus, Polybius again appears inadvertently to capture the Parthians attempting to implement their "Feign Retreat, Defeat in Detail" mode of warfare.[126] He states:

> Antiochus [III] traversed the worst part of the road in the manner I have described, safely but very slowly and with difficulty, only just reaching the pass of Mount Labus on the eighth day. The barbarians [that is, the Parthians] were collected there, convinced that they would prevent the enemy from crossing, and a fierce struggle now took place, in which the barbarians were forced back for the following reason. Formed in a dense mass they fought ardently against the phalanx face to face (συστραφέντες γὰρ ἐμάχοντο πρὸς τοὺς φαλαγγίτας κατὰ πρόσωπον ἐκθύμως), but while it was still night the light-armed troops had made a wide detour and occupied the heights in their rear, as soon as they became aware of what had happened, the barbarians grew immediately terrified and rushed into flight (εὐθέως πτοηθέντες ὥρμησαν πτὸς φυγήν).[127]

It appears Polybius here misrepresents the Parthians' intentions, again preferring to portray them ultimately as foolish and cowardly. Arsaces II had several days to reorganize his troops and form a new plan of action as Antiochus made slow progress through the mountain pass. The Parthians to this point had attempted unsuccessfully to engage the Seleucid phalanx on favorable terrain. Polybius' account makes it appear as though the Parthians out of desperation implemented their Overwhelm Strategy as Antiochus' army approached and executed their Massed Assault Tactic against the Seleucid phalanx until they became outmaneuvered and fled. Yet it is highly unlikely that the Parthians actually believed that they could suddenly defeat Antiochus' large army in a conventional battle and force him to retreat. The Parthians remained severely outnumbered, and they had no ability to flank the advancing Seleucid army. Instead, it appears Arsaces wanted the Seleucids to *think* that he was offering battle conventionally,

126. Overtoom 2017b.
127. Polyb. 10.31.1–3. Translation slightly altered.

while maintaining the Parthians' Harass Strategy. If the Parthians formed en masse for what appeared to be a major engagement, this might force Antiochus finally to act rashly and deploy his valuable phalanx on unfavorable, rocky ground, which he did. If the Parthians could put pressure on the phalanx and force it to break its ranks, they might still be able to damage a crucial portion of the Seleucid army, which might force Antiochus to reconsider his campaign.

Polybius states that the Parthians fought initially with great determination in a "dense mass" and "face to face" with the Seleucid phalanx for an entire day. Although the Parthians' attacks throughout the day were brave and spirited, it is impossible that the Parthian cavalry was able to sustain a continuous melee for several hours against pike infantry. Frontal assaults against dense pike formations would have devastated Arsaces II's army, especially his light-armed and unarmored horse archers. Meanwhile, horses, like most animals, are not inclined to impaling themselves. Therefore, Polybius' depiction of massed assaults by the Parthian cavalry against the Seleucid phalanx at the Battle of Mount Labus is unacceptable. Instead, the determined attacks of the Parthians at Mount Labus likely represent their aggressive and offensive Hit-and-Run Tactic.

Throughout the day the Parthian horse archers harassed the Seleucid army, attempting to force the phalanx to break its ranks. The length of this engagement and the determination of the Parthian attacks is further proof that the Parthians had developed a method of resupplying their horse archers on the battlefield long before the Battle of Carrhae. If a gap in the phalanx appeared, the Parthian cataphracts could mount a massed assault to try to exploit that gap. If the Seleucids tried to break out of the phalanx, the Parthians could counterattack. This tactical approach to the battle was the best way the Parthians could hope to damage the Seleucid army. Yet the rough, compact terrain of the mountain pass continued to work against the Parthians. The Parthians still could not maneuver freely or flank the dense formation of the Seleucids. Meanwhile, the Seleucids ultimately were able to maintain their formation and rely on the terrain to help protect them from the limited maneuverability of the Parthians. The battle brought the Seleucid advance to a halt, but it did not offer the Parthians enough of an opportunity to defeat Antiochus III's army.

The Parthian cavalry was unable to break the phalanx, and the phalanx was unable to advance without becoming vulnerable, creating a stalemate. Antiochus III realized the potential danger facing his phalanx and ordered his light-armed troops to flank the Parthians over the rocky heights. Polybius states that the Parthians at this point became panicked and fled; however, it appears instead that Arsaces II, understanding that assaults on the Seleucid phalanx had proved less effective than he had hoped and realizing that Antiochus had turned his flank, decided to test the discipline of the Seleucids once more by implementing the Parthians' Feigned Retreat Tactic. Thus, the Parthians did not simply panic and flee as Polybius would have us believe; but instead they feigned their flight to encourage the Seleucids to make an ill-advised night pursuit. On the more open ground of the mountain pass summit, Arsaces still could hope to encourage the Seleucids to break their dense formation and to overwhelm any isolated detachments with counterattacks, and, in fact, the tactic was almost successful. Polybius records, "The king [Antiochus] made every effort to restrain his men from continuing the pursuit, summoning them back by bugle-call, as he wanted his army to descend into Hyrcania unbroken and in good order. Having regulated his march in the manner he wished, he reached Tambrax, an unwalled city, but of large size and containing a large royal palace, and encamped there."[128] Thus, disorganized portions of the Seleucid army almost played directly into the Parthians' hands at the end of the battle; however, a critical factor in the battle was that Antiochus restrained his men.

Again, instead of accepting the generally negative portrayals of the Parthians in battle from our biased Greek and Roman sources, we should consider that the Parthians were acting in a calculated manner to obtain specific tactical and strategic objectives. Arsaces II's efforts finally to disrupt the dense formation of the Seleucid army almost worked at Mount Labus; however, the instincts and command of Antiochus III protected his army. When Antiochus' men impulsively began to pursue the Parthians, he sensed a trap, called for his men to stop their pursuit, wisely reformed his ranks, and eliminated any chance the Parthians had of counterattacking his superior force.

With numerous missed opportunities and frustrations in Parthia and Hyrcania, Arsaces II was running out of options. His continued withdrawals without a military victory meant that he had abandoned most of his kingdom with little to show for it. He could not continue giving ground in the face of Antiochus III's steady and determined advance unless he planned to abandon his kingdom completely, and he lacked allies on the Central Asian steppe and in Bactria to shelter him and his remaining forces. Therefore, Arsaces decided to shift his strategy drastically to a siege defense of what remained of his kingdom. Antiochus had occupied the royal residence at Tambrax; however, the strongest citadel in the region remained in Arsaces' possession, and therefore he decided to force Antiochus into a siege to halt his advance. Polybius records:

> Most of the enemy, both from the scene of the battle and from the surrounding country, had retreated to a town called Sirynx, which was at no great distance from Tambrax, and was as it were the capital of Hyrcania owing to its strength and favorable situation, and he [Antiochus] decided to take this city by storm. He advanced therefore with his army and encamping around it began the siege. The chief means he employed was the use of protective shelters for sappers. There were three moats, each

128. Id. 10.31.4–5.

> not less than thirty cubits broad and fifteen deep [roughly forty-five by twenty-two-and-a-half feet], and each defended at its edge by a double row of palisades, and behind all [these obstacles] there was a strong wall. There were constant combats at the works, in which neither side could bring off their dead and wounded, as the hand-to-hand fighting took place not only on the surface of the ground but beneath it in the mines.[129]

Sirynx (located near either modern Behshahr or Gorgan, Iran), with its three moats, six wooden walls, and strong central fortification, was an imposing defensive structure, and Arsaces had garrisoned Sirynx with a portion of his remaining force.[130] He hoped to bog down the Seleucid army and force Antiochus to come to terms. A similar strategy would later work for the Bactrians in defense of their fortress capital, Bactra-Zariaspa.[131] Yet in the first years of Antiochus' anabasis, the Seleucid army was well-supplied and had suffered few casualties. Moreover, Antiochus' resolve was unmatched in this early phase of his eastern expedition. He intended to reestablish Seleucid hegemony over the entire Iranian plateau, and therefore he had to assure the total submission of the Parthians.

Perhaps to capture the fortress before winter made the siege more difficult, Antiochus III combined frontal assaults with tunneling efforts to seize Sirynx. The fighting was desperate and the carnage considerable as the Parthians frantically defended the walls and dug counter-tunnels; however, Antiochus put the full force of his army and its engineers to work to overcome Sirynx and its defenders. Polybius concludes:

> But in spite of all, owing to the superiority of numbers and the personal activity of the king [Antiochus], the moats were very soon filled up and the wall was undermined and fell, upon which the barbarians [that is, the Parthians] were thoroughly discouraged, and after killing all the Greeks in the town and pillaging all the finest things they made off by night. When the king became aware of this he sent Hyperbas after them with the mercenaries, and the barbarians when overtaken by him threw away their encumbrances and fled again into the town. When the [Seleucid] peltasts now vigorously forced their way through the breach, they surrendered in despair.[132]

Considering the significant extent of the siege operations at Sirynx, the conflict must have lasted several weeks, and the Parthians fought the Seleucids to the point of exhaustion until the inner wall began to give way. The remaining defenders attempted a desperate breakout against the Seleucid siege lines but did

129. Id. 10.31.6–9. Translation slightly altered.
130. Bing and Sievers 2011; Kiani 2012.
131. Polyb. 10.49.15.
132. Id. 10.31.10–13.

not have the strength necessary to succeed. Polybius' depiction of the barbarian Parthians as murders, bandits, and cowards continues his mostly negative portrayal of the character of the Parthians in war and should give us some pause since it again emphasizes eastern stereotypes and since no other surviving account discusses these controversial events. If there was a massacre of the Greek population during the siege by the Parthians, there likely was a pragmatic reason that did not concern Polybius or his audience.

With the final defenses of the town falling and the Parthians readying for a desperate assault on the Seleucid siege lines, the Greek population in Sirynx could have posed a serious security threat to the remaining Parthian defenders. The Parthians did not want to surrender; the Seleucids eventually *forced* the Parthians to surrender. Therefore, the Parthians would not have wanted the Greeks in Sirynx to turn against them in favor of the Seleucids.[133] If the Parthians executed the Greeks in the town, this was a brutal and harsh act, but it reflects the brutal and harsh environment in which these ancient peoples lived and operated. This was not an act of senseless vengeance against the Greeks or a violent reaction against Hellenism.[134] In fact, the Parthians generally were inclusive and supportive when it came to Greek communities within their kingdom, and in eighty years the Parthians worked alongside Greek communities to undermine Seleucid power in Mesopotamia and Media.[135] Moreover, the Greek community at Sirynx had lived under the Parthians without issue for a generation, and therefore, if we can accept Polybius' account here, the desperation and savagery of the siege of Sirynx made this massacre possible and perhaps necessary.

Polybius never confirms the presence of Arsaces II at Sirynx, and in fact, it seems highly unlikely that Arsaces was there.[136] Unfortunately, Polybius abruptly ends his account of the campaign, and therefore, the details of Antiochus III's final operations against the Parthians have not survived. The Parthian breakout at Sirynx failed, and after a vigorous last assault, the city fell to Antiochus with the remainder of the Parthian defenders surrendering. Had Arsaces been among the prisoners of war, it seems improbable that Polybius and Justin would have ignored such a major event. Further, Antiochus' actions after the capture of Sirynx further suggest that Arsaces remained active in the field. Justin records, "His [that is, Arsaces I's] son and successor on the throne, whose name was also Arsaces [II], fought with the greatest bravery against Antiochus [III], the son of Seleucus [II], who was at the head of a hundred thousand foot and twenty thousand horse, and was at last taken into alliance with him."[137] Thus, although

133. Note Taylor 2013: 77; Olbrycht 2017b: 9–10.

134. Mommsen 1856 (1903): iii 286–90, iv 421, 433; v 157; Rawlinson 1876 (2002): 21, 24, 41, 97–98, 105, 118–19.

135. Note Justin 38.10.8; Diod. 34/35.15. Compare Dąbrowa 1994; id. 2005; id. 2005 [2006]; id. 2006–2007 [2008]; id. 2011a; id. 2011d; Shayegan 2011: 137–39; Wiesehöfer 2014; Olbrycht 2017b.

136. Bing and Sievers assume Arsaces was captured. Bing and Sievers 2011.

137. Justin 41.5.7. Note Grainger 2015: 69–70.

Arsaces lost the war, the terms of the peace were acceptable and lenient, making his capture even more unlikely.

After his losses in the Alborz Mountains and at the costly siege of Sirynx, Arsaces II had exhausted most of the military power of the Parthians. The efforts of the Parthians to escape Sirynx with its treasures also indicates the Parthians were low on funds to continue the conflict. There remained no scenario where Arsaces could win the war; however, the long pursuit of the Parthians, their determined defense of Sirynx, and the potential threat Arsaces still posed to Antiochus III's future plans also encouraged Antiochus to end the conflict. With his remaining mobile troops, Arsaces could continue to be a nuisance to Antiochus' extensive supply lines if the war against the Parthians was not brought to a definitive end. Antiochus moved his army from Sirynx into the Astuauene valley between the Kopet Dagh and Binalud mountain ranges, indicating that Arsaces had moved his remaining army to defend the important Parthian city of Nisa in southern Turkmenistan.[138] Instead of risking another prolonged siege and instead of punishing Arsaces further by removing him from power, Antiochus decided to bind Arsaces to his will diplomatically. This decision continued Antiochus' prior policy in Media Atropatene and Armenia. The peace agreement and alliance with Arsaces was a recognition of Antiochus' accomplishments in Parthia and Hyrcania, and it allowed Antiochus to consolidate his gains before continuing east against Bactria.

Therefore, by early 208 Arsaces II avoided destruction at the cost of submitting to Seleucid suzerainty as a subordinate ally.[139] Along with removing Arsaces' right to strike his own coinage, it is likely that part of Arsaces' peace settlement with Antiochus III included the Parthians supplying Antiochus with cataphracts, similar to how the Bactrians and Indians later had to supply Antiochus with war elephants.[140] The Seleucid army first employed the heavily armed and armored Parthian-style cataphracts in the west under Antiochus against the Ptolemies at the Battle of Panium in 200, and this heavy cavalry subsequently became a staple of the Seleucid army in its western conflicts.[141] Antiochus also reclaimed Parthia and Hyrcania south of the Kopet Dagh Mountains for the empire and left Arsaces in command of the mountainous terrain that separated the empire from the Central Asian steppe as a weak subordinate ally.[142] For Antiochus this settlement

138. Taylor 2013: 77. The great fortress of Dara also was in the area. Justin 41.5.2.

139. It is possible Antiochus III promised to marry one of his sons to one of Arsaces' daughters, Brittane. Assar 2011: 115. John Malalas, in his disorganized account of Seleucid history, perhaps confused the events of Antiochus III's anabasis with those of Antiochus VII's anabasis. Jo. Mal. 8.208. Antiochus III attempted to follow a similar policy in Bactria. Polyb. 11.34.9–10. Yet in both cases nothing came of the promised betrothals.

140. See Polyb. 11.34.10–12. For coinage, note Assar 2011: 115.

141. Polyb. 16.18.5–10, 30.25.6–10. Note Nikonorov 1994; id. 1995; id. 1998b; Mielczarek 1998; Olbrycht 2003: 94–96; Sekunda 2013: 1389; Overtoom 2017b; Johstono 2018.

142. See Taylor 2013: 77; Grainger 2015: 68–69.

nullified the threat of the Parthians to his empire, while leaving the burden of defending the interior of the Iranian plateau from nomadic raids on Arsaces.

The result of the war for the Parthians was a drastic reversal of fortune caused in large part by the military failures of their king. The Parthians had been humiliated, and they remained a marginal power in the region until the 160s.[143] Meanwhile, the initial result of the war for the Seleucids was mostly positive. Antiochus III did not have the time or the resources to subdue the Parthians completely. He still had a war to fight against Bactria, and the security of the western portion of the empire was always in jeopardy. His defeat of the Parthians had avenged the failure of his father; he had regained the best portions of Parthia for the empire, which included the many improvements that Arsaces I had commissioned; and he had forced the Parthians to accept Seleucid hegemony. It is unrealistic to expect that Antiochus could have accomplished anything more. He had won his hegemonic war against the upstart Parthians and had set the development of the Parthian state back a generation.[144] Yet the long-term results of the war were indecisive because Antiochus did not destroy the Arsacids.

The power of the Seleucid state revolved around the power of the central government, namely the king. Antiochus III could not remain in Parthia indefinitely, and therefore Seleucid power and authority in the region gradually began to wane as the Arsacids regained their former strength. For Antiochus, however, this was another problem for another time. He was pleased with his recent military and diplomatic successes against the Parthians and turned his attention to the punishment of the Bactrians.

143. Overtoom 2019a.
144. Taylor 2013: 78.

The Fall of Bactria, the Rise of Parthia

With the reconquest of much of Parthia and the submission of Arsaces II, Antiochus III had accomplished more militarily in the east than any Seleucid king since Seleucus I and Antiochus I. Yet Antiochus III's anabasis had greater objectives, and Seleucid retaliation next fell upon Bactria. After another challenging campaign, Antiochus forced the submission of Bactria as another subordinate allied kingdom of the Seleucid Empire. He then emulated Alexander the Great and Seleucus I by invading the Indus River valley before returning to the west. Antiochus' decision to establish Parthia and Bactria as subordinate allied kingdoms instead of completely reabsorbing these regions under the direct imperial rule of the Seleucid state maintained the integrity of the newly formed Iranian interstate system in the east; however, Antiochus' military and diplomatic successes temporarily made the Seleucid Empire the undisputed hegemon of that interstate system.

Unfortunately for the Seleucids, this renewed position of supremacy in the east was vulnerable because the power of the state was intertwined with the power and personality of the king. Once Antiochus III returned to the west, the influence of the Seleucids over the Iranian plateau began to wane. Parthia and Bactria once again began to act autonomously and to expand their power and influence regionally against the interests of the Seleucid state. Antiochus' successors found the challenge of maintaining Seleucid hegemony over the east perilous.

As Seleucid authority in the east began to fade in the early second century, the kings of Bactria exercised their autonomy by turning to campaigns of conquest in the northern Indus River valley. Yet dynastic instability and the growing threat of nomadic incursions created internal and external pressures that increasingly undermined their authority and overwhelmed their fledgling kingdom. In fact, although internal dynastic weaknesses and other external pressures, such as the renewed power of the Parthians, sapped Bactrian strength in the middle second century, nomadic attacks from the Central Asian steppe became the major threat to the survival of the Kingdom of Bactria, eventually bringing the kingdom to its knees in the 140s–130s.[1]

1. See Holt 1999: 133–38; Grainger 2013a: Ch. 5–6, 11. For the nomadic presence in Central Asia, note Sinor 1990a; Olbrycht 1996; id. 1998a; id. 2015a; id. 2015b.

Reign of Arrows. Nikolaus Leo Overtoom, Oxford University Press (2020). Oxford University Press.
DOI: 10.1093/oso/9780190888329.001.0001.

The decline of Seleucid authority and the rapid collapse of Bactria helped establish and perpetuate another period of geopolitical crisis in the Hellenistic Middle East. The power-transition crisis of the 160s–130s that emerged afforded Arsaces II's successors many opportunities to improve and expand the Parthian state.[2] After a generation of recovery and reconsolidation, a powerful, charismatic, ambitious, and talented man named Mithridates I became the new king of the Parthians. Under Mithridates the Parthians were determined to secure their survival through a series of major military expansions, and by the middle second century, the Parthians became the dominant power on the Iranian plateau and for the first time penetrated the wealthy lands of Mesopotamia.

The renewed decline of Seleucid authority in the east and the rapid emergence of the Parthians as a major rival encouraged the Seleucids once again to retaliate violently against the rising threat of Parthia. By 138 the Seleucid king, Demetrius II, had the opportunity and sufficient reason to conduct an eastern expedition against the Parthians. Yet Demetrius' campaign proved disastrous as he and his army fell victim to the Parthians' asymmetric mode of warfare. With this decisive victory, the Parthians established themselves firmly as the hegemonic rivals and geopolitical equals of the Seleucids within the Hellenistic Middle East.

Usurpers and Invaders

At the height of its power under Diodotus I and Diodotus II, the Kingdom of Bactria encompassed much of what is modern Afghanistan and Tajikistan and sizable portions of Turkmenistan, Uzbekistan, Kyrgyzstan, and Pakistan.[3] After the power-transition crisis of the 240s–230s, Bactria emerged briefly as the leading power in the east with extensive resources and military capabilities.[4] Yet the frontiers of the Kingdom of Bactria were continually vulnerable, especially in the north, because of the relative isolation and exposure of the region to movements of aggressive, warlike nomadic peoples. The Parni had attempted to penetrate the Bactrian frontier on two occasions before securing Parthia as a new stronghold, and the Parni were not alone in their interest to occupy the wealthy lands of Bactria. Similar to other Hellenistic states, strong kings were necessary to sustain and expand the power of Bactria within such a hostile international environment; however, equally similar to other Hellenistic states, dynastic conflicts and instability accelerated the deterioration of the Bactrian state.

Thus, the downfall of Bactria from its place of regional supremacy in the 230s–220s began and ended with usurpations and invasions. The rapid expansion of the

2. See Overtoom 2019a; id. 2019b; id. 2019/2020.

3. For the historiography of Hellenistic Bactria and the importance of numismatics to our evolving understanding of its history and archaeology, see Holt 2012a; Bordeaux 2018.

4. Overtoom 2016a.

Parthians under Arsaces I had created a regional rivalry that continually threatened to bring Parthia and Bactria into open conflict over the next several decades. Although the Seleucids under Antiochus III initially took advantage of the regional rivalry developing between the Parthians and Bactrians and exploited the dynastic conflicts within Bactria itself, the Parthians and the Central Asian tribal confederations ultimately capitalized on the crumbling power and authority of the Kingdom of Bactria. The rapid decline of Bactrian power from external pressures and internal dissension and the expanding capabilities of the Parthians meant that Bactria faded into obscurity as Parthia emerged as the rising power in the east by the beginning of the 150s.

The Battle for Bactria

In the face of Seleucus II's eastern expedition, the Parthians and Bactrians had put aside their differences temporarily to balance against a great threat to their survival.[5] Yet by 210 the Partho-Bactrian rivalry had escalated to a point that the two sides failed to form an alliance against Antiochus III's even greater threat. This was a monumental decision by the Parthians and Bactrians that left both regional powers vulnerable to the overwhelming force of Antiochus' invasion, and it facilitated the defeat of Arsaces II.

Two leading factors in the inability of Parthia and Bactria to put aside their differences to counter the imminent threat of Antiochus III were, first, the murder of Parthia's former ally Diodotus II and the usurpation of his throne by Euthydemus I and, second, the expanding power capabilities of the Parthians and Bactrians by the 210s. Euthydemus' successful rebellion and usurpation demonstrates the difficulties that the kings of Bactria faced in trying to hold together their disparate kingdom and the vulnerability of Diodotus' regime. It also is possible that Diodotus lost control of the lands north of the Gissar Mountains south of the Jaxartes River (now the Syr Darya River) to nomadic invaders before his death.[6] Diodotus' ineffective rule created an opportunity for Euthydemus, who was charismatic and ambitious. Euthydemus gained the support of local aristocrats in Sogdiana (modern northern Afghanistan) and seized the Bactrian throne in ca. 221.[7] Over the next decade, he consolidated his authority over his new kingdom, building a large army and fortifying his frontiers.[8] Euthydemus amassed an impressive force of around 10,000 cavalry, many of whom were from

5. Id. 2020.

6. Grainger 2015: 65.

7. There is considerable controversy over the position that Euthydemus held under Diodotus II. See Lerner 1999: 83–84. Compare Tod 1826: 321f.; Droysen 1878: ii 366; Cunningham 1884: 134; Grousset 1929: 53; Vallée-Poussin 1930: 233; Zabelina 1949: 101–2; Tarn 1951: 73–75; Masson 1955: 42–43; Narain 1957: 19; Smith 1979: 6–13; Holt 1999: 126–27. Lerner's conclusion that Euthydemus was the satrap of Sogdiana, who declared himself king of the country with the support of local aristocrats seems probable. Lerner 1999: 63–84.

8. Holt correctly rejects the depiction of Euthydemus as an "impotent Seleucid loyalist." Holt 1999: 127.

the Bactrian aristocracy.[9] He had learned the value of a strong cavalry wing and strategic frontier fortresses during his efforts to repulse nomadic incursions in Sogdiana.[10] He also maintained an infantry force large enough and loyal enough to withstand a two-year siege during Antiochus III's invasion of his kingdom.[11] It is a testament to the success of Euthydemus' authority and policies that he was able to retain the support of the local Bactrian aristocracy and his Greek troops during his intense conflict with Antiochus.[12]

Euthydemus I came to rule over an extensive and prosperous region; he commanded a sizable military; and he had the support of the local aristocracy.[13] Although the power and proximity of Parthia and Bactria made them natural rivals, Arsaces I and Diodotus II had put aside their differences to form an alliance against the aggression of Seleucus II in the 230s. Yet Arsaces II and Euthydemus did not renew this alliance when faced with the much larger invasion of Antiochus III in 210. One possible explanation for the unwillingness of the Parthians and Bactrians once more to work together to defeat the Seleucids is that the two powers had come to view one another as a major threat regionally on par with the Seleucid Empire. In terms of international relations theory, the expansion of Parthian power after the defeat of Seleucus and the sudden recovery of Bactria under Euthydemus likely heightened uncertainty and mistrust between the two powers within the Iranian interstate system. Antiochus' grand eastern campaign delayed any possible military confrontation between the Parthians and Bactrians; however, their unwillingness to work together to stop another Seleucid invasion illustrates that the relationship of the Parthians and Bactrians had deteriorated considerably since the 230s.

In 210 Arsaces II was unwilling to ask for aid, and Euthydemus I apparently viewed Antiochus III's invasion of Parthia as an opportunity. Jeffrey Lerner concludes, "Antiochus III must have been perceived from the Bactrian point of view as a mixed blessing: while he diminished any possible threat from Parthia, he himself was considered an outsider and his expedition into Bactria was that of a foreign invader, rather than the country's legitimate sovereign."[14] Certainly, Euthydemus understood the danger of Antiochus' anabasis; however, he also understood that Antiochus had to contend with the Parthians first before invading Bactria. Euthydemus did not view Antiochus as enough of a threat to aid his most immediate regional rival, the Parthians.

9. Lerner 1999: 50. Compare Tarn 1951: 82, 102, 124–25; Simonetta 1960: 52–62; Grainger 2015: 70.

10. Holt 1981: 34–35.

11. The Bactrian military perhaps was 30,000 soldiers strong. McLaughlin 2016: 76, 224. Justin records, however, that Demetrius II of Bactria commanded 60,000 men in the 170s. Justin 41.6.4.

12. Holt 1999: 128 n.7.

13. Justin records that there were a thousand cities in Bactria alone. Justin 41.4.5. The Kingdom of Bactria included Bactria, Sogdiana, Margiana, and possibly Aria at this time. See Lerner 1999: 48–50. For the vibrancy of civilization in Bactria for centuries, see Leriche 2007.

14. Lerner 1999: 51.

Euthydemus I could hope for the Parthians and Seleucids to exhaust one another, allowing Bactria to emerge once more as the leading regional power by default. It was a considerable gamble that offered the potential of the greatest of rewards and the most total of defeats; however, it reflected the evolving power relations of the Seleucids, Parthians, and Bactrians within the Iranian interstate system. With Antiochus III's defeat of Arsaces II in 209–208, the Parthians were no longer capable of rivalling Bactria, at least temporarily. Yet the submission of Parthia also left Bactria isolated against Antiochus' massive army, and Euthydemus faced potential destruction in the approaching hegemonic conflict.

After settling his affairs in Parthia and accepting Arsaces II's submission, Antiochus III invaded Euthydemus I's kingdom in 208.[15] The two sides fought a bloody battle along the Arius River (now the Hari River), where Antiochus was wounded severely in the mouth, but his bravery in battle and superior tactics allowed him eventually to rout the Bactrian cavalry.[16] Euthydemus then withdrew with the remainder of his army to his fortress capital, Bactra-Zariaspa (modern Balkh, Afghanistan).[17] If we are to accept Polybius' account, Euthydemus was "terror-stricken" at the loss of his cavalry. Whatever confidence Euthydemus possessed of winning the war in the field at the beginning of the campaign, he had lost it.

Although Euthydemus I had a strong cavalry force, he did not favor the asymmetric warfare of the Parthians. Instead, Euthydemus had hoped to defeat Antiochus III in a conventional engagement by blocking the Seleucid army with his forces along the Arius River.[18] Euthydemus' 10,000 horsemen blocked the river crossing; however, their idleness allowed Antiochus to cross the river unopposed at night. The next day Antiochus with a smaller force destroyed a large portion of the Bactrian cavalry, and Euthydemus decided to resist Antiochus to the last in his nearly impregnable capital city.

For two years Antiochus III conducted a spectacular siege of Bactra-Zariaspa, during which time he may have sacked other major urban centers in Bactria such as Ai Khanoum; however, unlike his prior siege of the Parthian stronghold, Sirynx, he was unable to take Bactra-Zariaspa by force.[19] The Bactrians proved

15. For Polybius' account of the expedition, see Polyb. 10.49, 11.34. Compare Walbank 1967: ii 264–65, 312–16; Will 1967: i 305ff.; id. 1982: 22, 51–54, 58–61. For recent accounts of the campaign, see Taylor 2013: 79–86; Grainger 2015: Ch. 4.

16. Polyb. 10.49.1–14. For the debate over the location of the battle, see Lerner 1999: 47–48. Compare Wilson 1841: 221; Cunningham 1884: 139–40; Tarn 1951: 89, 114–15; Walbank 1967: ii 265; Holt 1988: 23–24; Grainger 2015: 70.

17. Polyb. 10.49.15. For Bactra-Zariaspa, see P'yankov 1982; Masson 1985: 250ff.; Holt 1988: 11ff.

18. For the argument that the Bactrians' cavalry was a mixture of Greek and native elements and that their tactics were more suited to nomadic warfare, see Lerner 1999: 50–51. Compare Nikonorov 1992; Sherwin-White and Kuhrt 1993: 56; Nikonorov 1997; id. 2013. Euthydemus' choice to avoid asymmetric warfare in the campaign against Antiochus, even when it would have better suited his cavalry, helps illustrate that the Bactrian high command had a more conventional approach to warfare.

19. Polyb. 29.12.8. Note Martinez-Sève 2017. For Antiochus' sack of Ai Khanoum, see Lerner 2003–2004: 381–83, 397–99; id. 2013: 1013.

better equipped and more capable in siege defense, and finally in 206 Antiochus, frustrated with his lack of progress and aware that he could not remain in Bactria for much longer, came to favorable terms with Euthydemus I and ended the war.[20] In exchange for Antiochus officially recognizing Euthydemus as king of Bactria, Euthydemus agreed to become the subordinate ally of the Seleucid Empire.[21] With Bactria's recognition of Seleucid hegemony in 206, the Seleucids once again became the undisputed power throughout the Hellenistic Middle East.

Much like his campaign against Arsaces II in Parthia, Antiochus III had several good reasons for embracing Euthydemus I as a subordinate ally instead of removing Euthydemus and reestablishing direct Seleucid imperial control over Bactria. Seleucus II's failure in the 230s made the danger of eastern expeditions apparent, encouraging Antiochus to alter Seleucid policy to be more flexible and forgiving. He hoped a more moderate policy would cause less resistance to Seleucid hegemonic rule in the future.[22] Similarly, Euthydemus, like Arsaces before him, found this arrangement acceptable because of numerous practical concerns. The battle for Bactria was not fought in a vacuum and pressing geopolitical developments in the region encouraged both men to agree to peace.

The treaty allowed Antiochus III to resolve a costly and draining military endeavor favorably. Ancient sieges were not only costly in materials and men, but the idleness of soldiers could lead to disease or unrest.[23] The siege of Bactra-Zariaspa had dragged along for two years, and Polybius tells us that Euthydemus I still had enough excess grain to hand out generous rations to Antiochus' troops after the peace treaty.[24] With no end to the siege in sight, Antiochus needed to make a deal for the welfare of his army, which had begun to exhaust its supplies. Additionally, Antiochus' campaign was not finished once he subdued Parthia and Bactria. He planned to invade the Indus River valley to rival Alexander the Great and to reestablish Seleucid hegemony over the region to surpass Seleucus I.[25] The longer the war in Bactria lasted, the more difficult the rest of Antiochus' campaign would have become logistically.[26]

Antiochus III also could not afford to be absent from geopolitical developments in the west for much longer as his anabasis had already spanned five years. Because of the political weakness of Ptolemy IV in Egypt and the military distractions of Philip V in Macedon, Antiochus' western lands remained relatively safe during this period; however, there was no guarantee that this security

20. Polyb. 11.34.7.
21. Id. 11.34.8–10.
22. Grainger 2015: 57. Note Strootman 2011; id. 2015; id. 2018.
23. For Greek siege warfare and its limitations, see Kern 1999: Ch. 5–10, Campbell 2006: Ch. 2–5; Strauss 2007: 223–47; de Souza 2007: 434–60; Chaniotis 2013: 438–56. Compare Martin 2013: 671–87; Engels 2013: 351–68.
24. Polyb. 11.34.10.
25. Id. 11.34.11–13.
26. Antiochus also forced the Indian king, Sophagasenus, to provide elephants and provisions. Id. 11.13.12. Clearly, supplying his army concerned Antiochus by the latter stage of his anabasis.

would last.[27] In fact, immediately following Antiochus' return to the west in 204, Ptolemaic power rapidly collapsed, plunging the Eastern Mediterranean interstate system into a period of great chaos and violence. Arthur Eckstein identifies the collapse of the Ptolemies' standing in the Eastern Mediterranean interstate system at this time as a power-transition crisis that ultimately brought Rome into hegemonic conflict with Macedon and the Seleucid Empire.[28] Rome's subsequent victories against the Antigonids and Seleucids drastically altered the international environment in the Mediterranean, and Rome emerged suddenly as the undisputed hegemon of a new Pan-Mediterranean interstate system.

Rome's victory once again drastically reshaped the international environment. The Seleucids came to function within three distinct major interstate systems: the Roman-dominated Mediterranean system, the Seleucid-dominated Iranian system, and the emerging multipolar Near Eastern system that stretched from Egypt to eastern Anatolia over to the Caucasus and Mesopotamia. This new Near Eastern interstate system featured the rivalry of the Seleucids and Ptolemies but also included the actions of numerous middling and minor states, including the Hasmonean Kingdom in Judaea, Cappadocia in southeastern Anatolia, Pontus in northeastern Anatolia, Armenia, and various Arab tribes. As Rome continued to expand eastward and the Parthians began to expand westward throughout the second century, they came to dominate the lands of the Near East between them before establishing their own long-standing rivalry across a massive Irano-Mediterranean interstate system that encompassed the known world from Spain to India.[29]

In 206 a conflict with Rome did not yet concern Antiochus III. Yet his rivalries with the kings and city-states of the Eastern Mediterranean remained important. He could ill-afford to remain in the east for much longer.

Finally, the submission of Euthydemus I as a subordinate ally of the Seleucid Empire satisfied Antiochus III's desire to avenge the Bactrian revolt and the failure of his father. Euthydemus during the peace talks complained that Antiochus' desire to punish him was unfair because he had not rebelled against the Seleucids; rather, he had rebelled against the enemy of the Seleucids (that is, the Diodoti).[30] Although Antiochus had come to the east to retaliate against the Parthians and Bactrians, he also understood that Arsaces II and Euthydemus had not been the leaders of the rebellions or the commanders in the defeat of his father. Antiochus recognized the merit of Euthydemus' pleas during their negotiations, and he was pleased to establish a subordinate ally, resupply his army, and avoid the difficult

27. Grainger argues that Antiochus received frequent reports of political and religious events in the west and maintained his western political and military focus while on campaign in the east. Grainger 2015: 66–67, 71–72, 74–75.

28. See Eckstein 2012.

29. Note Overtoom 2016a; id. 2016c; id. 2016d; id. 2017a; id. 2017b; id. 2019a; id. 2019b; id. 2019c; is. 2019/2020; id. 2021.

30. Polyb. 11.34.1–2.

task of garrisoning and defending Bactria.[31] Although the hegemony of the Seleucids over Bactria was fragile and vulnerable, Antiochus' prudent policy of creating subordinate allied kingdoms along the frontier of his much-expanded empire continued to be a success, at least temporarily.

Meanwhile, the treaty offered Euthydemus I a great opportunity to salvage his regional authority and strength. Although Antiochus III could claim ultimate victory, Euthydemus had avoided total defeat. His determined defense of Bactra-Zariaspa and Antiochus' mounting logistical concerns facilitated the end of Antiochus' invasion of Bactria. In exchange for accepting subordinate status, which in reality meant little after Antiochus and his army returned to the west, Euthydemus gained Antiochus' recognition of his kingship and the promise of a marriage alliance with Antiochus' family.[32] Euthydemus had usurped the Bactrian throne, which Antiochus' invasion had called into question; however, this peace treaty reasserted the separate royal identity of Bactria and provided Euthydemus and his budding dynasty with legitimacy.[33]

Perhaps most important, the peace treaty removed the immediate threat of Antiochus III's army from Euthydemus I's lands and allowed him once again to focus on consolidating his power regionally. Bactria was a prosperous but unstable region. Its frontiers were vulnerable to attack on multiple fronts, and its aristocracy was powerful and ambitious. Euthydemus understood that his isolation in his capital during the siege and his inability to defeat the Seleucids created opportunities for rivals, both internally and externally, to challenge his increasingly vulnerable position. As a usurper, Euthydemus' authority derived directly from his leadership and the support of the local aristocracy. Antiochus' presence in Bactria increasingly damaged Euthydemus' authority; however, the peace treaty and Antiochus' concessions enhanced Euthydemus' prestige and allowed him to maintain his influence throughout his kingdom. Ultimately, Antiochus did not have the desire or the resources to reoccupy Bactria without great difficulty, and therefore he decided to leave Euthydemus in possession of most of his former lands.[34] Euthydemus' only tribute was to supply Antiochus' army with grain and elephants.[35]

Euthydemus I also never forgot the tremendous threat that the warlike Central Asian tribal confederations posed to his kingdom, and Antiochus III after two years in Bactria also came to appreciate the growing danger of nomadic incursions into the region. Both men agreed that their conflict jeopardized the survival of Bactria and the security of the entire Iranian plateau. Polybius states:

31. Id. 11.34.7.
32. Id. 11.34.9.
33. Euthydemus was able to save face and gain political recognition of his kingship. Grainger 2015: 71.
34. It is possible Antiochus reclaimed Aria and Margiana. Id. 72.
35. Polyb. 11.34.10.

> After speaking at some length in the same sense he [Euthydemus] begged Teleas to mediate between them [Euthydemus and Antiochus] in a friendly manner and bring about a reconciliation, entreating Antiochus not to grudge him the name and state of king, and if he did not yield to this request, neither of them would be safe. For considerable hordes of nomads were approaching, and this was not only a grave danger to both of them, but if they [the Seleucids] consented to admit them, the country would certainly relapse into barbarism. After speaking thus, he dispatched Teleas to Antiochus.[36]

Although Polybius perhaps exaggerates the threat of imminent nomadic invasions, Antiochus did not argue with Euthydemus' logic and agreed to peace negotiations.[37] Antiochus had no desire to defeat Euthydemus only to turn the region over to Central Asian invaders, and Antiochus had no desire to leave a large portion of his army in Bactria to secure the region.[38] He understood first-hand the trouble that nomadic warriors could cause in the eastern territories of the empire, having spent the first half of his anabasis suppressing Arsaces II and his mobile army in Parthia. Meanwhile, Euthydemus needed to secure his frontiers, and he understood that he could use the growing threat of the Central Asian tribal confederations as a warning to encourage Antiochus to end the siege. Antiochus, who wanted to emulate Alexander the Great in India but had no desire to emulate Alexander on the Central Asian steppe, could not afford to remain in Bactria fighting Central Asian invaders in an extended campaign.[39] The grueling expedition of Alexander to subdue Bactria and Sogdiana was not something that Antiochus wanted to repeat.[40] Instead, Antiochus left another submissive, yet regionally strong subordinate ally to bear the responsibility and cost of repulsing nomadic attacks.

By recognizing Euthydemus I officially as king, Antiochus III helped boost Euthydemus' authority in Bactria, which was in Antiochus' interest after the peace treaty.[41] Antiochus had established his dominance over the region but left Bactria strong enough to defend the eastern frontier of the Seleucid Empire. His

36. Id. 11.34.3–6.

37. Id. 11.34.7. The confederations of the powerful and aggressive Massagetae and Sacaraucae (or Saka) threatened Euthydemus' kingdom. Tarn 1951: 79–82, 116–17, 291–95; Simonetta 1960: 56–62; Holt 1981: 35ff.; Lerner 1999: 59; id. 2016: 107; Brüggemann 2017.

38. For a recent rejection of the modern criticisms of Antiochus for not annexing Bactria, see Taylor 2013: 81–82.

39. Grainger argues that, had Antiochus continued the siege, the Central Asian tribal confederations might have come to Euthydemus' aid out of fear that Seleucid control of Bactria would be a greater threat to them. Grainger 2015: 71. Since the Seleucids had created a strong eastern frontier prior to the power-transition crisis of the 240s–230s and since the Kingdom of Bactria was becoming increasingly vulnerable, it is likely that the tribal confederations viewed Antiochus' success in the east as a growing threat. Note Overtoom 2016a.

40. See Holt 2005; Antela-Bernardez 2014; Lerner 2015a: 305–6.

41. Grainger 2015: 72.

alliance with Euthydemus secured his supply lines and allowed Antiochus to finish his anabasis and return to the west without fearing the total collapse of the eastern portion of the empire under the weight of further nomadic invasions.

No other successive Seleucid king came close to achieving what Antiochus III accomplished in the east; however, scholars generally appear too critical of Antiochus' eastern accomplishments, viewing his campaign as vainglorious or ineffectual.[42] The debate hinges on a consideration of short-term successes versus long-term shortcomings. Antiochus' anabasis certainly was not a permanent solution to the empire's vulnerable eastern frontier, and in fact, Antiochus' establishment of subordinate allied kingdoms in the east demonstrates that his anabasis was not meant as such. Antiochus set out to address more immediate and pressing concerns, such as the Seleucids' deteriorating position within the Iranian plateau and the rising threat of Parthia and Bactria, both of which he overcame without exhausting his resources. The submission of Arsaces II and Euthydemus I established Seleucid unipolar hegemony over the Iranian interstate system, which remained in place until the 160s.[43]

Antiochus III's anabasis undeniably achieved critical short-term accomplishments, reestablishing Seleucid hegemony over the Iranian plateau and protecting the directly controlled lands of the empire in Media and Mesopotamia for two generations.[44] In fact, Antiochus' contemporaries viewed his anabasis as a resounding triumph. Polybius states, "In a word he put his kingdom in a position of safety (ἠσφαλίσατο), overawing all subject to him by his courage and industry. It was this expedition, in fact, which made him appear worthy of his throne not only to the inhabitants of Asia, but those of Europe likewise."[45] Notice Polybius' emphasis on the security that Antiochus provided for the empire. A primary goal of Antiochus' anabasis had been to reestablish Seleucid hegemony over the Hellenistic Middle East through the reduction of the threats that Parthia and Bactria posed to the Seleucid Empire. Antiochus unequivocally accomplished this goal, while also gaining wealth, glory, respect, prestige, and revenge.[46] Although Antiochus did not reestablish direct Seleucid control over

42. See Rawlinson 1876 (2002): 33; Will 1967: ii 348–53; Green 1990: 295–96; Lerner 1999: 52. To a lesser extent, see Grainger 2015: 194–95.

43. Overtoom 2019a.

44. Note Grainger 2015: 74–75. Media and Mesopotamia experienced one of the greatest periods of economic stability from ca. 220–140 in part because of Antiochus' success. Note Boiy 2004. For the economy of the Near East and Middle East under the Persians and Greeks, note Stolper 1985; Dandamaev and Lukonin 1989; Andreau, Briant, and Descat 1994; id. 1997; id. 2000; Bringmann 2000; Chankowski and Duyrat 2004; Aperghis 2004; Kuhrt 2010: Chs. 14–16; Archibald, Davies, and Gabrielsen 2011; van der Spek, van Leeuwen, and van Zanden 2014; van der Spek and van Leeuwen 2014; Waters 2014: Ch.6; Pirngruber 2017.

45. Polyb. 11.34.15–16.

46. The treasure Antiochus received by the end of his campaign was immense. See Id. 11.34.12. Taylor identifies the importance of the "physical exercise of coercive power over native people and their rulers." Taylor 2013: 85. Sherwin-White and Kuhrt contend that Antiochus' eastern expedition was substantive and important. Sherwin-White and Kuhrt 1993: 190, 200. Although Grainger criticizes Antiochus for the vulnerability of his treaties, he admits that the new sub-kingdoms in the east successfully protected Seleucid lands from the Central Asian tribal confederations. Grainger 2015: 78.

the entirety of Parthia and Bactria, his anabasis was successful in restoring the power and authority of the Seleucid state, initiating what we can call the "Second Seleucid Cycle" of hegemony over the Hellenistic Middle East (200s–160s). It was not until after Antiochus' sudden death in 187 that Seleucid hegemony in the east again declined.[47]

The major long-term shortcoming of Antiochus III's resettlement of the east was that it required continued diligence and, more important, military success by the Seleucids to succeed indefinitely. Renewed internal struggles and the continued western focus of the empire meant that neglect of the east once again created opportunities for the Parthians and Bactrians to challenge Seleucid hegemony. Because of the instability of the Seleucid dynasty and the western focus of its policy, maintenance of imperial power over the Iranian plateau was immensely difficult and continually frustrating.[48]

The volatility of Antiochus III's new network of subordinate allied kingdoms presented subsequent Seleucid kings with a major challenge. With severe limitations to the ability of states and statesmen to enforce agreements short of threats or renewed conflict, alliances in the ancient world were unstable and easily disregarded as power relations rapidly shifted and geopolitical considerations suddenly changed.[49] Moreover, even if an agreement remained in place, once Antiochus or one of his subordinate allies died, the previous arrangement had to be renewed diplomatically or by force.[50] Few of Antiochus' successors shared his diplomatic influence or military capability, and the resilience and proficiency of the Parthians played a fundamental role in undermining the sustainability of Antiochus' model of indirect imperialism in the east in the second century.[51] Since the competence of the Seleucid king in many ways dictated the ability of the state to maintain its hegemony, without a strong and determined central leader, the Seleucid Empire faltered, especially in the east. Once the Parthians and Bactrians recovered their strength or when new leaders emerged in Parthia and Bactria, there was little incentive to submit willingly to the Seleucids, and therefore, a new anabasis was necessary about once a generation to maintain or reestablish Seleucid hegemony in the east.[52] After the power-transition crisis of the 240s–230s, there were six attempted eastern expeditions over the course of a century by five different Seleucid kings: Seleucus II, Antiochus III, Antiochus IV,

47. Grainger 2016.

48. Sampson likely exaggerates the Parthians' fear of the Seleucids after 208, arguing that the Parthians thusly "kept a deliberately low profile." Sampson 2015: 44–45. Rather, the Parthians were militarily and financially exhausted; they had no choice but to keep a low profile.

49. Note Aron 1973: 98–99; Wheeler 2002: 287–88; Eckstein 2006: 1, 12, 20–22, 32, 39; Wheeler 2011: 86.

50. Note Grainger 2017b: Ch. 1.

51. Overtoom 2019a. Strootman associates the transition of Seleucid imperialism in the east with Seleucus II; however, he assumes Seleucus' anabasis was successful. Strootman 2011; id. 2015; id. 2018. Antiochus is a far more likely candidate.

52. Grainger 2015: 80–81; id. 2016: 1–2; id. 2017a: 38–39.

Demetrius II, and Antiochus VII.[53] This clearly demonstrates the strength of the Seleucids' resolve to contest the Parthians and reclaim their lost territories. Yet only one of those campaigns was successful, and it is a testament to Antiochus III's leadership and abilities that he was able to accomplish such a victory.

There was no way for Antiochus III to anticipate the future troubles of the Seleucid state, and he did not have the time or the resources to reoccupy all of Parthia and Bactria, while expanding Seleucid hegemony in the Eastern Mediterranean. He needed to make compromises to protect his extensive eastern frontier, and he hoped the diminished states of Arsaces II and Euthydemus I still could serve as reliable bulwarks against the tribes of the Central Asian steppe. Antiochus was able to reestablish the Seleucid Empire as the dominant power in the Hellenistic Middle East, while shifting the costs of defending the eastern frontier mostly upon the Parthians and Bactrians. Yet by the middle of the second century, civil war, the collapse of Bactria, and the resurgence of Parthia destabilized the favorable balance Antiochus had created in the Iranian interstate system.

A Short-lived Peace and Bactrian Decline

Despite the best intentions of the peace settlement in 206, Antiochus III's invasion of Bactria had weakened the Bactrian state at a time when the threat of nomadic invasions was expanding rapidly. After Antiochus and his army left Bactria, the new Seleucid subordinate ally, Euthydemus I, faced the challenge of reconsolidating his authority over his vulnerable kingdom and securing its ravaged frontiers. It was during Antiochus' siege of Bactra-Zariaspa that Euthydemus possibly lost control of Sogdiana in the north to a rebellion or Central Asian invaders and later had to campaign to recover it.[54] Yet, even with his eventual recovery of Sogdiana, Euthydemus was unable to expand his power into neighboring regions.[55] Euthydemus appears to have spent much of the rest of his reign consolidating his regional power and securing his frontiers as a nominally loyal subordinate ally of the Seleucid Empire.[56]

Euthydemus I had survived the Seleucid invasion and in the aftermath worked hard to stabilize his kingdom; however, by the late 190s, the policy of the Bactrians drastically shifted once more when Euthydemus' son, Demetrius I, became the new king of Bactria.[57] Euthydemus' death nullified

53. Overtoom 2016a; id. 2016d; id. 2019a; id. 2019b; id. 2019c; id 2019/2020; id. 2020. Antiochus III likely was preparing a second anabasis when he died trying to loot the Temple of Bel in Elymais in 187. Grainger 2015: 190–93; id. 2016: 1, 52–53.

54. Widemann 1989: 195–97; Bopearachchi 1991–1992: 1, 12–13; Grainger 2013a: 53–54. Compare Mitchiner 1973: 26–29. Antiochus' attacks on northern cities such as Ai Khanoum likely undermined the integrity of the northern frontier. Lerner 2003–2004: 381–83, 397–99.

55. Will 1962: 107.

56. Lerner 1999: 59–61. Euthydemus perhaps constructed defenses along his northern border. Rapin 2007; Grainger 2013a: 56.

57. The exact year of Euthydemus' death is uncertain, and it could range from 200 to 190. See Narain 1989: Appendix 1. Grainger favors the late 190s for his death. See Grainger 2015: 190.

any agreement made with Antiochus III, and Demetrius saw no need to renew a working relationship with the Seleucids. Like his father, Demetrius was a hugely ambitious man, adopting the epithets "Glorious in Victory" and "Invincible."[58] Antiochus had met Demetrius in Bactria during the siege of Bactra-Zariaspa and liked Demetrius enough to promise him one of his daughters as a bride; however, that match appears never to have materialized, perhaps souring their relationship.[59] Demetrius acted independently and tried to capitalize on the strength his father had been able to recover. He sought to expand the power of his kingdom through an invasion of Arachosia (modern southern Afghanistan and western Pakistan), perhaps in the early 180s.[60]

After signing a treaty with the Bactrians in 206, Antiochus III followed in the footsteps of Alexander the Great and Seleucus I, crossing into India, forging an alliance with the local Indian king, Sophagasenus, and leaving the region with a large amount of tribute.[61] Then on his return to the west in 205, Antiochus secured Seleucid hegemony over Arachosia.[62] Demetrius I's later invasion and occupation of Arachosia early in his reign was a direct challenge to Seleucid hegemony and Antiochus' authority. Demetrius' aggression would have demanded Seleucid retaliation against Bactria once again; however, Antiochus had become bogged down in a hegemonic war against the Romans to control the Eastern Mediterranean.[63]

The Roman defeat of Antiochus III at Magnesia in 189 drastically shaped power relations within the Mediterranean world; however, scholars (even within Parthian studies) still exaggerate its consequences for the Seleucid state as a whole.[64] For example, Philip Matyszak argues that after Magnesia "Seleucid power was irrevocably weakened by defeat" and that "after Magnesia there was little to limit the Parthian state's expansion."[65] Marek Olbrycht states that Magnesia, "followed by the miserable death of Antiochus III in Elymais in 187, marked the end of the Seleukids as a great power."[66] Meanwhile, Leonardo Gregoratti concludes that "after the defeat of Magnesia (190 BC), the Seleucids ceased to constitute a threat to Parthian independence."[67] Yet such conclusions overstate

58. Bopearachchi 1991; Bernard 2004; Holt 2012a: 124; Grainger 2015: 190.

59. Polyb. 11.34.9.

60. Demetrius' coins have been found throughout these regions. Narain 1989: Appendix 2. For Demetrius' occupation of Arachosia, see Schmitt 1986c; Shipley 2000: 283; Holt 2012a: 156–57; Mairs 2013b; Grainger 2015: 190–91.

61. Polyb. 11.34.11–12.

62. Id. 11.34.13.

63. See Eckstein 2012: Ch. 8.

64. Note Coşkun and Engels 2019. For the Battle of Magnesia, see Appian *Syr.* 6.30–36. Note Overtoom 2016b.

65. Matyszak 2008: xvii–xx.

66. Olbrycht 2016b: 459.

67. Gregoratti 2017b: 127.

the decline of the Seleucid state and overlook the great struggle of the Parthians to defeat the Seleucids.[68]

The Treaty of Apamea forged between the Romans and Antiochus III in 188 forced the Seleucids to pay an indemnity and relinquish all territorial rights to the lands beyond the Taurus Mountains.[69] Antiochus' defeat and the loss of Seleucid lands in Anatolia certainly hurt the power and prestige of the Seleucid state in the wider Mediterranean world; however, the power of the Seleucids in the Hellenistic Middle East remained considerable. In fact, Antiochus IV maintained an army of more than 50,000 men in Syria only two decades later, and Antiochus VII led a similarly sized army on an expedition to reclaim the east in the early 120s.[70] Moreover, Anatolia had been a source of constant conflict for the Seleucids and was far less important strategically and financially to the empire than Syria and Mesopotamia.[71] The Treaty of Apamea meant that Antiochus and his successors no longer had to concern themselves with the volatile geopolitical developments in Anatolia and Greece. Instead, the Seleucid kings could focus on their rivalry with Ptolemaic Egypt or the geopolitical developments within the Iranian plateau. After 188, Rome became the leading power in the Mediterranean; however, the Seleucid Empire remained a major player in the geopolitics of the Near East and Middle East for several decades.[72] It was in fact the Parthians, rather than the Romans, who eventually damaged Seleucid power irreparably.[73]

Antiochus III in 188 faced only his second major military setback during his long reign. Similar to his earlier policy after the Battle of Raphia in 217, Antiochus looked to the east to restore his reputation, power, and wealth. Antiochus' advantageous treaty with Ptolemy V remained in place following the Fifth Syrian War (202–195), and his network of subordinate allied kingdoms in the east remained mostly intact. Yet Euthydemus I's death had provided Demetrius I with an opportunity to end the submission of Bactria to the Seleucid Empire and act aggressively to expand his regional power and influence. Antiochus could not allow the

68. Compare also Shipley 2000: 291, 324–25, 386; Gabelko 2009: 52; Howarth 2013: 30; Strootman 2013a: 478; id. 2013b: 6122; Dąbrowa 2014b: 61; Sampson 2015: 22, 27–28, 44–5; Overtoom 2019a; id. 2019b; id. 2019c; Coşkun and Engels 2019.

69. Note Appian *Syr.* 7.37–9.

70. Polyb. 30.25.1–26.9. Antiochus IV even almost conquered Egypt during the Sixth Syrian War (170–168) before the Romans intervened. Polyb. 29.2.1–4, 26.1–2, 27.1–13; Livy 44.19.1–14, 45.11.9–12.8, 23.12; Diod. 31.1.1, 2.1–2; *II Maccabees* 5.1–4; Porph. 49–50; Vell. Pat. 1.10.1–2; Val. Max. 6.4.3. Antiochus VII commanded as many as 80,000 soldiers. Justin 38.10.2; Diod. 34/35.17. Compare Orosius 5.10.8, which records he had 100,000 soldiers, Eus. *Chron.* (Smith ed.): 255, which states he had 120,000 soldiers, and *I Maccabees* 15.13, which claims he commanded 128,000 soldiers.

71. Grainger 2002: 350–51; id. 2015: 188–89.

72. For the establishment of Roman hegemony over the Mediterranean after 188, see Eckstein 2012: Ch. 9. For a recent survey of the Hellenistic Near East, note van der Spek 2007.

73. Overtoom 2016a; id. 2016c; id. 2016d; id. 2017b; id. 2019b; id. 2019c. Some scholars fortunately view the aggression of the Parthians as a more important factor in the decline of the Seleucid state than that of the Romans. Note Gruen 1984: 671; Habicht 1989: 369ff.; Sherwin-White and Kuhrt 1993: 217–29; Grainger 2002: 350–51; Strootman 2004; Nabel 2017a: 25; Strootman 2018: 141.

actions of Demetrius to threaten Seleucid hegemony over the Iranian plateau, and therefore Antiochus' choice of action in 188/187 was simple. Antiochus immediately began preparing for a second anabasis.[74]

As he had done before, Antiochus III left his son and co-ruler, Seleucus, in Antioch to preside over the court and the western territories while he was away in the east. Antiochus then prepared for his eastern expedition in Babylonia in 187, making elaborate ceremonial rituals and sacrifices to emphasize his continued authority at Babylon, Borisippa, and Seleucia.[75] However, unlike his previous anabasis, Antiochus chose to march south through Elymais, in what is modern southwestern Iran, instead of through Media, the more direct route north.[76] He likely chose this alternate route because he needed a large amount of money to fund his new expedition.[77] His previous northward march through Media in 210 had allowed him to loot the Temple of Aene in Ecbatana; however, in 187 Antiochus realized that looting this temple a second time in such a short period would not yield the treasure he required.[78] Instead, Antiochus turned his attention to the large deposit of gold and silver at the Temple of Bel (Baal) in Elymais.

The Greek and Roman sources are highly critical of Antiochus III's actions in Elymais, associating his villainy in attempting to sack the temple with his desperation to pay his debts to the Romans.[79] Yet Antiochus' outstanding debt to the Romans, although sizable, was not unreasonable (1,000 talents annually for a term of twelve years).[80] In fact, Antiochus already had paid an advanced sum of 3,000 talents without issue.[81] The Seleucid Empire remained extensive under Antiochus, generating large amounts of silver and gold annually (for instance, the annual upkeep of the Seleucid army alone was 7,000–8,000 talents).[82] Debt to Rome certainly was a nuisance, but it could not have been the driving force behind Antiochus' decision to pillage the Temple of Bel in Elymais. Rather, the wealth from this temple made another eastern expedition to reinforce the Seleucids' position within the Iranian plateau possible.[83] Instead of viewing

74. Note Taylor 2013: 150; Grainger 2013a: 67; id. 2015: 190–93; id. 2016: 1.

75. See Sachs and Hunger 1989: no. -187A. Compare Sherwin-White and Kuhrt 1993: 216; Grainger 2015: 192.

76. Isidore of Charax in his *Parthian Stations* demonstrates that the northern route through Media was the most common overland trade-route. Isid. 1–19.

77. In marching through Elymais, Antiochus also might have planned to follow a more direct southern approach toward Arachosia through Carmania. Note Polyb. 11.34.13–15. His son, Antiochus IV, perhaps planned to follow a similar route. Note Grainger 2016: 35.

78. Polyb. 10.27.12–13.

79. Justin 32.2.1–2; Diod. 28.3.1, 29.15.1; Strabo 16.1.18. Compare *II Maccabees* 1.13–16.

80. The suggestion that the indemnity was "huge" is exaggerated. Strootman 2013b: 6122. For example, the Romans forced Carthage to pay an indemnity of 10,000 talents after the Second Punic War. Note Hoyos 2003: 179. After ten years Carthage offered to repay the entire debt, which the Romans refused. Livy 36.4.5–9. Even after Magnesia, Antiochus' empire was larger and wealthier than the much-diminished state of Carthage. For sacred plunder and the Seleucids, see Taylor 2014.

81. Appian *Syr.* 7.38–9.

82. Note Grainger 2015: 60–61.

83. The Parthians in the 120s looted 10,000 talents from the temples of Elymais. Strabo 16.1.18.

concern for Rome at the center of Antiochus' decision-making, it seems far more likely that Antiochus eagerly seized another opportunity to undertake an anabasis to enhance his military reputation, recover disputed lands, and forge new alliances. Demetrius I's independence in Bactria and his likely aggression against Arachosia justified Antiochus' expedition, and the recovery of Seleucid hegemony over Bactria and Arachosia was important to the security of the Iranian plateau and the maintenance of Antiochus' alliance network in the east. Unfortunately for the Seleucids, Antiochus' ill-fated attempt to sack the Temple of Bel in Elymais in 187 resulted in his violent death.[84]

Antiochus III's sudden death in Elymais was a shock to the Seleucid state and severely threatened its stability once again. The Seleucids had lost their most capable and charismatic leader since Seleucus I, and Antiochus' son, Seleucus IV, was mostly ineffective.[85] Back in Syria Seleucus immediately canceled his father's plans to campaign in the east as affairs in the Near East dominated his reign.[86]

Once again, the western concerns of the Seleucids took precedence, and the Seleucids never punished Demetrius I for his occupation of Arachosia. This in turn encouraged Demetrius to continue his aggressive policies to maximize his power and security. Furthermore, the sudden vulnerability of the Seleucid state encouraged Armenia and perhaps Elymais and Persis to declare their independence temporarily at this time. John Grainger and Khodadad Rezakhani suggest that these rebellions could have occurred after Magnesia in 189; however, Antiochus III's actions in 188–187 suggest otherwise.[87] It is highly unlikely that Antiochus ignored a rebellion in Armenia before marching east since the submission of Armenia and the establishment of a strong northern frontier had been a major point of emphasis before his first anabasis. He could not have left a rebellious Armenia at his back in 187. Moreover, Antiochus' decision to loot the Temple of Bel in Elymais with only a handful of soldiers indicates that Elymais was not yet in open rebellion. It is more likely that Antiochus' attempt to plunder the temple in 187 pushed Elymais toward rebellion.

Finally, the Parthians also were able to reassert more of their former autonomy. After losing their right to issue independent coinage when they submitted to Antiochus III in 208, the Parthians resumed the minting of their coinage from Hecatompylus in the early 180s.[88] Although Antiochus likely left minor garrisons

84. Justin 32.2.1–2; Diod. 28.3.1, 29.15.1; Strabo 16.1.18.

85. Appian *Syr.* 8.45.

86. It is possible Seleucus stopped making payments of silver to Rome as his father's unfavorable treaty with Rome was no longer valid. Grainger 2015: 193–94; id. 2016: 2. There is little reason to assume Seleucus' effort to tax the Jews heavily late in his reign was an attempt to pay his father's outstanding debt to Rome. See *II Maccabees* 3.2–40, 5.18; Hieron. *Daniel* 11: 20. After the death of Antiochus, the Seleucids ignored multiple components of the Treaty of Apamea, including the restrictions placed upon their navy and elephant corps. Appian *Syr.* 7.38–39, 8.46; Polyb. 31.2.11–15; Diod. 31.27a; Justin 34.3.6–8.

87. For Armenia, see Grainger 2015: 189–90, 193–94; Traina 2017. Compare Strabo 11.14.5. For Elymais and Persis, see Hansman 1998; Wiesehöfer 1994c; Rezakhani 2013: 773, 775; Dąbrowa 2014b; Wiesehöfer 2017.

88. Assar and Bagloo 2006: 25, 33; Assar 2011: 115–16.

in southern Parthia to maintain Seleucid authority in the region, it is possible these garrisons were removed in preparation for the clash with the Romans in Anatolia at Magnesia.[89] The Seleucids seemingly abandoned Hecatompylus by the early 180s, allowing the Parthians to reoccupy the region by the middle of the decade without issue. Therefore, the new coinage likely was an act of defiance to mark the end of the Parthians' submission to Antiochus once he had died.[90]

With Antiochus III's death, the hegemony of the Seleucid Empire that he had established throughout the Iranian interstate system remained in place; however, it was increasingly vulnerable because of the reemerging capabilities of the Parthians and Bactrians and because of Seleucus IV's unwillingness or inability to reassert the position of the Seleucids in the east by force. Moreover, in the 190s–180s, the geopolitical focus of the Bactrians began to shift as a great opportunity for expansion southward presented itself during Demetrius I's reign. For decades the Seleucid Empire and then the Kingdom of Bactria had shared an extensive frontier with the powerful Mauryan Empire of India, and the province of Arachosia had been an area of contention between Macedonian and Indian kings since the invasion of Alexander in 326.[91] Yet by the middle 180s, the Mauryan Empire had crumbled under the pressures of internal chaos and civil war, leaving the empire's former western provinces isolated and vulnerable.[92]

The rapid decline of the Mauryan Empire after the death of Asoka in the late 230s created a power-transition crisis in the separate Indian interstate system.[93] In 206/205 Antiochus III took advantage of the disintegration of Mauryan power, first, by forcing the regional king of Paropamisadai (modern northeastern Afghanistan and northern Pakistan), Sophagasenus, to accept an alliance, supply the Seleucids with war elephants, and offer tribute, and second, by occupying Arachosia.[94] In the early 180s, it is likely Demetrius I seized his own opportunity

89. Sampson argues the removal of these garrisons allowed the Parthians "to rebuild their own forces and re-establish her [Parthia's] independence from Seleucid interference." Sampson 2015: 44–45.

90. Assar and Bagloo suggest that the Parthians minted the new S7 (Figure 4) silver and bronze coinage as a response to Antiochus' failure at Magnesia in 189. Yet their argument that the defiant new coinage was meant to reinforce Arsaces II's rule in Parthia and to assure "the Parthians of no further Seleucid assault on their kingdom" works much better if we accept that the Parthians struck the coinage after receiving news of Antiochus' death in 187. Assar and Bagloo place the minting of the coinage somewhere between 189–185. Thus, the death of Antiochus works within that timeframe. See Assar and Bagloo 2006: 25, 33; Assar 2011: 115–16.

91. Mutinous soldiers halted Alexander's campaign just before he carried his war into what is modern India. Plut. *Alex.* 62.1–3. Compare Arr. *Anab.* 5.25. Seleucus I gave up his Indian expedition in exchange for an alliance and war elephants. Appian *Syr.* 9.55; Strabo 15.2.9. Antiochus III ended his Indian expedition in exchange for a renewed alliance and war elephants. Polyb. 11.34.11–12.

92. For the Mauryan Empire, see Salomon 1998; Mookerji 1999; Singh 2011; Olivelle, Leoshko, and Ray 2012; Thapar 2012; Allen 2012; Zambrini 2017; Beggiora 2017. The Sunga Empire, which was focused further east on the Ganges River, emerged as the new leading power in India after the fall of the Mauryans. For the Sunga Empire, see Olivelle 2006; Singh and Shrivatava 2011; Gupta 2013: 3447–48.

93. Note Overtoom 2016a: 986, 997.

94. Polyb. 11.34.11–12. Grainger argues that Antiochus knew he could occupy Arachosia with impunity because of the Mauryan collapse and that Antiochus perhaps made Sophagasenus hand over Arachosia as part of the treaty they forged. Grainger 2015: 65–66, 72–73. Antiochus' reoccupation of Arachosia seems likely since the Parthians and Bactrians also had to cede territories to Antiochus in recognition of Seleucid hegemony.

to campaign in Paropamisadai and Arachosia.[95] Although Demetrius died soon afterward, the success of his southern expedition encouraged other Bactrian kings to campaign in the Indus River valley. Preoccupation with Indian expeditions and a series of devastating civil wars over the next few decades became the legacy of Demetrius I's reign.

Demetrius I's own campaign in the south helped destabilize his kingdom and allowed a Graeco-Bactrian nobleman, Antimachus I, to usurp the throne of Bactria.[96] The series of civil wars that followed sapped the strength of Bactria and the authority of its kings so greatly that by ca. 180 the newly conquered lands in the south broke away under another usurper, Apollodotus I, to form a rival state known as the Indo-Greek Kingdom.[97] This new kingdom initially had wide-ranging success in India, conquering the Indus River valley and raiding deep into central and eastern India; however, its kings also remained long-standing rivals of the kings of Bactria, and debilitating warfare between them became common.[98] Continual dynastic conflicts and an ongoing rivalry with the Indo-Greek Kingdom gradually turned the attention of the Bactrian kings away from their precarious northern and western borders, and Bactria became increasingly vulnerable to nomadic and Parthian aggression in this chaotic environment.

The recurrent deterioration of the Bactrian state coincided with growing hardships and instability on the Central Asian steppe. In the 170s–160s a nomadic tribal confederation from what is modern Xinjiang in northwestern China known as the Yuezhi lost a series of conflicts with a neighboring tribe, the Hsiung-nu (or Xiongnu), and were forced to migrate to the southwest.[99] In so doing they displaced another tribal confederation known as the Saka, who also chose to migrate to the southwest, descending into Sogdiana.[100] The Saka, seeking security and recognizing the vulnerability of the Bactrians, began to put mounting pressure on the northern frontier of Bactria, and by the end of

95. Note Strabo 11.11.1. Demetrius even celebrated his victory with new coins that depicted him wearing an elephant head cap. Grainger 2013a: 56; id. 2015: 190–91; id. 2016 3.

96. Grainger 2013a: 56. Compare Narain 1989: 399–400; Lerner 2015a: 309.

97. For a brief account of the numerous usurpers and civil wars that followed the death of Demetrius I, see Grainger 2013a: 56–59, 70. There also was a later Indo-Parthian kingdom. Note Bopearachchi 1993; id. 1998b; Bivar 2007; Olbrycht 2017b: 17–18.

98. For the successes of the Indo-Greek kings in India and their rivalry with the Bactrian kings, see Narain 1957; Bopearachchi 1991; id. 1993; Bopearachchi and Rahman 1995; Bopearachchi 1998a; Holt 1999: 135; Bopearachchi 2003; Rtveladze 2011: 149–150; Grainger 2013a: 71–76; Lerner 2013; id. 2015a: 309–11; Stoneman 2019. The Indo-Greek king Menander conducted widespread conquests within India, even reaching Pataliputra (near modern Patna). Strabo 11.11.1; Justin *Prol.* 41.

99. See Mair 2014: 8–15, 23–26, 29, 90, 144, 161–63; Daryaee 2015: 288. For the culture of Xinjiang, see Yong and Binghua 1999. For the Hsiung-nu, see Yü 1990; Ishjamts 1999; Yong and Yutang: 1999; Di Cosmo 2004: Ch. 5; McLaughlin 2016: Ch. 3. For recent reconstructions of Yuezhi history, see Enoki, Koshelenko, and Haidary 1999; Benjamin 2007; Bivar 2009; Rtveladze 2011: 150; Olbrycht 2012b; Lerner 2015a: 311–18; McLaughlin 2016: 27, 41–91, 98–99, 101–2, 179, 188–90, 192–93, 199. The Han emperor Wudi later tried to make an alliance with the Yuezhi to defeat the Hsiung-nu. See Tao 2007: 91–92.

100. See Mair 2014: 17–18, 20, 144. For the Saka, see Puri 1999; Harmatta 1999; Callieri 2016.

the 130s, the Saka and Yuezhi had overrun what remained of the Kingdom of Bactria.[101]

The rapid decline of the Kingdom of Bactria and its final collapse in the 130s helps once again to demonstrate the inherent dangers and harsh realities facing states in the ancient world. Although at times strong and powerful, the Bactrians too often faltered in the face of their rivals in the Hellenistic Middle East and fell victim to mounting internal weakness and external pressures. The Central Asian tribal confederations played an important role in the final destruction of the Kingdom of Bactria; however, the resurgent Parthians, through resilience and determination, emerged as the true beneficiaries of the power void left by the Seleucids and Bactrians on the Iranian plateau.

The Resurgence of the Parthian State

Although Antiochus III's sudden death in 187 threatened to destabilize the Hellenistic Middle East, his prior anabasis had damaged the strength and standing of the Parthians and Bactrians. Arsaces II and Euthydemus I found it difficult to consolidate and expand the power of their diminished kingdoms. The process took several years for both men; however, their successors eagerly built upon their efforts to reassert the autonomy of Parthia and Bactria. While the Bactrians became increasingly concerned with wars in India and nomadic invasions, the Parthians steadily concentrated on rebuilding their power base in northeastern Iran. In the 180s–170s, the Seleucid Empire remained the leading power in the Iranian interstate system; however, numerous distractions in the west and a series of military and political setbacks provided the Parthians with many opportunities to regain and expand their former strength.[102] By the 160s, the Seleucids and Bactrians faced mounting difficulties that helped create another power-transition crisis in the Hellenistic Middle East, and the Parthians, especially under the leadership of Mithridates I, once again emerged as the great beneficiaries of this crisis. It was in this period that the Parthians not only became determined to establish a level of regional security that assured their survival and protection on the Iranian plateau, but also became determined to dominate the entire Hellenistic Middle East.[103] Under Mithridates I and his immediate successors, the

101. Mukherjee 1969a; Posch 1995; Olbrycht 2012b; Ellerbrock and Winkelmann 2012: Ch. 6; Grainger 2013a: 58–59; McLaughlin 2016: 50. Some scholars point to the sudden abandonment of the prosperous town, Ai Khanum, in this period as an indication of Bactria's collapse in the face of growing nomadic incursions. See Lerner 2010; id. 2011; Holt 2012a: 97, 99–112, 124–30, 132–33, 136, 138–43, 148, 154, 156, 164–67, 176–81, 183, 185–93, 195–96, 200, 206, 217, 219; id. 2012b; Grainger 2013a: 59–62; Lerner 2015a: 308–13; Olbrycht 2016c; Callieri 2016. For a recent reconstruction of life at Ai Khanum, see Lecuyot 2007. Compare Bernard 1985; Rapin 1992; Bernard 2008; id. 2011. Some scholars argue that the last Greek king of Bactria, Heliocles I, ruled over the city of Bactra as a tributary vassal of the Yuezhi (ca. 125–90), who did not forcefully annex the region until the middle-first century. See Cribb 2005: 212–14; Lerner 2010; id. 2015a: 313.

102. Note Dąbrowa 1999 [2000]: 9.

103. Overtoom 2016a: 1000; id. 2019a.

Kingdom of Parthia transformed into what international relations theorists call an "unlimited revisionist state."[104] The Parthians were no longer content to share power within the Hellenistic Middle East, and they suddenly and with great energy began to invade and occupy neighboring regions at the direct expense of the Bactrians and Seleucids.

The western distractions of the Seleucid Empire and the crumbling of the Kingdom of Bactria meant that Parthia came to dominate most of the Iranian plateau by the 130s. The Bactrians were too divided and weak to retaliate against the Parthians; however, the Seleucids were not going to surrender their eastern lands without a fight. After the Parthians conquered western Iran and penetrated southern Mesopotamia in the 140s, the Seleucids committed to a major military undertaking against the rising Parthian state in the form of Demetrius II's anabasis. This campaign was a hegemonic war to punish the Parthians and reclaim the lost lands of the east once more for the Seleucid Empire. However, Demetrius was ill-prepared for the power and effectiveness of the Parthian army under Mithridates I. The decisive defeat of Demetrius reinforced the Parthians' rising authority, legitimized their rule over the Iranian plateau, and firmly established a new balance of power between the Seleucids and Parthians within the expanding Iranian interstate system. The Parthians for the first time established an empire that became the most threatening rival of the Seleucids in the Hellenistic Middle East, and this new bipolar rivalry between the Seleucids and Parthians drastically shaped the international environment of the Iranian interstate system for the next several decades.[105]

Recovery

After the anabasis of Antiochus III in the 200s, our knowledge of geopolitical developments in Parthia unfortunately is quite limited until the ascension of Mithridates I to the Parthian throne in ca. 165/164.[106] The battle for Parthia had been a disaster for Arsaces II, and Antiochus' defeat of the Parthians had been more thorough and devastating than his defeat of the Bactrians. The Parthians had lost most of their lands in northeastern Iran in the war, and the position of Arsaces had been damaged severely.[107] For the remainder of his reign, he was a mostly docile ruler of a marginal subordinate kingdom. Although the Parthians took note of the sudden deterioration of Bactrian power to their east, it took over

104. Note Kissinger 1957; Schweller 1994: 93–95, 100, 107; id. 1996: 106–7; id. 1998: 75–89; id. 2015: 8–10.

105. Overtoom 2016a: 1000; id. 2016d: Chs. 2–3; id. 2019a; id. 2019b; id 2019c; id. 2019/2020. Note Assar 2011: 117.

106. For the year of Mithridates' ascension to the throne, see Assar 2004; id. 2005a; id. 2006c; id. 2011: 116; Overtoom 2019a: 121. For the usefulness of Moses of Chorene in reconstructing early Parthian chronology, see Assar 2006b.

107. Sherwin-White and Kuhrt have a minimalist view of Parthian territorial holdings before the second century. Sherwin-White and Kuhrt 1993: 88. However, their conclusions have drawn strong criticism. See Olbrycht 2010a: 233.

a generation for the Parthians to recover militarily from Antiochus' invasion before they once again could expand their territory by force of arms.[108]

In ca. 185, with the death of Arsaces II, a new king of the Parthians, named Phriapatius (Figures 5–8), became Arsaces III.[109] Phriapatius likely was the fraternal grandnephew of Arsaces I and the first cousin once removed of Arsaces II.[110] It is certainly possible that Arsaces II lost his eldest sons in the war against Antiochus III and died before his remaining son was of age, thus transferring the crown to Phriapatius.[111] Yet it is also possible that Arsaces deemed Phriapatius the better and more experienced candidate and selected him as his successor. Phriapatius' eldest son, Phraates I (Figures 10–11), did something similar in ca. 165/164 when he made his brother, Mithridates I, his successor over his own sons.[112] This arrangement between Arsaces II and Phriapatius also perhaps helps explain Phriapatius' choice to name Arsaces' grandson, Arsaces IV (Figure 9), his successor over his own sons.[113]

Once Phriapatius gained the throne, he reigned for fifteen years; however, little literary evidence of his long reign has survived. In replacing Arsaces II, Phriapatius certainly faced similar problems of trying to reconsolidate the authority of the Arsacids and the power of the Parthian state in the continually shifting international environment of the Hellenistic Middle East. Yet the sudden military successes of Phriapatius' successors likely would not have been possible without his efforts to rebuild the kingdom and rehabilitate the image of the king.

Phriapatius' primary concern throughout his reign likely was the restoration of the Parthians' regional power, which international relations theory helps support. The Parthians lived in a dangerous world, where survival was precarious and violence was unavoidable. The much diminished and weakened Parthian state in the 180s was immensely vulnerable to aggression from stronger neighbors, and the Parthians understood the importance of security, strength, and intimidation in international relations, especially within an international environment as hostile and fluid as the Iranian interstate system. Strabo captures the competitiveness, militarism, and aggression of the Parthians from their humble origin to their emergence as a world power, which was a partial consequence of the harsh systemic pressures of the international environment within the Hellenistic Middle

108. Note Justin 41.5.9.

109. For the complicated and much debated reconstruction of the early Arsacid dynasty, see Lerner 1999: 26–28; Assar 2005a; id. 2011: 113–22; Overtoom 2016a; id. 2016d; id. 2019a; id. 2019b; id. 2019c; id. 2019/2020; id. 2020; Faghfoury 2020. Compare Koshelenko 1976: 33–34; Frye 1984: 209; Gardiner-Garden 1987: 15; Wolski 1993: 14, 62–65, 146; id. 1996: 170ff; Lerner 1999: 26–28, 42; Assar 2000; id. 2004; id. 2006c. On Phriapatius, see Karras-Klapproth 1988: 152–53; Assar 2004; id. 2005a; id. 2011: 116.

110. Assar 2005a: 35–36; id. 2011: 116.

111. The early Arsacids did not follow strict primogeniture succession and did not allow minors (those under the age of fifteen) to become king. Id. 2005a: 38; id. 2006c: 88; id. 2006–2007: 12; id. 2011: 116.

112. Justin 41.5.10.

113. Note Assar 2005a: 38; id. 2006c: 88; id. 2006–2007.

East. He states, "Now at the outset Arsaces [I] was weak, being continually at war with those who had been deprived by him of their territory, both he himself and his successors, but later they [the Parthians] grew so strong, always taking the neighboring territory, through successes in warfare, that finally they established themselves as lords of the whole country inside the Euphrates."[114] Consolidation and expansion of power was necessary for state survival in the ancient world, and all ancient states faced similar serious security concerns and threats to their survival within the often grim and unforgiving interstate systems of antiquity. The Parthians in part were a product of this reality; however, they eventually excelled within this dangerous environment, and a major factor in their success was the generally strong leadership of the early Arsacid dynasty.

The focus of Phriapatius' policy was to restore the strength of the Parthian army and the prestige of the Arsacid dynasty. Arsaces I had placed great emphasis on expanding the Parthian military, making the Parthian state a regional power.[115] Yet Arsaces II's unsuccessful campaign against Antiochus III severely damaged the size and capability of the Parthian army.[116]

With the decline of Seleucid power and the sudden death of Antiochus III in the early 180s, Arsaces II recognized an opportunity to reassert some of his former autonomy. The reoccupation of Hecatompylus and the renewal of independent Parthian coinage in this period illustrate the growing momentum within Parthia to restore its full independence.[117] In fact, Phriapatius was the first Parthian king to adopt the epithets "Great King" and "Divine King" on his late coinage (S10.1, S10.15, S10.18–19 [Figures 7–8]).[118] Yet although the Parthians were able to occupy a few neighboring cities abandoned by the Seleucids, no major military operations occurred under Arsaces or Phriapatius.[119]

While Arsaces II's status as a subordinate ally of Antiochus III after 208 helps explain the prolonged inactiveness of the Parthians during the remainder of most of his extensive reign, the uneventfulness of Phriapatius' long reign (ca. 185–170) suggests that the Parthian state had remained relatively weak under Arsaces. Unlike Demetrius I in Bactria, who inherited a strong kingdom from his father, Phriapatius inherited a relatively weak kingdom still suffering from economic and military hardships, and therefore, unlike Demetrius, Phriapatius did not openly challenge Seleucid hegemony by aggressively expanding his kingdom. Instead, the task of conducting major military operations fell to Phriapatius' sons.

114. Strabo 11.9.2.

115. Justin 41.4.8. Note Overtoom 2016a.

116. Polyb. 10.28–31.

117. Assar 2004: 80–82; Assar and Bagloo 2006; Rezakhani 2013: 768.

118. Assar 2011: 116; Rezakhani 2013: 768.

119. The Parthians expanded the mints they were using to produce coinage in this period. This could indicate limited territorial expansion. Assar 2004: 80–82; Sampson 2015: 44–45.

The opportunity and motivation for Phriapatius to expand militarily was considerable during his reign. In the west the Seleucids found themselves fighting yet another round of internal and external conflicts, making Hyrcania and Media vulnerable.[120] Meanwhile, in the east the aggressiveness of Demetrius I's expansions into Arachosia and India, paired with the rising threat of nomadic invasions from the Central Asian steppe, increasingly threatened Phriapatius' small kingdom. Had Arsaces II been able to reestablish the strength of the Parthian state and military, the quietness of Phriapatius' long reign would be highly peculiar, and therefore, the limited resources of the Parthian state in this period likely were the primary obstacle restricting Phriapatius' ability to act aggressively throughout his reign. Thus, Phriapatius' great contributions to Parthian history were his determined domestic policy to restore the power and authority of the kingdom and his royal line (he likely had four sons, Phraates, Mithridates, Bagasis, and Artabanus, three of whom became future Parthian kings).[121]

Phriapatius died in ca. 170, and new epigraphic evidence from Nisa suggests that a previously unknown Parthian king, now known as Arsaces IV, who was the great-grandson of Arsaces I and Phriapatius' second cousin once removed, reigned briefly for two years.[122] Yet Arsaces IV, who appears to have perished suddenly in his early thirties, was an ineffective leader who died without an heir.[123] His death in ca. 168 allowed the Parthian throne to pass to his third cousin, the eldest son of Phriapatius, Phraates I, who became Arsaces V.[124] Phriapatius' policy of strengthening the kingdom and army over a period of fifteen years appears finally to have produced results under the leadership of his eldest son, who became the first king to expand the boundaries of his kingdom outside of Parthia proper since Arsaces I.

Phraates I's reign only lasted three years; however, in that short span he implemented aggressive military expansion against neighboring peoples for the first time in decades, conquering the strong Mardian tribe in the Alborz mountain range.[125] This campaign also reclaimed a large section of Hyrcania for the Parthians, reintroducing a direct threat to the holdings of the Seleucid Empire in Media. It is highly unlikely Phraates could have acted so boldly and enjoyed such sudden military success without the diligent preparations of his father over

120. In 175 a court official named Heliodorus assassinated the mostly ineffective Seleucus IV, which led to Antiochus IV seizing the throne from this usurper and fighting the Sixth Syrian War against Ptolemaic Egypt. Note Appian *Syr.* 8.45–46, 11.66; Porph. 48–49.

121. Assar 2011: 113–19. Compare id. 2005a; id. 2006c. It appears Phriapatius later was deified because his son Mithridates I minted coinage inscribed with "Son of a Divine Father" (S10.17 [Figure 12]). Id. 2011: 118.

122. See id. 2004: 82–87; id. 2005a: 38–41; id. 2006c: 88; id. 2006–2007.

123. Id. 2005a: 38; id. 2006c: 88; id. 2006–2007; id. 2011: 116. Compare Karras-Klapproth 1988: 131–32.

124. Assar utilized numismatics to shift and shorten Phraates' reign from the traditional 176–171 to 168–165/164. See Assar 2005a: 38; id. 2006c: 88; id. 2011: 116. By shortening Phraates' reign, it is even more likely that his military success stemmed from his father's diligent rebuilding of the Parthian army and state.

125. Justin 41.5.9. Compare Isid. 7; Herod. 1.125; Strabo 11.7.1, 8.1, 8.8; Pliny *NH* 6.18.48, 31.134; Curt. 6.5.11–21; Arr. *Anab.* 3.24.1–3. Assar suggest that Phraates perhaps died fighting the Mardians. Assar 2005a: 40.

the course of his fifteen-year reign. The rapid burst of Parthian aggression under Phriapatius' sons demonstrates that the Parthian state finally had recovered from the anabasis of Antiochus III by the 160s. The Parthians once again were ready to take advantage of a chaotic period in the geopolitics of the Hellenistic Middle East and were highly motivated to do so.

Before Phraates I died in ca. 165/164 he named his younger brother, Mithridates I (Arsaces VI), his successor. To do this Phraates set aside several of his adult sons.[126] It is possible that Phraates, fearing his rapidly declining health, left the kingdom in his brother's more capable hands to secure the positive momentum of the dynasty and state. Certainly, Mithridates shared his brother's emphasis on aggressive foreign policy. Yet Phraates also was following the examples of Arsaces II and Phriapatius in appointing a successor who was not his son. Phraates' decision proved critical as Mithridates built off the momentum of his father and brother to raise the Parthian state to new heights of power.[127]

In terms of international relations theory, under the long reign of Mithridates I (ca. 165/164–132) the Parthian state began its transition from a limited revisionist state, looking primarily to maximize its security regionally, to an unlimited revisionist state, looking to replace the current makeup of the Iranian interstate system with its own hegemony.[128] The Parthians became no longer satisfied with regional power and influence on the Iranian plateau, instead becoming increasingly determined to supplant the Bactrians and Seleucids as the leading power in the Hellenistic Middle East.[129] Mithridates' aggressive and capable leadership was at the center of this transition.[130]

Antiochus III's anabasis had devastated the Parthian kingdom. The aggression of the Seleucids, the failures of the Parthian military, and the drastic reversal of Parthian fortunes at the end of the third century served as a warning to the Parthians about the potential threat of neighbors and the need to maximize state power. Justin even emphasizes that the Parthians came to seek vengeance against Seleucid aggression.[131] Although Arsaces II was mostly docile after 208, his reoccupation of southern Parthia and his issuing of new coinage toward the end of his reign helped create the foundation for the restoration of Parthian power and authority. Moreover, his successors pushed the Parthian state in the direction of

126. Justin 41.5.9–10.

127. Olbrycht 2010a: 230.

128. Note Overtoom 2016a: 1000; id. 2019a: 113, 122, 138–39; id. 2019b: 13. Unlimited revisionist states, although more common in antiquity, are rare in world history. Eckstein 2006: 26. For the recently revised chronology of Mithridates' reign, see Assar 2005a: 41–45; id. 2006a; id. 2006c: 88–98; id. 2011: 117; Overtoom 2019a. Compare Grainger 2013a: 72. Sherwin-White and Kuhrt recognized a new "Parthian policy of conquest and expansion" that began to form in the 170s. Sherwin-White and Kuhrt 1993: 197.

129. Justin emphasizes that Mithridates forged an empire that stretched from "Mount Caucasus [in the Hindu Kush] to the river Euphrates" through determined conquest. Justin 41.5.9–6.3, 6–9.

130. Note Overtoom 2019a.

131. Justin 42.1.1.

even more aggressive expansion, first, through the likely efforts of Phriapatius to rebuild the Parthian military and, second, through the renewed conquests of Phraates I.

Mithridates I eventually looked not only to recover the lost lands of Arsaces I's kingdom, but also to establish Parthia as the leading power in the Iranian interstate system. This was a momentous period of Parthian history that demands further attention and consideration.[132] Opportunity, motivation, and capability all aligned for the Parthians as Mithridates settled old scores against Bactria and the Seleucid Empire through hegemonic war.

Mithridates I was a daring and gifted military leader, and like his brother, he wasted little time in capitalizing on the renewed strength of the Parthian military. He completed the reconquest of Hyrcania and then set his sights on the dwindling power of the Kingdom of Bactria. Although Bactria had faced numerous internal and external threats by the 160s, the Bactrian kings had a respected military reputation and the potential strength of Bactria was undeniable. If the Parthians hoped to secure their eastern frontier and surpass the power of the Bactrians on the Iranian plateau, then war was unavoidable. Mithridates wanted to alter the balance of power in Parthia's favor and recognized the immediate vulnerability of the Kingdom of Bactria. Justin records:

> Almost at the same time that Mithridates [I] ascended the throne among the Parthians, Eucratides [I] began to reign among the Bactrians; both of them being great men. However, the fortune of the Parthians, being the more successful, raised them, under this prince [Mithridates], to the highest degree of power; while the Bactrians, harassed with various wars, lost not only their dominions, but also their liberty. For having suffered from contentions with the Sogdians, the Arachosians, the Drancae, the Arei, and the Indians, they were at last overcome, as if exhausted, by the weaker Parthians.[133]

Justin here emphasizes that the Bactrians were the greater power with the greater reputation in the 160s; however, Mithridates and the Parthians were more successful and eventually overcame the Bactrians. We should question Justin's unfair attempt to disparage the Parthians, equating their success to a mixture of luck and Bactrian weakness. Again, Justin continues the long-standing Graeco-Roman literary tradition of recognizing the success of the Parthians, while criticizing their militarism.[134] By robbing the Parthians of their agency in supplanting

132. Mithridates' conquests in the east have gained only limited scholarly attention; see Tarn 1951: 222–3; Masson 1951; Daffinà 1967: 40–82; Mukherjee 1969b; Wolski 1980b; Schippmann 1980: 24; Olbrycht 1998b: 82–105; Assar 2005a: 42; id. 2006c: 88–89; Dąbrowa 2006a; Olbrycht 2010a; Overtoom 2019a.

133. Justin 41.6.1–3. Compare Strabo 15.1.3.

134. Overtoom 2016c; id. 2017a.

the Bactrians as the leading power on the Iranian plateau, Justin here can blame Fortune for the sudden reversal of Bactria's power. Yet this passage from Justin clearly records that the Parthians acted aggressively against the Bactrians in the 160s and that Mithridates was responsible for winning the hegemonic conflict.

Let us consider the war between Parthia and Bactria more closely. In ca. 168, Eucratides I, a former governor under Demetrius I, seized the contested throne of Bactria from another usurper, Antimachus I.[135] In ca. 165, Eucratides added the epithet "Great" to his titulature and coinage, celebrating his efforts to consolidate and expand his kingdom against his Bactrian rivals.[136] The strong position of Eucratides in 165 lends itself to Justin's conclusion that the Bactrians remained a leading power at this time.[137] Yet a series of rebellions, usurpations, and invasions had made Bactria increasingly vulnerable, especially along its western and northern frontiers as Bactrian kings became more distracted with conflicts in the southeast. Civil wars and the budding rivalry with the new Indo-Greek splinter kingdom along the Indus River had damaged the prestige and authority of the Bactrian kings, and Eucratides' tumultuous reign further destabilized the Bactrian monarchy.[138] This chaotic environment provided Mithridates I with a great opportunity to implement aggressive foreign policy and expand his kingdom at the expense of one of the Parthians' great rivals.

Mithridates I conducted a successful war against Bactria by the middle 150s (and perhaps as early as 163/162).[139] The Parthians conquered the western portions of Aria and Margiana in this conflict, significantly expanding their eastern territory and raising their profile within the Hellenistic Middle East.[140] Mithridates even implemented new imperial imagery on his coinage to signify his victory over the Bactrian Greeks.[141] His victory drastically shifted the power balance on the Iranian plateau in Parthia's favor, and Bactria never again emerged as a major actor in the geopolitics of this region.

135. The traditional date of 171 is far from certain, especially if Mithridates' reign is shifted to 165/164. See Wilson and Assar 2007: 24–25. Compare Hollis 1996: 161 n.2–3.

136. Hollis 1996: 161; Bernard 2012.

137. Justin 41.6.1–3.

138. For Eucratides I's reign, see Jakobsson 2009; Holt 2012a: 18, 25, 114, 120; Bernard 2012; Lerner 2015a: 309.

139. Strabo 11.9.2. For the controversy surrounding the dates of Mithridates' invasion of Bactria, see Olbrycht 2010a: 237; Lerner 2017: 11. Assar originally placed the war against Bactria in 163 after the sudden death of Antiochus IV, which seems appropriate. Assar 2005a: 42; id. 2006c: 89. Yet he later oddly placed the campaign around 150. Id. 2011: 117.

140. Mithridates annexed the Bactrian eparchies of Turiva and Aspionus. Strabo 11.9.2, 11.2. For the debated identity and location of these districts, see Tarn 1930: 122–26; Assar 2006c: 89 n.12; Olbrycht 2010a: 234–36; Rtveladze 2011: 149–50; Lerner 2015b: 46, 48–52; Olbrycht 2019b. For the uncertain date and scope of this campaign, see Tarn 1932: 579; Debevoise 1938: 19–20; Junge 1949: 1975–79; Jenkins 1951: 15–17; Bivar 1983: 33; Sherwin-White and Kuhrt 1993: 84; Torday 1997: 350–51; Dąbrowa 2006a: 38; Assar 2005a: 42; id. 2006a: 2; id. 2006c: 89; Olbrycht 2010a: 232–38; Assar 2011: 117; Lerner 2015b; Olbrycht 2019b; Overtoom 2019a: 127–28. For Aria, see Schmitt 1986d.

141. Lerner 2017.

The sudden strength and aggression of the Parthians surprised and overwhelmed Eucratides I, who agreed to peace with Mithridates I and perhaps even became a Parthian vassal.[142] After the Parthians conquered large portions of Aria and Margiana, both sides found peace attractive for several reasons. For Eucratides, first, rebellion and civil war always threatened his position in Bactria. He could not afford to continue the damaging conflict with the Parthians for fear of losing ground to other usurpers. Second, Eucratides recognized the power of the Parthians and the abilities of Mithridates. He preferred to concentrate on wars against his Indo-Greek rivals to help enhance his prestige and power. In fact, after conceding the western lands of his kingdom to Parthia and agreeing to a treaty with Mithridates, Eucratides invaded India, where he proved successful in a series of battles until his son assassinated him.[143] Finally, Eucratides' kingdom had considerable security concerns along its extensive frontiers. Eucratides could not afford to fight a multiple-front war. By conceding western lands that were already difficult for him to control, Eucratides gained Mithridates as an ally and forced the Parthians to undertake a greater responsibility in protecting the Iranian plateau from nomadic incursions.[144]

Meanwhile for the Parthians, first, the peace settlement with Eucratides I allowed Mithridates I to expand his kingdom to the Arius River with little cost to the Parthian state. The wealthy lands of Aria and Margiana were a great addition to the strength and wealth of his kingdom. Second, Mithridates' conquest of these lands was a great boon to his prestige. Mithridates' occupation of Margiana in particular had clear propagandistic value. Despite Arsaces I's success in securing Parthia and Hyrcania, the founder of the Arsacid dynasty had failed to conquer Margiana from the Bactrians.[145] Mithridates' success avenged that defeat and established Mithridates as one of the great warrior kings of the Parthians. In fact, Justin makes this comparison, stating, "Being then taken ill, he [Mithridates] died in an honorable old age, and not inferior in merit to his great-grandfather [really his great-granduncle] Arsaces [I]."[146] Third, the total conquest and occupation of Bactria in the late 160s and early 150s would have been difficult and time-consuming for the Parthians because of the political chaos of Bactria and the growing threat of nomadic incursions into the region. The peace with Eucratides left the Kingdom of Bactria responsible for defending the most vulnerable section of the northern boundary with the Central Asian

142. Olbrycht 2010a: 236–37; Grainger 2013a: 72. Lerner argues Eucratides "swore an oath of fidelity," but suggests Mithridates' victory was minor. Lerner 2015b: 52; id. 2017: 11.

143. Justin 41.6.4–5; Strabo 15.1.3. Note Jakobsson 2009; Olbrycht 2010a: 231–32.

144. Sections of the Kingdom of Bactria, most notably Aria, rebelled against Eucratides' rule. See Olbrycht 2010a: 234.

145. Hennig 1944: 222–23; Wolski 1947: 26–31; id. 1969: 253–54; id. 1974: 159ff; Robert 1984: 467–82; Lerner 1999: 13–14, 29. Note Strabo 11.9.3; Justin 41.4.9.

146. Justin 41.6.9. Note Assar 2005a: 55; id. 2006–2007: 12.

steppe. Finally, with the defeat of Bactria, Parthia had established itself as the new leading regional power. Parthia too was vulnerable to wars on multiple fronts so a favorable peace and alliance with Bactria in the east was crucial to Mithridates' growing western ambitions.[147]

With the threat of a two-front war minimized, the Parthians could focus on their retaliation against the still mighty Seleucid Empire. Although Seleucid interests in the Eastern Mediterranean began to give way to the authority of the Romans in the 180s, in the Hellenistic Middle East the Seleucid Empire remained the major power for decades and exercised considerable power and influence. The Parthians still had much to fear from Seleucid aggression as the Seleucids were determined to maintain their hegemony in the east throughout the second century. Antiochus III had died in 187 while preparing for a second anabasis.[148] Then in early 165, Antiochus' youngest son, Antiochus IV, began his own abortive eastern expedition.[149]

Although Antiochus IV was in the middle of suppressing the Maccabean Revolt in Judaea, the sudden and violent disturbances of the Parthians in the east diverted Antiochus' attention. The fifth book of *Maccabees* records:

> And it was told to king Antiochus [IV] what Mattathias and his son Judas had done. News of this [that is, the growing momentum of the Maccabean Revolt] came also to the king of the Persians [that is, the king of the Parthians]; so that he [likely Phraates I] played false with Antiochus, departing from his friendship, following the example of Judas. Which giving Antiochus a great deal of uneasiness, he called to him one of his household officers named Lysias, a stout and brave man, and said to him, "I have now determined to go into the land of Persia [that is, Parthia] to make war; and I wish to leave behind me my son [Antiochus V] in my stead; and to take with me half of my army, and to leave the remainder with my son."[150]

147. See Olbrycht 2010a: 232. Compare Wolski 1980b; Lerouge-Cohen 2007: 215–23. Lerner's dismissive statement that these conquests "amounted to little more than a Pyrrhic victory" is unconvincing. Lerner 2015b: 52.

148. Diod. 28.3.1, 29.15.1; Strabo 16.1.18; Justin 32.2.1–2.

149. Jos. *Ant.* 12.293. Note *I Maccabees* 3.31–32, 6.1–5; *II Maccabees* 1.12–16, 9.1–4; *IV Maccabees* 18.5; *V Maccabees* 3.3, 7.18, 8.1. For Antiochus IV, see Hoffmann 1873; Mørkholm 1966; Sherwin-White and Kuhrt 1993: 218f.; Mittag 2006; Bing and Sievers 2011; Taylor 2013: Ch. 10; Mittag 2013; Feyel and Graslin-Thomé 2014; Grainger 2016: Chs. 1–2. For Antiochus' planned anabasis, see Habicht 1989: 351; Grainger 1997: 24–25; Assar 2005a: 39; Olbrycht 2010a: 231; Assar 2011: 116; Taylor 2013: 163; Mittag 2013; Coloru 2014; Martinez-Sève 2014; Plischke 2014: 291–95; Grainger 2016: 32–35, 52–3.

150. *V Maccabees* 7.10–13. Note *I Maccabees* 1–6; *II Maccabees* 3–10. For recent studies of the Maccabean Revolt, see Grainger 2012; Doran 2016; Avemarie et al. 2017. Although a controversial work extant only in Arabic, *V Maccabees* offers a chronicle of Jewish history from the early second century to 6 BCE that possibly draws upon lost accounts by Jason of Cyrene, Justus of Tiberias, and most likely Nicolaus of Damascus. See Charlesworth 1981: 153–56. We should continue to approach *V Maccabees* with caution; however, it is worth considering the accounts of *V Maccabees* in comparison with our other available sources to help broaden our understanding of these events.

Meanwhile, Tacitus states, "King Antiochus [IV] endeavored to abolish Jewish superstition and to introduce Greek civilization; the war with the Parthians, however, prevented his improving this basest of peoples; for it was exactly at that time that Arsaces had revolted (*desciverat*)."[151] These accounts illustrate that Antiochus left his western territories hastily to pursue a war against the Parthians in the east late in his reign. However, the exact context of Antiochus' anabasis is debated, and some scholars reject Tacitus' comment as an error because of his use of the name "Arsaces." Scholars, beginning with Clifford Moore, have accused Tacitus, first, of not knowing that Arsaces I seized Parthia in the middle of the third century and, second, of confusing the actions of Arsaces I here with the Maccabean Revolt.[152] Yet there is good reason to reject such criticisms. Nothing about Tacitus' comment definitively connects this "Arsaces" to Arsaces I. In fact, the Romans knew that all Parthian kings regardless of their original name took the name Arsaces upon their ascension as a royal title, much like the Romans used the titles Caesar and Augustus.[153] It is far more likely that Tacitus here simply refers to the reigning Parthian king by his regal name, Arsaces, and therefore we must consider, first, who was the Parthian king in 165 and, second, what this man had done to gain the full attention of Antiochus IV.[154]

The traditional date for the accession of Mithridates I is ca. 171, which would mean Antiochus IV conducted his anabasis to challenge Mithridates' rising ambitions in the east; however, evidence that Mithridates became king in 171 is inconclusive. Instead, Gholamreza Assar recently has made a convincing argument to shift the beginning of Mithridates' reign forward to ca. 165/164 and to alter Phraates I's reign to ca. 168–165/164.[155] Therefore, Mithridates' older brother, Phraates, could have been king when Antiochus began his anabasis. In fact, the passages from *V Maccabees* and Tacitus provide further evidence for this new chronology. In *V Maccabees* the Parthian king betrayed Antiochus' "friendship," and Tacitus claims the Parthians had "revolted." These depictions make far more sense if we associate them with Phraates instead of Mithridates.[156]

The passages in *V Maccabees* and Tacitus perhaps illustrate that Arsaces II, Phriapatius, Arsaces IV, and Phraates I had renewed terms of friendship with Seleucus IV and Antiochus IV before 165. Although the Parthians reclaimed Hecatompylus and the surrounding countryside in the early 180s after it was abandoned by the Seleucids, it is possible that Seleucus, who wished to abandon

151. Tac. *Hist.* 5.8.

152. See Moore 1931 (2005): 188–89; Marcus 1943: 153; Wellesley 1964: 284; Chilver and Townend 1985: 94. Note Assar 2005a: 39.

153. Justin 41.5.8; Dio 40.14.3; Amm. Mar. 23.6.5–6. Note Dąbrowa 2016b.

154. Justin 41.5.1–6; Strabo 15.1.36.

155. Assar 2005a: 38–45; id. 2006c: 88–89; id. 2011: 116. Compare id. 2004; id. 2006a; Wilson and Assar 2007: 24–25.

156. Assar 2005a: 39–40; id. 2006c: 88–89; Overtoom 2019a: 121–24.

his father's eastern expedition and secure his position in the west, and then Antiochus IV, who had a kingdom to consolidate and a war to fight in Egypt, agreed to recognize the new holdings of the Parthians and the heightened autonomy of the Arsacids to avoid a costly eastern war.[157] Moreover, even with the recovery of Hecatompylus and the surrounding countryside, the relative weakness and vulnerability of the Parthians in the 180s–160s helps explain why Arsaces II and his immediate successors would have agreed to and upheld a renewal of friendship to secure their heightened standing in the region and protect their expanded lands in northeastern Iran from possible Seleucid retaliation. Yet after a long period of general peace, the Parthians acted with aggressive force against the interests of the Seleucids in early 165 when Phraates I attacked the Mardians and began to reoccupy Hyrcania, once again directly threatening Media.[158] With the attack against Hyrcania taking place while the Seleucids were occupied in Judaea, Phraates' actions were perhaps even a deliberate exploitation of the Seleucids' overtaxed logistical and military commitments.

The sudden western expansion of Phraates I was a blatant violation of the long-standing status quo between the Parthians and Seleucids.[159] Thus, Phraates likely altered the relationship of the Parthians and Seleucids drastically, not Mithridates I, finally casting off "friendly" relations and violently "rebelling" against Seleucid suzerainty. The sudden belligerence and success of Phraates concerned Antiochus IV and demanded a rapid Seleucid response as Parthian aggression destabilized the Iranian plateau and directly threatened the important lands of Media. With half of the Seleucid military, Antiochus undertook a major retaliatory campaign aimed to punish the Parthians and restore Seleucid hegemony over the east.[160]

Antiochus IV closely followed the example of his father, Antiochus III, in preparing his anabasis. First, he organized his large army, placed trusted officials in charge of his western lands, and protected the position of his young son, Antiochus V.[161] Second, he secured his northern frontier by subduing Armenia.[162] Finally, he sought out a great sum of money to support his eastern expedition.

In need of money to finance a major eastern expedition and perhaps motivated by a desire to avenge the violent death of his father, Antiochus IV chose to attempt to plunder a temple in Elymais.[163] His assault also faced stiff resistance

157. Note Assar 2004: 80–82; Assar and Bagloo 2006: 25, 33; Assar 2011: 115–16; Sampson 2015: 44–45.

158. Justin 41.5.9. Note Gregoratti 2014b.

159. Phraates' attack on the Mardians perhaps was part of a larger Parthian strategy to conquer Media, see Assar 2006c: 89; Olbrycht 2010a: 230.

160. Antiochus had considerable economic and military resources at his disposal that he used to strengthen the Seleucid Empire. See Olbrycht 2010a: 231. Compare Sherwin-White and Kuhrt 1993: 57; Mittag 2006; Coşkun and Engels 2019. For the argument that Antiochus also used his anabasis as an opportunity to subdue Armenia, Media, and Persis, see Shayegan 2011: 161–65.

161. Appian *Syr.* 8.45; *V Maccabees* 7.10–13. Note *I Maccabees* 3.27–37.

162. Diod. 31.17a; Appian *Syr.* 8.45, 11.66; Porph. 38, 55–56.

163. Polyb. 31.9; Jos. *Ant.* 12.354–59; Appian *Syr.* 11.66; *II Maccabees* 9.1–3; Porph. 56.

from the Elymaeans and ended in abysmal failure. Antiochus did not die in the attack like his father; however, his failure in Elymais derailed his eastern expedition. He lacked the money and no longer had the men to attack the Parthians immediately. Although the cause is much debated in the sources, Antiochus suddenly died, likely from disease, near Gabae (modern Isfahan, Iran) in late 164 while trying to salvage his eastern campaign.[164]

With the sudden death of Antiochus IV in the east, the Seleucid throne passed to his nine-year-old son, Antiochus V, whose short reign (164–161) was dominated by conflict, political intrigue, and Roman influence.[165] The boy's regent, Lysias, had far too many concerns in the west to follow up on Antiochus IV's plans to subdue the Parthians. Thus, the burgeoning Parthian state avoided a major invasion that likely would have severely jeopardized its newly reacquired independence, and this respite from Seleucid retaliation allowed Mithridates I to pursue his aggressive foreign policy and military operations throughout the Iranian plateau. The collapse of the Seleucid government after the unexpected death of Antiochus IV exactly fits the theory of "power-transition crisis," where one pillar of the interstate system suddenly weakens (while another expands in power).

The Parthians took the news of Antiochus IV's anabasis seriously, fully appreciating the potential threat that the Seleucid Empire posed to their survival. Phraates I's reoccupation of Hyrcania had motivated Antiochus to march east, and when Phraates was dying in 165/164, he chose his experienced brother Mithridates I to succeed him. Justin records, "[Phraates] died not long after [conquering the Mardians], leaving several sons, whom he set aside, and left the throne, in preference, to his brother Mithridates, a man of extraordinary ability, thinking that more was due to the name of king than to that of father, and that he ought to consult the interests of his country rather than those of his children."[166] Thus, Phraates made a calculated decision to protect the interests of his kingdom, and he passed over his sons to choose his capable brother as his successor at least in part because of the imminent threat that Antiochus' anabasis posed to Parthia in 165/164.[167] Phraates understood that the security and power of Parthia depended on the maintenance of dynastic stability and strong leadership. He also understood that Parthia could not afford to put forth another inexperienced king,

164. Polybius states Antiochus died in Persia from madness. Polyb. 31.9. Josephus records that Antiochus died of anxiety and grief in Babylon. Jos. *Ant.* 12.354–9. Note *I Maccabees* 6.1–16; Porph. 56. Appian states Antiochus died of disease. Appian *Syr.* 11.66. Note *II Maccabees* 9.5–28. See Dąbrowa 1999 [2000]: 9; Assar 2005a: 41–42. The Hellenistic King List and the Babylonian *Astronomical Diaries* record that word of Antiochus' death and his body traveled quickly to Mesopotamia, making it highly unlikely that Antiochus died in Babylon. Id. 41 n.79–80. Note Sachs and Wiseman 1954: 204, 208; Sachs and Hunger 1996: no. -164B, no. -163C1.

165. Appian *Syr.* 8.46–47; Jos. *Ant.* 12.360–61.

166. Justin 41.5.9–10.

167. Assar 2005a: 41; id. 2011: 116. Assar also puts forth the argument that the Parthian Council (noted in Strabo 11.9.3) might have elected Mithridates as king. Id. 2006c: 89.

such as Arsaces II, to fight the Seleucids. Mithridates' proven military ability and experience made him a good match for Antiochus and secured him the throne. Yet as Mithridates consolidated his brothers' gains in Hyrcania and prepared his army to resist the Seleucid invasion, Antiochus suddenly died, and his anabasis ended abruptly.

The sudden death of Antiochus IV and the rapid expansion of Parthian power under Phraates I and Mithridates I drastically changed the geopolitical situation in the Hellenistic Middle East. With Antiochus dead, Mithridates was free to direct his military resources elsewhere, namely against Bactria. Meanwhile, chaos once again enveloped the Seleucid Empire in the west as Roman meddling, the usurpation of Demetrius I, the murders of Antiochus V and Lysias, and a series of subsequent civil wars severely sapped the strength and standing of the Seleucids.[168] A second, more devastating power-transition crisis emerged in the Hellenistic Middle East.

Much like the power-transition crisis of the 240s–230s that followed the setbacks of Antiochus II's reign, the power-transition crisis of the 160s–130s that followed the setbacks of Antiochus IV's reign provided the Parthians with an immense opportunity to expand their strength and standing drastically at the direct expense of the damaged and distracted Seleucid Empire.[169] Moreover, much like the rebellions of Andragoras in Parthia and Diodotus I in Bactria during the power-transition crisis of the 240s–230s, the power-transition crisis of the 160s–130s afforded satraps in Media, Elymais, Persis, and Characene the opportunity to rebel. As the Seleucid Empire once again began to fragment, Mithridates I established Parthia as the undisputed power on the Iranian plateau and the leading rival of the Seleucids within the expanding Iranian interstate system.

A New Crisis

After becoming king in 175, Antiochus IV appointed his close friend Timarchus to the major command of viceroy over the Upper Satrapies.[170] While Antiochus fought the Ptolemies and Jews in the west, Timarchus was the chief official in charge of maintaining the strength and influence of the Seleucids in the east. From his headquarters in Media, Timarchus witnessed the sudden aggression of Phraates I as he attacked the Mardians and began to reoccupy Hyrcania. In fact, it is likely that Timarchus was the official who sent urgent word to Antiochus in Judaea, stressing the seriousness of the Parthian threat.[171] As one of Antiochus' closest friends and most powerful advisors, Timarchus' warning would have

168. Rome took advantage of the weak position of Antiochus V and forced him to destroy the Seleucids' navy and elephant corps. See Appian *Syr.* 8.45–47; Polyb. 31.2.11–15; Diod. 31.27a; Justin 34.3.6–8. Note Grainger 2016: Chs. 2–4. Antiochus IV's death also caused chaos in Babylonia. Note Finkel, van der Spek, Pirngruber 2020c.

169. See Overtoom 2016a; id. 2019a.

170. Appian *Syr.* 8.45; Diod. 31.27a.

171. *V Maccabees* 7.10–13.

carried considerable weight and helps explain Antiochus' swift response to the deteriorating situation in the east. Although Antiochus likely marched his army from Judaea through Syria, Armenia, Babylonia, Elymais, and finally to Persis before his sudden death, he also appears to have included Media in his plans for attacking the Parthians and likely had been in communication with Timarchus during the campaign.[172] It is possible that Antiochus' strategy was to attack Parthia from two directions, attempting to trap the smaller, more mobile Parthian army between two forces. Yet it is also possible that Antiochus wanted to secure his position in Elymais and Persis before consolidating his forces in Media and invading Parthia en masse. The objective of the campaign was grand, but the result was debilitating. Antiochus' sudden death in 164 swiftly ended his plans of eastern conquest, left the Parthians unmolested, and isolated Timarchus.

With Antiochus IV dead, the boy king Antiochus V was not capable of maintaining his position or managing the kingdom. His father's advisors, Lysias, Philip, Timarchus, and Heracleides, and Antiochus V's twenty-two-year-old cousin Demetrius all vied for power and influence within the wavering empire. Much like the eastern satraps Andragoras, Diodotus, Molon, and Alexander before him, without a strong central authority to help protect the eastern lands of the empire and with mounting pressures threatening the security of his lands, Timarchus soon decided to declare independence from his position of power in Media. Another series of civil wars threatened to fracture the Seleucid state.

In terms of international relations theory, the rapid deterioration of Bactria under the strain of rebellions and civil war, the sudden aggression of Parthia, and the turmoil that followed the death of Antiochus IV caused another power-transition crisis in the Hellenistic Middle East.[173] This crisis, which lasted from the late 160s to the early 130s, facilitated extensive Parthian conquests, expanding the bounds of the Iranian interstate system and causing it to overlap with the lands of the Near Eastern interstate system for the first time. By the late 160s, the rapidly shifting geopolitical situation in the Hellenistic Middle East had helped foster a dangerous international environment of heightened uncertainty and anxiety between polities. In particular the sudden resurgence of the Parthians in the Iranian interstate system drastically altered power relations. Widespread conflict and rapid change facilitated and perpetuated the power-transition crisis of the 160s–130s as the hegemony of the Seleucids fractured temporarily into a multipolar system of numerous competing polities. The systemic pressures of the interstate anarchy within the Iranian interstate system (for example, heightened

172. For his movement through Mesopotamia, note Monerie 2019. Before dying Antiochus commanded one of his companions, Philip, to act as a guardian of his young son. Philip was to deliver the regalia of the king to Antiochus V, and he was to return to the young king the second half of the royal army that had accompanied Antiochus IV to the east. Philip's new command included royal forces stationed in Persia and Media. Jos. *Ant.* 12.360–61; *I Maccabees* 6.55–6.

173. See Overtoom 2019a.

militarism, uncertain power capabilities, lack of security, and fear of destruction) encouraged aggression and open conflict between numerous states and statesmen during the crisis to eliminate potential threats and to establish a new, more reliable distribution of power throughout the Hellenistic Middle East. The hostile and unstable international environment of the Hellenistic Middle East during the power-transition crisis of the 160s–130s helped encourage the aggressive foreign policies of several leaders, including Eucratides I in Bactria, Timarchus in Media, and Mithridates I in Parthia.

Timarchus had spent over a decade in Media consolidating his power and wealth; however, the sudden death of Antiochus IV left him in a vulnerable position. Timarchus had no ability to influence Antiochus' young son, Antiochus V, who was under the control of the royal advisor Lysias in Syria. When Antiochus V's cousin, Demetrius I, escaped from his captivity at Rome, executed Antiochus V and Lysias, and seized the Seleucid throne in 162/161, Timarchus was unable to intervene and unwilling to accept this usurper, declaring himself king in Media soon afterward.[174] Timarchus quickly raised "an army of considerable size" and forged a military alliance against Demetrius with King Artaxias I of Armenia, who had taken advantage of the crisis to reassert his independence.[175]

Timarchus utilized his large army and new alliance to rapidly expand his territory outside of Media. Diodorus states, "Having, moreover, intimidated the neighboring peoples by an impressive display of force, and brought many of them under his sway, he marched against Zeugma [on the Euphrates], and eventually gained control of the kingdom."[176] Although Diodorus exaggerates Timarchus' success in the war against Demetrius I, Timarchus began to call himself "Great King" and possibly gained control of Media Atropatene and Elymais before occupying Babylonia in 161/160.[177]

Scholars continue to debate the actions of the Parthians during this Seleucid civil war. The crisis eventually encouraged the Parthians to invade Media; however, it is unclear if Mithridates I attacked Media before Timarchus marched west to fight Demetrius I. Recently, Marek Olbrycht has argued that Timarchus probably repulsed Parthian attacks in the late 160s, which allowed him to secure his eastern frontier before invading Babylonia.[178] Meanwhile, John Grainger suggests that Timarchus and Mithridates made an agreement that limited Parthian expansion westward.[179] Finally, Michael Taylor claims that Timarchus "scored a major

174. See Appian *Syr.* 8.45–47; Polyb. 31.11–15; *I Maccabees* 7.1. Timarchus had many supporters at Rome. Diodorus states, "by launching many accusations against Demetrius, [Timarchus] persuaded the senate to enact the following decree concerning him: 'To Timarchus, because of . . . to be their king.'" Diod. 31.27a. Thus, it appears the Romans supported Timarchus' bid for power.

175. Diod. 31.27a.

176. Ibid.

177. Olbrycht 2010a: 232. Compare Plischke 2017.

178. Olbrycht 2010a: 232.

179. Grainger 2013a: 129–30.

victory over the Parthians and used this victory to proclaim himself king."[180] Yet there simply is no evidence that directly links Timarchus to a conflict or a treaty with the Parthians.

To connect Timarchus to the Parthians, scholars have cited a passage from Justin, which states, "During the course of these proceedings among the Bactrians [that is, the Indian wars of Eucratides I], a war arose between the Parthians and Medes, and after fortune on each side had been some time fluctuating, victory at length fell to the Parthians. Mithridates [I], enforced with this addition to his power, appointed Bagasis over Media, while he himself marched into Hyrcania."[181] Justin here illustrates that there was a long struggle for Media; however, Justin plainly states that this conflict did not occur until Eucratides had invaded India, which most likely occurred after Mithridates' successful war against the Bactrians in the late 160s or early 150s.[182] Moreover, after invading Babylonia in 161, Timarchus' reign was short. Demetrius I occupied Babylonia and Media soon after his defeat of Timarchus in 160.[183] Therefore, the available window for a conflict between Timarchus and the Parthians is extremely small.

The evidence does not support Taylor's assertion that Timarchus decisively defeated the Parthians and used that victory to declare himself king. In fact, Diodorus demonstrates clearly that Timarchus declared himself king in direct opposition to the usurpation of Demetrius I in 162/161.[184] Meanwhile, Grainger's conclusion that Timarchus would not have been able to rebel in Media if the Parthians had been free to attack him ignores that Andragoras *and* Diodotus had done exactly that in the face of the aggression of the Parni under Arsaces I in the 240s and that Molon and Alexander had declared their independence and campaigned in the west, just like Timarchus, in the 220s without first subduing the Parthians to their east.[185] Instead, the collapse of Seleucid authority after Antiochus IV's death and the growing power of Mithridates I were the exact reasons for Timarchus' rebellion.[186] Moreover, there also is little reason to accept Grainger's suggestion that Timarchus and Mithridates forged a treaty.

Timarchus had been the strong ally of Antiochus IV, who had threatened to attack and punish the Parthians in 164. Yet Demetrius I's usurpation of Antiochus V's throne encouraged Timarchus to declare his kingship and necessitated a civil war. Timarchus was hostile toward the Parthians; however, he could not afford to attack Parthia in 162/161 before dealing with Demetrius in the west. Meanwhile,

180. Taylor 2013: 155.

181. Justin 41.6.6–7. For the convincing argument that Bagasis (or Bacasis) was Mithridates' brother, see Del Monte 1997: 55–57; Assar 2005a: 48; id. 2006c: 89; Olbrycht 2010a: 239; Assar 2011: 117; Shayegan 2011: 72–73.

182. Overtoom 2019a: 127–28.

183. Demetrius killed Timarchus in Babylonia and gained the epithet *Soter* ("Savior") from the Babylonians. Appian *Syr.* 8.47; Diod. 31.27a; Justin *Prol.* 34.

184. Diod. 31.27a.

185. Note Overtoom 2016a.

186. Id. 2019a: 129.

Mithridates I had little reason to befriend the hostile Timarchus or, more important, to limit his own western military ambitions willingly. A favorable treaty between Timarchus and Mithridates was plausible only after a decisive engagement, for which no evidence exists.

Despite the assumptions of recent scholars, it seems highly unlikely that Timarchus clashed with the Parthians in the late 160s. If Timarchus declared himself king in 162/161, he would have needed time to organize his army, forge his alliance with Armenia, and consolidate his power over his immediate neighbors before invading Babylonia in 161/160. Meanwhile, Mithridates I was not ignorant of the considerable power Timarchus wielded in Media even after the death of Antiochus IV. Timarchus had spent over a decade strengthening the defenses of Media, and his diligent efforts of course help explain why it later took the Parthians so long to subdue the region. Timarchus was one of the most powerful men in the Hellenistic Middle East in the late 160s, and he used this strong position to frighten and coerce his regional rivals.[187] In fact, the Parthians likely were one of the neighboring peoples whom Timarchus intimidated with his impressive display of force early in his reign.

In the late 160s, the Parthians remained a minor power just beginning to reemerge from decades of recovery. After consolidating the recent territorial gains of his brother, Mithridates I readied for the defense of Hyrcania and Parthia in 165/164.[188] The failure of Antiochus IV's anabasis saved Parthia from invasion; however, Timarchus' position in Media remained strong. Mithridates simply did not have the resources in 163/162 to invade Media, and the unraveling crisis within the Seleucid Empire encouraged Timarchus to remain cautious in Media.[189]

Timarchus and Mithridates I found themselves in a stalemate. Neither leader could hope to overwhelm the other without first securing more resources, so they turned their attentions to other targets. Timarchus became involved in the Seleucid civil war in the west, and Mithridates quickly turned his attention to the vulnerable frontier of Bactria. By the time Mithridates completed his war against Eucratides I and occupied large sections of Aria and Margiana, he did not have time to organize and conduct major operations against Media before Timarchus' occupation of Babylonia in 161 and his death in 160. Thus, the long and difficult campaign of Mithridates to conquer Media most likely did not occur until the 150s.[190]

Even though Timarchus and Mithridates I did not go to war in the late 160s, large-scale conflict between the Parthians and Seleucids became increasingly

187. Diod. 31.27a.
188. The Parthians had begun to expand west of the Caspian Gates at this time. Note Olbrycht 2010a: 239.
189. Overtoom 2019a: 130.
190. Note id. 130-34.

likely as the Hellenistic Middle East descended into the power-transition crisis of the 160s–130s. The eastern lands of the Seleucid Empire became vulnerable to the rising power of the Parthians, and the renewed aggression of the Parthians on the Iranian plateau demanded Seleucid retaliation. It was in this period that a new phase of hegemonic warfare between the Parthians and Seleucids began to determine the new balance of power in the Iranian interstate system as the Parthians gradually strove to replace Seleucid hegemony and dominate the Hellenistic Middle East.[191]

By the end of the 160s, the Parthians controlled Parthia, Hyrcania, Aria, and Margiana, adding significantly to their logistical and financial capabilities. With new resources and a stronger eastern frontier, Mithridates I was in a better position to challenge the Seleucids in the west. Western expansion into Media, Persia, and Mesopotamia offered major political and financial incentives for the Parthians; however, the conquest and occupation of these regions proved immensely difficult as the Seleucids and regional dynasts challenged Parthia's rising hegemony frequently.

With the defeat and death of Timarchus in 160, Demetrius I regained control of Babylonia and Media, restoring the integrity of the empire at least temporarily. Demetrius' success in this civil war led Grainger to suggest recently that Mithridates I waited ten years to attack Media after Timarchus' defeat because "the Seleukid state under Demetrios I was strong enough to deter any adventure by the Parthian King."[192] However, this stance is too dismissive of the evidence and exaggerates Demetrius' position in the 150s. Although Demetrius was able to overcome Timarchus, his control over the empire was fragile and western concerns dominated his attention.

Demetrius I had poor relations with the Romans after his escape from captivity, which his success in seizing power in Syria did not alleviate.[193] In 160 Demetrius placed generals in charge of the defense of his eastern satrapies and immediately returned to the west, where he sent considerable gifts to the Romans to appease their anger.[194] Yet the gifts did little to satisfy the Romans, and when Demetrius attempted to intervene in Cappadocia in 159, the Romans quickly overruled his decision.[195] Justin states, "Demetrius, having possessed himself of the throne of Syria, and thinking that peace might be dangerous in the unsettled state of his affairs, resolved to enlarge the borders of his kingdom, and increase his power, by

191. The aggression of Arsaces I and of Phraates I had been limited to regional objectives for regional power and security. Id. 2016a. Note Justin 41.4.6–9, 5.1–5, 9–10.

192. Grainger 2013a: 130.

193. Appian *Syr.* 8.45–47; Polyb. 31.11–15; *I Maccabees* 7.1.

194. Demetrius sent a crown valued at 10,000 pieces of gold and offered to turn over the man who had murdered the Roman ambassador, Octavius, in Syria. Appian *Syr.* 8.47; Diod. 31.29–30.

195. Demetrius wanted to replace King Ariarathes V with the king's brother, Orophernes II, in exchange for a payment of 1,000 talents; however, the Romans determined both brothers should reign together. Appian *Syr.* 8.47; Justin 35.1.1–2; id. *Prol.* 34; Polyb. 32.10, 33.6; Diod. 31.31–32b.

making war upon his neighbors."[196] Justin illustrates that Demetrius recognized his vulnerable position, and it is not surprising that he chose to act aggressively to expand his security and power against a weak neighboring state. Yet Demetrius was unable to invade Cappadocia or install a puppet ruler because of the severe limitations of his power and influence within the Roman-dominated Mediterranean interstate system.[197] The Romans' decision to protect Cappadocia was meant to reassert their hegemony at the direct expense of Demetrius' regime, and the situation in Cappadocia was an embarrassment for Demetrius that called into question his strength and legitimacy, severely limiting his effectiveness in the 150s.

After the fiasco in Cappadocia, the capital city of Antioch rebelled against Demetrius I's rule, eventually leading to Alexander Balas openly challenging Demetrius for the Seleucid throne in 152.[198] Despite the weak claim to the throne of Alexander, Demetrius continued to mismanage his affairs, and Alexander eventually gained the support of the Jews and Ptolemaic Egypt in the civil war.[199] Demetrius was unable to repeat his success against Timarchus and died in battle against Alexander in 150.[200]

Thus, Demetrius I spent his entire tumultuous reign (162–150) suppressing revolts, fighting rivals to his throne, and trying to reconsolidate the power of the empire. He had every reason and desire to act aggressively against neighboring states, which included Parthia; however, he lacked the capability to do so. Justin tells us that Mithridates I's conquest of Media was a long affair with multiple setbacks, and Moses of Chorene indicates that Mithridates fought Demetrius' forces during this struggle before later fighting Demetrius' son.[201] Demetrius was never strong enough to "deter" the Parthians from attacking Media. In fact, his ineffectiveness and vulnerability encouraged the Parthians to attack his isolated generals in the east.

Grainger's recent conclusions, first, that Mithridates I did not attack Media until after Alexander Balas became king in 150 to avoid Demetrius I's power, second, that Mithridates justified his attack against Alexander because he was a Seleucid usurper, and third, that Mithridates hoped to revive Achaemenid legitimacy under the Arsacid dynasty are not tenable.[202] There simply is no convincing

196. Justin 35.1.1.

197. Note Eckstein 2006: Ch. 6; id. 2012: Ch. 9.

198. Justin 35.1.3–11. Timarchus' brother, Heracleides, aided Alexander in his bid for power, as did King Attalus II of Pergamum. Polyb. 33.15.1; Diod. 31.32a.

199. *I Maccabees* 10.1, 21, 46–47, 51–58; Appian *Syr.* 11.67.

200. Justin 35.1.9–2.2; *I Maccabees* 10.48–50; Jos. *Ant.* 13.116–19.

201. Justin 41.6.6; Moses 2.2. Note Assar 2005a: 42. For the Parthians in Moses of Chorene, see Hackl, Jacobs, and Weber 2010c: 402–55.

202. Grainger 2013a: 130, 136; id. 2016: 68–70, 77–78. Recently, Assar also oddly associated Mithridates' invasion of Media with "the lethargic and unpopular reign of the Seleukid usurper Alexander I Balas." Assar 2011: 117. Contra id. 2005a: 42; id. 2006c: 89. For the inadequate "unit-attribute" explanation that Parthian success stemmed from their eager "restoration" of the image of the Achaemenid Persian Empire championed by Wolski, see Wolski 1966; id. 1976a; id. 1983a; id. 1985a; id. 1993. Note Overtoom 2016d: 5–12.

evidence to support such conclusions. Demetrius' regime was vulnerable, the Arsacids were not yet intimately concerned with the dynastic politics of the Seleucids, and the Parthians' interest in an Achaemenid revival for their imperial propaganda arguably did not develop until their much later conflict with imperial Rome.[203] Instead, Mithridates began his campaign to conquer Media and Media Atropatene as early as 158 and no later than 155.[204] Mithridates did not need to justify his aggression against the Seleucids in Media along strong ideological or propagandistic lines; rather, he had far more compelling practical concerns, such as the expansion of his power against a vulnerable rival.

Although the western affairs of the empire during the crisis demanded Demetrius I's attention, the Parthians found the conquest of Media slow and difficult because of a determined resistance by various Seleucid generals made possible in part by the prior efforts of Timarchus to establish the region as a military stronghold. Mithridates I likely subjugated Media Atropatene as a tributary kingdom in the north; however, the strong defensive positions of the Seleucids in the south and their successful counterattacks turned the campaign into a war of attrition.[205] An unfinished Greek-Aramaic inscription on a carving of Heracles Triumphant at the Bisitun Pass in what is western Iran today, dated 148, gives us a good indication of the back-and-forth Seleucid and Parthian contest during the long conquest of Media.[206] The inscription asks for the safety of Cleomenes, the Seleucid viceroy of the Upper Satrapies in Media at the time.[207] The association of the inscription with Heracles Triumphant perhaps indicates that Cleomenes had won a victory against the Parthians as late as 148, signifying one of the many reversals of the Parthians' fortunes during this conflict mentioned by Justin.[208] The inscription also illustrates that the Seleucids still occupied parts of Media in 148 and that the permanent Parthian conquest of the region was not complete until after this date.[209] Mithridates marked his final annexation of Media by making his brother the new satrap of the region in ca. 147 and by issuing a series of commemorative coins.[210]

203. See Shayegan 2011: 244, 330–31; id. 2017.

204. Note Assar 2006c: 89; Olbrycht 2010a: 238–40; Overtoom 2019a: 131–34. Demetrius' failure in Cappadocia perhaps helped encourage Mithridates to act aggressively in Media.

205. See Marquart 1901: 109; Koshelenko 1966: 56; Assar 2006c: 142 n.172; Olbrycht 2010a: 239–40.

206. For recent evaluations of the political and propagandistic value of this carving and several other ancient Iranian rock reliefs, see Canepa 2014a; id. 2015.

207. Robert 1963: 76; id. 1967: 283, 291; Bivar 1983: 33.

208. See Grainger 2013a: 130; Callieri and Chaverdi 2013: 693.

209. Assar 2005a: 42. For the argument that the Seleucids had lost eastern Media to the Parthians by 148, see Le Rider 1965: 338ff; Schippman 1980: 24; Bivar 1983: 33; Frye 1984: 210; Olbrycht 2010a: 238; Assar 2011: 117. Compare Ehling 2008: 182–83.

210. Justin 41.6.7; Moses 1.8, 2.68. See Daryaee 2015: 286. A Median nobleman perhaps married his daughter Rīnnu to Mithridates after the Parthians had expelled the Seleucids from the region. The Parthians controlled all of Media no later than 145. Assar 2005a: 42–43. Mithridates issued a series of silver obols (S12.4–5 [Figure 16]) and copper coins (S12.13, S12.17–18, and S12.23–24) in Ecbatana. Id. 2006c: 89–90. For monetary production in Media under the Parthians, note Boillet 2016. For an introduction to the cultural developments in Media under the Seleucids and Parthians, see Callieri and Chaverdi 2013: 691–95.

The continued aggression of the Parthians and an ongoing series of Seleucid civil wars perpetuated the power-transition crisis of the 160s–130s in the Hellenistic Middle East.[211] Although Alexander Balas killed Demetrius I in battle in 150, his rule similarly was vulnerable and dominated by western concerns.[212] Alexander had been a usurper of questionable lineage, and his efforts to gain legitimacy through a marriage alliance with Ptolemaic Egypt ultimately failed.[213] Further, his generals in the east, although they continued to frustrate Mithridates I's advances in Media, were unable to eliminate the threat of the Parthians to the eastern lands of the empire.[214] In 147, as Media finally fell to the Parthians, Demetrius' eldest son, Demetrius II, arrived in Syria with the support of Ptolemy VI to contest Alexander's throne, and the Seleucid Empire again descended into civil war.[215]

In 145, Demetrius II and Ptolemy VI defeated Alexander Balas decisively in battle and secured his assassination.[216] Yet although Demetrius won the war, Media was lost, and he had to hand over control of Coele-Syria to Ptolemaic Egypt in exchange for Ptolemy's military support and a marriage to his daughter, Cleopatra Thea. Further, dynastic strife, ineffective administration, and poor military leadership plagued Demetrius' regime.[217] Demetrius quickly found that the growing factionalism of the Seleucid state presented him with numerous potential rivals and several unhappy communities. Widespread unrest in Syria encouraged the general Diodotus Tryphon to make a bid for power as the guardian of Alexander's young son, Antiochus VI, and the Seleucid Empire descended into an even longer, more difficult civil war from 145 to 138.[218]

The power, prestige, and influence of the Seleucids was in jeopardy, and to make matters worse, Rome, Ptolemaic Egypt, and Parthia were not the only concerns of the Seleucids during the crisis. In the 160s, Elymais and Persis in southern Iran appear to have followed the examples of Parthia, Bactria, Armenia, and Media, asserting their local autonomy and briefly breaking away from the

211. Overtoom 2019a: 134–36.

212. Justin 35.1.9–2.2; *I Maccabees* 10.48–50; Jos. *Ant.* 13.116–19.

213. *I Maccabees* 10.51–58; Diod. 32.9c.

214. Cleomenes, the Seleucid general who left the inscription to Heracles Triumphant at the Bisitun Pass in 148, would have been a trusted general of Alexander. Note Canepa 2014a; id. 2015.

215. *I Maccabees* 10.67–68, 11.1–12; Jos. *Ant.* 13.116–19; Diod. 32.9c–d. Note Grainger 2013a: Ch. 7; id. 2016: Ch. 5.

216. *I Maccabees* 11.14–17; Jos. *Ant.* 13.116–19; Diod. 32.9c–d, 10.1; Justin 35.2.2–4.

217. Justin calls Demetrius spoiled and lazy. Justin 36.1.1. Diodorus also calls him cruel and hated. Diod. 33.4, 4a, 9.

218. Note Grainger 2016: Ch. 6. Tryphon proclaimed himself king in early 140, killing Antiochus VI soon after. See *I Maccabees* 11.39–40, 54–56, 12.39, 13.31–32; Diod. 33.4a, 28, 28a; Appian *Syr.* 11.68; Justin 36.1.7; Orosius 5.4.18. For another tradition that maintains that Antiochus VI died of illness due to surgery, see Jos. *Ant.* 13.218; Livy *Epit.* 55.11. This likely was propaganda from Tryphon's camp to remove the taint of regicide. Tryphon perhaps did not kill Antiochus VI until the middle of 138. Shayegan 2003 [2007]: 88–90. Antiochus VI was at least alive until early 140, see Sachs and Hunger 1996: no. -143A.

Seleucid Empire.[219] Then in the 140s the mounting troubles of the Seleucid state allowed Elymais and Persis to assert their independence once again.[220] Meanwhile, Characene, which controlled the Euphrates and Tigris delta, also actively began asserting its autonomy in this period (ca. 141).[221] Moreover, the vulnerability of the Seleucid state encouraged Arab raids to begin penetrating the southern frontier.[222]

Yet the Parthians had emerged suddenly as the most pressing threat to the survival of the Seleucid state. The decline of Seleucid hegemony and the rapid rise of conflict throughout the Hellenistic Middle East during the crisis created a power vacuum that the Parthians eagerly began to fill.[223] Mithridates I's conquest of Media, although difficult, and his control over the passes of the Zagros Mountains were crucial to further Parthian expansion to the west and south. Moreover, control of Media also gave the Parthians direct access to the important breeding grounds of the famous Nisaean horses of the Medes.[224] The Parthian military increasingly required large numbers of quality horses (especially for their cataphracts) and, although there is no evidence to suggest that the Parthians targeted this region strictly to gain direct access to this resource, control of these breeding grounds would have strengthened the Parthian military.[225] Media quickly became a center of Parthian power and wealth, and as the crisis continued to unfold, Mithridates began to target the wealthy, urbanized, and vulnerable lands of Mesopotamia in the late 140s.[226]

Unfortunately, our sources for this period of Mithridates I's reign are vague and often at odds in the reconstruction of events. Justin records that Mithridates returned to Hyrcania after finalizing his conquest of Media, later returning to the west to conquer Elymais and then Mesopotamia.[227] Yet a fragment of the Babylonian *Astronomical Diaries* states that Mithridates conquered Babylonia by the summer 141 and then returned to Hyrcania, before marching to conquer Elymais.[228]

219. See Shayegan 2011: 155–76; Grainger 2013a: 130–31, 136–37. Compare Le Rider 1965: 347; Harmatta 1981: 189–217. It is possible that Persis ruled itself autonomously throughout much of the first half of the second century. The rulers of Persis intermittently dominated the region of the Persian Gulf, briefly occupying Characene and conducting a mass killing of 3,000 Greeks. See Callieri 1998; id. 2003; Wiesehöfer 2007a; Callieri 2007: 115–46; Curtis 2010; Olbrycht 2010a: 229–30; Wiesehöfer 2011; Shayegan 2011: 155–65, 168–87; Wiesehöfer 2012; Callieri and Chaverdi 2013: 691; Wiesehöfer 2013a; Rezakhani 2013: 775; Grainger 2015: 76; Strootman 2017.

220. For recent accounts of the history of Elymais in this period, see Assar 2004–2005: 27–91; Dąbrowa 2005; Shayegan 2011: 62, 65–67, 77–83, 85, 88–104, 107–8, 114, 116–18, 122, 131, 156, 164, 183–87, 204–5, 207, 324–25; Rezakhani 2013: 772–74; Plischke 2014: 287–90. For Persis, see Shayegan 2011: 155–59, 161, 168–82; Rezakhani 2013: 775–77; Engels 2018.

221. For Characene, see Schuol 2000; Wiesehöfer 2007a; Hansman 2011; Gregoratti 2011b; Shayegan 2011: 82–85, 101, 110–16, 114, 120, 152, 156–57, 160–61, 165–68, 171, 176–77, 183–86. For the Arabs, see id. 120, 205–6.

222. Sachs and Hunger 1996: no. -145. Note Grainger 2013a: 80.

223. Overtoom 2019a: 134–46.

224. Assar 2006c: 120.

225. Note Hauser 2006; Burris-Davis 2014; Olbrycht 2016a; Overtoom 2017b.

226. Assar 2006c: 89; Olbrycht 2010a: 230, 238–40; Shayegan 2011: 74; Callieri and Chaverdi 2013: 691–95; Boillet 2016.

227. Justin 41.6.7–8.

228. See Sachs and Hunger 1996: no. -140A, no. -140C. Note Shayegan 2003 [2007]: 84; Dąbrowa 2005; Assar 2006c: 93; id. 2011: 117; Dąbrowa 2014b: 61–63; Olbrycht 2017b: 10. For an introduction to cultural developments

The difficult Parthian conquest and occupation of Media was complete by the end of 147; however, consolidating Parthian control over the region took several more years to accomplish. While Mithridates I and his brother, Bagasis, began the challenging work of strengthening Parthia's new western frontier, Mithridates had to monitor developments in the east closely.[229] Mithridates likely returned to the east in 145 in response to two new threats. First, the Bactrian king Eucratides I died in 145 at the hands of his son.[230] Therefore, Mithridates needed to return east to make sure that the new king of Bactria (there were three possible competing candidates: Heliocles I, Eucratides II, and Platon) had no intentions to act aggressively toward him.[231] Second, and more important, the Kingdom of Bactria was beginning to crumble under the mounting pressures of the invasions of the Saka and Yuezhi.[232] In particular the wealthy and prosperous northern city Ai Khanoum likely fell to these invaders in ca. 146/145.[233] Bactria had always been a key bulwark against the tribal confederations of this region; however, as the Bactrians sapped their strength with dynastic conflicts and wars in India and as the violent displacement of the Yuezhi initiated a widespread migratory period for both them and the Saka toward Sogdiana, the Bactrians increasingly were unable to defend their northern and eastern frontiers. With Eucratides I dead and his kingdom rapidly deteriorating, Mithridates could not ignore the growing vulnerability of Parthia's eastern frontier. Since becoming king in 165/164, Mithridates had quadrupled the size of the Parthian state and had made Parthia the leading power on the Iranian plateau; however, the Parthians' hegemony in the east remained vulnerable. From 147–141 Mithridates worked diligently to consolidate and secure the expanded frontiers of the Parthian state, also perhaps subduing tribes in southeastern Iran and southwestern Pakistan while he was in the east.[234]

Mithridates I's continued efforts to strengthen and protect his eastern frontier were successful, at least temporarily; however, the wealthy lands of Mesopotamia, Elymais, and Persis remained tempting targets along the Parthians' extensive western frontier. In 141 Mithridates decided to risk the stability of his eastern frontier to strike at the heart of the Seleucid Empire. Late that spring he invaded

in Elymais under the Seleucids and Parthians, see Callieri and Chaverdi 2013: 695–98. Compare Potts 1999. For the Parthians in Babylonia, note Dąbrowa 1998; id. 2005; id. 2005 [2006]; id. 2006; id. 2006–2007 [2008]; id. 2008 [2009]; id. 2011; Clancier 2012; id. 2014.

229. Justin 41.6.6–7.

230. Id. 41.6.5. Note Holt 2012b; Lerner 2015b: 52; id. 2017: 11.

231. Heliocles perhaps is the most likely candidate. Lerner 2013: 1014; id. 2015b: 48.

232. Olbrycht 2012b; Grainger 2013a: 137, 170; Lerner 2015a: 311–13.

233. Bernard 1985: 97–105; Rapin 1992: 292; Holt 1999: 25 *et passim*; id. 2012b. Contra Narain 2003: 421, 292 n.159; Lerner 2010: 69–72; id. 2011.

234. Note Orosius 5.4.16; Diod. 33.18; Strabo 15.2.11. Orosius claims that Mithridates' kingdom stretched from the Hydaspes River in Media to the Indus River. Orosius 5.4.18. For the Parthians in Orosius, see Hackl, Jacobs, and Weber 2010b: 294–300. The Hydaspes River that Orosius mentions is the river identified by Virgil in Media. See Virg. *Geog.* 4.211. Compare Bivar 1983: 35; Dąbrowa 2005; Assar 2011: 117. For the argument that the bounds of the Parthian state eventually reached the mouth of the Indus River in Sind, see Daffinà 1967: 41–43; Olbrycht 2019b. For Bagasis in Media, note Shayegan 2011: 74.

and occupied Babylonia, which the Seleucids had mostly abandoned during the ongoing civil war between Demetrius II and Diodotus Tryphon in Syria, and Mithridates entered the symbolically powerful cities of Seleucia and Babylon as a triumphant conqueror, appointing commanders of Greek descent to maximize support in the region.[235]

It is also likely that Persis fell under Parthian control at this time.[236] Mithridates I's strategy could have been to organize his forces in Media, perhaps near Ecbatana, and then to strike rapidly in a two-pronged expedition. He clearly led the main Parthian force to conquer Babylonia; however, a trusted general, perhaps Bagasis, seemingly subdued Persis. These conquests expanded the bounds of the Iranian interstate system further west across the vast lands of Mesopotamia and eastern Syria, which had been a part of the separate Near Eastern interstate system since the 180s, creating for the first time what international relations theorist call "system overlap" between the separate Iranian and Near Eastern interstate systems. Although the Seleucids continued to contest Parthian hegemony in Mesopotamia for decades, this region was now firmly established within the bounds of the expanding Iranian interstate system, and control of Mesopotamia was another significant step in the rapid growth of Parthia as an unlimited revisionist state within that interstate system.[237]

The campaign in 141 was Mithridates I's most aggressive and direct challenge to the deteriorating hegemony of the Seleucid Empire in the Hellenistic Middle East. The Parthians' control of the royal capital of Seleucus I was a glaring representation of their new position of power. In fact, control of Media, Persis, and Babylonia made Parthia far more than just a regional power, and the occupation of Babylonia's great cities provided the Parthians with great prestige and immense wealth. Mithridates immediately struck a new series of silver tetradrachms (S13.1–2 [Figure 14]) in Seleucia on the Tigris, in which he adopted the epithet "Admirer of the Greeks," to commemorate his victory and appease the large Greek population in the area.[238]

With their conquests of Babylonia and Persis, which had been the administrative centers of the Achaemenids, Alexander the Great, and Seleucus I, the Parthians for the first time could claim to be the hegemonic rivals of the Seleucids. Moreover, the power-transition crisis of the 160s–130s had provided Mithridates

235. Mithridates appointed Antiochus, son of King Ar'abuzana, as his high commander with Nikanor serving as one of Antiochus' subordinates. Sachs and Hunger 1996: no. -140A, no. -140B, no. -140C, no. -140D; Shayegan 2003 [2007]: 84; Sartre 2005: 25; Assar 2005a: 43–44; id. 2006c: 90–91; Olbrycht 2010a: 240; Grainger 2016: 82–83. Note Orosius 5.4.16; Moses 2.2. The Parthians later placed other high commanders of Greek descent in charge of operations in Mesopotamia, such as Philinus and Theodosius. Sachs and Hunger 1996: no. -137C, no. -137E, no. -136B, no. -134B, no. -133B/C, no. -132A, no. -132B, no. -129A2, no. -124A.

236. See Alram 1986a: 162–63; id. 1987: 128; Wiesehöfer 1994a: 113, 118, 129; id. 2007a: 44–45; Shayegan 2011: 169; Wiesehöfer 2013a; Strootman 2017. Note Pliny *NH* 6.28.111; Strabo 15.3.3, 24. For an introduction to cultural developments in Persis under the Seleucids and Parthians, see Callieri and Chaverdi 2013: 698–709.

237. Note Overtoom 2019a: 138.

238. Assar 2006c: 91.

I with an immense opportunity to transform Parthia from a minor kingdom into an imperial power. The success of the Parthians and the threat they posed to the Seleucids assured further conflict between the two powers. The Seleucids could not let the aggression of the Parthians and, in particular, the loss of Babylonia, go unanswered, and the Parthians, who continued to expand westward for another half-century, had no intentions to limit their western ambitions to this region as the rising hegemon in the expanding Iranian interstate system and as a newly formed unlimited revisionist state.[239]

Although further major conflict between the two leading powers of the Hellenistic Middle East was on the horizon, the Seleucids and Parthians had several other concerns threatening their security in this period. After the occupation of Babylonia in 141, the Babylonian *Astronomical Diaries* record that Mithridates I again abruptly returned to the east.[240] Mithridates' immediate return to the Iranian plateau helps illustrate that, first, the conquests of Babylonia and Persis in 141 had been aggressive and opportunistic and, second, the eastern frontier continued to be in jeopardy. Gholamreza Assar, utilizing a passage from Strabo, even suggests that Mithridates returned to the east at this time to counter steppe invaders.[241] Although we have no definitive evidence of military encounters between the Parthians and the Saka at this time, Mithridates understood the considerable threat of the encroaching nomadic warriors and believed that his eastern lands were vulnerable.[242]

Mithridates I's decision to return to the east also illustrates that he did not anticipate the immediate challenges the Parthians faced to their occupation of Babylonia. The Babylonian *Astronomical Diaries* record that almost immediately following his departure from the region the recently independent Elymaeans invaded and began ravaging the territory, forcing Mithridates to return.[243] The Elymaeans even burned Apamea on the Tigris before Mithridates and his generals counterattacked toward their capital, Susa.[244]

The power-transition crisis of the 160s–130s threw Mesopotamia into chaos with the region changing hands on no fewer than eleven occasions in this period (Timarchus in 161–160, Demetrius I in 160, Alexander Balas ca. 150, Demetrius

239. Justin 38.3.1, 41.6.8–42.1.1, 2.3–6; Strabo 11.14.15, 14.5.2; Appian *Syr.* 8.48; Jos. *Ant.* 13.369–71, 384–86. Note Overtoom 2019a: 136–46.

240. See Sachs and Hunger 1996: no. -140C.

241. Assar 2005a: 43; id. 2006c: 91. Note Strabo 11.9.2. Although he is right to reject Tarn's argument that Mithridates returned to Hyrcania to invade Bactria, Jenkins' assumption that Mithridates was doing nothing more than returning to his royal headquarters in Hyrcania likely is too dismissive. Jenkins 1951: 15–16.

242. Grainger's conclusion that the Parthians' invasion of Mesopotamia would not have been possible without the collapse of Bactria under nomadic pressures is unconvincing. Grainger 2013a: 183–84. Mithridates had already defeated Bactria, severely limiting the threat that the Bactrians posed to Parthia's eastern frontier. In fact, the collapse of Bactria made Parthia's eastern frontier far more vulnerable because of the heighten nomadic threat that came with it. Overtoom 2019a; id. 2019b; id. 2019c; id. 2019/2020.

243. Sachs and Hunger 1996: no. -140C.

244. Ibid. See Dąbrowa 2014b: 63.

II ca. 145, the Parthians in 141, the Elymaeans in 141/140, the Parthians in 140, Demetrius II in 139/138, the Parthians in 138, the Elymaeans in 138/137, and the Parthians in 137).[245] Rebellions, raids, and a series of invasions destabilized and devastated the region, creating opportunity and incentive for further violence. The Parthians recognized the troubled state of Babylonia and the surrounding territories, conducting aggressive conquests.

Even though his chronology of events is confused, Justin records that Mithridates I defeated the Elymaeans and conquered Elymais.[246] Yet the Parthians' conquest of Elymais also was quite complicated. While the Parthians attempted to counter the advances of the Elymaeans, it is possible that the Seleucid usurper Diodotus Tryphon tried unsuccessfully to reestablish Seleucid control over Babylonia in 140.[247] Moreover, although Mithridates seized Susa and issued a series of bronze coins (S12.26–28) from its mint in 140–138, Rahim Shayegan recently has demonstrated that Elymais and Parthia had an ongoing conflict over Mesopotamia and the region around Susa until the Parthians finally forced Elymais to recognize Parthian suzerainty in 132 and accept Parthian direct rule in 124.[248]

For several years prior to the conflict with Parthia, Elymais had acted independently of the Seleucid Empire. In 147 in reaction to the destructive civil war between Demetrius II and Alexander Balas, the rulers of Elymais had declared themselves kings and began raiding Babylonia for the next fifteen years.[249] Thus, Elymais was one of many states within the expanding Iranian interstate system taking advantage of the decline of Seleucid hegemony during the power-transition crisis of the 160s–130s, pursuing power-maximizing policies to increase state security and authority. Much like Bactria, Parthia, and Media before them, Elymais and the other middling and minor states in the Hellenistic Middle East, such as Media Atropatene, Persis, Characene, and Armenia, chafed under Seleucid suzerainty in the first half of the second century. These states desired to rule themselves autonomously; however, until the sudden deterioration of Seleucid power, beginning in the late 160s and continuing into the 130s, they did not have the capabilities to resist Seleucid retaliation.[250]

245. Appian *Syr.* 8.47; Diod. 31.27a; Justin 36.1.4–5, 41.6.8; id. *Prol.* 34; Sachs and Hunger 1996: no. -140C, no. -140D, no. -137B, no. -137C, no. -137D. Note Shayegan 2011: 79–80; Dąbrowa 2014b: 63.

246. Justin states that the Parthians conquered Elymais before conquering Babylonia. Justin 41.6.8.

247. Shayegan 2011: 67. Compare Dąbrowa 2006a.

248. For the prolonged Parthian conflict with Elymais, see Sachs and Hunger 1996: no. -140C, no. -140D, no. -137D; Assar 2006c: 91–93; Shayegan 2011: 96–98. For the expansionistic aggression of Elymais, see id. 62–65, 67, 77–98. Note Sachs and Hunger 1996: no. -144. For the Kamnaskirid dynasty and their rule over Elymais in this period, see Shayegan 2011: 88–101, 103, 105–10, 183–87, 325; Dąbrowa 2014b. Note Strabo 15.3.12, 16.1.18.

249. Le Rider 1965: 340, 351; Dąbrowa 2014b: 61–63.

250. Note Marquart 1901: 109; Le Rider 1965: 347; Koshelenko 1966: 56; Harmatta 1981: 189–217; Callieri 1998; Schuol 2000; Callieri 2003; Assar 2004–2005: 27–91; Dąbrowa 2005; Assar 2006c: 89, 142 n.172; Wiesehöfer 2007a; Callieri 2007: 115–46; Curtis 2010; Olbrycht 2010a: 229–30, 232, 238–40; Wiesehöfer 2011; Shayegan 2011: 62, 65–67, 77–85, 88–104, 107–8, 110–18, 120, 122, 131, 152, 155–87, 204–7, 324–25; Wiesehöfer 2012; Callieri and Chaverdi 2013: 691; Wiesehöfer 2013a; Rezakhani 2013: 772–77; Grainger 2013a: 130–31, 136–37; Plischke 2014: 287–90; Grainger 2015: 76; Sampson 2015: 44–45; Grainger 2016: Chs. 4–6.

The temporary independence of these middling and minor states during the crisis and their aggressive efforts to secure their own power and safety further destabilized the international environment. In an unforgiving system of interstate anarchy like the Iranian interstate system in the 160s–130s, minor states needed to be highly militarized and bellicose to survive. Thus, it is not surprising that smaller powers, such as the Hasmonean Kingdom, Commagene, Cappadocia, Armenia, Elymais, Characene, Persis, Media Atropatene, Bactria, the Indo-Greek Kingdom, various Arab and Central Asian tribes, and especially Parthia, all emphasized aggressive militarism against neighboring powers in this period of crisis. Parthia under the leadership of Mithridates I emerged from the crisis as the most successful of these competing polities, and the Parthians' rapid hegemonic rise as an unlimited revisionist state within the expanding Iranian interstate system further threatened these middling and minor states, encouraging them to act even more violently to acquire state security.[251] The fracturing of Seleucid hegemony in the middle second century meant that the Seleucids and Parthians not only had to reckon with one another, but they also had to contend with several highly militarized, expansionistic middling and minor states in this period.

It was in this uncertain, fluid, and dangerous international environment that the Seleucid king Demetrius II determined to retaliate in the hegemonic struggle against Parthia. Demetrius decided to undertake an anabasis to punish the Parthians, to salvage the deteriorating prestige of the Seleucid state, and to restore the empire to its former glory. Although recent civil wars, rebellions, and territorial losses to the Parthians had severely damaged the authority of the Seleucid kings and the perceived power of the empire, the Seleucid state remained the preeminent military power in the Hellenistic Middle East. The Parthians had annexed Media, Persis, and Babylonia; however, each of these recent successes had been difficult and none of them had come at the expense of the main Seleucid royal army. The Parthians' conquest of Media against limited Seleucid forces had taken years to accomplish, and the recent Elymaean raids into Babylonia illustrated the fragility of the Parthians' occupation of this region. The newly acquired power of Parthia in the east remained quite fragile in 140. A determined, well-executed anabasis like that of Antiochus III in 210 could have reversed the recent gains of the Parthians swiftly and reestablished Seleucid hegemony over the eastern territories, at least temporarily.

The Disaster of Demetrius

Despite his many troubles in the west, Demetrius II set lofty goals and felt confident about his new eastern campaign. Josephus states, "Yet Demetrius passed

251. Note Overtoom 2019a: 142–46.

over [the Euphrates], and came into Mesopotamia, as desirous to retain that country still, as well as Babylon; and should he have obtained the dominion of the upper provinces [that is, Media], [he planned] to lay a foundation for recovering his entire kingdom (ὅλης τῆς βασιλείας)."[252] Josephus continues that Demetrius had high hopes of overthrowing the Parthians.[253] Thus, there is no doubting the ambition of Demetrius. He seemingly expected to regain control of Mesopotamia and Media, subdue the Parthians, and reclaim the hegemony of the Seleucids in the east.[254]

Demetrius II recognized the damage the Parthians had done to the empire but viewed their defeat as assured if he concentrated his forces against them. He had the desire and the confidence to follow the example of Antiochus III in part because his financial, logistical, and military resources remained considerable despite the ongoing troubles of the Seleucid Empire. The major eastern expeditions of Demetrius II and his brother, Antiochus VII, in the 130s provide the most striking evidence of the substantial potential power that the Seleucid Empire retained during the power-transition crisis of the 160s–130s even after a generation of debilitating internal chaos and external pressures.[255]

As early as 140, Demetrius II prepared to retaliate against Parthia and to conduct a hegemonic war to reclaim the empire's lost eastern lands.[256] What makes Demetrius' anabasis unique is that he was still embroiled in a civil war against the usurper Diodotus Tryphon. The prior eastern expeditions of Seleucus II, Antiochus III, and Antiochus IV had occurred in times of relative stability and security in the west. Therefore, it is worthwhile to consider Demetrius' motivations for undertaking a major eastern campaign.

The long civil war against Diodotus Tryphon had not gone well for Demetrius II. His many harsh policies, abuses, and military setbacks in Syria and Judaea had allowed Tryphon to seize control of the Seleucid lands along the eastern coast of the Mediterranean and force Demetrius to retreat into western Syria and northern Mesopotamia.[257] Yet Tryphon was unable to capitalize on Demetrius' vulnerability because of his own political and military blunders. Tryphon's betrayal of his Jewish allies, the near destruction of his army by bad weather near Ptolemais (modern Acre, Israel), and his execution of the child king Antiochus VI quickly undermined his new position of power considerably in Syria and

252. Jos. *Ant.* 13.184–5. Translation slightly altered.

253. Id. 13.186.

254. Other scholars have noted the lofty goals of Demetrius for his anabasis. See McDowell 1935: 56; Jenkins 1951: 19. However, Jenkins's opinion that Demetrius' invasion was a "forlorn hope" is too dismissive.

255. Note Overtoom 2019a: 142–46.

256. For a recent reevaluation of Demetrius' anabasis and the consequences of his failure, see Shayegan 2003 [2007]: 83–103. Compare Lerouge-Cohen 2005; Grainger 2016: Chs. 6–7.

257. Demetrius massacred the inhabitants of Antioch and sacked the city in 145. He also lost his alliance with the Jews and quickly found them to be his enemies. Diod. 33.4, 9.1; *I Maccabees* 11.41–58, 67–74, 12.24–34, 13.33–42; Jos. *Ant.* 13.133–42, 144–47, 158–63, 174–80, 213–14; id. *Bell.* 1.53; Livy *Epit.* 52.9–13; Justin *Prol.* 35–36.

Judaea.[258] Thus, the circumstances of the Seleucid civil war in the late 140s help explain Demetrius' decision to attack the Parthians.

Demetrius II could not afford to lose the important tax revenues of central and southern Mesopotamia if he hoped finally to overcome Diodotus Tryphon in Syria. Moreover, by reclaiming Babylonia and Media from the Parthians, Demetrius drastically would increase his prestige and resources. In fact, Justin argues that Demetrius attacked the Parthians to salvage his damaged reputation. He states, "As the cities, in consequence, began everywhere to revolt from his government, he resolved, in order to wipe off the stain of effeminacy from his character, to make war upon the Parthians."[259] Meanwhile, the explanations found in Josephus and *I Maccabees* claim that Demetrius wanted to defeat Parthia to gain more support and supplies for his war against Tryphon. Josephus records, "So he was elevated with these hopes, and came hastily to them, as having resolved, that if he had once overthrown the Parthians, and gotten an army of his own, he would make war against Tryphon, and eject him out of Syria," and *I Maccabees* states, "Demetrius the king assembled his forces and marched into Media to secure help, so that he could make war against Tryphon."[260] Each of these explanations is an accurate reflection of at least part of Demetrius' overall motive. If Demetrius defeated the Parthians in Babylonia and Media, he then could use his enhanced military, political, and financial position to crush Tryphon once and for all in the west.[261] Finally, by late 140 Demetrius was confident that the sudden devastation of Tryphon's army near Ptolemais and his tenuous position in Antioch after murdering Antiochus VI meant that Tryphon no longer had the capability to act aggressively in Syria. The Parthians became the most immediate threat to Demetrius' remaining lands and the most ideal target to bolster his standing and position as king to help secure the integrity of the state in a period of great turmoil.[262]

The Parthians' recent conquests of Seleucid territory in Media and Mesopotamia demanded Seleucid retaliation, and the rapid destabilization of their occupation of Babylonia by Elymaean raids in 140 severely damaged the perceived strength of the Parthians in the region. For Demetrius II the failure of the Parthians to maintain order in Babylonia signified vulnerability and weakness that could be exploited. Demetrius' eagerness to attack the Parthians during the Seleucid civil war demonstrates his confidence in that vulnerability. The

258. Tryphon betrayed the Jewish leader, Jonathan, in 143 and then unsuccessfully invaded Judaea. In 142 Tryphon's army defeated Demetrius' general, Sarpedon, near Ptolemais; however, in the aftermath of the battle a large wave washed over Tryphon's camp and drowned his men. *I Maccabees* 11.39–40, 12.39–53, 13.12–32; Jos. *Ant.* 13.187–89, 203–12, 218, 20.239; id. *Bell.* 1.49; Strabo 16.2.26; Athen. 8.7; Posid. 29; Diod. 33.4a, 28, 28a; Appian *Syr.* 11.68; Justin 36.1.7; Orosius 5.4.18; Livy *Epit.* 55.11.

259. Justin 36.1.2. Appian states that Demetrius wished to emulate his forefathers. Appian *Syr.* 11.67.

260. Jos. *Ant.* 13.186; *I Maccabees* 14.1.

261. Ehling 1998a: 228 n.13; Dąbrowa 1999 [2000]: 9–17; Shayegan 2003 [2007]: 86; id. 2011: 70–71.

262. Ehling 1998a: 228; id. 2008: 183.

Seleucids had mostly abandoned Babylonia because of their ongoing civil war, allowing the Parthians to seize the region without much resistance. Yet the position of the Parthians in the region was fragile. Antiochus IV had settled more Greeks in Babylonia, and this large Greek population played an important role in the subsequent eastern expeditions of Demetrius and Antiochus VII.[263] Josephus records, "For those Greeks and Macedonians who dwelt there frequently sent ambassadors to him [Demetrius], and promised, that if he would come to them, they would deliver themselves up to him, and assist him in fighting against Arsaces [that is, Mithridates I]."[264] Thus, the Parthians already faced considerable external and internal pressures in Babylonia, and Demetrius became convinced that he could reoccupy the region swiftly and successfully, increasing his military reputation and the integrity of the empire drastically and with ease.[265]

Demetrius II's successful anabasis would have restored his legitimacy as king, which he needed to regain the loyalty of the soldiers and communities of Syria, and it would have given him access to important recruits for his army. In addition to the levies that Demetrius hoped to gain from the Greek communities in Babylonia and Media, the defeat of the Parthians and their submission to Seleucid suzerainty would have secured for him valuable Parthian cavalry to utilize in his western wars.[266] Unfortunately for the Seleucid Empire, Demetrius' anabasis was a catastrophic failure. Although he had grand ambitions of reclaiming the lost lands of the east and subjugating the Parthians, Demetrius and his army made it no further east than Babylonia.[267]

Regrettably, the details of the campaign are negligible and often contradictory. Mithridates I was not in Babylonia at the beginning of Demetrius II's invasion, and therefore, Mithridates sent his trusted brother, Bagasis, whom he had made governor of Media with authority over the supreme command of Babylonia, to defend the region.[268] By summer 138, the Parthians had crushed Demetrius' army and taken him captive.[269] Yet it is perhaps possible to reconstruct the course of Demetrius' failed anabasis more definitively.

Elymaean raids into Babylonia in 140 had forced Mithridates I suddenly to put aside his continuing efforts to strengthen his eastern frontier.[270] By late 140,

263. See van der Spek 2005; Finkel, van der Spek, Pirngruber 2020c.

264. Jos. *Ant.* 13.185. Note Justin 36.1.3.

265. Jos. *Ant.* 13.186. Note Dąbrowa 1999 [2000]: 15. For the characteristics of Hellenistic kingship and its primary emphasis on militarism and military reputation, see Austin 1986; Sherwin-White and Kuhrt 1993: Ch. 5; Messina 2017, Grainger 2017a; Engels 2017.

266. Note Polyb. 16.18.5–10, 30.25.6–10.

267. See Sachs and Hunger 1996: no. -137B. For Shayegan's rejection of Dąbrowa's argument that Demetrius invaded Media, see Shayegan 2011: 71–72, 74. Compare Dąbrowa 1999 [2000]: 13–16.

268. See Shayegan 2011: 72–4.

269. See Sachs and Hunger 1996: no. -137A. For varying scholarly opinions on the dates and course of Demetrius' expedition, see van der Spek 1997–1998: 172–73; Ehling 1998a: 227–29; Dąbrowa 1998: 37–42; id. 1999 [2000]: 12–16; Potts 2002: 356–57; Shayegan 2003 [2007]: 87; id. 2011: 71–72.

270. See Sachs and Hunger 1996: no. -140C; Justin 41.6.7–8.

Mithridates had returned to Babylonia and successfully repulsed the Elymaeans, possibly defeating them significantly enough to limit their military activity considerably for the next couple of years.[271] With the Elymaean threat temporarily neutralized and the Parthian occupation of Babylonia tentatively restored, Mithridates returned once more to the east in 140/139 to renew his efforts to strengthen the frontier.[272] Diodorus praises Mithridates' efforts in the east, stating:

> Arsaces king of the Parthians, being a mild and gracious prince, was exceedingly prosperous and successful, and greatly enlarged the bounds of his empire. He conquered all before him, as far as to India, where Porus reigned formerly, with a great deal of ease; and though he had achieved that degree of power and authority, yet he inclined not in the least to pride and luxury, as is common with princes in such cases. He was kind to his subjects, and valiant in warfare against his enemies; and having subdued many nations, he collected the best of their customs, and imparted them to the Parthians.[273]

Diodorus here does not specify the Parthian king; however, his description of a prosperous and successful Parthian military leader and his placement of this short passage between a discussion of Pompey's attack on the Numantines in Spain in 141 and the consulship of Marcus Popillius Laenas in 139 make the association clear.[274] Although Diodorus perhaps exaggerates the extent of Mithridates' eastern conquests, he illustrates that Mithridates placed great emphasis on his eastern frontier.

Mithridates I's frequent trips to the east were a necessary reaction to the continued disintegration of the Kingdom of Bactria in the 140s–130s; however, they were not good for the stability of the Parthians' western frontier. His campaign against the Elymaeans had not been sufficient to secure the borders of Babylonia, and the Parthians had not had enough time to appease the unrest of the Greek communities in this region.[275] In 140/139 Demetrius II recognized an opportunity to reverse the recent territorial gains of the Parthians and began preparing for a major eastern expedition. The following year Demetrius invaded Babylonia while Mithridates was still in the east.[276]

Mithridates I ordered Bagasis to march south from Media, where he had been consolidating Parthian power since his appointment as governor over the

271. Justin tells us that Mithridates made war on Elymais and conquered the region. Justin 41.6.8. However, any influence Mithridates gained over Elymais quickly dissolved. In 138 Elymaean troops perhaps served alongside Demetrius' army in Babylonia, and Elymais independently raided Babylonia later that year. See Justin 36.1.4; Sachs and Hunger 1996: no. -137A.

272. Shayegan 2011: 72–74. Sachs and Hunger 1996: no. -137A.

273. Diod. 33.18. Note Strabo 15.2.11.

274. Diod. 33.17, 19.

275. Jos. *Ant.* 13.185–86; Justin 36.1.3.

276. Sachs and Hunger 1996: no. -137A; Eus. *Chron.* (Smith ed.): 255.

region in 147, to prepare the defenses of Babylonia and raise troops.[277] Yet the sources indicate that the early stage of Demetrius II's anabasis was highly successful. Justin records, "Being assisted, accordingly, by auxiliary troops from the Persians, Elymaeans, and Bactrians, he [Demetrius] routed the Parthians in several pitched battles."[278] Recently, Rahim Shayegan has challenged Justin's claim that the Persians, Elymaeans, and Bactrians came to the aid of Demetrius in 138. He contends that there is no other evidence of Parthia's enemies coordinating their attacks and that Parthia retained its control of Babylonia in this period.[279] A coordinated attack by the four strongest enemies of the Parthians in this period is indeed unlikely; however, Justin's account reflects the numerous challenges the Parthians faced to their rising hegemony during the crisis. Justin inadvertently recognizes that, while Demetrius invaded Babylonia, the Parthians had major security concerns along their southern and eastern frontiers that divided their attention. Underscored in Justin's account is the hostility of competing states within the much-expanded Iranian interstate system toward the ascending power of the Parthians and Parthia's considerable vulnerability in the 130s.

In 138 Demetrius II had a good chance to strike a major blow against the ascending power of the Parthians; however, his eastern expedition quickly turned disastrous. Justin records, "After making war, as has been said above, upon the Parthians, and gaining victory in several battles, he [Demetrius] was suddenly surprised by an ambuscade, and, having lost his army, was taken prisoner."[280] Note that this account differs slightly from Justin's earlier explanation of how the Parthians defeated Demetrius. There Justin states, "At length, however, being deceived by a pretended offer of peace, he [Demetrius] was made prisoner, and being led from city to city, was shown as a spectacle to the people that had revolted, in mockery of the favor that they had shown him."[281] In both of these accounts, Justin criticizes the Parthian victory as devious and cowardly, failing to appreciate that misdirection and mobility were the great strengths of the Parthian army. Again, we find evidence of the Graeco-Roman literary tradition disparaging Parthian militarism through stereotypes of eastern dishonesty.[282] Although the Parthians managed to outmaneuver and overwhelm Demetrius' superior force with great success, Justin here offers only censure for their actions. Justin, who otherwise has a negative opinion of Demetrius, does not blame him for this disaster but rather criticizes the duplicity of the Parthians.[283] Justin makes little

277. See *I Maccabees* 14.2; Sachs and Hunger 1996: no. -137A; Eus. *Chron.* (Smith ed.): 255. Note Justin 41.6.7; Moses 1.8, 2.68.

278. Justin 36.1.4. Translation slightly altered.

279. Shayegan 2011: 81–82. Contra Grainger 2016: 83–85.

280. Justin 38.9.2. Note id. *Prol.* 35–36; Appian *Syr.* 11.67; Jos. *Ant.* 13.186, 218–19; *I Maccabees* 14.2–3; Diod. 33.28.1; Eus. *Chron.* (Smith ed.): 255.

281. Justin 36.1.5.

282. See Isaac 2006: Chs. 4–5, 8. Compare Overtoom 2011; id. 2012; Kennedy, Roy, and Goldman 2013: Ch. 10; Gregoratti 2015a: 203–4; Overtoom 2016c, Müller 2017b; Overtoom 2017a; id. 2017b.

283. Justin calls Demetrius spoiled, lazy, prideful, and effeminate. Justin 36.1.1–2.

effort to understand the Parthians' tactics or strategy even though his account potentially says a great deal about the Parthians' asymmetrical approach to warfare. If we put aside Justin's cultural bias and constructively engage the evidence, Justin unknowingly describes another example of the successful execution of the Parthians' "Feign Retreat, Defeat in Detail" mode of warfare.[284]

The larger strategic objectives of the Parthian military relied heavily upon mobility, flexibility, deception, intimidation, and concentration of force. Justin's account clearly illustrates that the Parthian military eventually caught Demetrius II off-guard, destroying his army and capturing him in the process. Thus, the Parthians successfully implemented their asymmetric strategic approach in this campaign. In 138 the Parthians in Babylonia were outnumbered, but they had the advantage of mobility and put it to good use.

At the start of Demetrius II's invasion, Mithridates I needed time to bring his main force from the east to Babylonia, and since Mithridates did not want to abandon his gains in Mesopotamia, he sent his experienced brother, Bagasis, to fight a delaying action against the Seleucids.[285] Thus, after preparing the defenses of the region, Bagasis began to skirmish with the Seleucids, implementing the Parthians' "Harass Strategy." Bagasis attempted to force Demetrius through coercion into making mistakes during his advance into Babylonia that might create an opportunity for the Parthians to exploit. Justin records that Demetrius' initial invasion was highly successful after several victories; however, in reality these victories must have been quite minor.[286] Demetrius was unable to advance beyond Babylonia, only briefly retaking Seleucia, and Bagasis remained in the field.[287]

Ultimately, Bagasis successfully stalled Demetrius II's advance, skirmishing with the Seleucid army but avoiding climatic battles. The Parthians' asymmetric mode of warfare encouraged overconfidence in their enemies through misdirection, deception, and confusion to make enemy forces complacent or overly aggressive. By skirmishing with the Seleucids and "losing" these engagements, Bagasis reinforced Demetrius' opinion that the Parthians were weak and militarily inept, encouraging Demetrius to underestimate the threat his army faced in Babylonia. Demetrius had no prior experience fighting the Parthians, and he did not recognize the Parthians' larger strategic objectives, namely the delay and sudden destruction of his army. Seemingly unimpressed with the Parthian military, Demetrius appears to have fallen victim to complacency. As the Seleucids became increasingly distracted in Babylonia, Mithridates I approached rapidly

284. Note Overtoom 2017b.

285. Mithridates' generals in Babylonia, Antiochus, Nikanor, and then Philinus, likely aided Bagasis in the defense of the region. Sachs and Hunger 1996: no. -140A, no. -137C. Grainger suggests Demetrius defeated and perhaps killed Antiochus. Grainger 2016 85–87. Grainger is far too dismissive of the subsequent Parthian victory over Demetrius.

286. Justin 36.1.4, 38.9.2.

287. Lorber and Iossif 2009: 99; Monerie 2019.

with the main Parthian army. By the end of summer 138, the Parthians' trap was set, and Mithridates prepared to close it with devastating results.

Justin's account illustrates that he and his source, Trogus, like many Greeks and Romans, misunderstood or disregarded the Parthians' asymmetric approach to warfare. Because the Parthians did not fight and win large, conventional set-piece battles in early 138, Justin viewed the Parthians' initial defense of Babylonia as a resounding failure and exaggerated the military successes of Demetrius II. Yet by considering Justin's account more carefully with an appreciation for the uniqueness of the Parthians' strategy and tactics, we can recognize the intent of Bagasis and Mithridates I. Bagasis slowly drew Demetrius deeper into Babylonia while Mithridates advanced on the Seleucid flank and rear from Media. The skirmishes Bagasis lost were meant to distract Demetrius from Mithridates' approach and the evermore dangerous position of his army.

From the Parthians' perspective, Bagasis had conducted a well-planned and well-executed delaying campaign, utilizing their "Harass Strategy." Mithridates I completed his march through Media and arrived suddenly in Babylonia in July/August 138.[288] Demetrius was caught partially, if not completely unaware, and the Parthians quickly implemented their "Overwhelm Strategy" with an aggressive assault upon the Seleucid army. The Parthians' implementation of their unique asymmetric mode of warfare was a resounding success as they destroyed Demetrius' army and took him prisoner.[289]

With an understanding of the Parthians' successful delaying action and counterattack against Demetrius II, let us also attempt to reconcile the apparent disparity in Justin's account of Demetrius' final defeat and capture in passages 36.1.5 and 38.9.2. The issue remains whether the Parthians captured Demetrius at their decisive victory or soon after the battle. Justin's account in 36.1.5 perhaps is evidence of the latter scenario. In late summer 138, the Parthians ambushed and destroyed the Seleucid army in Babylonia; however, it is possible Demetrius escaped the battlefield. Without his army and desperate to secure a truce with the Parthians, Demetrius would have wanted to open negotiations with Mithridates I. Demetrius' attempt to negotiate with Mithridates would explain Justin's insistence in 36.1.5 that the Parthians captured Demetrius during dubious peace talks. Yet Justin's harsh criticism of the Parthians again appears biased and framed by Graeco-Roman stereotypes of dishonest easterners.[290] There is no reason to

288. Sachs and Hunger 1996: no. -137A; Eus. *Chron.* (Smith ed.): 255. Note Shayegan 2003 [2007]: 84; Assar 2005a: 43.

289. Justin 36.1.5, 38.9.2; id. *Prol.* 35–36; Appian *Syr.* 11.67; Jos. *Ant.* 13.186, 218–19; *I Maccabees* 14.2–3; Diod. 33.28.1; Eus. *Chron.* (Smith ed.): 255. Note Nabel 2017a. It seems undeniable that Mithridates left Hyrcania and was present at the climactic battle. See Shayegan 2011: 75–76. Compare Wolski 1993: 81–82; van der Spek 1997–1998: 173.

290. For similar stereotypes associated with the Parthians after Carrhae, see Plut. *Crass.* 28.3–33.4; id. *Pomp.* 76.5–6; Dio 40.26–27; Strabo 16.1.23; Ruf. Fest. 17.2–3; Orosius 6.13; Livy *Epit.* 106; Polyaen. 7.41.

assume that Mithridates considered peace after his great victory. Instead, the Parthians seized Demetrius before he could escape to northern Mesopotamia.

Mithridates I recognized that the capture of Demetrius II was an important statement regionally and internationally. Mithridates had already introduced new imperial imagery on his coinage to signify his victory over the Bactrian Greeks, and he now displayed the captured Seleucid king as a token of his power and as a strong warning to the potentially rebellious Greek communities of Babylonia that had shown Demetrius favor prior to his invasion.[291] Thus, Demetrius became a high profile and effective example of the consequences of resistance to Parthian rule.[292] Mithridates also likely adopted the epithet Philhellene ("Admirer of Greeks") to placate the Greek communities in Babylonia at this time, and he used Demetrius to help avoid further Greek resistance in Babylonia, helping stabilize what had been a turbulent region for several years.[293] Moreover, the capture of Demetrius was a further devastating blow to the power, prestige, and influence of the Seleucid king and state within the Hellenistic Middle East, while acting as a great boon to that of Mithridates and Parthia. Mithridates viewed the capture of Demetrius as a means to further legitimize his reign and the rule of the Arsacid dynasty. Demetrius remained an honored captive of the Parthians for the remainder of the decade, and in fact, Demetrius married one of Mithridates' daughters, Rhodogune, directly connecting the Arsacid and Seleucid dynasties.[294]

The destruction of Demetrius II's army and his capture was an important moment in the continued development of the Parthians' identity. For the first time since Arsaces I, the Parthians had defeated the royal Seleucid army. Moreover, the Parthians had defended their territorial gains in Media and Mesopotamia in a direct confrontation with the Seleucid king. By defeating Demetrius and then marrying him into his family, Mithridates I placed himself in a long line of Hellenistic warrior kings who had claimed legitimacy through "spear-won" land and family ties. The Arsacids were now the equals, if not the superiors, of the Seleucid kings, and the Parthian state emerged for the first time as the true hegemonic rival of the Seleucid Empire in the much-expanded Iranian interstate system. Although it took the Parthians another generation to emerge as the unrivaled hegemon in this interstate system and two generations finally to dominate the Seleucids, their victory over Demetrius brought an end to the power-transition crisis of the 160s–130s. A new system of bipolar rivalry, where Parthia and the Seleucid Empire were the two leading states of the Hellenistic Middle East, replaced the system of multipolar anarchy that had existed since the beginning of the crisis in the 160s.

291. Jos. *Ant.* 13.185. Note Justin 36.1.3–5. For the imagery of Mithridates' coinage, see Assar 2011: 118; Lerner 2017.

292. Assar 2011: 117; Grainger 2013a: 181.

293. Dąbrowa 1998; Assar 2011: 118; Dąbrowa 2011a; Olbrycht 2017b: 10.

294. Justin 36.1.6, 38.9.3; Appian *Syr.* 11.67. Note Dąbrowa 2018.

Yet, despite the great success of Mithridates I, the Parthians' new position of power and authority in the Hellenistic Middle East remained fragile and hotly contested.[295] In the east the further disintegration of the Kingdom of Bactria and the rising power and aggression of the Central Asian tribal confederations created major security concerns along the Parthians' extensive eastern frontier. Meanwhile, in the west the important task of securing Babylonia from numerous internal and external threats persisted.

The Parthians still needed to secure the loyalty of numerous Greek communities in the region, and Mithridates I made a forceful effort to accomplish this goal when he paraded Demetrius II from city to city as a warning and as a symbol of his power.[296] However, there was no guarantee of the obedience of these Greek communities if Mesopotamia remained an unstable, war-torn region. In particular, the kingdoms of Elymais and Characene made this process difficult as they continued to challenge Parthia's newly won regional hegemony.

Mithridates I had defeated the Elymaeans in 140 after their attacks on Babylonia.[297] Yet the invasion of Demetrius II had encouraged the Elymaeans to renew their attacks on the Parthians.[298] Mithridates' great victory over Demetrius in 138 must have made the Elymaeans fearful of Parthian retaliation; however, immediately following his greatest triumph Mithridates almost disappears from our historical record. It now appears that Mithridates did not die suddenly in late 138, as was the traditional argument; instead, he seems to have returned to the east and suffered a debilitating illness, perhaps a stroke, that did not claim his life until ca. 132.[299] Mithridates' severe illness helps explain the relative lack of Parthian expansion in this period. It sapped the momentum of the Parthians and created an opportunity for regional dynasts to once again challenge Parthian hegemony in Babylonia.

Late in 138 Elymaean forces renewed raids into Babylonia, perhaps encouraged by news of Mithridates' illness.[300] Elymais, although a minor kingdom, was another highly militarized and bellicose polity in the much-expanded Iranian interstate system, and the Elymaeans sought to increase their power and security at the expense of their neighbors, despite the considerable power disparity between Elymais and Parthia. The continued vulnerability of Babylonia, paired

295. Grainger's recent assumption that the Parthians were the dominant, unstoppable power in the Hellenistic Middle East, in essence the unipolar power, as early as 140 and his conclusion that Rome and Parthia already shared a binary world in the second century does not reflect the geopolitical realities of the 140s–120s. Grainger 2013a: 185–86. Compare Assar 2011: 118; Sampson 2015: 46. See instead, Overtoom 2016a; id. 2016c; id. 2019a; id. 2019b; id. 2019c; id. 2019/2020; id. 2021. Note Tac. *Hist.* 5.8.

296. Justin 36.1.5. Note Nabel 2017a: 31.

297. Justin 41.6.8; Sachs and Hunger 1996: no. -140C, no. -140D.

298. Justin 36.1.4. Note Dąbrowa 2014b: 63.

299. See Assar 2005a: 43–45; id. 2006c: 95, 98; id. 2011: 117. Compare Dąbrowa 2005: 73. For the argument that Mithridates died between 135–133, see Shayegan 2011: 76. For the traditional date of 138, see Wroth 1903: xxi; McDowell 1935: 201; Debevoise 1938: 26; Bivar 1983: 36; Assar 2001a: 21; Grainger 2016: 107.

300. Sachs and Hunger 1996: no. -137B. Note Shayegan 2011: 79–80.

with major security concerns, including the threat of Parthian retaliation and a famine in the region, encouraged the Elymaeans to act aggressively and test the Parthians' strength regionally. Yet the Parthians responded to the raids with determination and drove off the attackers, and although great fear of further Elymaean incursions into the region remained for the Parthians, they demonstrated that their power in the region was superior.[301]

The Elymaeans' miscalculation and defeat in Babylonia in 138/137 made them even more vulnerable to the aggression of the Parthians and other minor kingdoms in the region. The crisis had encouraged another Seleucid satrap named Hyspaosines to act independently in Characene (roughly modern southeastern Iraq).[302] Hyspaosines understood the need to expand the power and security of his new state and decided to take advantage of the recent Elymaean defeat in Babylonia to occupy the regions of southern Mesopotamia held by Elymais.[303] Characene's attacks on the vulnerable Elymaean state in this period further emphasize the war-prone, insecure, and dangerous existence of ancient polities.[304] Both Elymais and Characene were in competition among themselves and with the Parthians for regional power in a struggle where destruction was an ongoing possibility. As the Parthians attempted to replace Seleucid hegemony in Mesopotamia and southern Iran, loyalties and the balance of power remained fluid in these regions throughout the 130s–120s.

In fact, in the middle 130s Elymais and Characene temporarily put aside their differences and formed a military alliance in an effort to balance power relations in the region against the Parthians.[305] Years of Parthian military inactivity in Mesopotamia following the defeat of the Elymaean raids in 138, the continued deterioration of Mithridates I's health, and the expansion of Characene's power created geopolitical uncertainty in the region. Despite recent hostilities, Elymais saw an opportunity once again to occupy Babylonia, this time with the aid of Characene. Elymais clearly still viewed Parthia as its greatest threat and Babylonia as the most rewarding prize, and therefore, Elymais and Characene forged an alliance and made a destructive joint invasion of Babylonia in 133.[306]

With Mithridates I incapacitated, Bagasis appears to have acted in his brother's name successfully from 138 to 132.[307] A cuneiform tablet from ca. 132 describes sacrifices being made in Babylon for the life of Mithridates; however, sacrifices where also made for the life of Bagasis, indicating that Bagasis was considered

301. Sachs and Hunger 1996: no. -137C, no. -137D. Note Dąbrowa 2014b: 63.

302. For a recent account of Hyspaosines, see Schuol 2000: 291–300.

303. Hyspaosines also built a fortified capital at Charax. Pliny *NH* 6.31.149. Note Hansman 2011; Shahbazi 2011.

304. For the campaign, see Shayegan 2011: 80–81. For the failures of Elymais, giving rise to Characene as a regional power, see id. 101, 103.

305. Shayegan emphasizes that fear of Parthian power motivated the alliance, see id. 82, 103.

306. Sachs and Hunger 1996: no. -132B. Note Dąbrowa 2014b: 63.

307. Assar 2011: 117.

Mithridates' equal.[308] In his position of power, Bagasis held together the much-expanded Parthian Empire and maintained a strong position in Media. Although the combined invasion of Elymais and Characene seriously destabilized Babylonia, Bagasis responded definitively and pushed back the invaders.[309] In fact, another set of cuneiform tablets describe Bagasis conducting a violent campaign in Babylonia likely after the Elymais and Characene invasion had disrupted the region.[310]

With the defeat of the joint invasion of Elymais and Characene in 133, the Parthians reaffirmed their position of power in Mesopotamia; however, the victory had been costly, and the Parthians appreciated the continued threat that Elymais and Characene posed to their hegemony in the region. Thus, later that year the Parthians resolved to avenge the recent invasion of their territory with determination and severity, setting out on a campaign to eliminate the threat of Elymais to Babylonia.[311] The Parthians became determined to replace Elymaean independence with Parthian suzerainty. Such a harsh response was necessary in 133 because of the potential threat that the alliance between Elymais and Characene posed to the regional authority and security of the Parthians.

Recently, Shayegan has argued convincingly that after a decisive victory near Susa, the Parthians installed a pro-Parthian candidate on the throne of Elymais in 133/132, known as Kamnaskires the Younger.[312] This pro-Parthian king fought on behalf of the Parthians in the region and turned Elymais into a loyal Parthian tributary kingdom. The Parthian campaign against Elymais in 133/132 was so successful that Babylonian scribes began to refer to the Arsacids for the first time as "king[s] of the lands."[313] It was also at this time that the Parthians likely installed a vassal in Persis.[314] The practice of the Arsacids installing vassals over difficult to manage peripheral regions of their growing empire became a common aspect of the political and administrative organization of the Parthian Empire moving forward, providing the Parthians with a flexible and resilient form of imperialism that became a major factor in their long-standing success.[315] The Arsacids quickly

308. Finkel, van der Spek, Pirngruber 2020b.

309. Shayegan 2011: 82–88.

310. Finkel, van der Spek, Pirngruber 2020a .

311. Sachs and Hunger 1996: no. -132D2.

312. Shayegan 2011: 88–91, 93–94, 98, 104, 110. Compare Potts 2002: 358; Assar 2004–2005: 50–52, 70–73; id. 2011: 117–18; Dąbrowa 2014b: 63; Martinez-Sève 2015. Note Lucian *Macr.* 16.

313. Shayegan 2011: 104.

314. Strabo records that the Parthians significantly weakened the power of Persis but acknowledged a local vassal. Strabo 15.3.3, 24. Note Shayegan 2011: 178.

315. Note Keall 1994: 271–72; Dąbrowa 2005; id. 2005 [2006]; Tao 2007: 91; Dąbrowa 2006–2007 [2008]; id. 2008 [2009]; Olbrycht 2010b: 147; Grajetzki 2011: 11, 15; Dąbrowa 2011a; Shayegan 2011: 91–93; Hauser 2013: 734–39; Dąbrowa 2013; Wiesehöfer 2016: 217–18, 227; Gregoratti 2016a: 5; id. 2017a; Olbrycht 2017b; Overtoom 2019a: 143–45. For the arguments that the *Xong-e Nōrūzī* relief depicts either Mithridates I or Phraates II investing a local vassal with authority, possibly Kamnaskires the Younger, see Vanden Berghe 1983: 46; Shayegan 2011: 105–9. Compare Mathiesen 1992: ii 119–21; Invernizzi 1998: 224–25. For other Arsacid period rock reliefs, see Kawami 2013.

realized that loyal tributary kingdoms allowed them to enhance their prestige as the ultimate authority in the empire, while solidifying their control over troublesome regions at the smallest possible cost to the Parthian state.

Albeit briefly, the defeat of the alliance of Elymais and Characene in 133 and the suppression of Elymais in 132 secured the Parthians' position in Babylonia.[316] However, one major threat to Parthian hegemony in the region remained, the Seleucid Empire. With Demetrius II's defeat and capture, the Seleucids had been bloodied but not destroyed. The strength of the Seleucid Empire remained potentially strong, and the threat of further Seleucid aggression remained considerable.

The Parthians and Seleucids had become intense adversaries, and neither power was content with their new rivalry within the Hellenistic Middle East. The Parthians did not intend to end their western conquests in Babylonia, and the Seleucids rejected the notion that the Parthians had won the right to claim dominion over Media and Mesopotamia. Demetrius II's failure in 138 once again had embarrassed the Seleucids; however, the memory of Antiochus III's success in the east still gave the Seleucids hope of regaining their eastern hegemony. The great hegemonic struggle between the Seleucids and Parthians continued, and the last great Seleucid king sought vengeance for his family and kingdom.

316. Elymais appears to have participated in a sacrifice to honor Mithridates and Bagasis in ca. 132. See Finkel, van der Spek, Pirngruber 2020b.

5

The Climax of the Seleucid-Parthian Rivalry

The diligent efforts and unrivaled success of Mithridates I during the power-transition crisis of the 160s–130s had transformed Parthia from a minor state to a major empire.[1] Moreover, Demetrius II's decisive defeat and capture legitimized the Parthians as the leading rival of the Seleucid Empire in the much-expanded Iranian interstate system, the bounds of which now stretched from Syria to the Indus River. Yet the chaotic international environment and this new, tense rivalry encouraged further conflict between the Parthians and Seleucids. Although a series of political and military blunders had damaged the standing of the Seleucids, in the 130s the empire remained a powerful force in the region with great wealth and military resources.[2] There remained the possibility that the Seleucid state once again could recover fully from the crisis and reclaim its lost eastern lands. More important, the two major eastern expeditions of the Seleucids in the 130s demonstrate that their ambition to regain their unrivaled hegemonic status throughout the Hellenistic Middle East remained strong. Although Demetrius had failed, his brother, Antiochus VII, eagerly followed his brother's lead, looking to emulate his great namesake on a grand anabasis of his own.[3]

Antiochus VII demonstrated from the beginning of his reign that he had lofty designs to restore the prestige and power of the Seleucid state through a major expedition against the Parthians.[4] He wanted to conduct an extensive campaign against the Parthians to restore the stability and standing of the Seleucid Empire, to exact vengeance, and to gain control of his captured brother. The initial stages of his anabasis were a success; however, he too eventually fell victim to the Parthians' well-executed "Feign Retreat, Defeat in Detail" mode of warfare.[5]

1. The Parthians revered Mithridates so much that they deified him. Assar 2011: 118.

2. Some scholars have been too pessimistic about the irreversible decline of the Seleucid state after Demetrius' defeat. Note Dąbrowa 1999 [2000]: 16; Grainger 2013a: 182.

3. For Antiochus VII, see Will 1967: ii 410f.; Shayegan 2003 [2007]: 87–92; Bing and Sievers 2011; Grainger 2016: Chs. 7–8.

4. Antiochus wanted to restore the Parthians to tributary status within the confines of their "ancestral realm." Diod. 34/35.15. Compare *I Maccabees* 15.3, *V Maccabees* 21.19.

5. Note Overtoom 2017b.

Reign of Arrows. Nikolaus Leo Overtoom, Oxford University Press (2020). Oxford University Press.
DOI: 10.1093/oso/9780190888329.001.0001.

Antiochus VII's anabasis was the last great gasp of the Seleucid Empire. The Parthians' victory devastated the Seleucid state, providing the Parthians with an immense opportunity to push their advantage into the lands of the Near East for the first time. The Parthians looked as though they might finally emerge as the new hegemons over the entire Hellenistic Middle East. Yet the continued defiance of the Seleucids, instability in Mesopotamia and Media, and the near collapse of their eastern frontier kept the Parthians from acting upon their immediate desires to expand further west.

The total disintegration of the Kingdom of Bactria left the Parthians' eastern frontier vulnerable. For decades widespread conflict and large migrations on the Central Asian steppe had put an increasingly dangerous amount of pressure on Bactria, and once Bactria fell it became the Parthians' full responsibility to protect the vulnerable Iranian plateau. The full weight of the "nomadic problem" fell at the feet of the Arsacids.[6] Desperate conflicts with the Central Asian tribal confederations in the 120s–110s tested the power and authority of the Parthian state, claiming the lives of no fewer than two Parthian kings.

Through their major conflicts with the Seleucids and the Central Asian tribal confederations in the 130s–110s, the Parthians experienced firsthand the major difficulties of dominating the Hellenistic Middle East and maintaining imperial power. It took no small amount of diligence and persistence for the Parthians to overcome the numerous geopolitical challenges they faced both in the west and the east in this period as they continued to secure their new empire and battle for hegemony. The survival of the Parthian state remained in jeopardy.

The Last Great Seleucid

Antiochus VII was the last great Seleucid king.[7] Although he came to the throne in the chaotic aftermath of his brother's defeat in the east, he quickly demonstrated his considerable ambitions and capabilities by winning a civil war in Syria and subduing the Jews in Judaea. With his western lands secure, Antiochus prepared for a major eastern expedition that he desired to rival Antiochus III's in size and scope.

Although Antiochus VII's anabasis was a total disaster, it began with considerable momentum and potential. Antiochus commanded a relatively stable empire and a strong royal army.[8] Meanwhile, the Parthians faced severe internal and external pressures that made them vulnerable to Antiochus' concerted invasion. His

6. For recent evaluations of Parthian conflicts and interactions with Central Asian peoples, note Olbrycht 2015a; Dąbrowa 2016a; Overtoom 2019b; id. 2019c; id. 2019/2020; id. 2020.

7. Note Strootman 2019.

8. Although an exaggeration, *Maccabees* states that Antiochus commanded 128,000 well-trained soldiers. *I Maccabees* 15.13. Meanwhile, Justin records that Antiochus took 80,000 soldiers with him on his anabasis. Justin 38.10.2. Compare Diod. 34/35.17.

determined anabasis illustrates the continued power of the Seleucid state in the 130s and the strong motivations of the Seleucid kings to reclaim the hegemony of the empire through force. In fact, at the height of his invasion, Antiochus even regained Mesopotamia and Media before threatening to invade Parthia proper in 129. In desperation the new Parthian king, Phraates II (Figures 17–18), released his prized captive, Demetrius II, under guard to contest the Seleucid throne in Syria to delay Antiochus' attack.[9] Yet a series of rebellions and the asymmetric warfare of the Parthians took Antiochus by surprise and overwhelmed him. The Parthians isolated and destroyed the core of the Seleucid army in the mountain passes between Media and Mesopotamia, killing the last of the great Seleucid kings in the melee.

The death of Antiochus VII at the hands of the Parthians and the subsequent destruction or capture of much of the royal Seleucid army was the most decisive defeat in the history of the Seleucid Empire, the consequences of which outstripped those of Magnesia.[10] It was a disaster from which the Seleucid state never recovered. Although the Seleucids and Parthians continued their hegemonic struggle for another four decades, the Parthians never again had to suffer a Seleucid invasion of their lands. The great Middle Eastern empire of Seleucus I and Antiochus III was a memory and the ability to reestablish it was no more.

Another Ambitious Antiochus

With the defeat and capture of Demetrius II in 138, civil war in Syria escalated rapidly. No fewer than five generals contested the throne from their regional positions of power.[11] Meanwhile, the usurper Diodotus Tryphon, who had been feuding with Demetrius for several years, finally seized this opportunity to gain the Seleucid throne through treachery and bribery in that year; however, he quickly abused his power and lost the support of his soldiers.[12] Tryphon's unpopularity helped encourage Demetrius' brother, Antiochus VII, to return to Syria and assert his claim to the throne.[13] After a brief but difficult campaign, Antiochus defeated Tryphon, who soon after perished, and Antiochus became the sole ruler of a much diminished Seleucid state in early 137.[14]

Antiochus VII's new position as king initially was precarious. A series of civil wars had demonstrated the volatility of the Seleucid throne, and the defeat and capture of Demetrius II by the Parthians had damaged the reputation

9. Overtoom 2020.

10. Note Taylor 2013: 157.

11. Diod. 33.28.

12. Id. 33.28–28a; Jos. *AJ.* 13.218–21; Justin 36.1.7; Strabo 16.2.10, 19; Porph. 48. Note Shayegan 2003 [2007]: 90.

13. Jos. *AJ.* 13.222–23; Appian *Syr.* 11.68.

14. *I Maccabees* 15.10–14, 25–26, 37, 39; Jos. *AJ.* 13.223–24; id. *Bell.* 1.50–54; Appian *Syr.* 11.68; Justin 36.1.8; Strabo 14.5.2; Front. *Strat.* 2.13.2; Hieron. *Chron.* 160.3–4; Syncellus 553.

and standing of the Seleucids severely.[15] Although Antiochus had returned to Syria to defeat the usurper Diodotus Tryphon, Demetrius' captivity meant that Antiochus technically was a usurper to his brother's throne.[16] Antiochus even decided to marry his brother's wife, the politically shrewd Cleopatra Thea, before he proclaimed himself king.[17]

Although Antiochus VII capitalized on his opportunity to gain power in Syria, the severe pressures he faced and his considerable ambitions pushed him toward an aggressive policy of expansion to increase his strength, build his reputation, and secure his kingdom. He understood that the best way to accomplish his goals was through successful military conquest, and his defeat of Diodotus Tryphon allowed him to act aggressively. For example, while in Phoenicia, Antiochus decided to break his alliance with the Jews, invade Judaea, besiege Jerusalem, and force the Jews to submit to Seleucid hegemony.[18] The sudden, violent change in the geopolitical relationship between the Jews and the Seleucids in the middle 130s is another example of the uncertainty and instability of state interactions in the ancient world.

Antiochus VII eagerly had sought out Jewish help early in his war against Diodotus Tryphon and offered the Jews several concessions for their military aid. As recorded in *I Maccabees*:

> Antiochus [VII], the son of Demetrius [I] the king, sent a letter from the islands of the [Aegean] sea to Simon, the priest and ethnarch of the Jews, and to all the nation; its contents were as follows: "King Antiochus to Simon the high priest and ethnarch and to the nation of the Jews, greetings. Whereas certain pestilent men have gained control of the kingdom of our fathers [that is, Tryphon and his supporters], and I intend to lay claim to the kingdom so that I may restore it as it formerly was (ἀντιποιήσασθαι τῆς βασιλείας ὅπως ἀποκαταστήσω αὐτὴν ὡς ἦν τὸ πρότερον ἐξενολόγ ησα), and have recruited a host of mercenary troops and have equipped warships, and intend to make a landing in the region so that I may proceed against those who have destroyed our country and those who have devastated many cities in my kingdom, now therefore I confirm to you all the tax remissions that the kings before me have granted you, and release from all the other payments from which they have released you. I permit you to mint your own coinage as money for your country, and I grant freedom to Jerusalem and the sanctuary. All the weapons which you have

15. Dąbrowa 1999 [2000]: 16.

16. Bouché-Leclercq 1913–1914: i 378; Shayegan 2003 [2007]: 90; id. 2011: 124.

17. *I Maccabees* 15.1–4; Jos. *AJ*. 13.220–23; Appian *Syr*. 11.68; Justin 36.1.9; Eus. *Chron*. (Smith ed.): 255. Antiochus also sent gifts to appease the Romans. Livy *Epit*. 57.8. Note Shayegan 2003 [2007]: 87.

18. *I Maccabees* 15.25–16.10; *V Maccabees* 21.1–18; Diod. 34/35.1; Jos. *AJ*. 13.223–29, 236, 240–49; id. *Bell*. 1.50–54, 61; Eus. *Chron*. (Smith ed.): 255; Hieron. *Chron*. 162.1; Plut. *Reg. Imp. Apophtheg*. 184E–F. For Antiochus' Jewish Wars, see Bevan 1902: ii 239–41; Bouché-Leclercq 1913–1914: i 374–77; Abel 1952: i 200–9; Ehling 1998a: 234–41; Ehling 2008: 193–99.

prepared and the strongholds which you have built and now hold shall remain yours. Every debt you owe to the royal treasury and any such future debts shall be canceled for you from henceforth and for all time. When we gain control of our kingdom, we will bestow great honor upon you and your nation and the temple, so that your glory will become manifest in all the earth."[19]

This letter helps illustrate the level of destruction that multiple civil wars during the power-transition crisis of the 160s–130s had brought upon the Seleucid Empire. Since the early stages of the Seleucid dynasty, Syria was the political, military, and financial center of the Seleucid state; however, years of war had ravaged the Syrian countryside. Antiochus here shows great concern for the destruction of this region during the crisis because he understood that he could not restore the Seleucid Empire to its former strength without first restoring the productivity of Syria. Further, this letter demonstrates that Antiochus, even before his arrival in Syria, had grand plans "to lay claim to the kingdom so that I may restore it as it formerly was." Ultimately, he wanted to reclaim the empire of Seleucus I and Antiochus III, which involved a hegemonic war against the Parthians. Yet this letter also underscores Antiochus' vulnerability in 138 and the strong position of the Jews within the region. Before the royal army deserted Tryphon in favor of Antiochus, Antiochus had only a modest force of mercenaries and ships, encouraging him to secure a military alliance with the heavily militarized Jewish state. Meanwhile, the Jews stood to gain political, financial, and military freedom and, thus, agreed to the alliance. The alliance promised regional security and enhanced the prestige of the Jewish state, which was attractive to the Jews in part because state reputation was linked directly to perceived power and state security. With a new military ally in the south, Antiochus could put pressure on Tryphon on two fronts, and with an enhanced military and political reputation, the Jews could hope to bolster their security and standing within a highly volatile region.

Initially, this military alliance was a success. Antiochus VII quickly reclaimed Syria, pinning Diodotus Tryphon in Phoenicia between his forces. However, once Tryphon was defeated and Antiochus no longer needed Jewish aid, he quickly reneged on his agreement. Since there was no enforceable international law in the ancient world and since the Romans remained infrequently involved in geopolitical developments in the Near East at this time, there was little, short of the threat or use of military force, to hold Antiochus to his promises.[20] After

19. *I Maccabees* 15.1–9. Compare Jos. *AJ*. 13.223–24. Although it is difficult to say whether this letter is genuine, *I Maccabees* is a relatively contemporary historical account of these events and generally reliable. For the composition and content of *I Maccabees*, see Goldstein 1976; Mittmann-Richert 2000.

20. It is possible the Jews had brokered friendly relations with Rome by this time. *I Maccabees* 8.1–31, 12.1–4, 16, 14.24, 40, 15.15–24; Justin 36.3.9. Yet Roman involvement in Jewish affairs appears suspect. Note Gruen 1984: 749–50. If an agreement of friendship was in place, the Romans took little interest in intervening. Note Coşkun 2018; Dąbrowa 2019; Coşkun and Engels 2019.

defeating Tryphon and gaining the support of the Seleucid royal army, Antiochus had a strong enough force to make war against the Jews, and the Jews could do nothing to force Antiochus to honor their agreement. These were the grim realities of the international environment.

Antiochus VII's original concessions to the Jews reflect his vulnerability early in the war against Diodotus Tryphon. Yet his betrayal of the Jews toward the end of the conflict demonstrates his new position of power. Moreover, as the new king of Syria, Antiochus had reason for concern in the south since Judaea was a strategically important region and the Jews traditionally were long-standing antagonists of the Seleucids.

A strong, autonomous Jewish state was a threat to Syria and a challenge to the hegemony of the Seleucids in the region.[21] Antiochus VII's letter, in fact, mentions stockpiles of Jewish weapons and Jewish strongholds. Meanwhile, the Jews fought well in the war against Diodotus Tryphon, even sending Antiochus "two thousand picked men to fight for him, and silver and gold and much military equipment."[22] With the defeat of Tryphon, Antiochus recognized the need to subdue his former allies to secure his position in Syria and enhance his military reputation.

Thus, Antiochus VII participated in brazen power politics and expressed his demands through the abrasive rhetoric of ancient diplomacy. As recorded in *I Maccabees*:

> He [Antiochus] sent to him [that is, Simon] Athenobius, one of his friends, to confer with him, saying, "You hold control of Joppa and Gazara and the citadel in Jerusalem; they are cities of my kingdom. You have devastated their territory, you have done great damage in the land, and you have taken possession of many places in my kingdom. Now then, hand over the cities which you have seized and the tribute money of the places which you have conquered outside the borders of Judah; or else give me for them five hundred talents of silver, and for the destruction that you have caused and the tribute money of the cities, five hundred talents more. Otherwise we will come and conquer you."[23]

This is an excellent example of the aggressive and harsh diplomatic exchanges of the ancient world, known to international relations theorists as "compellence diplomacy." In the absence of permanent embassies, ancient states had no way to communicate with one another consistently, and because of the infrequency of diplomatic interactions, ancient states mostly lacked the ability to defuse

21. Antiochus' generals later faced a Jewish army of perhaps 20,000 soldiers. *I Maccabees* 16.4–10.
22. Id. 15.26.
23. Id. 15.28–31.

potential points of contention between polities before conflict became unavoidable. Thus, compellence diplomacy, like the example above, was the normal diplomatic exchange between two estranged states in the ancient world. Antiochus' envoy demanded the return of land and taxes or a substantial ransom, and he threatened the Jews with war for noncompliance. Moreover, Athenobius did not offer Simon any option to negotiate these terms. The message was clear; submit willingly or by force. In fact, when Simon claimed that the cities he held were the rightful property of the Jewish state and attempted to negotiate a lower payment, Athenobius promptly broke off communication and reported to Antiochus, who became "violently angry."[24] For Antiochus his message to the Jews was a manifestation of his power and to challenge that meant war.

Josephus tells us that Antiochus VII invaded Judaea in ca. 134, ravaged the countryside, surrounded Jerusalem with encampments, and assaulted the north wall with "a hundred towers of three stories high."[25] The Jewish commander, Hyrcanus, after a stout but costly defense, agreed to come to terms with Antiochus in ca. 132.[26] Antiochus rejected the advice of his counselors, who wanted to "utterly destroy the [Jewish] nation," and instead demanded that the Jews hand over their arms, pull down the walls of Jerusalem, deliver up hostages, pay 500 talents of silver in tribute, surrender control of Joppa and the surrounding cities, and accept Seleucid hegemony.[27] Finally, Antiochus forced Hyrcanus to spend another 2,500 talents to raise a mercenary force to accompany the Seleucids on their subsequent invasion of Mesopotamia.[28]

Antiochus VII's victory over the Jews accomplished three important objectives for his wider ambitions to restore the position of the Seleucid Empire in the Hellenistic Middle East. First, it enhanced his military prestige. The Jews in Judaea were highly militarized and warlike, and they had destabilized the southern frontier of the Seleucid Empire for decades. With the violent submission of Judaea, Antiochus could claim victory over a traditional enemy of the Seleucids.[29] This lent legitimacy to Antiochus' rule and garnered support for him within the army and state. Second, the submission of Judaea secured the southern frontier of Antiochus' realm. A strong show of force in Judaea discouraged further resistance by the Jews and outside interference in the region by Ptolemaic Egypt. By regaining control of the strategically important cities and fortifications in Judaea, Antiochus secured his position in Syria, making an eastern expedition

24. Id. 15.32–6.

25. Jos. *Ant.* 13.236–39. For the campaign, note Grainger 2016: 95–98.

26. The siege lasted about a year, which forced Hyrcanus to remove all noncombatants from the city to conserve supplies. Much like Caesar at Alesia, Antiochus did not let the civilians past his siege lines, and many died until Hyrcanus readmitted them to the city. Jos. *Ant.* 13.240–45. Note Caes. *BG* 7.78.

27. Jos. *Ant.* 13.245–48; Diod. 34/35.1.

28. Hyrcanus and his troops accompanied Antiochus into Mesopotamia and helped remove the Parthians from this region. Jos. *Ant.* 13.249–52; *V Maccabees* 21.19–23.

29. Antiochus possibly minted gold coins celebrating his success against the Jews, see Assar 2005a: 46.

possible. Finally, the war allowed Antiochus to raise the soldiers and revenue necessary to conduct his anabasis. Thus, Antiochus' expedition against the Jews was a major success that prepared him and his army for his hegemonic war against the Parthians.

Before discussing Antiochus VII's anabasis, it is worth considering his motivations to conquer the Parthians. Antiochus' eastern expedition was a retaliatory campaign to satisfy both long-standing and recent grudges, to secure and enhance Antiochus' position, and to eliminate the most threatening rival of the Seleucids in the east. It was a hugely ambitious undertaking; however, in the late 130s it was a realistic objective. Antiochus had the resources, the drive, and the *casus belli* to pursue and accomplish his lofty goal of restoring the Seleucid Empire to its leading position within the Hellenistic Middle East.[30]

Antiochus III had subdued Parthia and made it a subordinate allied kingdom; however, the Parthians under Phraates I and Mithridates I had created an aggressive rival imperial state. Antiochus IV, Antiochus V, Demetrius I, Alexander Balas, Demetrius II, and Diodotus Tryphon all were unable to exact retribution against the Parthians during the power-transition crisis of the 160s–130s, while the Parthians occupied important Seleucid lands in Media and Mesopotamia.[31] If Antiochus VII wished to be a strong leader and the true king, he had a duty to reclaim the lost eastern lands of the empire.

Antiochus VII also had a personal stake in the fight against the Parthians. Demetrius II's defeat and capture in Babylonia had brought shame to the dynasty and kingdom. The Parthians' control of such a high-profile prisoner was unacceptable. The captivity of Antiochus' older brother and the stain of Demetrius' defeat were embarrassments that Antiochus wished to eliminate.

The recovery of Demetrius II not only would have allowed Antiochus VII to reclaim the dignity of his family, it also would have removed the last major rival to his throne.[32] As long as Demetrius remained in Parthian hands, he could be used as a weapon against Antiochus, and indeed, eventually Demetrius was used against him.[33] Justin records, "But it was not compassion, or respect for ties of blood, that was the cause of this extraordinary clemency of the Parthians toward Demetrius; the reason was, that they had some designs on the kingdom of Syria, and intended to make use of Demetrius against his brother Antiochus, as circumstances, the course of time, or the fortune of war, might require."[34] Although there may be an element of hindsight in Justin's explanation, he underscores the reality that the conflict between the Seleucids and Parthians

30. See *I Maccabees* 15.13; Justin 38.10.2–4; Diod. 34/35.17. Note Grainger 2016: 105, 108–9.

31. Note Overtoom 2019a.

32. Note Shayegan 2011: 124; Grainger 2016: 107–8.

33. The Parthians eventually released Demetrius from captivity to contest the Seleucid throne. Justin 38.10.7, 11; Appian *Syr.* 11.68. Note Overtoom 2020.

34. Justin 38.9.10.

was ongoing and that the looming Parthian threat to deploy Demetrius as a rival against Antiochus was a serious danger.[35] Antiochus needed to bring the hegemonic war against the Parthians to a successful conclusion and secure his position as king. For Antiochus it did not matter that Demetrius lived reluctantly under the thumb of the Parthian king or that Demetrius seemingly garnered no ill will toward him.[36] Antiochus could not allow Demetrius to remain in Parthian captivity if he hoped to solidify his authority and legitimacy, making an anabasis necessary.

The prospect of world-renowned military glory also attracted Antiochus VII. For example, Alexander and Antiochus III had demonstrated that a successful anabasis brought with it "Great" prestige.[37] Directly emulating Alexander the Great, Seleucus the Victor, and Antiochus the Great was a bold undertaking; however, Antiochus VII clearly viewed himself as their equal and wanted others to make this association.[38] He had attacked the Jews in part to enhance his military prestige, but the suppression of the Jews was a minor victory compared to the defeat of the Parthians and the reconquest of the east. Antiochus understood that subduing the Parthians would give him the glory and prestige he sought, while destroying the Seleucids' most threatening rival in the east.

Antiochus VII's anabasis also was an attempt to seize the initiative in the conflict against the Parthians during a window of opportunity. After seizing Babylonia and defeating Demetrius II, the Parthians threatened northern Mesopotamia and Syria, and Antiochus recognized that he could protect these lands best by acting aggressively. Justin states, "Antiochus, having heard of their [that is, the Parthians' western] designs, and thinking it proper to be first in the field, led forth an army, which he had inured to service by many wars with his neighbors, against the Parthians."[39] Because of his success in the 130s, Antiochus could concentrate a large portion of the Seleucid military against the Parthians before the Parthians could pursue further expansion to the west.[40]

The sources certainly exaggerate the size of Antiochus VII's army in the east; however, it is possible that Justin's figure of 80,000 soldiers reflects a reliable total for the entire Seleucid military including mercenaries and subordinate allied forces in the late 130s. Although Antiochus could not take this entire force with him to Babylonia, it is reasonable to argue that he took at least half (and

35. Bing and Sievers 2011.

36. Demetrius apparently tried to escape his captivity twice, despite his marriage to Mithridates I's daughter and his life of luxury in the east. Justin 36.1.6, 38.9.3–9. Demetrius married Phraates II's sister, Rhodogune. Appian *Syr.* 11.67. Note Polyaen. 27. For the argument that there was little hostility between the two brothers, see Mittag 2002: 377–80.

37. Note Appian *Syr.* 1.1.

38. See Justin 38.10.6; Diod. 34/35.15; *I Maccabees* 15.3, *V Maccabees* 21.19. Note Shayegan 2003 [2007]: 90–91.

39. Justin states that there were also 300,000 camp followers in Antiochus' army. Justin 38.10.1. Diodorus places the entire force at 300,000. Diod. 34/35.17. Note Orosius 5.10.8.

40. Justin 38.10.2. For larger military figures, see Orosius 5.10.8; Eus. *Chron.* (Smith ed.): 255; *I Maccabees* 15.13.

perhaps as many as three quarters) of these men on campaign as Antiochus III and Antiochus IV had done before him.[41] In fact, Antiochus VII's eventual defeat in the east was ruinous for the overall strength of the Seleucid military, making a larger percentage more likely. Thus, Antiochus' army at the height of his anabasis could have numbered as many as 60,000 men, and even if we accept that the entire force of the Seleucid military in the late 130s was three quarters of Justin's figure, Antiochus reasonably had around 45,000 soldiers on campaign.[42]

Meanwhile, the Parthians were not "the unquestioned dominant power in the region" in the late 130s.[43] Their control over Media and Mesopotamia remained precarious because of Arab raids and conflicts with Elymais and Characene; the stability of their eastern frontier was a major concern; and the death of Mithridates I in 132 after years of severe illness left an untried young man, Phraates II (Arsaces VII), on the Parthian throne. In fact, Phraates was young enough (perhaps in his middle to late teens) that it appears he initially shared power with his mother, Rīnnu, and his early coinage (S14.1–2) illustrates an adolescent with a small beard.[44] Susan Sherwin-White and Amélie Kuhrt correctly recognized that, in the conflict between the Seleucids and Parthians in the 130s–120s, both powers were matched evenly and the outcome "hung in the balance."[45] With the Seleucid bogeyman, Mithridates, dead and the youthful, unproven Phraates left to hold together a wide-ranging, newly won kingdom that faced internal unrest and severe external pressures, Antiochus VII had every reason to be optimistic about his anabasis' chances of success. Unfortunately for the Seleucids, Antiochus was unable to realize his dreams and reach his potential because he underestimated the effectiveness of the leadership of the Arsacids and the capabilities of the Parthian military.

The King Slayers

Although inexperienced, Phraates II recognized the vulnerability of his position in the late 130s and enacted several policies to secure his western frontier. He began his reign by consolidating Parthian hegemony over Elymais in 132/131, and he also initiated extensive military preparations in Babylonia in

41. Justin states Antiochus III's army contained 120,000 soldiers; however, this too likely reflects the entire strength of the Seleucid military including mercenaries and subordinate allied forces. Justin 41.5.7. It appears Antiochus III took around 70,000 men on his anabasis. Bar-Kochva 1987: 10; Taylor 2013: 72; Grainger 2015: 60–63. Antiochus IV took half of his 50,000 soldiers in Syria to link up with his eastern forces under Timarchus. Polyb. 30.25.1–26.9; *V Maccabees* 7.10–13. Note *I Maccabees* 1–6. Grainger assumes Antiochus took every available soldier on campaign. Grainger 2016: 109. Yet clearly the court in Syria maintained a portion of the army. Eus. *Chron.* (Smith ed.): 257; Justin 39.1.1–2.

42. Although Assar conservatively surmises that Antiochus' army in the east was closer to 30,000 soldiers, even this figure is an impressive military force. Assar 2011: 118.

43. Sampson 2015: 46. Compare Grainger 2013a: 185–86.

44. See Sachs and Hunger 1996: no. -131D; Assar 2005a: 45–47; id. 2006c: 98; id. 2006–2007: 12; id. 2011: 118. Note Valverde 2017.

45. Sherwin-White and Kuhrt 1993: 224. Note Grainger 2016: 106–9.

131.[46] Antiochus VII's major eastern campaign was not a secret, and Phraates understood that Babylonia, with its resources and large Greek population, was Antiochus' first target. Thus, it was necessary for the new Parthian king to ensure the loyalty and security of this region.

The Greek population in Babylonia was one of the most potentially volatile groups in the region, and therefore, to secure its support in the looming conflict, Phraates II met with representatives from the various Greek communities and appointed a Greek as mayor of Babylon.[47] Phraates' campaign to win over the support of local Greek leadership in the region was a prudent decision that paid dividends in the approaching conflict with Antiochus VII. The harsh criticisms of our Greek and Roman sources of Parthian rule in the region are exaggerated and again likely reflect negative Graeco-Roman stereotypes of despotic eastern rule.[48] Instead, these Greek communities continued to work with Phraates enthusiastically before, during, and after Antiochus' invasion of the region. Thus, I agree with Rahim Shayegan's conclusion that the cities of Mesopotamia joined Antiochus in 130 by "dint of conquest" and lacked "Hellenic fervor" for the Seleucid reoccupation.[49] Moreover, a closer evaluation of the geopolitical developments in the region through the framework of Realist Theory strengthens the case that the cities in Mesopotamia sided with Antiochus in 130 because of systemic pressures. With the approach of Antiochus' large army and the withdrawal of the Parthians, all the communities "defecting (*deficientibus*)" to Antiochus did so because of immediate security concerns, rather than out of enthusiasm to rid themselves of despotic Parthian rule.[50] Without Parthian military support, armed resistance to Antiochus' invasion of Babylonia risked destruction. Therefore, these communities made practical and calculated decisions to surrender, at least temporarily. The later eagerness of these cities to betray Antiochus and their devoted collaboration with the Parthians in 130–129 underscores the lack of "Hellenic fervor" in these communities, the relative popularity of the Parthians in the region after a decade of occupation, and the abuses of the Seleucid troops to these communities.

Yet Phraates II had less success in keeping the loyalties of the various eastern dynasts in the region under his authority. Antiochus VII invaded Mesopotamia in summer 130 and occupied the region until the end of autumn 129.[51] Justin states:

46. Assar 2006c: 98–9.

47. Sachs and Hunger 1996: no. -129A. Compare Dąbrowa 2006–2007 [2008]; id. 2011a; Shayegan 2011: 125–27; Olbrycht 2017b: 12–17. Note van der Spek 2005.

48. Diod. 34/35.19, 21; Justin 38.10.5–6; id. *Prol.* 42; Athen. 11.15b–c.

49. Shayegan 2011: 136.

50. Justin 38.10.6.

51. Note Assar 2006c: 99–104; id. 2011: 118. Compare Fischer 1970: 39–41, 43–44, 47; Bing and Sievers 2011; Grainger 2016: 109–10.

> But his [Antiochus'] preparations for luxury were not less than those for war, for three hundred thousand camp followers, of whom the greater number were cooks, bakers, and stage-players, attended on eighty thousand armed men. Of silver and gold, it is certain, there was such an abundance, that the common soldiers fastened their boots with gold, and trod upon the metal for the love of which nations contend with the sword. Their cooking instruments, too, were of silver, as if they were going to a banquet, not to a field of battle. Many kings of the east met Antiochus on his march, offering him themselves and their kingdoms, and expressing the greatest detestation of Parthian pride.[52]

Although Justin here again exaggerates the circumstances, he emphasizes the great power and wealth of Antiochus at the beginning of his anabasis.[53] As the large Seleucid army moved eastward, other powerful men began to flock to Antiochus' banner. It is unclear who these eastern kings were; however, they recognized the rising position of the Seleucids in the region and seized an opportunity to shake off Parthian hegemony.

In 130 the Parthians only recently had defeated the military alliance of Elymais and Characene and forced Elymais to become a tributary kingdom.[54] Their control over these regions remained fragile, and the Parthians continued to face resistance from rivals in Mesopotamia and southern Iran. These eastern rulers had come to view the Parthians as the most immediate threat to their security, and therefore they eagerly came to Antiochus VII's support.[55] The decision of these eastern kings to join Antiochus' fight against the Parthians is a process known to international relations theorists as "balancing behavior."[56] These "kings" helped shift the regional balance of power in the Seleucids' favor in the hope that they would benefit from Antiochus' new settlement of the eastern territories as his allies.

Even if Antiochus VII defeated the Parthians, eventually he would have to return to Syria and concern himself with the always troublesome geopolitics of the Eastern Mediterranean. Unlike the Parthians, who were making Media and Mesopotamia the new power centers of their growing empire, it was well-understood that the Seleucids were never free from major western concerns that limited their interference in the geopolitics of Mesopotamia and the Iranian plateau. In particular, Elymais, Persis, and Characene had made diligent efforts to

52. Justin 38.10.2–5. Translation slightly altered.

53. For Antiochus' extravagance, see Athen. 5.46d, 12.56b–c.

54. See Shayegan 2011: 110–11, 131 n.375.

55. These eastern dynasts perhaps offered their support to Antiochus after his conquest of Mesopotamia, see Fischer 1970: 42. Compare Ehling 2008: 203.

56. For balancing behavior, see Waltz 1979: 168; Walt 1987; Waltz 1988: 625; Strauss 1991; Sheehan 1996; Mastanduno 1997; Beck 1997: 231–32; Mastanduno and Kapstein 1999; Wohlforth 1999; id. 2002; Eckstein 2006: 65–67.

assert their independence for decades. By joining the war against the Parthians, these eastern kings hoped to secure Antiochus' favor and official recognition of their regional positions of power.

Much like the campaign of his brother, Antiochus VII's anabasis appears initially to have enjoyed great success. Justin states, "Nor was there any delay in coming to an engagement. Antiochus, being victorious in three battles, and having got possession of Babylon, began to be thought a great man. All the neighboring people, in consequence, deserting to him, nothing was left to the Parthians but their own country."[57] Meanwhile, Josephus adds, "Nicolaus of Damascus is a witness for us; who in his [Augustan Age] history writes thus: 'When Antiochus had erected a trophy at the river Lycus [that is, the Great Zab River in northern Iraq], upon his conquest of Indates, the general of the Parthians, he stayed there two days.' "[58] Thus, in late summer and early autumn 130, Antiochus won three engagements against the Parthians in northern Mesopotamia; he seized Babylonia and occupied its major cities, minting celebratory coinage at Seleucia; and he invaded Elymais, removing its pro-Parthian vassal from power.[59]

In 129 Antiochus VII continued eastward and subdued much of Media, which led Justin to exaggerate, "nothing was left to the Parthians but their own country."[60] Yet the approach of winter meant that Antiochus had to postpone his campaign into Parthia until the following year. Over the course of the campaign, Antiochus had billeted his soldiers in the prosperous cities of Mesopotamia and Media, dividing his large army into several garrisons. Justin notes how this decision had disastrous results for the Seleucids, stating:

> On account of the number of his forces, Antiochus had distributed his army, in winter quarters, through several cities; and this dispersion was the cause of his ruin; for the cities, finding themselves harassed by having to furnish supplies, and by the depredations of the soldiers, revolted to the Parthians, and, on an appointed day, conspired to fall upon the army divided among them, so that the several divisions might not be able to assist each other.[61]

Instead of concentrating his forces against the Parthians' main army, Antiochus decided to spread his soldiers out into isolated pockets across the cities of the reoccupied eastern territories. With the sudden and violent support of these communities, especially in Babylonia, the Parthians cut off Antiochus and his

57. Justin 38.10.5–6. Translation slightly altered.

58. Jos. *Ant.* 13.251. Compare *V Maccabees* 21.21–23.

59. See Assar 2006c: 102–4; id. 2011: 118; Shayegan 2011: 131 n.375; Dąbrowa 2014b: 63; Monerie 2019; Faghfoury 2020. Characene likely stayed aloof from the conflict but used the chaos that followed Antiochus' death to invade Babylonia. Shayegan 2011: 110–11.

60. Justin 38.10.6. The Parthians still maintained control over most of the Iranian plateau.

61. Id. 38.10.8. Compare Diod. 34/35.17.2.

much-reduced force in southern Media late in 129. This allowed Phraates II to ambush and destroy the core of the Seleucid army, leaving Antiochus among the dead.[62]

Before considering the major consequences of Antiochus VII's defeat and death, it is worth considering his anabasis further because once again we find evidence of the Parthians successfully implementing and executing their "Feign Retreat, Defeat in Detail" mode of warfare.[63] Antiochus' war against the Parthians shares numerous similarities to the earlier campaigns of the Seleucids and the later campaigns of the Romans against the Parthians. This is not a coincidence, but rather further evidence that the Parthians developed a long-standing military tradition that had great strategic and tactical capabilities. Antiochus, like so many Macedonian and Roman generals who fought the Parthians, found himself outmaneuvered and overwhelmed by the highly mobile, cunning, and opportunistic Parthian army.

When Antiochus VII came to the throne, the Seleucids still maintained control over portions of northern Mesopotamia.[64] Yet in the time it took Antiochus to secure his position in Syria, Phoenicia, and Judaea, it appears the Parthians had begun to make inroads into northern Mesopotamia north of the Great Zab River. Like his brother, Antiochus recognized an immediate need to reestablish firm Seleucid control over Mesopotamia and Media to stabilize and expand his power.[65] In early summer 130, he moved across the Euphrates into northern Mesopotamia with a large, eclectic army. Phraates II had spent the early portion of the year strengthening his position in Babylonia, preparing for Antiochus' imminent invasion, and when the Seleucid army crossed into northern Mesopotamia, Phraates likely still remained in Babylonia near Seleucia.[66] Like Mithridates I in the early 130s and Orodes II in the middle 50s, Phraates delegated the initial defensive campaign in Mesopotamia to one of his trusted generals, Indates, and like Bagasis in the early 130s and Surena in the middle 50s, it was Indates' responsibility to probe, harass, and delay the invading enemy. The Parthians had enjoyed immense success earlier in the decade against Demetrius II in Babylonia, and Phraates and Indates likely planned initially to follow a similar strategy against Antiochus. Thus, Indates implemented the Parthians' Harass Strategy and contested the Seleucids in three minor engagements, testing their strength and resilience. Again, one of the major objectives of the Parthians' asymmetric

62. Justin 38.10.9–10; Diod. 34/35.16–17.1; Jos. *Ant.* 13.253–54, 271; Appian *Syr.* 11.68; Athen. 10.53; Hieron. *Chron.* 163.1; Orosius 5.10.8; Moses 2.2; *V Maccabees* 21.23–24; Sebeos in Thomson 1978: 364–65. John Malalas erroneously records that Antiochus VII forced the Parthians to accept a truce and married his son to the daughter of the Parthian king, Brittane. Yet Malalas appears to confuse Antiochus VII with Antiochus III here. Jo. Mal. 8.208. Note Assar 2011: 115.

63. Note Overtoom 2017b.

64. Note Diod. 33.28.

65. Dąbrowa 1999 [2000]: 15–16.

66. Sachs and Hunger 1996: no. -129A1, no. -129A2. Note Shayegan 2011: 127–28.

mode of warfare was to encourage overconfidence in their enemies through misdirection, deception, and confusion to make enemy forces complacent or overly aggressive. The Parthians knew that overcoming Antiochus' large army while it was concentrated would be immensely difficult; however, they could hope to coerce Antiochus into making a military blunder that would provide them with an opportunity to counterattack decisively. It seems likely that the Parthians initially had hoped to draw Antiochus' army into a vulnerable position within Babylonia between Indates' and Phraates' forces, at which point they could counterattack and overwhelm yet another Seleucid army. Yet the Parthians did not anticipate the determination and diligence of Antiochus' initial expedition.

The Seleucid victories in northern Mesopotamia granted Antiochus VII access to Babylonia; however, they were not decisive in helping him win the war. Justin, who exaggerated the victories of Demetrius II in Mesopotamia and misunderstood the strategic goals of the Parthians, made similar oversights in his account of Antiochus' campaign against the Parthians.[67] The resources and manpower of the Parthian military in the 130s remained quite limited (perhaps as few as 20,000 soldiers).[68] They could not have endured three defeats of any significance early in the campaign against Antiochus. Rather they hoped to delay the Seleucids and create an opportunity to strike at Antiochus while giving ground.

Although his victories must have been minor, unlike his brother, Antiochus VII did not yet provide the Parthians with the opportunity they needed to counterattack decisively. He successfully protected his large army as he entered Babylonia and approached the major urban centers in the region. Like Arsaces II's decision to abandon Hecatompylus in the face of Antiochus III's overwhelming advance, Phraates II decided in early autumn to implement the Parthians' Deceptive Withdrawal Strategy to lure Antiochus VII away from the major cities of Babylonia and into an unfavorable position further east.[69] Justin hints at this change of strategy when he states, "In the meantime, since he [Phraates] could not overthrow Antiochus by open force, he made attempts upon him everywhere by stratagem (*insidiis*)."[70] Although Justin here uses the term *insidiae* as a pejorative to censure the Parthians, he recognized that the Parthians were attempting to manipulate Antiochus strategically.[71]

Justin's brief account of Antiochus VII's anabasis unfortunately condenses the separate Seleucid campaigns in Mesopotamia, Elymais, and Media into one series of events; however, what Justin here identifies as Parthian "stratagem" was in

67. Justin 36.1.4, 38.9.2.

68. Note Potter 2010: 157; Olbrycht 2016a 295; McLaughlin 2016: 223–24. Eusebius of Caesarea and Moses of Chorene place Phraates' army at 120,000 men. Eus. *Chron.* (Smith ed.): 255; Moses 2.2. Compare Sebeos in Thomson 1978: 364–65. This figure is an immense exaggeration.

69. Note Polyb. 10.28.6–7; Appian *Syr.* 9.57.

70. Justin 38.10.7.

71. Note Shayegan 2011: 135.

fact the Parthians adapting to the rapidly evolving geopolitical situation in the region from late 130 to late 129 following well-established military traditions.[72] Although Antiochus had not eliminated the threat of the Parthians by late 130, their seemingly poor showing in the skirmishes with the Seleucids in northern Mesopotamia and their abandonment of Babylonia served to lower Antiochus' opinion of the capabilities of the Parthian military moving forward in the campaign. With Antiochus' conquests of Mesopotamia and Elymais almost complete, he divided his army into numerous garrisons across an extended front in winter 130/129.

Despite Phraates II's continued presence in the field with his army, Antiochus VII became increasingly less concerned with the threat of the Parthian military, which was in part a result of the Parthians' successful execution of their asymmetric approach to warfare.[73] The continued withdrawal and apparent weakness of the Parthians throughout much of 130–129 drew the Seleucids even deeper into enemy territory, encouraging Antiochus eventually to make a critical mistake. Like Marc Antony's much later blunder in Media, Antiochus once again divided his large force into vulnerable detachments directly in the face of the enemy.[74] In late 129, with Antiochus exposed and isolated, the Parthians quickly recognized their opportunity and counterattacked decisively, utilizing their Overwhelm Strategy.

Phraates II's diplomatic initiatives during this campaign also played a crucial role in enhancing his military capabilities. In winter 130/129, Antiochus VII's forces abused the captured cities of Mesopotamia, especially in Babylonia, allowing Phraates' agents to communicate with these disgruntled communities over the next several months and enlist them in a well-planned and coordinated uprising against their Seleucid garrisons in late 129.[75] It is astonishing that such an extensive and complex plan was kept secret and successfully executed, and it is a testament to the Parthians' effective use of diplomacy and espionage. In fact, only Phraates and Mithridates VI of Pontus successfully organized and implemented such wide-ranging, synchronized uprisings against their foes.[76]

72. Antiochus' anabasis consisted of two phases. See Fischer 1970: 39–48; Shayegan 2003 [2007]: 90–92; Ehling 2008: 201–5; Bing and Sievers 2011; Shayegan 2011: 125 n.341, 128–37. Note that Plutarch records that Antiochus twice made an inroad into Parthian territory. Plut. *Reg. Imp. Apophtheg.* 184D. Justin's incorrect compression of events still adversely affects modern studies. For example, Taylor assumes Antiochus' anabasis took one year and began in 129. Taylor 2013: 156–57.

73. Phraates' later efforts to supplement his forces with a large band of Central Asian mercenaries and captive Greeks demonstrates that the Parthian military remained relatively small and in need of soldiers. Note Justin 42.1.1–2, 4.

74. Note Vell. Pat. 2.82; Plut. *Ant.* 38.2–3; Dio 49.25–26; Florus 2.20.3; Livy *Epit.* 130.

75. Note Justin 38.10.8; Diod. 34/35.15. These communities revolted to the Parthians, making Phraates' involvement highly likely. Note Shayegan 2011: 129, 136. Grainger is too dismissive of Seleucid abuses and the resentment toward Antiochus' occupation of Mesopotamia and Media. Grainger 2016: 111–12.

76. Mithridates' uprising in Anatolia killed 80,000–150,000 Roman citizens and allies. Memnon 22.9; Appian *Mithr.* 4.22–23; Plut. *Sul.* 24.4; Dio 30–5.101; Cic. *Man.* 5.11. Note Mayor 2010: 13–26.

Further, the eagerness of these communities to aid Phraates, their continued secrecy, and their successful rebellions speak to their continued support for the Parthians and their displeasure with Antiochus' reoccupation of the region. The relatively mild rule of the Parthians and the recent efforts of Phraates to work with Greek communities in the region to gain their support paid off when these communities aided the Parthians in isolating Antiochus.[77]

While Phraates II worked to retain the support of the communities in Babylonia, Antiochus VII began his invasion of Media in spring 129. Antiochus' imminent threat to Media encouraged Phraates to engage in further diplomatic negotiations, this time with Antiochus himself. Diodorus records:

> The warm spring heat had begun to melt the snow; the crops, after the long cold of winter, were showing their first buds; and men were going to the work of agriculture; when Arsaces [that is, Phraates], wishing to test the enemy (ἀποπειραθῆναι βουλόμενος τῶν πολεμίων), sent envoys to negotiate peace. Antiochus replied that he would grant peace on these conditions: that his brother Demetrius [II] was freed from captivity and released, that Arsaces evacuated the territory which he had occupied, and that, content with his ancestral realm, he paid tribute to Antiochus. Provoked by the harshness of this response, Arsaces marched against Antiochus.[78]

In Antiochus' severe terms of peace, we find another prime example of "compellence diplomacy." Antiochus' response to Phraates contains the standard, abrasive rhetoric of diplomatic exchanges in the ancient world. He demanded his brother's release into his custody, the return of all Seleucid territory occupied by the Parthians, and the payment of tribute, leaving no room for further negotiation. Moreover, his demands help underscore his larger objectives and ambitions. Antiochus was attempting to secure his unrivaled position throughout the Hellenistic Middle East by restoring the conditions of Antiochus III's settlement of the Iranian plateau.[79] Yet Phraates was not yet in the desperate position in which Arsaces II found himself in 208; such terms were unacceptable.

In opening diplomatic communication with Antiochus VII in early 129, Phraates II delayed the Seleucids' advance, allowing him to further organize resistance within Babylonia and defenses within Media. Phraates did not actually

77. Shayegan argues that the Parthians not only retained the loyalty of Greek leaders in Babylonia, but also the native population. He argues that the *Dynastic Prophecy* links Phraates to Darius III as the successful successor and avenger of the Persian Empire. He concludes that this prophecy was propaganda to encourage pro-Parthian rebellions against Antiochus in Mesopotamia and that it demonstrates local support of the Parthians as the second coming of the Achaemenid Persians. Shayegan 2011: 137–39. For the *Dynastic Prophecy*, note Neujahr 2005.

78. Diod. 34/35.15. Translation slightly altered.

79. Athenaeus associates Antiochus' anabasis directly with that of Antiochus III, arguing that Antiochus VII wanted to "drink up the kingdom of Arsaces." Athen. 10.53e.

desire peace in these negotiations; rather, this was a ploy to "test" the resolve of Antiochus and to stall his momentum.[80] Although to Antiochus the position of Phraates in early 129 appeared weak and desperate, Antiochus failed to appreciate that Phraates was attempting to outmaneuver him. With Antiochus' ultimatum, Phraates' choice in 129 was to submit or fight, and having not been defeated himself, he easily chose to carry on the war.

Although Antiochus VII's penetration of Media could not be avoided, this diplomatic exchange bought Phraates II precious time, delaying the renewal of Antiochus' invasion until ca. March 129.[81] After leaving garrisons in Mesopotamia to maintain his lines of communication and supply, Antiochus undertook the second phase of his anabasis.[82] Still unable to defeat the concentrated force of Antiochus' army, the Parthians continued to implement their Harass and Deceptive Withdrawal strategies, biding their time for the opportunity they needed to counterattack. By autumn 129, Antiochus likely had reoccupied much of Media and began to consider his push into Parthia proper.[83] Yet by autumn 129, numerous communities in Babylonia had secretly allied themselves with the Parthians to overthrown Seleucid control in the region. If the Parthians hoped to utilize these allies in Babylonia, they needed to continue to delay Antiochus' invasion of Parthia proper.

In an aggressive political maneuver, Phraates II decided to utilize one of his most valuable remaining assets to impede and distract Antiochus VII. Phraates released his prized prisoner, Demetrius II, under a Parthian escort to contest the Seleucid throne in Syria.[84] Justin records, "It was then that Phraates sent Demetrius into Syria, with a body of Parthians, to seize the throne, so that Antiochus might be recalled from Parthia to secure his own dominions."[85] Meanwhile, Josephus states, "And his brother Demetrius succeeded in the kingdom of Syria, by the permission of Arsaces [Phraates], who freed him from his captivity at the same time that Antiochus attacked Parthyene [that is, Parthia]."[86] Thus, Phraates

80. Grainger assumes Antiochus' victory in Media was "so comprehensive" that the Parthians asked for terms. Grainger 2016: 110–11. The swift reversal of Antiochus' position in 129 demonstrates that his invasion of Media was anything but comprehensive.

81. Note Shayegan 2011: 133.

82. Although I disagree that Antiochus returned to Babylonia in late 129 before the uprising, I agree with Shayegan's conclusion that the Babylonian communities spearheaded the revolt after further abuses. Id. 135–37.

83. Jos. *Ant.* 13.253; Plut. *Reg. Imp. Apophtheg.* 184D; Ael. *NA* 10.34; id. *VH* 2.41; Livy *Obseq.* AUC 624; Diod. 34/35.15. Note Shayegan 2011: 132–33.

84. Many scholars maintain that Phraates released Demetrius as a last resort to destabilize the Seleucid Empire, a decision he later came to regret; see Saint-Martin 1850: ii 50–52; Bevan 1902: 247; Bouché-Leclercq 1913–1914: i 382–84; Bellinger 1949: 58–59; Will 1967: ii 414, 432–34; Dąbrowa 1992: 46–48; Ehling 1998b: 142; Bing and Sievers 2011; Overtoom 2020. Mittag rejects that Phraates released Demetrius as part of his strategy to win the war, arguing instead that Demetrius escaped Parthian captivity. Mittag 2002. Yet Shayegan strongly refutes Mittag. See Shayegan 2011: 140–45.

85. Justin 38.10.7.

86. Jos. *Ant.* 13.253.

likely released Demetrius in early autumn 129 (probably August/September) as Antiochus threatened to invade the Parthians' homeland.[87]

Demetrius II's sudden release and the approach of winter encouraged Antiochus VII to delay his invasion of Parthia proper until spring 128.[88] Antiochus understood that Demetrius potentially posed a severe threat to the stability of Syria and that the large Seleucid army could not cross the difficult terrain of western Parthia without new supplies.[89] Phraates II's shortsighted but aggressive decision to release Demetrius at least in part again stifled Antiochus' momentum. Not fearing the capabilities of the Parthian military and not realizing the disloyalty of the reoccupied eastern cities, Antiochus again divided his large army into several small commands and dispersed them throughout the communities of southern Media and Babylonia in mid-autumn. Antiochus' division of the Seleucid army and the arrival of new garrisons into the mutinous communities in the region was the opportunity Phraates and his allies had been seeking to overwhelm the invaders. Parthian agents worked with local officials to finalize plans for a major uprising against the Seleucids, and in ca. October/November 129, a widespread revolt surprised and overtook numerous isolated Seleucid garrisons.[90]

Contrary to Shayegan's recent argument, it is not necessary to reject Justin's account that Antiochus VII likely wintered in Media in 129, nor is it necessary to assume that Antiochus actually wintered in Babylonia.[91] Justin records, "News of the attack [in the cities] being brought to Antiochus, he hastened with that body of troops, which he had in winter quarters with him, to succor the others that lay nearest."[92] Although Justin does not here specify the location of these events, he previously argued that "nothing was left to the Parthians but their own country," suggesting that Antiochus was in Media when he heard news of the rebellion.[93] Justin also here emphasizes that Antiochus had entered winter quarters. Meanwhile, there is an interesting passage on the possible location of these events from the *Primary History*, which is a jumbled summary of Armenian history recorded by the seventh century CE Armenian bishop Sebeos.[94] It states:

> Arshak [Phraates II] released Demetrius [II] after ten years and sent him to his brother to tell him what he would do to him. Demetrius did not go

87. Note Shayegan 2011: 129–30; Bing and Sievers 2011.

88. Disparity in the sources has led scholars to disagree widely on the reconstruction of the end of Antiochus' anabasis. See Saint-Martin 1850: ii 38; Fischer 1970: 44–48; Ehling 2008: 204; Bing and Sievers 2011; Assar 2011: 118; Shayegan 2011: 134–40.

89. Note Polyb. 10.28.1.

90. Justin 38.10.8. Compare Eus. *Chron.* (Smith ed.): 255; Diod. 34/35.17.2. See Assar 2006c: 104; Shayegan 2011: 134.

91. Shayegan 2011: 134–35.

92. Justin 38.10.9.

93. Id. 38.10.6.

94. For Sebeos (or Pseudo-Sebeos) and the *Primary History*, see Hewson 1975. Shayegan mistakenly credits Moses of Chroene for this passage. Shayegan 2011: 134–35.

> to his brother in Babylon but moved on to Asiastan. Then Arshak marched on Babylon with one hundred thirty thousand [troops]. In the one hundred twenty-eighth year of his reign, when he was close to Babylon, Antiochus [VII] suddenly fell on him in the wintertime in a narrow spot. They [the Greeks] were worsted and their army was destroyed. They [the Parthians] smote and humbled Antiochus and killed him, and they captured Seleucus, Antiochus' son, whom the king, he says, held at his own royal court.[95]

Sebeos' account is far too unreliable to favor it over Justin's; however, his emphasis that Phraates was on his way to attack Antiochus in Babylonia when he ambushed the Seleucids in a narrow defile and destroyed Antiochus' army is an important insight into the possible movements of the opposing forces late in 129.

Justin's account led Thomas Fischer to argue that Antiochus VII established winter quarters in Media in 129 and that the newly conquered cities of Media had in fact revolted against him, not the cities of Mesopotamia.[96] Shayegan recently has rejected this notion, arguing instead that the cities of Babylonia rebelled and that Antiochus withdrew into Babylonia late in 129 before the uprisings in this region occurred.[97] Shayegan concludes, "Antiochos, having penetrated Media and the Parthyene in search of the elusive Arsacids, may have been forced, with the approach of winter, to withdraw back to Babylonia, unable to confront them in a decisive battle."[98] Although the Parthians were utilizing their asymmetric approach to warfare to avoid a decisive battle until it was in their favor to engage the enemy, Shayegan exaggerates the frustrations of Antiochus in late 129, who had gained control over much of Media in recent months. It is hard to believe that Antiochus willingly abandoned his gains in Media late in 129 to return to Babylonia. Moreover, Antiochus planned to invade Parthia and force the Parthians into submission the following year.[99] The abandonment of Media in late 129, allowing the Parthians the opportunity to regain the region before the next spring, would have worked against the larger objectives of Antiochus' anabasis. Therefore, it is highly likely that the "several cities" Antiochus occupied with garrisons in late 129 included important cities in Babylonia *and* southern Media. Meanwhile, although Sebeos' passage hints at the possible location of Antiochus' final demise, by Shayegan's own admission this account is distorted since it does not mention any Seleucid expedition beyond Babylonia.[100] It can only serve as a clue as to where the armies were moving in late 129.

95. Sebeos in Thomson 1978: 364–65.
96. Fischer 1970: 44–48.
97. Shayegan 2011: 134–35.
98. Id. 135.
99. See Diod. 34/35.15
100. Shayegan 2011: 135.

Phraates II had withdrawn into Parthia proper as Antiochus VII had surged forward toward the region in autumn 129, at which point Phraates had released Demetrius II to delay Antiochus in Media. Phraates only moved against Antiochus in southern Media after the uprisings in Babylonia had isolated the divided Seleucid army. Thus, the mutinous *civitates* mentioned by Justin indeed were the cities in Babylonia, which Antiochus hoped to quell.[101] However, part of the Seleucid army, including Antiochus, likely had billeted in Media.[102] This would mean that both Antiochus and Phraates were moving through Media toward Babylonia before the climactic battle.

Antiochus VII had several practical reasons for billeting his soldiers in both southern Media and Babylonia in late 129, and Antiochus' winter command post likely was in Media (perhaps Ecbatana), not Babylon. A winter base of operations in southern Media would have allowed Antiochus potentially to accomplish several key objectives: first, maintain his authority throughout the region; second, dissuade any efforts of the Parthians to regain territory in the region; third, maintain a strong line of communication and supply with Mesopotamia and Syria; and finally, minimize his logistical burden of maintaining his large army during the winter by quartering soldiers throughout the major cities of Media *and* Babylonia. Although Antiochus likely wintered a large portion of his army in southern Media, he already had established strategic garrisons to control the prosperous cities of Babylonia, which were important logistical bases to maintain in 129 if he hoped to continue his anabasis in 128.

By late 129, Antiochus VII no longer feared a major Parthian counterattack and appeared oblivious to severe unrest within Babylonia. His fateful decision to divide his army into numerous, widespread garrisons was the final motivation the communities in Babylonia needed to rebel and the military blunder the Parthians desired. As the uprisings began to seize his garrisons in Babylonia and cut off his supplies, Antiochus was forced to act suddenly to alleviate the deteriorating situation in Mesopotamia without proper military intelligence and force of arms.

When news of the massed uprising against his garrisons reached Antiochus VII at his winter headquarters in southern Media, he underestimated the severity of the situation and the vulnerability of his position, deciding to move swiftly with his limited command to relieve his southern garrisons. The boldness of this decision illustrates Antiochus' unpreparedness for the rebellion and his disregard for the military capabilities of the Parthians by 129. Yet as news of the rebellions reached the Parthians, Phraates II immediately implemented the Parthians' aggressive Overwhelm Strategy, arriving in southern Media with great speed and determination to ambush Antiochus' much-reduced force while they were en

101. Id. 135–36.
102. Note McLaughlin 2016: 152.

route to Babylonia. Justin records, "On his way he [Antiochus] was met by the king of the Parthians, with whom he himself fought more bravely than his troops; but at last, as the enemy had the superiority in valor, he was deserted, through fear on the part of his men, and killed."[103] Thus, once the uprisings had distracted Antiochus and forced him into a vulnerable position, the Parthians utilized their considerable mobility and stealth to enter Media undetected and quickly outpace Antiochus as he marched through the passes of the Zagros Mountains toward Babylonia.

Phraates II maintained superior military intelligence during this final phase of the campaign to track the movements of Antiochus VII as he rushed southward. With winter swiftly approaching, the Parthians needed to act quickly and decisively to secure victory.[104] Under the shadows of the Zagros, the Parthians closed their trap around Antiochus, destroying his army and claiming his life.

Diodorus offers another account of the final moments of Antiochus VII's life that also helps reflect some of the important aspects of the Parthians' unique mode of warfare. Diodorus states:

> The friends of Antiochus urged him not to engage in combat against the Parthians, who were so superior in numbers; for they [the Seleucids] could retreat to the nearby mountains, where the difficult ground would protect them from the danger of the enemy cavalry. Antiochus paid no heed to this advice, saying it was shameful that the victors should fear the audacity of those they had already conquered. So he urged his friends to face the dangers and boldly withstand the attack of the barbarians.[105]

Diodorus here underscores the complete success of Phraates II's strategy to isolate and overwhelm Antiochus. The measured efforts of the Parthians to appear weak and vulnerable in 130–129 to encourage carelessness in their enemy had worked, and the sudden arrival of the Parthian army surprised Antiochus and his officers. Despite the examples of Seleucus II, Antiochus III, and Demetrius II, Antiochus VII had not recognized that the deceptive withdrawals of the Parthians into their kingdom were in fact a tried and true method of asymmetric warfare that the Parthians had utilized for a century to create military opportunities from their enemies' complacency and overconfidence.[106] By 129 Antiochus held the capabilities of the Parthian military in contempt. Diodorus even emphasizes Antiochus' arrogance as he viewed the large Parthian army on the field. Antiochus found it shameful to fear what he considered a defeated enemy. Although he had not

103. Justin 38.10.9–10.

104. Dio 40.15.4.

105. Diod. 34/35.16.

106. Hundreds of years later the Romans also struggled to understand the larger strategic objectives of the Parthians' unique mode of warfare. For example, note Suet. *Caes.* 44.3; Herodian 4.15, 6.3.7. See Overtoom 2016c; id. 2017a; id. 2017b.

actually vanquished the Parthian military, Antiochus' perception of his own recent successes and the apparent cowardice of the Parthians throughout 130–129 had encouraged him to assume that the Parthians were incapable of fighting with resolve. The perceived unwillingness of the Parthians to fight a traditional decisive battle had diminished Antiochus' respect for the Parthians' power and military reputation, demonstrating in part the importance and fluctuation of perceptions of power in the ancient world. Antiochus' eagerness to engage a vastly superior Parthian force on unfavorable terrain directly reflects the Parthians' successful manipulation of their enemy through their unique mode of warfare.

While Diodorus' account underscores the hubris of Antiochus VII and the great stock that Antiochus placed in his reputation and military prowess, it also provides a window into the extremely difficult decisions that state leaders had to make in the ancient world under the considerable pressures of the international environment. Antiochus refused to be labeled a coward, despite facing a greatly superior enemy force in late 129, in part because he could not afford to appear weak to his soldiers, allies, and enemies. Since Antiochus held the Parthian military in contempt, his own military prestige, his authority as king, and the perceived power of the Seleucid state was at risk if he retreated in the face of a "conquered" foe.

Antiochus VII also understood that he could not flee before the Parthians while Babylonia was in rebellion and while Demetrius II was free to challenge his throne in Syria because it drastically threatened his international reputation and standing, and therefore systemic pressures helped encourage Antiochus to risk battle against a superior force in unfavorable terrain to save face. Meanwhile, Antiochus also understood that if he scored a resounding victory against such unfavorable odds, he could win the war, cementing his unrivaled reputation and standing. Thus, larger concerns about perceptions of power within the harsh international environment of the Hellenistic Middle East influenced both Antiochus' disdain for the Parthian military and his enthusiasm to commence battle. In such a grim, unforgiving environment, it was better to risk open conflict than admit weakness, and therefore what might seem like a foolish military decision to us and his officers was an easy choice for Antiochus.

Despite Antiochus VII's courage and determination, the battle was a total disaster for the Seleucids. Eusebius adds an important detail about the final battle, stating, "But at the onset of winter Antiochus met the barbarians in a confined space; bravely attacking them, he was injured and killed, in the 35th year of his life."[107] The various descriptions of the battlefield strongly indicate that Phraates II likely surprised Antiochus as he tried to pass through the Zagros Mountains on

107. Eus. *Chron.* (Smith ed.): 255. Compare Moses 2.2.

his way to relieve his garrisons in Babylonia.[108] In fact, Diodorus further supports this conclusion, stating:

> Athenaeus, Antiochus' general, soon met with a just reward for the wrongs he had committed when he put the army in quarters. After being the first to flee, forsaking Antiochus in the heat of battle, he came to some of the villages which he had mistreated when he used them for winter quarters. They all shut their gates on him and refused to help him with either food or drink, so that he wandered up and down the country, till at length he died from starvation.[109]

Since the victorious Parthian army blocked the passage north back into Media, Athenaeus must have fled south and came upon the hostile communities of Babylonia. The wrongs Athenaeus had committed against these communities here refer to the abusive winter quarters of the Seleucid garrisons in Babylonia during winter 130/129. The communities of Media clearly do not fit this description, and therefore this is further evidence that in late 129 Antiochus and his men were rushing back to Babylonia from Media to quell the unrest in this region when Phraates appeared and overwhelmed them with his army.

It is possible to reconstruct an outline of the climactic battle between Antiochus VII and Phraates II using the brief accounts of Justin, Diodorus, and Eusebius, and in fact, the unfavorable position of the Seleucid army, their difficulties against the more mobile Parthians, and their destruction on the battlefield has numerous possible parallels with the much later Roman disaster at Carrhae. This again is not a coincidence. Rather, it further reflects a long-standing military tradition of the Parthians as they implemented their "Feign Retreat, Defeat in Detail" mode of warfare with devastating results.[110]

As Antiochus VII marched south through the Zagros Mountains with only a portion of his army in ca. November 129, the Parthians suddenly emerged at their rear in full force. Antiochus' officers advised him to retreat to the safety of the mountainsides.[111] Here, much like Antiochus III's experience in the approach toward Mount Labus, the terrain would have nullified the advantages of the cavalry-based Parthian army, and the Seleucid light infantry could have gained the advantage.[112] However, not respecting the Parthians' militarism and wanting to protect and advance his military reputation, Antiochus VII decided to engage

108. It is likely that Antiochus was marching on the main passage through the Zagros Mountains connecting Media to Babylonia, known today as the Baghdad-Khurasan Road. Kawami 2013: 752. Although Aelian records that Antiochus committed suicide, he maintains that Antiochus "threw himself over a precipice." Ael. *NA*. 10.34. This further supports the conclusion that Antiochus died in isolation while crossing the Zagros.

109. Diod. 34/35.17.2.

110. Note Overtoom 2017b.

111. Diod. 34/35.16.

112. See Polyb. 10.29.5–31.3.

the enemy directly. Justin's use of *ad postremum* ("at last") to describe Antiochus' final moments supports the argument that the battle had various stages and was not over in moments.

Since Antiochus VII did not utilize the protection of the mountainsides, the open terrain of the valley was ideal for the Parthian cavalry. The Parthians likely implemented a mixture of their Massed Assault and Hit-and-Run tactics to hem in and harass the Seleucid position at the start of the battle. By all accounts Antiochus fought bravely despite the wavering confidence of his men as the Parthian assaults became more ferocious.[113] Finally, Eusebius records that Antiochus attacked the Parthians, and Justin and Diodorus state that Antiochus' soldiers eventually deserted him because they feared the onslaught of the Parthians.[114] These are interesting clues that might help us understand the final moments of the battle.

Surrounded by an enemy with superior numbers, mobility, and range, Antiochus VII appears to have attempted a counterattack as his situation became more desperate. Justin records that the Parthians fought with superior valor, and whatever misconceptions Antiochus had about the weakness of the Parthian military vanished quickly. In a final, desperate attempt to drive off the enemy and avoid disaster, Antiochus, like Crassus' son Publius, appears to have charged the Parthian horsemen.[115] This charge helps explain how Antiochus became separated from the main Seleucid line and how many of his men were able to flee or defect without being slaughtered. Again, like Publius at Carrhae, Antiochus eventually found himself overwhelmed and destroyed by the relentless attacks of the Parthians' horse archers and cataphracts.

If Eusebius' account describes a desperate, yet disastrous charge by Antiochus VII to drive the Parthians from the field, then we get a better sense of the possible ebb and flow of this battle. After placing the Seleucids under a barrage of arrows and pinning them in place with devastating charges by the cataphracts, the Parthians were on the verge of overwhelming the Seleucid position.[116] In desperation, Antiochus sought to gain the initiative in the battle, and with a select force of mobile troops, he advanced against the Parthians.[117] The Parthians likely then implemented their Feigned Retreat Tactic to draw Antiochus' detachment away from the main Seleucid line, and once Antiochus was isolated, the Parthians turned about and destroyed this detachment with their Massed Assault Tactic.[118] Antiochus either fell fighting in the ensuing melee or committed suicide to avoid

113. Diod. 34/35.16; Justin 38.10.9.
114. Eus. Chron. (Smith ed.): 255; Justin 38.10.10; Diod. 34/35.17.2.
115. Note Eus. *Chron.* (Smith ed.): 255. Compare Moses 2.2.
116. Diod. 34/35.16; Justin 38.10.9.
117. Eus. Chron. (Smith ed.): 255.
118. Justin 38.10.10; Eus. Chron. (Smith ed.): 255; Sebeos in Thomson 1978: 364–65.

capture once all hope was lost.[119] Perhaps to avoid the shame that had befallen his brother, Antiochus decided to end his life with a semblance of honor.

Justin records that Antiochus VII's men deserted him at the end of the battle, and this likely refers to the main body of infantry that did not participate in Antiochus' final charge.[120] Before the battle Antiochus' officers had expressed their reluctance to fight against the approaching Parthian cavalry, and once Antiochus had charged off into the distance, these officers saw no need to continue the battle.[121] Diodorus again supports this conclusion when he records that Athenaeus was the first of these officers to flee during the battle.[122] Athenaeus' escape would not have been possible if the Seleucid force had been surrounded by Parthian cavalry, lending further support to the argument that Antiochus drove off the Parthians only to be overwhelmed by them on a separate portion of the battlefield.

Without Antiochus VII present to hold together the loyalty and resolve of his men, the exhausted and terrified soldiers eagerly withdrew from the field, leaving Antiochus to his fate. Although Athenaeus' flight allowed him to escape the Parthians, most of the outnumbered and immobile Seleucid force did not make in back to Babylonia. As the Parthian cavalry returned from overwhelming Antiochus, the remaining Seleucid soldiers and officers surrendered and, eventually, agreed to serve under Phraates II as mercenaries.[123] As a token of their submission to the Parthians, they surrendered Antiochus' son Seleucus and his brother's daughter Laodice to Phraates, who made the former an honored prisoner and married the latter.[124]

With the defeat of Antiochus VII, the Parthians had overcome their third Seleucid king; however, for the first time in their history the Parthians could claim to be king slayers.[125] Phraates II through patience and cunning had outmaneuvered and destroyed the last great Seleucid ruler, ending the last great Seleucid invasion of Parthian lands. By the end of 129, the Parthians had made a violent statement about their standing within the Hellenistic Middle East. Within the course of a decade, they twice had defeated their major rival within the much-expanded Iranian interstate system decisively. What remained of Antiochus' grand royal

119. Appian *Syr.* 11.68; Ael. *NA.* 10.34. Note Kosmin 2013a: 686. Publius also committed suicide. Plut. *Crass.* 25.11–12; Dio 40.21.3.

120. Justin 38.10.10.

121. Diod. 34/35.16.

122. Id. 34/35.17.2.

123. Justin 42.1.4.

124. This Seleucus could be Demetrius II's son, the future Seleucus V. Ogden 1999: 150–51. Yet the sources favor Antiochus VII also having a son named Seleucus who became a Parthian hostage and agent in northern Syria, while Cleopatra Thea later had Seleucus V murdered at Ptolemais. Eus. *Chron.* (Smith ed.): 257; Athen. 4.38a–b; Jos. *Ant.* 13.268–69; Justin 38.10.10, 39.1.7–9; id. *Prol.* 39; Appian *Syr.* 11.68–69; Livy *Epit.* 60.11; Sebeos in Thomson 1978: 364–65; Roberto 2005: i F 144. Note Shayegan 2011: 146–48; Overtoom 2020. Further, it is unnecessary to assume that Cleopatra Thea bore Antiochus all five of his recorded children. Eus. *Chron.* (Smith ed.): 257. Rather, she perhaps only bore Antiochus his last child, the future Antiochus IX, after their marriage in 138, making this Seleucus a son of Antiochus from a prior relationship. App. *Syr.* 11.68; *I Maccabees* 15.1–4; Jos. *AJ.* 13.220–23; Justin 36.1.9; Eus. *Chron.* (Smith ed.): 255. Phraates likely later married one of his daughters to this Seleucus. Roberto 2005: i F 144; Shayegan 2011: 150.

125. The Parthians also later killed Antiochus X in battle. Jos. *Ant.* 13.371.

army quickly became the prisoners of Phraates. The Seleucid Empire never recovered from this catastrophic defeat, and the Parthians finally were poised to dominate the Hellenistic Middle East.[126] In a public ritual that mimicked the actions of Alexander the Great toward Darius III, Phraates honored Antiochus with full funeral rites.[127] Phraates perhaps respected Antiochus as a worthy foe; however, by honoring Antiochus and marrying Demetrius II's captured daughter, the larger message Phraates was sending to his Greek and Persian subjects was that he was a worthy Hellenistic ruler and the true successor to the Seleucids' hegemony.

From Triumph to Disaster

By 128 the Parthians had emerged as the de facto leading power in the Hellenistic Middle East. Their defeat of Demetrius II had established a temporary bipolar rivalry with the Seleucids; however, their destruction of Antiochus VII finally ended the threat of the Seleucids to their eastern lands. For the first time in their history, the Parthians considered expanding their hegemony over Armenia, Syria, and the regions along the Eastern Mediterranean coast, thus firmly establishing their unrivaled hegemony. Yet any hopes of immediately occupying these regions quickly vanished because of calamities and miscalculations in the early 120s. Phraates II's release of Demetrius to contest the Seleucid throne in Syria became a political debacle that hindered Parthian influence in the region. Moreover, the Parthians could do little to intervene in the chaotic geopolitics of the diminished Seleucid state in the 120s–110s because of chronic instability in Mesopotamia and the collapse of their eastern frontier.

The position of the Parthians remained fragile, and the "nomadic problem" that had been developing along the eastern frontier since the reign of Mithridates I created a highly volatile international environment within the Iranian plateau that almost destroyed the Parthian state. Although the Parthians and Bactrians had forged working relations with numerous tribal groups for generations, even recruiting them into their armies, in the 120s highly militarized, aggressive warriors poured into the vulnerable eastern territories of the Parthian Empire and devastated these regions.[128] The Parthians' wars against the Central Asian tribal confederations were some of the most costly and difficult in their history. No fewer than two Parthian kings, including Phraates II, died in the conflict, encouraging Elymais and Characene once more to challenge Parthian hegemony in Mesopotamia and further nomadic incursions to penetrate the Iranian plateau. Within a few years of their greatest victory, the Parthians found themselves

126. Note Diod. 34/35.17.1, 18. Antiochus' defeat was so devastating to the strength and prestige of the Seleucid state that the Chinese envoy, Zhang Qian, who was traveling among the tribes of the Central Asian steppe in the aftermath of Antiochus' death, believed the Parthians had subjugated the Seleucids. Mair 2014: 26–28, 87, 154.

127. Justin 38.10.10; Athen. 10.53d–e. For Alexander, note Arr. *Anab.* 3.22.1.

128. Debevoise 1938: 36; Wolski 1965; Bivar 1983: 38; Wolski 1996; Gaslain 2005; Assar 2005: 47; id. 2006c: 111; Mairs 2013a; Dąbrowa 2016; Overtoom 2019a; id. 2019b; id. 2019c; id. 2019/2020. Note Strabo 11.8.8; Justin 42.1.2.

beleaguered and nearly broken, temporarily losing control of the Iranian interstate system.

Fallout in the West

With the death of Antiochus VII and the destruction or capture of much of his army, the Parthians finally damaged the strength and standing of the Seleucid state within the Hellenistic Middle East beyond repair. Antiochus' defeat not only guaranteed another civil war in Syria, but also, it was a major statement of Parthian power. The Seleucids never again acted as world leaders, and even their hegemony along the Eastern Mediterranean coast began to unravel.[129] The near complete loss of Antiochus' grand royal army in the east was particularly detrimental to the viability of the Seleucid state. Diodorus notes that every family in Antioch lost a family member in this immense failed expedition, stating:

> When the death of Antiochus became known at Antioch, the whole city mourned, and every house was full of wailing, especially from women, who bemoaned this great loss. Three hundred thousand men had been lost, including those who did not serve in the ranks. Every family had some loss to grieve: among the women, some had to mourn the death of a brother, others that of a husband or a son; and many girls and boys, left as orphans, lamented that they were bereaved of their fathers.[130]

Although Diodorus exaggerates the casualties, the losses of Antiochus' campaign were catastrophic. The Seleucids lost nearly an entire generation of soldiers and exhausted their Greek and Macedonian recruitment pool, forcing successive Seleucid kings to rely increasingly on short-term levies and mercenaries.[131] There were no more "grand" royal armies to assemble and no more great leaders to stabilize the state. Instead of making concerted efforts to rebuild the diminished Seleucid kingdom, no fewer than a dozen Seleucid claimants struggled for control over Syria for the next sixty-five years.

In 128 Phraates II had the opportunity to follow up on his resounding victory over Antiochus VII to dominate the Seleucids completely by conquering northern Mesopotamia and Syria. Diodorus states, "Arsaces [Phraates], king of the Parthians, after defeating Antiochus expected to invade Syria and easily make himself master of the country, but he was not able to make this expedition, since fate had placed him in grave danger and many perils."[132] Meanwhile, Justin adds, "After the death of Mithridates [I], king of the Parthians, Phraates his son was

129. For instance, the Jewish leader Hyrcanus began taking cities and subjugating communities in Judaea and southern Syria when he heard about Antiochus' death. Jos. *Ant.* 13.254–58; id. *Bell.* 1.62–63; Hieron. *Chron.* 165.2.

130. Diod. 34/35.17.1.

131. See Hoover and Iossif 2009: 48.

132. Diod. 34/35.18.

made king, who, having proceeded to make war upon Syria, in revenge for the attempts of Antiochus on the Parthian dominions, was recalled, by hostilities on the part of the Scythians [that is, the Saka and Yuezhi], to defend his own country."[133] Thus, partly motivated by vengeance, Phraates wanted to conduct a retaliatory campaign in the west to conclude the long hegemonic struggle between the Parthians and the Seleucids favorably and definitively. Phraates saw the need not only to defeat the Seleucids, but also to dominate them by punishing their aggression and subduing what remained of their kingdom.[134] Even after the decisive defeat of Antiochus, Phraates viewed the Seleucids as a potentially dangerous rival within the Hellenistic Middle East, and it was his intention to end this threat.

Yet Phraates II quickly realized that preparing an invasion of Syria was not his only concern. The defeat of Antiochus VII had established the Parthians as the new hegemons within the much-expanded Iranian interstate system; however, that hegemony was fragile and volatile. Although Diodorus goes on to blame the fickleness of Fortune for bringing about "such a reversal in the course of the whole war, that those who were previously successful were in the end brought low," there emerged several serious domestic and foreign concerns that stifled the momentum of the Parthians in the 120s.[135]

Like the consequences of Demetrius II's anabasis ten years prior, Antiochus VII's invasion had ravaged and destabilized the western lands of the Parthian Empire. Phraates II could not hope to invade Syria without first reconsolidating his authority over Media and Mesopotamia and repairing the damages from the war.[136] Meanwhile, thousands of new prisoners of war and disgruntled mercenaries created major political and logistical complications for the Parthians that could not be resolved quickly. Moreover, the mounting vulnerability of the eastern frontier made further aggression westward highly risky because warriors from the Central Asian steppe threatened the Iranian plateau. Finally, Phraates also suddenly faced a diplomatic fiasco in the west because of his decision to release Demetrius from custody late in 129.[137]

Phraates II had released Demetrius II to distract and delay Antiochus VII in Media; however, with Antiochus' defeat and death, Phraates immediately regretted his decision to send Demetrius to Syria and ordered soldiers to cut off Demetrius' advance and return him to captivity. Justin states, "He [Phraates] then began to regret having sent away Demetrius, and hastily dispatched some

133. Justin 42.1.1. Compare id. 38.9.10.

134. Note Shayegan 2011: 145.

135. Diod. 34/35.18.

136. Severe brutality and destruction often accompanied Seleucid conquests. Sherwin-White and Kuhrt 1993: 58–59. Babylonia seemingly suffered terribly from the 140s–120s. See Fischer 1970; Oelsner 1975; id. 1986: 274–76; Sherwin-White and Kuhrt 1993: 225.

137. Note Overtoom 2020.

troops of horse to fetch him back; but they found that prince, who had been in fear of pursuit, already seated on his throne, and, after doing all they could to no purpose, returned to their king."[138] Thus, Phraates was unable to recapture Demetrius, who used his brother's death to secure support in Syria. Phraates ultimately lamented his initial decision to release Demetrius because the geopolitical situation by 128 had changed drastically. Before Antiochus' death Phraates had hoped Demetrius could destabilize Syria to the Parthians' benefit; however, after Antiochus' death Phraates realized that Demetrius instead threatened to stabilize Syria to the Parthians' detriment.

Recently, scholars have tried to reconsider the political fiasco surrounding Demetrius II's return to Syria. Peter Mittag made a radical argument, rejecting that Phraates released Demetrius as part of a larger strategy to defeat Antiochus VII. Instead, Mittag argued that Demetrius finally escaped his captivity in late 129 because of the Parthians' carelessness.[139] Yet Rahim Shayegan later countered Mittag's arguments, reasoning that Phraates' release of Demetrius and the uprisings against Antiochus were two parts of a larger strategy.[140] Shayegan instead concludes that Phraates released Demetrius because of a long-term, farsighted strategic policy to place him on the Seleucid throne as a Parthian vassal.[141]

Mittag's argument appears mostly untenable and does not correspond with any of the available evidence.[142] It is undeniable that Phraates II released Demetrius II intentionally and that this decision served immediate strategic ends. However, Shayegan's conclusion that Demetrius' release was "the important component of an elaborate stratagem aimed at establishing Arsacid authority over Syria, once Antiochus Sidetes' campaign was thwarted" goes too far.[143] Rather, although Demetrius' release was an intentional aspect of the Parthians' strategy to win the war against Antiochus, the strategy was shortsighted, and the consequences were haphazard.[144]

After his defeat and capture in 138, Demetrius II acted neither as an outspoken enemy, nor as a compliant stooge toward the Parthians. Instead, he found himself in a difficult situation full of complex relationships. Mithridates I had humiliated him in Babylonia but honored him in Hyrcania as a friend and son.[145] Demetrius had two children with his new Parthian wife and even began styling his beard in the Parthian manner, which he later featured on his coinage during his second reign in Syria.[146] Yet Demetrius did not otherwise embrace his

138. Justin 38.10.11.

139. See Mittag 2002.

140. Shayegan 2011: 143.

141. Shayegan cites the Parthians' use of other captives as vassals. Id. 144–45. Taylor also supports the argument that Phraates released Demetrius to rule as his vassal in Syria. Taylor 2013: 157.

142. Jos. *Ant.* 13.253; Appian *Syr.* 11.68; Justin 38.10.7; Eus. *Chron.* (Smith ed.): 255.

143. Shayegan 2003 [2007]; id. 2011: 145.

144. Overtoom 2020.

145. Justin 36.1.6; Appian *Syr.* 11.67.

146. For Demetrius' coinage, see Leake 1856: 30, 32; Gardner 1878: 58–62, 76–78; Houghton 1983; Lorber and Iossif 2009: 105. For Demetrius' second reign, see Bevan 1902: 247–50; Bouché-Leclercq 1913–1914: i 388–94;

captivity, or his forced relationship with the Arsacids. Instead, Demetrius considered himself the true king of the Seleucid Empire and longed to return to his position of power. Despite lenient treatment, access to luxury, and his new Parthian family, Demetrius twice attempted to escape to Syria.[147] He first tried to escape soon after his capture in early 137 when he heard that his younger brother Antiochus VII had defeated the usurper Diodotus Tryphon.[148] Justin claims that, before Demetrius tried to escape, Mithridates had "promised (*promittit*) to recover for him the throne of Syria, which Tryphon had usurped in his absence."[149] This statement appears quite suspect as it is unclear why Mithridates would make such a promise to Demetrius without the intention or the means to fulfill it. At most this statement illustrates that Mithridates recognized that Demetrius could be utilized to manipulate the geopolitics of Syria in Parthia's favor; however, Mithridates did not implement a concerted new strategy to establish a Parthian vassal over Syria. In fact, Demetrius' attempted escape demonstrated to Mithridates that Demetrius was self-serving and potentially dangerous, forcing the Parthians to place him under stricter confinement.[150] Several years later Demetrius again attempted to escape, likely after the death of Mithridates in 132 had created temporary disorder at court; however, Phraates II recaptured him, sparing his life because of their familial ties.[151]

Justin emphasizes that boredom and frustration, rather than malice toward the Parthians, motivated Demetrius II's attempted escapes; however, the relationship between Phraates II and Demetrius was distant and distrustful.[152] Justin then argues that the Parthians mostly showed Demetrius clemency because they intended to utilize him against the threat of Antiochus VII because "they had designs on the kingdom of Syria."[153] Justin even claims that the Parthians' intentions toward Syria forced Antiochus to attack the Parthians preemptively.[154] Yet Justin here utilizes heightened drama, foreshadowing, and hindsight to manipulate his account. Justin knew that the Parthians eventually released Demetrius to contest Antiochus' throne and that the Parthians ultimately became involved in the geopolitics of Syria, and therefore, Justin here projects the consequences of the war back upon its beginnings.

Bellinger 1949: 58–65; Will 1967: ii 432–36; Ehling 1998b: 144–47; Ehling 2008: 208–9; Hoover and Iossif 2009: 48–49; Shayegan 2011: 148; Grainger 2016: Ch. 9; Overtoom 2020.

147. Justin 38.9.3–9.

148. Id. 38.9.4–7. Justin incorrectly claims that Phraates recaptured Demetrius at this time and forced him into stricter confinement.

149. Id. 38.9.3.

150. Id. 38.9.7.

151. Id. 38.9.8–9.

152. Phraates put Demetrius under guard and reproached him for his "childish levity (*puerilis levitatis*)." Id. 38.9.9.

153. Id. 38.9.10.

154. Id. 38.10.1.

Phraates II in fact did not trust Demetrius II and did not have any intention to release Demetrius until the successes of Antiochus VII in 129 forced his hand. Meanwhile, Antiochus clearly wanted to gain control over his brother; however, this was not the primary motivation for his grand anabasis to restore the eastern hegemony of the Seleucid Empire. When Phraates released Demetrius under guard in late 129, he did so cautiously and out of desperation to accomplish an immediate strategic objective, namely the delay and derailment of Antiochus' invasion of Parthia proper. Phraates had made no long-term strategic plans to use Demetrius as a puppet in Syria, which his immediate efforts to recapture Demetrius after Antiochus' death clearly demonstrate. Further, Demetrius had no intention of ruling over Syria as a Parthian vassal, which explains his immediate efforts to escape his Parthian guards and secure his throne against Phraates' wishes.[155]

Demetrius II's actions while on the throne in Syria also strongly support the conclusion that he was not a cooperative Parthian vassal.[156] Although he did not make war against the Parthians during his second reign, he did not act on their behalf or to their benefit in the west. For example, the evidence does not support Shayegan's conclusion that Demetrius made war upon Ptolemaic Egypt because of a "tacit entente with Frahād II that limited the sphere of Demetrios II's operations to the west."[157] Rather, Demetrius went to war with the Ptolemies and avoided further conflict with the Parthians to suit his own agenda.

Demetrius II entered Syria in ca. September/October 129, and most of what remained of Antiochus VII's household, including his youngest son (later known as Antiochus IX), fled to Cyzicus (modern northwestern Turkey) in fear of Demetrius' approach.[158] Demetrius found no resistance in Antioch and easily seized the vacant throne, remarrying his former wife Cleopatra Thea as news of Antiochus VII's disaster reached the city in ca. November/December 129.[159] Demetrius used his new position of power to distance himself from his Parthian guards and then blocked the Parthian horsemen sent to recapture him, compelling all Parthian forces in Syria to return to Phraates II in Mesopotamia.[160] Finally free from his captors, Demetrius immediately decided to make war against Ptolemaic Egypt in early 128. Justin records:

155. Id. 38.10.11.

156. Note Nabel 2017a; Overtoom 2020.

157. Shayegan 2011: 145.

158. The Parthians likely still controlled Media Atropatene, at least nominally, late in 129, making it probable that Demetrius and his Parthian escort rode to Syria following a northerly route to avoid Antiochus' men in southern Media and Mesopotamia. Eus. *Chron.* (Smith ed.): 257. For the date, note Bing and Sievers 2011.

159. Jos. *Ant.* 13.253, 268, 271; Justin 38.10.11; id. *Prol.* 39; Eus. *Chron.* (Smith ed.): 257; Hieron. *Chron.* 163.1; Livy *Epit.* 60.11.

160. Justin 38.10.7, 11.

> After Antiochus and his army were cut off in Persia, his brother Demetrius, being delivered from confinement among the Parthians, and restored to his throne, resolved, while all Syria was mourning for the loss of the army, to make war upon Egypt, (just as if his and his brother's wars with the Parthians, in which one was taken prisoner and the other killed, had had a fortunate termination). Cleopatra [II] his mother-in-law promised him the kingdom of Egypt, as a recompense for the assistance that he should afford her against her brother [and husband, Ptolemy VIII].[161]

Demetrius had several potential targets that he could have pursued in 128. He could have retaliated against the Jews, who were aggressively expanding their power in Judaea, or the Parthians, who had tried to recapture him; however, there was greater opportunity for success and reward if Demetrius attacked the much disliked and vulnerable Ptolemy VIII.[162]

Cleopatra II had used her brother's unpopularity to seize control of Egypt in 131, forcing him to escape to Cyprus; however, in 129 Ptolemy VIII reclaimed his position of power in Egypt and forced Cleopatra to flee to Syria where her daughter Cleopatra Thea was queen.[163] Justin continues, "Ptolemaeus [Ptolemy VIII], king of Egypt, too, who was threatened with a war by him [Demetrius II], having learned that his sister Cleopatra [II] had put much of the wealth of Egypt on ship-board, and fled into Syria to her daughter [Cleopatra Thea] and son-in-law Demetrius, sent an Egyptian youth [Alexander Zabinas], the son of a merchant named Protarchus, to claim the throne of Syria by force of arms."[164] Thus, not only had Cleopatra II offered Demetrius control over the Kingdom of Egypt, she also brought with her from Egypt a large war chest to entice Demetrius to action.

The Ptolemies' long-standing rivalry with the Seleucids in the Eastern Mediterranean also enticed Demetrius II to action since the Seleucids, even at this late stage, remained primarily focused on political entanglements in the west. The Seleucids and Ptolemies had fought six major wars, known as the Syrian Wars, to control the Eastern Mediterranean from 274–168, and during the power-transition crisis of the 160s–130s, the Ptolemies had meddled frequently in the civil wars within Syria.[165] Considerable tension remained between these two dynasties in the early 120s as Demetrius looked to stabilize his kingdom,

161. Id. 39.1.1–2. Compare id. 38.8.2, 9.1; Eus. *Chron.* (Smith ed.): 257; Diod. 33.6a, 34/35.14; Jos. *Ant.* 12.388, 13.63–64, 69–70, 20.236.

162. Demetrius considered retaliating against the Jews, but the war against Ptolemy VIII took precedence. Jos. *Ant.* 13.254–58, 267–69; id. *Bell.* 1.62–63; Hieron. *Chron.* 165.2. Ptolemy was notoriously cruel and hated by many of his subjects. Note Justin 38.2–15; Diod. 33.6–6a, 12; 34/35.14. For a recent evaluation of Ptolemy VIII, see Nadig 2007.

163. Livy *Epit.* 59.14; Justin 38.3.11.

164. Justin 39.1.4.

165. Note Grainger 2010; Overtoom 2019a.

and the family ties between the Seleucid and Ptolemaic dynasties made further conflict unavoidable. Demetrius' sons with Cleopatra Thea had the pedigree to wear both crowns; and once Cleopatra II offered Demetrius control over Egypt, he had a justified cause to seize Alexandria and install one of his sons as the new king of Egypt.[166]

Another leading reason Demetrius II immediately attacked Ptolemy VIII is that in early 128 Demetrius desperately needed a military victory to secure and bolster his prestige and position as king. Factionalism within the Seleucid court during the power-transition crisis of the 160s–130s had begun to undermine the state, and Demetrius not only faced stiff resistance from the former supporters of his brother, but also the former supporters of Diodotus Tryphon. Meanwhile, Demetrius' campaign against the Parthians in 140–138 and his decade-long captivity had been a humiliation that had severely damaged his military reputation and legitimacy as a ruler. Although Demetrius had seized the throne during the chaos that immediately followed his brother's death, his influence within the court was limited and tremendously vulnerable. In fact, within a year the usurper Alexander Zabinas challenged Demetrius for his throne and found many supporters within Syria.[167] It is perhaps ironic that Demetrius' attack on Ptolemy facilitated Alexander's rebellion; however, the considerable pressures facing Demetrius in 129/128 left him little choice. It is not surprising that Demetrius acted aggressively against a similarly vulnerable enemy in 128. He wanted to use his war against Ptolemy to win over the army, regain his reputation, and protect his throne.

Unfortunately for Demetrius II, his poor generalship and immense unpopularity quickly removed any hope of salvaging his second reign. In 128, he marched his army along the coast into Egypt, perhaps reaching Pelusium before his soldiers mutinied and forced him to retreat to Syria.[168] The sudden failure of Demetrius' expedition and the mutiny of his soldiers severely damaged his already vulnerable authority, leading to several rebellions in Syria and the rise of Alexander Zabinas as a rival.

Although our other ancient accounts blame the mutinies and rebellions against Demetrius II on his unpopularity and poor reputation, Justin offers an interesting take on the widespread rejection of Demetrius in 128, stating:

> Yet, as is often the case, while he [Demetrius] was grasping at what belonged to others [that is, Egypt], he lost his own [kingdom] by a rebellion in Syria. For the people of Antioch, in the first place, under the

166. Cleopatra Selene later claimed the throne of Egypt for her sons from her Seleucid husband, Antiochus X; however, the illegitimate Ptolemy XII seized the kingdom. Cic. *Ver.* 4.61; Dio 39.12–14. Note Llewellyn-Jones 2013; Dumitru 2016.

167. Jos. *Ant.* 13.267–68; Justin 39.1.3–5; id. *Prol.* 39; Eus. *Chron.* (Smith ed.): 257.

168. Eus. *Chron.* (Smith ed.): 257; Justin 39.1.1–2.

> leadership of Trypho, and from detestation of the pride (*superbiam*) of their king (which, from his intercourse with the unfeeling Parthians (*Parthicae crudelitatis*), had become intolerable), and afterward the Apamenians and other people, following their example, revolted from Demetrius in his absence.[169]

Justin here argues that, from his perspective and from the perspective of the Syrians, Demetrius chose to pursue the wrong war. Thus, Justin underscores the weaknesses plaguing Demetrius' reign and his own critical opinion of Demetrius.

Demetrius II's lack of authority because of his past abuses and failures meant that his people did not respect him, making it easy for them to criticize his judgment and rebel against his rule. In particular, the Syrians detested Demetrius' pride, which appeared worse since his captivity. It is important to remember that early in 128 almost all of Syria was in mourning following Antiochus VII's disastrous defeat and death at the hands of the Parthians, and Demetrius' sudden return with Parthian guards and a large beard in the Parthian style did little to curry favor with the Seleucids.[170] Even though Demetrius escaped his Parthian guards, the taint of his captivity under the Parthians remained in part because the Parthians were a despised enemy of the Seleucids, which brings us to our final and most important point. Both Justin and the Syrians detested Demetrius, not because he started a war, but because he started the wrong war. For them, Demetrius had failed to seek necessary vengeance against the Parthians, which was unforgivable.

Justin's contempt is clear when he snipes, "While all Syria was mourning for the loss of the army, [Demetrius II decided] to make war upon Egypt, (just as if his and his brother's wars with the Parthians, in which one was taken prisoner and the other killed, had had a fortunate termination)."[171] For Justin and the Syrians, Demetrius had a duty to avenge the recent disasters in the east, and they considered the conflict against the Parthians unresolved. Justin adds to this sentiment when he then criticizes Demetrius for "grasping at what belonged to others" when he attacked Egypt instead of Parthia.[172] Thus, Justin justifies the rebellions in Syria against Demetrius because Demetrius ignored the *real* enemy, the Parthians. Justin and the Syrians did not criticize Demetrius' aggression; rather, they criticized his misplaced aggression. Despite the resent disasters, Justin and the Syrians wanted Demetrius finally to punish the Parthians and reclaim the lost eastern territories; they wanted another anabasis.

Thus, we should consider again why Demetrius II did not pursue another eastern expedition in 128. There simply is no good evidence to support the

169. Justin 39.1.3. Note Jos. *Ant.* 13.267; Eus. *Chron.* (Smith ed.): 257.
170. Diod. 34/35.17.1. Note Lorber and Iossif 2009: 105.
171. Justin 39.1.1–2.
172. Id. 39.1.3.

conclusion that Phraates II controlled Demetrius' actions in Syria and encouraged him to attack Egypt while avoiding a new war in Mesopotamia.[173] Further, the suggestion that Demetrius relied on Parthian support in his conflict with Ptolemaic Egypt is unfounded and contrary to the available evidence.[174] If Phraates released Demetrius late in 129 to establish a tributary kingdom in Syria, the plan was shortsighted and failed immediately. By 128 Demetrius had numerous good reasons and pressing concerns that pushed him into war against Ptolemy VIII instead of against Phraates. Perhaps the least convincing explanation is that Demetrius was a vassal of the Parthians.[175]

Despite Justin's harsh criticisms of Demetrius II and the anger of the Syrians for Demetrius' failure to retaliate against the Parthians, another war against Parthia was a military, logistical, and political impossibility in 128. Even if Demetrius had wanted to invade Mesopotamia in 128 to punish the Parthians at the behest of his people, he lacked the forces and funds to do so. Antiochus VII's ruinous anabasis finally had exhausted the Seleucid state. The tens of thousands of soldiers and immense wealth that Antiochus had lost in 129 were never recovered.[176] Demetrius gained control of the soldiers that had remained in Syria (perhaps 15,000–20,000 men); however, to invade Egypt he had to hire mercenaries that he struggled to pay even with Cleopatra II's financial support.[177]

The Seleucid Empire was not the Roman Republic, with its seemingly inexhaustible recruitment pool and unique ability to absorb catastrophic defeats; rather, the Seleucid army relied on the recruitment of emigrated Greeks and Macedonians, and once these men were lost in battle, it was difficult to replace them.[178] In fact, Demetrius II had conducted his own anabasis in the early 130s in part because he had hoped to gain more Greek soldiers in the east.[179] It is quite astonishing that the Seleucid state was able to recover from Demetrius' disaster so quickly in the 130s. Antiochus VII's ability to mount a major eastern expedition later in the decade is a testament to his capabilities as a ruler and the continued strength of the Seleucid state before his defeat. In theory the Seleucids could have recovered their strength even after Antiochus' defeat to reemerge as a major force in the geopolitics of the Hellenistic Middle East; however, they needed stability, good leadership, and time to do so, none of which was available to Demetrius.

Demetrius II understood that he could not hope to conduct another major eastern expedition against the Parthians without first consolidating his power

173. Note Shayegan 2011: 145.

174. See Ehling 1998b: 144; id. 2008: 208; Shayegan 2011: 145.

175. Overtoom 2020.

176. Josephus records that Demetrius III commanded 17,000 soldiers in ca. 89. Jos. *Bell.* 1.93. Compare id. *Ant.* 13.377–78. He only commanded 11,000 by 87. Id. 384.

177. Note Hoover and Iossif 2009: 48.

178. See Bar-Kochva 1987: 19–48; Grainger 2010: 40, 83, 205–7, 233, 257, 261; id. 2017a: Ch. 9. For the Romans, note Eckstein 2006: Ch. 7.

179. Jos. *Ant.* 13.186; *I Maccabees* 14.1.

along the Eastern Mediterranean coast because he did not have enough men and supplies to protect Syria while he campaigned in the east. Moreover, the uprisings in Babylonia and troop mutinies in Media against his brother had demonstrated that the Seleucids could no longer expect to gain military and financial support in this region without difficulty, and therefore, if Demetrius ever wanted to invade Mesopotamia again, he needed to secure other sources of support. The war against Ptolemy VIII was Demetrius' best option to reestablish his power because he stood to gain Cleopatra II's wealth and, if successful, the immense resources of Egypt.

Further, Demetrius II's family ties to the Ptolemaic dynasty meant that he could not simply ignore the pleas of his mother-in-law to go to war. To do so immediately would have strained his already precarious relationship with his wife Cleopatra Thea, who was an influential and ambitious woman within the Seleucid court.[180] His remarriage to Cleopatra Thea after his return to the throne had lent Demetrius much-needed legitimacy because she reconnected him to his sons and helped reinstitute his line of the Seleucid dynasty. Demetrius had little choice but to rely on the political and financial support of his strong female relatives, and therefore he could not refuse Cleopatra II without alienating his wife.

There is one final important point to consider that further discredits the argument that Demetrius II was a strategically placed agent of the Parthians during his second reign. The Parthians actively worked against Demetrius' rule in Syria. Phraates II had released Demetrius to start a civil war in Syria; however, after Antiochus VII's death, Phraates tried to recapture Demetrius. With the death of Antiochus, Demetrius' release was no longer necessary, and therefore Phraates tried to abort his short-term strategy to destabilize Syria during Antiochus' invasion and instead considered a more permanent solution through an invasion of the region. Once Demetrius escaped his Parthian guards and established himself on the throne, he became a potentially dangerous liability. Thus, Demetrius' vulnerable regime was in fact the intended target of Phraates' expected invasion of Syria.[181]

After Antiochus VII's death, there is simply no evidence that Phraates II influenced Demetrius II's policies to the benefit of Parthia. Phraates also never provided Demetrius with any money or soldiers, which Demetrius desperately needed to attack Ptolemy VIII, combat Alexander Zabinas, and put down the rebellions in Syria. In fact, after Demetrius retreated from Egypt to Syria, Alexander eventually arrived with an army and defeated Demetrius near Damascus in ca. 126.[182] Phraates not only made no effort to aid his supposed

180. For Cleopatra Thea, see *I Maccabees* 10.51–58, 11.12, 15.10; Diod. 32.9c; Jos. *Ant.* 13.80, 109, 116, 270, 365; Appian *Syr.* 11.68; Justin 36.1, 39.1.2, 7, 9, 2.7, 2.8.

181. Diod. 34/35.18; Justin 42.1.1. Compare id. 38.9.10. Note Overtoom 2020.

182. Eus. *Chron.* (Smith ed.): 257; Justin 39.1.7; Jos. *Ant.* 13.268. Soon after defeating Demetrius, Alexander made an alliance with the Jewish leader Hyrcanus and captured Laodicea in Syria. Jos. *Ant.* 13.269, 273; Diod. 34.22.1.

vassal in Demetrius' greatest hour of need, but he also chose this moment to send the body of Antiochus back to Syria. Justin records:

> Meanwhile the body of Antiochus, who had been killed by the king of the Parthians, arrived in Syria, being sent back in a silver coffin for burial, and was received with great respect by the different cities as well as by the new king, Alexander, in order to secure credit to the fiction [of his legitimate rule]. This show of affection procured him extraordinary regard from the people, everyone supposing his tears not counterfeit but real.[183]

I agree with Shayegan's argument that Phraates did not send Antiochus' body back to Syria to lend legitimacy to Alexander; however, I would like to offer an alternative to Shayegan's speculative conclusion that Phraates sent Antiochus' body, under the escort of Antiochus' captured son Seleucus, to replace his "pro-Parthian" vassal, Demetrius, with a new candidate.[184]

Shayegan questions the validity of Justin's passage because he finds it illogical that the Parthians would have sent Antiochus VII's body back to Syria "against the interests of their own protégé Demetrios II," and therefore, Shayegan concludes that, before Alexander Zabinas captured Antioch and gained control over Antiochus' body, Phraates II sent Seleucus under guard with his father's body to win over support in Antioch as the new pro-Parthian vassal of Syria.[185] Shayegan convincingly uses the jumbled comments of John of Antioch to establish the likelihood that Seleucus accompanied his father's body to Syria to act as a Parthian vassal before enemy forces compelled him to flee back to Parthia, where he remained the rest of his life.[186] However, the major issue with Shayegan's reconstruction is that Demetrius clearly was not a Parthian "protégé," and therefore Phraates indeed sent Seleucus to Syria with his father's body in direct opposition to Demetrius *and* Alexander in an attempt to establish an actual vassal on the Seleucid throne.[187]

By 127 the Parthians' eastern frontier had collapsed as the Saka invaded the Iranian plateau, ending any plans Phraates II had to invade Syria to contest Demetrius II's position and forcing Phraates to implement a new plan to establish Seleucus as a Parthian vassal on the Seleucid throne.[188] Again, this was not part of a long-term strategic policy, but rather, another short-term reaction to immediate geopolitical circumstances. While Phraates tried to restore his eastern frontier, continued chaos in Syria was to his great benefit. As much as possible Phraates wanted to keep Mesopotamia safe from possible Seleucid retaliation.

183. Justin 39.1.6.

184. Shayegan 2011: 149–50.

185. Id. 149.

186. Id. 150. Note Roberto 2005: i F 144. Compare Bouché-Leclercq 1913–1914: i 393 n.2; Fischer 1970: 54. For John of Antioch and the Parthians, see Hackl, Jacobs, and Weber 2010b: 199–202.

187. Note Nabel 2017a; Overtoom 2020.

188. Note Overtoom 2019c.

Although Phraates had failed to control Demetrius in late 129, Demetrius' unpopularity and mismanagement had led to another Seleucid civil war in 128. Phraates recognized that sending Seleucus to Syria with his father's body was an opportunity to exploit this developing situation. Phraates could hope to secure the region in his favor at little cost, and even if that plan failed, Phraates could hope to further destabilize the region, thus diminishing any possible threat the Seleucids posed to the Parthians' western frontier.

Thus, Phraates II instructed the teenaged Seleucus to take his father's body through several cities that had rebelled against Demetrius II's authority until he reached Antioch. Again, Shayegan likely is correct that Phraates and Seleucus hoped that these communities, and especially the Antiochenes, would show sympathy and affinity toward Seleucus because of their hatred for Demetrius and their continued mourning after Antiochus VII's defeat.[189] However, Phraates and Seleucus had not anticipated the sudden arrival of the usurper Alexander Zabinas in northern Syria.

Ptolemy VIII had supplied Alexander Zabinas with an army at the behest of Demetrius II's mutinous soldiers and the rebellious Syrian communities. When Alexander entered Syria in ca. 127, he found little resistance as he marched north toward Antioch and Apamea, at which point he seized the caravan transporting Antiochus VII's body. Seleucus and his guards were able to escape back to Mesopotamia; however, Alexander used Antiochus' body to secure his position in Antioch. With a strong base of support in the north, Alexander then defeated Demetrius near Damascus in ca. 126. Demetrius first fled to Cleopatra Thea's stronghold at Ptolemais before attempting to flee to the fortress city of Tyre, where he was betrayed and killed in 125.[190]

Unfortunately for Phraates II, his decision to send Seleucus to Syria with Antiochus VII's body failed to accomplish either of his primary objectives, namely to establish Seleucus as a vassal on the throne or further complicate the Seleucid civil war. In fact, Alexander Zabinas used Antiochus' captured body to help secure the Seleucid throne for himself, and Phraates never successfully established a vassal in Syria. He had released Demetrius II and Seleucus to destabilize the Seleucid state; however, Phraates did not commit the military or financial support necessary to make these short-term strategies successful. To be fair, his difficult conflicts, first with Antiochus VII and second with the Saka, did not allow him to make a major military commitment in the west. However, the haphazard conduct of these strategies illustrates their shortsightedness. In the 120s, the Parthians began to intervene in the geopolitics of Syria for the first time;

189. Shayegan 2011: 149. Note Diod. 34/35.17.1. This Seleucus' eagerness to replace Demetrius II makes his association with Seleucus V, Demetrius' son, even less likely. Ogden 1999: 150–51; Shayegan 2011: 146–50; Overtoom 2020. Note Eus. *Chron.* (Smith ed.): 257; Athen. 4.38a–b; Sebeos in Thomson 1978: 364–65. John of Antioch states that Demetrius forced Seleucus to flee; however, it was Alexander Zabinas. Roberto 2005: i F 144; Shayegan 2011: 149–50.

190. Jos. *Ant.* 13.268; Justin 39.1.7–8; Eus. *Chron.* (Smith ed.): 257.

however, they had not yet committed to a viable, long-term strategy to dominate this region.[191] Such a strategy was impossible until the newly formed Parthian Empire was stable, and the empire was anything but stable in the aftermath of Antiochus' anabasis.

Collapse in the East

Destruction and disruption in Mesopotamia were major factors obstructing Phraates II's desire to intervene militarily in Syria. Antiochus VII's anabasis had destabilized the region and called Parthian authority into question. Numerous cities had violently revolted against their Seleucid garrisons, and the difficult task of reorganizing these communities and managing thousands of prisoners of war fell to the Parthians.[192] Although the rebellious communities in Babylonia had worked with the Parthians to overthrow Seleucid power late in 129, returning these volatile communities to Parthian hegemony early in 128 was not a simple task.[193] Phraates conducted tense negotiations with Seleucia, and in fact, the Parthians' relationship with Seleucia became so difficult that they founded a new, fortified imperial capital named Ctesiphon across from Seleucia on the Tigris River to undermine Seleucia's standing in the region.[194] Phraates also had to navigate a strained relationship with Babylon, which he tried to control by appointing a harsh disciplinarian named Himerus as viceroy over the region.[195] Similar to the wide-ranging command Mithridates I gave his brother, Bagasis, Phraates perhaps entrusted Himerus with command over the western territories. In fact, Justin states that Phraates left Himerus "to take care of his kingdom," making it likely that Himerus' responsibility was to maintain Parthian authority in the west while Phraates managed developments in the east.[196]

A major conflict against the Saka that erupted across the Iranian plateau also helped encourage an even more chaotic geopolitical situation in Mesopotamia as Hyspaosines, the ruler of Characene, decided to declare his autonomy in direct opposition to Parthian hegemony in late summer 128.[197] The sudden collapse of the Parthians' eastern frontier earlier that year under the pressure of nomadic invasion had forced Phraates II to march into the Iranian plateau with the main Parthian army; and therefore, Phraates' representative in Mesopotamia,

191. For later possible political interventions in Syria by the Parthians, see Bellinger 1948: 65–67; id. 1949: 67; Ehling 2008: 228; Shayegan 2003 [2007]: 97; id. 2011: 150 n.449; Overtoom 2016d: Ch. 3; id. 2019b.

192. Shayegan and Assar assume most of the captured Seleucid soldiers were executed. Shayegan 2003 [2007]: 92; Assar 2006c: 112.

193. The Parthians regained control of Babylonia no later than April/May 128. Assar 2006c: 105.

194. Diod. 34/35.19; Pliny *NH* 6.30.122; Strabo 16.1.16. Diodorus might refer to a later incident in ca. 124. Assar 2006c: 124. Ctesiphon became a major imperial residence, administrative center, and trade hub. See Kröger 2011; Iossif 2013; Lendering 2019. Note Bergamini 1987.

195. Diod. 34/35.21; Justin 42.1.3; id. *Prol.* 42; Athen. 11.15b–c.

196. Justin 42.1.3. For the Parthians' division of their kingdom into upper and lower regions, note Pliny *NH* 6.29.

197. Assar 2006c: 105–7. Hyspaosines had restored the strength of Charax. Pliny *NH* 6.139.

Himerus, was left to lead an unsuccessful expedition against Characene in late 128.[198] Himerus not only bungled his invasion of Characene, but also, he completely mismanaged the situation in Babylonia by abusing its inhabitants.[199] In spring 127, Hyspaosines seized his opportunity to invade and occupy Babylonia, where he began to destroy symbols of Parthian imperial rule and mint royal coinage.[200] The collapse of the Parthians' eastern frontier and Hyspaosines' success in Babylonia also helped encourage rebellions in Elymais against Parthian hegemony in 127.[201] Thus, the Parthians' western and eastern frontiers were in major crisis at the same time. This forced Phraates to split his army, sending a large force under his general, Timarchus, from Media to reclaim Babylonia in autumn 127.[202]

By late 127, the Parthians had stemmed the tide of Hyspaosines' aggression; however, Mesopotamia remained vulnerable to threats from Characene, Elymais, and Arab tribes. It was not until 125 that Characene once again began offering tribute to the Parthians, with Hyspaosines accepting Parthian suzerainty; however, even this did not end hostilities between the two rivals as the following year the Parthians decided to install their own governor over Characene.[203] Meanwhile, the Elymaeans continued to rebel against Parthian authority, forcing the Parthians to conduct another major expedition into Elymais to capture Susa in 124.[204] As we shall discuss further, the Parthians struggled greatly to stabilize their western frontier, and the simultaneous collapse of their eastern frontier made this task all the more difficult. Despite their resounding victory over Antiochus VII, the Parthians found themselves beset by enemies on all sides in the 120s. The instability of their empire called the power of the Parthians into question and encouraged further aggression from their highly militarized neighbors. Throughout much of the 120s, military distractions in the west hamstrung the Parthians' military capabilities in the east, resulting in almost total ruin for the Parthian state.[205]

The collapse of the Kingdom of Bactria and the prior efforts of Mithridates I to secure a much-expanded and vulnerable eastern frontier foreshadowed a major crisis for the Parthian state. Perhaps by the early 130s, the Saka confederation had advanced into what is modern Turkmenistan and soon after began to

198. Justin 42.1.1; id. *Prol.* 42. For the Parthians' difficult wars against various Central Asian invaders, see Overtoom 2019b; id 2019c.

199. Diod. 34/35.21; Justin 42.1.3; id. *Prol.* 42; Athen. 11.15b–c.

200. Sachs and Hunger 1996: no. -125A; Potts 2002: 359; Assar 2006c: 108; Shayegan 2011: 110–11, 151, 157.

201. Assar 2004–2005; id. 2006c: 108; Shayegan 2011: 111, 118; Dąbrowa 2014b: 63.

202. Sachs and Hunger 1996: no. -126A; Assar 2006c: 108–12; Shayegan 2011: 110–11, 151, 157. Shayegan assumes Phraates had already conducted his eastern campaign and died when Timarchus was successful. Id. 114. Yet it is highly unlikely that Characene would have risked another invasion of Babylonia in early 126 without the failure of Phraates' expedition in late 127. Overtoom 2019c.

203. Sachs and Hunger 1996: no. -124B; Shayegan 2011: 112–14, 168.

204. Shayegan 2011: 116–19. Compare Strabo 16.1.18.

205. Overtoom 2019b; id. 2019c; id. 2019/2020.

impinge upon the Parthians' frontier.[206] Soon after Phraates II's decisive victory over Antiochus VII, conflict between the Saka and the Parthians erupted.

To help overcome Antiochus VII's invasion, Phraates II had hired a large band of Saka mercenaries; however, this relationship quickly soured.[207] Justin states:

> For the Scythians [that is, the Saka], having been induced, by the offer of reward (*mercede*), to assist the Parthians against Antiochus king of Syria, and not having arrived till the war was ended, were disappointed of the expected reward (*mercede*), and reproached with having brought their aid too late; and when, in discontent at having made so long a march in vain, they demanded that either some payment (*stipendium*) for their trouble, or another enemy to attack, should be assigned them, being offended at the haughty reply (*superbo responso*) which they received, they began to ravage the country of the Parthians.[208]

Phraates' decision to hire a large group of nomadic mercenaries to fight the Seleucids is another example of shortsighted, haphazard strategic policy. Much like his decision to release Demetrius II, Phraates had no long-term plans when it came to hiring the Saka warriors and allowing them to penetrate the Iranian plateau. Rather, Phraates initially viewed these mercenaries as a possible solution to an immediate problem that eventually had major unintended consequences.

Before the first century, the size of the Parthian field army remained quite limited, and Phraates II's use of mercenaries and prisoners of war to bolster his army in the early 120s clearly demonstrates his desperate need for more soldiers.[209] Recently, some scholars have argued that the potential military power of the Parthian state became immense and matched the military might of imperial Rome; however, there was a considerable difference between the potential strength and the actual active force of the Parthian military, especially in the third to first centuries.[210] Marek Olbrycht's recent conclusion that the Parthian military eventually had a defensive capability of 300,000 soldiers and an offensive capability of 150,000 soldiers appears highly optimistic, and at best it reflects the potential capabilities of the entire Parthian state after it obtained hegemony throughout the Hellenistic Middle East.[211] Rather, the Parthians likely had 20,000–50,000 soldiers for active combat duty throughout most of their history; however, this figure still may be optimistic for much of the second century.[212]

206. Bivar 1983: 36. It is unlikely that "the Saca mercenaries hired for the war against Antiochus were probably an advanced group of this eastern horde." Debevoise 1938: 35. The Saka were well established in the region by the 120s. See Bernard 1999: 103; Koshelenko and Pilipko 1999: 132; Mair 2014: 29.

207. Debevoise 1938: 36; Bivar 1983: 38; Assar 2005a: 47; id. 2006c: 111.

208. Justin 42.1.2. Translation slightly altered.

209. Note id. 42.1.4.

210. Sheldon 2010: 3; Olbrycht 2016a.

211. Olbrycht 2016a: 326–29.

212. Id. 295; McLaughlin 2016: 223–24. Potter places the Parthian field army at roughly 30,000 soldiers even in the first to third centuries CE. Potter 2010: 157.

Meanwhile, the Central Asian tribal confederations, such as the Saka and Yuezhi, had immense military resources. Although exaggerated, contemporary Chinese sources put the military strength of these confederations between 80,000–200,000 trained bowmen.[213] In fact, the Chinese envoy Zhang Qian viewed the Yuezhi as far more powerful than the Parthians and recommended that the Han dynasty try to gain the loyalty of the Yuezhi through bribes.[214] As more nomadic peoples advanced southward toward Bactria, the potential threat their warriors posed to the Parthians' eastern frontier expanded considerably, and therefore Mithridates I and Phraates tried to foster working relationships with these new tribes, which helps explain how Phraates was able to hire a large force of Saka mercenaries on such short notice.[215]

Before late 129, Phraates II had been unable to overcome Antiochus VII's large army, and therefore, as the Seleucids threatened to invade Parthia proper after occupying much of Media, Phraates hired a large band of Saka warriors to supplement his army. With these new soldiers, Phraates could hope to harass and distract Antiochus if he moved deeper into the Iranian plateau, creating a possible opportunity to counterattack the Seleucids decisively before the war truly was lost. Thus, a coordinated campaign with the Saka mercenaries in 128 was Phraates' latest plan to defeat the Seleucids if the release of Demetrius II or the uprisings in Babylonia failed to halt Antiochus' advance. The fact that the mobile Saka army did not arrive until after Antiochus' sudden defeat in late 129 demonstrates that Phraates did not hire them until late in the campaign, likely when the Parthians lost control of Media.[216]

Justin's account offers interesting insight into Phraates II's negotiations with the Saka. Phraates offered the Saka the reward of spoils if they agreed to fight for the Parthians but clearly did not agree to pay them. Further, Phraates only enlisted the Saka to fight the Seleucids; however, the Saka clearly had not limited their agreement with Phraates strictly to the war against Antiochus VII. This eventually created major tension between the Parthians and the Saka after Phraates defeated Antiochus because Phraates' hurried and desperate negotiations with the Saka in 129 left considerable ambiguity in their agreement. For Phraates, his sudden defeat of Antiochus had nullified his prior agreement with the Saka and made their further employment unnecessary; however, for the Saka, Phraates still owed them military spoils as a reward for their agreed-upon

213. See Mair 2014: 22–23, 159, 161, 168, 170, 178, 646. The Saka perhaps could mobilize around 20,000 horsemen. McLaughlin 2016: 76.

214. See Mair 2014: 31. For the longstanding concerns of the Chinese for their northern and western frontiers against the threat of nomadic incursions, see Barfield 1989, Di Cosmo 2004; Tao 2007.

215. The argument that Phraates was absent from Babylonia when Antiochus VII attacked because the Saka invaded in 130 is dubious and unsupported by evidence. Tarn 1932: 581ff.; Debevoise 1938: 35–36. Phraates was near Seleucia. Shayegan 2011: 128.

216. Note Overtoom 2019c.

service. This explains why the Saka asked for either a buyout of the agreement or another enemy to attack after Antiochus' defeat. Justin claims that Phraates' haughty response offended the Saka and encouraged them to ravage the Iranian plateau; however, there is more to Phraates' response than stereotypical Parthian arrogance.

Both the Saka and Phraates II here clearly engaged in the abrasive yet common rhetoric of compellence diplomacy in the ancient world. In these negotiations the Saka used the threat of force to demand payment or reassignment to a new conflict. Phraates unsurprisingly refused them, likely demanded their immediate return to the Central Asian steppe, and prepared for war. Phraates responded harshly to the demands of the Saka in part because he felt they were breaking their original agreement, which for him only concerned the defeat of Antiochus VII, and in part because he found the demands of the Saka unacceptable. Yet Phraates' equally harsh response offended the Saka, who believed Phraates had reneged on his promise of spoils. After these negotiations ended unsuccessfully, the Saka began to ravage the Iranian plateau extensively. The Saka felt they had a right to acquire loot as a reward for their original pact with Phraates, and his refusal of their demands made the Parthians their enemy. This new understanding of the separate intentions of Phraates and the Saka in their negotiations helps explain why the mercenaries, "content with their victory, and with having laid waste Parthia, returned home" after their decisive victory over Phraates in 127.[217] Unlike subsequent nomadic invasions in the 120s, these warriors were not attacking the Parthians to gain territory; they were settling the debt they felt the Parthians owed them.[218]

The Saka mercenaries began to devastate the vulnerable lands of the Iranian plateau early in 128, and they used their mobility to ravage huge swaths of the Parthian Empire without much resistance, raiding perhaps as far west as Media (and less likely Mesopotamia).[219] Phraates II also had reason to feel betrayed after negotiations with the Saka devolved into violence, and he became determined to retaliate against them immediately. Phraates could not allow the Saka to destabilize his eastern territories and challenge his authority for fear of losing control of his fragile empire. He wanted to act swiftly to stamp out the threat of the Saka before opposition to the Parthians spread, and therefore he placed Himerus in charge of the western territories and marched east to crush the rebels.[220] Yet news of the mercenary rebellion in the east spread quickly and helped encourage

217. Justin 42.2.1.

218. Note Overtoom 2019c.

219. John of Antioch states, "While the Scythians were overrunning Mesopotamia at this time and devastating the kingdom of Arsaces, the Parthian [king] himself fell in the war and his successor had to pay tribute to the Scythians." See Mariev 2008: Jo. Antioch, Frag. 97, pp. 108–9. Compare Bivar 1983: 38; Koshelenko and Pilipko 1999: 132; Assar 2005a: 48. Debevoise found this doubtful. Debevoise 1938: 36.

220. Justin 42.1.3.

Hyspaosines' uprising in Characene in late summer 128 and the rebellion in Elymais in 127. For the first time in their history, the Parthians faced the difficulties of a two-front war.

Although Phraates II's campaign against the Saka was successful initially, it ended in utter disaster, and one of the major problems he faced during the campaign was a shortfall of soldiers.[221] Phraates could no longer rely on mercenaries from the Central Asian steppe to supplement his forces, and therefore he decided to enlist into his army the only other readily available pool of recruits, Antiochus VII's captured and mutinous soldiers. Justin records, "Phraates himself, meanwhile, took with him to the war a body of Greeks, who had been made prisoners in the war against Antiochus, and whom he had treated with great pride and severity, not reflecting that captivity had not lessened their hostile feelings, and that the indignity of the outrages which they had suffered must have exasperated them."[222] Again, Justin here exaggerates the stereotypical cruelty and arrogance of the Parthians; however, Phraates clearly hoped to utilize a large force of Greek soldiers trained in the Macedonian style of warfare to supplement the mobile Parthian army for the first and only time in its history.[223]

Most of Antiochus VII's grand royal army had perished in the uprisings and during the Parthian counterattack in late 129; however, many thousands of men also deserted or became prisoners.[224] The pool of deserters and captives was so large in fact that eventually these men were able to betray and destroy Phraates II and his Parthian troops.[225] Yet Gholamreza Assar recently suggested that only a small group of Greek mercenaries defected to the Parthians "because to maintain a large hostile force in an empire constantly at war with different foes would have been ill-advised and reckless."[226] Certainly, Phraates' decision to enlist deserters and captives into his army was risky; however, I find Assar's conclusion here too conservative. A force of 10,000 Parthians captured a Roman force of similar size during Crassus' failed Carrhae campaign in 53, and the Parthians incorporated these men into garrisons along their eastern frontier.[227] It is reasonable to argue that Phraates gained control over at least several thousand Greek soldiers in 129/128 that he later conscripted into his army.

221. Note Assar 2006c: 112. Sampson's portrayal of Phraates as a weak leader is unfair. Sampson 2015: 47–49.

222. Justin 42.1.4.

223. Note Müller 2017b.

224. Justin 38.10.10; Diod. 34/35.17.1; Jos. *Ant.* 13.253; Orosius 5.10.8; Moses 2.2; Sebeos in Thomson 1978: 364–65.

225. Justin 42.1.5.

226. Assar 2006c: 112.

227. Plut. *Crass.* 31.7; Pliny *NH* 6.18.47; Solinus 48.3; Dio 40.27.4. Note Engels 2017: 56–57. These Romans married native women and perhaps served to protect Parthia's eastern frontier. Hor. *Od.* 3.5.5–8; Vell. Pat. 2.82.5; Florus 2.20.4. Note Plinval 1948: 491–95; Pigulevskaja 1963; Wolski 1965: 103–15; Frumkin 1970: 146; Warry 1995: 156–57; McLaughlin 2016: 94, 161, 179. For the argument that some of these Romans became soldiers in the east, see Dubs 1975; Ferguson 1978: 599–601; Dauge 1981; McLaughlin 2016: 63–64.

Although conscripting these men indeed turned out to be ill-advised and reckless, Phraates II had several understandable and pressing reasons for trying to control and utilize these men to his benefit. First, he needed more soldiers. After the rebellion of the Saka mercenaries in early 128, and especially after Hyspaosines' rebellion in Mesopotamia later that year, Phraates needed a larger military to secure his western and eastern frontiers. The well-trained and well-equipped Greek captives of Antiochus VII's army were a welcome recruitment pool. Second, many of Antiochus' men had deserted their king, including several of Antiochus' leading officers, to serve the Parthians. Although Phraates misjudged their reliability, he at least initially could have hoped to use his control over the Seleucid high command to influence the Greek troops in his favor.[228] Third, Phraates planned to deploy these soldiers along his eastern frontier. Phraates did not send these soldiers to fight in Babylonia against Hyspaosines because he knew this theater of war was too close to their homes in Syria. By sending these men to fight deep within the Iranian plateau, Phraates hoped to use their fear of an unfamiliar place and an unfamiliar foe to help maintain their allegiance.[229] Fourth, once Phraates defeated the Saka he could use the Greek soldiers to garrison and protect his eastern frontier far from their former homes and any hope of return to Syria.[230] Finally, once Phraates secured his eastern frontier he could always hope to use these captives as a bargaining chip in later negotiations with the Seleucids.[231]

Ultimately, the rebellion of the Saka mercenaries and their devastation of the Iranian plateau forced Phraates II to make another shortsighted, haphazard decision to counter an immediate threat. Phraates' decision to conscript foreign captives, many of whom had already deserted their former king, was reckless but necessary. In fact, the haphazardness of Phraates' decision is borne out in the lack of integration that we find between his Parthian and Greek troops during the subsequent campaign. Phraates made no efforts to reform the Parthian military along more traditional Hellenistic models when he incorporated these Greek soldiers.[232] Phraates simply viewed these Greek recruits as a means to an end, which helps explain the tense relationship between the two sides recorded by Justin.

Unfortunately, little detail of Phraates II's campaign against the Saka survives; however, a general outline of it is possible. By spring 128, negotiations between

228. Justin 38.10.10; Diod. 34/35.16; 17.2.

229. Note Debevoise 1938: 37; Bivar 1983: 38.

230. Alexander the Great had established a similar precedence, installing Greek garrisons in Bactria. Holt 1999: 24; Lerner 2015a: 306. The Parthians later followed a similar policy with Crassus' captured soldiers after Carrhae. Plut. *Crass.* 31.7; Pliny *NH* 6.18.47; Solinus 48.3; Dio 40.27.4.

231. The Parthians later utilized Crassus' captured soldiers in their negotiations with the Romans. Note Overtoom 2016c; id. 2017a; id. 2019c.

232. The Parthians did not adopt the equipment and methods of the Seleucids as Colledge claimed. Colledge 1967: 65. Note Hauser 2006; Olbrycht 2016a; Overtoom 2017b.

Phraates and the Saka had ended, and the Saka began to ravage the Iranian plateau.[233] These events encouraged Phraates to begin conscripting Greek captives in Babylonia as soldiers to bolster his forces, and by summer he had appointed Himerus as his viceroy in Mesopotamia and moved the main Parthian army into Media to secure the region.[234] Assar argues that Phraates likely was campaigning in Hyrcania by late summer because he did not return to Mesopotamia to suppress Hyspaosines' rebellion at this time; however, there is an alternative explanation that considers the unstable situation in Media and the threat of the Saka.[235]

If Phraates II lived until ca. October/November 127 as Assar convincingly argues, then placing the start of his campaign in summer 128 would mean that he would have campaigned against the Saka for over a year while only fighting one major engagement.[236] Yet with the extent of the Saka raids, this relative lack of conflict over two campaign seasons appears odd unless we consider that Phraates likely did not actively campaign against the Saka mercenaries in Hyrcania until early 127 because he needed time to organize his expedition before the onset of winter in 128. Thus, Phraates likely spent most of the latter half of 128 consolidating his control over Media after the considerable damages of recent invasions and organizing his army after incorporating more captive troops.[237] Although Phraates had captured Greek soldiers as he entered Mesopotamia, a large portion of Antiochus' army also likely had wintered in Media before deserting or surrendering.[238] Since the garrisons in Media likely did not face the violent uprisings experienced in Babylonia, they would have been healthier and more substantial. Phraates would have needed time to collect and organize these various forces.

Although the success of the Saka in the east and Phraates II's movement away from Babylonia helped encourage Hyspaosines to rebel in summer 128, the regional challenge of Characene could not replace the extensive threat of the Saka to the eastern territories of the empire. Even after Himerus' series of failures in Mesopotamia, Phraates chose to delegate the responsibility of ending the conflict with Hyspaosines to his generals, Timarchus and Indupanē.[239] Thus, Phraates recognized that the collapse of his eastern frontier demanded his full attention in 128–127.

233. Justin 42.1.2. Note John of Antioch in Mariev 2008: Jo. Antioch, Frag. 97, pp. 108–9. Assar's suggestion that the Saka advanced as far as Mesopotamia after Phraates' death appears unlikely. Assar 2005a: 48. Although John of Antiochus' account is ambiguous, Justin clearly states that the Saka returned home after their defeat of Phraates. Justin 42.2.1.

234. Diod. 34/35.21; Justin 42.1.3–4; id. *Prol.* 42; Athen. 11.15b–c.

235. Assar 2006c: 108; Overtoom 2019c.

236. Assar 109–12; id. 2011: 119. See Sachs and Hunger 1996: no. -126B, no. -125A; Justin 42.1.5. Compare Debevoise 1938: 37; Bivar 1983: 38; Assar 2005a: 47; Valverde 2017. Unfortunately, the likely incorrect traditional date of Phraates' death in 128 remains in use. Lerner 2015a: 312.

237. Note Overtoom 2019c.

238. Justin 38.10.8–9.

239. Sachs and Hunger 1996: no. -126A; Assar 2006c: 109.

Early in 127, Phraates II likely began his reoccupation of Parthia proper and his pursuit of the Saka. There is no indication that Phraates reinforced Himerus after his failed invasion of Characene late in 128. Yet when Hyspaosines invaded and occupied Babylonia in spring and summer 127, Phraates could no longer overlook the threat of Characene to the security of his western frontier. He decided to split his army and send Timarchus with a large force from Media to reclaim Babylonia by autumn.[240] Yet rather than wait for the return of Timarchus, Phraates decided to continue his pursuit of the Saka with a much-reduced force toward Margiana.

Phraates II initially conducted a successful campaign against the Saka in 127. Phraates possibly drove the Saka back as far as the Murghāb River in modern Turkmenistan before news arrived of the deteriorating situation in Babylonia.[241] The aggressiveness of Phraates' pursuit of the Saka indicates that he implemented the Parthians' Overwhelm Strategy. He hoped to force a major engagement against the Saka before they reached the wide-open steppe of Central Asia to reclaim the immense spoils the rebellious mercenaries had seized, punish their treachery, and annihilate the threat they posed to his frontier though their destruction. Meanwhile, the Saka, laden with loot from their raids, initially wanted to avoid a major confrontation with Phraates' concentrated army before they could return to the Central Asian steppe. The Saka understood that they were vulnerable and isolated deep within the Iranian plateau, and they sought the safety and protection of the steppe, where reinforcements were available.[242] This helps explain why the Saka did little to stop Phraates' reoccupation of his eastern territories before autumn 127 when the course of the campaign changed drastically.[243]

Although the Greek conscripts obeyed Phraates II throughout most of 127, they played a pivotal role in his ultimate destruction when they betrayed him in battle.[244] Justin states that the Parthians and Greeks in Phraates' army had a tense relationship that ended in violence; however, we must consider why the Saka finally attacked Phraates in autumn 127 and why the Greeks suddenly betrayed Phraates. The answer lies in large part in Phraates' decision to split his army in summer 127 and continue his advance eastward that autumn.

Before Timarchus departed with a large force to reclaim Babylonia in summer 127, Phraates II's Parthian soldiers were numerous enough to ensure the complicity of the outnumbered Greeks within the army; however, by autumn the composition of Phraates' army was quite different. Phraates understood that he could not send the Greeks back to Mesopotamia, and therefore he decided to retain the foreign conscripts in the east and send Timarchus to the west with a

240. Sachs and Hunger 1996: no. -126A, no. -125A.
241. Assar 2005a: 47; id. 2006c: 112; id. 2011: 119. Note Sellwood 1995: 98–101; Dąbrowa 2006a: 38.
242. Justin 42.2.1. Note Assar 2006c: 112.
243. Note Overtoom 2019c.
244. Justin 42.1.5.

large contingent of Parthian soldiers. Suddenly, the Greeks represented a much larger portion of Phraates' army in the east, and despite the inherent danger of trusting this large body of foreign soldiers, Phraates thought he could successfully maintain a productive relationship with them. Yet Phraates made a major miscalculation when he decided to continue his aggressive pursuit of the Saka into Margiana without Timarchus' soldiers in late 127.

Phraates II's prior success that year had made him overconfident in his ability to control the Greeks and in the unwillingness of the Saka to join battle. Phraates' eclectic army was atypical and not well-suited to accomplish the traditional strategies and tactics of the Parthians' unique mode of warfare, especially against the mobile cavalry-based army of the Saka. Phraates had no advantage of speed or maneuverability during the campaign, which helps explain the lack of engagements earlier in 127 despite the aggressiveness of the Parthians' advance. Phraates' slower army could not force an engagement against the more mobile Saka, and his superior numbers meant that the Saka initially were uninterested in attacking the Parthian army. However, when Phraates eliminated his numerical advantage and isolated his reduced force in autumn 127, he provided his enemies with an opportunity to destroy him.[245] As the reduced Parthian army advanced through Margiana, the Saka almost immediately recognized the Parthians' vulnerability and counterattacked.

Justin's description of the climactic battle is interesting because it underscores the lack of integration within Phraates II's vulnerable army and provides further evidence of the Parthians trying to implement their traditional tactical approach to warfare despite their reliance on a large body of Greek infantry. Justin records, "Therefore as they saw the Parthians' battle line giving ground (*inclinatam Parthorum aciem vidissent*), the [Greek] soldiers went over to the enemy [that is, the Saka], and executed that revenge for their captivity, which they had long desired, by a sanguinary destruction of the Parthian army and of king Phraates himself."[246] Although Justin would have us believe that hatred of Parthian cruelty and arrogance motivated the Greek defectors, self-preservation was a more pressing concern.[247] In an ironic turn of events, Phraates and his men found themselves caught off-guard by a faster, more maneuverable enemy as they moved through Margiana in late autumn. The Greeks had seen a similar disaster befall Antiochus VII two years prior, and they once again favored desertion over destruction.[248]

Although it is possible that the Greeks served in the Parthian army reluctantly, there were two more important factors that encouraged their desertion in this

245. Note Assar 2006c: 112; Overtoom 2019c.
246. Justin 42.1.5. Translation slightly altered.
247. Id. 42.1.4.
248. Id. 38.10.9–10; Diod. 34/35.16–17.1–2.

battle, namely their sudden fear of the Saka and their confusion over Parthian tactics. This was the first major engagement of the campaign, and the Parthians and Greeks did not work well together on the field of battle. The abrupt aggression of the Saka surprised Phraates II and forced his less mobile army into a defensive position. Meanwhile, the unexpected arrival of thousands of hostile warriors rattled the resolve of the Greeks, who had little reason to die fighting for the Parthians. Yet Justin's explanation of how the battle unfolded is key to our greater appreciation of these events.

The Parthians often utilized speed and misdirection tactically to outmaneuver and overcome their enemies, and therefore again I would like to interpret Justin's negative portrayal of the Parthians in a more constructive light.[249] When Justin states that the Parthians began the battle by "giving ground," he in fact identifies the Parthians implementing their Feigned Retreat Tactic. If the Parthian cavalry was trying simply to flee the battle, the ability of the less mobile Greek infantry to take part in the slaughter of Phraates II and his men is peculiar. Moreover, Justin clearly states that the Greeks worked with the Saka to destroy the Parthians, which was not possible without some sort of coordination. Thus, it appears Justin severely condenses a major battle that had five distinct phases.[250]

In the first phase of the battle, the Saka suddenly arrived to attack the unprepared Parthian army. After realizing his precarious position, Phraates II hoped to outmaneuver the Saka in the second phase of the battle by implementing the Feigned Retreat Tactic with his Parthian cavalry. The Greek infantry did not take part in this action and, instead, likely was meant to maintain a strong defensive position. It is possible Phraates hoped to draw in the Saka toward the Greek infantry before wheeling around with his cavalry and smashing the Saka between two hostile forces; however, Phraates in his haste did not clearly express his full intentions to the Greeks, whom he wrongly assumed would loyally hold their position. In the third phase of the battle, the Greeks began to turn on the Parthians out of fear, confusion, and anger. These men continued to have little understanding or appreciation of the Parthians' asymmetric tactics, and therefore Phraates' feigned retreat appeared to be a legitimate rout and betrayal. It looked as though Phraates planned to abandon the Greeks to the enemy, and this immediate sense of terror and treachery is a far more satisfactory explanation of the Greeks' enthusiasm to seek violent reprisals against the Parthians in the battle than Justin's stereotypical explanation of continuous Parthian cruelty and arrogance.

If Phraates II had decided to flee the battle, it would have been impossible for the Greek infantry to attack and annihilate the Parthian cavalry. Instead, Phraates, realizing his mistake, likely called off the cavalry maneuver to try to restore order

249. Note Overtoom 2017b.
250. Note id. 2019c.

among the riotous Greeks in the fourth phase of the battle. However, Phraates was unsuccessful, and the Greeks violently fell upon the bewildered Parthian cavalry as they returned. In the final phase of the battle, the approaching Saka recognized and exploited the violent defection of the Greeks by utilizing their mobility to hem in the Parthians and help destroy Phraates and his men. It is unclear what happened to the Greek troops after the battle; however, the unsubstantiated claim that they marched back to Syria appears highly dubious.[251] Instead, it is likely some of them fought as mercenaries for the Saka, while others settled into various Greek cities in Margiana and Bactria.[252]

The death of Phraates II in battle severely damaged the power and prestige of the Parthians within the Hellenistic Middle East, encouraging other nomadic warriors to invade the Iranian plateau and further resistance to Parthian hegemony in Characene and Elymais. In particular, the destruction of thousands of Parthian horsemen made the empire vulnerable. Recruitment shortfalls had already been a major issue during Phraates' reign, forcing him to hire mercenaries and conscript captives. The limitations of the Parthian military in the 120s also hamstrung Phraates' immediate successors and made their war on two fronts a near impossible challenge to overcome.[253]

In late 127, the Parthians' hegemony over the Iranian interstate system was in jeopardy as they tried to recover from Phraates II's death and widespread disturbances along their western and eastern frontiers. Traditionally scholars, following Justin 42.2.1–2, have assumed Phraates' uncle, a man named Artabanus (Figure 19), became the next king and immediately went to war with the Central Asian tribal confederations.[254] Yet Babylonian cuneiform records and numismatic evidence illustrates that between the reigns of Phraates (ca. 132–127) and Mithridates II (ca. 121–91), two other men also possibly reigned.[255]

Although Phraates II likely reigned as Arsaces VII until ca. 127 and although an Artabanus (Figures 20–23) clearly reigned for a few years in the 120s and died at the hands of the Central Asian invaders, it is possible another Artabanus also reigned in the 120s. The S18.1 tetradrachms (Figure 19) minted at Seleucia in ca. 126 portray an older, fully bearded man, who looks drastically different than the Parthian kings featured on S17 and S19 coins (Figures 17, 20).[256] Assar identified this elderly ruler as Arsaces VIII (late 127–late 126), and he argued originally that this Arsaces VIII was another of Phraates II's uncles, the experienced Bagasis.[257]

251. Rawlinson 1876 (2002): 61; McLaughlin 2016: 42.

252. Assar 2006c: 127 n.123; Olbrycht 2010b: 146–47; Assar 2011: 120.

253. Note Overtoom 2019b; id. 2019c.

254. Scholars generally have placed the reign of this "Artabanus" tentatively in 128–124. See Wroth 1903: xxiv 20–21, pl. v, no. 1–8; Sellwood 1980: 56–62; id. 1983: 283; Shore 1993: 97–99, no.57–65; Shayegan 2011: 114; Grainger 2016: 115.

255. See Assar 2005a; id. 2006c; id. 2011; Overtoom 2019b; id. 2019c.

256. Assar 2005: 47–48; id. 2006: 112–16; id. 2011: 119. Compare id. 2001a: 20, 25–26, 41; id. 2001b: 17–22.

257. For Bagasis as king, see id. 2005a: 47; id. 2006c: 112–16; Valverde 2017.

Bagasis would have been quite old by late 127; however, the rapid deterioration of the Parthian Empire in the early 120s helps explain the possible appointment of Bagasis as king. Bagasis had been a successful general and administrator for decades, and his elder brother, Mithridates I, had entrusted him with command over Media starting in the 140s.[258] Moreover, Mithridates also had entrusted Bagasis with the difficult task of preparing the defense of Babylonia in the face of Demetrius II's anabasis, and Bagasis had been vital to the defeat of the Seleucids in that campaign. Finally, Bagasis had been fundamentally important to maintaining stability within the empire from ca. 138–132 as Mithridates succumbed to illness.

However, there are a few glaring problems with the Bagasis reconstruction.[259] First, the literary evidence works against the identification of Bagasis as king because there is no record of it. Second, Bagasis' son later appears as a commander-in-chief in the western territories under his younger cousin Mithridates II in 120.[260] If Bagasis became Arsaces VIII, this would mean that after his death his son was passed over in the line of succession. Although sons did not always succeed their fathers in the Arsacid dynasty, it seems highly peculiar that a well-positioned and accomplished adult son of the former king was passed over without mention or issue in 126. Finally, Bagasis does not appear to have served under his nephew, Phraates II, who favored generals such as Indates, Timarchus, Himerus, and Indupanē. This either indicates that Bagasis had retired from service after Mithridates I's death, or it more likely suggests that Bagasis also died in ca. 132.[261] In fact, the sudden death of Bagasis around the time of Mithridates' death helps explain why he was not Mithridates' immediate successor over the inexperienced Phraates, and it helps explain the initially strong position of Rīnnu, the primary wife of Mithridates, at court when Phraates became king as a young adult.[262]

Perhaps because of these difficulties with the Bagasis reconstruction, Assar recently has favored a new explanation that Justin "correctly identified the successor of Phraates II with his paternal uncle, Artabanos II (late 127–late 126 BC), but conflated the latter's reign with that of the next king who was probably also called Artabanos."[263] Although this new reconstruction remains mostly hypothetical, it appears plausible. The Artabanus in Justin, who fought the Central Asian invaders, cannot be the short-reigning Arsaces VIII, who appears to have struck the S18.1 tetradrachms to commemorate his defeat of Characene in the region.[264]

258. Justin 41.6.6–7. See Assar 2005a: 48; Shayegan 2011: 72–73.

259. Note Overtoom 2019c.

260. Sachs and Hunger 1996: no. -119A2+B1, no. -119C; Del Monte 1997: 147–48.

261. Interestingly, public sacrifice was made in Babylon in ca. 132 for the lives of Mithridates *and* Bagasis. This perhaps indicates that the health of both men was failing. Finkel, van der Spek, Pirngruber 2020b.

262. Sachs and Hunger 1996: no. -131D; Assar 2005a: 45–47; id. 2006c: 98; id. 2011: 118.

263. Assar 2006c: 112–16.

264. Justin 42.2.2. Note Assar 2005: 47–48; id. 2006: 115–16; id. 2011: 119; Overtoom2019c. Compare Assar 2001a: 20, 25–26, 41; id. 2001b: 17–22.

Moreover, the portrait on a handful of rare drachms from Ecbatana bear a close resemblance to the issuer of the S18.1 tetradrachms, identifying the issuer as the "Son of a Divine Father" and perhaps linking Arsaces VIII to Phriapatius as one of his younger sons.[265] Although Justin states that Phriapatius left behind two sons, Phraates I and Mithridates I, he simply meant that Phriapatius only had two adult sons upon his death in ca. 170.[266] It is clear from the cuneiform and numismatic evidence that Phriapatius had younger sons, namely Bagasis and perhaps Arsaces VIII, and Assar's conclusion that Justin likely conflated the reigns of Arsaces VIII and Arsaces IX because the two kings shared the same name is worth consideration.[267] In this reconstruction, Arsaces VIII likely was Artabanus (presumably I or II), the youngest uncle of Phraates II (Arsaces VII) and the youngest son of Phriapatius (Arsaces III), and Arsaces IX likely was Artabanus (presumably II or III), whom we later find fighting the Tochari in Justin and who likely was Arsaces VIII's son and the elder brother of Mithridates II (Arsaces XI).[268]

Although the eastern frontier remained in jeopardy in late 127, the victorious Saka returned to Central Asia with their spoils.[269] John of Antioch mentions that Phraates II's successor "had to pay tribute to the Scythians."[270] John, like Justin, perhaps conflates the reigns of Artabanus the father and Artabanus the son, making it possible that Artabanus I/II decided to pay off the Saka in the immediate aftermath of Phraates' death to help encourage them to leave the Iranian plateau. This policy satisfied the Saka because they finally had received their *merces* and *stipendium* from the Parthians, and it temporarily stabilized the war in the east and allowed the much-reduced Parthian army to concentrate on the renewed geopolitical crisis in the west.[271]

By the end of 127 with the withdrawal of the Saka, the most pressing threats to the Parthians were the ongoing rebellions of Characene and Elymais. Moreover, when news of Phraates II's death reached Mesopotamia, Hyspaosines began to ravage Babylonia once again in early 126.[272] Artabanus I/II could not ignore these new disturbances, and therefore he focused on reclaiming and stabilizing

265. Assar 2006c: 115–16; id. 2011: 119.

266. Justin 41.5.9.

267. See Del Monte 1997: 55–57; Assar 2005: 48 no.118, 52; id. 2006: 89, 140; Olbrycht 2010a: 239; Assar 2011: 117, 119; Shayegan 2011: 72–73.

268. The later coinage of the Artabanus noted in Justin (S20, S22.1–2, S22.4 [Figures 22–23]) bore the epithet "Brother-Loving." Assar 2011: 119. Justin records that Mithridates II succeeded his father because he likely conflated the reigns of Mithridates' father and brother. Justin 42.2.1–3. The Babylonian *Astronomical Diaries* also indicate that Artabanus II/III was Mithridates II's brother. Sachs and Hunger 1996: no. -118A. Compare van der Spek 2001: 453–54; Olbrycht 2010b: 150–51; Assar 2011: 119; Overtoom 2019b; id. 2019c. Shayegan's conclusion that the evidence is contradictory is unconvincing. Shayegan 2011: 114 n.309. Much controversy surrounds the possible identity of Arsaces II as Artabanus I. Note Wolski 1962; Lerner 1999: 26–28; Assar 2005a: 29–35; id. 2008; id. 2009a; 2011: 114–15.

269. Justin 42.2.1.

270. See Mariev 2008: Frag. 97, pp. 108–9.

271. Justin 42.1.2. Note Overtoom 2019c.

272. Sachs and Hunger 1996: no. -125A; Assar 2006c: 115; Shayegan 2011: 111–12.

Mesopotamia by defeating Characene.[273] Yet after overcoming Hyspaosines, Arsaces VIII disappears from the record by late 126. Since Artabanus I/II would have been an older man, it is possible that he died of old age or that the challenges of a major command complicated his health and facilitated his sudden death, at which point his eldest son, Artabanus II/III, became Arsaces IX.[274]

Artabanus I/II's successful reoccupation of Babylonia in 126 was an important step in the Parthians' efforts to reestablish their hegemony over their western frontier; however, his sudden death after a brief reign again jeopardized the stability of the empire.[275] Although his treaty with the Saka temporarily saved the eastern territories from further destruction, he had not been able to restore Parthian authority throughout much of the Iranian plateau before he died. The new king, Artabanus II/III, needed to secure both frontiers of the empire, and from his base in Media, he began reoccupying the ravaged eastern territories in 126/125.

Recently, Assar suggested that Arsaces VIII did not control most of the Iranian mints during his brief reign because the Saka seized the Iranian plateau after Phraates II's death.[276] Yet the brevity of Artabanus I/II's reign and the devastation of the eastern territories because of the Saka's prior raids satisfactorily explain his lack of eastern issues. He could not have invaded Babylonia if the Saka were threatening Media in 126. Instead, his policy of finally paying off the Saka mercenaries so that they would return to the Central Asian steppe temporarily relieved the eastern territories of the empire, eventually allowing the Iranian mints to recover under his son.[277] This explains how the new king, Artabanus II/III, began minting issues in the east early in his reign without a major campaign.[278]

With the eastern territories tentatively under his control, Artabanus II/III seemingly decided to resolve the lingering disturbances in the west. He appears to have returned to Babylonia and forced Characene to offer tribute in 125 when Hyspaosines likely submitted to Parthian suzerainty to save his rule and protect his realm.[279] Artabanus probably also prepared a major invasion of Elymais that allowed him to capture territory and decisively defeat the Elymaeans under the rebel leader, Pittit, in 124.[280]

273. To commemorate his victory, Arsaces VIII overstruck Hyspaosines' tetradrachm from Seleucia (S18.1). Assar 2005a 47–48; id. 2006c: 115; id. 2011: 119. For the mint-towns of the Parthian Empire, see Sellwood 1972; Gregoratti 2012a; Rezakhani 2013.

274. Assar 2011: 119; Overtoom 2019b; id. 2019c.

275. For example, Arabs raided Babylonia throughout the 120s. Sachs and Hunger 1996: no. -125A, no. -124A, no. -123A, no. -123C, no. -122A, no. -122D. Note Assar 2006c: 125; Overtoom 2019b.

276. Assar 2005a: 48; id. 2006c: 115–16.

277. Note Mariev 2008: Frag. 97, pp. 108–9.

278. Note Assar 2006c: 117–22; Overtoom 2019c.

279. Sachs and Hunger 1996: no. -124B; Shayegan 2011: 112–14. Hyspaosines soon after died in summer 124 at the age of eighty-five. Sachs and Hunger 1996: no. -123; Lucian *Macr.* 16.

280. Sachs and Hunger 1996: -124B. Pittit could be the Pitthides mentioned by Diodorus, which would mean Artabanus II/III punished Seleucia instead of Phraates II. Diod. 34/35.19. Note Assar 2006c: 117–20, 123–26; id. 2011: 119.

While in Elymais, the Parthians sacked wealthy temples in retribution for the Elymaeans' rebellion. Strabo records:

> In later times the king of Parthia, though warned by what had happened to Antiochus [III], hearing that the temples in that country contained great wealth, and seeing that the inhabitants were disobedient subjects, made an invasion with a great force, and took both the temple of Athena and that of Artemis, the latter called Azara, and carried off treasures valued at ten thousand talents. And Seleuceia near the Hedyphon River [in southern Elymais], a large city, was also taken.[281]

The Parthians not only gained vast amounts of much-needed wealth in Elymais, but also they appear to have annexed the region at this time and ruled over it directly for a generation until a vassal eventually reemerged around the beginning of the tumultuous Parthian "Dark Age" period (91–55).[282]

Rahim Shayegan, following the arguments of Georges Le Rider, maintains that Mithridates II, not Artabanus II/III, was king in 125 and that Mithridates conducted the campaign against Pittit, arguing that Artabanus could not have fought in Elymais at this time because he died fighting against Central Asian invaders in the east.[283] However, Shayegan does not consider the successive reigns of Arsaces VIII (Artabanus I/II) and Arsaces IX (Artabanus II/III). The elder Arsaces VIII clearly did not fight the Central Asian invaders before his death in 126, and if his son, Artabanus, in fact fought the Central Asian invaders, this campaign likely occurred in 122, not 126.[284] Meanwhile, the slain "Artabana" mentioned in the Babylonian *Astronomical Diaries* cannot be Mithridates II's father; however, despite Olbrycht's objections, it could be Mithridates' older brother, the former king.[285]

The ascension date of Mithridates II is not definitive in the literary records, and therefore numismatic evidence is key in trying to reconstruct the chronology of his early reign. Le Rider used tetradrachms of Artabanus II/III from Seleucia (S21.1-4 (Figure 21) and a *dichalkoi* of Mithridates (S23.4) to contend that Mithridates became king between 125/124 and 122/121.[286] Meanwhile, Shayegan assumes that Artabanus died after he issued his tetradrachms at Seleucia in 125/124, and he argues that two undated issues of tetradrachms by Mithridates belong to his early reign, sometime around 125/124, suggesting that a younger-looking Mithridates on the undated S23.1–2 coins (Figure 24) means that these coins

281. Strabo 16.1.18.

282. Assar 2006c: 141; Shayegan 2011: 118. Compare Alram 1986a: 143–44.

283. Shayegan 2011: 114 n.309. Compare Le Rider 1965: 386. Note Sachs and Hunger 1996: no. -118A.

284. Numismatic evidence illustrates that Artabanus likely reigned until 122, see Assar 2005a: 49; id. 2006c: 128–29; id. 2011: 119; Overtoom 2019b; id. 2019c.

285. Olbrycht 2010b: 150–51.

286. Le Rider 1965: 386. Note Assar 2011: 119–20.

should precede the *dichalkoi* of Mithridates (S23.4).[287] However, we should not assume that the S23.1–2 coins depict Mithridates. Assar argues convincingly that "the sudden and pronounced facial disparity between the obverse portraits of the S23.1–2 large silver on the one hand and those of S23.4 bronze and S24 coinage [Figure 25] on the other is unparalleled in the Parthian series," and concludes that these disparities indicate that "a prince other than Mithridates II issued the S23.1–2 tetradrachms. He may well have been son of Artabanus."[288] Moreover, it appears that Artabanus in fact issued coins at Susa commemorating his victory there in 124, as well as in the east at Ecbatana, Rhagae, and Margiane during his later campaign against the Central Asian tribal confederations.[289] Therefore, Artabanus II/III, not Mithridates, likely subdued Characene, conquered Elymais, and kept Arab raids in check in 125/124.[290]

Artabanus I/II's treaty with the Saka in winter 127/126 bought the Parthians precious time to secure their western frontier; however, the Iranian plateau remained immensely vulnerable to further incursions. Although the Parthians established tentative control over the eastern territories in 126/125, they had made no major show of force in the east to secure the eastern frontier permanently or deter aggression from other tribes in the region. One of these tribes, the Tochari, who perhaps were a branch of the approaching Yuezhi, had occupied parts of Bactria and in 123 invaded Parthia.[291] Artabanus II/III likely was in Media when news arrived of the Tochari invasion, and he immediately set out to face this new threat.[292]

Artabanus II/III also appears to have implemented the Parthians' Overwhelm Strategy as he aggressively pursued the marauding Tochari, initially reversing their penetration of the Iranian plateau in 123/122 and temporarily restoring control over Parthia and Margiana. As Artabanus advanced eastward, he minted coins to mark his success and advertise his authority. Most notably, Artabanus minted a series of silver drachms in Rhagae and Margiane (S20.4, S20.5–6, S22.4).[293] The S22.4 coins (Figure 23) included the epithet Philhellene ("Admirer of Greeks") because Artabanus likely wanted to ensure the support of Greek settlers in the region, especially the Greeks who had defected from Phraates II's army and settled in the region.[294] Yet similar to Phraates' experience, Artabanus' eastern campaign

287. Shayegan 2011: 114 n.309.

288. Assar 2005a: 50; id. 2006c: 129–34; id. 2011: 120. Contra Olbrycht 2010b: 144–46.

289. Specifically, S18.2, S20.3, S20.4–5, S22.4. See Assar 2005a: 49; id. 2006c: 116–29.

290. Id. 2005a: 48; id. 2006c: 118–27; Overtoom 2019b; 2019c. For the raids, note Sachs and Hunger 1996: no. -124B. Compare van der Spek 2001: 451–53.

291. Strabo 11.8.2; Justin 42.2.2; id. *Prol.* 41. Tarn rejected that the Tochari had reached Parthia by this point. Tarn 1930: 115–16. However, Tarn's conclusions are unconvincing and widely rejected. See Debevoise 1938: 37–38; Bivar 1983: 39; Olbrycht 2012b; Rtveladze 2011: 150. For the Tochari, see Enoki, Koshelenko, Haidary 1999; Piankov 2010; Mair 2014: 17, 19.

292. Assar 2005a: 49; id. 2006c: 126–27.

293. Id. 2006c: 127.

294. Id. 127 n.123. Compare Loginov and Nikitin 1996: 40; Nikitin 1998: 14–15; Dąbrowa 2008 [2009]; id. 2011a; Olbrycht 2017b: 10–12.

came to an abrupt and disastrous end. Justin records, "Artabanus, making war upon the Tocharii, received a wound in the arm, of which he immediately died."[295] It is possible Artabanus also acted too aggressively in the east against a mobile enemy, exposing his army to a devastating counterattack as he reached the frontier of the Central Asian steppe.

Phraates II had lost a sizable portion of the Parthian military in his defeat at the hands of the Saka in late 127, leaving his successors a much-reduced force to command in the middle and late 120s.[296] Although Artabanus II/III must have made efforts to enlist new recruits into his army, he could not have replenished the entire Parthian military in only three years. Moreover, even though the invasion of the Tochari demanded a strong retaliation, Artabanus would have been forced to leave garrisons in Mesopotamia and Media to maintain his authority in the west. In fact, following his departure to the east, violence once again gripped Babylonia as local powers, perceiving the vulnerability of the Parthians, once again tried to challenge Parthian hegemony within the region.[297] Thus, Artabanus pursued the Tochari with a limited force that became increasingly vulnerable and isolated as he reached Margiana, and when the Tochari counterattacked, they defeated the Parthians and mortally wounded Artabanus in autumn 122.[298]

The sudden absence of Parthian-issued drachms from Iranian mints over the next few years indicates that Parthian authority in the east nearly evaporated following Artabanus II/III's defeat and death.[299] Unlike the previous Saka invasion, the Tochari did not return to the Central Asian steppe. Instead, they began to occupy the Iranian plateau, filling the power void left by the decisive defeats of Phraates II and Artabanus. Parthian power and prestige continued to plummet as the eastern frontier collapsed once again. The empire was in crisis, and the survival of the Parthian state was at stake. It would take yet another great leader to stabilize the frontiers and finally establish the Parthians as the dominant force in the Hellenistic Middle East.

295. Justin 42.2.2.

296. Note Overtoom 2019b; id. 2019c.

297. Sachs and Hunger 1996: no. -122D.

298. It is likely that the other tribes in the area aided the Tochari in the defeat of Artabanus. Sachs and Hunger 1996: no. -118A. Note Assar 2005a: 51; id. 2006c: 128–29; id. 2011: 119; Shayegan 2011: 114 n.309; Overtoom 2019b; id. 2019c. Contra Olbrycht 2010b: 150.

299. Assar 2005a: 50.

6

Parthian Hegemony

Although the decisive defeat of Antiochus VII created the Parthians' first opportunity to extend their hegemony into Syria, diplomatic missteps in the west and the collapse of their eastern frontier prevented the Parthians from capitalizing on this opportunity. The Parthians scarcely got to enjoy their finest victory in the west before their vulnerable position in the east became disastrous. Moreover, the subsequent deaths of two Parthian kings at the hands of Central Asian invaders drastically reduced the power and prestige of the Parthian military and brought the survival of the state into question. Thus, in the 120s the Parthian state endured an immense reversal of fortune that threatened to spiral out of control. As the decade neared an end, the Parthians were in desperate need of a new great leader, one who could defeat their many enemies and restore their power over the Iranian plateau. Mithridates II emerged as that leader, and through his leadership, Mithridates not only saved the Parthian state from possible ruin, but also, he finally established unrivaled Parthian hegemony over the entire Hellenistic Middle East.

Mithridates II conducted a series of successful wars against the various Central Asian tribal confederations that had come to occupy large portions of the Iranian plateau and reestablished a strong eastern frontier. In fact, his wars against the tribal confederations and his efforts to strengthen the eastern frontier were so successful that no major nomadic threat materialized in the east for two centuries. Yet his punishment of the numerous eastern enemies of the Parthians did not satisfy his wider ambitions to create an unrivaled Parthian state.

By the 100s, Mithridates II also stabilized the continually volatile situation in Mesopotamia and expanded the network of vassal kings under his authority, resurrecting the old Achaemenid title of "King of Kings" and portraying himself as the supreme ruler of the greatest power in the eastern world.[1] The stability of Mesopotamia and the Iranian plateau under Mithridates finally allowed the

1. Mithridates was responsible for a "breakthrough" in Parthian royal ideology. He emphasized Achaemenid tradition in his name, dress, and coins. Olbrycht 2009: 165. The use of the title was not meant to be anti-Seleucid; rather it helped connect the Arsacids to the previous ruling dynasties in the east, including the Seleucids. See Strootman 2011–2012; id. 2016; Shayegan 2017; Strootman 2019.

Reign of Arrows. Nikolaus Leo Overtoom, Oxford University Press (2020). Oxford University Press.
DOI: 10.1093/oso/9780190888329.001.0001.

Parthians to pursue their desire to expand further west to subdue their long and bitter rivals, the Seleucids. After a long war to dominate Armenia, which established Parthian hegemony over the region for the first time, the Parthians turned their sights to the diminished Seleucid state in Syria.

Under Mithridates II the Parthians extended their hegemony to the western reaches of the Euphrates and beyond by involving themselves in the geopolitical developments of northern Mesopotamia, Commagene, Cappadocia, Cilicia, and Syria. Mithridates put these policies of aggressive western expansion into place, which his sons brought to a successful conclusion in the early 80s. The Parthians' defeat of two more Seleucid kings and their appointment of another Seleucid king to the throne in Antioch marked the end of the century-and-a-half-long hegemonic struggle between the Parthians and Seleucids. Although major conflicts with the Armenians and Romans were on the horizon, the Parthians finally emerged as the masters of the entire Hellenistic Middle East.

From Ruin to Unrivaled Power

Mithridates II likely came to the throne in ca. 121 at a time of great peril for his kingdom.[2] Recent military setbacks and devastating raids had diminished the strength of the Parthian state severely and allowed a fractured, chaotic, and highly militarized international environment (a system of multipolar interstate anarchy) to reemerge temporarily in the Iranian interstate system.[3] Despite the claims of recent scholarship, the Parthians were not yet an unparalleled, dominant power within the Hellenistic Middle East.[4] Rather, several warlords and kings continued to contest the tenuous position of the Parthians as the second century neared its close. It took a generation of diligent military operations, administrative reform, and political maneuvering before the Parthians finally claimed unrivaled hegemony over an enormous interstate system that stretched from western Anatolia, Syria, and the Levant in the west to the Central Asian steppe and the Indus River valley in the east, and even that position of power remained vulnerable well into the first century.[5]

By 121 the faltering Parthian state needed a savior. Mithridates II's wide-ranging, successful campaigns and his ability to stabilize and renew the vitality of the Parthian state and military were monumental accomplishments. It is reasonable to argue that the wavering Parthian Empire could have disintegrated in the late second century without the resolute and effective leadership of Mithridates. His policies and actions in the east and west had a significant influence on the

2. Note Assar 2006c: 129–34; Olbrycht 2010b; Assar 2011: 120; Overtoom 2019b; id. 2019c.
3. See Overtoom 2019a; id. 2019b; id. 2019c; id. 2019/2020.
4. Note Grainger 2013: 185–86. Compare Assar 2011: 118; Sampson 2015: 46.
5. See Overtoom 2016a: 1000; id. 2016c; id. 2016d; id. 2017a.

rapidly changing geopolitical climate of the Near Eastern and Middle Eastern worlds in the late second and early first centuries.[6]

A Savior Emerges

Despite his many efforts to stabilize the empire from ca. 126–122, Artabanus II/III left his immediate successors a disastrous geopolitical situation to overcome throughout the Iranian plateau. Traditionally, scholars, following the lead of Justin 42.2.3, have assumed that the celebrated Mithridates II, whom Justin calls the son of Artabanus, immediately succeeded his father; however, numismatics and cuneiform records appear to expand the line of succession.[7] Justin likely conflates the successive reigns of Mithridates' father and brother (both named Artabanus) in the period following Phraates II's death.[8] Yet there is a third possible king, known simply as Arsaces X (Figure 24), who could have reigned briefly (late 122–early 121) before Mithridates.[9] This otherwise unknown Parthian king appears to have issued a short series of coins at Seleucia (S23.1–2) that depict a young man with a small beard, which clash drastically with Artabanus II/III's and Mithridates' imagery of a fully bearded older man.[10]

Although this coin series traditionally is associated with Mithridates II, numerous scholars have noted the considerable disparity of the profiles of the young man featured on the S23.1–2 silver tetradrachms issued at Seleucia when compared to Mithridates' other coinage, and therefore some scholars have attempted to identify a different issuer.[11] Most recently, Gholamreza Assar has identified this young man as Arsaces X, suggesting that he was the young son of Mithridates' older brother, Artabanus II/III, which helps explain Arsaces X's coronation before that of Mithridates and the youthfulness of Arsaces X's portraiture when compared to that of Mithridates.[12] Yet if Arsaces X ruled prior to Mithridates II and was Mithridates' nephew, he only reigned for about half a year before Mithridates ascended to the throne in ca. April 121.[13] Although Arsaces X remains

6. Note id. 2019b.

7. Olbrycht mistakenly states that Justin records that Mithridates succeeded his paternal uncle. Olbrycht 2010b: 144. For the traditional view, see Newell 1938b: 479; Brett 1955: 290; Le Rider 1965: 86–88, 366, 386; Sellwood 1980: 59, 65–66, 71. For Mithridates II, see Daffinà 1967: 69–75; Wolski 1980a; id. 1993: 88–96; Olbrycht 1998b: 96–104; Assar 2005a: 51–52; id. 2006c: 134–49; Olbrycht 2009; id. 2010a; id. 2010b; Shayegan 2011: 114–19, 193–200, 203–7, 241–46, 388–409; Assar 2011: 120–21; Overtoom 2019b.

8. Note Sachs and Hunger 1996: no. -118A; van der Spek 2001: 453–54; Olbrycht 2010b: 150–51; Assar 2011: 119.

9. For Arsaces X, see Assar 2005a: 49–51; id. 2006c: 129–34; id. 2011: 120; Overtoom 2019b: 9–11.

10. See Assar 2006c: 129–134.

11. Rapson 1893: 214–15, pl. XVI.5; Wroth 1900: 194, pl. 8.6; id. 1903: xxi, 23, n.1, pl. V.9; Newell 1924: 141–42; Dayet 1925a; id. 1925b: 131; Newell 1938b: 479; Thompson et al. 1973: 261, no.1813; Assar 2005a: 50; id. 2006c: 129–30; id. 2011: 120.

12. Assar 2011: 120. Assar originally argued that Arsaces X and Mithridates were brothers, but he has since abandoned this stance in favor of the more likely nephew-uncle-relationship. Assar 2011: 120. Compare id. 2004: 89; id. 2005a: 49–51; 2006c: 132. Contra Olbrycht 2010b: 144–6, 149 n.21. Justin also easily could have overlooked or conflated the insignificant reign of Arsaces X. Note Overtoom 2019b: 9–11.

13. See Sachs and Hunger 1996: no. -118A; van der Spek 2001: 453–54; Assar 2005a: 49–51; id. 2006c: 131–32; id. 2011: 120.

a hypothetical figure, Marek Olbrycht's recent rejection of Assar's reconstruction of Mithridates' early coinage and the existence of Arsaces X seems equally speculative. Olbrycht argues that the inconsistencies found in the early coinage of Mithridates stemmed from "the fact that this king, in the difficult moments immediately following Artabanos I's sudden death, had not yet had time to define his own iconography."[14] Unfortunately, there is not yet a definitive answer to the major disparity in the portraiture of the S23.1–2 silver tetradrachms; however, the existence of Arsaces X remains a possibility and, therefore, his sudden death could reflect the dangerous international environment he inherited. In fact, the brevity of his reign immediately following the military disaster of his father has led Assar to suggest that Arsaces X also perhaps died in battle.[15] The violent death of another Parthian king in the 120s only would have served to further weaken the position of the Parthians within the Hellenistic Middle East.

When Mithridates II (Arsaces XI) finally inherited the throne in ca. 121, it appears that he understood the precariousness of his position and the gravity of the situation facing the Parthian state. He lost no time in aggressively seeking a military solution to the numerous geopolitical threats facing his dwindling empire. Like his immediate predecessors, Mithridates needed to demonstrate his power in his western lands if he hoped to campaign extensively in the east, and he first concentrated his attention on matters in and around Babylonia.[16] Overstruck Characenean bronze coinage (S23.4) suggests that in early 121 Mithridates even campaigned in Characene and quickly suppressed another uprising there.[17] Although it is possible that Mithridates installed a Parthian vassal in Characene at this time, the region remained unstable for several more years.[18]

Yet Mithridates II's early show of force in Mesopotamia allowed him to turn his attention toward the major crisis in the east. For almost a decade, armies had ravaged the eastern territories of the Parthian Empire. Phraates II and Artabanus II/III had restored Parthian hegemony in the east temporarily; however, their violent deaths had plunged the Iranian plateau into disorder and encouraged further penetration of the Iranian plateau by numerous bands of nomadic warriors.[19]

From his power base in Media, Mithridates II struck rapidly against the Central Asian invaders in Parthia proper, and late in 121 Mithridates issued a drachm (S23.3) in Margiana, illustrating that he successfully campaigned against the tribes in the region.[20] Like Artabanus II/III before him, Mithridates used the

14. Olbrycht 2010b: 144–46.
15. Assar 2005a: 51; id. 2006c: 138. Contra Olbrycht 2010b: 149 n.21.
16. Olbrycht 2010b: 145–46.
17. See Assar 2006c: 135.
18. Ibid.; Olbrycht 2010b: 147–48.
19. Note Overtoom 2019c.
20. Assar 2006c: 136. Compare Loginov and Nikitin 1996: 40–44; Nikitin 1998: 14–15.

epithet Philhellene ("Admirer of Greeks") on his issues in Margiana because he hoped to gain the support of the local Greek population and because he wanted to ease tensions between the Arsacids and the remaining Greek defectors of Antiochus VII's army, who had settled in the region after betraying Phraates II.[21] The last thing Mithridates wanted to encourage in the east was another alliance between the Central Asian invaders and these Greek soldiers against Parthian interests.

Thus, Mithridates II established himself as a capable military commander early in his reign; however, at the height of the "nomadic problem," it was near impossible for one man to combat all the threats facing the Parthian state. Mithridates faced severe military pressures on opposite frontiers with a limited military force, and neglect of one region in favor of another often encouraged the numerous rivals of the Parthians to challenge their hegemony. In the east the frontier had disintegrated under the pressure of multiple incursions, and in the west years of military setbacks and dynastic instability had brought the power of the Parthian state into question.

As long as the tribal confederations of the Central Asian steppe threatened the eastern frontier of the empire, the Parthians could not hope to dominate the Hellenistic Middle East. In fact, power relations within Mesopotamia and southern Iran remained fluid throughout much of the 120s–110s because of the unsettled situation in the east. It is unsurprising that minor powers, such as Characene, Elymais, and various Arab tribes, acted aggressively in this period of wide-ranging international chaos to maximize their power and security at the expense of their most threatening rival, Parthia. Because of their many recent failures in the east, the Parthians had to pursue an ad hoc and inconsistent policy of maintaining order throughout their western lands. Mithridates II's campaign in early 121 against Characene had been one of many recent attempts by the Parthians to find a permanent solution to the instability of their western frontier; however, major distractions in the east worked against the temporary success of Mithridates' early western campaign. Thus, when Mithridates moved most of the Parthian army out of Babylonia to campaign in the east, Arab tribes began to plunder this vulnerable region relentlessly in 120–119, and Characene and Elymais possibly rebelled yet again in 120.[22]

The uncertainty and danger of Mithridates II's position placed great pressure on him also to act violently. Despite its recent military setbacks, the Parthian Empire under Mithridates remained an unlimited revisionist state that aggressively pursued the complete dominance of the much-expanded Iranian interstate

21. See Olbrycht 2010b: 146–47; Assar 2011: 120; Olbrycht 2017b: 10–12. Compare Dąbrowa 2008 [2009]; id. 2011a.

22. Sachs and Hunger 1996: no. -119A2+B1, no. -118A. Compare Olbrycht 2010b: 146–49. The vulnerability and relative weakness of the remaining Parthian garrison in Babylonia likely encouraged further violence in the region. Assar 2006c: 137; id. 2011: 120.

system.[23] The Parthians were no longer content to share power within the Hellenistic Middle East; however, the task at hand to dominate this region was tremendous.

As Justin records, Mithridates II was a highly ambitious and courageous man, whose "achievements procured the surname of Great; for, being fired with a desire to emulate the merit of his ancestors, he was enabled by the vast powers of his mind to surpass their renown."[24] The menacing systemic pressures of the violent and unforgiving international environment within the Hellenistic Middle East encouraged Mithridates, who already was a militaristic and imperialistic leader, to expand the strength and influence of the Parthian state at the expense of his many militarized neighbors. Justin underscores the aggressive military focus of Mithridates' reign, stating, "He [Mithridates] carried on many wars, with great bravery, against his neighbors, and added many provinces to the Parthian kingdom."[25] Mithridates' skilled and determined leadership was integral to the turnabout of the Parthians' fortunes, and he provided a much-needed stabilizing force upon the Parthian throne.

Before leaving Babylonia in 121 to campaign in the east, Mithridates II had appointed or confirmed five generals to oversee the western territories.[26] The commander-in-chief was the son of the accomplished commander, Bagasis, which implies not only that some high offices within the Arsacid court could become hereditary, but also that certain clans within the Parthian aristocracy had become highly influential within specific regions.[27] As Mithridates prepared for further military operations in the east from his power base in Media in early 120, his commander-in-chief in the west visited Mithridates, perhaps to obtain more instructions and supplies against mounting Arab raids in Babylonia.[28] Although the instability of Mesopotamia was a major concern of Mithridates in early 120, he decided to remain in Media and to entrust the defense of Mesopotamia to his western generals.[29] This decision demonstrates that the threat of the Central Asian invaders remained considerable throughout the eastern territories even after Mithridates' first successful campaign in Parthia and Margiana.

Certainly, Mithridates II's initial success in reasserting Parthian power over portions of the Iranian plateau late in 121 encouraged him to push his advantage in the east in 120; however, he misjudged the situation in Babylonia. Mithridates' western generals failed to protect the region, forcing him to dismiss both Bagasis'

23. Note Overtoom 2019a; id. 2019b.

24. Justin 42.2.3.

25. Id. 42.2.4.

26. Sachs and Hunger 1996: no. -119A2+B1, no. -119C; Del Monte 1997: 147–48.

27. Olbrycht 2010b: 148–49; Dąbrowa 2013. Bagasis likely was Mithridates' uncle, and therefore the commander-in-chief in the west would have been Mithridates' cousin. Note Overtoom 2019b: 9–13.

28. Sachs and Hunger 1996: no. -119A2+B1.

29. Olbrycht is probably right that the Arab raids were not meant to occupy Babylonia, and therefore Mithridates could commit most of his army to his campaign in the east. Olbrycht 2010b: 148.

son as commander-in-chief and Urrahšu as general in Babylonia in summer 120.[30] This unexpected setback in the west compelled Mithridates to intervene, and he sent a portion of his army to drive out the Arabs in Babylonia in spring 119, once again securing the region temporarily for the Parthians.[31] In fact, it is possible that Mithridates himself returned to Mesopotamia in early 119 and celebrated his success in temporarily halting the Arab raids by issuing tetradrachms at Seleucia (S24).[32] Yet the presence of this expeditionary force in Babylonia was short-lived, and it appears to have returned to Media almost immediately to partake in Mithridates' major eastern campaign.[33]

By summer 119, Mithridates II was ready to concentrate his military might against the Central Asian invaders to restore the integrity of the empire's eastern frontier. He became determined to end the threat of the Central Asian tribal confederations to the Iranian plateau definitively. Moreover, the Babylonian *Astronomical Diaries* tell us that one of Mithridates' main motivations for another determined campaign against the Saka and Yuezhi was revenge. They record:

> A18: That [month], the 15th, a leather document of king Arsaces
> A19: [which] was written to the governor of Babylon and the citizens who were in Babylon, was read in the house of observation; accordingly, many troops assembled and went to fight against the son of the king and his troops of the cities [. . .]
> A20: [. . . of the G]utians who killed my brother Artabana, and I set up (troops) opposite them, and fought them; a great killing I performed among them; except two men [. . .]
> A21: [. . .] were not killed; and the king's son and his troops fled from the fight and withdrew to the difficult mountains. That month, the general who is above the four generals for damming [?]
> A22: [. . .] . . . departed. That month, the Arabs became hostile, as before, and plundered. That month, king Arsaces [went] to the remote cities of the Gutian country in order to fight.[34]

Thus, Mithridates conducted an extensive retaliatory campaign to reclaim the disputed eastern territories of the Parthian Empire. He not only wanted to restore Parthian hegemony throughout the Iranian plateau, but also, he desired the destruction of Parthia's enemies in the east to restore the prestige and reputation of the Arsacid dynasty.[35] Within the framework of Realist Theory, the reputation

30. Sachs and Hunger 1996: no. -119C.
31. Id. no. -118A.
32. Assar 2006c: 139. Compare Newell 1938b: 479–80; Simonetta 1979: 363.
33. Olbrycht 2010b: 149; Overtoom 2019b: 13–14. This encouraged the Arabs to raid Babylonia once again in late 119. Sachs and Hunger 1996: no. -118A.
34. Sachs and Hunger 1996: no. -118A.
35. Compare Shayegan 2011: 242.

of states (or leading statesmen) is linked directly to perceptions of power in interstate systems, and therefore states must strive to protect and advance their reputations to heighten their security. Two Parthian kings had died fighting the tribal confederations in the east, severely diminishing the military reputation of the Parthian state and the Arsacids.[36] The faltering position of the Parthians within the Hellenistic Middle East and the diminishing perception of their military capabilities made the Parthians increasingly vulnerable within a highly militarized and aggressive international environment, and therefore Mithridates' ferocity and determination in the east was in part a calculated response to numerous hegemonic pressures within the Iranian interstate system that encouraged him to pursue a bloody campaign of vengeance in the east.

In the above text, Mithridates II mentions the death of his brother Artabana (likely Artabanus II/III, Arsaces IX) at the hands of the Central Asian invaders and emphasizes the "great killing" he performed on the enemy to avenge his family.[37] Yet Mithridates' slaughter of the enemy's main force was not enough. He then decided to root out the remaining pockets of resistance in the east with unyielding resolve.

Over the course of his eastern war, Mithridates II made several expeditions into difficult terrain and against remote cities to defeat the tribal confederations along the eastern frontier of the empire.[38] Although the name "Gutians" was a term often used by Mesopotamians to indicate diverse non-Mesopotamian peoples, and therefore it does not indicate the true identity of the peoples resisting the Parthian attacks in the east, the tribes Mithridates defeated likely were a part of the larger Saka confederation.[39] Meanwhile, the Babylonian *Astronomical Diaries* record that these "Gutians" were working alongside an undisclosed prince and his army, and it is possible this other army was the Tochari.[40]

Mithridates II likely annihilated the main force of unspecified "Gutians" as he moved eastward through Margiana in October/November 119, at which point the Tochari fled into the mountainous regions of Bactria and Sogdiana.[41] Over the next few campaign seasons, Mithridates pursued the Tochari and the remnants of other tribes throughout Bactria and Sogdiana, eventually destroying their bases of power. Mithridates' war in the east was so successful that it "led to the liquidation of the Sacae and saved the empire from disintegration."[42] The

36. Note Overtoom 2019c.

37. There has been much debate about the identity of "Artabana" in this text. See Del Monte 1997: 150; van der Spek 2001: 453–54; Assar 2005a: 48 n.118, 52; id. 2006c: 140; Olbrycht 2010b: 150–51; Shayegan 2011: 114 n.309. Yet it now seems possible and perhaps likely that Artabana (Artabanus II/III) and Mithridates were the sons of Arsaces VIII (Artabanus I/II). Note Assar 2011: 119–20; Overtoom 2019b; id. 2019c.

38. Justin 42.2.5.

39. For the Gutians, see Zadok 1985: 143–44; Del Monte 1997: 4 n.12, 150 n.12; van de Mieroop 2002. Note also Assar 2006c: 139.

40. Justin 42.2.2. Note Olbrycht 2010b: 151.

41. Olbrycht 2010b: 150; Assar 2011: 120.

42. Assar 2005a: 52.

Parthians once again were the dominant power on the Iranian plateau and the leading force within the larger Iranian interstate system.[43]

With the threat of the tribal confederations destroyed, Mithridates II appears to have occupied all of lands of the former Kingdom of Bactria (likely including Sogdiana and Arachosia), extending the Parthian frontier in the east.[44] Strabo states, "And they [the Parthians] also took a part of Bactriana, having forced the Scythians [that is, the Saka and Yuezhi], and still earlier Eucratides [I] and his followers, to yield to them."[45] Mithridates' annexation of these eastern territories in the early 110s was a necessary precaution because the prior fall of the Kingdom of Bactria to the incoming Central Asian invaders had made the Parthians' original eastern frontier untenable. Further, the numerous wealthy and well-positioned cities in these regions had helped make the Bactrian kingdom a major force in the Hellenistic Middle East for several generations.[46] The Seleucids had introduced the policy of establishing Bactria as a major defensive bulwark to protect the Iranian plateau from the tribes of the Central Asian steppe, and Mithridates especially recognized the need to control the strategically important valleys and mountain passes of Bactria directly.

Yet the Parthians' occupation of these eastern territories was not simply a defensive decision. It appears that the Parthians began to utilize their eastern bases at Rhagae, Nisa, Merv, and in southern Bactria to prevent nomadic threats and occasionally to penetrate the Central Asian steppe.[47] The Parthians also successfully pacified the remaining Central Asian peoples, who had settled throughout much of the Iranian plateau in the 120s, under their rule.[48] Finally, the restoration of Parthian hegemony throughout the eastern territories also helped Media become a center of Parthian wealth, cultural evolution, and political identity.[49] Mithridates II's new settlement of the eastern frontier stabilized these regions for almost two centuries.

Mithridates II's depiction of his successful eastern war in his imperial propaganda was a public declaration of his salvation of the Parthian Empire and the

43. Overtoom 2019b: 13–15.

44. Olbrycht 2010b: 151–53; Overtoom 2019b: 14–15. Compare Pilipko 1976; Koshelenko and Sarianidi 1992; Rtveladze 1992: 33; id. 1994: 87; Zeymal 1997; Rtveladze 2000; Biriukov 2010; Litvinskii 2010; Gorin 2010; Olbrycht 2012b.

45. Strabo 11.9.2.

46. Note Overtoom 2016a.

47. See Watson 1961: 268; Rtveladze 1992: 34; Vainberg 1992: 37; Olbrycht 1998b: 101–2, 122–23; Nokandeh et al. 2006; Olbrycht 2010b: 152, 154–55; James 2013: 108. Nisa perhaps served as the first capital of Parthia. Chaumont 1968; id. 1971; Bader 1996; Invernizzi 2007; Sampson 2015: 41. For the restoration of Nisa and its importance under Mithridates as a mint, see Pilipko 1976; Pilipko and Loginov 1980; Bader 1996; Olbrycht 2010b: 154. For Merv, see Herrmann, Kurbansakhatov, et al. 1994: 62; Smirnova 2007: 382–83; Olbrycht 2010b: 154–55.

48. Many Central Asians had settled southeast of Parthia proper, for example. This region became known as Sakastan ("land of the Saka"), modern Sistan. Note Herzfeld 1931–1932; Olbrycht 1998b: 96–100; Shipley 2000: 285; Olbrycht 2010b: 152–53; Rezakhani 2013: 769; Lerner 2015a: 312; Callieri 2016. Compare Senior 2001.

49. The Arsacids began to adopt Median heritage and Achaemenid traditions. Olbrycht 2010b: 152–53. Note Tac. *Ann.* 11.10; Jos. *Ant.* 20.91. Compare Nikitin 1983; Olbrycht 1997; id. 2010a: 238–39; id. 2010b: 155.

Arsacid dynasty.[50] In celebration of his victory and the restoration of Parthian hegemony throughout the Iranian plateau, Mithridates issued a series of drachms in Ecbatana and Rhagae (S25) with the epithet "Savior."[51] Moreover, Justin states, "He [Mithridates] fought successfully, too, several times, against the Scythians, and avenged the injuries received from them by his forefathers."[52] Similar to the numerous Seleucid kings who had made war upon Parthia in the past to avenge and emulate their predecessors, Mithridates actively avenged and emulated his predecessors to demonstrate his hegemonic power. Justin also records, "[Mithridates] being fired with a desire to emulate the merit of his ancestors, he was enabled by the vast powers of his mind to surpass their renown."[53] It is unsurprising that Mithridates especially emulated the other great expansionistic king of the Parthians, Mithridates I.[54]

Mithridates II's eastern war was a sweeping success, and it firmly restored the standing of the Parthians throughout much of the Hellenistic Middle East. Moreover, Mithridates' portrayal of himself as the savior of the Parthian Empire certainly was important propaganda to emphasize his vital role in defeating the nomadic menace; however, the new epithet "Savior" accurately reflected the astounding accomplishments of Mithridates in his early reign. Through his aggressive militarism and determined leadership, he had brought the Parthian state back from the brink of ruin and reestablished it as the undisputed power on the Iranian plateau. With the "nomadic problem" solved and the eastern frontier secure, Mithridates could realize his wider imperial ambitions in the west.

The New King of Kings

Unfortunately, there are few details concerning the remainder of Mithridates II's long reign (ca. 121–91). Justin simply records that Mithridates fought many wars, conquered many regions, and for the first time in Parthian history made war on Armenia.[55] Yet there are enough clues in the surviving Greek and Roman sources, cuneiform archives, and numismatic records to reconstruct Mithridates' reign approximately. The 130s–120s had been a period of considerable violence and destruction throughout the Parthian Empire, and it was Mithridates' responsibility not only to restore the integrity of the empire's frontiers, but also to stabilize and revive the prosperity of the empire itself. Thus, Mithridates set forth numerous domestic and foreign policies to make the Parthian state strong once

50. Note Overtoom 2019b.

51. Previously, Mithridates' eastern coinage had featured war emblems like the horse and gorytos (bow-case) in preparation for his eastern campaigns. See Olbrycht 2010b: 153–54. Compare Nikitin 1983; Assar 2005a: 52; id. 2006c: 140; id. 2011: 120.

52. Justin 42.2.5.

53. Id. 42.2.3.

54. See Olbrycht 2010a; id. 2010b: 146, 151–52.

55. Justin 42.2.4–6.

again. After defeating the tribal confederations, he established powerful military and administrative centers in Hyrcania, Margiana, and Bactria to protect the Iranian plateau.[56] His widespread and diverse coinage also demonstrates that he rejuvenated the various mints within the empire.[57] Finally, he worked to integrate the multicultural population of the empire by settling Parthians, Medes, Persians, Greeks, and peoples from the Central Asian steppe into his newly pacified and expanded eastern territories.[58]

Mithridates II's eastern war was a difficult operation that took several years to complete. Justin records that Mithridates conducted frequent campaigns and added many provinces to the empire.[59] This statement in part reflects the determined operations of Mithridates in the east as he subdued the numerous remote strongholds of the tribal confederations.[60] The conquest, occupation, and resettlement of Margiana, Bactria, Sogdiana, and Arachosia would have taken years to accomplish, and it is possible that the Parthians also began making inroads into the northern Indus region at this time.[61] Further, Mithridates undertook several campaigns against the various nomadic groups that had settled in the east over the past two decades. We know that in 116/115 a Chinese envoy named Zhang Qian from the Han court made first contact with the Parthians while Mithridates still was campaigning in the east and that Mithridates sent 20,000 horsemen to greet Qian and sent envoys of his own to China.[62] Thus, Mithridates' responsibilities in the east were extensive, and they dominated his attention throughout much of the early and middle 110s.

In fact, geopolitical developments in Mesopotamia reinforce the argument that Mithridates II spent most of the 110s in the east. In 119, while Mithridates was pursuing the tribal confederations in Bactria, Arab tribes yet again plundered Babylonia.[63] Although Mesopotamia was relatively peaceful in the 110s when compared to the tumultuous 120s, Arab raids continued to menace the region as late as 112.[64] Mithridates' western generals were able to manage the situation in Mesopotamia while he was securing the eastern territories; however, the raids came to an abrupt halt when Mithridates finally completed his eastern responsibilities and returned to Media and Mesopotamia with the main Parthian army to focus on his western ambitions in 112.[65]

56. Watson 1961: 268; Rtveladze 1992: 34; Vainberg 1992: 37; Olbrycht 1998b: 101–2, 122–23; Nokandeh et al. 2006; Olbrycht 2010b: 152, 154–55; James 2013: 108.

57. Note Sellwood 1972; id. 1980; Assar 2006c; id. 2011: 120–21.

58. Olbrycht 1998b: 96–100; id. 2010b: 152–53; Rezakhani 2013: 769; Lerner 2015a: 312.

59. Justin notes that Mithridates especially targeted the "Scythians." Justin 42.2.4–5.

60. Sachs and Hunger 1996: no. -118A; Overtoom 2019b.

61. Bivar 1983: 41; Schmitt 1986c; Olbrycht 2010b: 151–53; Rtveladze 2011; Callieri 2016.

62. Mair 2014: 158. Compare Olbrycht 1998b: 102. For the political and economic relationship of the Parthians and the Chinese, note Eiland 1996; Tao 2007; Gregoratti 2012b; Juping 2013; Gregoratti 2014a; Daryaee 2015: 288; McLaughlin 2016.

63. Sachs and Hunger 1996: no. -118A. Note Assar 2006c: 141; Olbrycht 2010b: 149.

64. Sachs and Hunger 1996: no. -111B.

65. Id. no. -111B, no. -110.

When Mithridates II returned to the west, he brought with him the numerous lessons he had learned in the east as a warrior and administrator and began to apply them to his western policies. Since the reign of Mithridates I, the Parthians had desired to conduct a decisive hegemonic war against the Seleucids and expand their hegemony into the lands of the Near East. Phraates II even had begun plans to dominate Syria before the collapse of the eastern frontier of the empire in the early 120s.[66] Although the Parthians struggled to recover their position within the Hellenistic Middle East throughout the 120s–110s, they never lost their desire to expand further west and finally to eliminate the threat of the Seleucids. After Mithridates II's successful eastern war and his restoration of the eastern territories, the Parthians once again had the opportunity and the resources to pursue aggressive foreign policies in the west. Mithridates' immediate objective was to establish firm control over all of Mesopotamia so that he could begin to pressure the Seleucids in Syria. Yet to secure northern Mesopotamia and truly threaten Syria, Mithridates recognized the importance of dominating Armenia.

Armenia was an important border region for the Achaemenids, Seleucids, Parthians, and Romans in part because it provided direct access to Anatolia, Syria, Mesopotamia, and Media and because control of Armenia also helped protect these regions from invasion.[67] Further, an independent Armenia was a considerable threat itself. Armenia was a highly militarized and potentially powerful state in the Near East that had long battled the aggression of larger neighboring states.[68] For generations, Seleucid kings, such as Antiochus III and Antiochus IV, had attempted to dominate Armenia to help maintain their hegemony over their eastern territories.[69] Yet, as the Seleucid state dwindled in the late second century, Armenia increasingly became a major player in the geopolitics of the Near East. By the middle 80s, the Armenians began to utilize their geographically advantageous position to harass and devastate the heartland of the Parthian Empire, and the Romans and Parthians later enlisted the Armenians to challenge one another in the long-standing Romano-Parthian rivalry.[70] Finally, control of the mountain passes in Armenia, especially those over the Caucasus Mountains, were crucial to mitigating the threat of nomadic incursions from the wide-ranging Eurasian steppe.[71] As the international environment in the Hellenistic Middle East became

66. Justin 42.1.1; Diod. 34/35.18. Note Overtoom 2020.

67. Note Manandyan 1940 (2007); Chaumont 1976; Lang 1983; Schmitt 1986a; Chaumont 1986a; Chahin 1987; Redgate 1998; Olbrycht 2009; Gregoratti 2013c; Olbrycht 2015b; id. 2016c; Toumanoff 2016; Gregoratti 2017c.

68. See Chaumont 1986a; Chahin 1987; Sherwin-White and Kuhrt 1993: 190–92; Garsoian 2004; Overtoom 2016d: Chs. 4–6.

69. Polyb. 8.23; Diod. 31.17a; Appian *Syr.* 8.45, 11.66; Porph. 38, 55–6.

70. Tigranes II eventually conquered large sections of northern Mesopotamia and Media. Strabo 11.14.15. See Overtoom 2016d: Chs. 5–6. Compare Armen 1940; Manandyan 1940 (2007); Arnaud 1987; Garsoian 2005. Influence over Armenia was critical to the two major Roman invasions of the Parthian Empire in the first century, and control of Armenia became a focus of Roman and Parthian imperial policy for centuries. See Plut. *Crass.* 19.1–3, 21.5; id. *Ant.* 37.3, 38.1; Dio 49.24–29. Note Overtoom 2016c; id. 2017a; id. 2021.

71. For centuries the tribal confederations of the Eurasian steppe, known collectively as the Scythians, harassed the states of the ancient Near East and Middle East by crossing the Caucasus Mountains. See Cernenko 1983; Gregoratti

more unstable after the death of Antiochus VII, the Parthians quickly came to view the domination of Armenia as fundamental to the protection of their empire in the west.[72]

The course of Mithridates II's conquest of Armenia is difficult to reconstruct; however, many scholars place the beginning of the war too early. For example, some scholars argue that the Parthians subjugated Armenia as early as 120.[73] However, this would mean Mithridates attacked Armenia while Babylonia and the eastern territories of the empire were extremely destabilized, which seems highly unlikely. Meanwhile, Rahim Shayegan places the earliest date for the first Parthian campaign against Armenia in 118.[74] Yet this too appears too early because of Mithridates' ongoing campaigns in the east at this time.[75]

Mithridates II seemingly replaced Bagasis' son as commander-in-chief in the west with a man named Mitradatā perhaps as early as 120, and Mithridates placed great confidence in his new commander both to manage the affairs of the western territories and to expand the hegemony of the Parthians in the west.[76] Yet the numerous disturbances throughout the 120s–110s in Mesopotamia and the abrupt dismissal of Bagasis' son from the empire's second highest position of power demonstrate that this was an immensely difficult and volatile command. Mitradatā and his generals had to protect Babylonia and Media from attack and maintain authority over Characene, Elymais, and Persis, and therefore it again is highly unlikely that Mithridates began a new major conflict on the opposite side of the empire while he carried out his duties in the east in the first half of the 110s. Instead, it is probable that Mithridates began the war against Armenia in the middle to late 110s after he had settled affairs in the east.

Justin ends his summary of Mithridates II's reign, stating, "At last he turned his arms against Artoadistes, king of Armenia."[77] Although this suggests that Mithridates led the campaign against Armenia, the identity of "Artoadistes" is unclear, making it uncertain against whom Mithridates initiated the war. There is considerable debate as to the correct reconstruction of the chronology for the early Armenian kings in this period because of the fractured and contradictory nature of the surviving sources.[78] Scholars have assumed that Justin meant Artavasdes

2013a; Olbrycht 2015a, id. 2015b. For example, the nomadic Alans crossed the Caucasus Mountains in the 70s CE and terrorized the Parthian Empire. See Jos. *Bell.* 7.244–51; Suet. *Dom.* 2. Later tribal confederations from the Eurasian steppe, such as the Goths, Huns, and Turks, also used the passes over the Caucasus Mountains to bring widespread destruction to the Near East and Middle East for centuries. See, e.g., Heather 1998; Thompson 1999; Findley 2004.

72. Pliny the Elder described the Parthian state as "shut up by doors," emphasizing the important mountain ranges and passes of this region. Pliny *NH* 6.17.

73. Schottky 1989: 219; Olbrycht 2009: 165, 168.

74. Shayegan 2011: 243.

75. Overtoom 2019b.

76. Sachs and Hunger 1996: no. -111B. Note Shayegan 2011: 224.

77. Justin 42.2.6.

78. Note Debevoise 1938: 41–42, 45; Manandyan 1940 (2007): 19–20; Seyrig 1955; Bedoukian 1968; Lang 1983: 513; Bivar 1983: 40–41; Chaumont 1986a; Chahin 1987: 225–26; Chaumont 1988: 23; Schottky 1989: 219; Redgate 1998: 69; Mousheghian and Depeyrot 1999: 31; Assar 2006c: 142; Olbrycht 2009: 165, 168; Assar 2011: 121.

I when he recorded the name Artoadistes; however, it is certainly possible that Justin did not know which Armenian king Mithridates attacked and, therefore, confused the account. Moreover, some scholars also assume Mithridates in fact defeated Artavasdes; however, Justin does not make this claim.[79]

Artavasdes I reigned either ca. 160–123 or ca. 123–96, with a man named Tigranes I also reigning either ca. 160–123 or ca. 123–96.[80] If we accept Justin's account, Mithridates II could not have attacked Artavasdes unless he ruled from 123–96; however, a further complication in the reconstruction of Artavasdes' reign is the identity of the father of a later Armenian king, Tigranes II. Over the course of the first Armeno-Parthian war, Tigranes (Tigranes II) became a hostage of the Parthians.[81] Cuneiform records confirm a father-son relationship between Tigranes and the man who preceded him on the Armenian throne, but they do not identify the man specifically.[82] Although Moses of Chorene records in his jumbled account of Tigranes II's reign that Artavasdes was his father, the far more reliable Appian states that Tigranes' father was a man also named Tigranes (Tigranes I).[83]

With the available evidence, Artavasdes I most likely reigned from 160–123; his son or younger brother, Tigranes I, then reigned from 123–96; and finally, Tigranes I's son, Tigranes II, became king of Armenia with the aid of the Parthians in 96/95.[84] The only piece of evidence that does not fit this reconstruction is Justin's claim that Mithridates II made war against Artoadistes (presumably Artavasdes); however, Assar put forth an interesting argument, stating, "As for Justin's statement, he may well have confused Mithridates I, who probably wrested Media-Atropatene from Artavasdes I [in the middle 150s], with Mithridates II."[85] The argument that Justin here conflates events in Mithridates I's reign with those in Mithridates II's reign, while also confusing the name of the Armenian monarch, appears sound since both Parthian kings campaigned in Media Atropatene. Yet it is unlikely that Mithridates I actually made war against Armenia. The Seleucids appear to have controlled Media Atropatene under Timarchus and Demetrius I, and the evidence

79. For example, Chaumont 1986a; Assar 2011.

80. For Artavasdes' former dates, note Lang 1983: 513; Coloru 2013: 6752. For Artavasdes' latter dates, note Mousheghian and Depeyrot 1999: 31. For Tigranes' former dates, note Lang 1983: 513. For Tigranes' latter dates, note Mousheghian and Depeyrot 1999: 31; Coloru 2013: 6752.

81. Strabo 11.14.15; Justin 38.3.1; Appian *Syr.* 8.48.

82. Sachs and Hunger 1996: no. -95C, no. -95D. Compare Assar 2006c: 142–43. See Schottky 1989; Mousheghian and Depeyrot 1999: 31.

83. Appian *Syr.* 8.48; Moses 2.14.

84. Manandyan 1940 (2007): 19–20; Mousheghian and Depeyrot 1999: 31; Assar 2006c: 142; Nurpetlian 2008-2009; Coloru 2013: 6752. Compare Seyrig 1955; Bedoukian 1968; Lang 1983: 513. For the year of Tigranes II's ascension, note Plut. *Luc.* 21.1. For Tigranes II's alliance with Parthia, see Justin 40.1.3. Note Traina 2016.

85. Assar 2006c: 142 n.172. Assar oddly later abandoned this reconstruction, denying the existence of Tigranes I and claiming Tigranes II was Artavasdes' eldest son. Id. 2011: 121. Compare Debevoise 1938: 41–42, 45; Bivar 1983: 40–41; Chahin 1987: 225–26; Coloru 2013: 6752.

suggests the Parthians seized this region from the Seleucids, not the Armenians.[86] Moreover, in the 150s the Parthians were fighting a difficult war in Media against the Seleucids, and a further conflict with the Armenians would not have been desirable.[87] Thus, although both Parthian kings campaigned in the region, it is mostly likely that Mithridates I fought the Seleucids and Mithridates II fought the Armenians. The Romans knew the Armenians and Parthians eventually fought over this region, making Justin's mistake of associating Mithridates I with a war against Armenia to control Media Atropatene understandable; however, Justin's confused and condensed account leaves much to be desired.[88] It only should be utilized to demonstrate that Mithridates II fought a successful war against Armenia. One must look elsewhere to reconstruct the events of this conflict.

Mithridates II started his Armenian war likely against Tigranes I, sometime between 121–96.[89] In fact, it is most likely that the first Armeno-Parthian war began in the latter half of the 110s. The war against the Central Asian invaders consumed Mithridates' early reign, and a second major war was not desirable or possible until after the destruction of the tribal confederations in 119/118.[90] Yet Mithridates' eastern war and resettlement of the eastern frontier was not complete in 118. He spent several more years in the east reestablishing Parthian hegemony over the Iranian plateau, in which time he met the Chinese envoy, Zhang Qian, with 20,000 horsemen in 116/115.[91] If Mithridates already had been engaged in a protracted conflict in Armenia, this major show of force along the eastern frontier in 116/115 likely would not have been possible.

Further, before Mithridates II could attack Armenia directly, the Parthians needed to establish firm control over northern Mesopotamia and Media Atropatene.[92] By the late 110s the Parthians were advancing steadily into northern Mesopotamia, putting increased pressure on Seleucid Syria and southern Armenia. For example, the Parthians conquered the Seleucid fortress city of Dura on the western bank of the Euphrates in ca. 113.[93] The important task of expanding the western frontier of the empire appears to have fallen initially to the western commander, Mitradatā.

86. Olbrycht 2010a: 232, 238–40; Grainger 2013a: 130. Note Diod. 31.27a.
87. Overtoom 2019a: 131–4.
88. Id. 2016d: Chs. 5–6. Note Dio 36.14.2; Eutrop. 6.8; Orosius 6.4.9; Isid. 6.
89. Appian *Syr.* 8.48.
90. Overtoom 2019b. Note also Shayegan 2011: 243.
91. Mair 2014: 158.
92. Strabo records that Tigranes II later surrendered seventy valleys to the Parthians, which were likely located throughout northern Mesopotamia and northwestern Media Atropatene. Strabo 11.14.15. See Marquart 1901: 109; Manandyan 1940 (2007): 18–20; Sherwin-White 1984: 223; Chaumont 1986a.
93. See Bellinger 1948: 65; Welles 1957; Leriche 1987; Millar 1993: 445–52; Sartre 2005: 26; Olbrycht 2009: 165; Shayegan 2011: 313; Leriche 2011; Gaslain 2012. Contrary to Bellinger, Ehling, and Shayegan, an alliance between the Parthians and Antiochus IX against Antiochus VIII appears dubious. Bellinger 1948: 67; Ehling 2008: 228; Shayegan 2011: 313. Such an alliance was unnecessary for the Parthians to exert their power over Dura, and the claim that Antiochus IX formed a marriage alliance with the Parthians is unconvincing. Jo. Mal. 8.208. Note Assar 2011: 115.

The earliest evidence we have of a possible conflict between Parthia and Armenia during Mithridates II's reign comes from the Babylonian *Astronomical Diaries*, which mention Mitradatā in close association with disturbances in Media in 112.[94] Then in 111 the *Astronomical Diaries* perhaps indicate that Mithridates conducted a successful campaign against the "land of Habigalbat," which here likely refers to a region of the Kingdom of Armenia.[95] Shayegan even argues that this victory likely marked the end of the first phase of Mithridates' war against Armenia.[96] Thus, Mithridates could have ordered his trusted second-in-command to initiate conflict with Armenia in Media Atropatene in 113/112 to prepare for his larger invasion of southern Armenia in 111. This new chronology also coincides with the end of Arab raids into Babylonia in 112 with the return of Mithridates and the main Parthian army to the west. Parthian hegemony along the western frontier suddenly became more stable and extensive in this period.

With his successful invasion of Armenia, Mithridates II forced the Armenian king to surrender his son as a political hostage.[97] When the Armenian king later died in 96, his successor, Tigranes II, left from Babylon, where he had sojourned at the Parthian court, and with the military support of the Parthians he became the pro-Parthian candidate on the Armenian throne.[98] Thus, the evidence suggests that Mithridates conducted a hegemonic war against Armenia that culminated in a partial victory in ca. 111 and a more complete victory in 96/95 when he established Tigranes II as a Parthian vassal king.[99] In an attempt to mitigate the potential threat of Armenia further, Mithridates confiscated seventy valleys from the kingdom in exchange for his support of Tigranes.[100] This war placed Armenia and the surrounding regions of the Caucasus, which had been a part of the separate Near Eastern interstate system since the 180s, firmly within the bounds of

94. Sachs and Hunger 1996: no. -111C.

95. Id. no. -110. Note id. 1989: no. -164B; Gera and Horowitz 1997: 243, 245, 247; Del Monte 1997: 80–81, 153–54; Mittag 2006: 296 n.1; Shayegan 2011: 244. The region of "Habigalbat (or Hanigalbat)" could refer to territory along the Tigris River south of Lake Van known in the Parthian period as Gordyene, meaning the Parthians could have seized Gordyene from Armenia at this time. Note Marciak 2012b; id. 2013; Blasweiler 2015; Da Riva 2016; Marciak 2017.

96. Shayegan 2011: 244. Assar argues that there is "nothing to justify a military expedition" here. Assar 2006c: 141. However, Shayegan makes a compelling argument that Mithridates' association with the "King of Kings" title coincided with a major victory in Armenia. Shayegan 2011: 241.

97. Strabo 11.14.15; Justin 38.3.1; Appian *Syr.* 8.48. Note Manandyan 1940 (2007): 19–20; Chahin 1987: 225–26; Chaumont 1988: 23; Redgate 1998: 69.

98. Sachs and Hunger 1996: no. -95C, no. -95D. Redgate's suggestion that Tigranes was never a Parthian vassal and that the Romans favored him because they wanted a buffer state between them and the Parthians is untenable. Redgate 1998: 69. Note Sullivan 1990: 116–17; Olbrycht 2009: 167. However, Olbrycht's conclusion that Mithridates II installed Tigranes as his vassal "to meet Mithridates Eupator's wishes" goes too far. Olbrycht 2009: 169. Note Overtoom 2016d: Chs. 4–5.

99. Strabo's opinion that the Parthians never ruled over the Armenians is mistaken. Strabo 16.1.19.

100. Id. 11.14.15. These seventy valleys were some of the most prosperous and well positioned valleys in the Armenian Kingdom. See Marquart 1901: 109; Manandyan 1940 (2007): 20; Sherwin-White 1984: 223; Chaumont 1986a.

what had become the Parthian-dominated Iranian interstate system, which now encompassed most the lands of the Hellenistic Middle East.

Mithridates II's emphasis on expanding Parthian hegemony into the Near East also drastically changed the position of southern Mesopotamia within the Parthian Empire. Under Mithridates, southern Mesopotamia transitioned from a chaotic frontier zone to the new administrative and military center of the Parthian state, with Ctesiphon eventually becoming the leading city within the empire by the end of the first century.[101] Decades of regional instability and violence helped convince Mithridates that a different system of imperial rule was necessary to control the new center of his expanding empire.

From the late 110s to the end of his reign, Mithridates II concentrated on implementing foreign and domestic policies in the west that would strengthen the Parthian state and heighten his prestige. After stabilizing and expanding the eastern frontier, Mithridates found it advantageous to create a larger system of satrapies and vassal kingdoms under his authority in the west.[102] For example, vassals, such as Apodakos, Kamnaskires, and Tiraios, all struck coins between 109–94, ruled over the kingdoms of Elymais and Characene, and served Mithridates.[103] Many of the regions Mithridates maintained as tributary subkingdoms, such as Media Atropatene, Persis, Elymais, and Characene, had been seeking local autonomy, sometimes violently, for generations, and he recognized an opportunity to win over the local aristocracies in these regions through a less direct form of imperial coercion that still reinforced his power and authority.[104] This new system of loyal vassals in and around Mesopotamia helped stabilize what had been an untenable region for the Parthians in recent decades, and in 96/95 Mithridates eagerly extended this system by installing Tigranes II as a vassal king on the Armenian throne.[105] Mithridates' creation of a larger network of vassal kings in the 100s–90s drastically enhanced his reputation, prestige, and the perceived power of the Parthians, helping Mithridates create an image of himself as the supreme ruler of the supreme power in the Hellenistic Middle East.

Another important aspect of this new imperial agenda for Mithridates II in this period was the adoption of new regalia and titles to reflect his new position of unrivaled dominance. Mithridates incorporated a new decorative tiara into his imperial imagery (S28 [Figure 27]), and more spectacularly, embraced the Achaemenid Persian title of "King of Kings."[106] Babylonian scribes began

101. Strabo 16.1.16; Jos. *Ant.* 18.374–79. Note Kröger 2011. Sampson argues that Mithridates established Ctesiphon as the new Parthian capital to provide better protection for the royal court, to secure better access to the lands of the Near East, and to mimic the Achaemenids. Sampson 2015: 51.

102. This process began around 110. Assar 2011: 121.

103. Note Le Rider 1959: 251; id. 1969: 22–24; Dilmaghani 1986: 217 and pl. 24.2; Assar 2006c: 141; Dąbrowa 2014b: 63–64. Compare Schuol 2000: 299.

104. Bernard 1990: 41–3; Olbrycht 2010b: 147.

105. By 94 the Parthians were attempting to revitalize the prosperity of Babylonia with new irrigation by digging out the Euphrates. Finkel, van der Spek, Pirngruber 2020i.

106. Note Mithridates' two final coin issues (S27 and S28 [Figures 26–27]) and his rock monument at Bisitun. Assar 2006c: 143, id. 2011: 121. Compare Ionescu 2017.

associating Mithridates with this imperial title in ca. 111, and Mithridates had adopted this new imperial image into his official titulature no later than 109.[107] Thus, the sudden and drastic change in Mithridates' imperial image coincided with his defeat of Armenia and the establishment of his larger vassalage network in the west, and it was meant to reinforce Mithridates' aggressive western ambitions to establish unrivaled hegemony throughout the entire Hellenistic Middle East.[108]

Armenia became an important key to the protection of the Parthians' western and northern frontiers and control of this region facilitated the Parthians' eagerness to dominate the rest of the Near East.[109] Mithridates II's control of Armenia was a challenge to Seleucid prestige and a direct threat to what remained of the Seleucid state. For two centuries Armenia had recognized the Seleucids as the hegemonic power in the Near East.[110] However, the defeat and eventual submission of Armenia to the Parthians had symbolic significance to Mithridates and signified a changing of the guard in the region.[111] Syria, the last stronghold of Seleucid power and influence, at last was vulnerable to Mithridates' grand ambitions.

A New Power in the Near East

By the 90s the Seleucid state was in sharp decline. Unable to recover from the staggering losses of Antiochus VII's failed anabasis, the Seleucids further undermined their potential strength through another series of devastating civil wars. The two competing branches of the Seleucid dynasty that developed through the sons of Demetrius II and Antiochus divided the resources and loyalty of the Seleucids and allowed foreign powers, such as the Parthians, Armenians, and Romans, to manipulate the political and military affairs of Syria.[112] Phraates

107. Sachs and Hunger 1996: no. -110, no. -108B. Note Assar 2006c: 141; id. 2011: 121; Shayegan 2011: 43–44 n.22, 241; Dąbrowa 2012; Grainger 2016: 171.

108. For the argument that the revival of the old Achaemenid title was of Babylonian origin and followed Mithridates' successful first invasion of Armenia, see Shayegan 2011: 45–59, 241, 244, 247, 292. For indices on Arsacid knowledge of the Achaemenids, see Wiesehöfer 2002a: 112–13; id. 2005: 120; Fowler 2005: 125–55. For the argument that the Arsacids revived Achaemenid traditions, see Wolski 1964a: 156–57; id. 1966: 74; id. 1977; Dąbrowa 1983: 103–17; Wolski 1984: 373–79; Wiesehöfer 1986: 177–81; Panitschek 1990: 459–61; Wolski 1990a: 8–9; id. 1990b: 15; id. 1990c: 108–9; id. 1991: 53–55; id. 1993: 152–60; Wiesehöfer 1994b: 39; Olbrycht 1997; Wiesehöfer 2000: 714; Wheeler 2002: 288–99; Wiesehöfer 2002b: 296; id. 2007b: 128; Shayegan 2011: 41–60; Assar 2011: 121; Gregoratti 2015b: 14–15. Compare Strootman 2018. For the argument that Mithridates II adopted the title in 111 as an indication of his great power and not as an Achaemenid revival, see Dąbrowa 2008 [2009]; Shayegan 2011: 244. Shayegan argues instead that the Arsacids did not adopt the Achaemenid legacy into their political ideology until their conflict with Rome and, at that time, embraced the imperial propaganda Mithridates VI of Pontus had developed. Id. 330–31. Contra Olbrycht 2012a. Daryaee incorrectly states that Mithridates I adopted this title. Daryaee 2015: 286. Note also, Ballesteros-Pastor 2014.

109. Note Justin 42.1.1; Diod. 34/35.18; Plut. *Ant.* 30.1; Tac. *Ann.* 6.31; Amm. Mar. 23.6.5–7, 25.4.23–24.

110. Sherwin-White and Kuhrt 1993: 190–92.

111. Id. 218.

112. Note Overtoom 2016d: Chs. 5–6.

II had been the first Parthian king to attempt to interfere in Syria; however, Mithridates II made the manipulation of the Seleucid dynasty in Syria a major policy of his later reign.[113] Although it was left to his immediate successors to achieve the full submission of the Seleucids under Parthian hegemony in the early 80s, Mithridates' reign underscored the strong and determined leadership of the Arsacids, the cultural flexibility and administrative inclusiveness of the Parthians, and the innovative and deadly force of the Parthian military that established the Parthian state as one of the greatest world empires in history.

Wars in Syria

Mithridates II's success in establishing the Parthians' firm control over the Iranian plateau, Mesopotamia, and Armenia, which coincided with the new imperial image of Mithridates as the King of Kings, initiated what we may call the "First Arsacid Cycle" of hegemony over the Hellenistic Middle East (100s–80s).[114] Although rivals in Armenia and Syria remained independent at the end of the 110s, no coalition of states could overcome Mithridates' power in the Hellenistic Middle East, and Mithridates utilized his new position of power to begin dominating potential rivals in the Near East. After consolidating the gains of his vast territorial expansions for several years, the focus of Mithridates' foreign policy by the 90s was the domination of Syria and its surrounding territories. The submission of Armenia in 96/95 made this task more manageable, and with Armenia under their control, the Parthians could pressure the Seleucids in Syria along multiple fronts, further isolating the region.

After Mithridates II established a network of vassal kingdoms in and around Mesopotamia, which culminated in his domination of Armenia, the only notable polity remaining in the Hellenistic Middle East that had the potential to rival the Parthians was the much-diminished Seleucid state. Many of the important lands of the once great Seleucid Empire, such as Syria, Anatolia, and the Levant, remained outside the Parthians' sphere of influence. Yet this fragile geopolitical situation in the Near East changed drastically in the 90s–80s as Mithridates and his sons began to maneuver politically and militarily to dominate the Parthians' longest-standing rival.

Since the death of Antiochus VII in late 129 at the hands of the Parthians, the Seleucids had suffered chronic dynastic intrigue and civil strife that continued to sap their potential strength and made them vulnerable to foreign influence.[115] Traditionally, the Ptolemies of Egypt had benefited the most from periods of weakness and turmoil for the Seleucids; however, a series of feeble leaders and a debilitating civil war between Ptolemy IX and Ptolemy X had crippled the

113. Note id. 2019/2020.
114. Note id. 2016d: Ch. 4.
115. For a recent reevaluation of the difficult chronology of the late Seleucids, see Hoover 2007.

power of Egypt, making Ptolemaic foreign policy mostly ineffective.[116] Thus, the Parthians had a great opportunity to extend their hegemony over the lands of the eastern Mediterranean coast for the first time, and two major factors helped motivate Mithridates II's operations against the Seleucids. First, although much-reduced since the 120s, the Seleucids remained a threat to Parthian hegemony. In living memory, the Parthians had suffered two major Seleucid invasions and had experienced a major reversal of fortune in the east against the Central Asian invaders. What international relations theorists call the "uncertainty principle" and the "security dilemma" encouraged the Parthians and Seleucids to continue to act aggressively to heighten their security and expand their power in this period. Although recent conflicts had allowed the Parthians to emerge as the leading power in the Hellenistic Middle East, they would have understood that power relations could suddenly shift dramatically (as they did in the 80s–50s).[117] There was little way for the Parthians to understand the military capabilities or designs of the Seleucids in the 90s–80s without testing them in war, and this uncertainty helped motivate Mithridates' new policy to isolate and subdue Syria. Moreover, the Seleucids never lost their desire to reclaim their lost empire. Even during an intense civil war in the late 90s and early 80s, Antiochus X pursued a war against the Parthians.[118] In fact, there was a major increase in coinage production under Antiochus X that was similar to the preparations of Antiochus III and Antiochus IV for their eastern expeditions.[119] Oliver Hoover is right to point out that the campaign of Antiochus X did not come near to matching previous Seleucid efforts to conduct hegemonic war against the Parthians; however, the effort in and of itself is significant.[120] For the Parthians there was a considerable risk involved in allowing potential rivals, such as Armenia and Syria, to remain autonomous, and Mithridates had experienced firsthand that power was fluid and fragile. Therefore, aggression against Syria became necessary in the 90s to cement the unrivaled hegemony of the Parthians throughout the Hellenistic Middle East. Second, although diminished, the prestige of the Seleucids in the Hellenistic Middle East still carried with it considerable authority. If the Parthians wanted their subjects and neighbors to view them as the true masters of the Hellenistic Middle East and if Mithridates wanted to be the true "King of Kings," then a definitive offensive campaign against the Seleucids was important to reinforcing that image.

116. See Jos. *Ant.* 12.235, 243, 13.267–68, 284–87, 324–64, 370, 14.250; id. *Bell.* 1.86; Justin 38.8, 39.2–5; Diod. 34.39a; Paus. 1.9.3; Athen. 12.550a; Eus. *Chron.* (Smith ed.): 163. For the conflicts of the Ptolemies and Seleucids, note Grainger 2010. For Ptolemy VIII and his sons, note Hölbl 2001: 181–221; Nadig 2007.

117. Note Overtoom 2016d: Chs. 4–6; id. 2021.

118. Jos. *Ant.* 13.371.

119. Aperghis 2004: 240–42; Hoover 2007: 292–93; Aperghis 2011: 94.

120. Hoover 2007: 292–93.

By no later than the early 80s, the Parthians had become involved in Syria militarily and established their hegemony over the Seleucids firmly, capturing yet another Seleucid king as a political prisoner and gaining influence over his rival. Josephus records:

> But when Demetrius [III] was departed out of Judea, he went to Beroea, and besieged his brother Philip [I], having with him ten thousand footmen, and a thousand horsemen. However, Strato, the tyrant of Beroea, the confederate of Philip, called in Azizus, the chief (φύλαρχον) of the Arabian tribes, and Mithridates Sinaces, the local governor (ὕπαρχον) of the Parthians, who coming with a great number of forces, and besieging Demetrius in his encampment, into which they had driven them with their arrows, they compelled those that were with him by thirst to deliver up themselves. So, they took a great many spoils out of that country and Demetrius himself they sent to Mithridates, who was then king of the Parthians; but as to those whom they took captive of the people of Antioch, they restored them to the Antiochenes without any reward. Now Mithridates, the king of the Parthians, had Demetrius in great honor, until Demetrius ended his life by sickness. So, Philip, presently after the fight was over, came to Antioch, and took it, and reigned over Syria.[121]

It appears Josephus provides us with yet another possible example of the Parthians implementing their unique "Feign Retreat, Defeat in Detail" mode of warfare.[122] In 87 the Parthians answered the request of Philip and his allies to attack Philip's brother, Demetrius, while he besieged Beroea (modern Aleppo, Syria). Demetrius immediately found himself in a vulnerable position between two enemy forces. The Parthians recognized his vulnerability, and it appears they implemented their Overwhelm Strategy, striking quickly at Demetrius. In the ensuing battle, the Parthians likely executed their Massed Assault and Hit-and-Run tactics, driving Demetrius and his men into their camp under a barrage of arrows. Demetrius found himself trapped and unable to break out against the more mobile and longer-ranged Parthian cavalry. Josephus even notes that the Parthians compelled Demetrius' men to surrender because of their great thirst. It is possible the Parthians circled their cavalry around the camp, intentionally clouding the air with dust to blind and suffocate Demetrius' men, a tactic of psychological warfare that the Parthians later implemented at Carrhae against the Romans.[123] Exhausted and unwilling to carry on the fight, Demetrius' men offered him to the Parthians as a prisoner, the latest in a long line of captured Seleucid royalty.[124]

121. Jos. *Ant.* 13.384–6. Translation slightly altered. Shayegan associates Mithridates Sinaces with Mitradatā, concluding Josephus mistakenly credits Mitradatā for deeds accomplished by his successor, Mitrāṭu. Shayegan 2011: 150 n.449, 198–204. However, this association is not clear or necessary, and likely Mithridates Sinaces indeed was the local Parthian governor (*hyparchos*) in northern Mesopotamia, making him the subordinate of Mitrāṭu. Sachs and Hunger 1996: no. -90, no. -87C, no. -83, no. -82B.

122. Note Overtoom 2017b.

123. Plut. *Crass.* 25.3–6; Dio 40.23.4.

124. Note Nabel 2017a.

Scholars traditionally have assumed that Mithridates II died soon after this victory because Josephus states that Demetrius III became the prisoner of king "Mithridates."[125] However, Assar has argued convincingly that the Mithridates mentioned here by Josephus was not Mithridates II, King of Kings; rather it was Mithridates II's son, Mithridates III (ca. 87–80) [Figure 30].[126] In fact, numismatic and cuneiform evidence now likely illustrates that Mithridates II died in 91, not 87 as previously thought.[127] This important realignment of Parthian chronology perhaps indicates that the Parthians did not conduct hegemonic war against the Seleucids until after Mithridates II's death in 91.[128] Yet if we reexamine the chaotic geopolitical developments of this period carefully, it seems likely that Mithridates initiated the hegemonic conflict with the Seleucids before he died.

The violent deaths of Demetrius II and his eldest son, Seleucus V, in 125 left the Seleucid throne to Demetrius' youngest son, Antiochus VIII.[129] Yet Antiochus had many rivals, including the usurper, Alexander Zabinas, his own mother, Cleopatra Thea, and his half-brother and cousin, Antiochus IX, which severely limited the effectiveness of Antiochus VIII's regime.[130] Antiochus VIII and Antiochus IX had the pedigree necessary to reinvigorate the Seleucids and to make war against the Parthians; however, the half-brothers were evenly matched in a back-and-forth battle over Antioch that further subverted the power of the Seleucid state and damaged the prestige of the Seleucid crown.[131] Although both their fathers had conducted unsuccessful wars against the Parthians, making a retaliatory campaign against the Parthians attractive to both men, control of Antioch changed hands between the two claimants as many as seven times in less than twenty years, making a major eastern expedition impossible.[132] Antiochus IX outlived Antiochus VIII, who died in 96; however, Antiochus IX barely held the throne for a year before his nephew, Seleucus VI, overthrew him.[133] The Seleucid

125. See Gardner 1877: 7; Debevoise 1938: 48–50; Simonetta 1953–1957: 115; Sellwood 1962: 73; Le Rider 1965: 391; Simonetta 1966: 20 n.1; Sellwood 1976: 6; Bivar 1983: 42–44. Compare Newell 1939: 82, nos. 130–31; Houghton and Spaer 1998: 378–82. The last coins of Demetrius are dated 88/87. Note Hoover 2007: 294–96.

126. Assar 2006d: 69–75; id. 2011: 122. Compare Newell 1918: 117; Bellinger 1949: 75–77.

127. Assar 2005a: 51–52; id. 2006c: 145–49; id. 2006d: 70; id. 2011: 120–21; Valverde 2017.

128. Assar is rather conservative and limits the advance of Mithridates' western expansion to northern Mesopotamia. Assar 2006c: 145; id. 2011: 121.

129. Seleucus likely was killed by his mother, Cleopatra Thea. Jos. *Ant.* 13.268–69; Justin 39.1.7–9; id. *Prol.* 39; Eus. *Chron.* (Smith ed.): 257; Appian *Syr.* 11.68–69; Livy *Epit.* 60.11.

130. Justin 39.2.1–4, 7–8; Appian *Syr.* 11.69. Antiochus VIII defeated and killed Alexander Zabinas in 123/122. Diod. 34.28.1–3; Jos. *Ant.* 13.269; Justin 39.2.1–6; Eus. *Chron.* (Smith ed.): 257. Chahin argues that Antiochus VIII was "the last of the Seleucids with any credence." Chahin 1987: 227. For Antiochus VIII and his cities, note Athen. 5.210e–f, 6.246d, 12.540a-b; *ChronPasc.* 448a; Welles 1934: *RC* 70–72.

131. Josephus states that the half-brothers fought a long war in Syria and describes them as evenly matched wrestlers. Jos. *Ant.* 13.270–77, 282–3, 327; id. *Bell.* 1.65. Compare Justin 39.2.9–10, 3.3–12; id. *Prol.* 39; Appian *Syr.* 11.69; Eus. *Chron.* (Smith ed.): 257–59; Plut. *Mor.* 486A; Hieron. *Chron.* 1905.

132. Note Hoover 2007: 284–88. There is no evidence to support Grainger's claim of an alliance between Antiochus IX and the Parthians against Antiochus VIII. Grainger 2016: 140–41.

133. Jos. *Ant.* 13.365–68, 14.38; Appian *Syr.* 11.69; Justin *Prol.* 39–40; Athen. 4.153b; Diod. 34.34.1; Arnob. 6.21; Eus. *Chron.* (Smith ed.): 259, 263; Hieron. *Chron.* 1923; *ExcBarb.* 46b; *ChronSynt.* 92. Note Houghton 1993: 93; Hoover 2006: 28–29; id. 2007: 285 n.19.

state soon descended into chaos as six men, including five sons of Antiochus VIII, fought over the throne from the middle 90s to the late 80s.[134] Yet it is in this period of chaos that we find evidence of the hegemonic war initiated by Mithridates II against the Seleucids. Josephus states:

> But when Antiochus [X], the son of Cyzicenus, was king of Syria, Antiochus [XI], the brother of Seleucus [VI], made war upon him, and was overcome, and destroyed, he and his army. After him, his brother Philip [I] put on the diadem and reigned over some part of Syria; but Ptolemy [IX] Lathyrus sent for his [that is, Philip's] fourth brother Demetrius [III], who was called Eucerus, from Cnidus, and made him king of Damascus. Both these brothers did Antiochus [X] vehemently oppose, but swiftly died (ταχέως ἀπέθανεν); for when he came to the military aid (σύμμαχος) of Laodice, queen of the Samenians (Σαμηνῶν), when she was making war against (πολεμούσῃ) the Parthians, and he [Antiochus X] was fighting courageously, he fell, and so Demetrius and Philip governed Syria, as hath been elsewhere related.[135]

Josephus illustrates the unraveling political situation in Syria and demonstrates that the Parthians actively were involved in the region's geopolitical developments. Further, Josephus records that Parthian forces counterattacked and killed Antiochus X, who had aggressively advanced against the Parthians. Yet it is necessary to clarify other aspects of this passage to appreciate its content fully.

The identity of Queen Laodice and the location of the Samenians are ambiguous, leading some scholars to contend, rather tenuously, that the Samenians were the inhabitants of Samosata in Commagene (modern Samsat, Turkey).[136] In fact, Olbrycht used this assumption to argue that this Queen Laodice was Laodice VII, who had married King Mithridates I Callinicus of Commagene.[137] However, after further consideration it seems highly unlikely that Laodice VII of Commagene was the Laodice here mentioned by Josephus.

Laodice VII's father was Antiochus VIII, who was the bitter rival of Antiochus IX, the father of Antiochus X. Further, Laodice's brothers were Seleucus VI, Antiochus XI, Philip I, and Demetrius III, all of whom were the enemies of Antiochus X. It makes little sense that Antiochus X would have come to the

134. Jos. *Ant.* 13.367–71, 384–86, 14.38; Appian *Syr.* 11.69–70; Justin *Prol.* 40; Eus. *Chron.* (Smith ed.): 259–61; Hieron. *Chron.* 1923. Note Hoover 2007: 288–99; Grainger 2016: Chs. 10–13.

135. Jos. *Ant.* 13.369–71. Translation slightly altered. Ptolemy IX Lathyrus was expelled from the throne by his mother Cleopatra III in favor of his younger brother Ptolemy X. Ptolemy IX fled to Cyprus where he reigned from 106/105 until his return to Egypt to reclaim the throne in 88. He seemingly aided Demetrius while in exile. See Mitford 1959: 104; Bennett 2002: 147. Compare Paus. 1.9.1–3; Athen. 12.5550b; Justin 39.4.1–2, 5.1; id. *Prol.* 39; Eus. *Chron.* (Smith ed.): 163–65, 171; Hieron. *Chron.* 1929; *ChronSynt.* 91; *ChronPasc.* 449a.

136. Bouche-Leclercq 1913–1914: i 421 n.1; Shayegan 2011: 314. Ralph Marcus in his Loeb translation notes the various translations used for Σαμηνῶν. Marcus 1943: 411.

137. Olbrycht 2009: 166.

military aid of the daughter and sister of his sworn enemies. Moreover, Laodice VII, who assumed the epithet "Brother-Loving," had living brothers, namely Philip and Demetrius, to whom she could have turned for military aid against the Parthians. Finally, there is the issue of Laodice VII's high profile as a Seleucid princess. She was the daughter of Antiochus VIII, the granddaughter of Ptolemy VIII, the wife of Mithridates I of Commagene, and the mother of Antiochus I Theos of Commagene. Laodice's notable family ties make Josephus' rather vague reference to "Laodice, queen of the Samenians" an unlikely match for Laodice VII. Laodice, like Cleopatra, was a common royal name in the Near East, and Josephus had much better and clearer options for identifying Laodice VII if she was involved in the conflict with the Parthians. Instead, Josephus here likely refers to another Laodice, who was queen of an Arab tribe from the Syrian Desert named the Samenians.[138]

The identity of this tribe again is not well known. The eighteenth-century historian William Whiston, in his translation of Josephus, labels the Σαμηνῶν as the Gileadites, a tribe from Gilead (modern northern Jordan); however, this association also appears highly unlikely because of the contexts of the passage.[139] First, Josephus later makes a clear distinction between the Samenians and the Gileadites (Γαλααδίτας) in his text.[140] Second, Josephus states that the Parthians were making war upon the Samenians. To attack the Gileadites, the Parthians would have needed to move through Syria without conflict past Damascus, a Seleucid stronghold, to sustain a campaign south of the Wadi Yarmuk. This would have isolated the Parthian army far from its base of operations in northern Mesopotamia in hostile and unfavorable terrain. Further, Antiochus X's rival, Demetrius III, used Damascus as his base of power. It seems impossible that Antiochus X would have abandoned his position in northern Syria, dangerously bypassing Demetrius in Damascus, to attack the Parthians in Gilead. Instead, the proximity of the Parthians in northern Mesopotamia and Antiochus X in Antioch is the best indication of the location of the Samenians in northeastern Syria, perhaps between Beroea, Palmyra, and Dura.[141]

Antiochus X's eagerness to aid the Samenians militarily against the Parthians means that Laodice was his vassal or ally, whose important responsibility it was to protect the eastern and southern frontier of Antiochus' portion of the dwindling Seleucid state. Thus, the Parthians' conflict with the Samenians demonstrates that they had penetrated Seleucid territory or at least the Seleucid sphere of influence in and around Syria south of the Euphrates. The Parthians were not yet

138. See Dobiáš 1931: 221–23; Hoover 2007: 295. Arab tribes had been encroaching upon Seleucid territory in Syria for at least a generation. Justin 39.5.5–6; id. *Prol.* 39.

139. Whiston 1737.

140. Jos. *Ant.* 13.373.

141. For Palmyra, note Colledge 1987; Aruz 2018. For Dura, note Leriche 1987; id. 2011; Wójcikowski 2013; Kaizer 2016.

prepared to attack Antioch directly, so their war against the Samenians in eastern Syria likely was a continuation of Mithridates II's policy to surround and isolate the Seleucids in western Syria.

Antiochus X thought the conflict with the Parthians was so important that he temporarily disregarded his ongoing wars against Demetrius III and Philip I. Moreover, Antiochus' increased coinage production at this time illustrates the considerable resources he invested in this campaign.[142] Clearly, the advances of the Parthians in recent years into eastern Syria became a major concern of Antiochus, who wanted to defeat the Parthians to strengthen his position in Syria and heighten his prestige in his rivalry with his cousins. Josephus states that Laodice was making war against the Parthians and that Antiochus joined this aggressive campaign. Thus, Antiochus' likely objective was the restoration of Seleucid control over the western bank of the Euphrates.

Unfortunately for the Seleucid state, Antiochus X's campaign against the Parthians was yet another disaster. Josephus records that Antiochus suddenly died fighting courageously, and therefore it appears the Parthians once again utilized their Overwhelm Strategy to destroy another Seleucid army and kill another Seleucid king. Yet the date of this disaster for the Seleucids is unclear. Appian's account of Antiochus' end makes no mention of a Parthian attack and, instead, insists that Tigranes II of Armenia drove Antiochus out of Syria.[143] However, there is no epigraphic or numismatic evidence to suggest that Antiochus lived into the late 80s, and therefore it is highly likely that Appian here confuses the later Antiochus XIII with his father Antiochus X, making his account less reliable than that of Josephus.[144]

Traditionally, scholars have assumed that Antiochus X died in 92, in which case he perished at the hands of Mithridates II's soldiers.[145] Yet a recent reevaluation of Seleucid coinage from the late 90s and early 80s suggests that Antiochus was alive until ca. 89/88, at which point he answered the call of the Samenian Arabs and died fighting the Parthians.[146] Hoover used this new information to argue further that the Parthians defeated and captured Demetrius III in 87 in a continuation of the Arab-Parthian war. He states, "The involvement of Arabs and Parthians in both cases is notable, making it tempting to suggest that the apparent close proximity of Aziz and Mithridates [Sinaces] during the conflict between Philip [I] and Demetrius [III] may have been caused by the same

142. Hoover 2007: 292–93.

143. Appian *Syr.* 8.48, 11.69.

144. See Bellinger 1949: 75; Brodersen 1989: 229–30; Hoover 2007: 291–92. A third account, shared by Eusebius and Jerome, where Antiochus X fled the advances of Philip I to the Parthians before returning to beg Pompey to return his kingdom, is even more confused and should be disregarded. Id. 292. Note Nabel 2017a.

145. Bouche-Leclercq 1913–1914: i 420; Newell 1918: 117; Will 1967: ii 380. See Assar 2006c: 144; Hoover 2007: 290.

146. See Hoover 2007: 294–96.

Arab-Parthian war that claimed the life of Antiochus X."[147] Thus, Hoover offers a convincing reconstruction that aligns with the culmination of Mithridates II's foreign policy against the Seleucids, namely the submission of the Seleucids under Parthian hegemony through the Parthians' defeats of Antiochus and Demetrius in the early 80s.

After the defeat of Demetrius III, the Parthians also appear to have gained control of Philip I. Olbrycht argues that Philip agreed to become the pro-Parthian vassal king of Syria in 87 in exchange for Parthian military aid against his brother.[148] However, John Grainger recently suggested that "enmity between the brothers was a later invention," proposing that Demetrius III and Philip in fact were allies fighting a Parthian vassal named Straton at Beroea.[149] Grainger also maintains that when the Parthians captured Philip, he became a Parthian vassal in exchange for his freedom.[150] Yet if Demetrius and Philip both fought the Parthians and became their captives, the Parthians' widely different treatment of the brothers is peculiar. The Parthians clearly favored Philip, allowing him to seize the throne at Antioch, while keeping Demetrius in confinement. The available evidence still favors Olbrycht's reconstruction, and it appears likely that Philip served as king in northern Syria at the pleasure of the Parthians, at least initially.

Thus, the growing presence of the Parthians in the geopolitics of Syria by the early 80s is notable. In a two-year period, the Parthians killed a Seleucid king, captured a second Seleucid king, and placed a third Seleucid king on the throne at Antioch, unequivocally establishing their hegemony over the Seleucids in Syria. Although the defeat of Antiochus X likely occurred during the reign of Mithridates II's eldest son, Gotarzes I (ca. 91–87) [Figure 29], and the defeat of Demetrius III and the establishment of Philip I at Antioch likely occurred during the reign of Mithridates' younger son, Mithridates III (ca. 87–80), the momentum behind this successful hegemonic conflict was the efforts of Mithridates II in the 90s.[151] The Parthians' involvement in Syria was a major legacy of Mithridates' reign and their continued interest in influencing the geopolitical developments within the Near East would have monumental ramifications for the rapidly evolving international environment in the region throughout the first century.[152]

147. Id. 295. Note Jos. *Ant.* 13.384–86.

148. Olbrycht 2009: 165.

149. Grainger 2016: 178–79.

150. Id. 179–81.

151. For Gotarzes' lineage and his role under his father, see Assar 2006d: 62–66; id. 2011: 121–22; Shayegan 2011: 196–97, 225–26; Overtoom 2016d: Ch. 4–5. For Mithridates III, see Sellwood 1976: 4–9; Mørkholm 1980: 35; Assar 2006d: 69–75; id. 2011: 122–23; Overtoom 2016d: Chs. 4–5; Valverde 2017; Faghfoury 2020.

152. Note Overtoom 2016d: Chs. 4–6; id. 2021.

The End of One Rivalry and the Beginning of Another

When Mithridates II began a major military and administrative program to establish the Arsacid dynasty as the unrivaled ruling force throughout the entire Hellenistic Middle East, he put into place policies to extend Parthian hegemony for the first time over Armenia, the Caucasus, northern Mesopotamia, Syria, and portions of southern Anatolia and northern Phoenicia.[153] Justin even emphasizes that Mithridates added many regions to the Parthian state and made war against the Armenians, arguing that he "surpassed" the renown of his ancestors.[154] After finalizing the conquest of northern Mesopotamia and the submission of Armenia in the middle 90s, Mithridates utilized his momentum to expand Parthian hegemony into eastern Syria and southern Anatolia, and for the first time, Parthian influence spread as far west as Cappadocia and Cilicia.[155] Note especially Strabo, who states:

> And at the same time the [Cilician] pirates, pretending to be slave-dealers, carried on their evil business unchecked. Neither were the Romans concerning themselves as yet so much about the peoples outside the Taurus [i.e., the peoples living in and beyond Cilicia]; but they sent Scipio Aemilianus, and again certain others, to inspect the tribes and the cities; and they decided that the above mentioned piracy was due to the incompetence of the [Seleucid] rulers, although they were ashamed, since they themselves had ratified the hereditary succession from Seleucus [I] Nicator, to deprive them of it. And this is what made the Parthians masters of the country, who got possession of the region on the far edge of the Euphrates (τοῦτο δὲ συμβὰν τῆς μὲν χώρας ἐποίησε κυρίους Παρθυαίους, οἳ τὰ πέραν τοῦ Εὐφράτου κατέσχον); and at last made also the Armenians masters, who not only seized the country outside the Taurus even as far as Phoenicia, but also, so far as they could, overthrew the kings and the whole royal stock; the sea, however, they gave over to the Cilicians. Then, after these people had grown in power, the Romans were forced to destroy them by war and with an army, although they had not hindered their growing power.[156]

Thus, according to Strabo, the Parthians took advantage of Roman neglect and Seleucid incompetence to extend their power and influence into the lands of the

153. Mithridates made Iberia and Albania tributary states. Olbrycht 2009: 170–71. Compare Chaumont 1985; Schippmann 1987. For the importance of the Caucasus as a frontier region, see Braund 1986; Gregoratti 2013a.

154. Justin 42.2.3–6. Olbrycht's conclusion that Mithridates II added little new territory to the empire after the conquests of Mithridates I is too dismissive. Olbrycht 2010a: 240.

155. See Plut. *Sul.* 5; Livy *Epit.* 70.6–7; Ruf. Fest. 15; Vell. Pat. 2.24.3; Justin 38.9.3, 10.7, 11, 42.1.1; Diod. 34/35.18; Jos. *Ant.* 13.365–71, 384–86. Note Bouché-Leclercq 1913–1914: i 421. Note Olbrycht 2009; Shayegan 2011: 317–18.

156. Strabo 14.5.2.

Near East in this period. Strabo's criticism of Parthian imperialism as parasitic is exaggerated; however, he captures the hectic and fluid international environment in the Near East in the early first century. The Romans were not yet involved heavily in the Near East, and the decline and collapse of the Seleucids after the 120s created a power void in the region. The Parthians not only seized the lands to the east of the Euphrates, but also temporarily became "masters of the country" between the Euphrates and the Taurus. Strabo also indicates that the Parthians ruled this territory in part by vassalizing the Seleucids, unlike the Armenians who subsequently "overthrew the kings and the whole royal stock."

It was under the leadership of Mithridates II that the Parthians finally emerged as a leading power in the Near East. By the end of his reign, Mithridates had extended Parthian hegemony over Armenia, Gordyene, Adiabene, Sophene, Osrhoene, Commagene, and Cilicia, all of which had been subject territories of the Seleucid state.[157] Further, Josephus demonstrates that the Parthians began pressing upon the Arab tribes of the Syrian Desert, further closing the trap around Antioch in the early 80s under Mithridates' sons.[158] With the death of Antiochus X in battle against the Parthians, the capture of Demetrius III in battle against the Parthians, and the elevation of Philip I to the throne in Antioch by the Parthians, they had achieved the successful culmination of Mithridates' western policy.

Modern international relations theory again can help explain the sudden momentum of the Parthian state under Mithridates II in the west as he initiated his program of expansion in the late 110s–90s. For two and a half decades, Mithridates consolidated and expanded his power and influence in the west, and Justin records that he fought many wars with great bravery.[159] Yet Mithridates also created an extensive network of allies and vassals, who generally supported him in his efforts to establish unrivaled Parthian rule throughout the entire Hellenistic Middle East. These men supported Mithridates' regime in the hope of gaining local geopolitical advantage and security, a process known to international relations theorists as "bandwagoning."[160] In competitive and violent international environments, such as the Hellenistic Middle East, minor and middling states normally do not have the capability to overcome determined aggression by major states, and therefore minor and middling states will attempt to balance against the growing power of a potential hegemon by joining forces or

157. Note Sartre 2005: 26–27. For Parthian control of Gordyene, Adiabene, and Sophene, see Marciak 2011; id. 2012a; id. 2012b; id. 2013; Witakowski 2013; Marciak 2015; id. 2017. Compare Luther 2015. For Osrhoene, see Edwell 2017. For Commagene, see Weiskopf 1992; Shayegan 2016. The Parthians also likely maintained loose hegemony over Judaea. Gaslain 2008.

158. Compare Strabo 16.1.28. The Parthians perhaps established a vassal king at Edessa in this period. Segal 1970: Ch. 1; Grainger 2016: 171.

159. Justin 42.2.4.

160. For bandwagoning, see Kaufman 1992: 417–47; Schweller 1994: 72–107. For examples of bandwagoning in the ancient world, see Strauss 1991; Eckstein 2006: 65–66, 68; id. 2012: 23, 219–20, 229, 268.

bandwagon with the rising hegemon to avoid destruction.[161] Mithridates worked tirelessly to establish the Parthian Empire as the unrivaled power throughout the entire Hellenistic Middle East. The deterioration of the Seleucid state was so widespread and damaging that most of the numerous minor and middling states throughout the Near East did not view balancing against the rising power of the Parthians as a viable option by the 100s, and no coalition of states attempted to halt the advances of the Parthians in the Near East until Antiochus X's failed campaign.

It appears that by the 100s the Parthians had passed what international relations theorists call the "threshold point" in the growth of their power, meaning the power of Parthia had surpassed a level that was acceptable for minor and middling states to pursue balancing behavior against the Parthians with confidence.[162] Instead, the momentum of the Parthians in this period convinced numerous minor and middling states to join forces with the ascending Parthian Empire. One might even argue that some of these bandwagoning states, in particular Tigranes II's Armenia, were pursuing a policy known to international relations theorists as "jackal bandwagoning," where ambitious minor or middling states join a rising hegemon to gain a share in the spoils from a new systemic configuration of the international environment.[163] Thus, as long as Mithridates II could maintain the perception of Parthian dominance within the Hellenistic Middle East through the expansion of his power and prestige, he could coerce neighboring peoples and kings to support his regime, rather than oppose it. This too increasingly left the Seleucids isolated and vulnerable. It was in this favorable international environment that Mithridates and his immediate successors conducted and successfully concluded their last hegemonic struggle with the Seleucids, finally establishing the Parthian Empire as the unrivaled hegemon of the much-expanded Iranian interstate system, which came to encompass the entirety of the Hellenistic Middle East in the 90s.

Mithridates II had saved the Parthian state from ruin and had established it as an unrivaled power at least temporarily. His leadership and policies were fundamentally important to the identity of the Parthian Empire over the next three centuries, but they built upon the legacy of the early Arsacids and the resilience of the Parthians. To introduce his account of Parthian history, Justin emphasizes the amazing success of the Parthians in overcoming such daunting odds in their struggle to create an empire, stating:

> It must seem wonderful to everyone, that they [the Parthians] should have reached such a height of good fortune as to rule over those nations under

161. For geopolitical balancing, see Waltz 1979: 168; Walt 1987; Waltz 1988: 625; Sheehan 1996; Beck 1997: 231–32; Wohlforth 1999; id. 2002.

162. For threshold point, see Wohlforth 2002: 103–6.

163. Note Schweller 1994: 93–5; Eckstein 2012: 23.

> whose sway they had been merely slaves. Being assailed by the Romans, also, in three wars, under the conduct of the greatest generals, and at the most flourishing period of the republic, they alone, of all nations, were not only a match for them, but came off victorious; though it may have been a greater glory to them, indeed, to have been able to rise amidst the Assyrian, Median, and Persian empires, so celebrated of old, and the most powerful dominion of Bactria, peopled with a thousand cities, than to have been victorious in war against a people [the Romans] that came from a distance; especially when they were continually harassed by severe wars with the Scythians and other neighboring nations, and pressed with various other formidable contests.[164]

Justin here identifies the harsh and unforgiving world in which the Parthians had survived and thrived. He labels the Parthians as the successors and equals of the greatest eastern empires, and he champions the significance of the Parthians' rise to power, stressing the continued success of the Parthians in their numerous military confrontations. He especially emphasizes the Parthians' ability to rival the Romans, knowing that the success of the Parthians' westward advances under Mithridates into the lands of the Near East and their new relationship with Armenia for the first time brought Parthia to the attention of Rome.[165]

Yet, despite his numerous accomplishments and accolades, Mithridates II's reign ended in tragedy. In ca. 93 it appears the remaining son of Mithridates I, Sinatruces (Figure 28), rebelled against Mithridates II in an attempt to seize the throne, foreshadowing the devastating dynastic strife and cycles of civil war that hamstrung the Parthian Empire for much of the remainder of its long existence.[166] Mithridates was unable to overcome this usurper and in 91 died in the effort, plunging the empire into what Parthian scholars call a "Dark Age" of geopolitical turmoil.[167] The sudden and dramatic decline of the Parthian Empire during the "Dark Age" period is yet another example of the vulnerability and fragility of ancient states and the violence inherent in their international environments. It is perhaps ironic that the foremost architect of Parthian imperialism and unipolar hegemony also oversaw the beginning of the empire's drastic decline in the first half of the first century. Although the Parthians eventually stabilized their position within the Hellenistic Middle East, ruling for another three centuries, this difficult period of Parthian history

164. Justin 41.1.6–9.

165. Note Schneider 2007; Gregoratti 2015c; Overtoom 2016c; id. 2017b; id. 2021.

166. Note Assar 2005a: 53; id. 2005b; id. 2006d: 56–62; id. 2011: 121–22; Valverde 2017. Strong factionalism emerged between Parthian nobles in the east and west that spurred on civil strife. Dąbrowa 2013; Gregoratti 2013b. Sinatruces appears to have gained the support of the eastern nobles. Note Olbrycht 1997.

167. Assar 2006d: 56–60; id. 2011: 121. For the Parthian Dark Age, see id. 2009b. Compare Simonetta 1953–1957: 111–21; id. 1966: 15–40; Dobbins 1974; Sellwood 1976: 2–25; Mørkholm 1980: 33–47; Simonetta 2001: 69–108.; Assar 2006d: 55–96; Fowler 2013: 5073.

also coincided with the emergence of the long-standing Romano-Parthian rivalry.[168] Although it took forty years of confused, awkward, and infrequent interaction, by the middle first century the Romans emerged as the last great rival of the Parthians, and the Hellenistic Middle East yet again became a battlefield of clashing empires.

168. Note Overtoom 2016c; id. 2016d; id. 2017a; id. 2017b; id. 2021.

Bibliography

Abdullaev, K. "Nomad Migration in Central Asia." *After Alexander*. Oxford, 2007. 73–98.

Abel, P. *Histoire de la Palestine depuis la conquête d'Alexandre jusqu'a l'invasion Arabe*. Paris, 1952.

Adler, E. "Who's Anti-Roman? Sallust and Pompeius Trogus on Mithridates." *Classical Journal* 101.4 (2006): 383–407.

Adler, W., and P. Tuffin. *The Chronography of George Synkellos: A Byzantine Chronicle of Universal History from the Creation*. Oxford, 2002.

Ager, S. "An Uneasy Balance: From the Death of Seleukos to the Battle of Raphia." *A Companion to the Hellenistic World*. Ithaca, 2003. 35–50.

Ager, S. "Roman Perspectives on Greek Diplomacy." *Diplomats and Diplomacy in the Roman World*. Leiden, 2009. 15–43.

Allen, C. *Ashoka: The Search for India's Lost Emperor*. New York, 2012.

Allen, L. *The Persian Empire*. Chicago, 2005.

Allen, R. *The Attalid Kingdom: A Constitutional History*. Oxford, 1983.

Allison, J. *Power and Preparedness in Thucydides*. Baltimore, 1989.

Allotte de la Fuÿe, F. "Monnaies arsacides surfrappées." *Revue Numismatique* 8 (1904): 174–96.

Alonso-Núñez, J. "An Augustan World History: The *Historiae Philippicae* of Pompeius Trogus." *Greece & Rome* 34.1 (1987): 56–72.

Alonso-Núñez, J. *La Historia Universal de Pompeyo Trogo: Coordenadas espaciales y temporales*. Madrid, 1992.

Alram, M. *Nomina propria iranica in nummis: Materialgrundlagen zu den iranischen Personennamen auf antiken Münzen*. Vienna, 1986a.

Alram, M. "Arsacids iii—Arsacid Coinage." *Encyclopaedia Iranica Online Edition* (1986b). Last accessed 1/2020. http://www.iranicaonline.org/articles/arsacids-iii.

Alram, M. "Die Vorbildwirkung der Arsakidischen Münzprägung." *Litterate Numismaticae Vindobonensis* 3 (1987): 117–46.

Alram, M. "Stand und Aufgaben der arsakidischen Numismatik." *Das Partherreich und seine Zeugnisse*. Stuggart, 1998. 365–87.

Altheim, F., and R. Stiehl. *Geschichte Mittelasiens im Altertum*. Berlin, 1970.

Anderson, E. *Cataphracts: Knights of the Ancient Eastern Empires*. Barnsley, 2016.

Andreau, J., P. Briant, and R. Descat, eds. *Économie Antique. Les échanges dans l'Antiquité: le rôle de l'état*. St. Bertrand de Comminges, 1994.

Andreau, J., P. Briant, and R. Descat, eds. *Économie Antique. Prix et formation des prix dans les économies antiques*. St. Bertrand de Comminges, 1997.

Andreau, J., P. Briant, and R. Descat, eds. *Économie Antique. La guerre dans les économies antiques*. St. Bertrand de Comminges, 2000.

Anson, E. "Fortress Egypt: The Abortive Invasions of 320 and 306 BC." *Alexander's Legacy*. Rome, 2016. 85–96.

Antela-Bernardez, B. "Simply the Best. Alexander's Last Words, and the Macedonian Kingship." *Eirene* 47 (2011): 118–26.

Antela-Bernardez, B. "World Is Not Enough: Alexander the Great's Campaigns against the 'Guerrillas' in Sogdiana." *Central Asia in Antiquity*. Oxford, 2014. 77–84.

Anthony, D. *The Horse, the Wheel, and Language: How Bronze-Age Riders from the Eurasian Steppes Shaped the Modern World*. Princeton, 2007.

Aperghis, M. *The Seleukid Royal Economy*. Cambridge, 2004.

Aperghis, M. "Population—Production—Taxation—Coinage: A Model for the Seleucid Economy." *Hellenistic Economies*. New York, 2011. 69–102.

Apicella, C. "Antiochos III et les cités de Phénicie." *Antiochos III et l'Orient*. Nancy, 2017. 143–62.

Archibald, Z., J. Davies and V. Gabrielsen, *The Economies of Hellenistic Societies, Third to First Centuries BC*. Oxford, 2011.

Arendt, H. *On Violence*. New York, 1970.

Armen, H. *Tigranes the Great: A Biography*. Detroit, 1940.

Arnaud, P. "Les guerres des Parthes et de l'Arménie dans la première moitié du premier siècle av. n.è. Problèmes de chronologie et d'extension territoriale, 95 BC–70 BC." *Mesopotamia. Rivista di archeologia, epigrafia e storia orientale antica* 22 (1987): 129–46.

Arnaud, P. "Le guerres parthiques de Gabinius et de Crassus et la politique occidentale des Parthes Arsacides entre 70 et 53 av. J.-C." *Electrum* 2 (1998): 13–34.

Aron, R. *Peace and War: A Theory of International Relations*. Garden City, 1973.

Aruz, J. *Palmyra: Mirage in the Desert*. New York, 2018.

Assar, G. R. F. "Recent Studies in Parthian History: Part I." *The Celator* 14.12 (2000): 6–22.

Assar, G. R. F. "Recent Studies in Parthian History: Part II." *The Celator* 15.1 (2001a): 17–27, 41.

Assar, G. R. F. "Recent Studies in Parthian History: Part III." *The Celator* 15.2 (2001b): 17–22.

Assar, G. R. F. "Genealogy and Coinage of the Early Parthian Rulers I." *Parthica* 6 (2004): 69–93.

Assar, G. R. F. "History and Coinage of Elymais During 150/149–122/121 BC." *The International Journal of Ancient Iranian Studies* 8 (2004–2005): 27–91.

Assar, G. R. F. "Genealogy and Coinage of the Early Parthian Rulers II: A Revised Stemma." *Parthica* 7 (2005a): 29–63.

Assar, G. R. F. "The Genealogy of the Parthian King Sinatruces." *Journal of the Classical & Medieval Numismatic Society* 6.2 (2005b): 16–33.

Assar, G. R. F. "The Terminal Date of the Reign of Mithridates I of Parthia." *Bulletin of Ancient Iranian History* 2 (2006a): 1–16.

Assar, G. R. F. "Moses of Chorene and the Early Parthian Chronology." *Electrum* 11 (2006b): 61–86.

Assar, G. R. F. "A Revised Parthian Chronology of the Period 165–91 BC." *Electrum* 11 (2006c): 87–158.

Assar, G. R. F. "A Revised Parthian Chronology of the Period 91–55 BC." *Parthica* 8 (2006d): 55–104.

Assar, G. R. F. "An Early Parthian 'Victory' Coin." *Parthica* 8 (2006e): 25–35.

Assar, G. R. F. "Arsaces IV (c. 170–168 BC) the 1st 'Missing' Parthian King." *The International Journal of Ancient Iranian Studies* 6.1–2 (2006–2007): 3–14.

Assar, G. R. F. "The Inception and Termina Dates of the Reigns of Seleucus II, Seleucus III, and Antiochus III." *Nouvelles Assyriologiques Brèves et Utilitaires* 3 (2007): 49–53.

Assar, G. R. F. "The Proper Name of the 2nd Parthian Ruler." *Bulletin of Ancient Iranian History* 4 (2008): 1–7.

Assar, G. R. F. "Artabanus of Trogus Pompeius' 41st Prologue." *Electrum* 15 (2009a): 119–40.

Assar, G. R. F. "Some Remarks on the Chronology and Coinage of the Parthian 'Dark Age.'" *Electrum* 15 (2009b): 195–234.

Assar, G. R. F. "Iran under the Arsacids, 247 BC–AD 224/227." *Numismatic Art of Persia*. Lancaster and London, 2011. 113–71.

Assar, G. R. F., and M. Bagloo. "An Early Parthian 'Victory' Coin." *Parthica* 8 (2006): 25–35.

Austin, M. "Hellenistic Kings, War, and the Economy." *The Classical Quarterly* 36.2 (1986): 450–66.

Avemarie, F., et al., eds., *Die Makkabäer*. Tübingen, 2017.

Babelon, M. *Les Rois de Syrie d'Arménie et de Commagène*. Paris, 1890.

Babnis, T. "Augustan Poets on the Roman-Parthian Treaty of 20 BC." *Classica Cracoviensia* 20 (2017): 5–44.

Bader, A. "Parthian Ostraca from Nisa: Some Historical Data." *Convegno internazionale sul tema: La Persia e l'Asia Centrale da Alessandro al X secolo*. Roma, 1996. 251–76.

Balakhvantsev, A. *Political History of Early Parthia* (Политическая история ранней Парфии). Moscow, 2017.

Ballesteros-Pastor, L. *Pompeyo Trogo, Justino, y Mitrídates: Comentario al Epítome de las Historias Filípicas (37,1,6–38,8,1)*. Hildesheim and New York, 2013.

Ballesteros-Pastor, L. "Mithridates, God-King? Iranian Kingship in a Greek Context." *Divinizzazione, cultodel sovrano e apoteosi. Tra Antichità e Medioevo*. Bologna, 2014. 179–92.

Bar-Kochva, B. *Seleucid Army: Organization and Tactics in the Great Campaigns*. Cambridge, 1987.

Barfield, T. *The Perilous Frontier: Nomadic Empires and China 221 BC to AD 1757*. Cambridge, 1989.

Barnes, T. *Ammianus Marcellinus and the Representation of Historical Reality*. Ithaca, 1998.

Barnett, G. *Emulating Alexander: How Alexander the Great's Legacy Fuelled Rome's Wars with Persia*. Barnsley, 2017.

Bartlett, B. "Justin's Epitome. The Unlikely Adaptation of Trogus' World History." *Histos* 8 (2014): 246–83.

Baumer, C. *The History of Central Asia: The Age of the Steppe Warriors*. London, 2012.

Beck, H. *Polis und Koinon: Untersuchungen zur Geschichte und Struktur der griechischen Bundesstaaten im 4. Jahrhundert v.Chr.* Stuttgart, 1997.

Beck, H. "Pompeius Trogus." *The Encyclopedia of Ancient History*. Malden, 2013. 5408.

Beck, M., ed. *A Companion to Plutarch*. Hoboken, 2014.

Beckwith, C. *Empires of the Silk Road: A History of Central Eurasia from the Bronze Age to the Present*. Princeton, 2009.

Bederman, E. *International Law in Antiquity*. Cambridge, 2001.

Bedoukian, P. "A Classification of the Coins of the Artaxiad Dynasty of Armenia." *American Numismatic Society Museum Notes* 14 (1968): 41–66.

Beggiora, S. "Indian Ethnography in Alexandrian Sources: A Missed Opportunity." *With Alexander in India and Central Asia*. Oxford and Philadelphia, 2017. 238–54.

Bellinger, A. "Seleucid Dura: The Evidence of the Coins." *Berytus* 9.1 (1948): 51–67.

Bellinger, A. "The End of the Seleucids." *Transactions of the Connecticut Academy of Arts and Sciences* 38 (1949): 51–102.

Beloch, K. *Griechische Geschichte*. 4.2. Berlin and Leipzig, 1927.

Bemmann, J., and M. Schmauder, eds. *Complexity of Interaction along the Eurasian Steppe Zone in the First Millennium* CE. Bonn, 2015.

Bengston, H. *Griechische Geschichte: Von den Anfängen bis in die römische Kaiserzeit*. Munich, 1969.

Benjamin, C. *The Yuezhi: Origin, Migration, and the Conquest of Northern Baktria*. Turnhout, 2007.

Bennett, B., and M. Roberts. *The War of Alexander's Successors 323–281* BC: *Volume 1: Commanders & Campaigns*. Barnsley, 2012a.

Bennett, B., and M. Roberts. *Twilight of the Hellenistic World*. Barnsley, 2012b.

Bennett, C. "The Chronology of Berenice III." *Zeitschrift für Papyrologie und Epigraphik* 139 (2002): 142–48.

Bennison, A., and A. Gascoigne, *Cities in the Pre-Modern Islamic World: The Urban Impact of Religion, State and Society*. London, 2007.

Bergamini, G. "Parthian Fortifications in Mesopotamia." *Mesopotamia. Rivista di archeologia, epigrafia, e storia orientale antica* 22 (1987): 195–214.

Bernard, P. *Fouilles d'Ai Khanoum IV: Les monnaies hors trésors questions d'histoire Gréco-Bactrienne*. Paris, 1985.

Bernard, P. "Vicissitudes au gré de l'histoire d'une statue de bronze d'Héraclès entre Séleucie du Tigre et la Mésène." *Journal des Savants* 1–2 (1990): 3–68.

Bernard, P. "The Greek Kingdoms of Central Asia." *History of Civilizations of Central Asia*. Delhi, 1999. 99–130.

Bernard, P. "The Greek Colony at Ai Khanum and Hellinism in Central Asia; Ai Khanum Catalog." *Afghanistan: Hidden Treasures from the National Museum, Kabul*. Washington, 2008. 81–130.

Bernard, P. "ĀY ḴĀNOM." *Encyclopaedia Iranica Online Edition* (2011). Last accessed 5/2018. http://www.iranicaonline.org/articles/ay-kanom-or-a-khanum-tepe-a-local-uzbek-name-lit.

Bernard, P. "Eucratides." *Encyclopaedia Iranica Online Edition* (2012). Last accessed 5/2018. http://www.iranicaonline.org/articles/eucratides.

Bernard, P., G. Pinault, and G. Rougemont. "Deux nouvelles inscriptions grecques de l'Asie central." *Journal des Savants* 2 (2004): 227–356.

Bevan, E. *The House of Seleucus*. London, 1902.

Biagi, P. "Uneasy Riders: With Alexander and Nearchus from Pattala to Rhambakia." *With Alexander in India and Central Asia*. Oxford and Philadelphia, 2017. 255–78.

Bickerman, E. *Institutions des Séleucides*. Paris, 1938.

Bickerman, E. "Notes on Seleucid and Parthian Chronology." *Berytus* 8 (1944): 73–83.

Bickerman, E. "The Seleucid Period." *Cambridge History of Iran*. 3.1. Cambridge, 1983. 3–20.

Billows, R. *Antigonos the One-Eyed and the Creation of the Hellenistic State*. Berkeley, 1997.

Billows, R. "International Relations." *Cambridge History of Greek and Roman Warfare*. 1. Cambridge, 2007. 303–24.

Bing, D., and J. Sievers. "Antiochus." *Encyclopaedia Iranica Online Edition* (2011). Last accessed 6/2017. http://www.iranicaonline.org/articles/antiochus-1--thirteen-kings-of-the-seleucid-dynasty.

Biriukov, D. "Pandakheion i Parfavnisa (evristicheskoe znaczenie arshakidskikh monet iz Kampyrtepa)." *NTsA* 9 (2010): 34–48.

Bishop, M. *Lucius Verus and the Roman Defence of the East*. Barnsley, 2018.

Bivar, A. "The Achaemenids and the Macedonians: Stability and Turbulence." *Central Asia*. London, 1969. 9–34.

Bivar, A. "The Political History of Iran under the Arsacids." *Cambridge History of Iran*. 3.1. Cambridge, 1983. 21–99.

Bivar, A. "Gondophares and the Indo-Parthians." *The Age of the Parthians*. London, 2007. 26–36.

Bivar, A. "Kushan Dynasty i. Dynastic History." *Encyclopaedia Iranica Online Edition* (2009). Last accessed 5/2018. http://www.iranicaonline.org/articles/kushan-dynasty-i-history.

Bivar, A. "Euthydemus." *Encyclopaedia Iranica Online Edition* (2012). Last accessed 5/2018. http://www.iranicaonline.org/articles/euthydemus.

Blainey, G. *The Causes of War*. New York, 1988.

Blasweiler, J. "Hanigalbat and the Land Hana." *Anatolia in the Bronze Age* 3 (2015): 1–13.

Boardman, J. "Central Asia: West and East." *After Alexander*. Oxford, 2007. 9–28.

Boillet, P. "Quantifying Monetary Production: Ecbatana and Media in Parthian Times." *The Parthian and Early Sasanian Empires*. Oxford and Philadelphia, 2016. 109–22.

Boiy, T. *Late Achaemenid and Hellenistic Babylon*. Leuven, 2004.

Bopearachchi, O. *Monnaies gréco-bactriennes et indo-grecques, Catalogue raisonné*. Paris, 1991.

Bopearachchi, O. "The Euthydemus Imitations and the Date of Sogdian Independence." *Silk Road Art and Archaeology* 2 (1991–1992): 1–21.

Bopearachchi, O. *Catalogue of Indo-Greek, Indo-Scythian and Indo-Parthian Coins of the Smithsonian Institution*. Washington, 1993.

Bopearachchi, O. "Diodotus." *Encyclopaedia Iranica Online Edition* (1995). Last accessed 12/2015. http://www.iranicaonline.org/articles/diodotus.

Bopearachchi, O. *Sylloge Nummorum Graecorum: The Collection of the American Numismatic Society, Part 9: Graeco-Bactrian and Indo-Greek Coins*. New York, 1998a.

Bopearachchi, O. "Indo-Parthians." *Das Partherreich und seine Zeugnisse*. Stuttgart, 1998b. 389–406.

Bopearachchi, O. *An Indo-Greek and Indo-Scythian Coin Hoard from Bara (Pakistan)*. Seattle, 2003.

Bopearachchi, O. *From Bactria to Taprobane: Selected Works of Osmund Bopearachchi, vol. 1: Central Asian and Indian Numismatics*. New Delhi, 2015.

Bopearachchi, O., and M. Boussac, ed. *Afghanistan: Ancien carrefour entre l'est et l'ouest*. Turnhout, 2005.

Bopearachchi, O., and A. Rahman. *Pre-Kushana Coins in Pakistan*. Karachi, 1995.

Bordeaux, O. *Les Grecs en Inde: politiques et pratiques monétaires (IIIe s.a.C.–Ier s.p.C.)*. Bordeaux, 2018.

Borgna, A. "Scrivere del nemico: Pompeo Trogo e la storia dei Parti (Iust. XLI—XLII)." *Dialogues d'histoire ancienne* 41.2 (2015): 87–116.

Bostock, J., and H. Riley, *The Natural History. Pliny the Elder*. London, 1855.

Bosworth, A. *The Legacy of Alexander: Politics, Warfare and Propaganda under the Successors*. Oxford, 2005.

Boucharlat, R. "L'Iran à l'époque hellénistique et parthe: un état des données archéologiques." *Art et civilisations de l'Orient hellénisé*. Paris, 2014. 123–38.

Bouché-Leclercq, A. *Histoire des Séleucides (323–64 J.-C.)*. Paris, 1913–1914.

Boyce, M. "Parthian Writings and Literature." *Cambridge History of Iran*. 3.2. Cambridge, 1983. 1151–65.

Boyce, M. "The Sedentary Arsacids." *Iranica Antiqua* 29 (1994): 241–51.

Braund, D. "The Caucasian Frontier: Myth, Exploration and the Dynamics of Imperialism." *The Defense of the Roman and Byzantine East*. Oxford, 1986. 31–49.

Breasted, J. *Ancient Times: A History of the Early World*. Boston. 1914 (1944).

Brecher, M., and J. Wilkenfeld. "Crises in World Politics." *World Politics* 34 (1982): 380–417.

Brett, A. *Museum of Fine Arts–Boston. Catalogue of Greek Coins*. New York, 1955.

Briant, P. *Antigone le Borgne: Les débuts de sa carrière et les problèmes de l'assemblée macédonienne*. Paris, 1973.

Briant, P. *Alexandre le Grand*. Paris, 1987.

Briant, P. *From Cyrus to Alexander: A History of the Persian Empire*. University Park, 2002.

Bringmann, K. "Hellenistic Economies in the Post-Finley Era." *Hellenistic Economies*. New York, 2000. 11–62.

Brodersen, K. "The Date of the Secession of Parthia from the Seleucid Kingdom." *Historia* 35 (1986): 378–81.

Brodersen, K. *Appians Abriß der Seleukidengeschichte*. Munich, 1989.

Brosius, M. *The Persians: An Introduction*. London, 2006.

Brosius, M. "Women i. In Pre-Islamic Persia." *Encyclopaedia Iranica Online Edition* (2010). Last accessed 9/2017. http://www.iranicaonline.org/articles/women-i.

Brown, A. "The Tyranny of a Construct: Feudalism and Historians of Medieval Europe." *Debating the Middle Ages*. Hoboken, 1998. 148–69.

Brüggemann, T. "The Anabasis of Antiochus III and the Tribal Populations of the Upper Satrapies." *Antiochos III et l'Orient*. Nancy, 2017. 341–76.

Brun, P. "From Arrows to Bullets: The Fortifications of Abdullah Khan Kala (Merv, Turkmenistan)." *Antiquity* 79.305 (2005): 616–24.

Brunt, P. "On Historical Fragments and Epitomes." *The Classical Quarterly* 30 (1980): 477–94.

Brunt, P. *The Fall of the Roman Republic and Related Essays*. Oxford, 1988.

Bucciantini, V. "From the Indus to the Pasitigris: Some Remarks on the Periplus of Nearchus in the Arrian's *Indikê*." *With Alexander in India and Central Asia*. Oxford and Philadelphia, 2017. 279–304.

Bull, M. *Thinking Medieval: An Introduction to the Study of the Middle Ages*. Basingstoke, 2005.

Burris-Davis, B. "Parthian Horses and Parthian Horse Archers." *Heritage, Parthian Military History* (2014). Last accessed 4/2019. http://kavehfarrokh.com/heritage/parthian-horses-and-parthian-horse-archers/

Butterfield, H. *History and Human Relations*. London, 1951.

Buzan, B., C. Jones, and R. Little. *The Logic of Anarchy*. New York, 1993.

Callieri, P. "A proposito di un'iconografia monetale dei dinasti del Fars post-achemenide." *Ocnus* 6 (1998): 25–38.

Callieri, P. "Some Notes on the So-Called Temple of the Fratarakas at Persepolis." *Studi in onore di Umberto Scerrato: per il suo settantacinquesimo compleanno*. 1. Naples, 2003. 153–65.

Callieri, P. *L'archéologie du Fars à l'époque hellénistique*. Paris, 2007.

Callieri, P. "Sakas: In Afghanistan." *Encyclopaedia Iranica Online Edition* (2016). Last accessed 5/2018. http://www.iranicaonline.org/articles/sakas-in-afghanistan.

Callieri, P., and A. Chaverdi. "Media, Khuzestan, and Fars between the End of the Achaemenids and the Rise of the Sasanians." *Oxford Handbook of Ancient Iran*. Oxford, 2013. 690–717.

Cameron, G. *History of Early Iran*. New York, 1936.

Campbell, B. "War and Diplomacy: Rome and Parthia, 31 BC–AD 235." *War and Society in the Roman World*. London, 1993. 213–40.

Campbell, D. *Besieged: Siege Warfare in the Ancient World*. Oxford, 2006.

Canali De Rossi, F. *Iscrizioni dello Estremo Oriente Greco: Un repertorio (Inschriften griechischer Städte aus Kleinasien, Bd. 65)*. Bonn, 2004.

Canepa, M. "Topographies of Power: Theorizing the Visual, Spatial and Ritual Contexts of Rock Reliefs in Ancient Iran." *Of Rocks and Water*. Oxford, 2014a. 53–92.

Canepa, M. "Seleukid Sacred Architecture, Royal Cult and the Transformation of Iranian Culture in the Middle Iranian Period." *Iranian Studies* 48.1 (2014b): 1–27.

Canepa, M. "Dynastic Sanctuaries and the Transformation of Iranian Kingship between Alexander and Islam." *Of Architecture and Kingship*. London and New York, 2015. 65–117.

Canepa, M. "Cross-Cultural Communication in the Hellenistic Mediterranean, and Western and South Asia." *Mercury's Wings*. Oxford, 2017a. 249–72.

Canepa, M. "Rival Images of Iranian Kingship and Persian Identity in Post-Achaemenid Western Asia." *Persianism in Antiquity*. Stuttgart, 2017b. 201–22.

Canepa, M. *The Iranian Expanse: Transforming Royal Identity through Architecture, Landscape, and the Built Environment, 550 BCE–642 CE*. Berkeley and Los Angeles, 2018.

Capdetrey, L. "Séleucos, satrape d'Akkad: Réflexions sur l'origine du pouvoir séleucide." *Scripta Anatolica: Hommages à Pierre Debord*. Bordeaux, 2007. 193–214.

Carey, S. *Pliny's Catalogue of Culture: Art and Empire in the Natural History*. Oxford, 2006.

Carr, E. *The Twenty Years' Crisis, 1919–1939*. London, 1939.

Carsana, C. *Commento storico al libro II delle Guerre Civili di Appiano. (parte I). Pubblicazioni della Facoltà di Lettere e Filosofia dell'Università di Pavia 116*. Pisa, 2007.

Cary, E., trans. *Cassius Dio's Roman History Vols. 1–9*. Cambridge, 1914–1927.

Cernenko, E. *Scythians 700–300 BC*. Oxford, 1983.

Chahin, M. *The Kingdom of Armenia*. New York, 1987.

Champion, C. *Cultural Politics in Polybius's Histories*. Berkeley, 2004.

Champion, C. "Review of Arthur Eckstein's *Rome Enters the Greek East*." *Classical Philology* 104.2 (2009): 253–57.

Champion, J. *Antigonus the One-Eyed: Greatest of the Successors*. Barnsley, 2014.

Chaniotis, A. "Greeks under Siege: Challenges, Experiences, and Emotions." *Oxford Handbook of Warfare in the Classical World*. Oxford, 2013. 438–56.

Chankowski, V., and F. Duyrat, *Le roi et l'économie. Autonomies locales et structures royales dans l'économie de l'empire séleucide*. Orléans and Lille, 2004.

Charles River Editors. *The Parthian Empire: The History and Culture of One of Ancient Rome's Most Famous Enemies*. CreateSpace Independent Publishing Platform, 2015.

Charles River Editors. *Legendary Enemies of Rome: The History of the Carthaginians, Parthians, Goths, and Vandals*. CreateSpace Independent Publishing Platform, 2016.

Charles River Editors. *The Empires of Ancient Persia: The History and Legacy of the Achaemenids, Parthians, and Sassanids in Antiquity*. CreateSpace Independent Publishing Platform, 2017.

Charlesworth, J. *The Pseudepigapha and Modern Research with a Supplement*. Chico, 1981.

Chaumont, M. "Les ostraca de Nisa. Nouvelle contribution à l'histoire des Arsacides." *Journal Asiatique* 256 (1968): 11–35.

Chaumont, M. "Études d'histoire parthe. I. Documents royaux à Nisa." *Syria* 48 (1971): 143–64.

Chaumont, M. "L'Arménie entre Rome et l'Iran I. De l'avènement d'Auguste à l'avènement de Dioclétien." *Aufstieg und Niedergang der romischen Welt* 2.9.1 (1976): 71–194.

Chaumont, M. "Albania." *Encyclopaedia Iranica Online Edition* (1985). Last accessed 3/2016. http://www.iranicaonline.org/articles/albania-iranian-aran-arm.

Chaumont, M. "Armenia and Iran ii: The Pre-Islamic Period." *Encyclopaedia Iranica Online Edition* (1986a). Last accessed 2/2016. http://www.iranicaonline.org/articles/armenia-ii.

Chaumont, M. "Antony, Mark." *Encyclopaedia Iranica Online Edition* (1986b). Last accessed 2/2016. http://www.iranicaonline.org/articles/antony-mark-roman-gencral-ca.

Chaumont, M. "Apollodorus of Artimita." *Encyclopaedia Iranica Online Edition* (1986c). Last accessed 12/2017. http://www.iranicaonline.org/articles/apollodorus-of-artimita-historian.

Chaumont, M. "Appianus." *Encyclopaedia Iranica Online Edition* (1986d). Last accessed 12/2017. http://www.iranicaonline.org/articles/appianus-alexandria-historian.

Chaumont, M. "A propos des premières interventions parthes en Arménie et des circonstances de l'avènement de Tigrane le Grand." *Acta Antiqua Academiae Scientiarum Hungaricae* 31 (1988): 13–25.

Chaumont, M. "Dio Cassius." *Encyclopaedia Iranica Online Edition* (1995). Last accessed 12/2017. http://www.iranicaonline.org/articles/dio-cassius.

Chilver, G., and G. Townend. *A Historical Commentary on Tacitus' Histories IV and V*. Oxford, 1985.

Chrubasik, B. *Kings and Usurpers in the Seleukid Empire: The Men Who Would Be King*. Oxford, 2016.

Clancier, P. "Les compétences judiciaires des temples babyloniens à l'époque hellénistique et parthe." *Transferts culturels et droits dans le monde grec et hellénistique*. Paris, 2012. 255–68.

Clancier, P. "La longue mise en place de la domination parthe en Babylonie au IIe siècle." *Les Arsacides, héritiers des Séleucides? Ktèma 39*. Strasbourg, 2014. 186–98.

Clinton, H. *Fasti Hellenici: The Civil and Literary Chronology of Greece and Rome from the CXXIVth Olympiad to the Death of Augustus*. Oxford, 1881.

Cohen, S. *Josephus in Galilee and Rome: His Vita and Development as a Historian*. Leiden, 1979.

Cohen, S. "Justice, Interest, and Political Deliberation in Thucydides." *Quad. Urb.* 16 (1984): 35–60.

Colburn, H. "Connectivity and Communication in the Achaemenid Empire." *Journal of the Economic and Social History of the Orient* 56 (2013): 29–52.

Colledge, M. *The Parthians*. New York, 1967.

Colledge, M. *Parthian Art*. London, 1977.

Colledge, M. *The Parthian Period (Iconography of Religions XIV Ser: No. 3)*. Leiden, 1986.

Colledge, M. "Parthian Cultural Elements at Roman Palmyra." *Mesopotamia. Rivista di archeologia, epigrafia, e storia orientale antica* 22 (1987): 19–28.

Collins, S. *Parthia: The Forgotten Ancient "Superpower" and Its Role in Biblical History*. Royal Oak, 2002.

Coloru, O. "Tigranes II–IV of Armenia." *The Encyclopedia of Ancient History*. Vol. 12. Malden, 2013. 6752–54.

Coloru, O. "Antiochos IV et le royaume de Médie Atropatène: nouvelles considérations sur un mariage dynastique entre Séleucides et la maison d'Atropatès." *Le projet politique d'Antiochos IV*. Nancy, 2014. 395–414.

Coloru, O. "La forme de l'eau: idéologie, politique, et stratégie dans l'Anabase d'Antiochos III." *Antiochos III et l'Orient*. Nancy, 2017. 303–18.

Comploi, S. "Frauendarstellungen bei Fremdvölkern in den «Historiae Philippicae» des Pompeius Trogus/Justin." *Geschlechter—Frauen—Fremde Ethnien in antiker Ethnographie, Theorie, und Realität*. Innsbruck, 2002: 331–59.

Connor, W. *Thucydides*. Princeton, 1987.

Copeland, D. "Neorealism and the Myth of Bipolar Stability." *Security Studies* 5.3 (1996): 29–89.

Copeland, D. *The Origins of Major War*. Ithaca, 2000.

Cornell, T. *The Fragments of the Roman Historians*. Oxford, 2013.

Corò, P. "'Kislīmu Day 10, Year 31, Seleucus and Antiochus the Kings': Greek Elements in Babylonian Sources." *With Alexander in India and Central Asia*. Oxford and Philadelphia, 2017. 2–16.

Coşkun, A. "Laodike I, Berenike Phernophoros, Dynastic Murders, and the Outbreak of the Third Syrian War (253–246 BC)." *Seleukid Royal Women*. Stuttgart, 2016. 107–35.

Coşkun, A. "Friendship and Alliance between the Judaeans under Judas Maccabee and the Romans (1Macc 8: 17–32): A Response to Linda Zollschan's Rome and Judaea." *Electrum* 25 (2018): 85–125.

Coşkun, A. and D. Engels, eds. *Rome and the Seleukid East: Selected Papers from Seleukid Study Day V, Brussels, 21–23 August 2015. Collection Latomus, volume 360.* Leuven, 2019.

Coşkun, A., and A. McAuley, eds. *Seleukid Royal Women: Creation, Representation and Distortion of Hellenistic Queenship in the Seleukid Empire*. Stuttgart, 2016.

Coşkun, A., and A. McAuley, eds. "The War of the Brothers, the Third Syrian War, and the Battle of Ankyra (246–241 BC): A Re-appraisal." *The Seleukid Empire, 281–222 BC: War within the Family*. Swansea, 2018. 197–252.

Cotton, H., trans. *The Five Books of Maccabees in English*. London, 1832.

Coulston, J. "Roman, Parthian and Sassanid Tactical Developments." *The Defense of the Roman and Byzantine East*. Oxford, 1986. 59–75.

Crane, G. *Thucydides and the Ancient Simplicity*. Berkeley, 1998.

Crescioli, L. "The Scythians and the Eastern Limits of the Greek Influence: The Pazyryk Culture and Its Foreign Artistic Influences." *With Alexander in India and Central Asia*. Oxford and Philadelphia, 2017. 122–51.

Cribb, J. "The Greek Kingdom of Bactria, Its Coinage and Its Collapse." *Afghanistan: Ancien carrefour entre l'est et l'ouest*. Turnhout, 2005. 207–25.

Cribb, J., and E. Errington. *The Crossroads of Asia: Transformation in Image and Symbol*. Cambridge, 1992.

Culham, P. "Review of Arthur Eckstein's *Mediterranean Anarchy, Interstate War, and the Rise of Rome*." *The American Historical Review* 113.2 (2008): 552.

Cunningham, A. *Coins of Alexander's Successors in the East*. London, 1884.

Cunningham, A. "Coins of the Indo-Scythian King Miaus or Heraus." *Numismatic Chronicle* 3.8 (1888): 47–58.

Curtis, V. "Parthian Culture and Costume." *Mesopotamia and Iran in the Parthian and Sasanian Periods*. London, 2000. 23–34.

Curtis, V. "The Iranian Revival in the Parthian Period." *The Age of the Parthians*. London, 2007. 7–25.

Curtis, V. "The Fratáraka Coins of Persis: Bridging the Gap between Achaemenid and Sasanian Persia." *World of Achaemenid Persia*. London, 2010. 379–96.

Curtis, V., R. Hillenbrand, and J. Rogers, eds. *The Art and Archaeology of Ancient Persia: New Light on the Parthian and Sasanian Empires*. London, 1998.

Curtis, V., and A. Magub. *Rivalling Rome: Parthian Coins and Culture*. London, 2020.

Curtis, V., and S. Stewart. "Introduction." *The Age of the Parthians*. London, 2007. 1–6.

D'Agostini, M. "Asia Minor and the Many Shades of Civil War. Observations on Achaios the Younger and His Claim to the Kingdom of Anatolia." *The Seleukid Empire, 281–222 BC*. Swansea, 2018. 59–82.

Da Riva, R. "A New Attestation of Habigalbat in Late Babylonian Sources." *Welt des Orients* 47 (2016): 259–64.

Dąbrowa, E. *La politique de l'État Parthe à l'égard de Rome: d'Artaban II à Vologèse I (ca 11–ca. 79 de n.è.) et les factures que la conditionnaient*. Kraków, 1983.

Dąbrowa, E. "Könige Syriens in der Gefangenschaft der Parther. Zwei Episoden aus der Geschichte der Beziehungen der Seleukiden zu den Arsakiden." *Tyche* 7 (1992): 45–54.

Dąbrowa, E. "Dall'autonomia alla dipendenza. Le città greche e gli Arsacidi nella prima metà del I secolo d.C." *Mesopotamia* 29 (1994): 185–98.

Dąbrowa, E. "Philhellên. Mithridate Ier et les Grecs." *Electrum* 2 (1998): 35–44.

Dąbrowa, E. "L'Expédition de Démétrios II Nicator contre les Parthes (139–138 avant J.-C.)." *Parthica* 1 (1999 [2000]): 9–17.

Dąbrowa, E. "'. . . ostentasse Romana arma satis . . .': The military Factor in Roman-Parthian Relations under Augustus and Tiberius." *Limes XVIII*. Oxford, 2002. 275–80.

Dąbrowa, E. "Les Seleucides et l'Elymaide." *Parthica* 6 (2004 [2005]): 107–15.

Dąbrowa, E. "Les Aspects politiques et militaires de l'invasion de la Mésopotamie par les Parthes." *Electrum* 10 (2005): 73–88.

Dąbrowa, E. "Les Grecs sous les drapeaux des Arsacides." *Parthica* 7 (2005 [2006]): 65–70.

Dąbrowa, E. "The Conquests of Mithridates I and the Numismatic Evidence." *Parthica* 8 (2006a): 37–40.

Dąbrowa, E. "Marc Antoine, les Parthes et l'Arménie." *Studi sull'eta di Marco Antonio, "Rudiae" 18, Galatina*. Congedo, 2006b. 343–52.

Dąbrowa, E. "Greeks under the Arsacids Rule (2nd century BC)." *Iranistik: Deutschsprachige Zeitschrift für iranische Studien (Festschrift für Erich Kettenhofen)* 5 (2006–2007 [2008]): 1–8.

Dąbrowa, E. "The Political Propaganda of the First Arsacids and Its Targets: From Arsaces I to Mithridates II." *Parthica* 10 (2008 [2009]): 25–31.

Dąbrowa, E. "Mithridates I and the Beginning of the Ruler-cult in Parthia." *Electrum* 15 (2009): 41–51.

Dąbrowa, E. "The Parthian Kingship." *Concepts of Kingship in Antiquity*. Padova, 2010a. 123–34.

Dąbrowa, E. "The Parthians and the Seleucid Legacy." *Interkulturalität in der Alten Welt: Vorderasien, Hellas, Ägypten und die vielfältigen Ebenen des Kontakts*. Wiesbaden, 2010b. 583–89.

Dąbrowa, E. "Hellenistyczne elementy partyjskiej monarchii." *Hortus Historiae*. Kraków, 2010c. 257–61.

Dąbrowa, E. *Studia Graeco-Parthica: Political and Cultural Relations between Greeks and Parthians*. Wiesbaden, 2011a.

Dąbrowa, E. "ΑΡΣΑΚΕΣ ΕΠΙΦΑΝΗΣ. Were the Arsacids Deities 'Revealed'?" *Studi Ellenistici* 24 (2011b): 223–30.

Dąbrowa, E. "ΑΡΣΑΚΕΣ ΘΕΟΣ. Observations on the Nature of the Parthian Ruler-cult." *Un impaziente desiderio di scorrere il mondo*. Firenze, 2011c. 247–53.

Dąbrowa, E. "Greek: A Language of the Parthian Empire." *Studia Graeco-Parthica: Political and Cultural Relations between Greeks and Parthians*. Wiesbaden, 2011d. 153–63.

Dąbrowa, E. "The Arsacids and Their State." *Altertum und Gegenwart*. Innsbruck 2012. 21–52.

Dąbrowa, E. "The Parthian Aristocracy: Its Social Position and Social Activity." *Parthica* 15 (2013): 53–62.

Dąbrowa, E. "Hellenistic Elements in Parthian Kingship: The Numismatic Portrait and Titulature." *Kulturkontakte in Antiken Welten*. Leuven, 2014a. 301–12.

Dąbrowa, E. "A Troublesome Vassal? Elymais and Parthia (141 BC–AD 228)." *Parthica* 16 (2014b): 61–68.

Dąbrowa, E. "The Arsacids: Gods or Godlike Creatures?" *Divinizzazione, cultodel sovrano e apoteosi. Tra Antichità e Medioevo*. Bologna, 2014c. 149–160.

Dąbrowa, E. "L'histoire des Parthes dans la Geographie de Strabon." *Studi Ellenistici* 29 (2015): 285–303.

Dąbrowa, E., ed. *Central Asia and Iran: Greeks, Parthians, Kushans and Sasanians*. Kraków, 2016a.

Dąbrowa, E. "Roman Authors on the Honours of Arsaces I: Observations on the Transmission of a Historical Tradition." *Latomus* 75.3 (2016b): 573–84.

Dąbrowa, E. "Sacral Kingship in Parthia." *Studi Ellenistici* 31 (2017a): 287–96.

Dąbrowa, E. "Tacitus on the Parthians." *Electrum* 24 (2017b): 171–89.

Dąbrowa, E. "Arsacid Dynastic Marriages." *Electrum* 25 (2018): 73–84.

Dąbrowa, E. "The Seleukids, Rome and the Jews (134–76 BCE)." *Rome and the Seleukid East*. Brussels, 2019. 389–99.

Daffinà, P. *L'immigrazione dei Saka nella Drangiana*. Rome, 1967.

Dandamaev, M. *A Political History of the Achaemenid Empire*. Leiden, 1989.

Dandamaev, M., and V. Lukonin. *The Culture and Social Institutions of Ancient Iran*. Cambridge, 1989.

Daryaee, T. "Western and Central Eurasia." *Cambridge World History*. 4. Cambridge, 2015. 271–99.

Daryaee, T. "From Terror to Tactical Usage: Elephants in the Partho-Sasanian Period." *The Parthian and Early Sasanian Empires*. Oxford and Philadelphia, 2016. 36–41.

Dauge, Y. *Le barbare: Recherches sur la conception romaine de la barbarie et de la civilisation*. Brussels, 1981.

Davis, B. "Timeline of the Development of the Horse." *Sino-Platonic Papers* 177 (2007): 1–186.

Davis, J. "Hellenistic Economies." *Cambridge Companion to the Hellenistic World*. Cambridge, 2006. 73–92.

Dayet, M. "Un tétradachme arsacide inédit." *Arethuse* 7 (1925a): 63–66.

Dayet, M. "Une trouvaille de monnaies séleucides et arsacides." *Arethuse* 9 (1925b): 131–39.

de Souza, P. "Naval Battles and Sieges." *Cambridge History of Greek and Roman Warfare*. 1. Cambridge, 2007. 434–60.

Debevoise, N. *A Political History of Parthia*. Chicago, 1938.

Del Monte, G. *Testi dalla Babilonia Ellenistica*. Vol. I. Pisa, 1997.

Di Cosmo, N. *Ancient China and Its Enemies: The Rise of Nomadic Power in East Asian History*. Cambridge, 2004.

Diakonoff, I., and V. Livshits. "Novie Nakhodki Dokumentov v Staroy Nise." *Peredneaziatskiy Sbornik* 2 (1966): 134–57, 169–73, pls. II–XVIa.

Diakonoff, I., and V. Livshits. *Parthian Economic Documents from Nisa*. London, 1976–2001.

Diakonoff, I., and E. Zeimal. "Pravitel 'Parfii Andragor i ego monet.'" *Vestnik drevnei istorii* 4 (1988): 4–19.

Dignas, B., and E. Winter. *Rome and Persia in Late Antiquity: Neighbors and Rivals*. Cambridge, 2007.

Diller, A. *The Textual Tradition of Strabo's Geography*. Amsterdam, 1975.

Dilmaghani, J. "Parthian Coins from Mithridates II of Parthia to Orodes II." *Numismatic Chronicle* 146 (1986): 216–24.

Dirven, L., ed. *Hatra: Politics, Culture and Religion between Parthia and Rome*. Stuttgart, 2013.

Dixon, M. "Review of Arthur Eckstein's *Rome Enters the Greek East*." *The American Schools of Oriental Research* 356 (2009): 95–97.

Dobbins, K. "Mithridates II and His Successors: A Study of the Parthian Crisis." *Antichthon* 8 (1974): 63–79.

Dobiáš, J. "Les premiers rapports des Romains avec les Parthes et l'occupation de la Syrie." *Archiv Orientální* 3.2 (1931): 215–56.

Doran, R., "Resistance and Revolt: The Case of the Maccabees." *Revolt and Resistance in the Ancient Classical World and the Near East: In the Crucible of Empire*. Leiden, 2016. 175–88.

Downey, S. *Mesopotamian Religious Architecture: Alexander through the Parthians*. Princeton, 1988.

Doyle, M. *Empires*. Ithaca, 1986.

Doyle, M. "Thucydides: A Realist?" *Hegemonic Rivalry*. Boulder, 1991. 169–87.

Drijvers, J. "Strabo on Parthia and the Parthians." *Das Partherreich und seine Zeugnisse*. Stuggart, 1998. 279–93.

Droysen, J. *Geschichte des Hellenismus*. Gotha, 1878.

Dubs, H. "A Roman City in Ancient China." *Greece and Rome* 2.4 (1975): 139–48.

Dueck, D. *Strabo of Amasia: Greek Man of Letters in Augustan Rome*. New York, 2000.

Duff, T. *Plutarch's Lives: Exploring Virtue and Vice*. Oxford, 2002.

Dumitru, A. "Kleopatra Selene - A Look at the Moon and Her Bright Side." *Seleukid Royal Women*. Stuttgart, 2016. 253–72.

Dumke, G. "Anker gesetzt? Überlegungen zur Finanzierung der Anabasis Antiochos III." *Antiochos III et l'Orient*. Nancy, 2017. 319–40.

Ecker, A., et al. "The Southern Levant in Antiochos III's Time: Between Continuity and Immediate or Delayed Changes." *Antiochos III et l'Orient*. Nancy, 2017. 163–210.

Eckhel, I. *Doctrina Numorum Veterum*. 3. Paris, 1888.

Eckstein, A. *Moral Vision in the Histories of Polybius*. Berkeley, 1995.

Eckstein, A. "Thucydides, the Outbreak of the Peloponnesian War, and the Foundation of International Systems Theory." *International History Review* 23 (2003): 757–74.

Eckstein, A. "Bellicosity and Anarchy: Soldiers, Warriors, and Combat in Antiquity." *International History Review* 27.3 (2005): 481–97.

Eckstein, A. *Mediterranean Anarchy, Interstate War, and the Rise of Rome*. Berkeley, 2006.

Eckstein, A. "Conceptualizing Roman Imperial Expansion under the Republic: An Introduction." *A Companion to the Roman Republic*. Hoboken, 2007. 567–89.

Eckstein, A. *Rome Enters the East: From Anarchy to Hierarchy in the Hellenistic Mediterranean, 230–170 BC*. Hoboken, 2012.

Eckstein, A. "What Is an Empire and How Do You Know When You Have One? Rome and the Greek States after 188 BC." *Culture, Identity and Politics in the Ancient Mediterranean World*. Canberra, 2013. 173–90.

Edwell, P. "The Euphrates as a Boundary between Rome and Parthia in the Late Republic and Early Empire." *Culture, Identity and Politics in the Ancient Mediterranean World*. Canberra, 2013a. 191–206.

Edwell, P. "Sasanians." *The Encyclopedia of Ancient History*. Vol. 11. Malden, 2013b. 6051–56.

Edwell, P. "Osrhoene and Mesopotamia between Rome and Arsacid Parthia." *Arsacids, Romans and Local Elites*. Oxford and Philadelphia, 2017. 111–36.

Ehlert, H., et al., eds. *The Schlieffen Plan: International Perspectives on the German Strategy for World War I*. Lexington, 2014.

Ehling, K. "Probleme der seleukidischen Chronologie und Geschichte der Jahre zwischen 139 and 131 v.Chr." *Stephanos nomismatikos: Edith Schönert-Geiss zum 65. Geburtstag*. Berlin, 1998a. 227–41.

Ehling, K. "Seleukidische Geschichte zwischen 130 und 121 v. Chr." *Historia* 47.2 (1998b): 141–51.

Ehling, K. *Untersuchungen zur Geschichte der späten Seleukiden (164–63 v. Chr.): Vom Tode des Antiochos IV, bis zur Einrichtung der Provinz Syria unter Pompeius*. Stuttgart, 2008.

Eiland, M. "Ceramics of the Silk Road: Parthia and China." *Transactions of the Oriental Ceramic Society* 60 (1996): 105–20.

Eiland, M. "Parthians and Romans at Nineveh." *Electrum* 2 (1998): 55–68.

Eilers, C., ed. *Diplomats and Diplomacy in the Roman World*. Leiden, 2009.

Ellerbrock, U. *The Parthians: The Forgotten Empire*. London, (Forthcoming) 2021/2022.

Ellerbrock, U., and S. Winkelmann. *Die Parther: Die vergessene Großmacht*. Darmstadt, 2012.

Elman, C., and M. Elman. "Diplomatic History and International Relations Theory: Respecting Differences and Crossing Boundaries." *International Security* 22 (1997): 5–21.

Engels, D. *Alexander the Great and the Logistics of the Macedonian Army*. Berkeley, 1980.

Engels, D. "Middle Eastern 'Feudalism' and Seleucid Dissolution." *Seleucid Dissolution: The Sinking of the Anchor*. Wiesbaden, 2011. 19–36.

Engels, D. "Logistics: Sinews of War." *Oxford Handbook of Warfare in the Classical World*. Oxford, 2013. 351–68.

Engels, D. *Benefactors, Kings, Rulers: Studies on the Seleukid Empire between East and West*. Leuven, 2017.

Engels, D. "Iranian Identity and Seleukid Allegiance: Vahbarz, the Frataraka and Early Arsakid Coinage." *The Seleukid Empire, 281–222 BC*. Swansea, 2018. 173–96.

Engels, J. *Augusteische Oikumenegeographie und Universalhistorie im Werk Strabons von Amaseia*. Stuttgart, 1999.

Engels, J. "Strabon aus Amaseia und Apollodoros aus Artemita." *Parthika*. Wiesbaden, 2017. 29–46.

Enoki, K., G. Koshelenko, and Z. Haidary. "The Yueh-chih and Their Migrations." *History of Civilizations of Central Asia*. Delhi, 1999. 171–90.

Erikson, K. "Antiochos Soter and the Third Syrian War." *The Seleukid Empire, 281–222 BC*. Swansea, 2018. 253–74.

Errington, E., and V. Curtis. *From Persepolis to the Punjab: Exploring the Past in Iran, Afghanistan and Pakistan*. London, 2007.

Erskine, A. "Review of Arthur Eckstein's *Mediterranean Anarchy, Interstate War, and the Rise of Rome*." *Journal of Roman Studies* 98 (2008): 187–88.

Evans, G., and J. Newnham. *The Penguin Dictionary of International Relations*. London, 1998.

Faghfoury, M., ed. *Ancient Iranian Numismatics in Memory of David Sellwood*. Irvine, 2020.

Farrokh, K. *The Armies of Ancient Persia: The Sassanians*. Barnsley, 2017.

Farrokh, K., et al. "An Examination of Parthian and Sasanian Military Helmets (2nd century BC–7th century CE)." *Crowns, Hats, Turbans and Helmets: The Headgear in Iranian History, Volume I: Pre-Islamic Period*. Siedlce and Tehran, 2017. 121–63.

Farrokh, K, and G. Karamian. "Weapons in the Tombs of Parthian Era Women in Northern Iran: A Preliminary Report." *Fezana Journal* 32.3 (2018): 18–21.

Ferguson, J. "China and Rome." *Aufstieg und Niedergang der romischen Welt* 2.9.2 (1978): 581–603.

Ferguson, R. "Rome and Parthia: Power Politics and Diplomacy across Cultural Frontiers." *Centre for East-West Cultural & Economic Studies Research Papers* 12 (2005). Last accessed 1/2020. https://pure.bond.edu.au/ws/portalfiles/portal/27882809/Rome_and_Parthia.pdf.

Ferrar, L. *Arrogance and Anxiety: The Ambivalence of German Power, 1848–1914*. Iowa City, 1981.

Feyel, C., and Graslin-Thomé, eds. *Le projet politique d'Antiochos IV*. Nancy, 2014.

Feyel, C., and Graslin-Thomé, eds. *Antiochos III et l'Orient*. Nancy, 2017.

Findley, C. *The Turks in World History*. Oxford, 2004.

Finkel, I., R. van der Spek, and R. Pirngruber. "BCHP 18B/A Chronographic Document Concerning Bagayasha B/A." *Babylonian Chronographic Texts from the Hellenistic Period (BCHP)* (2020a). Last accessed 1/2020. https://www.livius.org/sources/content/mesopotamian-chronicles-content/bchp-18b-a-chronographic-document-concerning-bagayasha-b-a/.

Finkel, I., R. van der Spek, and R. Pirngruber. "BCHP 18C Astronomical Diary Concerning Bagayasha and Timotheus." *BCHP* (2020b). Last accessed 1/2020. https://www.livius.org/sources/content/mesopotamian-chronicles-content/bchp-18c-astronomical-diary-concerning-bagayasha-and-timotheus/.

Finkel, I., R. van der Spek, and R. Pirngruber. "BCHP 14 (Greek Community Chronicle)." *BCHP* (2020c). Last accessed 1/2020. https://www.livius.org/sources/content/mesopotamian-chronicles-content/bchp-14-greek-community-chronicle/.

Finkel, I., R. van der Spek, and R. Pirngruber. "BCHP 12 (Seleucus III Chronicle)." *BCHP* (2020d). Last accessed 1/2020. https://www.livius.org/sources/content/mesopotamian-chronicles-content/bchp-12-seleucus-iii-chronicle/.

Finkel, I., R. van der Spek, and R. Pirngruber. "BCHP 10 (Seleucid Accessions Chronicle)." *BCHP* (2020e). Last accessed 1/2020. https://www.livius.org/sources/content/mesopotamian-chronicles-content/bchp-10-seleucid-accessions-chronicle/.

Finkel, I., R. van der Spek, and R. Pirngruber. "BCHP 11 (Invasion of Ptolemy III Chronicle)." *BCHP* (2020f). Last accessed 1/2020. https://www.livius.org/sources/content/mesopotamian-chronicles-content/bchp-11-invasion-of-ptolemy-iii-chronicle/.

Finkel, I., R. van der Spek, and R. Pirngruber. "BCHP 7 (Antiochus, Bactria, and India Chronicle)." *BCHP* (2020g). Last accessed 1/2020. https://www.livius.org/sources/content/mesopotamian-chronicles-content/bchp-7-antiochus-bactria-and-india-chronicle/.

Finkel, I., R. van der Spek, and R. Pirngruber. "BCHP 5 (Antiochus I and Sin Temple Chronicle)." *BCHP* (2020h). Last accessed 1/2020. https://www.livius.org/sources/content/mesopotamian-chronicles-content/bchp-5-antiochus-i-and-sin-temple-chronicle/.

Finkel, I., R. van der Spek, and R. Pirngruber. "BCHP 20 (Euphrates Chronicle)." *BCHP* (2020i). Last accessed 1/2020. https://www.livius.org/sources/content/mesopotamian-chronicles-content/bchp-20-euphrates-chronicle/.

Fischer, T. *Untersuchungen zum Partherkrieg Antiochos' VII: im Rahmen der Seleukidengeschichte*. Tübingen, 1970.

Fliess, P. J. *Thucydides and the Politics of Bipolarity*. Baton Rouge, 1966.

Forster, E., trans. *Florus' Epitome of Roman History*. Cambridge, 1929.

Fowler, R. "Most Fortunate Roors: Tradition and Legitimacy in Parthian Royal Ideology." *Imaginary Kings*. Stuttgart, 2005. 125–218.

Fowler, R. "Parthians, Rulers." *The Encyclopedia of Ancient History*. Vol. 9. Malden, 2013. 5071–75.

Foy-Vaillant, J. *Arsacidarum Imperium, sive Regum Parthorum Historia, ad fidem Numismatum Accommodata, Tomus Primus*. Paris, 1725.

Frankel, B. *Roots of Realism*. London, 1996a.

Frankel, B., ed. *Realism: Restatements and Renewal*. London, 1996b.

Fraser, P. *Cities of Alexander the Great*. Oxford, 1996.

Fratantuono, L. *Roman Conquests: Mesopotamia and Arabia*. Barnsley, 2019.

Frechette, J. "Review of Arthur Eckstein's *Rome Enters the Greek East*." *H-Net: H-War* (2009). Last accessed 1/2020. http://www.h-net.org/reviews/showrev.php?id=23965.

Frendo, D. "Roman Expansion and the Graeco-Iranian World: Carrhae, Its Explanation and Aftermath in Plutarch." *Bulletin of the Asia Institute* 17 (2007): 71–81.

Froelich, E. *Annales compendiarii regum et rerum Syriae*. Vienna, 1744.

Frumkin, G. *Archaeology in Soviet Central Asia, Handbuch der Orientalistik Abt. 7, Bd. 3/1*. Leiden and Cologne, 1970.

Frye, R. "The Political History of Iran under the Sasanians." *Cambridge History of Iran*. 3.1. Cambridge, 1983. 116–89.

Frye, R. *The History of Ancient Iran*. Munich, 1984.

Frye, R. "Andragoras." *Encyclopaedia Iranica Online Edition* (1985). Last accessed 5/2018. http://www.iranicaonline.org/articles/andragoras-seleucid-satrap-of-parthia-and-hyrcania-known-primarily-from-his-coins-1.

Frye, R. "Parthian and Sasanian History of Iran." *Mesopotamia and Iran in the Parthian and Sasanian Periods*. London, 2000. 17–22.

Fuhrmann, C. *Policing the Roman Empire: Soldiers, Administration, and Public Order*. Oxford, 2012.

Gabelko, O. "The Dynastic History of the Hellenistic Monarchies of Asia Minor." *Mithridates VI and the Pontic Kingdom*. Aarhus, 2009. 47–62.

Galimberti, A. and G. Zecchini, ed. *Studi sull'epitome di Giustino. III. Il tardo ellenismo. I Parti e i Romani*. Milan, 2016.

Gardiner-Garden, J. *Apollodorus of Artemita and the Central Asian Skythians*. Bloomington, 1987.

Gardner, P. *The Parthian Coinage. International Numismata Orientalia, Part V*. London, 1877.

Gardner, P. *Catalogue of Greek Coins: The Seleucid Kings of Syria*. London, 1878.

Gariboldi, A. "The Birth of the Sasanian Monarchy in Western Sources." *The Parthian and Early Sasanian Empires*. Oxford and Philadelphia, 2016. 47–52.

Garlan, Y. "War and Siegecraft." *Cambridge Ancient History*. 7.1. Cambridge, 1984. 353–62.

Garnsey, P., and C. Whittaker, *Imperialism in the Ancient World*. Cambridge, 1978.

Garsoian, N. "Armeno-Iranian Relations in the Pre-Islamic Period." *Encyclopaedia Iranica Online Edition* (2004). Last accessed 3/2016. http://www.iranicaonline.org/articles/armeno-iranian-relations-in-the-pre-islamic-period.

Garsoian, N. "Tigran II." *Encyclopaedia Iranica Online Edition* (2005). Last accessed 6/2015. http://www.iranicaonline.org/articles/tigran-ii.

Garthwaite, G. *The Persians*. Hoboken, 2005.

Gaslain, J. "Arsaces I, the First Arsacid King? Some Remarks on the Nature of Early Parthian Power." *Central Asia from the Achaemenids to the Timurids*. St. Petersburg, 2005a. 221–24.

Gaslain, J. "Le *bachlik* d'Arsace Ier ou la représentation du nomade-roi." *Bulletin of Parthian and Mixed Oriental Studies* 1 (2005b): 9–30.

Gaslain, J. "Réflexions sur la signification des armes des premières monnaies arsacides." *Arms and Armour as Indicators of Cultural Transfer*. Wiesbaden, 2006: 233–57.

Gaslain, J. "Les 'élites militaries' des Parthes Arsacides et la conquête de la Judée au Ier siècle av. J.-C." *Les élites dans le monde biblique*. Paris, 2008. 75–98.

Gaslain, J. "A propos d'Arsace Ier." *Electrum* 15 (2009): 27–39.

Gaslain, J. "Quelques remarques sur la politique impériale des Parthes Arsacides et la prise d'Europos-Doura." *Europos-Doura: Varia* 1. Beirut, 2012. 255–66.

Gaslain, J. "Some Aspects of Political History: Early Arsacid Kings and the Seleucids." *The Parthian and Early Sasanian Empires*. Oxford and Philadelphia, 2016. 3–7.

Geer, R., trans. *Diodorus Siculus' Library of History, Volume IX: Books 18–19.65*. Cambridge, 1947.

Geller, D., and J. Singer. *Nations at War: A Scientific Study of International Conflict*. Cambridge, 1998.

Gera, D. "Review of Arthur Eckstein's *Rome Enters the Greek East*." *The Classical Review* 60.1 (2010): 204–7.

Gera, D., and W. Horowitz. "Antiochus IV in Life and Death: Evidence from the Babylonian Astronomical Diaries." *Journal of the American Oriental Society* 117.2 (1997): 240–52.

Gerardin, F. "D'un grand roi à l'autre: la Syrie-Coélé entre rivalités idéologiques et transition impériale de Ptolémée IV à Antiochos IV." *Antiochos III et l'Orient*. Nancy, 2017. 81–106.

Ghodrat-Dizaji, M. "Remarks on the Location of the Province of Parthia in the Sasanian Period." *The Parthian and Early Sasanian Empires*. Oxford and Philadelphia, 2016. 42–46.

Gholami, K., and G. R. F. Assar. *Parthian Coins*. Pazineh, 2013.

Gibbs, L., trans. *Aesop's Fables*. Oxford, 2002.

Gibson, B. and T. Harrison. *Polybius and his World: Essays in Memory of F.W. Walbank*. Oxford, 2013.

Gibson, R., and R. Morello, *Pliny the Elder: Themes and Contexts*. Leiden, 2011.

Gilpin, R. *War and Change in World Politics*. Cambridge, 1981.

Gilpin, R. "Theory of Hegemonic War." *Journal of Interdisciplinary History* 18 (1988): 591–613.

Glaser, C. "Political Consequences of Military Strategy: Expanding and Refining the Spiral and Deterrence Models." *World Politics* 44 (1992): 497–538.

Glaser, C. "The Security Dilemma Revisited." *World Politics* 50 (1997): 171–201.

Gochman, C., and Z. Maoz. "Militarized Interstate Disputes, 1816–1976: Procedures, Patterns and Insights." *Journal of Conflict Resolution* 28 (1983): 585–616.

Godley, A., trans. *Herodotus' The Histories*. Cambridge, 1920.

Golden, P. *Central Asia in World History*. Oxford, 2011.

Goldstein, J. *I MACCABEES: A New Translation with Introduction and Commentary*. Garden City, 1976.

Goldsworthy, A. *The Roman Army at War 100 BC–AD 200*. Oxford, 1998.

Goldsworthy, A. *How Rome Fell*. New Haven, 2009.

Goodyear, E. "On the Character and Text of Justin's Compilation of Trogus." *Goodyear: Papers on Latin Literature*. London, 1992. 210–33.

Gorin, A. "Parthian Coins from Kampyrtepa." *Anabasis* 1 (2010): 107–34.

Gorshenina, S. "Alexandre le Grand et les Russes: Un Regard sur le Conquérant Porté depuis l'Asie Centrale." *With Alexander in India and Central Asia*. Oxford and Philadelphia, 2017. 152–93.

Gourevitch, P. "The Second Image Reversed: The International Sources of Domestic Politics." *International Organization* 32.4 (1978): 881–912.

Graham, D. *Rome and Parthia: Power, Politics and Profit*. CreateSpace Independent Publishing Platform, 2013.

Grainger, J. *A Seleukid Prosopography and Gazetteer*. Leiden, 1997.

Grainger, J. *The Roman War of Antiochos the Great*. Leiden, 2002.

Grainger, J. *Alexander the Great Failure: The Collapse of the Macedonian Empire*. New York, 2007.

Grainger, J. *The Syrian Wars*. Leiden, 2010.

Grainger, J. *The Wars of the Maccabees*. Barnsley, 2012.

Grainger, J. *Rome, Parthia, India: The Violent Emergence of a New World Order 150–140 BC*. Barnsley, 2013a.

Grainger, J. *Seleukos Nikator: Constructing a Hellenistic Kingdom*. London, 2013b.

Grainger, J. *The Rise of the Seleukid Empire (323–223 BC): Seleukos I to Seleukos III*. Barnsley, 2014.

Grainger, J. *The Seleukid Empire of Antiochus III (223–187 BC)*. Barnsley, 2015.

Grainger, J. *The Fall of the Seleukid Empire 187–75 BC*. Barnsley, 2016.

Grainger, J. *Kings and Kingship in the Hellenistic World 350–30 BC*. Barnsley, 2017a.

Grainger, J. *Great Power Diplomacy in the Hellenistic World*. London, 2017b.

Grajetzki, W. *Greeks and Parthians in Mesopotamia and Beyond 331 BC–224 AD*. London, 2011.

Grant, J. "A Note on the Tone of Greek Diplomacy." *Classical Quarterly* 12 (1962): 261–66.

Graslin-Thomé, L. "La Babylonie hellénistique: le point de vue des «dominés»." *Communautés locales et pouvoir central dans l'Orient hellénistique et romain*. Nancy, 2012. 237–58.

Graslin-Thomé, L. "Le règne d'Antiochos III vu depuis Babylone: Antiochos III dans les sources cunéiformes." *Antiochos III et l'Orient*. Nancy, 2017. 211–44.

Green, P. *Alexander to Actium: The Historical Evolution of the Hellenistic Age*. Berkeley, 1990.

Gregoratti, L. "Fighting an Ever Dying Enemy: Western Perspectives on Persians and Parthians." *Myth-Making and Myth-Breaking in History and the Humanities*. Bucharest, 2011a. 25–36.

Gregoratti, L. "A Parthian Port on the Gulf Coast: Characene and Its Trade." *Anabasis* 2 (2011b): 209–25.

Gregoratti, L. "The Role of the Mint of Seleucia on the Tigris in the Arsacid History." *Mesopotamia* 47 (2012a): 129–36.

Gregoratti, L. "The Parthians between Rome and China: Gan Ying's Mission into the West (1st century AD)." *Academic Quarter* 4 (2012b): 109–20.

Gregoratti, L. "The Caucasus: A Communication Space between Nomads and Sedentaries (1st BC–2nd AD)." *Mountain Areas as Frontiers and/or Interaction and Connectivity Spaces*. Arachne, 2013a. 477–93.

Gregoratti, L. "The Journey East of the Great King: East and West in the Parthian Kingdom." *Parthica* 15 (2013b): 43–63.

Gregoratti, L—. "Between Rome and Ctesiphon: The Problem of Ruling Armenia." *Armenia-Iran: Proceedings of the Conference of Armenia—Iran*. Moscow, 2013c. 134–41.

Gregoratti, L. "The Parthian Empire: Romans, Jews, Nomads, and Chinese on the Silk Road." *The Silk Road: Vol. 1*. Cambridge, 2014a. 43–70.

Gregoratti, L. "The Mardians: A Note." *Anabasis* 5 (2014b): 75–84.

Gregoratti, L. "A Tale of Two Great Kings: Artabanus and Vologaeses." *Studies on the Iranian World I, Before Islam*. Kraków, 2015a. 203–10.

Gregoratti, L. "The Kings of Parthia and Persia, Some Considerations on the 'Iranic' Identity in the Parthian Empire." *Dabir Journal* 1.1 (2015b): 14–16.

Gregoratti, L. "In the Land West of the Euphrates: The Parthians in the Roman Empire." *Soma 2011 Proceedings of the 15th Symposium on Mediterranean Archaeology, Held at the University of Catania 3–5 March 2011*. Oxford, 2015c. 731–36.

Gregoratti, L. "Parthian Empire." *The Encyclopedia of Empires*. Hoboken, 2016a. 1–6.

Gregoratti, L. "Legendary and Real Wealth in the Arsacid Kingdom." *Studies on Wealth in the Ancient World*. London, 2016b. 83–92.

Gregoratti, L. "Sinews of the Other Empire: The Parthian Great King's Rule over Vassal Kingdoms." *Sinews of Empire*. Oxford, 2017a. 95–104.

Gregoratti, L. "The Arsacid Empire." *King of the Seven Climes*. Irvine, 2017b. 125–53.

Gregoratti, L. "Corbulo versus Vologases: A Game of Chess for Armenia." *Electrum* 24 (2017c): 107–21.

Grousset, R. *Histoire de l'Extréme-Orient*. 1. Paris, 1929.

Gruen, E. *The Hellenistic World and the Coming of Rome*. Berkeley, 1984.

Gruen, E. "Romans and Others." *A Companion to the Roman Republic*. Hoboken, 2007. 459–77.

Gruen, E. "Josephus' Image of the Parthians." *Parthika*. Wiesbaden, 2017. 223–40.

Gupta, S. "India." *The Encyclopedia of Ancient History*. Vol. 6. Malden, 2013. 3444–50.

Gutschmid, A. *Geschichte Irans und seiner Nachbarländer*. Tübingen, 1888.

Gyselen, R. "The Parthian Language in Early Sasanian Times." *The Parthian and Early Sasanian Empires*. Oxford and Philadelphia, 2016. 61–68.

Habicht, C. "The Seleucids and Their Rivals." *Cambridge Ancient History*. 8.2. Cambridge, 1989. 324–87.

Hackl, U., B. Jacobs, D. Weber, eds. *Quellen zur Geschichte des Partherreiches: Textsammlung mit Ubersetzungen und Kommentaren*. Vol. 1. Göttingen and Oakville, 2010a.

Hackl, U., B. Jacobs, D. Weber, eds. *Quellen zur Geschichte des Partherreiches: Textsammlung mit Ubersetzungen und Kommentaren*. Vol. 2. Göttingen and Oakville, 2010b.

Hackl, U., B. Jacobs, D. Weber, eds. *Quellen zur Geschichte des Partherreiches: Textsammlung mit Ubersetzungen und Kommentaren*. Vol. 3. Göttingen and Oakville, 2010c.

Hansen, E. *The Attalids of Pergamon*. New York, 1971.

Hansen, W., trans. *Phlegon of Tralles' Book of Marvels*. Exeter, 1996.

Hansman, J. "Elymais." *Encyclopaedia Iranica Online Edition* (1998). Last accessed 6/2015. http://www.iranicaonline.org/articles/elymais.

Hansman, J. "Characene and Charax." *Encyclopaedia Iranica Online Edition* (2011). Last accessed 5/2018. http://www.iranicaonline.org/articles/characene-and-charax-spasinou-in-pre-islamic-times.

Harmatta, J. "Parthia and Elymais in the Second Century BC." *Acta Antiqua Academiae Scientiarum Hungaricae* 29 (1981): 189–217.

Harmatta, J. "Languages and Scripts in Graeco-Bactria and the Saka Kingdoms." *History of Civilizations of Central Asia*. Delhi, 1999. 397–416.

Harris, W. *War and Imperialism in Republican Rome*. Oxford, 1979.

Harris, W. *Roman Power: A Thousand Years of Empire*. Cambridge, 2016.

Hartmann, U. "Das Bild der Parther bei Plutarch." *Historia* 56 (2008): 426–52.

Hartmann, U. "Herrscher mit geteilten Loyalitäten. Vasallenherrscher und Klientelkönige zwischen Rom und Parthien." *Amici—socii—clientes? Abhängige Herrschaft im Imperium Romanum*. Berlin, 2015. 301–62.

Hartmann, U. "Die Parthischen Stationen des Isidor von Charax: eine Handelsroute, eine Militärkarte, oder ein Werk geographischer Gelehrsamkeit?" *Parthika*. Wiesbaden, 2017. 87–126.

Haruta, S. "Aramaic, Parthian, and Middle Persian." *Oxford Handbook of Ancient Iran*. Oxford, 2013. 779–94.

Haubold, J. "Hellenism, Cosmopolitanism and the Role of Babylonian Elites in the Seleucid Empire." *Cosmopolitanism and Empire*. Oxford, 2016. 89–102.

Haubold, J., J. Steele, K. Stevens, eds. *Keeping Watch in Babylon: The Astronomical Diaries in Context*. Leiden, 2019.

Hauser, S. "Die ewigen Nomaden? Bemerkungen zu Herkunft, Militär, Staatsaufbau und nomadischen Traditionen der Arsakiden." *Krieg-Gesellschaft-Institutionen: Beiträge zu einer vergleichenden Kriegsgeschichte*. Berlin, 2005. 163–208.

Hauser, S. "Was There No Paid Standing Army? A Fresh Look on Military and Political Institutions in the Arsacid Empire." *Arms and Armour as Indicators of Cultural Transfer*. Wiesbaden, 2006. 295–319.

Hauser, S. "The Arsacids (Parthians)." *Oxford Handbook of Ancient Iran*. Oxford, 2013. 728–50.

Hauser, S. "Isidor von Charax *Σταθμοὶ Παρθικοί*—Annäherungen an den Autor, den Routenverlauf, und die Bedeutung des Werkes." *Parthika*. Wiesbaden, 2017. 127–88.

Head, B. *Historia Numorum: A Manual of Greek Numismatics*. Oxford, 1911.

Heather, P. *The Goths*. Hoboken, 1998.

Heckel, W. *Justin: Epitome of the Philippic History of Pompeius Trogus: Volume I: Books 11–12: Alexander the Great*. Trans. J. Yardley. Oxford, 1997.

Heil, M. "Die Parther bei Tacitus." *Parthika*. Wiesbaden, 2017. 259–78.

Heller, A. "Antiochos Hierax." *The Encyclopedia of Ancient History*. Vol. 2. Malden, 2013. 482–83.

Hennig, R. *Terrae Incognitae. Eine Zusammenstellung und kritische Bewertung der wichtigsten vorcolumbischen Entdeckungsreisen an Hand der darüber vorliegenden Originalberichte. Teil 1: Altertum bis Ptolemäus*. Leiden, 1944.

Herrmann, G. "Parthian and Sassanian Saddlery: New Light from the Roman West." *Archaeologia Iranica et Orientalis* 2 (1989): 757–809.

Herrmann, G., and J. Cribb, eds. *After Alexander: Central Asia before Islam*. Oxford, 2007.

Herrmann, G., K. Kurbansakhatov, et al. "The International Merv Project. Preliminary Report onthe Second Season (1993)." *Iran* 32 (1994): 53–75.

Herz, J. "Idealist Internationalism and the Security Dilemma." *World Politics* 2 (1950): 157–80.

Herzfeld, E. "Sakestan, Geschichtliche Untersuchungen zu den Ausgrabungen am Kūh-e Khwādja." *Archäologische Mitteilungen aus Iran* 4 (1931–1932): 1–116.

Hewson, R. "'The Primary History of Armenia': An Examination of the Validity of an Immemorially Transmitted Historical Tradition." *History in Africa* 2 (1975): 91–100.

Hill, S. *Defining the alter orbis: The Roman View of Parthia in the Early Principate*. (Diss.) University of Wales, 2013.

Hind, J. "Mithridates." *Cambridge Ancient History*. 9.2. Cambridge, 1994. 129–64.

Hobbes, T. *Leviathan*. New York, 1959.

Hoffmann, J. *Antiochus IV Epiphanes, König von Syrien*. Leipzig, 1873.

Hölbl, G. *A History of the Ptolemaic Empire*. Trans. T. Saavedra. London, 2001.

Hölkeskamp, K. "Review of Arthur Eckstein's *Mediterranean Anarchy, Interstate War, and the Rise of Rome*." *The Classical Review* 59.1 (2009): 211–14.

Holleaux, M. "Rome and Macedon: The Romans against Philip." *Cambridge Ancient History*. 8.1. Cambridge, 1930. 138–98.

Hollis, A. "Laodice Mother of Eucratides of Bactria." *Zeitschrift für Papyrologie und Epigraphik* 110 (1996): 161–64.

Holsti, K. *Peace and War: Armed Conflicts and International Order, 1648–1989*. Cambridge, 1991.

Holsti, O. *Crisis, Escalation, War*. Montreal, 1972.

Holt, F. "The Euthydemid Coinage of Bactria: Further Hoard Evidence from Ai Khanoum." *Revue Numismatique* 23 (1981): 7–44.

Holt, F. *Alexander the Great and Bactria: The Formation of a Greek Frontier in Central Asia*. Leiden, 1988.

Holt, F. *Thundering Zeus: The Making of Hellenistic Bactria*. Berkeley, 1999.

Holt, F. *Into the Land of Bones: Alexander the Great in Afghanistan*. Berkeley, 2005.

Holt, F. *Lost World of the Golden King: In Search of Ancient Afghanistan*. Berkeley, 2012a.

Holt, F. "When Did the Greeks Abandon Aï Khanoum?" *Anabasis* 3 (2012b): 161–72.

Hoover, O. "A Late Hellenistic Lead Coinage from Gaza." *Israel Numismatic Research* 1 (2006): 28–29.

Hoover, O. "A Revised Chronology for the Late Seleucids at Antioch (121/0–64 BC)." *Historia: Zeitschrift für Alte Geschichte* 56.3 (2007): 280–301.

Hoover, O., and P. Iossif. "A Lead Tetradrachm of Tyre from the Second Reign of Demetrius II." *Numismatic Chronicle* 169 (2009): 45–50.

Houghton, A. *Coins of the Seleucid Empire from the Collection of Arthur Houghton*. New York, 1983.

Houghton, A. "The Reigns of Antiochus VIII and Antiochus IX at Antioch and Tarsus." *Schweizerische numismatische Rundschau* 72 (1993): 87–106.

Houghton, A., and A. Spaer. *Sylloge Nummorum Graecorum: Israel I: The Arnold Spaer Collection of Seleucid Coins*. Jerusalem, 1998.

Houghton, A., and C. Lorber. *Seleucid Coins: A Comprehensive Catalogue. Part I: Seleucus I through Antiochus III*. New York, 2002.

Howarth, R. "War and Warfare in Ancient Rome." *Oxford Handbook of Warfare in the Classical World*. Oxford, 2013. 29–45.

Hoyland, R. *In God's Path: The Arab Conquests and the Creation of an Islamic Empire*. Oxford, 2015.

Hoyos, D. *Unplanned Wars: The Origins of the First and Second Punic Wars*. Berlin, 1998.

Hoyos, D. *Hannibal's Dynasty: Power and Politics in the Western Mediterranean, 247–183 BC*. London, 2003.

Hunger, H., and A. Sachs. *Astronomical Diaries and Related Texts from Babylonia, Vol. 5, Lunar and Planetary Texts*. Vienna, 2001.

Huntington, S. "Why International Primacy Matters." *International Security* 17 (1993): 68–83.

Huyse, P. "Die Begegnung zwischen Hellen und Iraniern. Griechische epigraphische Zeugnisse von Griechenland bis Pakistan." *Iran und Turfan*. Wiesbaden, 1995. 99–126.

Huyse, P. "Die Rolle des Griechischen im 'hellenistischen' Iran." *Hellenismus*. Berlin, 1996. 57–76.

Hyland, A. *The Horse in the Ancient World*. Westport, 2003.

Invernizzi, A. "Elymaeans, Seleucids, and the Hung-e Azhdar." *Mesopotamia* 33 (1998): 219–59.

Invernizzi, A. "The Culture of Parthian Nisa between Steppe and Empire." *After Alexander*. Oxford, 2007. 179–212.

Invernizzi, A. "L'Iran arsacide tra Achemenidi e Sasanidi." *Civiltà dell'Iran: passato, presente, futuro*. Rome, 2013. 99–114.

Invernizzi, A. "A Note on Architectural Traditions in Arsacid Parthia: The Round Hall at Nisa." *The Parthian and Early Sasanian Empires*. Oxford and Philadelphia, 2016. 83–89.

Ionescu, D. "The Use of the Tiara as a Symbol of Persian Achaemenid Kingship: Why Alexander the Great Didn't Adopt It?" *Crowns, Hats, Turbans and Helmets: The Headgear in Iranian history, Volume I: Pre-Islamic Period*. Siedlce and Tehran, 2017. 21–33.

Iossif, P. "Seleukeia." *The Encyclopedia of Ancient History*. Vol. 11. Malden, 2013. 6125–26.

Isaac, B. *The Invention of Racism in Classical Antiquity*. Princeton, 2006.

Ishjamts, N. "Nomads in Eastern Central Asia." *History of Civilizations of Central Asia*. Delhi, 1999. 151–70.

Jakobsson, J. "Indo-Greek Chronology c. 200–145." *Journal of the Oriental Numismatic Society* 198 (2009): 8–12.

Jakubiak, K. "Arsacids viii. Military Architecture of Parthia." *Encyclopaedia Iranica Online Edition* (2008). Last accessed 3/2016. http://www.iranicaonline.org/articles/arsacids-viii-military-architecture-of-parthia.

Jal, P. "À propos de *Historiae Philippicae*: Quelques Remarques." *Revue des Etudes Latines* 65 (1987): 194–209.

James, S. "The Archaeology of War." *Oxford Handbook of Warfare in the Classical World*. Oxford, 2013. 91–127.

Jenkins, F. *Ammianus Marcellinus: An Annotated Bibliography 1474 to the Present*. Leiden, 2016.

Jenkins, G. "Notes on Seleucid Coins." *Numismatic Chronicle* 6.11 (1951): 1–21.

Jervis, R. *Perception and Misperception in International Politics*. Princeton, 1976.

Jervis, R. "Cooperation under the Security Dilemma." *World Politics* 30 (1978): 167–214.

Jervis, R. "Variation, Change, and Transitions in International Politics." *Review of International Studies* 27 (2001): 281–95.

Jettmar, K. *Art of the Steppes*. Trans. A. Keep. New York, 1967.

Johnson-Bagby, L. "The Use and Abuse of Thucydides in International Relations." *Int. Org.* 48 (1994): 131–53.

Johstono, P. "'No Strength to Stand': Defeat at Panium, the Macedonian Class, and Ptolemaic Decline." *Brill's Companion to Military Defeat in Ancient Mediterranean Society*. Leiden, 2018. 162–87.

Jones, K. "Marcus Antonius' Median War and the Dynastic Politics." *Arsacids, Romans and Local Elites*. Oxford and Philadelphia, 2017. 51–64.

Jones, T., and A. Ereira. *Terry Jones' Barbarians*. London, 2006.

Junge, P. "Parthia II A. Das Partherreich in hellenistischer Zeit." *Paulys Realencyclopädie der classischen Altertumswissenschaft* 18.4 (1949): 1968–86.

Juping, Y. "Hellenistic World and the Silk Road." *Anabasis* 5 (2013): 73–91.

Justi, F. *Iranisches Namenbuch*. Marburg, 1895.

Kagan, D. *Thucydides: The Reinvention of History*. New York, 2009.

Kahrstedt, U. *Artabanos III und seine Erben*. Bern, 1950.

Kaim, B. "Women, Dance and the Hunt: Splendour and Pleasures of Court Life in Arsacid and Early Sasaian Art." *The Parthian and Early Sasanian Empires*. Oxford and Philadelphia, 2016. 90–108.

Kaizer, T., ed. *Religion, Society and Culture at Dura-Europos*. Cambridge, 2016.

Karras-Klapproth, M. *Prosopographische Studien zur Geschichte des Partherreiches auf der Grundlage antiker literarischer Überlieferung*. Bonn, 1988.

Katouzian, H. *The Persians: Ancient, Medieval, and Modern Iran*. New Haven, 2009.

Kaufman, R. "To Balance or Bandwagon? Alignment Decisions in 1930s Europe." *Security Studies* 1.3 (1992): 417–47.

Kauppi, M. "Contemporary International Relations Theory and the Peloponnesian War." *Hegemonic Rivalry*. Boulder, 1991. 91–124.

Kawami, T. *Monumental Art of the Parthian Period in Iran*. Leiden, 1987.

Kawami, T. "Parthian and Elymaean Rock Reliefs." *Oxford Handbook of Ancient Iran*. Oxford, 2013. 751–65.

Keall, E. "Qal'eh-i Yazdigird, a Sasanian Palace Stronghold in Persian Kurdistan." *Iran* 5 (1967), 99–121.

Keall, E. "Parthian Nippur and Vologases' Southern Strategy: A Hypothesis." *Journal of the American Oriental Society* 95.4 (1975): 620–32.

Keall, E. "Political Economic and Social Factors on the Parthian Landscape of Mesopotamia and Western Iran: Evidence from Two Case Studies." *Mountains and Lowlands*. Malibu, 1977a. 81–9.

Keall, E. "Qal'eh-i Yazdigird: The Question of Its Date." *Iran* 15 (1977b): 1–9.

Keall, E. "Qal'eh-i Yazdigird: An Overview of the Monumental Architecture." *Iran* 20 (1982): 51–72.

Keall, E. "How Many Kings Did the Parthian King of Kings Rule?" *Iranica Antiqua* 29 (1994): 254–272.

Keeley, L. *War Before Civilization: The Myth of the Peaceful Savage*. Oxford, 1999.

Kegley, C. "The Neoidealist Moment in International Studies? Realist Myths and the New International Realities: ISA Presidential Address March 27, 1993, Acapulco, Mexico." *International Studies Quarterly* 37.2 (1993): 131–46.

Kelly, G. *Ammianus Marcellinus: The Allusive Historian*. Cambridge, 2008.

Kennedy, D. "Parthia and Rome: Eastern Perspectives." *The Roman Army in the East*. Ann Arbor, 1996. 67–90.

Kennedy, H. *When Baghdad Ruled the Muslim World: The Rise and Fall of Islam's Greatest Dynasty*. Cambridge, 2006.

Kennedy, H. *The Great Arab Conquests: How the Spread of Islam Changed the World We Live In*. Cambridge, 2008.

Kennedy, R., C. Roy, and M. Goldman, eds. *Race and Ethnicity in the Classical World: An Anthology of Primary Sources in Translation*. Indianapolis, 2013.

Keohane, R., and J. Nye. "Power and Interdependence Revisited." *International Organization* 41.4 (1987): 725–53.

Kern, P. *Ancient Siege Warfare*. Bloomington, 1999.

Kiani, M. "Gorgan iv. Archeology." *Encyclopaedia Iranica Online Edition* (2012). Last accessed 9/2018. http://www.iranicaonline.org/articles/gorgan-iv.

Kidd, I. *Posidonius: Volume Two: The Commentary: (i) Testimonia and Fragments 1–149*. Cambridge, 1988.

Kissinger, H. *A World Restored: Castlereagh, Metternich, and the Problem of Peace, 1812–1822*. Boston, 1957.

Klein, K., and P. Wirtz. "Parthia." *The Encyclopedia of Ancient History*. Vol. 9. Malden, 2013. 5068–71.

Klotz, A., and C. Lynch. *Strategies for Research in Constructivist International Relations*. Armonk and London, 2007.

Koshelenko, G. *Kul'tura Parfii*. Moscow, 1966.

Koshelenko, G. "Genealogiya pervîkh Arshakidov (eshche raz o nisiyskom ostrake)." *Istoriya i kul'tura narodov Sredneĭ Azii*. Moscow, 1976. 31–37.

Koshelenko, G. "Les cavaliers parthes. Aspects de la structure sociale de la Parthie." *Dialogues d'histoire ancienne* 6 (1980): 177–99.

Koshelenko, G. "Zakliuchenie." *Drevneĭshie gosudarstva Kavkaza i Sredneĭ Azii*. Moscow, 1985a. 338–50.

Koshelenko, G., ed. *Drevneĭshie gosudarstva Kavkaza i Sredneĭ Azii*. Moscow, 1985b.

Koshelenko, G., and I. Sarianidi. "Les monnaies de la nécropole de Tillia-tepe (Afghanistan)." *Studia Iranica* 21.1 (1992): 21–32.

Koshelenko, G., V. Gaibov, and A. Bader. "Evolution of the Settlement Patterns in the Merv Oasis (Turkmenistan) from Alexander the Great to Arab Conquest." *La Persia e l'Asie centrale: Da Alessandro al X secolo*. Roma, 1996. 305–17.

Koshelenko, G., and V. Pilipko. "Parthia." *History of Civilizations of Central Asia*. Delhi, 1999. 131–50.

Kosmin, P. "Alexander the Great and the Seleucids in Iran." *Oxford Handbook of Ancient Iran*. Oxford, 2013a. 671–89.

Kosmin, P. "Rethinking the Hellenistic Gulf: The New Greek Inscription from Bahrain." *Journal of Hellenic Studies* 133 (2013b): 61–79.

Kosmin, P. *The Land of the Elephant Kings: Space, Territory, and Ideology in the Seleucid Empire*. Cambridge, 2014.

Kosmin, P. *Time and Its Adversaries in the Seleucid Empire*. Cambridge, 2018.

Kritt, B. *New Discoveries in Bactrian Numismatics*. London, 2015.

Kröger, J. "Ctesiphon." *Encyclopaedia Iranica Online Edition* (2011). Last accessed 6/2017. http://www.iranicaonline.org/articles/ctesiphon.

Kuhrt, A. *The Persian Empire: A Corpus of Sources from the Achaemenid Period*. New York, 2010.

Kuhrt, A., and H. Sancisi-Weerdenburg. "Aluaka." *Brill's New Pauly* (2006). Last accessed 1/2020. http://referenceworks.brillonline.com/entries/brill-s-new-pauly/aluaka-e116850.

Kuhrt, A., and S. Sherwin-White, *Hellenism in the East: The Interaction of Greek and Non-Greek Civilizations from Syria to Central Asia after Alexander*. London, 1987.

Kuranga, D. "International Organizations: Wielders of Power in the Emerging International Order." (Diss.) Rutgers University, 2010.

Labs, E. "Beyond Victory: Offensive Realism and the Expansion of War Aims." *Security Studies* 6 (1997): 1–49.

Lamberton, R. *Plutarch*. New Haven, 2001.

Lang, D. "Iran, Armenia and Georgia." *Cambridge History of Iran*. 3.1. Cambridge, 1983. 505–36.

Lange, C., and J. Madsen. *Cassius Dio: Greek Intellectual and Roman Politician—Historiography of Rome and Its Empire*. Leiden, 2016.

Layne, C. "The Unipolar Illusion: Why New Great Powers Will Arise." *International Security* 17 (1993): 5–51.

Le Rider, G. "Monnaies de Characène." *Syria* 36 (1959): 229–53.

Le Rider, G. *Suse sous les Séleukides et les Parthes*. Paris, 1965.

Le Rider, G. "Monnaies grecques récemment acquises par le cabinet de Paris." *Revue Numismatique* 11 (1969): 7–27.

Leake, W. *Numismata Hellenica: A Catalogue of Greek Coins*. London, 1856.

Lebow, R. "Thucydides, Power Transition Theory, and the Cause of War." *Hegemonic Rivalry*. Boulder, 1991. 125–65.

Lebow, R., and B. Strauss, eds. *Hegemonic Rivalry: From Thucydides to the Nuclear Age*. Boulder, 1991.

Lecuyot, G. "Ai Khanum Reconstructed." *After Alexander*. Oxford, 2007. 155–62.

Lemke, D., and J. Kugler. "The Evolution of the Power Transition Perspective." *Parity and War*. Ann Arbor, 1996. 3–33.

Lendering, J., trans. "First Book of Maccabees." *Livius* (2006). Last accessed 3/2016. http://www.livius.org/maa-mam/maccabees/1macc01.html.

Lendering, J. "Ctesiphon (Parthian: Tyspwn), The capital of the Parthians and the Sassanids." *Iran Chamber Society* (2019). Last accessed 4/2019. http://www.iranchamber.com/history/ctesiphon/ctesiphon.php.

Lendon, J. "Primitivism and Ancient Foreign Relations." *The Classical Journal* 97.4 (2002): 375–84.

Lendon, J. "Xenopon and the Alternative to Realist Foreign Policy: 'Cyropaedia' 3.1.14–31." *The Journal of Hellenic Studies* 126 (2006): 82–98.

Lepper, F., and J. DeVoto. *Trajan's Parthian War and Arrian's Parthika*. Palos Heights, 1985.

Leriche, P. "Doura Europos grecque, parthe, et romaine." *Mesopotamia* 22 (1987): 57–66.

Leriche, P. "Bactria, Land of a Thousand Cities." *After Alexander*. Oxford, 2007. 121–54.

Leriche, P. "Dura Europos." *Encyclopaedia Iranica Online Edition* (2011). Last accessed 11/2017. http://www.iranicaonline.org/articles/dura-europos.

Lerner, J. *The Impact of Seleucid Decline on the Eastern Iranian Plateau: The Foundations of Arsacid Parthia and Graeco-Bactria*. Stuttgart, 1999.

Lerner, J. "Correcting the Early History of Ay Kanom." *Archäologische Mitteilungen aus Iran und Turan* 35–36 (2003–2004): 373–410.

Lerner, J. "Revising the Chronologies of the Hellenistic Colonies of Samrakand-Marakanda (Afrasiab II–III) and Ai Khanoum (northeastern Afghanistan)." *Anabasis* 1 (2010): 58–79.

Lerner, J. "Reappraisal of the Economic Inscriptions and Coin Finds from Aï Khanoum." *Anabasis* 2 (2011): 103–47.

Lerner, J. "Bactria." *The Encyclopedia of Ancient History*. Vol. 2. Malden, 2013. 1012–15.

Lerner, J. "Regional Study: Baktria—The Crossroads of Ancient Eurasia." *Cambridge World History*. 4. Cambridge, 2015a. 300–24.

Lerner, J. "Mithridates I's Conquest of Western Greek-Baktria." *Journal of History, Philology, and Cultural Studies* 47.1 (2015b): 45–55.

Lerner, J. "The Emergence of Wakhan Fortresses in the Hellenistic Period." *Anabasis* 7 (2016): 107–30.

Lerner, J. "Mithridates I and the Parthian Archer." *Arsacids, Romans, and Local Elites*. Oxford and Philadelphia, 2017. 1–24.

Lerner, J. "Alexander's Settlement of the Upper Satrapies in Policy and Practice." *Anabasis* 9 (2018): 110–28.

Lerouge-Cohen, C. "Les guerres parthiques de Démétrios II et Antiochos VII dans les sources gréco-romaines, de Posidonios à Trogue/Justin." *Journal des Savants* 2 (2005): 217–52.

Lerouge-Cohen, C. *L'image des Parthes dans le monde gréco-romain: Du début du Ier siècle av. J.-C. jusqu'à la fin du Haut-Empire romain*. Stuttgart, 2007.

Lerouge-Cohen, C. "Les livres 41–42 des *Histoires Philippiques* de Trogue-Pompée résumées par Justin." *Iranica Antiqua* 44 (2009a): 361–92.

Lerouge-Cohen, C. "L'image des Parthes à l'époque d'Auguste: tentative de confrontation des sources littéraires et iconographiques." *Figures de l'étranger autour de la Méditerranée antique 'à la rencontre de l'Autre'*. Paris, 2009b. 295–303.

Lerouge-Cohen, C. "Les Parthes sont-ils des nomads comme les autres?" *Portraits de migrants, portraits de colons II*. Paris, 2010. 161–68.

Lerouge-Cohen, C. "Le banquet des Arsacides d'après les sources grecques." *Le banquet du monarque dans le monde antique*. Rennes and Tours, 2013. 275–89.

Lerouge-Cohen, C., ed. *Les Arsacides, héritiers des Séleucides? Ktèma 39*. Strasbourg, 2014.

Lerouge-Cohen, C. "L'image des Parthes chez Arrien. Réflexions sur quelques fragments attribués aux *Parthika*." *Parthika*. Wiesbaden, 2017. 279–305.

Levy, J. *War in the Modern Great Power System*. Lexington, 1983.

Levy, J. "Theories of General War." *World Politics* 37.3 (1985): 344–74.

Levy, J. "Domestic Politics and War." *Journal of Interdisciplinary History* 18.4 (1988): 653–73.

Levy, J. "Preferences, Constraints, and Choices in July 1914." *Military Strategy and the Origins of the First World War*. Princeton, 1991. 226–61.

Lewis, T. *The History of the Parthian Empire: From the Foundation of the Monarchy by Arsaces, to Its Final Overthrow by Artaxerxes the Persian; Contained in a Succession of Twenty Nine Kings*. London, 1728.

Lindsay, J. *A View of the History and Coinage of the Parthians*. Cork, 1852.

Linfert, A. "Bärtige Herrscher." *Jahrbuch des Deutschen Archäologischen Instituts* 91 (1976): 157–74.

Liska, G. *Career of Empire: America and Imperial Expansion over Land and Sea*. Baltimore, 1978.

Liska, G. *The Ways of Power: Pattern and Meaning in World Politics*. Oxford, 1990.

Little, R. "Structure and Logic of Anarchy." *The Logic of Anarchy*. New York, 1993. 132–54.

Litvinskii, B. "Parfiano-baktriiskie perekrestki." *Problemy istorii, filologii, kul'tury* 1.27 (2010): 84–103.

Llewellyn-Jones, L. "Cleopatra Selene." *The Encyclopedia of Ancient History*. Vol. 3. Malden, 2013. 1572–73.

Loginov, S., and A. Nikitin. "Parthian Coins from Margiana: Numismatics and History." *Bulletin of the Asia Institute* 10 (1996): 39–51.

Lorber, C., and P. Iossif. "Seleucid Campaign Beards." *L'Antiquité Classique* 78 (2009): 87–115.

Lozinski, B. *The Original Homeland of the Parthians*. Berlin, 1959.

Lukonin, V. "Political, Social, and Administrative Institutions: Taxes and Trade." *Cambridge History of Iran*. 3.2. Cambridge, 1983. 681–746.

Lund, H. *Lysimachus: A Study in Early Hellenistic Kingship*. London, 1992.

Luther, A. "Das Königreich Adiabene zwischen Parthern und Römern." *Amici—socii—clientes? Abhängige Herrschaft im Imperium Romanum*. Berlin, 2015. 275–300.

Lyall, J. *Paths of Ruin: Why Revisionist States Arise and Die in World Politics*. (Diss.) Cornell University, 2005.

Lynn-Jones, S. "Realism and America's Rise: A Review Essay." *International Security* 23.2 (1998): 157–82.

Lyonette, B. "Les rapports entre l'Asie Centrale et l'Empire achéménide d'après les données de l'archéologie." *Achaemenid History IV*. Leiden, 1990. 77–92.

Macdonald, G. "The Hellenic Kingdoms of Syria, Bactria, and Parthia." *Cambridge History of India: Ancient India*. Cambridge, 1922. 427–66.

Mair, V., ed. *A Concise Commentary on Memoirs on the Western Regions in the Official Histories of the Western and Eastern Han, Wei, Jin, and Southern and Northern Dynasties*. Trans. Y. Taishan. Beijing, 2014.

Mairs, R. "Waiting for the Barbarians: The 'Fall' of Greek Bactria." *Parthica* 15 (2013a): 9–30.

Mairs, R. "Euthydemos of Bactria." *The Encyclopedia of Ancient History*. Vol. 5. Malden, 2013b. 2583–84.

Manandyan, H. *Tigranes II and Rome: A New Interpretation Based on Primary Sources*. Trans. G. Bournoutian. Costa Mesa, 1940 (2007).

Manning, J. "Hellenistic Trade(rs)." *Traders in the Ancient Mediterranean*. Chicago, 2015. 101–40.

Marciak, M. "Seleucid-Parthian Adiabene in the Light of Ancient Geographical and Ethnographical Texts." *Anabasis* 2 (2011): 179–208.

Marciak, M. "The Historical Geography of Sophene." *Acta Antiqua Academiae Scientiarum Hungaricae* 52 (2012a): 295–338.

Marciak, M. "The Historical Geography of Gordyene. Part 1: Classical Sources." *Anabasis* 3 (2012b): 173–213.

Marciak, M. "The Historical Geography of Gordyene. Part 2: Oriental Sources." *Anabasis* 4 (2013): 149–59.

Marciak, M. "Das Königreich Adiabene in hellenistisch-parthischer Zeit." *Gymnasium. Zeitschrift für Kultur der Antike und Humanistische Bildung* 122.1 (2015): 57–74.

Marciak, M. *Sophene, Gordyene, and Adiabene: Three Regna Minora of Northern Mesopotamia Between East and West*. Leiden, 2017.

Marcus, R., trans. *Josephus' Jewish Antiquities*. 7. Cambridge, 1943.

Mari, M. "A 'Lawless Piety' in an Age of Transition. Demetrius the Besieger and the Political Uses of Greek Religion." *Alexander's Legacy*. Rome, 2016. 157–80.

Marić, N., ed. *Parthian Empire: A Captivating Guide to the Enemy of the Roman Republic and Roman Empire*. CreateSpace Independent Publishing Platform, 2018.

Mariev, S., trans. *Ioannis Antiocheni fragmenta quae supersunt omnia*. Berlin, 2008.

Marquart, J. *Ērānšahr: nach der Geographie des Ps. Moses Xorenac'i*. Berlin, 1901.

Martin, T. "Demetrius 'the Besieger' and Hellenistic Warfare." *Oxford Handbook of Warfare in the Classical World*. Oxford, 2013. 671–87.

Martinez-Sève, L. "Laodice, femme d'Antiochos II: du roman à la reconstruction historique." *Revue des Études Grecques* 116 (2003): 690–706.

Martinez-Sève, L. "Antiochos IV en Susiane, dans le Golfe Persique et en Élymaïde." *Le projet politique d'Antiochos IV*. Nancy, 2014. 363–93.

Martinez-Sève, L. "Susa iv. The Hellenistic and Parthian Periods." *Encyclopaedia Iranica Online Edition* (2015). Last accessed 5/2018. http://www.iranicaonline.org/articles/susa-iv-hellenistic-parthian-periods.

Martinez-Sève, L. "Les operations d'Antiochos III en Bactriane-Sogdiane: l'apport de la documentation archéologique." *Antiochos III et l'Orient*. Nancy, 2017. 271–302.

Mason, S., ed. *Flavius Josephus: Translation and Commentary*. Leiden, 2000.

Masson, V. "O severo-vostochnykh predelach parfyanskogo gosudarstva." *Krakie soobshcheniya instituta materyal'noy kul'tury* 38 (1951): 145–51.

Masson, V. "Denejznoe khoziaistvo drevnei Srednei Azii po numizmaticheskim dannym." *Vestnik drevnei istorii* 52.2 (1955): 37–47.

Masson, V. "Severnaia Baktriia." *Drevneĭshie gosudarstva Kavkaza i Sredneĭ Azii*. Moscow, 1985. 250–72.

Mastanduno, M. "Preserving the Unipolar Moment: Realist Theories and US Grand Strategy after the Cold War." *International Security* 21 (1997): 49–88.

Mastanduno, M., and E. Kapstein. "Realism and State Strategies after the Cold War." *Unipolar Politics*. New York, 1999. 1–27.

Mathiesen, H. *Sculpture in the Parthian Empire*. Aarhus, 1992.

Mattern, S. *Rome and the Enemy: Imperial Strategy in the Principate*. Berkeley, 1999.

Matthews, J. *The Roman Empire of Ammianus Marcellinus*. Baltimore, 1989.

Matyszak, P. *Mithridates the Great: Rome's Indomitable Enemy*. Barnsley, 2008.

May, T. *The Mongol Art of War*. Yardley, 2007.

Mayor, A. *The Poison King: The Life and Legend of Mithridates Rome's Deadliest Enemy*. Princeton, 2010.

McAuley, A. "The House of Achaios: Reconstructing an Early Client Dynasty of Seleukid Anatolia." *The Seleukid Empire, 281–222 BC*. Swansea, 2018. 37–58.

McDowell, R. *Coins from Seleucia on the Tigris*. Ann Arbor, 1935.

McGing, B. *Polybius' Histories*. Oxford, 2010.

McGushin, P., trans. *Sallust: The Histories, Volume 1*. Oxford, 1992.

McGushin, P., trans. *Sallust: The Histories, Volume 2*. Oxford, 1994.

McLaughlin, R. *The Roman Empire and the Silk Routes: The Ancient World Economy and the Empires of Parthia, Central Asia and Han China*. Barnsley, 2016.

Meadows, A. "The Administration of the Achaemenid Empire." *Forgotten Empire. The World of Ancient Persia*. London, 2005. 181–88.

Meadows, A. "The Spread of Coins in the Hellenistic World." *Explaining Monetary and Financial Innovation*. Heidelberg, 2014. 169–95.

Mearsheimer, J. "The False Promise of International Relations." *International Security* 19.3 (1994–1995): 5–49.

Mearsheimer, J. *The Tragedy of Great Power Politics*. New York, 2001.

Mehl, A. *Seleukos Nikator und sein Reich: Teil 1: Von Triparadeisos bis Pydna*. Leuven, 1986.

Mehrkiyan, J. "The Elymaian Rock-carving of Shaivand, Izeh." *Iran* 35 (1997): 67–72.

Menegazzi, R. "Seleucid, Parthian Mesopotamia, and Iran, Archaeology of." *Encyclopedia of Global Archaeology*. New York, 2014. 6554–64.

Mercer, J. "Independence or Interdependence: Testing Resolve Reputation." *Coping with Complexity in the International System*. Boulder, 1993. 163–91.

Merkelbach, R., and J. Stauber. *Jenseits des Euphrat: Griechische Inschriften. Ein epigraphisches Lesebuch*. Munich and Leipzig, 2005.

Messina, V. "Aspects of Seleucid Iconography and Kingship." *With Alexander in India and Central Asia*. Oxford and Philadelphia, 2017. 17–36.

Meulenbroek, L. *The Parthian Shot: Kingship and Coinage in the Early Arsacid Empire*. (Thesis) Utrecht University, 2014.

Midlarsky, M. *The Onset of World War*. Boston, 1988.

Mielczarek, M. "Cataphracts—A Parthian Element in the Seleucid Art of War." *Electrum* 2 (1998): 101–6.

Militký, J. and M. Mašek, eds. *Sylloge Nummorum Graecorum Czech Republic. Vol. 1. The National Museum Prague. Part 10: Baktria and India*. Prague, 2019.

Millar, F. *A Study of Cassius Dio*. Oxford, 1964.

Millar, F. *The Roman Near East 31 BC–AD 337*. Cambridge, 1993.

Millett, P. "Part I Greece: Winning Ways in War." *Oxford Handbook of Warfare in the Classical World*. Oxford, 2013. 46–73.

Mineo, B. and G. Zecchini. *Abrégé des Histoires Philippiques de Trogue Pompée. Tome I: Livres I–X*. Paris, 2016.

Mineo, B. and G. Zecchini. *Abrégé des Histoires Philippiques de Trogue Pompée. Tome II: Livres XI–XXIII*. Paris, 2018.

Minns, E. "Parchments of the Parthian Period from Avroman in Kurdistan." *Journal of the Hellenic Studies* 35 (1915): 22–65.

Mitchell, S. "Dispelling Seleukid Phantoms: Macedonians in Western Asia Minor from Alexander to the Attalids." *The Seleukid Empire, 281–222 BC*. Swansea, 2018. 11–36.

Mitchiner, M. *The Early Coinage of Central Asia*. London, 1973.

Mitford, T. "Helenos, Governor of Cyprus." *Journal of Hellenic Studies* 79 (1959): 94–131.

Mittag, P. "Beim Barte des Demetrios: Überlegungen zur parthischen Gefangenschaft Demetrios' II." *Klio* 2 (2002): 373–99.

Mittag, P. *Antiochus IV Epiphanes: Eine politische Biographie*. Berlin, 2006.

Mittag, P. "Antiochos IV Epiphanes." *The Encyclopedia of Ancient History*. Vol. 2. Malden, 2013. 479–80.

Mittmann-Richert, U. *Einführung zu den historischen und legendarischen Erzählungen. Jüdische Schriften aus hellenistisch-römischer Zeit 6.1.1*. Gütersloh, 2000.

Mommsen, T. *The History of Rome*. Trans. William P. Dickson. 3–5. New York, 1856 (1903).

Monerie, J. "Invading Mesopotamia, from Alexander the Great to Antiochus VII." *Literary Change in Mesopotamia and Beyond and Routes and Travellers between East and West*. Münster, 2019. 155–85.

Mookerji, R. *Chandragupta Maurya and His Times*. Delhi, 1999.

Moore, C., trans. *Tacitus: The Histories Books IV–V*. Cambridge, 1931 (2005).
Moore, C., and J. Jackson, trans. *Tacitus' Histories and Annals*. Cambridge, 1925–1937.
Moore, K., ed. *Brill's Companion to the Reception of Alexander the Great*. Leiden, 2017.
Morgenthau, H. *Politics among Nations: The Struggle for Power and Peace*. New York, 1973.
Mørkholm, O. *Antiochus IV of Syria*. Oslo, 1966.
Mørkholm, O. "The Parthian Coinage of Seleucia on the Tigris, c. 90–55 BC." *Numismatic Chronicle* 140 (1980): 33–47.
Motyl, A. *Imperial Ends: The Decay, Collapse, and Revival of Empires*. New York, 2001.
Mousheghian, A., and G. Depeyrot. *Hellenistic and Roman Armenian Coinage (1st. c. BC–1st. c. AD)*. Wetteren, 1999.
Mukherjee, B. "Ta-hsia and the Problem Concerning the Advent of Nomadic Peoples in Greek Bactria." *East and West* 19.3–4 (1969a): 395–400.
Mukherjee, B. "An Examination of the Theory of the Occupation of the Greek Bactria by Mithridates I." *Journal of Asiatic Society* 11 (1969b): 1–5.
Müller, S. "Visualizing Political Friendship, Family Ties, and Links to the Argead Past in the Time of the Successors." *Alexander's Legacy*. Rome, 2016. 121–40.
Müller, S. "Apollodoros als Historiograph parthischer Geschichte." *Parthika*. Wiesbaden, 2017a. 59–70.
Müller, S. "Das Bild der Parther bei Trogus-Justin." *Parthika*. Wiesbaden, 2017b. 241–58.
Murison, C. *Rebellion and Reconstruction: An Historical Commentary on Cassius Dio's Roman History*. Oxford, 1999.
Murphy, T. *Pliny the Elder's Natural History: The Empire in the Encyclopedia*. Oxford, 2004.
Musti, D. "Syria and the East: 175–220." *Cambridge Ancient History*. 7.2.1. Cambridge, 1984. 175–220.
Mynott, J., ed. *Thucydides: The War of the Peloponnesians and the Athenians*. Cambridge, 2013.
Nabel, J. "The Seleucids Imprisoned: Arsacid-Roman Hostage Submission and Its Hellenistic Precedents." *Arsacids, Romans and Local Elites*. Oxford and Philadelphia, 2017a. 25–50.
Nabel, J . "Alexander between Rome and Persia: Politics, Ideology, and History." *Brill's Companion to the Reception of Alexander the Great*. Leiden, 2017b. 197–232.
Nabel, J. "Lucan's Parthians in Nero's Rome." *Classical Philology* 114.4 (2019): 604–625.
Ñaco del Hoyo, T., and F. Sánchez, eds. *War, Warlords, and Interstate Relations in the Ancient Mediterranean. Brill's Impact of Empire Series, 28*. Leiden and Boston, 2018.
Nadig, P. *Zwischen König und Karikatur: Das Bild Ptolemaios' VIII. im Spannungsfeld der Überlieferung*. Munich, 2007.
Narain, A. *The Indo-Greeks*. Oxford, 1957.
Narain, A. "The Greeks of Bactria and India." *Cambridge Ancient History*. 8.2. Cambridge, 1989. 388–421.
Narain, A. *The Indo-Greeks, Revisited and Supplemented*. Delhi, 2003.
Nawotka, K. "Strabon aus Amaseia und Apollodoros aus Artemita." *Parthika*. Wiesbaden, 2017. 47–58.

Negmatov, N. "States in North-western Central Asia." *History of Civilizations of Central Asia*. Delhi, 1999. 441–56.

Nelson, B., ed. *Numismatic Art of Persia. The Sunrise Collection, Part I: Ancient—650 BC to AD 650*. Lancaster and London, 2011.

Neugebauer, O. *Astronomical Cuneiform Texts: Babylonian Ephemerides of the Seleucid Period for the Motion of the Sun, the Moon and the Planets—Introduction: The Moon*. London, 1955a.

Neugebauer, O. *Astronomical Cuneiform Texts: Babylonian Ephemerides of the Seleucid Period for the Motion of the Sun, the Moon and the Planets—Plates*. London, 1955b.

Neujahr, M. "When Darius Defeated Alexander: Composition and Redaction in the Dynastic Prophecy." *Journal of Near Eastern Studies* 64.2 (2005): 101–7.

Neusner, J. "Parthian Political Ideology." *Iranica Antiqua* 3 (1963): 40–59.

Neusner, J. *A History of the Jews in Babylonia, 1, The Parthian Period*. Leiden, 1965.

Neusner, J."Jews in Iran." *Cambridge History of Iran*. 3.2. Cambridge, 1983. 909–23.

Newell, E. *The Seleucid Mint of Antioch*. New York, 1918.

Newell, E. "A Parthian Hoard." *Numismatic Chronicle* 4 (1924): 141–80.

Newell, E. *The Coinage of the Western Seleucid Mints from Seleucus I to Antiochus III*. New York, 1938a.

Newell, E. "The Coinage of the Parthians." *A Survey of Persian Art*. 1. London, 1938b. 475–92 and pls. 140–44.

Newell, E. "Late Seleucid Mints in Ake-Ptolemais and Damascus." *American Numismatic Society Numismatic Notes and Monographs* 84 (1939): 1–107 and pls. I–XVII.

Niebuhr, R. *Moral Man and Immoral Society*. New York, 1937.

Nikitin, A. "The Mint at Rhagae Early in the Reign of Mithridates II." *Journal of Ancient History (Vestnik drevnej istorii)* 164.2 (1983): 95–100.

Nikitin, A. "Early Parthian Coins from Margiana." *The Art and Archaeology of Ancient Persia*. New York, 1998. 14–19 and pls. I–II.

Nikonorov, V. *Vooruzhenie i voennoe delo v Parfii*. Leningrad, 1987a.

Nikonorov, V. "O roli kochevnicheskogo plasta v voennom dele postellinisticheskogo Vostoka (na primere Parfii)." *Vzaimodeistvie kochevykh kultur i drevnikh tsivilizatsii*. Alma-ata, 1987b. 106–7.

Nikonorov, V. "Le cataphractaire d'Iluratum." *Journal of Ancient History (Vestnik drevnej istorii)* 180.1 (1987c): 201–13.

Nikonorov, V. "New Data on Ancient Bactrian Body-Armour (in the Light of Finds from Kampyr-Tepe)." *Iran* 30 (1992): 49–54.

Nikonorov, V. "Sredneaziatskie katafraktarii kak produkt vzaimodeistviia voennykh shkol Zapada i Vostoka v epokhu rannego ellinizma." *Vzaimodeistvie drevnikh kultur i tsivilizatsii i ritmy kulturogeneza*. St. Petersburg, 1994. 47–51.

Nikonorov, V. "K voprosu o parfianskoi taktike (na primere bitvy pri Karrakh)." *Voennoe delo i srednevekovaia arkheologiia Tsentral'noi Azii*. Kemerovo, 1995. 53–61.

Nikonorov, V. *The Armies of Bactria, 700 BC–450 AD*. Stockport, 1997.

Nikonorov, V. "Apollodorus of Artemita and the Date of His Parthica Revisited." *Electrum* 2 (1998a): 107–22.

Nikonorov, V. "Cataphracti, Catafractarii, and Clibanarii: Another Look at the Old Problem of Their Indentifications." *Military Archaeology*. St. Petersburg, 1998b. 131–38.

Nikonorov, V. "A Nomadic Layer in the Cultural Heritage of the Parthian Realm." *Turkmenistan Cultural Heritage*. St. Petersburg, 2000a. 31–33.

Nikonorov, V. "Parthian Kettledrums." *ΣΥΣΣΙΤΙΑ*. St. Petersburg, 2000b. 167–74.

Nikonorov, V. "On the Parthian Cavalry Saddles." *Voennoe delo nomadov Severnoj i Central'noj Azii*. Novosibirsk, 2002. 21–27.

Nikonorov, V. "On the Parthian Legacy in Sasanian Iran: The Case of Warfare." *Central Asia from the Achaemenids to the Timurids*. St. Petersburg, 2005. 141–79.

Nikonorov, V. "On the Contribution of the Central Asian Nomads to the Warfare of the Antique Civilization (by the Example of Iran)." *The Role of Nomads of the Eurasian Steppes in the Development of World Military Art*. Almaty, 2010. 43–65.

Nikonorov, V. "Kampyr-Tepe, More about Western Elements in the Armament of Hellenistic Bactria: The Case of the Warrior Terracotta from Kampyr-Tepe." *Zwischen Ost und West: Neue Forschungen zum antiken Zentralasien*. Darmstadt, 2013. 187–204.

Nikonorov, V. "A Unique Sword of the Parthian Period from Southern Turkmenistan." *Experience of Turkmenistan in Research and Museumification of Archaeological Findings*. Asgabat, 2014. 36–37.

Noble, D. *Dawn of the Horse Warriors: Chariot and Cavalry Warfare 3000–600 BC*. Barnsley, 2015.

Nokandeh, J., et al. "Linear Barriers of Northern Iran: The Great Wall of Gorgan and the Wall of Tammishe." *Iran* 44 (2006): 121–73.

Nurpetlian, J. "Ancient Armenian Coins, the Artaxiad Dynasty (189 BC - AD 6)." *Berytus* 51–52 (2008–2009): 117–67.

Oelsner, J. "Randbemerkungen zur arsakidischen Geschichte anhand von babylonischen Keilschrifttexten." *Altorientalische Forschungen* 3 (1975): 25–45.

Oelsner, J. *Materialien zur babylonischen Gesellschaft und Kultur in hellenistischer Zeit*. Budapest, 1986.

Ogden, D. *Polygamy, Prostitutes and Death: The Hellenistic Dynasties*. Oxford, 1999.

Ogden, D. "Seleucus, His Signet Ring and His Diadem." *Alexander's Legacy*. Rome, 2016. 141–56.

Olbrycht, M. "Some Remarks on the Hellenistic Influence upon Fortifications of Northeastern Iran in the Arsacid Period." *Folia Orientalia* 29 (1993): 131–51.

Olbrycht, M. "Die Beziehungen der Steppennomaden Mittelasiens zu den hellenistischen Staaten (bis zum Ende des 3. Jahrhunderts vor Chr.)." *Hellenismus*. Berlin, 1996. 147–69.

Olbrycht, M. "Parthian King's Tiara—Numismatic Evidence and Some Aspects of Arsacid Political Ideology." *Notae Numismaticae/Zapiski Numizmatyczne* 2 (1997): 27–65.

Olbrycht, M. "Die Kultur der Steppengebiete und die Beziehungen zwischen Nomaden und der sesshaften Bevölkerung (Der arsakidische Iran und die Nomadenvölker)." *Das Partherreich und seine Zeugnisse*. Stuggart, 1998a. 11–43.

Olbrycht, M. *Parthia et ulteriores gentes. Die politischen Beziehungen zwischen demarsakidischen Iran und den Nomaden der eurasischen Steppen*. Munich, 1998b.

Olbrycht, M. "Das Arsakidenreich zwischen der mediterranean Welt und Innerasien." *Electrum* 2 (1998c): 123–59.

Olbrycht, M. "Parthian Military Strategy at Wars against Rome." *Military Archaeology*. St. Petersburg, 1998d. 138–41.

Olbrycht, M. "The Significance of the Arsacid Kingdom in the History of Central Asia." *Izuchenie kulturnogo naslediia Vostoka*. St. Petersburg, 1999. 101–4.

Olbrycht, M. "A Nomadic Layer in the Cultural Heritage of the Parthian Realm." *Turkmenistan Cultural Heritage*. St. Petersburg, 2000a. 33–35.

Olbrycht, M. "Policy and Royal Propaganda in Parthia: Hellenistic Concepts versus Nomadic and Iranian Tradition under the Arsacids." *Kulturnoe nasledie Turmenistana (glubinnye istoki i sovremennye perspektivy)*. St. Petersburg, 2000b. 35–38.

Olbrycht, M. "The Origins of the Arsacid Parthian Cavalry: Some Remarks." *The Role of Ahalteke Horses in the Formation of World Horse-Breeding*. Ashgabat, 2001. 108–11.

Olbrycht, M. "Parthia and Nomads of Central Asia. Elements of Steppe Origin in the Social and Military Development of Arsacid Iran." *Militär und Staatlichkeit, Orientwissenschftliche Hefte 12.2003*. Halle, 2003. 69–110.

Olbrycht, M. *Aleksander Wielki i świat irański*. Rzeszów, 2004a.

Olbrycht, M. "Seleukidzi i Arsakidzi: aspekty propagandy w walce o hegemonię na 'hellenistycznym' Bliskim Wschodzie." *Ideologia i propaganda w starożytności*. Rzeszów, 2004b. 45–68.

Olbrycht, M. "Mithradates VI Eupator and Iran." *Mithridates VI and the Pontic Kingdom*. Aarhus, 2009. 163–90.

Olbrycht, M. "Mithradates I of Parthia and His Conquests up to 141 BC." *Hortus Historiae*. Kraków, 2010a. 229–45.

Olbrycht, M. "The Early Reign of Mithradates II the Great in Parthia." *Anabasis* 1 (2010b): 144–58.

Olbrycht, M. "Ethnicity of Settlers in the Colonies of Alexander the Great in Iran and Central Asia." *Bulletin of the International Institute of Central Asian Studies* 14 (2011): 22–35.

Olbrycht, M. "Shayegan, Arsacids and Sasanians (review)." *Gnomon* 84.8 (2012a): 718–22.

Olbrycht, M. "Eastern Baktria under Da Yuezhi Hegemony." *Glory of the Kushans*. New Delhi, 2012b. 79–86.

Olbrycht, M. "The Titulature of Arsaces I, King of Parthia." *Parthica* 15 (2013a): 63–74.

Olbrycht, M. "Iranians in the Diadochi Period." *After Alexander: The Time of the Diadochi (323–281 BC)*. Oxford, 2013b. 159–82.

Olbrycht, M. "Die Alexandergründungen in den nordiranischen Ländern im Lichte der geographischen Tradition der Antike." *The Periphery of the Classical World in Ancient Geography and Cartography*. Leuven, Paris, and Walpole, 2014. 95–121.

Olbrycht, M. "Arsacid Iran and the Nomads of Central Asia—Ways of Cultural Transfer." *Complexity of Interaction along the Eurasian Steppe Zone in the First Millennium CE*. Bonn, 2015a. 333–90.

Olbrycht, M. "Persia beyond the Imperial Frontiers: The Nomads of the South Ural Region Versus the Near East." *Anabasis* 6 (2015b): 257–75.

Olbrycht, M. "Manpower Resources and Army Organisation in the Arsakid Empire." *Ancient Society* 46 (2016a): 291–338.

Olbrycht, M. "Ruler Cult in the Parthian Empire." *Боги среди людей (Gods among People)*. Moscow, 2016b. 451–75.

Olbrycht, M. "Archaeological Discoveries at Tillya-tepe and Parthia's Relations with Bactria." *Parthica* 18 (2016c): 9–30.

Olbrycht, M. "Dynastic Connections in the Arsacid Empire and the Origins of the House of Sāsān." *The Parthian and Early Sasanian Empires.* Oxford and Philadelphia, 2016d. 23–36.

Olbrycht, M. "The Sacral Kingship of the Early Arsacids I. Fire Cult and Kingly Glory." *Anabasis* 7 (2016e): 91–106.

Olbrycht, M. "Alexander the Great at Susa (324 BC)." *Alexander's Legacy.* Rome, 2016f. 61–72.

Olbrycht, M. "Parthia, Bactria and India: The Iranian Policies of Alexander of Macedonia (330–323)." *With Alexander in India and Central Asia.* Oxford and Philadelphia, 2017a. 194–210.

Olbrycht, M. "Greeks in the Arsacid Empire." *Parthika.* Wiesbaden, 2017b. 3–28.

Olbrycht, M. "Augustus versus Phraates IV. Some Remarks on the Parthian-Roman Relations." *Emas non quod opus est, sed quod necesse est: Beiträge zur Wirtschafts-, Sozial-, Rezeptions- und Wissenschaftsgeschichte der Antike, Festschrift für Hans-Joachim Drexhage zum 70. Geburtstag.* Wiesbaden, 2018. 389–397.

Olbrycht, M. "The Aparnoi in Arsacid History." *Antiquities of Eastern Europe, Central Asia and Southern Siberia in the Context of Connections and Interactions in the Eurasian Cultural Space.* St. Petersburg, 2019a. 161–65.

Olbrycht, M. "Mithradates I of Parthia and India." *EstOvest: Confini e Conflitti fra Vicino Oriente e Mondo Greco-Romano.* Rome, 2019b. 243–51.

Olbrycht, M. "Contesting Seleukid Unity: Seleukos II, Antiochos Hierax, and Regional Rulers in Western Asia." (Forthcoming2020/2021) .

Olivelle, P., ed. *Between the Empires: Society in India 300 BCE to 400 CE.* New York, 2006.

Olivelle, P., J. Leoshko, and H. Ray. *Reimagining Asoka: Memory and History.* Oxford, 2012.

Omar, C. *Da Alessandro a Menandro: il regno greco di Battriana.* Pisa and Roma, 2009.

Organski, A. and J. Kugler. *The War Ledger.* Chicago, 1980.

Overtoom, N. L. *Contesting the Greatness of Alexander the Great: The Representation of Alexander in the Histories of Polybius and Livy.* (Thesis) University of Maryland, 2011.

Overtoom, N. L. "A Roman Tradition of Alexander the Great Counterfactual History." *Acta Antiqua Academiae Scientiarum Hungaricae* 52.3 (2012): 203–12.

Overtoom, N. L. "Six Polybian Themes Concerning Alexander the Great." *Classical World* 106.4 (2013): 571–93.

Overtoom, N. L. "The Power-Transition Crisis of the 240s and the Creation of the Parthian State." *International History Review* 38.5 (2016a): 984–1013.

Overtoom, N. L. "Magnesia." *Conflict in Greece and Rome.* Santa Barbara, 2016b. 1025–26.

Overtoom, N. L. "The Rivalry of Rome and Parthia in the Sources from the Augustan Age to Late Antiquity." *Anabasis* 7 (2016c): 137–74.

Overtoom, N. L. *Challenging Roman Domination: The End of Hellenistic Rule and the Rise of the Parthian State from the Third to the First Centuries.* (Diss.) Louisiana State University, 2016d.

Overtoom, N. L. "Polybius." *Conflict in Greece and Rome.* Santa Barbara, 2016e. 1122–24.

Overtoom, N. L. "Ammianus." *Conflict in Greece and Rome.* Santa Barbara, 2016f. 697–98.

Overtoom, N. L. "Julian." *Conflict in Greece and Rome.* Santa Barbara, 2016g. 987–88.

Overtoom, N. L. "The Parthian Rival and Rome's Failure in the East: Roman Propaganda and the Stain of Crassus." *Acta Antiqua Academiae Scientiarum Hungaricae* 57.4 (2017a): 415–35.

Overtoom, N. L. "The Parthians' Unique Mode of Warfare: A Tradition of Parthian Militarism and the Battle of Carrhae." *Anabasis* 8 (2017b): 99–122.

Overtoom, N. L. "The Power-Transition Crisis of the 160s–130s BCE and the Formation of the Parthian Empire." *Journal of Ancient History* 7.1 (2019a): 111–55.

Overtoom, N. L. "A Reconsideration of Mithridates II's Early Reign: A Savior Restores the Eastern Frontier of the Parthian Empire." *Parthica* 21 (2019b): 9–21.

Overtoom, N. L. "Considering the Failures of the Parthians against the Invasions of the Central Asian Tribal Confederations in the 120s BCE." *Studia Iranica* 48 (2019c): 77–111.

Overtoom, N. L. "The Parthians' Failed Vassalage of Syria: The Shortsighted Western Policy of Phraates II and the Second Reign of Demetrius II (129-125 BCE)." *Acta Antiqua Academiae Scientiarum Hungaricae* 60.1–2 (2020): 1–14.

Overtoom, N. L. "A Fight to Reclaim the Central Asian Frontier: The Seleucid and Parthian Rivalry in the 230s BC." *Studia Hercynia: Journal of the Institute of Classical Archaeology* 25.1 (2021a): 105–18.

Overtoom, N. L. "Reassessing the Role of Parthia and Rome in the Origins of the First Romano-Parthian War (56/5-50 BCE)." *Journal of Ancient History* 9.2 (2021b): 238–68.

Panitschek, P. "Zur Darstellung der Alexander- und Achaemenidennachfolge als politische Programme in kaiserzeitlichen Quellen." *Klio* 72 (1990): 457–92.

Paratore, E. "La Persia nella letteratura latina." *La Persia e il mondo greco-romano*. Rome, 1966. 505–58.

Parmeggiani, G., ed. *Between Thucydides and Polybius: The Golden Age of Greek Historiography*. Cambridge, 2014.

Pastor, J., P. Stern, and M. Mor, *Flavius Josephus: Interpretation and History*. Leiden, 2011.

Paton, W., trans. *Polybius' The Histories Vols. 1–6*. Cambridge, 1922–1927.

Pelling, C. *Plutarch and History*. Swansea, 2011.

Perrin, B., trans. *Plutarch's Lives, Volume II: Themistocles and Camillus, Aristides and Cato Major, Cimon and Lucullus*. Cambridge, 1914.

Perrin, B., trans. *Plutarch's Lives, Volume III: Pericles and Fabius Maximus, Nicias and Crassus*. Cambridge, 1916.

Perrin, B., trans. *Plutarch's Lives, Volume V: Agesilaus and Pompey, Pelopidas and Marcellus*. Cambridge, 1917.

Perrin, B., trans. *Plutarch's Lives, Volume VII: Demosthenes and Cicero. Alexander and Caesar*. Cambridge, 1919.

Petrowicz, A. *Sammlung Petrowicz: Arsaciden Münzen*. Wien, 1904.

Piankov, I. "The Tochari—Who Are They?" *Anabasis* 1 (2010): 97–106.

Pigulevskaja, N. *Les villes de l'état Iranien aux époques Parthe et Sassanide*. Paris, 1963.

Pilipko, V. "A Hoard of Parthian Coins from Garry-Kyariz (Parfiena)." *Journal of Ancient History (Vestnik drevnej istorii)* 136.2 (1976): 114–21.

Pilipko, V., and S. Loginov. "Klad parfianskikh drakhm iz Ashkhabada." *Izvestiia Akademii Nauk Turkmenistana SSR* 1 (1980): 77–83.

Pirngruber, R. *The Economy of Late Achaemenid and Seleucid Babylonia*. Cambridge, 2017.

Plinval, G. de. "Horace et le sort des prisonniers d'Orient." *Mélanges de philologie, de littérature, et d'histoire anciennes offerts à J. Marouzeau par ses collègues et élèves étrangers*. Paris, 1948. 491–95.

Plischke, S. *Die Seleukiden und Iran: Die seleukidische Herrschaftspolitik in den östlichen Satrapien*. Wiesbaden, 2014.

Plischke, S. "Persianism under the Early Seleukid Kings? The Royal Title 'Great King.'" *Persianism in Antiquity*. Stuttgart, 2017. 163–76.

Poirot, J. "The Romano-Parthian Cold War: Julio-Claudian Foreign Policy in the First Century CE and Tacitus' Annales." (Diss.) Louisiana State University, 2014.

Popov-Reynolds, N. "Justin, Roman Historian." *The Encyclopedia of Ancient History*. Malden, 2013. 3666–67.

Porada, E. "The Art of Parthians." *Iran Chamber Society* (2019). Last accessed 4/2019. http://www.iranchamber.com/art/articles/art_of_parthians.php.

Posch, W. *Baktrien zwischen Griechen und Kuschan. Untersuchungen zu kulturellen und historischen Problemen einer Übergangsphase. Mit einem textkritischen Exkurs zum Shiji 123*. Wiesbaden, 1995.

Potter, D. "The Transformation of the Empire: 235–337 CE." *A Companion to the Roman Empire*. Malden, 2010. 153–74.

Potts, D. *The Archaeology of Elam: Formation and Transformation of an Ancient Iranian State*. Cambridge, 1999.

Potts, D. "Five Episodes in the History of Elymais, 145–124 BC: New Data from the Astronomical Diaries." *Iran: Questions et connaissances*. Paris and Leuven, 2002. 349–62.

Pownall, F. "Alexander's Political Legacy in the West: Duris on Agathocles." *Alexander's Legacy*. Rome, 2016. 181–202.

Prandi, L. "Philodemus of Gadara on Callisthenes and Alexander (New Light from PHerc 1675 and 1050)." *Alexander's Legacy*. Rome, 2016. 203–14.

Price, J. *Thucydides and Internal War*. Cambridge, 2001.

Prontera, F. "The Indian Caucasus from Alexander to Eratosthenes." *With Alexander in India and Central Asia*. Oxford and Philadelphia, 2017. 212–21.

Puri, B. "The Sakas and Indo-Parthians." *History of Civilizations of Central Asia*. Delhi, 1999. 191–208.

P'yankov, I. *Baktriia v antichnoi traditsii (obshchie dannye o strane: nazvanie i territoriia)*. Dushanbe, 1982.

Questor, G. "Crisis and the Unexpected." *Journal of Interdisciplinary History* 18 (1988): 701–19.

Quillin, J. "Review of Arthur Eckstein's *Mediterranean Anarchy, Interstate War, and the Rise of Rome*." *Bryn Mawr Classical Review* (2009). Last accessed 1/2020. http://bmcr.brynmawr.edu/2009/2009-06-44.html.

Quinn, J. "The Counterinsurgency Dilemma: The Causes and Consequences of State Repression of Human Rights in Civil Wars." (Diss.) University of North Texas, 2010.

Rahe, P. "Thucydides' Critique of Realpolitik." *Roots of Realism*. London, 1996. 105–41.

Ramsey, G. "Review of Arthur Eckstein's *Rome Enters the Greek East*." *Bryn Mawr Classical Review* (2013). Last accessed 1/2020. http://bmcr.brynmawr.edu/2013/2013-07-05.html.

Ramsey, J., trans. *Sallust's Fragments of the Histories and Letters to Caesar*. Cambridge, 2015.

Rapin, C. *Fouilles d'Aï Khanoum VIII, La trésorerie du palais hellénistique d'Aï Khanoum*. Paris, 1992.

Rapin, C. "Nomads and the Shaping of Central Asia: From the Early Iron Age to the Kushan Period." *After Alexander*. Oxford, 2007. 29–72.

Rapin, C. "Alexandre le Grand en Asie Centrale: Geographie et Strategie de la Conquête des Portes Caspiennes à l'Inde." *With Alexander in India and Central Asia*. Oxford and Philadelphia, 2017. 37–121.

Rapson, M. "Markoff's Coins of the Arsacidae." *Numismatic Chronicle* 3.13 (1893): 203–19.

Rawlings, L. "War and Warfare in Ancient Greece." *Oxford Handbook of Warfare in the Classical World*. Oxford, 2013. 3–28.

Rawlinson, G. *The Sixth Great Oriental Monarchy or the Geography, History and Antiquities of Parthia*. London, 1873.

Rawlinson, G. *The Seven Great Monarchies of the Ancient Eastern World*. Vol. 3. Piscataway, 1876 (2002).

Rea, C. *The Rise of Parthia in the East: From the Seleucid Empire to the Arrival of Rome*. CreateSpace Independent Publishing Platform, 2013.

Rea, C. *Leviathan vs. Behemoth: The Roman-Parthian Wars 66 BC–217 AD*. CreateSpace Independent Publishing Platform, 2014.

Redgate, A. *The Armenians*. Hoboken, 1998.

Reinach, T. *Mithridate Eupator, roi de Pont*. Paris, 1890.

Rezakhani, K. "Arsacid, Elymaean, and Persid Coinage." *Oxford Handbook of Ancient Iran*. Oxford, 2013. 766–78.

Rezakhani, K. "From Aramaic to Pahlavi: Epigraphic Observations Based on the Persis Coin Series." *The Parthian and Early Sasanian Empires*. Oxford and Philadelphia, 2016. 69–75.

Richter, S. "Antiochos III and the Revolt of Molon." *Antiochos III et l'Orient*. Nancy, 2017. 255–70.

Robert, L. "Samothrace: Excavations Conducted by the Institute of Fine Arts, New York." *Gnomon* 35 (1963): 50–79.

Robert, L. "Encore une inscription Grecque de l'Iran." *Comptes rendus des séances de l'Académie des Inscriptions et Belles-Lettres* 111.2 (1967): 281–97.

Robert, L. "Pline VI 49, Démodamas de Milet et la reine Apamè." *Bulletin de Correspondance Hellénique* 108 (1984): 467–72.

Roberto, U., ed. *Ioannis Antiocheni Fragmenta ex Historia Chronica: Introduzione, Edizione Critica, e Traduzione*. Berlin and New York, 2005.

Rolfe, J., trans. *Sallust's the War with Catiline and the War with Jugurtha*. Cambridge, 1921.

Rolfe, J., trans. *Qunitus Curtius' History of Alexander Vols 1–2*. Cambridge, 1946.

Rolfe, J., trans. *Ammianus Marcellinus' History Vols 1–3*. Cambridge, 1939–1950.

Roller, D., trans. *The Geography of Strabo*. Cambridge, 2014.

Romm, J. *Ghost on the Throne: The Death of Alexander the Great and the Bloody Fight for His Empire*. New York, 2012.

Rose, C. "The Parthians in Augustan Rome." *American Journal of Archaeology* 109 (2005): 21–75.

Rose, G. "Neoclassical Realism and Theories of Foreign Policy." *World Politics* 51.1 (1998): 144–72.

Rostovtzeff, M. "Dura and the Problem of Parthian Art." *Yale Classical Studies* 5 (1935): 155–304.

Rostovtzeff, M. "Parthia: Foreign Policy." *Cambridge Ancient History*. 11.1. Cambridge, 1936. 104–24.

Rostovtzeff, M. *Dura-Europos and Its Art*. Oxford, 1938.

Rostovtzeff, M. *Social and Economic History of the Hellenistic World*. Oxford, 1941.

Roth, J. *Roman Warfare*. Cambridge, 2009.

Rougemont, G. *Inscriptions grecques d'Iran et d'Asie centrale (Corpus inscriptionum Iranicarum, Part II: Inscriptions in Non-Iranian Languages, 1)*. London, 2012a.

Rougemont, G. "Hellenism in Central Asia and the North-West of the Indo-Pakistan Sub-Continent: The Epigraphic Evidence 1." *Ancient Civilizations from Scythia to Siberia* 18.1 (2012b): 175–82.

Rougemont, G. "Les inscriptions grecques d'Iran et d'Asie central: Bilinguismes, interférences culturelles, colonisation." *Journal des Savants* 1 (2012c): 3–27.

Rougemont, G. "The Use of Greek in Pre-Sasanian Iran." *Oxford Handbook of Ancient Iran*. Oxford, 2013. 795–801.

Rtveladze, E. "O zone parfianskikh vladenii v zapadno Baktrii." *Merv v drevnei i srednevekovoi istorii Vostoka III*. Ashgabad, 1992. 33–34.

Rtveladze, E. "Coins of the Yuezhi Rulers of Northern Bactria." *Silk Road Art and Archaeology* 3 (1994): 81–95.

Rtveladze, E. "Parfiia i iuechizhskaia Baktriia." *Istoriia material'noi kul'tury Uzbekistana* 31 (2000): 86–90.

Rtveladze, E. "Parthians in the Oxus Valley: Struggle for the Great Indian Road." *Anabasis* 2 (2011): 149–78.

Ruzicka, S. *Trouble in the West: Egypt and the Persian Empire, 525–332 BCE*. Oxford, 2012.

Sachs, A. *Late Babylonian Astronomical and Related Texts*. Providence, 1955.

Sachs, A., and H. Hunger. *Astronomical Diaries and Related Texts from Babylonia: Diaries from 652 BC to 262 BC*. Vienna, 1988.

Sachs, A., and H. Hunger. *Astronomical Diaries and Related Texts from Babylonia: Diaries from 261 BC to 165 BC*. Vienna, 1989.

Sachs, A., and H. Hunger. *Astronomical Diaries and Related Texts from Babylonia: Diaries from 164 BC to 61 BC*. Vienna, 1996.

Sachs, A., and D. Wiseman. "A Babylonian King List of the Hellenistic Period." *Iraq* 15 (1954): 202–11.

Saint-Martin, A. *Fragments d'une histoire des Arsacides*. Paris, 1850.

Salomon, R. *Indian Epigraphy*. Oxford, 1998.

Sampson, G. *The Defeat of Rome: Crassus, Carrhae and the Invasion of the East*. Barnsley, 2015.

Sampson, G. *Rome and Parthia: Empires at War: Ventidius, Antony and the Second Romano-Parthian War, 40–20 BC*. Barnsley, 2020.

Sancisi-Weerdenburg, H. "Decadence in the Empire or Decadence in the Sources? From Source to Synthesis: Ctesias." *Achaemenid History I*. Leiden, 1987. 33–45.

Sartre, M. *The Middle East under Rome*. Trans. C. Porter and E. Rawlings. Cambridge, 2005.

Sartre, M. "Review of Eckstein, *Mediterranean Anarchy*." *Topoi* 15 (2007): 619–25.

Scheidel, W. "Review of Eckstein, *Mediterranean Anarchy, Interstate War, and the Rise of Rome*." *Journal of Interdisciplinary History* 39.1 (2008): 100–2.

Schelling, T. "The Diplomacy of Violence." *International Politics*. New York, 2000. 169–83.

Schippmann, K. *Grundzüge der parthischen Geschichte*. Darmstadt, 1980.

Schippmann, K. "Arsacids ii. The Arsacid Dynasty." *Encyclopaedia Iranica Online Edition* (1986). Last accessed 1/2020. http://www.iranicaonline.org/articles/arsacids-ii.

Schippmann, K. "Azerbaijan iii. Pre-Islamic History." *Encyclopaedia Iranica Online Edition* (1987). Last accessed 6/2015. http://www.iranicaonline.org/articles/azerbaijan-iii.

Schippmann, K. "Archaeology iii. Seleucid and Parthian." *Encyclopaedia Iranica Online Edition* (2011). Last accessed 12/2017. http://www.iranicaonline.org/articles/archeology-iii.

Schlude, J. "Rome, Parthia, and Empire: The First Century of Roman-Parthian Relations." (Diss.) University of California, 2009.

Schlude, J. "The Early Parthian Policy of Augustus." *Anabasis* 6 (2015): 139–56.

Schlude, J. *Rome, Parthia, and the Politics of Peace: The Origins of War in the Ancient Middle East*. Abingdon, 2020.

Schlude, J., and B. Rubin. "Finding Common Ground: Roman-Parthian Embassies in the Julio-Claudian Period." *Arsacids, Romans and Local Elites*. Oxford and Philadelphia, 2017. 65–92.

Schlumberger, D. "Parthian Art." *Cambridge History of Iran*. 3.2. Cambridge, 1983. 1027–54.

Schmitt, H. *Untersuchungen zur Geschichte Antiochos' des Grossen und seiner Zeit*. Stuttgart, 1964.

Schmitt, R. "Armenia and Iran i. Armina, Achaemenid Province." *Encyclopaedia Iranica Online Edition* (1986a). Last accessed 10/2017. http://www.iranicaonline.org/articles/armenia-i.

Schmitt, R. "Artavasdes." *Encyclopaedia Iranica Online Edition* (1986b). Last accessed 9/2017. http://www.iranicaonline.org/articles/artavasdes-old-iranian-male-personal-name-attested-as-greek-artaousdes-artabzes-artbazos-artozos-latin-artava.

Schmitt, R. "Arachosia." *Encyclopaedia Iranica Online Edition* (1986c). Last accessed 5/2019. http://www.iranicaonline.org/articles/arachosia.

Schmitt, R. "Aria." *Encyclopaedia Iranica Online Edition* (1986d). Last accessed 5/2019. http://www.iranicaonline.org/articles/aria-region-in-the-eastern-part-of-the-persian-empire.

Schmitt, R. "Ex Occidente Lux. Griechen und griechische Sprache im hellenistischen Fernen Osten." *Beiträge zur hellenistischen Literatur und ihrer Rezeption in Rom*. Stuttgart, 1990. 41–58.

Schmitt, R. "Isidors *Stathmoi Parthikoi* aus Sicht der Iranischen Toponomastik." *Parthika*. Wiesbaden, 2017. 189–220.

Schneider, R. "Friend and Foe: The Orient in Rome." *The Age of the Parthians*. London, 2007. 50–86.

Schottky, M. *Media Atropatene und Gross-Armenien in hellenistischen Zeit*. Bonn, 1989.

Schroeder, P. "History and International Relations Theory: Not Use or Abuse, but Fit or Misfit." *International Security* 22.1 (1997): 64–74.

Schuman, F. *International Politics*. New York, 1969.

Schuol, M. *Die Charakene: Ein mesopotamisches Königreich in hellenistisch-parthischer Zeit*. Stuttgart, 2000.

Schuol, M. "Isidor von Charax und die literarische Gattung der *stathmoi*." *Parthika*. Wiesbaden, 2017. 71–86.

Schweller, R. "Bandwagoning for Profit: Bringing the Revisionist State Back In." *International Security* 19 (1994): 72–107.

Schweller, R. "Neo-Realism's Status Quo Bias: What Security Dilemma?" *Realism*. London, 1996. 90–121.

Schweller, R. *Deadly Imbalances: Tripolarity and Hitler's Startegy of World Conquest*. New York, 1998.

Schweller, R. "Rising Powers and Revisionism in Emerging International Orders." *Valdai Papers* 16 (2015): 1–15.

Scott, W. "On Parthian Coins." *Numismatic Chronicle* 17 (1854): 131–73.

Seaman, M. "The Peloponnesian War and Its Sieges." *Oxford Handbook of Warfare in the Classical World*. Oxford, 2013. 642–56.

Segal, J. *Edessa, the Blessed City*. Oxford, 1970.

Sekunda, N. "The Aribazoi: A Family in Seleucid Service." *Hortus Historiae*. Kraków, 2010. 219–27.

Sekunda, N. "Cavalry, Hellenistic." *The Encyclopedia of Ancient History*. Vol. 3. Malden, 2013. 1388–89.

Sellwood, D. "The Parthian Coins of Gotarzes I, Orodes I, and Sinatruces." *Numismatic Chronicle* 7.2 (1962): 73–89.

Sellwood, D. "The Mint-Towns of Parthia." *The Memorial Volume of the VIth International Congress of Iranian Art and Archaeology*. Tehran, 1972. 293–98.

Sellwood, D. "The Drachms of the Parthian 'Dark Age.'" *Journal of the Royal Asiatic Society* (1976): 2–25.

Sellwood, D. *An Introduction to the Coinage of Parthia*. London, 1980.

Sellwood, D. "Parthian Coins." *Cambridge History of Iran*. 3.1. Cambridge, 1983. 279–98.

Sellwood, D. "Trade Routes Through Parthia." *Coinage, Trade and Economy, January 8th–11th, 1991, 3rd International Colloquium*. Maharashtra, 1991. 23–27.

Sellwood, D. "Parthians and Scythians." *Ex Moneta*. Nashik, 1995. 97–102.

Senior, R. *Indo-Scythian Coins and History*. London, 2001.

Seyrig, H. "Trésor monétaire de Nisibe." *Revue Numismatique* 17 (1955): 85–128.

Shahbazi, A. "Arsacids i. Origins." *Encyclopaedia Iranica Online Edition* (1986a). Last accessed 1/2020. http://www.iranicaonline.org/articles/arsacids-i.

Shahbazi, A. "Arsacids v. The 'Arsacid' Era." *Encyclopaedia Iranica Online Edition* (1986b). Last accessed 1/2020. http://www.iranicaonline.org/articles/arsacids-v.

Shahbazi, A. "ASB i. In Pre-Islamic Iran." *Encyclopaedia Iranica Online Edition* (1987). Last accessed 9/2018. http://www.iranicaonline.org/articles/asb-pre-islamic-iran.

Shahbazi, A. "Carrhae." *Encyclopaedia Iranica Online Edition* (1990). Last accessed 12/2015. http://www.iranicaonline.org/articles/carrhae-harran-town-in-mesopotamia-where-in-may-53-b.

Shahbazi, A. "Charax." *Encyclopaedia Iranica Online Edition* (2011). Last accessed 5/2018. http://www.iranicaonline.org/articles/charax-town-in-the-seleucid-and-parthian-province-of-rhagiana-the-area-around-modern-ray.

Shahbazi, A. "Parthian Army." *Iran Chamber Society* (2019). Last accessed 4/2019. http://www.iranchamber.com/history/parthians/parthian_army.php.

Shahin, T., ed. *Fragmente der Historiker: Nikolaos von Damaskus*. Stuttgart, 2018.

Shanske, D. *Thucydides and the Philosophical Origins of History*. Cambridge, 2006.

Shayegan, M. R. "On Demetrius II Nicator's Arsacid Captivity and Second Rule." *Bulletin of the Asia Institute 17* (2003 [2007]): 83–103.

Shayegan, M. R. *Arsacids and Sasanians: Political Ideology in Post-Hellenistic and Late Antique Persia*. Cambridge, 2011.

Shayegan, M. R. "The Arsacids and Commagene." *The Parthian and Early Sasanian Empires*. Oxford and Philadelphia, 2016. 8–22.

Shayegan, M. R. "Persianism: Or Achaemenid Reminiscences in the Iranian and Iranicate World(s) of Antiquity." *Persianism in Antiquity*. Stuttgart, 2017. 401–55.

Sheehan, M. *The Balance of Power: History and Theory*. London, 1996.

Sheldon, R. *Intelligence Activities in Ancient Rome: Trust in the Gods, but Verify*. London and New York, 2005.

Sheldon, R. *Rome's Wars in Parthia: Blood in the Sand*. London and Portland, 2010.

Sheppard, S. *Roman Soldier versus Parthian Warrior: Carrhae to Nisibis, 53 BC–AD 217*. Oxford, 2020.

Sherwin-White, A. *Roman Foreign Policy in the East 168 BC to AD 1*. Norman, 1984.

Sherwin-White, S. "Seleucid Babylonia: A Case Study for the Installation and Development of Greek Rule." *Hellenism in the East*. London, 1987. 1–31.

Sherwin-White, S., and A. Kuhrt. *From Samarkhand to Sardis: A New Approach to the Seleucid Empire*. Berkeley, 1993.

Shiping, T. "International System, Not International Structure: Against the Agent-Structure Problématique in IR1." *The Chinese Journal of International Politics* (2014): 483–506.

Shipley, G. *The Greek World after Alexander 323–30 BC*. London, 2000.

Shore, F. *Parthian Coins and History: Ten Dragons against Rome*. Quarryville, 1993.

Sidky, H. *The Greek Kingdom of Bactria*. Lanham, 2000.

Simonetta, A. "Notes on the Parthian and Indo-Parthian Issues of the First Century BC." *Actes du congrès international du numismatique*. Vol. 2. Paris, 1953–1957. 111–21.

Simonetta, A. "Some Hypotheses on the Military and Political Structure of the Indo-Greek Kingdom." *Journal of the Numismatic Society of India* 22 (1960): 56–62.

Simonetta, A. "Some Remarks on the Arsacid Coinage of the Period 90–57 BC." *Numismatic Chronicle* 7.6 (1966): 15–40.

Simonetta, A. "Numismatic Provinces and the Debasement of the Parthian Coinage." *South Asian Archaeology*. Berlin, 1979. 355–68.

Simonetta, A. "A Proposed Revision of the Attributions of the Parthian Coins Struck during the So-called 'Dark Age' and Its Historical Significance." *East & West* 52.1–2 (2001): 69–108.

Simonetta, A., and D. Sellwood. "Again on the Parthian Coinage from Mithradates II to Orodes II." *Quaderni Ticinesi di Numismatica e di Antichità Classiche* 7 (1978): 95–119.

Simpson, St. J. "Merv, an Archaeological Case-Study from the Northeastern Frontier of the Sasanian Empire." *Journal of Ancient History* 2.2 (2014): 1–28.

Singh, M. *Maurya Empire*. New Delhi, 2011.

Singh, M., and E. Shrivastava. *Gupta Empire*. New Delhi, 2011.

Sinisi, F. "The Coinage of the Parthians." *Oxford Handbook of Greek and Roman Coinage*. Oxford, 2012. 275–94.

Sinisi, F. "Sources for the History of Art of the Parthian Period: Arsacid Coinage as Evidence for Continuity of Imperial Art in Iran." *Parthica* 16 (2014): 9–59.

Sinisi, F. "Battriana e Partia." *Survey of Numismatic Research 2008–2013*. Taormina, 2015. 135–41.

Sinor, D. "Horse and Pasture in Inner Asian History." *Oriens Extremus* 19 (1972): 171–83.

Sinor, D. "The Inner Asian Warriors." *Journal of the American Oriental Society* 101 (1981): 133–44.

Sinor, D. "Introduction: The Concept of Inner Asia." *Cambridge History of Early Inner Asia*. Cambridge, 1990a. 1–18.

Sinor, D., ed. *Cambridge History of Early Inner Asia*. Cambridge, 1990b.

Smirnova, N. "Some Questions Regarding the Numismatics of Pre-Islamic Merv." *After Alexander*. Oxford, 2007. 377–88.

Smith, A., trans. "Memnon's History of Heracleia." *Attalus* (2004). Last accessed 3/2016. http://www.attalus.org/translate/memnon1.html.

Smith, A., trans. "Eusebius of Caesarea, Chronicon, Book 1." *Tertullian* (2008). Last accessed 3/2016. http://www.tertullian.org/fathers/eusebius_chronicon_01_text.htm.

Smith, C., trans. *Thucydides' History of the Peloponnesian War Vols. 1–4*. Cambridge, 1919–1923.

Smith, R. "The First Bactrian Coinage: An Introduction." *Cornucopiae* 4 (1979): 6–13.

Sonnabend, H. *Fremdenbild und Politik: Vorstellungen der Römer von Ägypten und dem Partherreich in der späten Republik und frühen Kaiserzeit*. Frankfurt, 1986.

Spirtas, M. "A House Divided: Tragedy and Evil in Realist Theory." *Realism*. London, 1996. 385–423.

Stadter, P., ed. *Plutarch and the Historical Tradition*. New York, 2011.

Stadter, P.. *Plutarch and His Roman Readers*. Oxford, 2015.

Stark, F. *Rome on the Euphrates: The Story of a Frontier*. London, 1966.

Stehle, E. "Arrian." *The Encyclopedia of Ancient History*. Vol. 2. Malden, 2013. 756–60.

Stevens, K. "Empire Begins at Home: Local Elites and Imperial Ideologies in Hellenistic Greece and Babylonia." *Cosmopolitanism and Empire*. Oxford, 2016. 65–88.

Stevenson, D. "Militarization and Diplomacy in Europe before 1914." *International Security* 22 (1997): 125–61.

Stolper, M. *Entrepreneurs and Empire: The Murašu Archive, the Murašu Firm, and Persian Rule in Babylonia*. Leiden, 1985.

Stoneman, R. *The Greek Experience of India: From Alexander to the Indo-Greeks*. Princeton, 2019.

Strauss, B. "Of Bandwagons and Ancient Greeks." *Hegemonic Rivalry*. Boulder, 1991. 189–210.

Strauss, B. "Naval Battles and Siege." *Cambridge History of Greek and Roman Warfare*. 1. Cambridge, 2007. 223–47.

Stride, S. "Regions and Territories in Southern Central Asia: What the Surkhan Darya Province Tells Us about Bactria." *After Alexander*. Oxford, 2007. 99–120.

Strootman, R. "Review of Grainger, *The Roman War of Antiochos the Great*." *Bryn Mawr Classical Review* (2004). Last accessed 1/2020. http://bmcr.brynmawr.edu/2004/2004-03-52.html.

Strootman, R. "Hellenistic Court Society: The Seleucid Imperial Court under Antiochus the Great, 223–187 BCE." *Royal Courts in Dynastic States and Empires*. Leiden and Boston, 2011. 63–89.

Strootman, R. "The Seleukid Empire between Orientalism and Hellenocentrism: Writing the History of Iran in the Third and Second Centuries BCE." *Name-ye Iran-e Bastan* 11.1–2 (2011–2012): 17–35.

Strootman, R. "Antiochos III Megas." *The Encyclopedia of Ancient History*. Vol. 2. Malden, 2013a. 476–79.

Strootman, R. "Seleucids." *The Encyclopedia of Ancient History*. Vol. 11. Malden, 2013b. 6119–25.

Strootman, R. "Hellenistic Imperialism and the Idea of World Unity." *The City in the Classical and Post-Classical World*. Cambridge, 2014. 38–61.

Strootman, R. "Seleucus." *Encyclopaedia Iranica Online Edition* (2015). Last accessed 4/2018. http://www.iranicaonline.org/articles/seleucus-kings.

Strootman, R. "Imperial Persianism: Seleukids, Arsakids and *Fratarakā*." *Persianism in Antiquity*. Stuttgart, 2017. 177–200.

Strootman, R. "The Coming of the Parthians: Crisis and Resilience in the Reign of Seleukos II." *The Seleukid Empire, 281–222 BC*. Swansea, 2018. 129–50.

Strootman, R. "The Great Kings of Asia: Universalistic Titulature in the Seleukid and Post-Seleukid East." *Seleukeia*. Berlin, 2019. 1–29.

Strootman, R., and J. Versluys., eds. *Persianism in Antiquity*. Stuttgart, 2017.

Sullivan, R. *Near Eastern Royalty and Rome*. Toronto, 1990.

Suren-Pahlav, S. "General Surena, The Hero of Carrhae." *Iran Chamber Society* (2019). Last accessed 4/2019. http://www.iranchamber.com/history/surena/surena.php.

Sykes, P. *History of Persia*. London, 1915.

Syme, R. *Tacitus*. Oxford, 1958.

Syme, R. *Ammianus and the Historia Augusta*. Oxford, 1968.

Syme, R. "The Date of Justin and the Discovery of Trogus." *Historia* 37 (1988): 358–71.

Syvänne, I. *Caracalla: A Military Biography*. Barnsley, 2017.

Taaffe, R. "The Geographic Setting." *Cambridge History of Early Inner Asia*. Cambridge, 1990. 19–40.

Taliaferro, J. "Security Seeking under Anarchy: Defensive Realism Revisited." *International Security* 25 (2000–2001): 128–61.

Tammen, R., et al. *Power Transitions: Strategies for the 21st Century*. New York, 2000.

Tao, W. "Parthia in China: A Re-examination of the Historical Records." *The Age of the Parthians*. London, 2007. 87–104.

Tarn, W. "The Struggle of Egypt against Syria and Macedonia." *Cambridge Ancient History*. 7.1. Cambridge, 1928. 699–731.

Tarn, W. "Seleucid–Parthian Studies." *Proceedings of the British Academy* 16 (1930): 105–35.

Tarn, W. "Parthia in the Time of the Roman Republic 133–44 BC." *Cambridge Ancient History*. 9.1. Cambridge, 1932. 574–614.

Tarn, W. *The Greeks in Bactria and India*. Cambridge, 1951.

Täubler, E. *Die Parthernachrichten bei Josephus*. (Diss.) Universität zu Berlin, 1904.

Taylor, D. *Roman Republic at War: A Compendium of Battles from 498 to 31 BC*. Barnsley, 2017.

Taylor, M. *Antiochus the Great*. Barnsley, 2013.

Taylor, M. "Sacred Plunder and the Seleucid Near East." *Greece & Rome* 61.2 (2014): 222–41.

Taylor, T., ed. *Approaches and Theory in International Politics*. London, 1978.

Teixidor, J. "Parthian Officials in Lower Mesopotamia." *Mesopotamia* 22 (1987): 187–94.

Thapar, R. *Asoka and the Decline of the Mauryas*. Oxford, 2012.

Thauer, C., and C. Wendt, *Thucydides and Political Order: Lessons of Governance and the History of the Peloponnesian War*. London, 2016.

Thompson, E. *The Huns*. Hoboken, 1999.

Thompson, M., et al. *An Inventory of Greek Coin Hoards*. New York, 1973.

Thompson, W. *On Global War: Historical-Structural Approaches to World Politics*. Columbia, 1988.

Thompson, W. "Why Rivalries Matter." *Great Power Rivalries*. Columbia, 1999. 3–28.

Thomson, R., ed. *Moses Khorenats'i: History of the Armenians*. Cambridge, 1978.

Thonemann, P., ed. *Attalid Asia Minor: Money, International Relations, and the State*. Oxford, 2013.

Thonemann, P. *The Hellenistic World: Using Coins as Sources*. Cambridge, 2015.

Timpe, D. "Die Bedeutung der Schlacht von Carrhae." *Museum Helveticum* 19 (1962): 104–29.

Tod, J. "An Account of Greek, Parthian and Hindu Metals Found in India." *Transactions of the Royal Asiatic Society* 1.2 (1826). 313–42.

Tolstov, S. *Drevnii Khorezm. Op't istoriko-arkheologicheskogo issledovaniia*. Moscow, 1948.

Torday, L. *Mounted Archers—the Beginnings of Central Asian History*. Durham, 1997.

Toumanoff, C. "Arsacids vii. The Arsacid Dynasty of Armenia." *Encyclopaedia Iranica Online Edition* (1986). Last accessed 1/2020. http://www.iranicaonline.org/articles/arsacids-vii.

Traina, G. *La resa di Roma: 9 giugno 53 a.C., battaglia a Carre*. Roma and Bari, 2010.

Traina, G. "Imperial Views on the Battle of Carrhae." *War in Words*. Berlin and New York, 2011. 209–17.

Traina, G. "L'impero di Tigran d'Armenia nella versione di Trogo-Giustino." *Studi sull'epitome di Giustino. III. Il tardo ellenismo. I Parti e i Romani*. Milan, 2016. 99–115.

Traina, G. "Rois ou dynastes? Les territoires arméniens à l'époque d'Antiochos III." *Antiochos III et l'Orient*. Nancy, 2017. 377–88.

Treves, P. "Balance of Power Politics in Classical Antiquity." *Proceedings of the Thirteenth International Congress of Historical Science*. Moscow, 1970. 55–63.

Troncoso, V. "Antigonus Monophthalmus and Alexander's Memory." *Alexander's Legacy*. Rome, 2016. 97–120.

Usmanova, Z., M. Filanovich, and G. Koshelenko. "Margiana." *Drevneĭshie gosudarstva Kavkaza i Sredneĭ Azii*. Moscow, 1985. 226–42.

Vainberg, B. "Parfiia i Khorezm." *Merv v drevnei i srednevekovoi istorii Vostoka III*. Ashgabad, 1992. 36–39.

Vallée-Poussin, L. *L'Inde aux Temps des Mauryas et des Barbares, Grecs, Scythes, Parthes, et Yue-Tchi*. Paris, 1930.

Valverde, L. "Algunas novedades sobre numismática parta desde Fraates II a Orodes II (132–38 a.C.)." *Gaceta Numismática* 193 (2017): 111–28.

van de Mieroop, M. "Gutians" *Encyclopaedia Iranica Online Edition* (2002). Last accessed 11/2018. http://www.iranicaonline.org/articles/gutians.

van der Spek, R. "New Evidence from the Babylonian Astronomical Diaries Concerning Seleucid and Arsacid History." *Archiv für Orientforschung* 44–45 (1997–1998): 167–75.

van der Spek, R. "The Seleucid State and the Economy." *Production and Public Powers in Antiquity*. Cambridge, 2000. 27–36.

van der Spek, R. "The Theatre of Babylon in Cuneiform." *Veenhoof Anniversary Volume*. Leiden, 2001. 445–56.

van der Spek, R. "Ethnic Segregation in Hellenistic Babylon." *Ethnicity in Ancient Mesopotamia*. Leiden, 2005. 393–408.

van der Spek, R. "The Hellenistic Near East." *Cambridge Economic History of the Greco-Roman World*. Cambridge, 2007. 409–33.

van der Spek, R. "The Latest on Seleucid Empire Building in the East." *Journal of the American Oriental Society* 138.2 (2018): 385–94.

van der Spek, R., and B. van Leeuwen. "Quantifying Integration of the Babylonian Economy in the Mediterranean World Using a New Corpus of Price Data, 400–50 BCE." *Quantifying the Greco-Roman Economy and Beyond*. Bari, 2014. 79–101.

van der Spek, R., B. van Leeuwen, and J. van Zanden, *A History of Market Performance from Ancient Babylonia to the Modern World*. New York, 2014.

van Evera, S. "Offense, Defense, and the Causes of War." *International Security* 22.4 (1998): 5–43.

van Wees, H. *Greek Warfare: Myths and Realities*. London, 2004.

Vanden Berghe, L. *Reliefs rupestres de l'Iran Ancien (vers 2000 av. J.C.–7e s. apres J.C.)*. Brussels, 1983.

Viotti, P., and M. Kauppi. *International Relations Theory*. New York, 2011.

Visconti, E. *Iconographie grecque*. Milan, 1808.

Vogelsang, W. "Parthian Pottery from Iran." *Archaeologische Mitteilungen aus Iran* 18 (1985): 157–72.

Vogelsang, W. "The Achaemenids and India: Two Worlds in Contact." *Achaemenid History IV*. Leiden, 1990. 93–110.

Vogelsang, W. *The Rise and Organisation of the Achaemenid Empire: The Eastern Iranian Evidence*. Leiden, 1992.

Vogt, J. "Die Tochter des Grosskönigs und Pausanias, Alexander, Caracalla." *Gesetz und handlungsfreiheit in der Geschichte*. Stuttgart, 1955. 55–80.

Volkmann, H. "Parthian." *Der kleine Pauly*. Vol. 4. Munich, 1972. 332–37.

Walbank, F. *A Historical Commentary on Polybius (Commentary on Books vii–xviii)*. Oxford, 1967.

Walbank, F. *A Historical Commentary on Polybius*. Vol. 1–3. Oxford, 1957–1979.

Walbank, F. *The Hellenistic World*. London, 1981.

Walbank, F. *Polybius*. Berkeley, 1990.

Walbank, F. *Polybius, Rome, and the Hellenistic World: Essays and Reflections*. Cambridge, 2002.

Walt, S. *The Origins of Alliances*. Ithaca, 1987.

Walton, F., trans. *Diodorus Siculus' Library of History, Volume XI: Fragments of Books 21–32 and Library of History, Volume XII: Fragments of Books 33–40*. Cambridge, 1957–1967.

Waltz, K. *Man, the State and War: A Theoretical Analysis*. New York, 1959.

Waltz, K. *Theory of International Politics*. New York, 1979.

Waltz, K. "The Origins of War in Neorealist Theory." *Journal of Interdisciplinary History* 18 (1988): 615–28.

Waltz, K. "The Emerging Structure of International Politics." *International Security* 18 (1993): 44–79.

Waltz, K. "Structural Realism after the Cold War." *International Security* 25 (2000): 5–41.

Wang, Y. *Harmony and War: Confucian Culture and Chinese Power Politics*. New York, 2011.

Ward, A. *Marcus Crassus and the Late Roman Republic*. Columbia, 1977.

Warner, A., and E. Warner, trans. *The Sháhnáma of Firdausí*. 6. London, 1912.

Warry, J. *Warfare in the Classical World*. Norman, 1995.

Waterfield, R. *Dividing the Spoils: The War for Alexander the Great's Empire*. Oxford, 2011.

Waters, M. *Ancient Persia: A Concise History of the Achaemenid Empire, 550–330 BCE*. Cambridge, 2014.

Watson, B. *Records of the Grand Historian of China, Translated from the Shih-chi of Ssu-ma Ch'ien*. New York, 1961.

Watson, J., trans. *Justin's Epitome of the Philippic History of Pompeius Trogus*. London, 1853.

Weiskopf, M. "Commagene." *Encyclopaedia Iranica Online Edition* (1992). Last accessed 7/2015. http://www.iranicaonline.org/articles/commagene-a-portion-of-southwestern-asia-minor-modern-turkey-.

Weggen, K. *Der lange Schatten von Carrhae: Studien zu M. Licinius Crassus*. Hamburg, 2011.

Welles, C. *Royal Correspondence in the Hellenistic Period: A Study in Greek Epigraphy*. New Haven, 1934.

Welles, C. "The Chronology of Dura-Europos," *Eos* 48 (1957): 467–74.

Welles, C. trans. *Diodorus Siculus' Library of History, Volume VIII: Books 16.66–17*. Cambridge, 1963.

Wellesley, K., trans. *Tacitus: Histories*. London, 1964.

Wendt, A. "Anarchy Is What States Make of It: The Social Construction of Power Politics." *Inernational Organization* 46.2 (1992): 391–425.

Wenghofer, R. "Rethinking the Relationship between Hellenistic Baktria and the Seleucid Empire." *The Seleukid Empire, 281–222 BC*. Swansea, 2018. 151–72.

Westad, O., ed. *Reviewing the Cold War: Approaches, Interpretations, Theory*. London, 2000.

Wheatley, P., and W. Heckel. *Justin: Epitome of the Philippic History of Pompeius Trogus: Volume II: Books 13–15*. Trans. J. Yardley. Oxford, 2012.

Wheeler, E. "Roman Treaties with Parthia: Völkerrecht or Power Politics." *Limes XVIII*. Oxford, 2002. 287–92.

Wheeler, E. "Greece: Mad Hatters and March Hares." *Recent Directions in the Military History of the Ancient World*. Claremont, 2011. 53–104.

Whiston, W., trans. *Josephus' Antiquities of the Jews*. London, 1737.

Whiston, W., trans. *Flavius Josephus: The Works of Flavius Josephus*. Auburn and Buffalo, 1895.

White, H., trans. *Appian's Foreign Wars*. New York, 1899.

Widemann, F. "Un Monnayage inconnu de type Gréco-Bactrien à légende araméenne." *Studia Iranica* 18 (1989): 193–97.

Widengren, G. "Sources of Parthian and Sasanian History." *Cambridge History of Iran*. 3.2. Cambridge, 1983. 1261–83.

Wiesehöfer, J. "Iranische Ansprüche an Rom auf ehemals achämenidische Territorien." *Archäologische Mitteilungen aus Iran, Neue Folge* 19 (1986): 177–86.

Wiesehöfer, J. *Die "Dunklen Jahrhunderte" der Persis: Untersuchungen zu Geschichte und Kultur von Fārs in frühhellenistischer Zeit (330–140 v. Chr.)*. Munich, 1994a.

Wiesehöfer, J. "'King of Kings' and 'Philhellen': Kingship in Arsacid Iran." *Aspects of Hellenistic Kingship*. Aarhus, 1994b. 55–66.

Wiesehöfer, J. *Ancient Persia from 550 BC to 650 AD*. Trans. A. Azodi. London, 1996.

Wiesehöfer, J., ed. *Das Partherreich und seine Zeugnisse*. Stuggart, 1998.

Wiesehöfer, J. "'Denn Orodes war der griechischen Sprache und Literatur nicht unkundig . . .': Parther, Griechen, und griechische Kultur." *Variatio Delectat: Iran und der Western*. Münster, 2000. 703–21.

Wiesehöfer, J. "Gebete für die 'Urahnen' oder: Wann und wie verschwanden Kyros und Dareios aus der historischen Tradition Irans?" *Tradition and Innovation in the Ancient World*. 6. Kraków, 2002a. 111–17.

Wiesehöfer, J. "Die 'Sklaven des Kaisers' und der Kopf des Crassus: Römische Bilder des Ostens und parthische Bilder des Westens in augusteischer Zeit." *Limes XVIII*. Oxford, 2002b. 293–300.

Wiesehöfer, J. "Fars under Seleucid and Parthian Rule." *The Age of the Parthians*. London, 2007a. 37–49.

Wiesehöfer, J. "From Achaemenid Imperial Order to Sasanian Diplomacy: War, Peace, and Reconciliation in Pre-Islamic Iran." *War and Peace in the Ancient World*. Malden, 2007b. 121–40.

Wiesehöfer, J. "Frataraka Rule in Seleucid Persis: A New Appraisal." *Creating a Hellenistic World*. Swansea, 2011. 107–21.

Wiesehöfer, J. "Frataraka." *Encyclopaedia Iranica Online Edition* (2012). Last accessed 5/2017. http://www.iranicaonline.org/articles/frataraka.

Wiesehöfer, J. "Frataraka and Seleucids." *Oxford Handbook of Ancient Iran*. Oxford, 2013a. 718–27.

Wiesehöfer, J. "Arsaces." *The Encyclopedia of Ancient History*. Vol. 2. Malden, 2013b. 761.

Wiesehöfer, J. "Greek Poleis in the Near East and Their Parthian Overlords." *Urban Dreams and Realities in Antiquity*. Leiden, 2014. 328–46.

Wiesehöfer, J. "Iranian Empires." *Oxford Handbook of the State in the Ancient Near East and Mediterranean*. Oxford, 2016. 199–233.

Wiesehöfer, J. "Antiochos III. und die Persis." *Antiochos III et l'Orient*. Nancy, 2017. 245–54.

Wiesehöfer, J., and S. Müller, eds. *Parthika: Greek and Roman Authors' Views of the Arsacid Empire*. Wiesbaden, 2017.

Wight, M. *Power Politics*. New York, 1978.

Wilcox, P. *Rome's Enemies (3): Parthians & Sassanid Persians*. Oxford, 1986.

Wilkinson, D. "Unipolarity without Hegemony." *Interdisciplinary Science Reviews* 1 (1999): 142–72.

Will, E. "Les premières années du regne d'Antiochus III (223–219 av. J.-C.)." *Revue des études grecques* 75 (1962): 72–129.

Will, E. *Histoire politique du monde hellénistique*. Nancy, 1967.

Willekes, C. *The Horse in the Ancient World: From Bucephalus to the Hippodrome*. London, 2016.

Williams, T. "Ancient Merv: Queen of Cities." *World Heritage* 24 (2002): 4–15.

Williams, T. "The City of Sultan Kala, Merv, Turkmenistan: Communities, Neighbourhoods and Urban Planning from the Eighth to the Thirteenth Century." *Cities in the Pre-Modern Islamic World*. London, 2007. 42–62.

Wilson, H. *Ariana Antiqua: A Descriptive Account of the Antiquities and Coins of Afghanistan*. London, 1841.

Wilson, L., and G. R. F. Assar. "Re-Dating Eukratides I Relative to Mithradates I." *Journal of the Oriental Numismatic Society* 191 (2007): 24–25.

Witakowski, W. "Adiabene, Ruling Dynasty of." *The Encyclopedia of Ancient History*. Vol. 1. Malden, 2013. 69–71.

Wohlforth, W. "Realism and the End of the Cold War." *International Security* 19 (1994–1995): 91–129.

Wohlforth, W. "The Stability of a Unipolar World." *International Security* 24 (1999): 5–41.

Wohlforth, W. "US Strategy in a Unipolar World." *America Unrivaled*. Ithaca, 2002. 98–118.

Wójcikowski, R. "Graffito from Dura Europos and the Hybrid Armor in Parthian-Sasanian Iran." *Anabasis* 4 (2013): 233–48.

Wolfers, A. *Discord and Collaboration: Essays on International Politics*. Baltimore, 1962.

Wolski, J. "La topographie de la Nouvelle Carthage et Polybe.: L'effondrement de la domination des Séleucides en Iran au IIIe siècle av. J.-C." *Bulletin international de l'Académie Polonaise des Sciences et des Lettres*. Kraków, 1947. 13–70.

Wolski, J. "The Decay of the Iranian Empire of the Seleucids and the Chronology of the Parthian Beginnings." *Berytus* 12 (1956–1957): 35–52.

Wolski, J. "L'historicité d'Arsace I." *Historia* 8 (1959): 222–38.

Wolski, J. "Les Iraniens et le royaume gréco-bactrien." *Klio* 38 (1960): 110–21.
Wolski, J. "Arsace II ou la généalogie des premiers Arsacides." *Historia* 11 (1962): 136–45.
Wolski, J. "Program polityczny panstwa partyjskiego." *Eos* 54 (1964a): 152–62.
Wolski, J. "Aufbau und Entwicklung des parthischen Staates." *Neue Beiträge zur Geschichte der Alten Welt*. 1. Berlin, 1964b. 379–88.
Wolski, J. "Le rôle et l'importance des mercenaires dans l'état parthe." *Iranica Antiqua* 5 (1965): 103–15.
Wolski, J. "Les Achéménides et les Arsacides: Contribution à l'histoire de la formation des traditions iraniennes." *Syria* 43 (1966): 65–89.
Wolski, J. "L'aristocratie parthe et les commencements du féodalisme en Iran." *Iranica Antiqua* 7 (1967): 133–44.
Wolski, J. "Der Zusammenbruch der Seleukidenherrschaft im Iran im 3. Jh. v. Chr.." *Der Hellenismus in Mittelasien. Wege der Forschung 91*. Darmstadt, 1969. 188–254.
Wolski, J. "Arsace I, fondateur de l'État parthe." *Acta Iranica* 3 (1974): 159–99.
Wolski, J. "Le classi inferiori della popolazione nel regno dei Parti." *Storia sociale ed economica dell'età classica negli studi polacchi contemporanei*. Milan, 1975. 55–61.
Wolski, J. "Iran und Rom. Versuch einer historischen Wertung der gegenseitigen Beziehungen." *Aufstieg und Niedergang der römischen Welt* 2.9.1 (1976a): 195–214.
Wolski, J. "Untersuchungen zur frühen parthischen Geschichte." *Klio* 58 (1976b): 439–557.
Wolski, J. "Les Parthes et la Syrie." *Acta Iranica* 12 (1977): 395–417.
Wolski, J. "L'Arménie dans la politique du Haut-Empire Parthe (env. 175–87 av. n. è.)." *Iranica Antiqua* 15 (1980a): 251–67.
Wolski, J. "La frontière orientale dans la politique de l'Iran des Arsacides." *Folia Orientalia* 21 (1980b): 235–44.
Wolski, J. "L'aristocratie foncière et l'organisation de l'armée parthe." *Klio* 63 (1981): 105–12.
Wolski, J. "Le problème de la fondation de l'État gréco-bactrien." *Iranica Antiqua* 17 (1982): 131–46.
Wolski, J. "Die Parther und ihre Beziehungen zur griechisch-römischen Kultur." *Klio* 65 (1983a): 137–149.
Wolski, J. "Les relations de Justin et Plutarque sur les esclavages et la population dépendante dans l'empire parthe." *Iranica Antiqua* 18 (1983b): 145–57.
Wolski, J. "Les monarchies hellénistiques et les Parthes." *Proceedings of VIIth Congress of the International Federation of the Societies of Classical Studies*. Budapest, 1984. 267–379.
Wolski, J. "Dans l'attente d'une nouvelle histoire de l'Iran arsacide." *Iranica Antiqua* 20 (1985a): 163–73.
Wolski, J. "Die abhängige Bevölkerung im Partherreich." *Antike Abhängigkeitsformen in den griechischen Gebieten ohne Polisskultur und den römischen Provinzen*. Berlin, 1985b. 80–87.
Wolski, J. "Die gesellschaftliche und politische Stellung der großen partischen Familien." *Tyche* 4 (1989): 221–27.
Wolski, J. "Alexandre le Grand et l'Iran: Contribution à l'histoire de l'époque séleucide et arsacide." *From Alexander to Kül Tegin*. Budapest, 1990a. 1–9.

Wolski, J. "Le titre de 'Roi des Rois' dans l'idéologie monarchique des Arsacides." *From Alexander to Kül Tegin*. Budapest, 1990b. 11–18.

Wolski, J. "Alexandre le Grand: Légende et réalité: De l'avènement des Seleucides à la chute des Arsacides." *Neronia IV: Alejandro Magno, modelo de los emperadores romanos*. Brussels, 1990c. 100–9.

Wolski, J. "L'époque parthe entre l'hellénisme et l'iranisme." *Histoire et cultes de l'Asie centrale préislamique*. Paris, 1991. 49–55.

Wolski, J. *L'Empire des Arsacides*. Leuven, 1993.

Wolski, J. "Les débuts de l'état parthe et ses contacts avec l'Asie Centrale." *La Persia e l'Asia centrale: Da Alessandro al X secolo*. Roma, 1996. 179–85.

Wolski, J. *Seleucid and Arsacid Studies: A Progress Report on Developments in Source Research*. Kraków, 2003.

Worthington, I. *By the Spear: Philip II, Alexander the Great, and the Rise and Fall of the Macedonian Empire*. Oxford, 2014.

Wozniak, M. *Armies of Ancient Persia: From the Founding of the Achaemenid State to the Fall of the Sasanid Empire*. Point Pleasant, 2018.

Wroth, W. "On the Rearrangement of Parthian Coinage." *Numismatic Chronicle* 3.20 (1900): 181–202 and pls. VII–IX.

Wroth, W. *A Catalogue of the Greek Coins in the British Museum, vol. 23, Catalogue of the Coins of Parthia*. London, 1903.

Yardley, J. *Justin and Pompeius Trogus: A Study of the Language of Justin's Epitome of Trogus*. Toronto, 2003.

Yardley, J., and R. Develin. *Justin: Epitome of the Philippic History of Pompeius Trogus*. Atlanta, 1994.

Yardley, J., and W. Heckel. *Justin: Epitome of the Philippic History of Pompeius Trogus, vol. 1: Books 11–12*. Oxford, 1997.

Yardley, J., W. Heckel, and P. Wheatley. *Justin: Epitome of the Philippic History of Pompeius Trogus, vol. 2: Books 13–15*. Oxford, 2011.

Yarrow, L. *Historiography at the End of the Republic: Provincial Perspectives on Roman Rule*. Oxford, 2006.

Yarshater, E., ed. *Cambridge History of Iran*. 3.1. Cambridge, 1983.

Yong, M., and S. Yutang. "The Western Regions under the Hsiung-nu and the Han." *History of Civilizations of Central Asia*. Delhi, 1999. 227–46.

Yong, M., and W. Binghua. "The Culture of the Xinjiang Region." *History of Civilizations of Central Asia*. Delhi, 1999. 209–26.

Yonge, C., trans. *Athenaeus: The Deipnosophists*. London, 1854.

Yü, Y. "The Hsiung-nu." *Cambridge History of Early Inner Asia*. Cambridge, 1990. 118–50.

Zabelina, N. "Novaia moneta s legendoi ΒΑΣΙΛΕΩΣ ΕΥΘΥΔΗΜΟΥ." *Kratkie soobshcheniia o dokladakh i polevykh issledovaniiakh Instituta istorii material'noi kul'tur' AN SSSR* v (1949): 101–2.

Zack, A. *Hegemonic War and Grand Strategy: Ludwig Dehio, World History, and the American Future*. London, 2017.

Zadneprovskiy, Y. "The Nomads of Northern Central Asia after the Invasion of Alexander." *History of Civilizations of Central Asia*. Delhi, 1999. 457–72.

Zadok, R. *Geographical Names According to New-and Late-Babylonian Texts. Répertoire Géographique des Textes Cunéiformes*. Vol. 8. Wiesbaden, 1985.

Zakaria, F. *From Wealth to Power: The Unusual Origins of America's World Role*. Princeton, 1998.

Zambrini, A. "Megasthenes Thirty Years Later." *With Alexander in India and Central Asia*. Oxford and Philadelphia, 2017. 222–37.

Zavyalov, V. "The Fortifications of the City of Gyaur Kala, Merv." *After Alexander*. Oxford, 2007. 313–29.

Zeymal, E. "Coins from the Excavations of Takht-i Sangin (1976–1991)." *Studies in Silk Road Coins Art and Culture*. Kamakura, 1997. 89–110.

Ziegler, K. *Die Beziehungen zwischen Rom und dem Partherreich: ein Beitrag zur Geschichte des Völkerrechts*. Wiesbaden, 1964.

Zuber, T. *Inventing the Schlieffen Plan: German War Planning 1871–1914*. Oxford, 2014.

Index

For the benefit of digital users, indexed terms that span two pages (e.g., 52–53) may, on occasion, appear on only one of those pages.